Critical Digital Studies: A Reader

Edited by

ARTHUR KROKER AND MARILOUISE KROKER

UNIVERSITY OF TORONTO PRESS
Toronto Buffalo London

ISBN 978-0-8020-9798-9 (cloth)
ISBN 978-0-8020-9546-6 (paper)

Printed on acid-free paper

Library and Archives Canada Cataloguing in Publication

Critical digital studies: a reader / edited by Arthur Kroker and Marilouise Kroker.

Includes bibliographical references.
ISBN 978-0-8020-9798-9 (bound)   ISBN 978-0-8020-9546-6 (pbk.)

1. Technology – Social aspects. 2. Technological innovations — Social aspects.
I. Kroker, Arthur, 1945– II. Kroker, Marilouise, 1943–

T14.5.C75 2008   303.48'3   C2008-904622-6

University of Toronto Press acknowledges the financial assistance to its publishing program of the Canada Council for the Arts and the Ontario Arts Council.

University of Toronto Press acknowledges the financial support for its publishing activities of the Government of Canada through the Book Publishing Industry Development Program (BPIDP).

Contents

POLITICS, GENDER, AND RELIGION

INFORMATION AND POWER

GENDER

Acknowledgments

Critical Digital Studies traces its origins to an interesting conflation of events. First and foremost, the world itself has been transformed by the question of the digital. Transformed not in a minor sense, but in the strikingly constitutive way by which politics, economy, culture, and identity are increasingly enabled, and sometimes constrained, by the historical triumph of digital society. Where this will lead us, whether or not the networked future will produce a new generation of upgraded minds, accelerated bodies, and perceptually sharpened subjects or perhaps the opposite, remains to be seen. However, what we do know is that the threshold event of critical digital studies has to do with writing and rewriting one's own technological autobiography. How could it be otherwise? What makes networked culture so fascinating is that its implications do not stop at the surface of communication, identity, and consciousness, but somehow slip beneath the human nervous system to become the real, living matter of the human sensorium. The question of technological autobiography, that point where we study the complexity of digital inflections at the level of culture and body and society and power, is the essence of *Critical Digital Studies: A Reader.*

Our exploration of Critical Digital Studies has taken place in the intellectually stimulating environment of the Pacific Centre for Technology and Culture at the University of Victoria in British Columbia. A research and teaching university where the life of the mind touches on the greater questions of the day, from climate change and indigenous struggle to theories of power and bodies and genders and technology, the University of Victoria and its Faculty of Social Sciences is a remarkably congenial setting for the study of technology and society. Arthur Kroker has been supported in his research by his appointment as Canada Research Chair in Technology, Culture, and Theory. Marilouise Kroker has engaged in critical digital studies within a research facility that has effectively repurposed 'streaming' into a new language for reflecting upon the human uses of technology. Here, noted scholars and digital visionaries including Stelarc, N. Katherine Hayles, Donna Haraway, Paul D. Miller (DJ Spooky), William Leiss, and Taiaiake Alfred have made appearances, sometimes in person, other times electronically, as part of a global initiative to write the technological biography of all of us that is *Critical Digital Studies.*

The editors owe an enormous debt of gratitude to the disciplined work and intellectual imagination of Ted Hiebert. His commitment to the very complex project involved in transforming the leading edge of contemporary digital consciousness into print is deeply appreciated both by the editors as well as all contributors to the reader. We would also like to thank Siobhan McMenemy for her excellent editorial contributions, and Frances Mundy, Kate Baltais, and Harold Otto for their care with the editing and production of the book. Most of all, we acknowledge the creative, intellectual singularity of each and every contributor. *Critical Digital Studies* represents emergent digital consciousness because its many writers have developed critical perspectives on the larger issues of digital reality in ways that are consistently scholarly, creative, and engaged.

We dedicate this reader to Claire and Lilly and to the memory of our friend, Jean Baudrillard.

Permissions

Bryson, Mary, Lori MacIntosh, Sharalyn Jordan, and Hui-Ling Lin. 'Virtually Queer? Homing Devices, Mobility, and Un/Belongings.' *Canadian Journal of Communication* 31.4 (2006): 791–814.

Dixon, Steve. 'Metal Performance: Humanizing Robots, Returning to Nature, and Camping About.' *TDR/The Drama Review* 48.4 (Winter 2004): 15–46. © 2004 New York University and the Massachusetts Institute of Technology.

Haraway, Donna Jeanne. 'A Game of Cat's Cradle: Science Studies, Feminist Theory, Cultural Studies.' *Configurations* 2.1 (1994): 59–71. © The Johns Hopkins University Press and Society for Literature and Science. Reprinted with permission of the Johns Hopkins University Press.

Hayles, N. Katherine. 'Traumas of Code.' *Critical Inquiry* 33.1 (Fall 2006): 136–57. © 2006 by The University of Chicago (0093-1896/2006/3301-0005). Reprinted with permission of the University of Chicago Press.

Jonker, Julian. 'Black Secret Technology (The Whitey on the Moon Dub).' © Julian Jonker. First published in *Chimurenga* 2 (2002). Reprinted with permission of the author.

Leeson, Lynn Hershman. 'Romancing the Anti-body: Lust and Longing in (Cyber)space.' (1995). © Lynn Hershman Leeson. Reprinted with permission of the author.

CRITICAL DIGITAL STUDIES: A READER

Critical Digital Studies: An Introduction

Arthur and Marilouise Kroker

Critical Digital Studies represents a creative search for a new method of understanding digitally mediated culture.

From the spectacular emergence of new media innovations such as blogging, podcasting, flashmobs, mashups, and RSS feeds to video-sharing websites (MySpace, YouTube), Wikipedia, and massively multiplayer online role-playing games (MMORPGs), the *how and what we know* of contemporary society, culture, and politics is continuously being creatively transformed by strikingly original developments in technologies of digital communication.[1] To the challenge of understanding the implications of technological innovations, *Critical Digital Studies* responds by developing a new method of critical digital studies: *its scope* – full-spectrum knowledge of the digital future; *its method* – media archaeology; *its practice* – crossing boundaries; and *its goal* – bending the digital future in the direction of creative uncertainty.

Conceived as a global forum for critical digital studies, this book represents a new style of thought directly emergent from Net culture itself. Inspired by the same digital spirit that gave rise to the Open Architecture Movement, Shareware, and Web 2.0, *Critical Digital Studies* may be visualized as a *creative mashup* – a method of critical digital studies that creatively mixes the very traditional human demand to understand the world in which we live with the new ways of analysing, relating, communicating, and living that are digital reality today.

Representing many of the leading digital theorists in the field of new media analysis, *Critical Digital Studies* links the digital future to the question of knowledge. Here, *digital knowledge* – knowledge of surveillance strategies, knowledge of meta-media, knowledge of advanced cyber-warfare, knowledge of information technology, knowledge of gendered information, knowledge of peer production, knowledge of 'cyborg mothers' and 'biophilosophies' – is placed in the service of a digital culture that is struggling to be born, survive, and flourish.

Understanding the Digital

Looking around the crowd, even during the liveliest numbers, there was an eerie silence. At times, the atmosphere was more like a high-Catholic service than a pop concert. In the velvety dark, 10,000 points of polychrome light glimmered as cellphone screens were lit and turned reverently, towards the stage.

A sizable part of the audience was photo- and sound-recording the event, and another sizable part of the audience was transmitting Coldplay's performance to absent friends via mobile phones.

To get the best image with a mobile you keep arms outstretched and the whole body rigid – as if in prayer. No jumping or jigging to the beat. At various points in the set the stage backscreen projected a reciprocal mobile image of the audience.

Aware of this new concert technology, (Coldplay's) Chris Martin routinely asks the audience to take a simultaneous camera-phone snapshot, creating a sheet-lightning effect. Like Bono, he will instruct them to fire off a barrage of mid-performance text messages on behalf of Fair Trade.

The phone becomes an umbilical connector between artist, audience and outside world.

John Sutherland, 'For those about to rock: We turn on our cell phones for you'[2]

The explosive growth of the Internet is already common knowledge. What is less noticed, however, is that the digital future is definitely not limited to the question of the Internet, but has now become a very complex aspect of life. In the 1960s, Marshall McLuhan could write with confidence of a modern culture in which the different historical phases of the oral versus the literate, the mechanical versus the electronic, could not only be theoretically distinguished from one another but with their clear boundary divisions could be subject to styles of critical interpretation relative to the cultural singularities of each. Consequently, McLuhan could speculate eloquently on the emergence of the 'global village,' analyse 'the medium as the massage,' and contrast tribal cultures with their privileged oral sense with electronic crowds worked over by technologies of visualization. What he did not do, and, in fact, at that epochal moment of division had no need of doing, was to write equally eloquently of what would succeed electronic culture, namely, the complex multiplicity that is the digital future with its porous and blurred boundaries, clashing global villages, multiple media, and often contradictory messages. In retrospect, McLuhan's lasting contribution may well have been to represent, in all its creative utopianism, that great technological division in which for the last time it would be possible to distinguish clear border lines among alternative media, to attest to the existence of firm boundaries among the human, the mechanical, and the organic, or to speak with confidence of the necessity of media literacy rather than the more ambitious, and certainly difficult, task of the plurality of media literacies required to negotiate today's increasingly dense digital matrix. While McLuhan could distinguish with considerable intellectual impact the difference between a culture of the ear and a culture of the eye, his thought did not anticipate a much more ambivalent technological future, namely, one in which technologies of the ear (iPods) and the eye (webcams) combine with hidden technologies of the clothes we wear (RIFFs), the food we eat (genomics), the secrets we keep (digital archives), the words we speak (podcasts, satellite radio) to produce a digital culture that is as complex in its implications as it is ambivalent in its meanings. If McLuhan's electronic culture succeeded the (industrial) world of mechanical technologies, then today the media world built on the house of analogue electricity has been displaced by the digital universe constructed of binary codework.

When technological society is no longer understandable simply in terms of the globalizing spectacle of electronic images but in the more invisible, pervasive, and embodied language of computer codes, then three immediate implications follow. First, digital culture literally remaps, rewires, and recodes life itself using complex algorithms. When the theorist Katherine Hayles noted in a recent interview that 99 per cent of all communication is not humanly understandable because it is machine-to-machine interaction, then there is an urgent necessity, if we are to understand what is happening to us as we are being worked over by the codes, to decipher the meaning of codework, and, more precisely, to understand what complex things happen when codes are actually embodied, when codework becomes the culture within which we thrive, the means by which we download the music we love, the invisible apparatus that supports the communications within which we live. Second, the movement from the (electronic) current to the (digital) code implies some very serious blurring of boundaries where clear distinctions among flesh, machine, and images become increasingly more difficult to ascertain. Third, accelerating the speed of electronic culture, the new digital universe moves in two opposite directions simultaneously. As codework, digitality moves at the speed of light. But when the digital universe interacts with the putatively solid objects of society – bodies, politics, economy, gender, sexuality – its speed is suddenly altered, inflected by the very real materiality of a world that is, for all its digitality, still all the more physical, concrete, stubborn, as regressive politically as it is progressive. In contrast to the infectious utopianism of the original visionaries of the electronic age, from Marshall McLuhan to Teilhard de Chardin, no necessary human future is implied by the emergence of the digital world. Although codeworks definitely exert a massive, structural influence on human affairs, influencing by programming design the how, what, when, where, and why we live in these coded times, immense room remains for contingency, chance, and sheer willpower in this world. Neither inevitably utopian nor dystopian, digital reality is an open future, determined in the final instance by the play of human interests, desires, and power that have always represented the elementary matter of the human condition.

As we find ourselves thrust from the electronic media into digital reality, we are not left without guides to our technological future. After McLuhan, the question of the digital has attracted the passionate attention of a large community of theorists who, speaking with often very different voices and certainly from dramatically unique national localities, have sought to understand the real world of digital culture. They have sought to understand digital reality not only in terms of its local manifestations, but to comprehend from its very interior a fast-changing culture within which they themselves are active participants in the larger discourse-change that is represented by this movement from the mechanical to the electronic, and thence to the digital. Themselves caught up within a technoculture that is literally moving at light-speed, these theorists of the digital have had of necessity to develop a style of thought, a method of inquiry, and a digital vocabulary that would not only illuminate the darkest recesses of digital reality but also express something of the power of the digital inflection.

It is certainly contrary to the (recombinant) spirit of digitality to assign genealogical naming rights to the founding mothers, fathers, sons, and daughters of critical digital studies. Nevertheless, there is one name that continues to haunt critical digital studies, that of the German philosopher Martin Heidegger. In his classic essay, 'The Question of Technology,' Heidegger posed the fateful question that ever since has represented the hauntology of the digital age. For Heidegger, technology was a paradox. Not self-birthing and certainly not self-generating, the question of technology could only be posed as part of a larger query, namely, to what should we ascribe the dynamic, seductive power of technology? For Heidegger, technology could not be understood technologically for the simple reason that technology is not simply technical, but has everything to do with the more powerful currents out of which contemporary society has been fashioned – the planetary drive to 'conquer' nature; the politics of subordinating human nature; the will to expand our society, culture, and, in the last instance, 'ourselves' by means of technologies of communication; the greater historical project of remaking ourselves as technological beings. Heidegger sought his own philosophical resolution of this question by means of an increasingly complex position on the question of the technological that came, in the end, to recognize technology as containing possibilities for intense human creativity ('in-dwelling') and utter human devastation ('completed nihilism').

Critical Digital Studies is about 'the question of technology.' How could it not be? The sheer intensity, volume, and accelerating effects of the question of technology in its contemporary manifestation as digital reality have about them an *urgency* that demands the most serious reflection. If we are not to be swept away as so much digital debris in the technological maelstrom, if thought itself is not to be terrorized into passive submission by ubiquitous technologies of surveillance, if critical reflection – one of the enduring hallmarks of *being human* – is not to be blasted apart by a culture of (technological) distraction, then there is a desperate need to rise again to the challenge of the question of technology.

When thinking refuses to accommodate itself passively to the narrative line created as part of the justificatory logic of technology itself, then critical digital studies must itself absorb fully the quality of technological paradox. Curiously faithful to the spirit of technology, thought must simultaneously expose the as yet unrevealed implications of the historical project of technology, while at the same time, represent, in all its incommensurability, the full dimensions of the greater technological destiny within which we now find ourselves carried along. This is exactly what successive generations of thinkers who have risen to the Sisyphean challenge of answering the question of technology have done.

McLuhan's Doubt: Pathways to the Digital

Approaches to understanding the impact of technology upon society, politics, and culture are often divided into the clashing perspectives of technology as utopia or domination; but these binary perspectives on the question of technology miss entirely the real-time history of the digital inflection: a dramatic history that has everything to do with digital reality as a story of complexity. In the industrial age of mechanical technology, and even in the modern era of electronic technology, it was permissible (perhaps even salutary) to seek understanding of technology in terms of the larger mythological terms of *utopia* and *domination*. When technology exhibited clear divisions, was easily distinguishable from the boundaries of the body, and could be decisively analysed in terms of its generative relationship to questions of class, race, and gender, that is, when the question of technology staked its claim to power on a world with unbroken borders, it was appropriate to inscribe technology within literary traditions pronouncing in favour of utopia or apocalypse. Thus, understanding technology could be framed in all its mythic intensity and implacable planetary drive using the imaginary spectres of Mary Shelley's *Frankenstein* or the essentially religious story of technology as human salvation that was Teilhard de Chardin's *Noosphere*.

In the digital age of intelligent machines, the question of technology becomes a much more complex story concerning the infiltration of seemingly every aspect of human and non-human life by the digital code. In a way never really anticipated by even the most dystopian or, for that matter, utopian of techno-visionaries, boundaries among machines, humans, animals, and inanimate nature have broken down, perhaps forever. For example, consider the fate of the body in the digital age. We have long been accustomed to thinking of the human body as something that is self-contained and relatively independent of its technological prostheses. In his most utopian moments, McLuhan could declaim that electronic technologies of communication represented 'extensions' of the human nervous system, just before, that is, his self-avowed sense of Catholic melancholy forced him to lament what he saw as human passivity in the face of technologies performing violent 'psychic surgery' on the human sensorium. Although McLuhan's affirmation of technology as a helpful extension of the human nervous system has continued to this day in increasingly triumphant announcements of the coming of the age of 'augmented media,' it should be noted that McLuhan's deeply felt ambivalence regarding the fate of technology, whether it result in a vast extension or a cataclysmic implosion of the human body, introduced a truly ambivalent sense of complexity into the story of technology. Now that we live after McLuhan, now that the media analysis so appropriate to the era of electronic technologies of communication has been eclipsed by the codework so necessary to digital reality, now that the supposedly externalized world of technological prostheses have actually invaded the human body, what might be called *McLuhan's doubt* – his prescient sense that technology contained a paradoxical story of augmentation and diminution – has amplified in importance, becoming the basis of a new way of understanding the real world of digital technology. Like a chain of thought that remains unbroken, McLuhan's doubt has created a new generation of digital thinkers who have succeeded in transforming his initial doubt about the ends of technology into a compelling story of digital complexity.

Digital Complexity

> In computationally intense culture such as Canada, the USA, other western but also Asian cultures like Japan, machine-to-machine communication has now progressed to the point where it's about 99% of all coded traffic. Most of that traffic takes place outside human awareness. Consequently, human awareness is the tiny tip of the pyramid of a huge amount of data flow, most of which happens between machines. There is a very unsettling aspect to this, revealed, for example, in the United States by President Bush's surveillance policy. However, that is only one small part of what is happening. The fact is that nobody knows the contents of these machine-to-machine communications, not even the National Security Agency. This gives one pause. It raises profound questions about the proper relation of human communication to all of these coded transmissions.[3]

Complexity is the essence of digital technology. In a culture of coded transmissions, diminished human awareness, and the entanglement of machines, humans, and animals in larger data flows that are often outside the range of traditional ways of understanding, the old (technological) world of automatic opposites has suddenly dissolved into complex fractures: those subtle, difficult to detect yet alone analyse, *folds* wherein we have literally become digital bodies, with our eyes wide open to the wonders and dangers of wired culture. In the twenty-first century, complexity is what is unique about critical digital studies.

First applied to the problem of understanding technology in the writings of Katherine Hayles, a contemporary theorist of the 'regime of computation,' the concept of complexity has spread around the digital world at light-speed. That such a wide diversity of thinkers interested in the future of technology – artificial intelligence (AI) researchers, technovisionaries, communication experts, software programmers, new media artists, digital designers, web creators, and gaming innovators – immediately recognized in complexity theory something very familiar, indeed something reflective of their own experience of digital reality, implies that with the concept of complexity we are in the presence of a paradigm shift in interpreting technology.

This makes sense in two quite different ways. First, as expressed by Hayles in her books – *My Mother Was a Computer, How We Became Posthuman*, and *Writing Machines* – complexity intimates that the regime of computation with its complex models of simulation is capable of generating 'reality' itself, as well as providing powerful metaphors by which we have come to understand the increasingly computational culture within which we live. Digital technology ceases to be merely representational of the world, but becomes instead an emergent reality principle in its own right, driving culture and society forward by ever-proliferating digital innovations while, at the same time, providing compelling new ways of thinking about the digital reality that surrounds us. With Hayles, McLuhan's 'global village' actually comes inside us, transforming each of us into a navigator of the digital storm. And navigate we must because the regime of computation is beautifully complex.

Unlike previous historical eras in which we could with some authenticity maintain a safe distance from the question of technology, we all now have a *technological autobiography*. From the moment of our medically enabled births to our inevitable deaths in increasingly high-tech intensive care units, from a lifetime of computer-assisted education to digitally enhanced workplace experience, from the mass data archives that literally 'bank' human memory to the screens and spools and keystrokes composing the materiality of the regime of computation, the question of individual autobiography has become deeply entangled with the 'companion species' of technology. This entanglement is most apparent, of course, in the end products of technology, in those widely debated public policy issues that emerge directly from the planetary drive to the fully realized technological society – the crisis of global warming; the global economic creativity released by the 'flat world' of digital communication;[4] the ambivalent legacy of the science of genomics; the impact of digital technology in simultaneously concentrating immense conglomerations of corporate ownership while providing multiple opportunities for an 'open architecture' of information flows. What is more subtle, and more complex, however, is that we are also deeply entangled in the algorithmic currents of digital reality. Outside of normal human awareness, our consciousness, language, dreams, conjectures, gestures – the most familiar ways we communicate with and relate to each other – are being powerfully shaped and influenced by the 'machine-to-machine' data flows within which we circulate, and on account of which our lives are often enhanced, and sometimes disabled.

Waking up to the shock of the new, until now we have not had an adequate vocabulary by which to begin to articulate the full dimensions of the digital culture that surrounds us. But we do know this. If science and the humanities and, by extension, the natural and social sciences, remain in isolation from one another, it is critical human consciousness itself that will be lost in the cracks of the digital. Quite explicitly, if our lives are to be 'streamed' by the new sciences of computation, if individual autobiography is to be pushed and pulled by the strange loops, fast data flows, and complicated mediations of this epochal meeting of computation and flesh, then there is a desperate requirement to do something that is as ancient as it is futurist: to find the 'words' by which to make familiar to our senses the new home of digital technology within which we have staked our identities, both individually and collectively.

Finding the 'words,' creating a new imaginative vocabulary by which to attune ourselves to the question of the digital is what complexity theory is all about. Not particularly romantic, complexity theory refuses to have anything to do with the quasi-religious theories now in circulation that elevate technology to a singularity moment. There is nothing transcendental about the question of complexity. How could there be? When boundaries dissolve, when crossing border lines is more natural than continuing to live in the solitudes of science and the humanities, then *being complex* requires us to consider precisely how the 'regime of computation' intermediates with very traditional questions of class, gender, race, ethnicity, and sexuality.

Moreover, we must consider anew the real *material* history of digital technology: software as ideology, the 'intermediation' of print and digitality, the global media apparatus as a 'vision machine,' and the reality studio as a 'simulacrum.' If digital reality has literally come alive in our technologically enhanced bodies, our computer-enabled economy, and our graphically intensified high-definition screens, then we might well want to begin to probe the new rules of communication by which the to date deeply divided 'companion species' of machines, humans, animals, inanimate nature, and future AI replicants, clones, and zombies can finally become acquainted with a growing sense of dynamic harmony. When cyborgs become, as Donna Haraway has brilliantly argued, a 'companion species' to the human, *being complex* assumes a larger importance as a basic strategy of cultural survival: 'Cyborgs and companion species each bring together the human and the non-human, the organic and the technological, carbon and silicon, freedom and structure, history and myth, the rich and the poor, the state and the subject, diversity and depletion, modernity and postmodernity, and nature and culture in unexpected ways. Besides, neither a cyborg nor a companion species pleases the pure of heart who long for better protected species boundaries and sterilization of category deviants.'[5]

If the technology of fire lit up the darkness of the night, if electricity illuminated the sky, and the power of words finally provided the human imagination with the means to communicate its innermost visions, then being complex does something different. Complexity allows us to communicate consciously in a culture where technology now inhabits the space-time fabric itself. Complexity compels us to be sensitive to the much-neglected fact that although the seasons of life (with its air, fire, water, and earth) have not gone away, the material history of the planet is only now beginning a new dialogue with the new realities of digital culture. We remain as yet unaware of what the results of that dialogue might eventually be. However, this one certainty drives us forward: only by learning how to be (digitally) complex will we hominids be capable of joining in this greater dialogue with a technology that will not be stopped and a nature that will not be long denied. Following Haraway, who has argued long and eloquently for changing the 'narrative line' of science from fantasies of self-birthing and self-generation, and Hayles, who has made of us all potentially creative 'writing machines' in the midst of the digital maelstrom, should we not finally honour the question of technology by making of it an opportunity for appreciating the complexity of the digital reality that is our present and our future, and perhaps already even our unknown past? Should we not respond then to the question of technology with a search for a method by which to make of that question a guide to the future of digital complexity?

Approaches to Critical Digital Studies

Critical digital studies represents a search for a new method of understanding the digital future. Confronted with the challenge of translating the concept of complexity into a new way of seeing digital reality, critical digital studies does not begin with an established agenda, but with an innovative series of questions. Here, the working premise is that the most important aspect of a search for a new method of understanding is the immediate challenge of posing the right question(s). Consequently, guided by four interpretive rules, critical digital studies sets out to ask four questions of the question of (digital) technology. First, how can we expand the scope of studying the digital future to include the full array of technological innovations, namely, the impact of digital technology on culture, society, economy, and politics? Second, how can we best interpret the fluid world of media archeology, those innovative media convergences that drive together traditional media (print, television, radio) with their digital counterparts from the Internet and the Web? Third, how can critical digital studies break beyond the disciplinary boundaries of traditional media interpretation to actually cross boundaries – boundaries of knowledge, of societies, of species, of machine-human interfaces – in search of a form of media practice that is itself reflective of the porous boundaries of the digital reality that it seeks to explore? And, fourth, how can critical digital studies achieve its desired aim of bending the digital future in the direction of creative uncertainty, that is, privileging the intermediations, inflections, and paradoxes that are so deeply characteristic of the digital flow? Not a prescriptive agenda, critical digital studies rises to the task of answering the question of technology with a series of complex questions of its own. It must do this because what is most interesting about the digital future is that its full dimensions remain unknown, its fate uncertain, its strategies unexplored, and its lasting consequences unanticipated. Today more than ever, it is surely time to ask some serious, creative questions of the enigmatic silence surrounding the question of technology.

This is precisely what *Critical Digital Studies* sets out to do. In keeping with the spirit of complexity, it focuses on four key contemporary intersections of the digital future: code breakers, technology, politics, and culture.

Code Breakers

What is truly *critical* about critical digital studies is the emphasis on not only understanding the dominant codes of technology, politics, and culture in the digital era, but also on digital studies that excel in breaking the codes and in introducing new visions of the digital future by disrupting the codes, disturbing boundaries, and adding uncertainty to established patterns of (code) behaviour. Each contribution to *Critical Digital Studies* has this double quality about it – namely, studying what Haraway has described as the 'informatics of domination' only in order to write possible new codes for the ways in which we do politics and gender and bodies and communication in the future. The creative act of code breaking reaches its apogee, however, in the writings of N. Katherine Hayles, Donna Haraway, Sara Diamond, and Lynn Hershman Leeson. Understood individually, these four introductory chapters bring to the surface of critical thought the deeper codes of information, gender, design, and bodies so characteristic of the supercharged environment of technological society. Understood collectively, these contributions represent something very different, not so much critical studies of digital experience, but profound, even foundational, efforts to make of the act of digital code breaking a new way of understanding technology.

Hayles, in 'Traumas of Code' (chapter 1), explores the double-edged benefits (and dangers) of code as the 'unconscious of language.' For Hayles, we are living now in the dense web of the 'technological non-conscious.' Both a powerful enabler and potential danger, code as the technological non-conscious implies for Hayles 'the dual promise and threat that intelligent machines pose to the uniquely human capacity to create meaning through language.' But, of course, when code becomes language to the extent that we can now speak about a 'technological non-conscious,' this also means that questions of (digital) trauma cannot be far behind. In transferring control of human communications to intelligent machines, have we not also invested the age of intelligent machines with our hopes and desires, our fears and anxieties, our vulnerabilities and resentments?

If this is the case, then the other field-defining chapters in 'Code Breakers,' the first part of this book, can be viewed as brilliant recommendations concerning how best to work through the *trauma* of the technological unconscious. In 'A Game of Cat's Cradle: Sign Studies, Feminist Theory, Cultural Studies' (chapter 2) Haraway argues that if we are not to be sucked into the 'gravity well of technoscience' we had better learn quickly how to *reconfigure* – 'how to trope and how to knot together key discourses about technoscience.' Setting up a game of cat's cradle for the social sciences and humanities, Haraway follows her own advice by literally 'reconfiguring' the language of technoscience with urgent questions focused on gender, sexuality, colonialism, and class, representing in all of their latent power and immediate vulnerability the *critical consciousness* of science studies, feminist theory, and cultural studies. Although written at different moments and certainly with different intentions, it is almost as if Haraway's game of cat's cradle constitutes an immediate response to Hayles's plea for a form of critical digital consciousness that would finally take account of the fact that code is not simply the operating language of intelligent machines but perhaps something more disturbing, a counter-unconscious – a 'technological unconscious' – parallelling in its mystery the still unknown realm of the human unconscious.

Writing from a cross-cultural perspective, Sara Diamond surveys the brilliant contributions of Chinese, Japanese, African, Latin American, and (North American) indigenous new media artists to understanding the futures of digital complexity. In 'Reframing the Cathedral: Opening the Sources of Technologies and Cultural Assumptions' (chapter 3) Diamond explores the question of the technological unconscious at the level of digital design. Here, the traditional languages of new media authoring tools, from Hypertext and MIDI to gaming software, are supplemented with the creative visions of new media designers from the multiplicity of cultures and nations and traditions and even continents normally ignored by the informatics of (design) domination. Refusing to believe that the world of new media design is flat, Diamond's perspective resonates with images of difference: Japanese aesthetics with its bias towards beauty including 'incompletions and imperfections'; west coast indigenous art with its (virtual) visions of the sacred; and Chinese new media representations of ancient traditions of anime and calligraphy. With this, Diamond does that which is most difficult, but ultimately most rewarding, namely, illuminating digital vision with those creative expressions of the human mind that seemingly have become lost with the triumph of the language of technoscience. Maintaining that the 'visual aesthetics of tools tend towards binary, linear, rectangular aesthetics,' she argues on behalf of a different design vision, one advanced by cultures that embrace 'complexity, discontinuity and asymmetry as organizing principles': 'This is a delicate negotiation – the recognition of cultures that have maintained a continuity with a natural science that speaks to dimensions beyond four, that sees time as a navigable object, that uses circular forms and narratives in which scientists close their eyes and imagine models beyond our perception, of a space perhaps linked to ritual, prayer rugs, and mosaics. This pace of invention, of imagination, is a space shared by art, non-Western mathematics, and science. It is as science surrounded by our imaginings of Nature, West and East, North and South' (65).

Working independently, renowned California new media artist Lynn Hershman Leeson intensifies Diamond's evocative insights related to possible new languages of digital design by actually reframing the cathedral of her own (digital) body. Hershman Leeson's new media creations (film, video, writing) have achieved such global acclaim because she is a world leader in exploring the *rematerialization* of the body in cyberspace. Understanding digital culture as a fluid, liquid space of networked relations that increasingly circulate around and through the bodies of its inhabitants, Hershman Leeson asks unsettling questions not only about the fate of the electronic body, but also about the once and future shape of human identity: 'Identity is the first thing you create when you log on to a computer service. By defining yourself in some way, whether it is through your name, a personal profile, an icon, or mask, you also define your audience, space, and territory. In the architecture of networks, geography shifts as readily as time. Communities are defined by software and hardware access. Anatomy can be readily constituted' (71).

For Hershman Leeson, masking through computer-mediated communication has immediate consequences:

> Not only do you not need a body, but entering cyberspace encourages a disembodied body language. Posing and emoting are some of the terms for phantom gestures that can be read through words, or seen in special video programs through simple movements such as waves. Codes of gestures can be read by attachments on the computer that articulates hidden meanings of voiceless and mute speech.
>
> Actions are constantly under surveillance, tracked, traced, digitized and stored. Icons such as masks are of particular importance because the disguises used today may determine an archetype of the present that will eventually reflect the ephemeral nature of a society geared towards images of manipulation and self recreation (71).

Not satisfied with exploring the real-time art by which we have actually masked our (electronic) bodies as we communicate within and across the spaces of YouTube, Google, and the Web, Hershman Leeson goes beyond the language of (cyber) bodies and masks to an impressive exploration of all the 'non-bodies' and 'anti-bodies' that await the unfolding of the digital future. Less focused on machine crashes than crashes of the human body under the pressure of information flows, Hershman Leeson investigates what it means to locate ourselves in the found environments and virtual spaces of digital culture. Like an artistic avatar of massive online role-playing games, her work explores the transformed landscape of identity at that point where we willingly become an 'objectified non-bodied alternative personality.' And her concerns are not simply with the world of gaming. For Hershman Leeson, what happens now in digital reality has long been prefigured by mass media with its violent image-based transformation of the last remnants of real bodies into a strange new world of 'phantom limbs, interactivity, and disappearances.' About this, her perspective is explicit: 'These each articulate references to the mutation of the female body through the seduction of media. Reproductive technological parts sprout from the image of the female, creating a cyborgian reformation as parts of the real body disappear' (79).

At stake in Hershman Leeson's perspective is this basic code breaker of a thought, namely, are we witnessing today the 'birth of the anti-body,' our Net identities as increasingly fictional personas who 'in reaction to an unhealthy natural environment ... reject what exists, and in order to survive, form another environment': 'This Internetted, plugged-in anti-body is a transitory construction of time, circumstances, and technology, a newly issued prescription of earlier impulses. She has chosen to negate the selfhood in which she was born. Instead she shows a marked preference for the artifice of technology' (82).

A futurist by practice but very much a student of more enduring patterns of culture by temperament, Hershman Leeson has a vision of bodies, non-bodies, and anti-bodies that returns us to something we thought we had finally surpassed at the speed of digital culture – the Faustian bargain involved in the question of technology. Or, as she concludes: 'If humans have become the interface to the larger communicative body, can soulful automatons be far behind?' (84).

Technology, Identity, and Surveillance

The verdict is still out on the future of technology and culture. While perhaps neither a perfect utopia nor a fearful dystopia, one thing is certain. Contemporary society is increasingly stressed out by accelerating rates of technological change. Confronted with the blast of technology moving at light-speed, the human nervous system seems, in the first instance, to have either gone numb for survival, adapted itself passively and fatalistically to the digital juggernaut, or become lost in a culture of (digital) distractions. Today email is clogged with spam. Electronic spyware is capable of tracking our every move on the Internet. Complex computer systems, whether in business or government, can suddenly be disabled by always mutating viruses. No sooner have individuals become accustomed to the wired world of personal computers, CD players, and VCRs than digital technology itself suddenly evolves in the direction of the wireless future of iPods, cell video phones, radio-frequency identification (RFID) tracking chips, and a dense, creative matrix of new forms of digital communications spearheaded by blogs and podcasting.

When everyday life comes to mean *digitally mediated* experience, serious consequences follow for individuals and societies remaining unaware of the rate and direction of technological change. Indeed, over and beyond the rapid digital change that we can see on the surface, what may now be occurring as a result of massive technological transformations of the basic structures of culture, politics, and economics is a gigantic shift of the deepest fault lines of society where the only constant is that the world as we know it today is unlikely to persist, even into the near future. Understanding technological complexity is a key survival strategy in the twenty-first century.

Focusing on key approaches to understanding real-time technology, the chapters in the second part of this book, 'Technology, Identity, and Surveillance' explore the data archive, showing in detail what happens to human vision, identity, consciousness, power, and perception as society and culture are increasingly wrapped in the digital membrane. Beginning with the tacit assumption that the new world of digital media, images, and networking is no longer understandable in forms of media analysis relevant to electronic mass media such as television and radio, the contributions about real-time technology actually create a basic vocabulary for understanding new digital realities such as 'tracking,' 'armed perception,' 'meta-tags,' 'precogs,' and 'hyperviruses.' With astonishing speed, events that until not long ago were the subject of science fiction now have technologies of visualization, surveillance, gaming, and viral (computer) crashes. It is as if a violent (digital) shudder has suddenly passed through the framework of reality itself, instantly exposing us to a new digital reality with its space-time fabric moving at the speed of light. We are accelerating at escape velocity in the light through space and light through time of the digital blast anxiously seeking new concepts and visions by which to make sense of the contemporary human predicament. To the complexity of the digital reality that is their subject matter, the contributors to 'Technology, Identity, and Surveillance' respond with intense, complex thought – boundary-crossing, fluid, bifurcated, and often paradoxical.

Bringing together some of the leading international scholars in new media analysis – Jordan Crandall, Lev Manovich, Alexander R. Galloway, Nate Burgos, Eugene Thacker, and Thierry Bardini – a fundamentally new approach to understanding new media is articulated in all its internal coherence, intellectual diversity, and media relevance. Here the emphasis is placed on a slow, patient, in-depth reading of the borderland between digital media, identity, and perception.

Counterposing seeing (or visualizing) versus tracking (or calculating), Jordan Crandall explores what happens to human vision and consciousness when the media apparatus becomes a vast tracking mechanism, capable of very real precision in mapping bodies in their (electronic) movements, transactions, and (archived) memories. Refusing to approach precision tracking technologies as something safely outside human identity, Crandall does something more intellectually risky, but ultimately amazingly rewarding. He demonstrates how the digital body has now become complicit in precision tracking technologies, sometimes as a voyeur of its own digital travels, at other points numbed into submission by the ubiquity of 'Precision + Guided + Seeing.'

In 'Understanding Meta-media,' Lev Manovich extends new media analysis to its next logical step, exploring the meta-media paradigm that is at the centre of contemporary computer culture (software interfaces, hypertext, downloads). Taking seriously Katherine Hayles's narrative of the 'regime of computation,' Manovich argues that meta-media as a way of understanding real-time technology have become the dominant sign of network culture, replacing the older, more conservative notion of media culture proper. The argument has to do with the capacity of meta-media to extrude, extend, link, and expand both the media they engage with as well as the environment in which these engagements occur. In a media scene where the borderlines among traditional (mass) media and new (digital) media have imploded, Manovich's media analysis is like an early warning system, alerting us to a profound paradigm shift in the deep framework of contemporary media.

Focusing on *Warcraft*, the very popular massively multiplayer online role-playing game (MMORPG), Alexander R. Galloway's '*Warcraft* and Utopia' examines the fateful consequences that follow from a meta-media culture of precision tracking technologies.

Again, like Crandall and Manovich, Galloway refuses to think of the question of digital utopia/dystopia in conventional binary terms; he redefines the meaning of utopia in a network culture by discussing in detail the positive and negative aspects of considering video games as forms of utopia. Here the mandate for imagining life before or after capitalism becomes a challenge of imagining life *within* a networked capitalist world, with its complex interplay of coding, decoding, and recoding.

That the digital future can only be explored from within the parameters of a networked capitalist world is the common thread linking the following three contributions: 'The Age of Blur and Technology' by Nate Burgos, 'Biophilosophy for the 21st Century' by Eugene Thacker, and 'Hypervirus: A Clinical Report' by Thierry Bardini. Written by digital scholars who have thought deeply about issues related to digital complexity, these chapters rub closely against the major currents of power, language, and technology in the present epoch. If Burgos can articulate so well how the politics of 'pre-emptive deterrence' has seemingly shifted in a nanosecond from the subject-matter of Hollywood sci-fi blockbusters to omnipresent technologies of contemporary anti-terrorist policing, it is probably due to his acute understanding of real-time technology as equivalent to the 'age of blur.' From projection to prediction, eyes wide open, scanning possibilities and making precognitive representations as a strategy for dealing with the intensifying visual pace, *being precog* has become as 'natural' to us as human vision itself. No time for understanding, fast forward, rewind, and make your predictions before it is too late: the 'age of blur' is a mandate for a pre-emptive human imagination.

Not only the creation of a pre-emptive human imagination as part of the cultural fall-out of digital culture, but perhaps now even life itself is becoming rapidly destabilized by that powerful conjuncture of high-speed computer sequencing and genomic biology that we have come to know as the 'biotech century.' Thacker's contribution is itself pre-emptive in drawing some hard conclusions from the seeming triumph of digital technology. For Thacker, the interface of computers and biology has transformed the concept of life itself, bringing life within the purview of bioengineering, performance, representation, and simulation. With this, classical distinctions between flesh and machines dissolve, and we find ourselves within a new borderless zone, a new body future, desperately in need of a way of articulating issues related to multiplicity, contingency, and dynamism that are the elementary matter of biopower today. If the language of biology works in conjunction with software coding to produce the biophilosophies guiding the construction of the bodies of tomorrow, then this lends great urgency to Thacker's project of pre-emptively understanding the bioaccidents towards which we are accelerating, without much in the way of public reflection.

Equally, the theme of the virus is central to the question of the digital future, as is the communicability of the virus in growing social, cultural, and political contagions. Bardini explores the 'virus' as the master trope of contemporary society. Beginning with the main thesis that understanding the viral contagions of culture and society does not exempt one from their impact, Bardini maintains that we think about the virus today from an already virally infected (socially, culturally, and politically) position. Historically situating his analysis in an exploration of the four medical tropes symptomatic of the different phases of capitalism – plague, tuberculosis, cancer, and virus – Bardini offers some creative insights concerning those viral contagions such as terrorism, AIDS, epidemics, and perhaps information itself that both infect and inflect twenty-first century society. Is it possible that Bardini's account of the virus as the master trope of contemporary culture is the real 'meta media' within which the digital future will unfold?

Politics, Gender, and Religion

In the culture of real-time globalization will the digital future be open or closed?

We know for certain that an open digital future is surging everywhere on the Net. Consider newly emergent technologies such as blogging, shareware, Wikipedia, mash-ups, and Web 2.0, all of which have the potential to transform digital reality in the direction of greater human innovation, creativity, and individuality. To the question of whether digital culture will be effectively captured and privatized by powerful multinational corporations whose agenda necessarily reflects only their own proprietary interests, the answer can only be ambivalent. Politically, the issue is as yet undecided. While blogging, with its multiplicity of self-confessions, on-line diaries, and deeply courageous independent journalism giving witness to political cruelties in many countries of the world, may seem to reflect the movement online of humanity in all its varieties, it has also changed *how* the future is envisioned, communicated, and contested. Although official power – governmental and corporate – may consider the script of digital communication to be running on automatic, blogging is like that beautiful error in the software program, a technological innovation that potentially makes of every digital citizen the creative interpreter of her own narrative construction. Precisely because it is a massive global phenomenon with an always open future – variously democratic, polemical, reasoned, demagogic, critical, and conservative – blogging represents a radical transformation in the actual relations of communication surrounding the democratic future. Consequently, to the question Will the digital future be open or closed? the answer is probably *neither*, the greater truth residing in a careful study of the complexity that is the world of politics, gender, and religion.

Indeed, digital politics cannot be adequately analysed outside its relation to the dramatic issues surrounding the interplay of religion, terrorism, and ideology at present. Even the most cursory reading of daily newspapers or the briefest exposures to the 24/7 news cycle of mass media provides an instant snapshot of the turbulent nature of digital politics. On a global scale, struggles over power have increasingly migrated online: witness both the vast expenditures by governments in creating complex surveillance systems (data mining electronic archives, chat rooms, cell phones, bank records, Internet service providers), and the increasingly creative ways in which the otherwise scattered forces arrayed against such governments have utilized online resources for communication, organization, and planning. Equally, the spectre of terrorism haunts the media scene, with government-issued allegations of possible terrorist attacks competing with al-Qaeda's own production of cinematic trailers in the form of regularly updated warnings of terrorist threats. To the viral terrorism of political forces resisting the Western agenda of globalization, the state today has responded with its own strategies of media terrorism.

The unfolding complexity that is digital politics today is captured in all of its diversity and violence by the contributors to part three of this book, 'Politics, Gender, and Religion.' For example, James Tully's essay, 'Communication and Imperialism' (chapter 13) sets the stage for the discussion of digital politics by arguing that a new form of insurgent imperialism is the driving force behind the communicative technologies of networked culture. For Tully, the language of imperialism frames the how, why, what, when, and where of the politics of communication – sometimes overtly in terms of the staging of media spectacles, and at other points much more subtly by way of the proprietary design of the communication apparatus itself. While very real strategies of imperialism may have interpolated the structure of communication, the media scene is always seduced by the spectacle of terrorism. This is why Michael Dartnell, in 'Grammar of Terrorism: Captivity, Media, and the Critique of Biopolitics' (chapter 15) can argue so convincingly that 'hostage narratives' are now the essence of digital politics. Although not particularly new – hostage narratives, for example, are a crucial locus of American political history – the media figure of hostages is fundamental to the grammar of terrorism. Noting that all politics today is 'biopolitics,' Dartnell deploys the trope of hostage narratives as a way of deconstructing the media story of power and captivity. It's quite the opposite with Stephen Pfohl's 'Technologies of the Apocalypse: The *Left Behind* Novels and Flight from the Flesh' (chapter 22), which examines the massive popularity of the *Left Behind* series of novels (sixty-two million copies sold to date) in the United States. Here the focus is on 'rapture' not captivity, with the *Left Behind* novels telling the dramatic story of an epochal struggle waged between Christians and the dark forces of the anti-Christ in the twenty-first century. For Pfohl, the popularity of the technologically astute *Left Behind* series provides a privileged glimpse of the forms of popular subjectivity supporting contemporary neoconservative politics. The series also provides an opening for a series of critical observations on the rise of religious rapture as the capstone of neoconservative politics, with its dark eschatology and visions of (political) apocalypse. Complementing Dartnell's 'captivity narratives' and Pfohl's analysis of technologies of rapture, three other chapters undertake critical studies of the real world of digital politics: 'The Passion of the Social,' by Andrew Wernick explores the grisly reality of nihilistic violence in advanced technological societies; 'Digital Cosmologies: Religion, Technology, and Ideology,' by Arthur Kroker develops an important political thesis, namely, one that predicts that the digital future will increasingly play itself out as a global crisis of clashing perspectives – born-again ideology and the informatics of (digital) hegemony; and Daniel White's 'Terri Schiavo: Bride of Compassionate Conservatism,' inscribes in words the seduction and perils of the politics of compassionate conservatism viewed from the Atlantic coastline of Florida.

That we are living now in the detritus of digital politics with all of its unfinished borders among religion, terrorism, and ideology is powerfully reinforced in 'Politics, Gender, and Religion' by other contributors, their choice of topics betraying a very material sense of urgency. The subject-matter of these chapters serves as a haunting talisman leading *Critical Digital Studies* into the raw materiality of contemporary political struggles. With 'Tell Us What's Going to Happen: Information Feeds to the War on Terror,' by Samuel Nunn, 'Infomobility and Technics: Some Travel Notes,' by Belinda Barnet, '21st Century Graffiti: Detroit Tagging,' by Jeff Rice, and 'When Taste Politics Meet Terror: The Critical Art Ensemble on Trial,' by Joan Hawkins, we are suddenly thrust into the violent storm-centre of digital politics. Sensitive to the subtle modalities of lived politics, refusing easy polemics, always capable of drawing the focal insight from the web of intersecting political events, these chapters ride the cutting edge of digital politics. Creating new analytical terms to describe a complex political circumstance that is *still* dynamically evolving, these contributions put the reader in the vortex of the political storm: thus the reader is *becoming* an information-feed to the war on terror, *exposing* the 'policing [of] the convergence,' *experiencing* anew the bitter frustration of 'taste politics' meeting the dark angel of terror.

That the broken boundaries and disturbed borders so characteristic of digital culture have given rise to a new form of digital studies – one sensitive to the impact of technology on gender and on the human body – is demonstrated by Jaimie Smith-Windsor, in 'The Cyborg Mother: A Breached Boundary' (chapter 17). In this technological autobiography, Smith-Windsor explores the ambivalent relationship between machines and humans, asking explicitly if after sixty-nine days in an incubator her baby daughter has become a cyborg – a being caught up in a deadly race between bodily health and technological overdependency. Writing as a mother, a theorist, and a feminist poet, Smith-Windsor pioneers another way of speaking about technology: a form of writing not from the outside of digital reality, but literally from within the complex mediation of life-giving incubation and maternal life that is, with all its ambiguities, the balance on which her baby's life is suspended. This reflection on technological complexity is taken one step further by Mary Bryson, Lori MacIntosh, Sharalyn Jordan, and Hui-Ling Lin, in 'Virtually Queer? Homing Devices, Mobility, and Un/Belongings.' On the surface this is a strikingly original, ground-breaking study of the relationship of lesbian and gay sexuality to network culture; however, the essay no sooner begins its exploration of being lesbian and being gay, which is to say begins to queer digital culture, than it opens onto a more general reflection on the question of technology. With a deft touch, 'Virtually Queer?' asks in effect whether the real world of digital technology does not have about it a curious sense of mobility and un/belongings, homing devices, and estrangement. Could the human condition of being 'virtually queer' represent something larger than its sexual register – being digital as always living between the edges of obsolescence and transformation, networked connectivity, and personal isolation? If this is the case, then is all digital politics necessarily a complex mixture of the personal and the public – a search not only for the ethical ends of technology but also for an ethical account of oneself?

Culture, Communication, and Media

Critical Digital Studies approaches real-time culture with acute sensitivity to the impact of digital technology on human subjectivity. *Thinking digitally* implies the creation of a form of writing in which technology is interiorized with such intensity that thought itself begins to illuminate the digital future from the inside. In the age of mechanical technology, writing could still be from the outside, hovering around the edges of industrial technology in order to assess its consequences for patterns of social and cultural development. Even in the era of electronic technologies of communication, studies of technology permitted themselves the luxury of believing that thought itself was representational, still at one critical remove from the (technological) object of its investigation. No such illusions are possible in digital culture. When digital technology wraps itself around the human sensorium, when the human nervous system is invaded by software codes, when the 'soft' matter of perception, imagination, and vision are worked over seductively and violently by the digital reality machine, then writing itself must become digital approximating in its gestures, methods, and speed the (digital) reality principle that it wishes to explore.

Thinking digitally is the essence of the contributions to the last part of this book, 'Culture, Communication, and Media.' In 'The Rebirth of the Author,' Nicholas Rombes discusses information society in terms of its *enhanced* cultural possibilities. In a world of political control and technological surveillance, the ruptures ('mistakes, errors, slippages, ambiguities, reversals, contradictions, irrationalities, and surprises') in the system allow for the resurgence of humanity, and enable an exciting future of proliferating authorship. For Rombes, digital culture facilitates freedom to voice one's position in the increasingly popular (and populist) world of iPods, blogcasts, web design, and instant messaging. Equally important is the cultural impact of digital technology in creating space for a new 'anti-aesthetic' possibility, as illustrated, for example, by the global success of Dogma films and other indie rough cuts. However hard powerful network corporations try to smooth out the world of digital disturbances, hyper-individualism, and other inflections of digital space, ruptures – mistakes, slippages, surprises, errors, and contradictions – are, and will continue to be, a continuing part of digital logic. The age of passive media audiences interacting on a one-way track with content producers has given way now to a creative proliferation of authorship – with unpredictable consequences.

Julian Jonker illustrates this in 'Black Secret Technology (The Whitey on the Moon Dub)' (chapter 34). Through the autobiographical lens of a Black South African growing up with science fiction, comics, hip-hop, and cyberpunk, the essay reinforces the ideological implications of technological living, both on the imagination itself and on the politics of race, class, and culture. Gravitating towards the ways in which living with technology (and growing up technological) provokes new and alternative ways of engaging with the world, Jonker examines how politics and the imagination are shaped by personal experiences with a digital world, and how individual intervention in standardized patterns of technological use can be transformed into new spaces of resistance, new ideological patterns, and new imaginative 'homes.' Like Rombes's 'ruptures' as a gateway to the proliferation of authorship, Jonker thinks digitally as a way of describing the emerging contours of a 'politics of the imagination.' Here, science fiction is retranslated as a 'paraliterature' – an allegory for cultural difference – and the 'street finds its own use for things' outside the original intentions of (corporate) digital designers.

It is not just 'the street' that finds its use for things, but digital artists as well. Stelarc, the internationally renowned performance artist, has taken the project of thinking digitally to its next stage: being digital. Viewing the prosthetic head as a kind of prosthetic consciousness – an 'administrative double' of sorts – Stelarc investigates how to understand consciousness in order to better 'communicate with computers.' If we are indeed living in the 'regime of computation,' then Stelarc's insights are not only visionary, but practical survival habits for a culture where intelligence itself is experienced now in the doubled form of the 'embodied' and the 'embedded.' Absorbing the reality of fast-paced technological change directly into his consciousness, Stelarc makes the powerful methodological point that, today, awareness is heightened by crises as intelligence moves from the (physically) embodied to the (AI) embedded. If 'uncertainty generates possibilities,' then we need new accounts of such strange technological paradoxes that are the new normal, such as 'disembodied embodiment,' the 'personalization' of AI, and the creative nuances of coded language. That Stelarc's vision of the 'Prosthetic Head' blurs boundaries between machines and (human) flesh is illustrated by Julie Clarke's eloquent response as she takes the opposite view that machines are 'not-human' and that the Prosthetic Head is embedded, but not embodied, and thus incapable of slipping away from its status as a prosthesis. What we have in this debate between Stelarc and Clarke is less different viewpoints on the consequences of an artist's vision of the Prosthetic Head than a major clash of perspectives on the nature of consciousness itself in the digital age. Has Stelarc's Prosthetic Head actually gone inside each of us as our 'administrative double' for the future – what software CEOs like to describe as 'digital assistants' – or is there still an unbroken border between embodied consciousness and its technological prosthetics? If we dissent from Stelarc's viewpoint concerning the transformation of embodied intelligence into 'extruded consciousness,' how can we be certain that this is not the form of digital thinking intended to make bearable the future of increasingly prosthetic minds?

After all, as William Bogard argues in 'Distraction and Digital Culture' (chapter 28), powerful forces are at work in digital technology that function to distract (human) intelligence from the challenge laid down by Stelarc to received, comfortable interpretations of embodied mind. Emphasizing the dynamic in which contemporary power (on both the individual and social levels) not only deploys distraction for purposes of control, but also fears losing control to other distractions, this chapter situates the phenomenon of distraction as central to specific negotiations of identity, art, the military, hyperreality, and technology. The assertion is ultimately that awareness of the various trajectories of distraction enables renewed insight into the polyphonic flows of contemporary living. In relationship to critical digital studies, this chapter is of substantial importance because it situates not only the question of the digital future on the ideological level, but also the negotiation of the cognitive consequences that follow from living in a distracted culture. Distraction is both a 'game of power' and a 'condition of survival.' If the triumph of the 'regime of computation' means that we have been launched at escape velocity into self-regulating chaotic systems, then distraction with its logic of 'escape and capture,' 'clutching and elusion,' is now the real world of thinking digitally.

Notes

1 For example, see wikileaks, available at http://www.wikileaks.org.
2 John Sutherland, 'For those about to Rock: We Turn on Our Cellphones for You,' *Guardian*, 7 Sept. 2005.
3 Katherine Hayles in conversation with Arthur Kroker, *CTheory Live* interview, 26 April 2006, available at http://www.pactac.net/pactacweb/web-content/video44.html.
4 Thomas Friedman, *The World Is Flat: A Brief History of the Twenty-first Century* (New York: Farrar, Straus and Giroux, 2005).
5 Donna Haraway, *The Companion Species Manifesto: Dogs, People, and Significant Otherness* (Chicago: Prickly Paradigm Press, 2003).

CODE BREAKERS

1 Traumas of Code

N. KATHERINE HAYLES

Language isn't what it used to be. In computer-mediated communication, including cell phone conversations, email, chat room dialogues, blogs, and all documents written on a computer, the language we learned at mother's knee is generated by computer code. Though computer-mediated language may appear to flow as effortlessly as speaking face to face or scribbling words on paper, complicated processes of encoding and decoding race up and down the computer's tower of languages as letters are coupled with programming commands, commands are compiled or interpreted, and source code is correlated with the object code of binary symbols, transformed in turn into voltage differences. Most of this code is inaccessible to most people. At the level of binary code, few individuals are equipped to understand it with fluency, and even fewer can reverse engineer object code to arrive at the higher-level languages with which it correlates.[1] As a result, contemporary computer-mediated communication consists of two categories of dynamically interacting languages: so-called natural language, which is addressed to humans (and which I will accordingly call human-only language), and computer codes, which (although readable by some humans) can be executed only by intelligent machines.

The vast majority of the literate public who are not computer programmers becomes aware of this dynamic interaction through ordinary experiences. The easy flow of writing and reading human-only languages on computers, increasingly routine for the millions who populate cyberspace, is regularly interrupted by indications that unseen forces are interacting with the language flow, shaping, disrupting, redirecting it. I mistype a word, and my word processing program rearranges the letters. I think I am making the keystroke that will start a new paragraph and instead the previous paragraph disappears. I type a URL into the browser and am taken to a destination I do not expect. These familiar experiences make us aware that our conscious intentions do not entirely control how our language operates. Just as the unconscious surfaces through significant puns, slips, and metonymic splices, so the underlying code surfaces at those moments when the program makes decisions we have not consciously initiated. This phenomenon suggests the following analogy: as the unconscious is to the conscious, so computer code is to language. I will risk pushing the analogy even further; in our computationally intensive culture, code is the unconscious of language.

How literally should we take this aphorism, hovering somewhere between an analogy and a proposition? If we take it seriously as a proposition, a sceptic may object that code is easily read and understood, whereas the unconscious is inherently unknowable. Such an objection depends on a naive notion of programming that supposes code is transparently obvious to anyone who knows the coding language. On the contrary, people who have spent serious time programming will testify that nothing is more difficult than to decipher code someone else has written and insufficiently documented; for that matter, code one writes oneself can also become mysterious when enough time has passed. Since large programs – say, Microsoft Word – are written by many programmers and portions of the code are recycled from one version to the next, no living person understands the programs in their totality. Indeed, the number of person-hours necessary to comprehend a large program suite such as Microsoft Office exceeds a working lifetime.[2] In the case of evolutionary algorithms where the code is not directly written by a human but evolves through variation and selection procedures carried out by a machine, the difficulty of understanding the code is so notorious as to be legendary. These examples demonstrate that in practice both code and the unconscious are opaque, although with code it is a matter of degree, whereas the opacity of the unconscious is assumed. Psychoanalysts position themselves as informed theorists and practitioners who can understand, at least partially, the workings of the unconscious; programmers constitute the group who can understand, at least partially, the workings of code.

A more cogent objection is articulated by Adrian Mackenzie in his ground-breaking study *Cutting Code*, where he considers code as the site of social negotiations that structure and organize human agency, behaviour, and intention.[3] His book illustrates the advantages of *not* black-boxing code. This stance is a valuable option, and the rich insights in his work testify to the need for more studies of this kind. Nevertheless, the argument Mackenzie makes for the agency of code – one of his major points – can be appropriated for the case I am making here for code as the unconscious of language. With admirable clarity, he shows that code is not merely a neutral tool but an ordered system of cognitions making things happen in the world, both among humans who can (sometimes) understand the code and those who cannot. The agency of code underscores its similarity to the unconscious in producing effects even when it remains hidden under a linguistic surface.

A framework extending code's effects into the non-linguistic realm is provided by Nigel Thrift's *technological unconscious*.[4] Thrift uses the term to reference the everyday habits initiated, regulated, and disciplined by multiple strata of technological devices and inventions, ranging from an artefact as ordinary as a wristwatch to the extensive and pervasive effects of the World Wide Web. Implicit in his argument is the idea that both the conscious and unconscious are influenced and shaped by the technological environments with which humans have surrounded themselves as far back as the domestication of fire. The argument suggests that the unconscious has a historical dimension, changing in relation to the artifactual environment with which it interacts. Thrift's vision resonates with recent arguments for thinking of cognition as something that, far from being limited to the neocortex, occurs throughout the body and stretches beyond body boundaries into the environment. Andy Clark and Edwin Hutchins, among others, see human thought as taking place within extended cognitive systems in which artefacts carry part of the cognitive load, operating in flexible configurations in which are embedded human thoughts, actions, and memories. For Hutchins, an anthropologist, an extended cognitive system can be as simple as a geometric compass, pencil, and paper.[5] It is not only a metaphor, he asserts, that drawing a line on a navigation chart constitutes remembering, and erasing it is forgetting. Clark carries the argument further to envision humans as natural-born cyborgs who have, since the dawn of the species, excelled in enrolling objects into their extended cognitive systems, from prehistoric cave paintings to the laptops, PDAs, and cell phones pervasive today.[6]

The shift from 'thinking' to 'cognizing' in this model is significant, for it blurs the boundary between conscious self-awareness and non-conscious processes. These include dreams (associated with the Freudian unconscious) as well as cognitions that occur in the limbic system, the central nervous system, and the viscera, which, as Antonio Damasio has argued, are integrally involved in feedback loops with the cortex and thus should legitimately be considered part of the human cognitive system.[7] The idea that the unconscious may be historically specific now appears considerably less contentious. If the dreaming part of cognition is seen in the context of an integrated system that includes, for example, the limbic system and its associated motor functions, it stands to reason that, as motor functions change in relation to a technologically enhanced environment, these changes would resonate through the entire cognitive system. Indeed, from this perspective the Freudian unconscious may appear as a fetishization that privileges the dreaming part of cognition as consciousness's shadowy other, while relegating to mere biological functions the rest of the extended cognitive system.

In view of the long association of the unconscious with dreams, I propose modifying Thrift's terminology to the *technological non-conscious*. The modification highlights a principal difference between humans and intelligent machines: humans have conscious self-awareness, and intelligent machines do not. Along with the capacity to feel emotions, self-awareness remains a distinctively biological characteristic. Nevertheless, contemporary computers perform cognitions of immense power, complexity, and sophistication. The technological non-conscious, impacting human cognition for millennia before the advent of the digital computer, now has a stronger cognitive component than ever before. Human cognition increasingly takes place within environments where human behaviour is entrained by intelligent machines through such everyday activities as cursor movement and scrolling, interacting with computerized voice trees, talking and text messaging on cell phones, and searching the Web to find whatever information is needed at the moment. As computation moves out of the desktop into the environment with embedded sensors, smart coatings on walls, fabrics, and appliances, and radio frequency ID (RFID) tags, the cognitive systems entraining human behaviour become even more pervasive, flexible, and powerful in their effects on human conscious and non-conscious cognition. Thomas Whalen references this entrainment when he calls the World Wide Web the *cognisphere*, a term that can be expanded to include many different kinds of human-machine cognitions, including wired, wireless, and electromagnetic communications.[8]

Enmeshed within this flow of data, human behaviour is increasingly integrated with the technological non-conscious through somatic responses, haptic feedback, gestural interactions, and a wide variety of other cognitive activities that are habitual and repetitive and that therefore fall below the threshold of conscious awareness. Mediating between these habits and the intelligent machines that entrain them are layers of code. Code, then, affects both linguistic and non-linguistic human behaviour. Just as code is at once a language system and an agent commanding the computer's performances, so it interacts with and influences human agency expressed somatically, implemented, for example, through habits and postures. Because of its cognitive power, code is uniquely suited to perform this mediating role across the entire spectrum of the extended human cognitive system. Through this multilayered addressing, code becomes a powerful resource through which new communication channels can be opened between conscious, unconscious, and non-conscious human cognitions.

Code and Trauma

A promising site for the possibility of new communication channels is trauma. In clinical accounts of trauma, such as those presented by Bessel van der Kolk and Onno van der Hart, trauma overwhelms the ability of a human to process it.[9] In this view, traumatic events are experienced and remembered in a qualitatively different way from ordinary experience. The characteristic symptoms of trauma – dissociation, flashbacks, re-enactments, frighteningly vivid nightmares – suggest that traumatic memories are stored as sensorimotor experiences and strong emotions rather than as linguistic memory. Dissociated from language, trauma resists narrative. When traumatic events are brought into the linguistic realm, they are frequently divorced from appropriate affect. As Dominick LaCapra puts it, 'trauma brings about a dissociation of affect and representation: one disconcertingly feels what one cannot represent; one numbingly represents what one cannot feel.'[10] Moreover, van der Kolk's and van der Hart's research indicates that when people experience traumatic re-enactments while sleeping, their brain waves differ significantly from those characteristic of REM dreams. In light of these results, LaCapra suggests that traumatic nightmares should not be considered dreams but a different kind of phenomenon; to recognize the distinction, I will call traumatic re-enactments and related experiences that occur outside and apart from conscious awareness the traumatic aconscious.

Experienced consciously but remembered non-linguistically, trauma has structural affinities with code. Like code, it is linked with narrative without itself being narrative. Like code, it is somewhere other than on the linguistic surface, while having power to influence that surface. Like code, it is intimately related to somatic states below the level of consciousness. These similarities suggest that code can become a conduit through which to understand, represent, and intervene in trauma. Code in this view acts as the conduit through which traumatic experience can pass from its repressed position in the traumatic aconscious to conscious expression, without being trapped within the involuntary re-enactments and obsessive repetitions that typically constitute the acting out of traumatic experience.

This possibility was explored in the early days of virtual reality, through simulations designed to help people overcome such phobias as fear of heights, agoraphobia, and arachnophobia. The idea was to present a simulated experience through which the affected person could encounter the phobia at a distance, as it were, where fear remained at a tolerable level. As the person grew habituated and less fearful, the simulated experience was gradually intensified, with habituation occurring at each step. When the stimulus reached real-life levels and the person could tolerate it, the therapy was considered successful.[11]

Useful as these therapies may have been for particular phobias, they focused on a narrow range of traumatic experiences and used code in a purely practical way without deeper theoretical resonances. More interesting from a theoretical perspective are recent cultural productions that explore through fictional narratives the ways in which code can be appropriated as a resource to deal with trauma. Precisely because these are works of the imagination, they can shape their narratives to probe the deeper implications of what it means for code to entrain human behaviour. They consequently have much to say about the ways in which the technological non-conscious operates with unprecedented cognitive power in conjunction with the performances of intelligent machines; they explore the implications of these enactments for the computational present and the even more computationally intensive future; and they meditate upon the ethical significance of enmeshing human agency within the optic fibres, data flows, and smart environments of the cognisphere.

To explore these interrogations of the role of code in the cultural imaginary, I will focus on three works, each setting up a different relationship between trauma and code and each produced within a different medium. First, William Gibson's print novel *Pattern Recognition* represents a complex transmission pathway for trauma in which code plays a central role, by breaking the cycle of obsessive repetition and allowing the trauma to reach powerful artistic expression that can touch others and even initiate a process of healing.[12] *Pattern Recognition* makes extensive use of ekphrasis, the verbal representation of a visual representation, creating through its verbal art the representation of video segments released on the Internet (and therefore mediated through code).[13] The footage, as the 135 segments are called by those who avidly seek them out, becomes a topic of intense interest and speculation for the online discussion site F:F:F (Fetish:Footage:Forum), leading to a confrontation with trauma staged on multiple levels. Second, Mamoru Oshii's film *Avalon* explores a different problematic: how code controls and delimits the space of representation.[14] Compared to the sensory richness and infinite diversity of reality, computer simulations are necessarily much more limited, typically evolving only within the parameters specified by the code. The film sets up a structural dichotomy between real life and the eponymous virtual reality war game Avalon. Death is the ultimate signifier separating the real world from the simulacrum, for in the game 'reset' can be called and the game replayed. Code lacks the seriousness of real life because it provides only a simulacrum of death, not the thing itself. Paradoxically, the inability to experience the ultimate trauma becomes itself the presenting trauma of *Avalon*, a condition generated by and mediated through code. Finally, Jason Nelson's online fiction *Dreamaphage* takes this implication to its logical conclusion, presenting code as an infectious agent that inevitably leads to death.[15] The three works thus present a spectrum of possibilities, from code opening the way to overcoming trauma, to code becoming so ubiquitous it threatens the very idea of real life, and finally to code as a virus eating away at life from the inside. Their differences notwithstanding, all three works entwine code with trauma and explore code's ability to influence and entrain human conscious, unconscious, and non-conscious cognition.

The different thematic significations of code in these works correlate with how deeply code entered into the work's production, storage, and transmission. As a print novel, *Pattern Recognition* was produced by manipulating electronic files. Indeed, digital encoding has now become so essential to the commercial printing process that print should properly be considered as a specific output form of digital text. Code thus generated the text but was not necessarily involved in its transmission or storage. Code was also used in the production of *Avalon*, created through a combination of filming live actors, generating special effects through computer graphics, and using non-digital effects such as hand mattes. In contrast to the print novel, code was also involved in transmission and storage processes, especially in marketing the film as a DVD. For the online work *Dreamaphage*, code is obviously crucial in all phases of creation, storage, and transmission. As code enters more deeply into the production and dissemination of these works, they become more concerned about the adverse effects of code on the fabric of reality. Thematic anxiety about code within the text thus appears to be reflexively entwined with how deeply code was involved in the production of the work as an artistic object. The more the work depends on code, the more it tends to represent code as not merely involved with traumatic pathways but itself the cause of trauma.

At crucial points in the narratives, each work highlights a doubled articulation, as if acknowledging the double address of code to humans and intelligent machines. The specific configuration of the doubling serves as a metaphor for the work's exploration of the ethical significance of coupling code with trauma. In *Pattern Recognition*, the doubled articulation connects a physical wound with the representational space of the footage, suggesting that the transmission pathways opened by code can overcome dissociation by forging new associations between life and fiction. In *Avalon*, doubling blurs the boundary between life and simulation; rather than promoting healing, the interpenetration of life and code troubles the quotidian assumption that there can be life apart from code. In *Dreamaphage*, doubling takes the form of imagining a physical virus that is indistinguishable from viral computer code. Here the transmission pathway opened by code is figured as an epidemiological vector along which disease travels, with fatal results for human agency, consciousness, and life. The implication is that code is a virulent agent violently transforming the context for human life in a metamorphosis that is both dangerous and artistically liberating. Notwithstanding the different ways in which the encounter with code is imagined, the works concur in seeing code as a central component of a complex system in which intelligent machines interact with and influence conscious, unconscious, and non-conscious human behaviour.

Pattern Recognition: Interpolating Code

'Only the wound, speaking wordlessly in the dark.'[16] This is Cayce Pollard's thought when she finally succeeds in tracking down the maker, the artist responsible for the compelling segments of the footage. Cayce's search for the maker leads her to Nora and Stella Volkova, whose parents were killed by a bomb planted by the political enemies of their powerful and very wealthy uncle, Andrei Volkova. Nora was severely injured in the explosion when the triggering device of the Claymore mine was driven deep into her brain. As a result, Nora is unable to speak or focus on anything around her, but Stella notices that Nora seems to attend to a nearby screen. She has a computer and monitor installed by Nora's bedside, and Nora, a student filmmaker before her injury, begins creating the images that become the footage. The only time she is intellectually and spiritually present is when she works on the footage; otherwise she lapses into an unresponsive state that Stella describes by saying Nora is simply not 'there.' The footage, then, is both antidote and witness to the trauma Nora has suffered.

The breakthrough in Cayce's search comes when a group of Japanese footageheads discover that the images are watermarked. (Watermarking is a computational version of steganography, defined as hiding a message within another message.)[17] When decrypted, the hidden message depicts a T-shaped city map, presumably the city where the footage's action takes place. A pattern-matching program discovers, however, that the shape corresponds to no known urban geography; instead it is a perfect match with the Claymore mine trigger. In this complex entanglement of signifiers, the hidden message points in two directions at once: inward to the physical object that is the immediate cause of Nora's injury and outward to a representation that promises to link the footage with the world. This doubleness is mirrored by the footage's effects on trauma. It helps to give Nora's life focus if not meaning. It also has a profound effect on others, particularly Cayce, for whom it initiates a chain of events that helps her partially overcome her own traumatic symptoms.[18] The transmission pathways associated with the footage depend for their construction and dissemination on computer code. Without the mediating code, Nora could not create, others could not be affected by her creation, and the footage could not become the glue binding together the globally dispersed community participating in the F:F:F discussion site. Like the doubleness of the T-shaped map, this insistence on the mediating role of code is articulated twice over: once in the computer code that, when executed, creates the footage by making visual images, and again in the steganographic message hidden within the executable code.

Although the footage segments are not numbered, many who follow their release believe they should be assembled to create a narrative, although in what order remains a matter of intense debate, as does whether they should constitute a narrative at all. The *articulated* narrative, of course, is the plot built around the ekphrasis that creates the footage through verbal representation. On this level too code plays a crucial mediating role. Cayce is able to make contact with Stella Volkova after she obtains her email address through a back-door connection to the National Security Agency, the branch of the U.S. government charged with overseeing the encryption and decryption of code. Sitting in a London park at the foot of a statue of Peter Pan, Cayce enters a trancelike state in which she writes an email to an unknown addressee, whom she presumes to be the footage's maker: 'We don't know what you're doing, or why. Parkaboy thinks you're dreaming. Dreaming for us. Sometimes he sounds as though he thinks you're dreaming us ... We become part of it. Hack into the system. Merge with it, deep enough that it, not you, begins to talk with us ... We may all seem to just be sitting there, staring at the screen, but really ... [we are] out there, seeking, taking risks.'[19] The passage hints at an unconscious connection between Cayce, her fellow footageheads, the wound-marked Nora, and the code that mediates their connection to 'the system' with which they merge on conscious, unconscious, and nonconscious levels. The connection remains latent until Cayce, still in a trancelike state, hits the send button. The gesture, taking place as a somatic action below awareness, initiates the events that create a transmission pathway between Cayce's individual traumatic symptoms, those of the community whose presence she evokes, and the healing possibilities of the footage.

Although we never learn the precise nature of the originating trauma, Cayce's symptoms bear witness to its existence. The triggering stimuli are commercial logos, especially Bibendum, known in the United States as the Michelin Man. The symptoms, including panic attacks, flashbacks, nausea, inappropriate affect, and uncontrollable repetitions of the talismanic phrase, 'He took a duck in the face,' exist before the death of Cayce's father, Win, in the 9/11 Twin Towers disaster, but become worse afterwards. The symptoms seem to be connected with Cayce's inability to follow her father's advice to 'secure the perimeter' – a phrase that summed up his strategy as a security expert, the profession he adopted after retiring as a CIA operative. After his death, the phrase connotes for Cayce a haunting sense of vulnerability. One of its manifestations is pervasive paranoia; another is a deep sense of a rift between body and spirit that makes Cayce feel her soul is trailing after her as she jets around the world, tethered to her body by an invisible thread she feels she must reel in to achieve a wholeness that nevertheless eludes her.

These intuitions are embedded in a narrative in which, for nearly three hundred pages, nothing much happens. The effect of delaying all the decisive action until the end is to envelop the reader in an atmosphere of murky apprehension, searching for the pattern amid a welter of precisely drawn details that do not quite cohere into plot.[20] The murkiness finds explicit articulation in the belief of Cayce's mother, Cynthia, that her dead husband is trying to communicate with Cayce through electronic voice phenomena (EVP). Cayce has been named, we learn, for Edgar Cayce, the 'sleeping prophet' famous for falling into a self-induced trance in which his mind could seemingly transcend the limitations of time and space.[21] Cayce follows her father in refusing to believe in EVP and other paranormal phenomena, debunking the mindset that Win called 'apophenia ... the spontaneous perception of connections and meaningfulness in unrelated things.'[22] Yet the narrative seems finally to validate EVP, for, as the action accelerates, Cayce perceives (receives?) messages from her dead father that intervene by rescuing her from harm. In all but one instance, the messages come to her amid electronic noise, mediated through electronic circuitry. Indeed, they can be seen as a special kind of steganography, for they are messages hidden within the noise of other texts.

The connections thus created between Nora's wound and her creation of the footage, on the one hand, and Cayce's traumatic symptoms and her EVP experiences, on the other, extend the scope of code's mediating function to transnational proportions. As the action jumps from New York City to London, Tokyo to Moscow, computer-mediated communication is pervasive, from the F:F:F website to email and electronic music to the creation and rendering of the footage. Representing the cognisphere in which, as a mass-market print novel, it is also enmeshed, *Pattern Recognition* brings to conscious articulation the pattern we are thereby enabled to recognize: the crucial role of code in allowing trauma to be released from the grip of obsessive repetition, emotional disconnection, and aconscious re-enactment so that it can achieve narrative expression. In this sense *Pattern Recognition* is a self-referential fiction, for its ability to create a narrative about creating a narrative through code reflexively points back to the role of code in its own production as a material artefact. At the same time, the possibility that the footage, compelling as it is, may not finally be a narrative at all hints at the vulnerability of narrative at a time when Lev Manovich, among others, asserts that the database has displaced narrative as the dominant cultural form.[23] The apprehension that permeates the novel thus operates on two levels at once: as the visible trace of trauma that bodies experience in the text and as the text's latent fear that the penetration by code of its own textual body could turn out to be traumatic for the print novel as a cultural form.[24]

Avalon: Traumatizing Code

In *Pattern Recognition,* there is never any doubt that the world of flesh and blood exists in its own right as something other than code. This is precisely the premise that Mamoru Oshii's *Avalon* draws into question. Filmed in Poland by a Japanese director and crew, featuring Polish dialogue and actors, and Japanese and English subtitles, the film was released in Japan, the United States, and Europe. It thus shares with *Pattern Recognition* an international milieu and the computer technology necessary to coordinate a transnational enterprise. Even before the titles play, the film presents action in which code does not merely mediate but actually creates the world of the illegal virtual reality game Avalon. The opening scenes depict the terrifying events of a war zone – bombs dropping, tanks rumbling down city streets, civilians screaming and running. The signs of potential trauma are everywhere. But when the film's protagonist Ash (Malgorzata Foremniak) turns and shoots a young soldier drawing a bead on her, his body explodes into pixilated fragments as she calmly remarks, 'You are not ready for Class A yet. You might want to spend a little bit more time in Class B.' In the Avalon war game, death is evacuated of the finality that makes it the ultimate signifier, for it means merely that a player is ejected from one level of the game and must start again at a lower level. Moreover, even that simulated death becomes a matter of choice, for when the pressure becomes too intense and threatens to overwhelm a player, he can always call 'reset,' whereupon the game is aborted.

No sooner are these ontological boundaries established, however, than the film renders them ambiguous. The game's dangers are not exclusively simulated; players who push too far too fast can experience brain death and become Unreturned, condemned to live as institutionalized vegetables. When Ash meets Stunner (Bartek Swiderski), one of her former teammates from Wizard Party (as one of the VR teams is called), she learns that their leader Murphy (Jerzy Gudejko) suffered this fate. Stunner suggests that Murphy was searching for the gate that would lead to Special A, a secret, ultra-high level where one cannot call 'reset' and must play the game to the end. The sign that signals proximity to the gate is the Ghost, a mysterious apparition manifested as a luminous, floating young girl. 'Killing' her opens the gate, but her appearance is also accompanied by grave danger. Murphy's mistake, Stunner suggests, was to go after the Ghost, and as a result he became Unreturned.

Although Wizard Party was so good that its exploits were legendary, it broke up when one of its members disobeyed orders, panicked, and called 'reset,' thereby bringing ignominy upon the team. Unaccustomed to defeat, the members thereafter loathed one another, and the team was dissolved. The guilty player, so rumour goes, was none other than Ash. Ironically, the 'reset' call, designed to abort the game when it threatens to become traumatic, itself becomes for Ash the source of her traumatic symptoms, associated with a potent brew of intense fear, shame, and repulsion at her inability to control her emotions. She exhibits classic indications of trauma, including dissociation, flashbacks, and isolation. Her sole companion is her dog, a lugubrious basset hound. The film's representation of her condition is heightened by the landscape of urban blight she inhabits, the dreary communal kitchens where she watches Stunner wolf down disgusting gruel, and the sepia-coloured cinematography. Given this grim world, it is no wonder that disillusioned young people prefer the excitement of the virtual reality game or that the authorities have declared it illegal. Entering the game world is a relief not least because it offers an objective correlative for trauma in a context where one has at least a theoretical possibility of winning the game. The game's addictive appeal is clearly evident in Ash's lifestyle. Surrounded by code, immersed in code, she experiences simulation as if it were life, investing in it all her emotional energy, and lives life as if it were a pale imitation of the virtual reality war game. The ironic motto of the U.S. Army's Program for Simulation Training and Instrumentation, All but War Is Simulation, has come true for her.[25]

After Ash's encounter with Stunner, she experiences in her next game a wrenching flashback, involuntarily returning to the traumatic experience in which Wizard Party fights its last battle together. The violent experience is so upsetting that she rips off the VR helmet and vomits, in a symmetrical inversion of the scene where the camera gives us a long close-up of Stunner's repulsive gorging on the food she bought for him as a bribe for information about Murphy. The entanglement of food with trauma continues as she compensates for her involuntary re-enactment by splurging on real meat, real vegetables, and real rice so she can lovingly prepare a magnificent feast – for her dog. But when she turns around to find him in her small one-room apartment, the animal has inexplicably disappeared. Since he was her only friend and companion, his disappearance precipitates her realization that she can no longer put off confronting the source of her symptoms. She accordingly decides to go in search of Murphy, which in a sense means going in search of death.

This decision prepares for her entry into the game's next level, a transition signified by the image of her body surrounded by concentric rings of flashing code, emphasizing the massive computations necessary to propel her into this realm. When she emerges, she finds herself not in the war-torn game world but, significantly, back in her own apartment. Previous shots had shown her reclining with her head encased in a VR helmet when she was in the game world, establishing a clear boundary between simulated action and the real world. Moreover, to access the VR equipment she went to a cavernous game hall, the locale's specificity emphasized with long shots of her walking down the hallway, riding a grungy trolley home, and trudging up a flight of steps to her apartment. Now that geography collapses, along with the distinction it created between the game world and her drab everyday existence.

Glancing at the computer screen, she is informed she is now in 'Class Real.' A screen interlocutor tells her that a rogue player has illicitly entered this level, and her task is to find and kill him, which corresponds, her interlocutor says, to acting as a debugger and eliminating a virus from the system. She and the intruder will be the only players; everyone else is a 'neutral.' If she kills or injures one of them, she loses the game. If she succeeds in terminating the intruder, she will be allowed to join the privileged group whose members are successors to the game's original programmers. Warned that 'Class Real' is a much more complex game level than any she has previously seen, she finds beside her computer an evening dress and a gun.

Now comes another rupture in the fabric of reality, for when she goes out, she discovers not the dark and sombre world where she has lived but a bright, bustling, European metropolis, filled with light, colour, and people. All this suggests that her supposedly 'real' world was merely another level of the game, and she has now graduated from being a creature within the game world and been allowed to enter the real world, the one we ourselves inhabit. In this 'Class Real' world, she sees a poster advertising a musical concert of Avalon; decorating it is a picture of her beloved basset hound, underscoring his function as a signifier of the real.[26] Following the breadcrumb trail of posters, she is led to the concert hall, where she discovers, mingling among the concertgoers, her old teammate Murphy.

This discovery reinforces the suspicion that she is now in the real world, in which case the instruction telling her that killing Murphy amounts to eliminating a virus appears as a lie designed to overcome any scruples she might have about murdering her comrade. The discrepancy between what she has been told and the audience's understanding of her task hinges on the meaning of the death Murphy would suffer. Is he a person or a bit of troublesome code? Would his death represent an irrevocable finality or merely another move in a simulated world where the game can always be played again? The ambiguity is heightened by the Avalon concert, sung by a magnificent soprano backed by a full chorus and orchestra. In the Arthurian myth, Avalon is of course the island where, as the words of the song remind us, 'departed heroes go' – departed from one world but somehow still living in another.

Ash confronts Murphy as he perches on a First World War cannon, a reminder of the war game in which they were comrades. As the camera pans around her and Murphy, the music rises towards a climax, with jump cuts between their confrontation on the lawn and the ongoing concert in the hall. She charges Murphy with deliberately arranging the disaster that tore apart Wizard so he could continue on alone and reach this level of the game, deserting his teammates after they had ceased to be useful and becoming, as she says, a hollow shell. 'Do I look like a hollow shell?' he asks incredulously. He ripostes with what the audience has already surmised, that he has escaped from the game and now chooses to inhabit this world. 'Reality is only what we tell ourselves it is,' he asserts.

As the tension mounts and the action moves towards the inevitable moment in which one will kill the other, Murphy tells Ash that when the body actually bleeds instead of disintegrating into pixels she will know they are no longer in the game. Anticipating that moment, he asks her to 'imagine what it's like to actually be shot ... to experience that pain.' When Murphy draws his weapon, Ash shoots him repeatedly in the chest, whereupon he opens his hand and drops the bullets that, unknown to Ash, he has refused to use. As he predicted, his body bleeds and he writhes in pain. Trauma returns, it appears, as the signifier of the real. At the next moment, however, this normalizing interpretation is subverted, for at his death his body does not simply become inert but rather dissolves into the concentric rings used to signify the game death of advanced players. The double signifiers of his bleeding body and its disintegration into code create an unresolvable ambiguity about whether this world is a simulation or reality. Somehow it is both at once, and death functions simultaneously as the ultimate trauma and as a disjunction separating one round of game play from another.

With Murphy dead and erased from the scene, the antagonist that Ash must face shifts to those who control the game. The shift has been anticipated in Murphy's final words. He tells Ash, 'Don't listen to what they tell you. Never go back. This world right here is where you belong.' That the game is continuing into another round (perhaps at another level) is further indicated by what Ash does when Murphy's body disintegrates. As a result of his sacrifice, she has something the programmers of the game could not have predicted – the unused bullets he left behind, which she loads into her gun. The implication is that she intends to make those who control the game pay for their deception. But what does a loaded gun mean when the status of death is ambiguous? How can Ash kill the makers of the game when she may still be inside the game, as Murphy's pixilated body suggested? These questions are not so much answered as intensified by the action that follows. She slowly walks into the now-deserted concert hall, at the front of which appears the Ghost. As the girl lifts her head and smiles with an expression that is somehow menacing, the camera cuts to a game screen with the message, 'Welcome to Avalon.'

What are we to make of these mysterious final moments? Does Ash make it to Avalon because she has a loaded gun and the will to use it or because she refrains from shooting? How can the Ghost, an unearthly apparition possible only within the simulation, appear in the concert hall previously understood as located in the real world? In an interview, Oshii commented that 'Hollywood films about virtual reality always end with a return to the real world. However, because those real worlds exist within film they themselves are lies. Reality is a questionable thing. I didn't want to do a movie where the characters return to reality.'[27] As his remarks suggest, the conundrums of the final moments are unresolvable as long as we cling to the belief that the world of simulation, the world generated and maintained by code, is separate from the real world in which we live. The appearance of the Ghost indicates that 'Class Real' is yet another level of the game. Since this new world is indistinguishable from our own, we are left with the conclusion that there is no escape from the simulation; we too are creatures of code. If the realm of code has expanded so that all death is simulated, this does not mean that trauma is absent. Although death has (perhaps) been divested of its pre-eminent position as the ultimate trauma, it is revealed as covering over the actual traumatic experience, which is nothing other than the discovery that reality itself is generated by code. Hence the double signifiers of Murphy's bleeding body and its pixilated disintegration, respectively identified with reality and code; their juxtaposition indicates that reality and simulation no longer constitute mutually exclusive realms but now interpenetrate one another. Derrida's famous aphorism, 'Il n'y a pas de hors-texte' has been replaced by its computational equivalent *Il n'y a pas de hors-code* (there is no outside to code).[28]

Dreamaphage: Infecting Code

In Jason Nelson's online digital fiction *Dreamaphage*, code penetrates reality by first colonizing the unconscious. The backstory is narrated by Dr Bomar Felt, investigating doctor for the Dreamaphage virus. People infected with the virus start dreaming the same dream every night; the dream differs from person to person, but for any one person it remains the same. Becoming increasingly obsessed with the dream, the infected person finds that it starts looping, a term significantly associated with the programming commands of machine cognition rather than the putative free will of humans. Soon the dream occupies waking thoughts as well as sleeping visions. Within three to four months after initial onset, the infected person slips into a coma and dies. Dr Felt has encouraged patients to keep dream journals, and he suggests that they may hold the key to understanding the virus.

The next screen, an interactive animation programmed in Flash, shows rectangles whirling within a frame, suggesting that the work proceeds as an exploration of this digital space rather than as a linear account. Represented in diminishing perspective, the space seems to recede from the screen, intimating that it is larger than the screen can accommodate, perhaps larger than anyone can imagine. The navigation requires the user to catch one of the rectangles and, with considerable effort, drag it into the foreground so it can be read. The task is difficult enough so that the user may feel relieved when she finally succeeds and finds the rectangle imaged as a small hand-made book. If so, the relief is short-lived, for she discovers that the book's contents can be accessed only by laboriously catching onto the lower page corner and carefully dragging it to the other side, as if the work was punishing her for her desire to return to the simplicity and robustness of a print interface.

The dream journal narratives are wildly incongruous, telling of chairs impossible to move, grocery coupons exploding under the shopper's hat, and skin cells inhabited by couch potatoes. They are accompanied by clever interactive animations that do not so much act as illustrations as performances accentuating the surrealistic mood. The following illustrates the logical disjunctions that the verbal narratives enact:

And by sunlight I mean those sparkling particles the super-intelligent viruses manipulating the fiery burst we call the sun use [sic] to control our, deceivingly harmless, aquarium fish. But then that's another story now isn't it? Moving on, this substance holds our world and all other worlds together. It makes us sad and happy and hungry for humping. [next page] Sometimes this goo collects between two people ... [next page] but love has nothing to do with goo. Instead love is governed by a complex system of ropes and wires haphazardly connected to cattle in the Texas panhandle. [next page] Lucky for us it seems the cattle haven't yet discovered their power over love.[29]

Although the text presents itself as narrating a linear causal chain, the connections it posits are preposterous, from sunbursts to aquarium fish to love controlled by wires and ropes running through Texas cattle. Recall the interactive animation from which this text was pulled; with its swirl of many different shapes receding into the distance, it suggests a large matrix of reading trajectories, which I have elsewhere called a possibility space.[30] The narratives make no sense qua narratives because they function as if they were constructed by making random cuts through the possibility space and jamming together the diverse elements, resulting in texts that present themselves as sequential stories but are socially illegible as such. This does not mean that the narratives (or, better, pseudonarratives) fail to signify. They do so, powerfully, testifying to a cognisphere too dense, too multiply interconnected, too packed with data flows to be adequately represented in narrative form.

This intricately coded work, with its interactive animations, accompanying sound files, and complex screen designs, testifies through its very existence to the extent to which code has become indispensable for linguistic expression. If, as noted earlier in the discussion of *Pattern Recognition*, database is displacing narrative as the dominant cultural form of our computationally intensive culture, here we see that process represented as an *infection* of narrative by data. Generating the linguistic surface, the code infects that surface with its own viral aesthetics. The symptomatic monologic dreams indicate that the unconscious has been colonized by the Dreamaphage virus, a screenic word generated by the underlying code (as are all the screen images). Readers of Neal Stephenson's *Snow Crash* will recognize in the Dreamaphage virus a remediation of the idea that computer viruses can be transmitted to humans and make them behave as if they were computers, here specifically by making them execute an endless programming loop consisting of the dream.[31] Since it is not clear in Nelson's text how the virus is transmitted, we may suspect that viewing the screens of computers infected with the virus is a disease vector for human transmission (as in *Snow Crash*). In this case, the word that appears on the screen, *Dreamaphage*, at once names the phenomenon and spreads the infection, an implosion of signifier into signified that is possible because code is the underlying causative agent for both the screenic word and the disease it signifies. In a certain sense, then, the disease consists of nothing other (or less) than collapsing the distinction between artificial and human cognitions and a consequent conflation of computer code and human-infectious virus. The code-virus pre-empts the normal processes that produce dreams and installs itself in their place, creating visions of the cognisphere, its native habitat, that appear nonsensical when forced into the linear sequences of human-only language. It is not the virus that is diseased, however, but the human agents who cannot grasp the workings of the cognisphere except through stories no longer adequate to articulate its immense complexity. The individual patients may die, but the cognisphere continues to expand, occupying more and more of the terrain that the unconscious used to claim. That at least is the story *Dreamaphage* enacts, a bittersweet narrative that exults in the power of code to create digital art even as it also wonders if that power has exceeded the capacity of humans to understand – and by implication, control – the parasitical ability of machine cognition, not merely to penetrate but to usurp human cognition.

Code/Coda

Although previous arguments have established that code is available as a resource to connect with trauma, they do not fully explain why, as our culture races over the millennium mark, this resource should be taken up by contemporary cultural productions. To explore that question, I want to reference a moment in Joseph Weizenbaum's *Computer Power and Human Reason: From Judgment to Calculation*, when his secretary becomes so engaged with the ELIZA computer program mimicking a psychoanalyst's routine that she asks him to leave the room so she can converse with the machine in private.[32] The moment is all the more extraordinary because, as he notes, she's fully aware how the program works and so is not deceived by the illusion that the machine in any way understands her problem.[33] Shocked by the intensity of her engagement, Weizenbaum feels compelled to issue a stern warning about the limits of computer intelligence. Humans must not, he argues, think that computers can make ethical, moral, or political judgments – or indeed engage in any judgment at all. Judgment, in his view, requires understanding, and that is a faculty only humans possess.

I propose to revisit the scene with the secretary and ask again why she was so intensely engaged with what she knew was a dumb program. Let us suppose she was suffering from a traumatic experience and was using the computer to explore the significance of that experience for her life. What qualities does the computer have that would make it the ideal interlocutor in this situation? It does not feel emotion and so cannot be shocked or repulsed by anything she might reveal; it does not betray anyone (unless programmed to do so) and so can be assumed to function in a perfectly logical and trustworthy manner; and – precisely the point that so bothered Weizenbaum – it does not judge because it lacks the rich context of the human life-world that would make it capable of judgment. In brief, it possesses the kind of cognitive state that psychoanalysts train for years to achieve.

After four decades of research, development, and innovation in information technology, computers are becoming more humanlike in their behaviours. Research programs are under way to give computers 'emotions' (although as software programs they remain very different from human emotions mediated by the endocrine system and complex cortical feedback loops). Object-oriented languages such as C++ are designed to mimic in their structure and syntax human-only languages, making possible more intuitive communication between humans and computers. Neural nets, within the parameters of their feedback information, can learn to make a wide variety of distinctions. Genetic programs use diversity and selection to create new emergent properties, demonstrating that computers can achieve *human-competitive results* in such creative endeavours as electronic circuit design.[34] In addition, more and more code is written by software programs rather than humans, from commercial software like Dreamweaver that does html coding to more sophisticated programs designed to bootstrap computer-written software through successive generations of code, with each program more complex than its predecessor.

The present moment is characterized, then, by a deep ambivalence in the roles that computers are perceived to play. In certain ways they remain like the relatively primitive machine on which Weizenbaum created the ELIZA program – unendingly patient, emotionless, and non-judgmental. In this guise they are seen as interacting positively with humans to provide transmission pathways for the articulation of trauma. In other ways, however, they are taking over from humans more of the cognitive load, a manoeuvre widely perceived as an implicit threat to human autonomy and agency. The double speaking that characterizes my three tutor texts – in *Pattern Recognition* the map/trigger, in *Avalon* the bleeding/pixilated body, and in *Dreamaphage* the code-virus – signifies more than the double addressing of code to humans and intelligent machines. Rather, it interrogates the ambivalence inherent in the double role that the computer plays, as the perfect interlocutor and as the powerful machine that can not only penetrate but actually generate our reality.

Increasingly computers are seen as evolutionary successors to humans that are competing for the same ecological niche humans have occupied so successfully for the past three million or so years. The evolutionary progression that gave humans the decisive advantage over other species – the development of language, the coordination of larger social groups and networks that language made possible, and the rapid development of technologies to make the environment more friendly to the species – is now happening with intelligent machines, as computers have ever more memory storage and processing speed, as they are networked across the globe, and as they move out of the box and into the environment through interfaces with embedded sensors and actuators dispersed across the world.

The issues at stake, then, go well beyond linguistic address (although this is, I would argue, the fundamental characteristic from which other behaviours evolve, just as language was the fundamental development that initiated the rapid development of the human species). As the technological non-conscious expands, the sedimented routines and habits joining human behaviour to the technological infrastructure continue to operate mostly outside the realm of human awareness, coming into focus as objects of conscious attention only at moments of rupture, breakdown, and modifications and extensions of the system. Trauma, the site in these fictions through which the ambivalent relations of humans to intelligent machines are explored with special intensity, serves as the archetypal moment of breakdown that brings into view the extent to which our present and future are entwined with intelligent machines. No longer natural, human-only language increasingly finds itself in a position analogous to the conscious mind that, faced with disturbing dreams, is forced to acknowledge it is not the whole of mind. Code, performing as the interface between humans and programmable media, functions in the contemporary cultural imaginary as the shadowy double of the human-only language inflected and infected by its hidden presence.

Acknowledgments

A version of this chapter was delivered as a keynote presentation at the 2005 Centre for Cultural Analysis, Theory, and History (CongressCath) conference on 'The Ethics and Politics of Virtuality and Indexicality,' 1 July 2005, in Bradford, England.

Notes

1   The immense difficulty of reverse engineering object code was the key factor in the Y2K crisis. Although the feared catastrophic failure did not materialize, attempts to correct the problem vividly demonstrated code's opacity.

2   Robert Bach, vice president of Microsoft's marketing desktop application division, reports that the company employed 750 people, working full-time for two years, to bring Office 97 to market; see 'Office 97 Q and A with Robbie Bach,' *Go Inside*, available at http://goinside.com/97/1/097qa.html. Assuming forty-hour weeks and fifty weeks per year, that amounts to 1.5 million person-hours. To put this number in context, the average person puts in 80,000 person-hours at work during a lifetime. Of course, my argument is concerned with the amount of time necessary to understand the code, whereas the above figures indicate the time required to create and test the Microsoft product. Nevertheless, the comparison gives an idea of why no one person can comprehend a complex large program in its totality.

3   See Adrian Mackenzie, *Cutting Code: Software and Sociality* (New York: Peter Lang, 2006).

4   See Nigel Thrift, 'Remembering the Technological Unconscious by Foregrounding Knowledges of Position,' *Environment and Planning D: Society and Space* 22/1 (2004): 175–90.

5   See Edwin Hutchins, *Cognition in the Wild* (Cambridge: MIT Press, 1996).

6   See Andy Clark, *Natural-Born Cyborgs: Minds, Technologies, and the Future of Human Intelligence* (Oxford: Oxford University Press, 2003).

7   See Antonio Damasio, *Descartes' Error: Emotion, Reason, and the Human Brain* (New York: Penguin, 2005).

8 See Thomas Whalen, 'Data Navigation, Architectures of Knowledge,' available at www.banffcentre.ca/bnmi/transcripts/living_architectures_thomas_whalen.pdf.

9 See Bessel van der Kolk and Onno van der Hart, 'The Intrusive Past: The Flexibility of Memory and the Engraving of Trauma,' in *Trauma: Explorations in Memory*, ed. Cathy Caruth, 158-82 (Baltimore: Johns Hopkins University Press, 1995).

10 Dominic LaCapra, *Writing History, Writing Trauma* (Baltimore: Johns Hopkins University Press, 2000), 57.

11 See, e.g., the study conducted at the Human Interface Technology Laboratory at the University of Washington, Seattle, 'VR Therapy for Spider Phobia,' available at http://www.hitl.washington.edu/projects/exposure/. For a comprehensive list of publications on the subject, see the Delft University of Technology and the University of Amsterdam website on collaborative research at a number of universities, especially Charles van der Mast, 'Virtual Reality and Phobias,' available at http://graphics.tudelft.nl/~vrphobia/.

12 See William Gibson, *Pattern Recognition* (New York: Putnam, 2003).

13 This definition and insight is offered in W. J.T. Mitchell, 'Ekphrasis and the Other,' *Picture Theory: Essays on Verbal and Visual Representation* (Chicago: University of Chicago Press, 1994), 152.

14 See *Avalon*, DVD, dir. Mamoru Oshii (Miramax, 2001).

15 See Jason Nelson, *Dreamaphage*, available at http://www.heliozoa.com/dreamaphage/opening.html.

16 Gibson, *Pattern Recognition*, 305.

17 For more information on steganography techniques and countermeasures, see Neil F. Johnson, Zoran Durig, and Sushi Jajodia, *Information Hiding: Steganography and Watermarking: Attacks and Countermeasures* (New York: Kluwer, 2000).

18 See Cathy Caruth, *Unclaimed Experience: Trauma, Narrative, and History* (Baltimore: Johns Hopkins University Press, 1996), in which she comments on the infectious power of trauma. Even more eloquent is Shoshana Felman's account of the devastating effects that reading about trauma and listening to interviews with Holocaust survivors had on the members of her graduate class; see Felman, 'Education and Crisis, or the Vicissitudes of Teaching,' in *Trauma: Explorations in Memory*, ed. Cathy Caruth (Baltimore: Johns Hopkins University Press, 1995), 13–60.

19 Gibson, *Pattern Recognition*, 255.

20 The contrast between the precise details that are everywhere in Gibson's novel and the lack of historical and geographical markers in the footage is remarked upon by Fredric Jameson, 'Fear and Loathing in Globalization,' *New Left Review*, no. 23 (Sept.–Oct. 2003): 113–14.

21 For more information on Cayce, see Thomas Sugrue, *There Is a River: The Story of Edgar Cayce* (New York: Time-Life, 1945), and Sidney Kirkpatrick, *Edgar Cayce: An American Prophet* (New York: Riverhead, 2000); the range of publication dates indicates enduring interest in this phenomenon.

22 Gibson, *Pattern Recognition*, 115.

23 Manovich comments that 'the database becomes the center of the creative process in the computer age.' Lev Manovich, *The Language of New Media* (Cambridge: MIT Press, 2001), 227.

24 Kathleen Fitzpatrick discusses at length the fears of print writers – especially young white male writers – that the novel is about to become obsolete. She interprets their fear symptomatically, seeing it as a move to claim the cachet of being an at-risk minority while still occupying a hegemonic position; see Kathleen Fitzpatrick, *The Anxiety of Obsolescence: The American Novel in the Age of Television* (Nashville: Vanderbilt University Press, 2006), chap. 1. Nevertheless, the evidence that a number of writers do fear the obsolescence of the print novel is overwhelming.

25 For a discussion of this motto, see Timothy Lenoir, 'All but War Is Simulation: The Military Entertainment Complex,' *Configurations* 8 (Fall 2000): 289–335.

26 Brian Ruh, whose interpretation of the ending is almost orthogonal to my own, cites Oshii's comments on the significance of the dog: 'For the main character, the dog can be considered as the symbol of "reality" itself. The meaning of the disappearance of the dog is important in the film, but whether or not the dog existed in the first place is an even more important question.' Quoted in Brian Ruh, *Stray Dog of Anime: The Films of Mamoru Oshii* (New York: Palgrave Macmillan, 2004), 181. While Ruh interprets this comment to mean that Ash may be fantasizing the dog's existence, it seems to me to allude to the possibility that her entire world is a simulation.

27 Mamoru Oshii, quoted in *Akadot*, available at http://www.akadot.com/article.php?a=109.

28 Jacques Derrida, *Of Grammatology*, trans. Gayatri Spivak (Baltimore: Johns Hopkins University Press, 1976), 158.

29 Nelson, 'Book 4,' *Dreamaphage*.

30 See N. Katherine Hayles, 'Narrating Bits,' *Vectors* 1 (Winter 2005), available at http://vectors .iml.annenberg.edu.

31 See Neal Stephenson, *Snow Crash* (New York: Spectra, 2000).

32 See Joseph Weizenbaum, *Computer Power and Human Reason: From Judgment to Calculation* (New York: Freeman, 1977).

33 The ELIZA program was designed to prompt its human interlocutor by picking up and repeating key phrases and words as questions or comments. For example, if the human mentioned, 'I saw my father yesterday,' the computer would respond, 'Tell me about your father.' See Joseph Weizenbaum, 'ELIZA – A Computer Program for the Study of Natural Language Communication between Man and Machine,' *Communications of the Association for Computing Machinery* 9 (Jan. 1966): 35–6.

34 See John Koza et al., *Genetic Programming III: Darwinian Invention and Problem Solving* (San Francisco: Morgan Kaufmann, 1998).

2 A Game of Cat's Cradle:
Science Studies, Feminist Theory, Cultural Studies

DONNA J. HARAWAY

The tradition of the oppressed teaches us that the 'state of emergency' in which we live is not the exception but the rule. We must attain to a conception of history that is in keeping with that insight. Then we shall clearly realize that it is our task to bring about a real state of emergency.[1]

(Nature(TM) + Culture(TM))dn = New World Order, Inc.
n = 0

'Nature' is a *topos*, or commonplace. Nature is a topic I cannot avoid. It is the imploded, densely packed location for the simultaneously ethnospecific, cultural, political, and scientific conversations about what the allowable structures of action and the possible plots in the sacred secular dramas of technoscience – as well as in the analysis of technoscience – might be. This nature, this common place and topical commons, has possessed me since I was a child. To inhabit this nature has not been a choice, but a complex inheritance. I was riveted by natural law and fixed in the time zones of the Christian liturgical year, and then set loose in the culture medium of the molecular biological laboratory. For people nurtured in the worlds in which I grew up, whatever else it also is, nature is good to think with.

Nature is also about figures, stories, and images. This nature, as *trópos*, is jerry-built with tropes; it makes me swerve. A tangle of materialized figurations, nature draws my attention. A child of my culture, I am nature-tropic: I turn to nature as a sun-loving plant turns to the sun. Historically, a trope is also a verse interpolated into a liturgical text to embellish or amplify its meaning. Nature has liturgical possibilities; its metaphoricity is inescapable, and that is its saving grace. This nature displaces me definitively by rooting me in its domain. The domain in which I am so organically rooted in the first years of the twenty-first century is the fully imploded, fully artefactual, natural-cultural gravity well of technoscience. We do not so much swerve into this well as get sucked into it irrevocably. We had better learn to think this nature, this common and shared place, as something other than a star wars test site or the New World Order, Inc. If technoscience is, among other things, a practice of materializing refigurations of what counts as nature, a practice of turning tropes into worlds, then how we figure technoscience makes an immense difference.

In this meditation, I want to suggest how to refigure – how to trope and how to knot together – key discourses about technoscience. Rooted in the (sometimes malestream and maelstrom) cross-stitched disciplines of science studies, this short essay is part of a larger, shared task of using antiracist feminist theory and cultural studies to produce worldly interference patterns. Because I think the practices that constitute technoscience build worlds that do not overflow with choice about inhabiting them, I want to help foment a state of emergency in what counts as 'normal' in technoscience and in its analysis. Queering what counts as nature is my categorical imperative. Queering specific normalized categories is not for the easy frisson of transgression, but for the hope for livable worlds. What is normal in technoscience, and in its analysis, is all too often war, with all its infinitely ramifying structures and stratagems. All too often, the war of words and things is the luminous figure for theory, explanation, and narrative.

A lurking question stalks the project of refiguration: How can science studies scholars take seriously the constitutively militarized practice of technoscience and not replicate in our own practice, including the material-semiotic flesh of our language, the worlds we analyse? How can metaphor be kept from collapsing into the thing-in-itself? Must technoscience – with all its parts, actors, and actants, human and not – be described relentlessly as an array of interlocking agonistic fields, where practice is modelled as military combat, sexual domination, security maintenance, and market strategy? How not? Let us work by learning to play an old game. After all, ever since the Second World War, game theory has had a very high profile in technoscience, much envied and imitated in the human sciences and popular culture alike.[2] Let us turn to a game made of figures – string figures. Here we might find some knots of interest for tying up approaches to technoscience.

Cat's Cradle

In setting up a game of cat's cradle for science studies aficionado/as who want time off from the video arcade shoot-em-ups of much scholarly practice, I need to hold onto two strands that structure all the figures:

(1) Feminist, multicultural, antiracist technoscience projects aim to intervene in what can count as a good primal story, reliable rational explanation, or promising first contact among heterogeneous selves and others. Feminist, multicultural, antiracist technoscience projects do not respect the boundaries of disciplines, institu-

tions, nations, or genres. The projects are as likely to be located in computer graphics labs as in community meetings, in biomedical worlds as in antitoxics work. Feminist, multicultural, antiracist technoscience projects include, for example, popular cultural production (film, TV, video, print fiction, advertising, music, jokes, theatre, computer games), diverse practices for apprehending and refiguring the ethnospecific categories of nature and culture, professional studies of technoscience (philosophy, anthropology, history, sociology, semiology), community organizing, labour practices and struggles, policy work at many levels, health politics, media interventions, environmental activism, technical design, engineering, and every sort of scientific research. These practices regularly do not respect boundaries between and among sacred categories, such as nature and society or human and non-human. But boundary crossing in itself is not very interesting for feminist, multicultural, antiracist technoscience projects. Technoscience provokes an interest in zones of implosion, more than in boundaries, crossed or not. The most interesting question is, What forms of life survive and flourish in those dense, imploded zones?

(2) Textual rereading is never enough, even if one defines the text as the world. Reading, no matter how active, is not a powerful enough trope; we do not swerve decisively enough. The trick is to make metaphor and materiality implode in the culturally specific apparatuses of bodily production. What constitutes an apparatus of bodily production cannot be known in advance of engaging in the always messy projects of description, narration, intervention, inhabiting, conversing, exchanging, and building. The point is to get at how worlds are made and unmade, in order to participate in the processes, in order to foster some forms of life and not others. If technology, like language, is a form of life, we cannot afford neutrality about its constitution and sustenance. The point is not just to read the webs of knowledge production; the point is to reconfigure what counts as knowledge in the interests of reconstituting the generative forces of embodiment. I am calling this practice *materialized refiguration*; both words matter. The point is, in short, to make a difference – however modestly, however partially, however much without either narrative or scientific guarantees. In more innocent times, long, long ago, such a desire to be worldly was called activism. I prefer to call these desires and practices by the names of the entire, open array of feminist, multicultural, antiracist technoscience projects.

Optical metaphors are unavoidable in figuring technoscience.[3] Critical vision has been central to critical theory, which aims to unmask the lies of the established disorder that appears as transparently normal.[4] Critical theory is about a certain kind of 'negativity' – that is, the relentless commitment to show that the established disorder is not necessary, nor perhaps even 'real.' The world can be otherwise; that is what technoscience studies can be about. Technoscience studies can inherit the bracing negativity of critical theory without resurrecting its Marxist humanist ontologies and teleologies. If the poison of metaphor-free facticity can be neutralized by the tropic materiality of worldly engagement – and again, engagement without narrative or scientific guarantees – then technoscience studies will have done its job. Perhaps cracking open possibilities for belief in more livable worlds would be the most incisive kind of theory, indeed, even the most scientific kind of undertaking. Perhaps this is part of what Sandra Harding means by 'strong objectivity'.[5] 'High' theory might be about pushing critical negativity to its extreme – that is, towards hope in the midst of permanently dangerous times. So, for me, the most interesting optical metaphor is not reflection and its variants in doctrines of representation. Critical theory is not finally about reflexivity, except as a means to defuse the bombs of the established disorder and its self-invisible subjects and categories. My favourite optical metaphor is diffraction – the non-innocent, complexly erotic practice of making a difference in the world, rather than displacing the same elsewhere.

Two coloured fibres run through my work:

(1) I draw on intersecting and often co-constitutive threads of analysis – cultural studies; feminist, multicultural, and antiracist theory and projects; and science studies – because each of them does indispensable work for the project of dealing with sites of transformation, heterogeneous complexity, and complex objects.

(2) For the complex or boundary objects in which I am interested, the mythic, textual, technical, political, organic, and economic dimensions implode. That is, they collapse into each other in a knot of extraordinary density that constitutes the objects themselves. In my sense, story-telling is in no way an 'art practice' – it is, rather, a fraught practice for narrating complexity in such a field of knots or black holes. In no way is story-telling opposed to materiality. But materiality itself is tropic; it makes us swerve, it trips us; it is a knot of the textual, technical, mythic/oneiric, organic, political, and economic.

I try to attend to the differently situated human and non-human actors and actants that encounter each other in interactions that materialize worlds in some forms rather than others. My purpose is to argue for a certain kind of practice of situated knowledges in the worlds of technoscience, worlds whose fibres reach deep and wide in the tissues of the planet. These are the worlds in which the axes of the technical, organic, mythic, political, economic, and textual intersect in optically and gravitationally dense nodes that function like wormholes to cast us into the turbulent and barely charted territories of technoscience.

Along with other science studies scholars, I use the terms *actors*, *agencies*, and *actants* for both human and non-human entities.[6] Remember, however, that what counts as human and as non-human is not given by definition, but only by relation, by engagement in situated, worldly encounters, where boundaries take shape and categories sediment. If feminist, antiracist, multicultural science studies – not to mention technoscience – have taught us anything, it is that what counts as human is not, and should not be, self-evident. The same thing should be true of machines, and of non-machine, non-human entities in general, whatever they are. Both technoscience and technoscience studies teach people like those likely to be reading this essay, who like me are kicking and screaming in symptomatic Western universalist objection, that there is no pan-human, no pan-machine, no pan-nature, no pan-culture. The saving negativity of critical theory teaches the same thing. There are only specific worlds, and these are irreducibly tropic and contingent.

The choice to use the terms *actors*, *agencies*, and *actants* invites trouble, but it circumvents worse trouble, I hope. The invited trouble is obvious. Actors and agents seem a lot like the self-moving entities of a cosmos furnished in enduring Aristotelian style. They look a lot like preformed, modular subjects or core substances, with adhering accidents. Actors and agents act; they author action; all real agency is theirs. All else is patient, if occasionally passionate. All else is ground, resource, matrix, screen, secret to be revealed, fair game to be hunted by the hero, who is, to repeat ad nauseam, the actor. Actants are a little better; they at least are collectives for a semiotic action-function in a narrative, and not just fictionally coherent, single substance-actors. Actants are bundles of action-functions; they are not Actors and Heroes. To understand a story, it is almost never a mistake to anthropomorphize an actor; it might be a big mistake to anthropomorphize an actant. Part of the legacy of all this Aristotelian furniture is that everything in the world not 'self-moving' (and guess who is most self-moving of all – our old friend, the self-invisible man) ends up having to be patient. Non-human nature (including most white women, people of colour, the sick, and others with reduced powers of self-direction compared to the One True Copy of the Prime Mover) has been especially patient. (As you can see, this little lesson in the history of philosophy is a bit eclectic. No matter, cosmic interior decorating in post-pomo essays shows worse taste than that.)

To insist that both those humans denied the power of self-motion in the history of Western philosophy and also all of non-human nature be seen to be lively, consequential, where the action is, agents, actors, etc. – in short, movers and shakers in the knowledge-production game – I am willing to risk the metaphysical chronic fatigue syndrome induced by the language of agencies and actors. I do not yet know how to insist on such things well enough by a means other than stressing one pole of a disreputable binary, while refusing to use the more patient pole for much of anything. This is an occupational hazard for feminists of my cultural history. We seem terribly afraid of patience; we mistake it for passivity. Hardly any wonder. Like the characters in Marge Piercy's *Woman on the Edge of Time*, I do not know how to leap out of my natural-cultural history to make it all come out right.[7]

I try to get out of the trouble my language invites by stressing that the agencies and actors are *never* preformed, prediscursive, just out there, substantial, concrete, neatly bounded before anything happens, only waiting for a veil to be lifted and 'land ho!' to be pronounced. Human and non-human, *all* entities take shape in encounters, in practices; and the actors and partners in encounters are not all human, to say the least. Further, many of these non-human partners and actors are not very natural, and certainly not original. And all humans are not the Same. This is a key difference from the way the humans and the non-human components of knowledge production are generally figured in scientific discourse. In that kind of discourse, the objects of discovery and explanation might be hidden, but they are preformed, there, ready for the first voyager to pronounce 'land ho!' and forever after pose as the ventriloquist (representor) to the way the world really is. And the subjects/actors who do the discovering are, at least ideally, interchangeable, all the Same, self-invisible, reliable, modest witnesses – self-invisible, transcendent Subjects, in short, out on a noble journey to report on embodied Nature. Traditional scientific realism depends on that kind of reality, where nature and society are 'really,' foundationally, there. It is really existing reality, a bit like actually existing socialism used to be – quite totalitarian, really, though said to be fully objective, that is, full of objects. I find such realism simply objectionable, and full of nothing but tricks. Expunging metaphoricity from the sacred realm of facticity depends on the conjuring trick of establishing the categorical purity of nature and society, non-human and human.

All that is needed for a game of cat's cradle is now in play. Drawn into patterns taught me by a myriad of other practitioners in technoscience worlds, I would like to make an elementary string figure in the form of a cartoon outline of the interknitted discourses named (1) cultural studies; (2) feminist, multicultural, antiracist science projects; and (3) science studies. Like other worldly entities, these discourses do not exist entirely outside each other. They are not preconstituted, nicely bounded scholarly practices or doctrines that confront each other in debate or exchange, pursuing wars of words or cashing in on academic markets, and at best hoping to form uneasy scholarly or political alliances and deals. Rather, the three names are place markers, emphases, or tool kits – knots, if you will – in a constitutively interactive, collaborative process of trying to make sense of the natural worlds we inhabit and that inhabit us, that is, the worlds of technoscience. I will barely sketch what draws me into the three interlocked webs. My intention is that readers will pick up the patterns, remember what others have learned how to do, invent promising knots, and suggest other figures that will make us swerve from the established disorder of finished, deadly worlds.

Cultural Studies: A set of discourses about the apparatus of bodily/cultural production; emphasis on the irreducible specificity of that apparatus for each entity. Not culture only as symbols and meanings, not comparative culture studies, but culture as an account of the agencies, hegemonies, counter-hegemonies, and unexpected possibilities of bodily construction. Deep debts to Marxism, psychoanalysis, theories of hegemony, communications studies, critical theory of the Frankfurt variety, the political and scholarly cauldron of the Centre for Cultural Studies at the University of Birmingham. Relentless attention to the ties of power and embodiment, metaphoricity and facticity, location and knowledge. Unconvinced by claims about insuperable natural divides between high and low culture, science and everything else, words and things, theory and practice.[8]

Feminist, Multicultural, and Antiracist Theory/Projects: The view from the marked bodies in the stories, discourses, and practices; marked positions; situated knowledges, where the description of the situation is never self-evident, never simply 'concrete,' always critical; the kind of standpoint with stakes in showing how 'gender,' 'race,' or any structured inequality in each interlocking specific instance gets built into the world – that is, not 'gender' or 'race' as attributes or as properties, but 'racialized gender' as a practice that builds worlds and objects in some ways rather than others, that gets built into objects and practices and exists in no other way. Bodies in the making, not bodies made. Neither gender nor race is something with an 'origin,' for example, in the family, that then travels out into the rest of the social world, or from nature into culture, from family into society, from slavery or conquest into the present. Rather, gender and race are built into practice, which is the social, and have no other reality, no origin, no status as properties. Feminist, antiracist, and multicultural locations shape the standpoint from which the need for an elsewhere, for 'difference' is undeniable. This is the unreconciled position for critical inquiry about apparatuses of bodily production. Denaturalization without dematerialization; questioning representation with a vengeance.[9]

Science Studies: reflexivity, constructionism, technoscience instead of science and technology, science in action, science in the making (not science made), actors and networks, literary/social/material technologies for establishing matters of fact, science as practice and culture, boundary objects, the right tools for the job, artefacts with politics, delegated labour, dead labour, confronting nature, the culture of no culture, the nature of no nature, nature fully operationalized, escape velocities, obligatory compared with distributed passage points, representing and intervening, how experiments end, social epistemology. All the disciplines of science studies: history, philosophy, sociology, semiology, and anthropology; but also the formation of science studies out of the histories of radical science movements, community organizing, and policy-directed work. These histories are regularly erased in the hegemonic accounts of disciplinary and interdisciplinary development in the academy and the professions.[10]

I seek a knotted analytical practice, one that gets tangled up among these three internally non-homogeneous, non-exclusive, often mutually constitutive, but also non-isomorphic and sometimes mutually repellent webs of discourse. The tangles are necessary to effective critical practice. Let me name this knot tendentiously and without commas: antiracist multicultural feminist studies of technoscience – that is, a practice of critical theory as cat's cradle games.[11] This is a game for inquiring into all the oddly configured categories clumsily called things like science, gender, race, class, nation, or discipline. It is a game that requires heterogeneous players, who cannot all be members of any one category, no matter how mobile and inclusive the category seems to be to those inside it. I want to call the problematic but inescapable world of antiracist feminist multicultural studies of technoscience simply 'cat's cradle.' Cat's cradle is a game for nominalists like me who cannot not desire what we cannot possibly have. As soon as possession enters the game, the string figures freeze into a lying pattern.

Cat's cradle is about patterns and knots; the game takes great skill and can result in some serious surprises. One person can build up a large repertoire of string figures on a single pair of hands; but the cat's cradle figures can be passed back and forth on the hands of several players, who add new moves in the building of complex patterns. Cat's cradle invites a sense of collective work, of one person not being able to make all the patterns alone. One does not 'win' at cat's cradle; the goal is more interesting and more open-ended than that. It is not always possible to repeat interesting patterns, and figuring out what happened to result in intriguing patterns is an embodied analytical skill. The game is played around the world and can have considerable cultural significance. Cat's cradle is both local and global, distributed and knotted together.

If we do not learn how to play cat's cradle well, we can just make a tangled mess. But if we attend to scholarly, as well as technoscientific, cat's cradle with as much loving attention as has been lavished on high-status war games, we might learn something about how worlds get made and unmade, and for whom. 'String theory' and 'super string theory' are names for high-status explanatory models in cosmology and physics. These theories of the universe are designated TOE, – that is, a theory of everything. TOE is a joke, of course, but a very revealing one about the deep ideological resonances and commitment to unified totality in the knowledge-power games of the 'hard' sciences, with physics and mathematics the 'hardest' cases of all.[12] Cat's cradle is not that kind of game; its string theories are not theories of everything. Cat's cradle is, however, a mathematical game about complex, collaborative practices for making and passing on culturally interesting patterns. Cat's cradle belongs to no one, to no 'one' culture or self, to no frozen subject or object. Cat's cradle is a wonderful game for demystifying notions like subject positions and fields of discourse. I like the trope embedded in this string theory. Cat's cradle players are very unlikely to think that war games give the best models of knowledge-building and the best tropes for one's own practice. Narrative structures built on miming cat's cradle patterns would not produce another Sacred Image of the Same.

Cat's cradle is where I think the action is in science studies, feminist studies, antiracism, and cultural studies – not in the mind-numbing militarized games of endless agonistic encounters and trials of strength passing as critical theory and as technoscience. If, as we must do, we are fruitfully to mistake the world for the trope, and the trope for our own method, in a spiralling mimesis, cat's cradle promises to be a less-deadly version for moral discourse, knowledge claims, and critical practice than heroic trials of strength. Tracing networks and configuring agencies/actors/actants in antiracist feminist multicultural studies of technoscience might lead us to places different from those reached by tracing actors and actants through networks in yet another war game. I prefer cat's cradle as an actor-network theory. The issues here are not 'mere' metaphors and stories; the issues are about the semiosis of embodiment, or, in Judith Butler's nicely punning phrase, about 'bodies that matter.'[13]

Notes

1 Walter Benjamin, *Illuminations: Essays and Reflections*, trans. Hannah Arendt (New York: Schocken, 1969 [1955]), 257.

2 In 'The Ontology of the Enemy,' a paper presented to the Berlin Summer Academy on Large Technical Systems, session on Computational Systems, 27 July 1993, Peter Galison discusses the mid-century constitution of the enemy-machine (the 'servomechanical enemy') in the convergence of war propaganda in the Second World War and the Cold War, game theory, operations research, and cybernetics. This cybernetic enemy was crucial to refiguring the human-machine boundary in American culture broadly, producing both technical and popular paradigms for human action and theoretical explanation in the natural and human sciences. See also Donna J. Haraway: 'The Biological Enterprise: Sex, Mind, and Profit from Human Engineering to Sociobiology,' *Radical History Review* 20 (Spring/Summer 1979): 206–37; 'The High Cost of Information in Post-World War II Evolutionary Biology: Ergonomics, Semiotics, and the Sociobiology of Communications Systems,' *Philosophical Forum* 13/2–3 (1981-82): 244–78; 'Signs of Dominance: From a Physiology to a Cybernetics of Primate Society, C.R. Carpenter, 1930-70,' *Studies in History of Biology* 6 (1983): 129-219; and 'Manifesto for Cyborgs: Science, Technology, and Socialist Feminism in the 1980s,' *Socialist Review* 80 (1985): 65–108.

3 See Donna J. Haraway, 'Situated Knowledges: The Science Question in Feminism as a Site of Discourse on the Privilege of Partial Perspective,' *Feminist Studies* 14/3 (1988): 575–99.

4 The classical locus for critical theory still necessary to apprehending technoscience remains Max Horkheimer and Theodor Adorno, *Dialectic of Enlightenment*, trans. John Cumming (New York: Continuum, 1972). For a strongly critical argument about the absence of such negativity in my work on the figure of the cyborg, see Marsha Hewitt, 'Cyborgs, Drag Queens, and Goddesses: Emancipatory-Regressive Paths in Feminist Theory,' *Method and Theory in the Study of Religion* 5/2 (1993): 135–54. I disagree with her reading of the cyborg and her particular doctrine of the human subject, but not with her grasp of the core issue of negativity. Such negativity is the tonic for cynicism and lethargy.

5 Sandra Harding, *Whose Science? Whose Knowledge? Thinking from Women's Lives* (Ithaca: Cornell University Press, 1992).

6 See Bruno Latour, *Science in Action: How to Follow Scientists and Engineers through Society* (Cambridge: Harvard University Press, 1987); Michel Callon, 'Some Elements of a Sociology of Translation: Domestication of the Scallops and the Fishermen of St Brieuc Bay,' in *Power, Action, and Belief: A New Sociology of Knowledge*, ed. John Law, 196-233 (London: Routledge and Kegan Paul, 1986); Michel Callon and Bruno Latour, 'Don't Throw the Baby Out with the Bath School!' in *Science as Practice and Culture*, ed. Andrew Pickering, 343 68 (Chicago: University of Chicago Press, 1992); Donna J. Haraway, 'The Promises of Monsters: Reproductive Politics for Inappropriate/d Others,' in *Cultural Studies*, ed. Larry Grossberg, Cary Nelson, and Paula Treichler, 295–337 (New York: Routledge, 1992).

7 Marge Piercy, *Woman on the Edge of Time* (New York: Knopf, 1976). See also Marge Piercy, *He, She, and It* (New York: Knopf, 1991).

8 A bibliography of cultural studies is impossible, but for a view of one concatenation of writing under that label, see Grossberg, Nelson, and Treichler, eds., *Cultural Studies*; the bibliographies in that book lead into most of the other webs. My sense of the historically specific, coconstitutive, cat's cradlelike quality of cultural studies, science studies, and antiracist feminist theory is indebted to Katie King, *Theory in Its Feminist Travels: Conversations in U.S. Women's Movements* (Bloomington: Indiana University Press, 1995). See Joseph Rouse, 'What Are Cultural Studies of Scientific Knowledge?' *Configurations* 1 (1993): 1–22, for a very helpful argument and genealogy.

9 How can I footnote such a pattern of debts? I will not try. Let me only point to a few new works in this web that focus on science: Evelyn Fox Keller, *Secrets of Life, Secrets of Death* (New York: Routledge, 1992); Harding, *Whose Science? Whose Knowledge? Thinking from Women's Lives*; Sandra Harding, ed., *The 'Racial' Economy of Science* (Bloomington: Indiana University Press, 1993); Susan Leigh Star, 'Power, Technology and the Phenomenology of Conventions: On Being Allergic to Onions,' in *A Sociology of Monsters: Power, Technology and the Modern World*, ed. John Law, 26-56 (Oxford: Basil Blackwell, 1991); Emily Martin, 'The End of the Body?' *American Ethnologist* 19/1 (1992): 121-40; Zoe Sofia, 'Virtual Corporeality: A Feminist View,' *Australian Feminist Studies* 15 (Autumn 1992): 11–24. For an ambitious, recent, and already outdated bibliography of feminist science studies/projects, a document with hundreds of entries ranging from activist analyses in the midst of social movements to dozens of monographs and extensive scholarly journal literatures, see the special issue of *Resources for Feminist Research / Documentation sur la Recherche Feministe*, 19/2 (1990), entitled 'Philosophical Feminism: A Bibliographic Guide to Critiques of Science,' ed. Alison Wylie, Kathleen Okruhlik, Sandra Morton, and Leslie Thielen-Wilson, Department of Philosophy, University of Western Ontario, London, Ontario. This large, diverse, and very incomplete bibliography gives one pause when considering the paucity of citations of the feminist science studies literature by most malestream science studies aficionado/as.

10 I have made this section of my string figure mostly out of purloined titles from recent science studies publications. As above, there is no way to delineate adequately the structure of debts for learning to play cat's cradle. Obviously, not all of the works I draw from so impressionistically here are in harmony with each other; neither are they at war. They play,

contest, and join (and many other action verbs) with each other in a complex pattern of inquiry. A minimum citation practice demands at least: Latour, *Science in Action*; Bruno Latour and Steve Woolgar, *Laboratory Life* (Beverly Hills: Sage, 1979); Joseph Rouse, *Knowledge and Power* (Ithaca: Cornell University Press, 1987); Helen Longino, *Science as Social Knowledge* (Princeton: Princeton University Press, 1990); Peter Galison, *How Experiments End* (Chicago: University of Chicago Press, 1987); Ian Hacking, *Representing and Intervening* (Cambridge: Cambridge University Press, 1983); Sharon Traweek, *Beamtimes and Lifetimes* (Cambridge: Harvard University Press, 1988); Pickering, ed., *Science as Practice and Culture*; Steve Woolgar, ed., *Knowledge and Reflexivity: New Frontiers in the Sociology of Knowledge* (Beverly Hills: Sage, 1988); W.E. Bijker, T.P. Hughs, and T. Pinch, eds., *The Social Construction of Technological Systems: New Directions in the Sociology and History of Technology* (Cambridge: MIT Press, 1987); David Bloor, *Knowledge and Social Imagery* (London: Routledge and Kegan Paul, 1976); H.M. Collins, *Changing Order: Replication and Induction in Scientific Practice* (Beverly Hills: Sage, 1985); Karin Knorr-Cetina, *The Manufacture of Knowledge* (Oxford: Pergamon, 1981); Evelyn Fox Keller, *Reflections on Gender and Science* (New Haven: Yale University Press, 1985); Trevor Pinch, *Confronting Nature* (Dordrecht: Reidel, 1986); Donna Haraway, *Simians, Cyborgs, and Women* (New York: Routledge, 1991); Steve Shapin and Simon Schaffer, *Leviathan and the Air-Pump* (Princeton: Princeton University Press, 1985); Steve Fuller, *Social Epistemology* (Bloomington: Indiana University Press, 1988); Adele Clarke and Joan Fujimura, eds., *The Right Tools for the Job* (Princeton: Princeton University Press, 1992); Michael Lynch, *Art and Artifact in Laboratory Science* (London: Routledge and Kegan Paul, 1985); Langdon Winner, 'Do Artifacts Have Politics?' in *The Whale and the Reactor: A Search for Limits in an Age of High Technology* (Chicago: University of Chicago Press, 1986), 19-39, 180–1; Sal Restivo, 'Modern Science as a Social Problem,' *Social Problems* 35/3 (1988): 206–25; Londa Schiebinger, *The Mind Has No Sex?* (Cambridge: Harvard University Press, 1989); Annemarie Mol, 'Wombs, Pigmentation, and Pyramids: Should Antiracists and Feminists Try to Confine "Biology" to Its Proper Place?' in *Shaping Difference*, ed. A. van Lenning and J. Hermsen, 149-63 (London: Routledge, 1991); Susan Leigh Star and James R. Griesemer, 'Institutional Ecology, "Translations," and Boundary Objects,' *Social Studies of Science* 19 (1989): 387–420; Geof Bowker, 'How to Be Universal: Some Cybernetic Strategies,' *Social Studies of Science* 23 (1993): 107–27. The end of the list is arbitrary; the flavour is not.

11 Bab Westerveld, *Cat's Cradle and Other String Figures*, trans. Plym Peters and Tony Langham; research and explanations, Hein Broos, photography; and layout, Miriam deVries (New York: Penguin, 1979). Thanks to Rusten Hogness for his unpublished article on cat's cradle written for the Science Writing Program at the University of California at Santa Cruz, 1993. I also owe to him the joking comparison of cat's cradle and physical string theory.

12 Sharon Traweek has paid a lot of attention to the joking culture built into the names of theories and machines in high-energy physics. See Sharon Traweek, 'Border Crossings: Narrative Strategies in Science Studies and among Physicists in Tsukuba Science City, Japan,' in Pickering, *Science as Practice and Culture*, 429-65. Biology is also full of this mode of signifying practice. A serious, culturally specific, psychoanalytic treatment of technoscience joke-names could be more than a little interesting.

13 Judith Butler, *Bodies that Matter* (New York: Routledge, 1993).

3 Reframing the Cathedral:
Opening the Sources of Technologies
and Cultural Assumptions

SARA DIAMOND

Technologies embody assumptions about both the designers who use them and the audience for the works created with them. As designers and artists from diverse communities begin to construct virtual spaces, they seek expression of the cultural differences that they live. These expressions require that technologies be available and that tools and design methods must be adaptable in culturally specific ways.

Many challenges confound the use of current creative tools by culturally diverse users. Mark Green, a computer scientist and inventor of such tools lays out the problem:

> Most artists do not deal with the underlying technology of digital media, but instead use some form of authoring tool to produce the digital content for their pieces. While authoring tools are of great assistance in the development of digital content, there is a price to be paid for their use. An authoring tool makes part of a technology accessible to the content designer. The amount of coverage varies from tool to tool, but it rarely covers all of the technology and in many cases it misses significant parts of it. In this way, the authoring tool introduces its own bias into the creative process by making certain types of content easier to produce and not supporting the production of other types of content.[1]

The visual aesthetics of these tools tends towards the binary, linear, and rectangular. Music tools employ MIDI, which is based on the Western keyboard. The Western bias is not intentional, but rather a result of where the tools themselves are designed. There is little incentive for commercial producers to invent culturally specific tools because their largest market is North America and Western Europe.[2] Creative users of these tools can therefore either unconsciously express a cultural bias that is far different from their own aesthetics or reprogram the tool. At the recent Dak'Art Biennale of African Contemporary Art there were a number of cross-disciplinary projects by young African artists (from Senegal, Nigeria, and Côte d'Ivoire) all of whom worked from traditional and contemporary music including hip-hop, which they authored, combined with graphics they generated. While the work was engaging, the artists struggled to make it within the rhythmic structures and instrumentation created by MIDI. Even MAX, a physical interface technology that is highly responsive, is based on MIDI.

Digital tools enable classical perspective, not rich planar perspectives or connotation of time and space that requires many transparent layers. It is hard to 'make mistakes' as part of a digital aesthetic that refers to history or craft, or have a sense of hand-tooling on the part of the artist – the products of digital tools are meant to be clean and without artefact. They favour symmetry over asymmetry. These tools are not easily accessible to the learner. Designers often need to be able to program in order to shift aesthetics, but some tools are almost impossible or illegal to reprogram and adjust. Tools are often designed for individual use and the results of their applications for individual experience, yet many cultures favour collaborative forms of expression. Finally, there is little ability to constrain access to knowledge for different groups, or create levels of security, for example, around sacred histories that a community needs to access but outsiders should not.

This said, there are benefits and apertures within the space of technology. Not all tools work against the aesthetics of difference. Hypertext and game-making software fit more accurately within Aboriginal Australian world-views than written English, argues Christine Morris.[3] Internet security tools, a result of commercial needs and the homeland security push might help communities protect their intellectual property and still permit access from within. Extreme programming is becoming a norm in the corporate software sector, and open source has become mainstream, allowing more collaborative technologies and processes to emerge. Open source remains biased towards the West but by its very nature permits tools to be adapted to context. Localization efforts of large-scale new media products are not always a success. Some manufacturers, such as Hewlett Packard and Samsung, are beginning to understand that they need to create from the culture up in order to seed products into these markets. HP has invested significantly in India to support indigenous graphics centres and new community-based printing technologies.[4]

The challenge of representing indigenous aesthetics in the context of the design bias of tools is evident in artworks by Aboriginal new media makers. It is also present in the aesthetics that artists from developing nations bring to new media design. There are productive tensions of adaptation and design as artists and designers from culturally diverse backgrounds challenge assumptions about perspective, navigation, form, and time. Globalization provides technologies, locales of training, and access. Youth music cultures are already hybrid, valuing influences from all over the world. There is a strong sense of visual culture and identity that many entering the creative digital world bring with them. As more and more cultures are online, digitized, and in communication, the pressures on toolmakers in the West to include open-ended aesthetics, and the competition from makers all over the world who will create tools that allow a diversity of beauty within digital culture is already occurring. As well, new cultural forms challenge a new media aesthetic that tends towards coolness, or an appropriation aesthetics that quotes from original cultures but does not integrate them into the production equation.

These challenges exist in designing from an African or Aboriginal perspective, from a Brazilian, Japanese, Chinese, or Indian perspective. Some of these domains have experienced a significant penetration of technology and have programming capacity. Brazilians, for example, have designed their own software, teach programming, and contribute to an international dialogue, but with some frustration. They have dealt with economic disparities by creating 'pocket caves' that are portable and cheap venues for virtual reality work.[5]

Certainly artists all over the world have become toolmakers as well, in an attempt to address the inadequacies of mass-produced software tools. Digital artists such as Elizabeth VanderZaag, Andre Ktori, Mary Flanagan, Sher Duff, Simon Pope, Hermani Diamante, and David Rokeby have developed tools, as a form and force for sociality. This is different from previous avant gardes. Olga Goriunova, a spokeswoman for code art, would argue that software is a culture in its own right. And that code, as a language system, reflects at least two cultures, that of software and that of the coder's context.

At the Bridges II Conference in 2002 in Banff, Alberta, artists, designers, and technologists from Hong Kong discussed the problem of traditional Chinese aesthetics and calligraphy and the lack of graphics tools capable of rendering these approaches into visual images. Teams of programmers working with traditional and contemporary artists lead incursions into graphics difference. Mark Green states the challenge: 'A good example of this is the impending disappearance of Chinese animation. Over the past 40 years a Chinese animation style has been developed, but it is in danger of disappearing since it isn't supported by modern animation software. The only way of producing this animation style on a computer is to produce it frame-by-frame using tools like Photoshop. Young animators in China are learning North American 3D animation packages, and are largely unaware of the animations that have been produced in their own country. If there were reasonable tools for producing Chinese style animation this might not be the case.'[6] China has the capacity to create its own technologies, as demonstrated by the creation of its unique wireless standard and its ten million programmers and engineers, so why not graphics software? The Beijing Millennium Project of 2004-05 is precisely such an initiative, bringing together all Chinese art and design schools, computer science faculties, and international new media centres and schools.[7]

Lawrence Paul Yuxweluptun is a graduate of the Emily Carr Institute of Art and Design, in Vancouver, BC. Yuxweluptun documents and promotes change in contemporary Canadian history in large-scale paintings, using Coast Salish cosmology, Northwest Coast formal design elements, and the Western landscape tradition. His painted works explore political, environmental, and cultural issues and his personal and sociopolitical experiences enhance this practice of documentation.[8] *Shaman Dancing in the Sunset* provides insight into Yuxweluptun's style – he draws from myths, cultural forms, and landscape to comment on the ongoing value of those histories.[9] Other works graphically cartoon the political and social crisis of the white/Aboriginal encounter, including the devastating and celebratory experiences of reservation life. His work resonates with respect for the environment and for his culture, and in the past five years is moving towards abstraction, away from explicit narrative or characters. 'Most recently, he has been transforming the abstract ovoids that are traditional northwest coastal imagery into colour field compositions that fit right into the new millennium's revived appetite for smart abstraction.'[10] Petra Watson curated a retrospective of Yuxweluptun's work. She says the following:

> *Colour Zone* presents an inquiry into the limits and myths of modernist painting and aesthetic 'primitivism.' Lawrence Paul Yuxweluptun's figurative and abstract paintings, and etchings construct a modern/'primitive' encounter that is as much a means of inscribing a new aesthetic concept of form and space, as it is an inquiry into colonial imperialism. Yuxweluptun has referred to his work as 'history painting.' The power to colonize is therefore positioned within these works as a partial, but unfinished, extension of modernism. Conditions reside as a 'zone' with both aesthetic and political meaning.[11]

In 1991–93 Yuxweluptun created *Inherent Rights, Vision Rights*, a PC platform virtual reality work, at the Banff Centre. It was revived for exhibition in the late fall of 2003 at the Banff Centre, having been shown in Paris at the Pompidou Centre and the National Gallery of Canada.[12] Yuxweluptun provided new insights into the limits and potentials of computer-generated imagery. His vivid, colourful paintings lent themselves to three-dimensional navigation. The challenge was to construct the images as graphics images (wire frames and then graphics) and then to create the appropriate ceremonial dance movements through the sacred space of the longhouse. The longhouse was inhabited by powerful figures that hovered, emitting sounds. The movement in the longhouse needed to be circular, from the formal values of the figures to the seating of the guests.

The second challenge was how to structure levels of access to the images through paths of movement that kept the viewer at a culturally appropriate distance from the spirit figures and respected protocol. Lawrence Paul Yuxweluptun assumed that the audience would be non-Aboriginal viewers who were not party to the traditions of his people and would not have permission to approach the spirits. The manipulation of distance and the physics of apprenticeship and hierarchy required by this were not easily available in the toolsets.

Yuxweluptun described virtual reality technology as 'very primitive' compared to Aboriginal science and art.[13] This said, *Vision Rights* remains a haunting and immersive piece of virtual reality art, despite its longevity, precisely because the issues of approach, graphic representation, and navigation were solved through careful programming.

A larger question about the role of language in structuring culture is fundamental to this case study. Aboriginal practitioners such as Cheryl L'Hirondelle, Candice Hopkins, and Luanne Neal underscore the ways that language shapes the telling of the story and its mode of expression, as well as its content. To tell Aboriginal stories using contemporary cultural forms, the work needs to remain embedded in its language of origin with all its richness, nuance, and modality.[14] Cree, for example, a language spoken across Western Canada and used for trading among different bands has sixty words for love and sixty words for suffering. According to Aboriginal cultural practitioners, keeping language alive is fundamental to keeping culture alive. This provides a direct challenge for artists, writers, and others from Aboriginal communities who wish to use digital tools to express culture. As well, many languages, such as Cree and Inuktitut, use visual syllabic forms of expression, which offer an exciting connection to other visual languages.

The CREE ++ project was conceived at the 'Skinning Our Tools Designing for Culture and Context' summit at the Banff New Media Institute. It links Aboriginal artists, linguists, and computer scientists and designers from various cultures who are interested in rebuilding tools from the linguistic concepts of Aboriginal and other languages that remain alive today. After L'Hirondelle, Hopkins, and I worked in Dakar, the project expanded to include non-Canadian Aboriginal languages, such as Wolof from French Africa. Wolof is the trading language that bridges across French Africa and is rooted in the original languages of Senegal, Côte d'Ivoire and other West African nations. The BNMI, Dak'Art Lab, Aboriginal Arts at the Banff Centre, and the University of California at Irvine are currently developing strategies and alliances to launch this research program.

African artists, in particular those from Senegal, Côte d'Ivoire, South Africa, Nigeria, Algeria, and Morocco, are beginning to design virtual spaces. The aesthetics of Senegalese design are visually rich, layered, and with a flat perspective. In bringing their specific aesthetics forward, artists reject the notion of a national culture, preferring to speak for subcultures and specific histories. One of the goals of this practice is for African artists to speak to Africans. The active trading up the west coast of Africa among tribal groups ended by the nineteenth century and traditional religion and culture became layered with Islamic traditions and then those of France, Spain, and Portugal. This shifted many dynamics, including gender, as the previous equality of the sexes was then layered with patriarchy. Africans had little control over the technology or its implementation and little effective science education. Technology remained mystified and activists rejected rather than embraced it. This is beginning to shift with a new generation of artists and designers who are a 'geek corps,' often female, who work in collaborative ways with the new tools, bringing forward their aesthetics.[15]

Taki E'Bwenze, a Senegalese art historian, describes new media art as a rite or instrument of 'passage,' a state of being, conscience, knowing, and development, holding the past and the future in a shared space. He notes, 'This is to say that passage means metamorphosis, evolution and transformation and above all that the qualities are recognized, their power of transformation recognized and the power of transformation is without doubt the characteristic fundamental of artistic expression that is intercultural and African.' He argues that technology redefines African experience at both the local and the global levels, opening up the potential to sustain a relationship with current practice and the future. He sees 'passage' as the movement from one full state of being to another, from a traditional aesthetic to a modern one, from the artisan to high technology, from fabrication to conceptualization. The challenge is to sustain these past states or characteristics of the culture within the new forms of expression. He states: 'The important aspect of work is the idea of the passage of time, the idea of evolution, not a rupture, but a set of continuities that are part of the future. A movement, a stable state that is a way of being, of development already accomplished. This is like traditional musical instruments that allow for development within the culture, that include pieces made with new technologies – rites of passage from one culture to another, a place of bridges and of fusion between different aesthetics and artistic practices.'[16] E'Bwenze's own project is to create a virtual museum of traditional African masks, within a three-dimensional architecture that carries the aesthetic values of Western Africa. He feels that the mask is the ideal portal because it is a reality in its own right, one that contains the energy of the organism that is represented, that of the wearer, and their transformation into one entity.

Ahasiw Maskegon-Iskwew was a Cree Métis artist who took early aesthetic strides forward in creating Aboriginal new media works that made use of the capacities of the technology of the time, 1996-97, using graphics, text, and audio as an envelope for a story-cycle form. *Speaking the Language of Spiders* engaged fourteen Aboriginal artists, writers, and composers in the development of a cycle that stretches from the beginning of time to infinity and then goes back to the beginning.[17] This powerful work speaks of the life cycle and different ways of living through experiences, immersed, contemplative, suffering, and filled with hope. It is a beautiful, multilayered interactive experience that still sustains its power many years later.

Christine Morris stresses the relationship between new media experience and respect for elders and the land, as she calls it, the Law. She says that we must 'fully comprehend that technology is subordinate to the culture and especially the Law. If you do not see the power of the culture you will never understand the place of technology.'[18] Access to traditional information requires that participants earn the right to the information through their behaviours within a larger physical community. It is, however, also imperative that Aboriginal people represent themselves with the new tools: 'In one of the most remote regions of the Australian continent and the world, Pitjantjatjara Yankunytjatjara Media faces the day-to-day challenge of using the latest tools and techniques of communication to preserve and enhance the culture of the people of the Pitjantjatjara Lands so that that culture may endure and continue to grow as a vital part of the global community.'[19]

Morris argues that hypertext, with its level playing field of association and fluid movement of time, provides an ample place for Aboriginal artists and producers. Games structures and visual language are more appropriate to Aboriginal cultural forms than written English, opening up creative territories for Aboriginal artists and learners. David Vadiveloo is a convergent media artist who works in Alice Springs, Australia, with Aboriginal youth who design tangible objects like bicycles and interactive graphics and video environments that afford dialogue and play-acting. What emerge are powerful hybrid images that hover between the spaces and historical time zones of Australia.

Collaborative Culture

Collective cultural identity is built on the basis of a shared archive, which requires the development of databases that incorporate our histories and tools that allow navigation. Databases are deep repositories or encyclopaedias of knowledge, written on silicon. How do database navigators make decisions? In response to this problem and to their own observations, artists have made local data navigation tools, or search engines, dedicated to picking out cultural references. For example, Mongrel has created a tool that finds signs of 'blackness' within the vast sentience of the Web and Net. Search engines are hierarchical, structured through an economy of use and positioning, with contingent meanings and identities drawn through associations. The database is levelled without the hierarchy of story; it is, in actuality, never neutral. Participants author from given sources, the story is re-authored again through each threading; the narrative is collective by its very nature.[20] To allow this, Mongrel's authoring solution is a software system entitled Linker that allowed the easy structuring of a key words database by communities of interest, and ease of assembly. Music and its phrasing could be used to link visual imagery.

A later extension of this work was the ambitious Container Project, now in its fifth year, led by Mervin Jarman and Camille Turner. Mervin and his team ship a basic computer learning/creation facility into a community, train a local group and community, either leave the technology there, shipping out an empty container, or find a local source of technology. The learning and creation and presentation situations are structured as community experiences. Rather than individual towers, groups gather to work and experience the results. They finance their ongoing work by training users in the technology, the design systems, and basic programming.

The LINCOS (Little. Intelligent. Communities and Tropical Architectures) project is a remarkable collaboration between scientists and engineers, educators, government, health care providers, computer companies, indigenous leaders and communities, and content developers.[21] It is a mobile, wireless dwelling or centre. It contains fundamental tools and infrastructure in a physical architecture that encourages community use of all sorts. The community decides the level of outside access that it wants and the form. The structure is built to withstand tropical conditions. Key to LINCOS is the development of community media literacy and adaptation of the LINCOS world.

When LINCOS was first tested in Costa Rica (its birthplace), families undermined the individual seating at desktops and forced organizers to let them sit in self-teaching groups.[22] One of the most intriguing elements of the LINCOS environment is a bicycle that pedals through the village daily, with cellular phone capacity. Villagers take turns calling their relations, etc. The shared cost of the telephone by the entire village makes the service possible. As well, villagers can plan when they receive calls from outsiders. Of course, LINCOS also provides new markets for games, information, and services and brings global culture to non–first world contexts. However, communities control the influx of these media through group decision-making. LINCOS also allows local farmers to leave and monitor their crops while away, creating physical mobility and a stronger economy.

For Aboriginal groups in Canada, wireless and Internet technologies have been the key way to communicate their issues in confrontational contexts. Internet radio has helped to create a virtual sense of community.[23] These movements are part of a fabric of local interventions. At times, technology development becomes a necessary companion to content and context creation. During the past decade, Radio 90 was developed at the Banff Centre. It concentrated at first on issues of workplace organization as well as the development of an alternate music culture. For 'Net Congestion' in Amsterdam, Radio 90 commissioned pieces from all over the world, including Croatia, Latvia, and other sources in Eastern Europe. Radio 90 also provided members of Aboriginal Arts with training in Internet radio, helping to create a station in Morley, Alberta. They collaborated with Shane Breaker, from Siksika First Nations to create a Blackfoot channel. They provided community news and entertainment. With the Internet, they could program for more hours of the day, allowing a connection with Aboriginal stations around the world. They worked with Aboriginal Arts to create 'Sleeping Buffalo,' a Banff indigenous station. To better share programs, Radio 90 created a piece of technology, a scheduling program, and the World Service Scheduler.

In 2001, Radio 90, together with their Aboriginal companions, attended an event organized by eLab in Irbene in western Latvia at a former Soviet radio intelligence station. Using the satellite antenna they created audio pieces that considered globalization on earth. They trained former Soviet army personnel, allowed to remain in Latvia when the Red Army left in 1994, in basic computer communications and net radio so that they could more easily maintain their links to their families and the world. Radio 90 concentrates on work in areas where there is little or no radio access. The group consists of Susan Kennard, Cindy Schatkoski, Yvanne Faught, and Heath Bunting.

Carlota Brito's background is as an architect and artist. She also studied anthropology. She is from Belém (Pará), Brazil, and works at the Museu Paraense Emílio Goeldi, an Amazonian museum in Belém. Of Aboriginal descent, she created a remarkable CD-ROM about the Ticuna Indians (Magüta Arü Inü) that was made with the indigenous group, while carefully guarding access to their sacred information and clearly communicating the process and duration of ritual. A beautiful, accessible, and ornate design work, it will be used within the community as a learning tool and in the museum. Brito is also the technical coordinator of a CD-ROM about the Goeldi Museum's scientific research. As VRML (virtual reality modelling language) has become open source, it has re-emerged as software that artists can employ to convey depth and multiple perspectives. Brito next created an artistic project in VRML that is based on the indigenous codices and symbols depicted in the collection of indigenous art at the museum. The fundamental design proposal of one user/one machine was antithetical to the ways that all of these communities related to technology. Fatoumata Kande noted a similar issue in Senegal, where communities insist on group access and group sharing of information. Rather than individuate into individualistic consumer culture, these collective societies are pressing technology to be redesigned for collaboration.

Different cultures engage different notions of symmetry and asymmetry in nature. Western science embraces symmetry, balance, and perspective as fundamental values. Walter Karl Heisenberg, in his book entitled *Across the Frontier*, states: 'Beauty is the proper conformity of the parts to one another and to the whole.'[24] Some population scientists even pose relationships between evolution and symmetry. Complexity theorists, on the other hand, argue that symmetry is a simple state and that it is only when symmetrical forms break into a morphological cascade that the development of complex systems and their understanding can occur. This process moves beyond historical lineages and considers generative forms as a source: 'Ordered complexity emerges through a self-stabilizing cascade of symmetry breaking bifurcations, through spatial detail.'[25]

Some cultures have embraced complexity, discontinuity, and asymmetry as organizing principles, holding that 'the radical unpredictability in the dynamics of non-linear systems leaves the possibility of unexpected novelty.'[26] For example, the bias of traditional Japanese aesthetics towards beauty includes incompletion and imperfection or imbalance. Beauty focuses on beginnings and endings, not the climactic moment. For instance, Yoshida Kenkō postulated that 'uniformity is undesirable. Leaving something incomplete makes it seem interesting.'[27] The viewer completes the perfection. Painters and sculptors embrace this notion of asymmetry, encouraging engagement. Henry Moore chose to work with biomorphic forms that were asymmetrical, noting that the initial symmetries of nature were shifted by the environment and gravity. This argument works well with interactive media that require audience participation, and with work that does not resolve but rather poses possibilities or questions. Social symmetries are reshaped by context. These problems offer design challenges in software that is made to erase 'artefacts' and ruptures and to work quickly and best when symmetrical. How can software systems adapt to express these values?

Those living within the richness of postmodern culture in Senegal, for example, speak of the specificity of their representational systems, the depth of these systems, and the lack of access to technology, as well as of the idealization of technology. Theorists such as Fatoumata Kande are aware of the gift that their culture carries, but she and many others want to consolidate the discourse within the context of African representation. They need the tools to produce new media works; they want to learn how to program as well as design in order to carry their aesthetics forward. This is a delicate negotiation – the recognition of cultures that have maintained a continuity with a natural science that speaks to dimensions beyond four, that sees time as a complex navigable object, that uses circular forms and narratives in which scientists close their eyes and imagine models beyond our perception, of a space perhaps linked to ritual, prayer rugs, and mosaics. This space of invention, of imagination, is a space shared by art, non-Western mathematics, and science. It is a space surrounded by our imaginings of Nature, West and East, North and South.

The moon is an optical illusion, created by the atmosphere, the lens of our eyes, the speed of light, and time. The moon expresses the pulls of gravity, the power of what we cannot see but can feel. Some of the most dynamic work in new media calls on visualization and simulation – the methods that scientists, computer scientists, and designers use to make visual what we cannot see, what we see within the limits of human capacities and the models that we imagine. This science is rooted in manipulating the large-scale data sets of planetary systems. How can discourse be opened up to allow the simulation of the unseen, whether emotion, natural processes, psychic states, or the semantics of natural structures and systems that have remained outside of the dialogues of science? Nanotechnology researchers who bring together biological and digital forms speak about the lack of metaphor and their need to rely on spiritual and language systems outside of Western culture to express the potentials of their discoveries. Mathematicians refer to mathematical systems and systems of visual representation that stem from North Africa, the Moorish tradition, and from India and China. It is probable that some forms of science and mathematics research share the demands of graphic arts computing for non-Western aesthetics.

Like her former student Carla Brito, Tania Fraga is a Brazilian architect and artist who specializes in the creation of interactive poetics based on three-dimensional modelling, animation, and VRML environments. Fraga completed a Ph.D. in the Communication and Semiotics program at the Catholic University of São Paulo in 1999. Currently, she is adjunct professor with the Visual Arts Department at the University of Brasilia and associated researcher at the Polytechnic School of Engineering at the University of São Paulo. Fraga works in the domain of interdisciplinary collaboration between contemporary scientific studies and ancient knowledge systems for the creation of art works. This type of collaboration could stimulate the development of productive communication among artists, scientists, and engineers, in particular pressing science towards considering other forms of scientific discovery. Fraga has issued a call for

> an extended debate on identifying possibilities for poetic explorations through the superposition of scientific concepts re-elaborated by ancient techniques for the production of artworks. This convergence aims to explore possibilities for the creation of inter-disciplinary approaches integrating fields apparently antagonistic. The overlay of analytical methods, utilized by science, with analogical modes, used by shamans, brings forth practical methods for artists. It permits new structures to surface generating useful strategies. This

attitude engenders skills and permits the construction of artworks, which weave and expand non-linear processes for their creation and establishes multiple threads towards structures successively more complex.[28]

Tania Fraga created the spectacular *Aurora 2001: Fire in the Sky and Hekuras*, in which the scientific visualizations of astrophysics phenomena meld into a dreamlike aesthetic. Journeys are made either into the vortices of plasma ejected by the sun, or into scientific concepts such as 'magnetosphere,' 'solar wind,' 'serapilheira,' and 'metabolism of the forest,' or, further, into the domain of mystical beings, represented within the artwork. Fraga's background positions her capabilities to bridge science and art, develop and then program her own tools, and create a work that is both critique and expression. Fraga is currently at work on *The Xmantic Web*, a sensitive 'place' where the fluctuations of the impermanent process of becoming unfold. Within this multidimensional reality, people will interact, connect, and 'transform this poetic space-time manifold. Inside the Xmantic Web, virtuality, the process of coming into being, and reality are complementary notions that may be expressed as visual experiences either in the form of images or mental perceptions.'[29] At 'Arte y Technologia,' a conference in Brazil, Fraga recently discussed her frustration with the world of computer programming and her many years of struggle to learn the tools herself and direct programmers to open their minds and VRML to her bold aesthetics.

Ahasiw Maskegon-Iskwew, who died in 2006, was a leader of Aboriginal thought in new media. His position parallels both of the discussions above in his call for aesthetics of magic realism in new media, one that would include access to the technologies of its realization in virtual reality:

> Magic realism as a cultural force that inhabits and creates literature, visual art and performance has, in virtual reality, a new and vital mode of expression, one that can accommodate Nehiyawewin and the Nehiyawewin and the expression of its visions. Cultures out of which magic realism arises are excluded from the sphere of virtual reality by its economics and its ownership by an inaccessible, industrially developed world, an academically focused hierarchy. The forces of post-modern critical discourse may be the most culpable agents in this since they have both failed and refused to recognize the crucial relevance of magic realism theory and practice to the most obvious parameters of new media, never mind the more subtle potentialities. The art, literature and oratory of magic realism flow and intersect in a manner that stings and corrodes the monolith of re-colonization. Even on a static page or in a still image, works in this genre dig into the surging currents of the indeterminate and shifting forces of our ancestors. Examine the contemporary discourses of time-based, interactive media art. How are metaphor and metonymy constructed? How does time visit, how does space welcome you and what does it say?[30]

What are the bridges and barriers between Western and non-Western understandings of culture and science? How do humans recognize and make use of visual patterns in other language forms? In other words, when is pattern recognized and how is it meaningful? Are abstract patterns as emotionally resonant as those that we recognize? Can we learn a history through pattern generation for topics, individuals, and power relationships in chat? Will people change their behaviours to produce certain patterns, to be allowed to join groups, play games?

Agency is the fundamental construct of the collectivist, of building a sense of participation. In a sense, collaboration and collective action are a performance, whether writing, speaking, remixing, or moving. We construct our identities through roles and transactions; new technologies implicate us into a network of pre-existing structures. These assume, if thinly, that those identities are ways of being in the world. So much of new media is a speech act, rules-based, and contingent. How can these nuances cross cultural spaces and barriers? So much of new media is exchange-based. Whose currency defines the standard? If software is the means of exchange, what roles does software afford us? This is a very exciting and challenging terrain for collective creation, one that recognizes complexity, self-organization, and unpredictability. Collective forms are equally strong across a variety of cultures.

On this issue, Mark Green has issued a call to arms: 'An ambitious scheme would be to develop a core package for each type of media that could be customized for the local culture. For each culture a team of artists and programmers can work together to define the interface and tool features required to support media development for that culture. This could be done in an open source fashion, or some other collaborative scheme could be used.'[31]

The Banff New Media Institute co-created a new media laboratory with the Dak'Art Biennale in June 2004. The lab ran on the Linux platform. At a meeting about creating ongoing new media research, young computer programmers spoke about their skills as hackers and open source programmers. The lack of resources, combined with the need and cultural commitment to improvisation (cars are belted together with old parts, engines refabricated, music melded from the old and the new), had already created a positive attitude about engineering from machine language up, if needed. All software was pirated, downloaded thanks to Hotwire, and shared among colleagues. Skipping continents, this open source friendliness has been formalized in Brazil by President Lula da Silva, who has made Linux the new official language of Brazil, running all the civil service on open source. Linux still draws from traditional computer science. The *attitude* of supporting collaborative, open source technological invention is what is needed to build ground-up technologies. One of my ongoing goals is to suture together alliances of programmers, institutions, and cultural producers who can create methods to invent technologies across these continental divides.

This essay demonstrates the small steps that have been made to date in this direction and the incredible richness of possibility before us when tools can enable the aesthetic principles of artists from a wide array of cultures.

Notes

1 Mark Green, 'Cultural Implications of Authoring Tools, An Opportunity for Collaboration Research and Development,' Bridges II, Conference proceedings (Banff: Banff New Media Institute [BNMI], 2002), available at http://www.banffcentre.ca/bmni/bridges. Accessed Nov. 2007.

2 The growth of software gaming and digital design in India and China may eventually challenge this statement.

3 Christine Morris, 'Aboriginal Collaborations – Within and between Nations, within and between Cultures, Indigenising the Effects of Media Globalization,' Bridges II, Conference proceedings (Banff: Banff New Media Institute, 2002), available at http://www.banffcentre.ca/bmni/bridges. Accessed Nov. 2007.

4 *The Sims*, a game where players live in a suburban neighbourhood, create disfunctional characters, and compete for wealth, was a failure when introduced into Asian markets.

5 Diana Domingues, 'Living Artifical Scapes, Virtual and Physical Spaces: Pocket Cave and Artifical Life Installation,' Carbon Versus Silicon: Thinking Small, Thinking Fast Summit (Banff: BNMI Archives, 2003), available at http://www.banffcentre.ca/bnmi/programs/archives. Accessed Nov. 2007.

6 Green, 'Cultural Implications.'

7 This massive initiative included an exhibition in 2004 of all the schools and institutions, including Pratt, Banff, V2, ZKM, and many others, culminating in a symposium, and massive show as part of the Beijing Biennial in 2005.

8 Gerald McMaster, ed., *In the Shadow of the Sun: Perspectives on Contemporary Native Art* (Hull: Canadian Museum of Civilization, 1993).

9 Lawrence Paul Yuxweluptun, available at http://www.yuxweluptun.com/index.html. Accessed May 2005.

10 Deirdre Hanna, 'Coastal Catch,' *Now* (2001), available at http://www.nowtoronto.com/issues/2001-12-06/art_reviews.html. Accessed June 2005.

11 Lawrence Paul Yuxweluptun, *Colour Zone*, curated by Petra Watson (Winnipeg: Plug In ICA, 2003), travelling exhibition.

12 M.A. Moser and D. MacLeod. 'Inherent Rights, Vision Rights,' in *Immersed in Technology: Art and Virtual Enviornments* (Cambridge: MIT Press, 1996). See also http://digitalarts.lcc.gatech.edu/unesco/vr/artists/vr_a_lyxuweluptun.html. Accessed June 2005.

13 Lawrence Paul Yuxweluptun, television interview, *Bravo* (2005).

14 See *Horizon Zero* 17 (Tell) for a discussion of narrative, Aboriginal story-telling and language with comparative studies of other language-based expressions, available at http://www.horizonzero.ca. Accessed Nov. 2007.

15 Fatoumata Kande Senghor, 'Collaboration Is a Language and Report on Bridges II, An African Perspective,' Report on Bridges II to Rockefeller Foundation, 2003.

16 Taki E'Bwenze, 'ART = INSTRUMENT DE PASSAGE d'un état à un autre (état d'être / de conscience / de connaissance / de développement),' Bridges II, Conference proceedings

(Banff: Banff New Media Institute, 2002), http://www.banffcentre.ca/bmni/bridges. Accessed Nov. 2007.

17 First produced at the Banff Centre, this very visual site has been presented at the Canadian Cultural Centre in Paris and is now hosted by the St Norbert Arts Centre in Winnipeg and the Dunlop Gallery in Regina, available at http://www.snacc.mb.ca/projects/spiderlanguage. Accessed Aug. 2007.

18 Morris. 'Aboriginal Collaborations.'

19 Ibid.

20 Lev Manovich, *The Language of New Media* (Boston: MIT Press, 2001).

21 LINCOS is led by Franklin Hernandez-Castro. This remarkable scientist researches the ways that 'the evolutionary process and brain architecture influence the perception of beauty.' He has applied this research in the design of tropical architectures appropriate to the culture and climate of Costa Rica, yet able to house sensitive computer technology. Franklin Hernandez-Castro, 'Desino y Consuccion, Lincos (Little. Intelligent. Communities and tropical architectures), Costa Rica.' Emotional Architectures / Cognitive Armatures / Cognitive Science in Interactive Design (Banff: BNMI Archives, 2001), available at http://www.banffcentre.ca/bnmi/programs/archives. Accessed Nov. 2007.

22 Hernandez-Castro underscored the division of labour on their team when he spoke at Banff. Anthropologists and indigenous people were responsible for the tough critique of the systems' impact on local life, not the engineering team. Hernandez-Castro, 'Desino y Consuccion, Lincos.'

23 A number of artists' works in the early twenty-first century indicate a move towards mobility, play with locative media and place, and the engagement of audiences as active participants. Matt Locke who currently leads the Innovation Laboratories at the BBC has curated a series of text-based dramatic experiences. See Matt Locke's website, available at http://www.newmedia.sunderland.ac.uk/hudders/locke.htm. Accessed June 2005.

Blast Theory have excelled in engaging audiences in games, such as *Can You See Me Now*, available at http://www.blasttheory.co.uk. Accessed Aug. 2007.

Canadian new media artists explored the use of GPS tracking systems to create personal diaries or contributory works. See http://kid.kibla.org/~intima/gps. Accessed June 2005. The growth of wireless access and mobile communication has opened the door to significant collaboration between artists in Canada and the rest of the world. Such projects have now become part of Canada's research and creative practice with large-scale initiatives such as the Mobile Digital Commons Network that links researchers at the BNMI, Ontario College of Art and Design, and Concordia University.

24 Werner Karl Heisenberg, *Across the Frontier* (New York: Harper, 1974), 183.

25 Brian Goodwin, *How the Leopard Changed Its Spots* (Princeton: Princeton University Press, 2001).

26 Ibid., 31.

27 As cited in Donald Keene, *The Pleasures of Japanese literature* (New York: Columbia University Press, 1998).

28 Tania Fraga, 'Skinning Our Tools: Designing for Culture and Context' (Banff: BNMI Archives, 2003), available at http://www.banffcentre.ca/bnmi/programs/archives. Accessed Nov. 2007.

29 Ibid.

30 Ahasiw Maskegon-Iskwew, biography on Drumbytes.org, available at http://drumbytes.org/about/ahasiw.php. Accessed June 2005.

31 Mark Green, 'Cultural Implications.'

4 Romancing the Anti-body: Lust and Longing in (Cyber)space

LYNN HERSHMAN LEESON

Prior to this decade, there have been no media available to dissolve the boundaries between art and life as effectively and as instantly as cyberspace, which can not only erase social boundaries but irrevocably alter the idea of what identity itself is.

A precondition for electronic access is being one or even several other people. There are many reasons for this. In his book *The Virtual Community, Homesteading on the Electronic Frontier*, Howard Rheingold notes that people seem to need to use depersonalized modes of communication in order to get personal with each other. It is a way to connect.

Plugging into cyberspace requires the creation of a personal mask. It becomes a signature, a thumb print, a shadow, and a means of recognition. Primitive tribes also use coverings. Masks camouflage the body and in doing so liberate and give voice to virtual selves. As personal truth is released, the fragile and tenuous face of vulnerability is protected.

One of the more diabolical elements of entering CMC (computer-mediated communication) or virtual reality is that people can only recognize each other when they are electronically disguised. Truth is precisely based on the inauthentic!

Masks and self-disclosures are part of the grammar of cyberspace. It is the syntax of the culture of computer-mediated identity which, by the way, can include simultaneous multiple identities, or identities that abridge and dislocate gender and age.

Identity is the first thing you create when you log on to a computer service. By defining yourself in some way, whether it is through your name, a personal profile, an icon, or mask, you also define your audience, space, and territory. In the architecture of networks, geography shifts as readily as time. Communities are defined by software and hardware access. Anatomy can be readily reconstituted.

Masking through computer-mediated communication is read differently than in real life. You can be anything you can imagine, instantly, with very few props or prompts. Self-created alternate identities become guides with which to navigate a deeper access of Internetting. You do not need a body to do this.

Not only do you not need a body, but entering cyberspace encourages a disembodied body language. Posing and emoting are some of the terms for phantom gestures that can be read through words, or seen in special video programs through simple movements such as waves. Codes of gestures can be read by attachments on the computer that articulates hidden meanings of voiceless and mute speech.

Actions are constantly under surveillance, tracked, traced, digitized, and stored. Icons as masks are of particular importance because the disguises used today may determine an archetype of the present that will eventually reflect the ephemeral nature of a society geared towards image manipulation and self recreation.

In the search for contact, computer mediated communication solicits two-way dialogues. These require mutual narrative s(t)imulations. While often subliminally fulfiling and inherently filled with amorous potential, there have been incidents that have caused disturbances. Let me describe three famous case studies in the cyberworld annals.

Case 1: The Strange Case of the Electronic Lover

A classic example is related in 'The Strange Case of The Electronic Lover,' by Linsy Van Gelder, which was published in *Ms* magazine in October 1985.[1]

Van Gelder met 'Joan' on Compuserve, and began to chat. It was learned that Joan was a neuropsychologist in her late twenties, living in New York, who had been disfigured – crippled in fact – and left mute by an automobile accident at the hands of a drunken driver. Joan's mentor, so the story went, had given her a computer, modem, and subscription to Compuserve where Joan blossomed into a celebrity. Her wit and warmth extended to many people.

Eventually, however, Joan was unmasked – defrocked (so to speak), and it was discovered that she was not disabled, disfigured, mute, or female. Joan was in real life a New York psychiatrist, Alex, who had become obsessed with his own experiments in being treated as a female.

The shock in the electronic world had a higher voltage than anywhere else. The assault of this discovery was coupled by the fact that Joan had achieved an intimacy with many people who trusted her. Joan's very skeleton was based on pure deception. Van Gelder is quoted as saying that 'through this experience, those who knew Joan lost their innocence.'[2]

In the real world, it could be thought of as a kind of rape – a deep penetration by a masked stranger. Questions of ethics and behaviour ensued so as to avoid further incidents of netsleazing and other repulsive forms of bad etiquette.

Alex had cleverly called on the icons and codes of a society that has learned to fantasize media-produced females in a particular way. He chose to be a woman, a gender marginalized in technology.

Most people logging on are men. When Joan logged in it was 1985, and women chatting was unusual. It still is so unusual that even today whenever someone logs on as a woman there is a barrage of questions in order to determine whether it really is a woman, or someone just trying on a new sex for size.

It is a kind of harassment that people logging on as men or animals do not experience. Furthermore, Alex chose to make Joan the epitome of vulnerability. Perhaps whetting desires even more by making her paralysed and mute. The fictional presumption was that in real life she had lost her body, yet she could still be seductive. She could even lure her responders, like the Sirens calling Odysseus, into lustful responses to her non-body.

Case 2: Vito

In February 1993 a housewife signed up for a computer service to access information and make friends. She found she was able to form online relationships that quickly became intense. She could form close connections that were hard to make in the busy world of real life. However, very quickly 'she found herself the target of an invisible high-tech predator who threatened to become an all-too-real menace to her children.'[3]

She began to have vile, unsolicited messages from someone known as Vito. She had no idea if Vito was a man or woman, a friend of her children and family, or a psychotic maniac. Vito was able to tap into all of her messages, get a bit-by-bit profile of her, and post wider messages to all Internetters. The targeted woman complained that it was like 'rape.' Again without a body.

She sought out a computer crimes detective. Vito became well known, even infamous. Many people claimed to be him, just as many people claim to have committed the crimes of Ted Bundy.

When a suspect was finally arrested, the district attorney was forced to release him because of 'insufficient evidence.' This raises the question of how to bring law and order to the information superhighway, a place where villains are invisible and users become unwitting victims in crimes of the non-body.

The Electronic Frontier is attempting to do this and have been enormously effective since their creation. A self-sponsored group, they are like what Ralph Nader was to ecology; a hacker posse who round up, capture, and hold virtual vigilantes accountable. These do not only include hackers. The group has also questioned the computer and privacy invasions launched by the United States government. New users are forming the largest immigration in history. What happens to this population's non-body is of critical importance.

Case 3: Terra

About 1990 Tom Ray created a virtual computer that had evolved creatures. As Kevin Kelly notes, in his book *Out of Control*, 'beginning with a single creature, programmed by hand, this 80 byte creature began to reproduce by finding empty RAM blocks 80 bytes big and then copying itself. Within minutes, the RAM was saturated with replicas. By allowing his program to occasionally scramble digital bits during copying, some had priority. This introduced the idea of variation and death and natural selection, and an ecology of new creatures with computer life cycles emerged. The bodies of these creatures consisted of program memory and space. A parasite, this creature could borrow what it needed in the RAM to survive.'[4]

Furthermore, to everyone's astonishment, these creatures very quickly created their version of sex – even without programming! Sometimes in 'Terra' (which is what Ray called this system) a parasite would be in the middle of asexual reproduction (genetic recombination), but if the host was killed midway, the parasite would assimilate not only that creature's space but also part of the dead creature's interrupted reproduction function. The resultant junior mutant was a wild, new recombination created without deliberate mutation; a kind of inbred vampiristic progeny, an unrestrained strain.

Body-less sex in an anti-body ecosystem for co-evolution, cultured in the digital pool! What could be more appealing?

Getting back to the rational non-reality we have learned to love and trust, or in other words, the real world, it becomes all too clear that much that is considered ground-breaking is not really new. Moreover, each perspective we have today derives from a point originally placed many years earlier.

Consider, for example, the rules for one-point perspective, written by Alberti five hundred years ago. His mathematical metaphor was first applied to painting and drawing and promulgated an age of exquisite illusionism. Artists who used his theories could paint windows onto imagined vistas with such precision that viewers were impressively deceived.

Was this ethical? What implications did it have? Did Donatello or Vermeer question the vistas of voyeurism their windows would invite?

In an effort to eschew illusion, Marcel Duchamp investigated the essentials of art production, including selfhood and the uncontrolled idiosyncratic inner impulses. The sine qua non of art, according to Duchamp, is not some essence or quality residing in the final work, but rather an infinitely subtle shifting of the intent of the artist. In works by Duchamp such as *Rrose Selavy*, the intent and body of the artist are the sine qua non of artistic practice. Rrose was a non-body through which Duchamp could escape fixed identity, becoming an 'other' in the process. Otherness refers in this case to something defined by what it is not.

There is a relationship between Duchamp and his contemporary, Heisenberg. The irrationality of Heisenberg's theories of the observer affecting what is observed in quantum mechanics at the interior of extreme physics metaphorically reflects Duchamp's 'experiments' regarding randomness and chance.[5] They were travelling to the same place, but on different roads. Both were looking for the path not taken.

Don't byte off more than you can eschew

This pre(r)amble has been leading up to the development of my own body of non-body and anti-body work produced in the past three decades.

I divide my work in two categories, B.C. and A.D., or Before Computers and After Digital. I will begin with the first. In the 1960s I lived quite literally in B.C. or, Berkeley, California. Ideals of community, alternative, reprocessed media, free speech, and civil rights were constantly in the air. I could hear amplified speeches of radical heroes such as Malcolm X through my open windows. In those volatile years, art and life fused, political performances took place in the streets. I didn't realize until a decade later that the attitude of that era was to form the basis of my psychological armature, the framework for all the work that followed that time.

Consistently, my most relevant ideas occur on the cusp of some disaster. In 1972 the University Art Museum in Berkeley closed an exhibition of mine because I used audiotape and sound in a sculpture titled *Self Portrait as Another Person*. The museum curators claimed that electronic media were not art and most certainly did not belong in a museum. This closure opened a second phase in my work and inspired my first radical act!

Early B.C. non-body works

From 1960 to 1970 I created various wax masks that both talked to viewers through audio tapes and dissolved, extinguished by fire.

A few years later, in 1972, I created my first non-body work in an actual hotel room in *The Dante Hotel*. The identity of the person was defined by the objects that surrounded her taste and background. In painting, it might be called negative space. Books, glasses, cosmetics, and clothing were selected to reflect the education, personality, and socioeconomic background of the provisional identities. Pink and yellow light bulbs cast shadows and audiotapes of breathing emitted a persistent counterpoint to the local news playing on the radio.

Thus my path to non-body works and interactivity began, not with technology, but with installations and performances. Visitors entered the hotel, signed in at the desk, and received keys to the rooms. Residents of the transient hotel became 'curators' and cared for the exhibition. I intended to keep the room permanently accessible, gathering dust, and being naturally changed through the shifting flow of viewers. But 'real life' intervened. Nine months after the opening, a man named Owen Moore came to see the room at 3 a.m. and phoned the police. They came to the hotel, confiscated the elements, and took them to central headquarters where they are still waiting to be claimed. It was, I thought, an appropriate narrative closure.

Yet even in its tenuous and short-lived existence, *The Dante Hotel* became one of the first alternative spaces or public artworks produced in the United States. It was site-specific four years before the term was coined. The identities of the non-bodies inside were formed by what was absent.

The drive to alter 'found environments' that existed in real life persisted. Eventually temporary works were installed in such unlikely places as casinos in Las Vegas,

Figure 4.1. *The Dante Hotel.* Lynn Hershman, 1974.

store windows in New York, even walls in San Quentin Prison. In each the idea was the same: to transform what already existed through an interactive negotiation of simulated or 'virtual' reality, and to define the 'identity' of each context in terms of the 'other' or what was not there.

Inside *The Dante Hotel* room 47 was the 'essence' of an identity. When the room closed, it seemed important to liberate the essence of the person who might have lived there, to flesh out experience through real life. This led to a ten-year project titled *Roberta Breitmore*; a private performance of a simulated persona. In an era of alternatives, she became an objectified non-bodied alternative personality.

Roberta was at once artificial and real. A non-person, the gene of the anti-body, Roberta's first live action was to place an ad in a local newspaper for a roommate. People who answered the ad became participants in her adventure. As she became part of their reality, they became part of her fiction.

I wanted Roberta to extend beyond appearance into a symbol that used gesture and expression to reveal the basic truth of character. She had credit cards, checking accounts, and more credit than I did (she still does). Roberta was an interactive vehicle with which to analyse culture. Her profile was animated through cosmetics applied to her face as if it were a canvas, and her experience reflected the values of her society. Roberta participated in trends such as EST and Weight Watchers, saw a psychiatrist, had her own language, speech patterns, handwriting, apartment, clothing, gestures, and moods. Most significantly, she witnessed and documented the resonant nuances of that culture's alienation.

Over time Roberta accumulated forty-three letters from individuals answering her ads, and she experienced twenty-seven independent adventures. Her most difficult test was staying in character during psychiatric sessions, and her most dangerous was being asked to join a prostitution ring.

Roberta's manipulated reality became a model for a private system of interactive performances. Instead of being kept on a disc or hardware, her records were stored as photographs and texts that could be viewed without predetermined sequences. This allowed viewers to become voyeurs into Roberta's history. Their interpretations shifted, depending on the perspective and order of the sequences.

In her fifth year of life, Roberta's adventures became so archetypically victimized that multiples were created. Even with four different characters assuming her identity, the pattern of her interactions remained constant and negative. After zipping themselves into Roberta's clothing, each multiple began to also have Robertalike experiences. They were, perhaps like Tom Ray's computer viruses that filled the RAM space of real life, taking with them the genetic codes of Roberta's non-embodiment.

Many people assumed I was Roberta. Although I denied it at the time and insisted that she was 'her own woman,' with defined needs, ambitions, and instincts, in retrospect, I feel we were linked. Roberta represented part of me as surely as we all have within us an underside, a dark, shadowy cadaver that we try with pathetic illusion to camouflage. Roberta's traumas became my own haunting memories. They would surface with no warning, with no relief. She was buried deep within me, a skin closer to my heart. The negativity in her life affected my own decisions. As a 'cure,' Roberta was exorcised.

Figure 4.2. *Roberta Breitmore*. Lynn Hershman, 1975.

The exorcism ritual took place in Lucretia Borgia's crypt in Ferrara, Italy. Before the ceremony, Roberta had been a sculptural life/theatre performance, a sociopsychological portrait of culture seen through an individual woman who metaphorically became everywoman. The exorcism and subsequent transformation through fire, water, air, and earth, incorporating the alchemical colours from white to red to grey to black, and her rebirth out of ashes, represented a symbolic invocation for change away from powerlessness. In completing the ritual, Roberta's non-body disintegrated, slowly dissolving into the smoke of her reincarnation.

Roberta was not my only work with alternative non-body images. Jerry Rubin had visited *The Dante Hotel*, knew about Roberta, and asked me to work with him on creating the visual elements of his public identity. There were similar elements in his reconstruction as were used in Roberta's deconstruction. It was a kind of non-body image cannibalization.

Roberta's exorcism took place in 1979. When the smoke cleared, it was 1980. That year I picked up my first video camera. Video and interactive systems became a tool for retracing the body of my personal history. It was a fortunate coincidence that as video was defining its language, I was finding my voice.

In each of the fifty-three videotapes I have completed since Roberta's exorcism, the idea of 'site' or medium becomes part of the content. Although each is quite different from the others in external appearance and content, many of the tapes are about surveillance, voyeurism, and the inherent dangers of technological systems and media-based reality in which identity is threatened.

In *Longshot* (1989), for instance, a video editor, Dennis, obsessively pursues the image of a woman whose identity is fleeting and fragmentary. As Dennis tries to edit together Lian's reality, it becomes more fractured and fragile. Lian is a non-person, marginalized in her culture. The romance begins without her, and the seduction continues on the tape, without her corporeal presence, in Dennis's editing room.

Seeing Is Believing (1991) is about a thirteen-year-old girl who uses a video camera to search for her missing father and lapsed history. Eventually she finds both but through the process dissolves her 'essence' into the 'negatives' of the film itself.

In *Desire Incorporated* (1990) actual seduction ads were aired on television. Those who responded were eventually interviewed as to why they wanted to meet a fantasy or artificial person. The answers were woven into a videotape about 'desire.'

Virtual Love (1993) is about a shy woman, Valerie, who, discouraged with her own real body, implants someone else's image into the computers of identical twins, one of whom (Barry) she is infatuated with. This surrogate non-body, Marie, causes Barry to fight with his girlfriend, as well as to reach into the system to find his perfect simulated, virus-free mate.

Seduction of a Cyborg (1994) is about the infection of technology into the body, and the addition this causes. In this, the female central character eventually becomes part of the technology, seduced into cyborghood, where she both participates in and witnesses the pollution of history. The effects were designed from digitized and manipulated images of computer chips.

Twists of the Cord (1994) is about the history of the telephone, but within the story, Michelle becomes involved in a phantom or virtual relationship with RU Sirius. Both have sex with non-bodies, using the screen as a simultaneous condom and connection.

Double Cross Click Click (1995) is about the RAMifications of cross-dressing on the Internet.

The Electronic Diary (1984-95) has many parts. This personal work talks about the relationship of the invisible body and a 'talking head.' Often the body will fracture or rupture in the process of coming to self-understanding.

Phantom Limbs, Interactivity, and Disappearances

For the past decade, I have been creating a series of photographs known as Phantom Limbs. These each articulate references to the mutation of the female body through the seduction of media. Reproductive technological parts sprout from the image of the female, creating a cyborgian reformation as parts of the real body disappear.

While video is like a reflection that does not talk back, interactive works are like a trick two-way mirror that allows you to have a dialogue with the other side. I find this deeply subversive!

I consider *Lorna*, the first interactive artist videodisc, my entrance into electronics. Unlike Roberta, who existed in the world, Lorna never leaves her one-room apartment. The objects in her room are very much like those in *The Dante Hotel*, except that there is a television set. As Lorna watches the news and ads, she becomes fearful, afraid to leave her tiny room. Viewers are invited to liberate Lorna from her web of fears by accessing a remote control unit that corresponds to numbers placed on the items in her room. Instead of being passive, viewers have the action literally in their own hands. Every object in Lorna's room contains a number and becomes a chapter in her life that opens into branching sequences.

The viewer/participant accesses information about Lorna's past, future, and personal conflicts via these objects. Many images on the screen are of the remote control device Lorna uses to change television channels. Because the viewer/participant uses a nearly identical unit to direct the disc action, a metaphoric link or point of identification is established, and surrogate decisions are made for Lorna.

The telephone is Lorna's link to the outside world. Viewers/participants choose to voyeuristically overhear conversations of different contexts as they trespass the cyberspace of her hard-pressed life. There are three endings: Lorna shoots her television set, commits suicide, or, what we northern Californians consider the worst of all, moves to Los Angeles.

The plot has multiple variations that include being caught in repeating dream sequences or using multiple soundtracks, and can be seen backwards, forwards, at increased or decreased speeds, and from several points of view. There is no hierarchy in the ordering of decisions. And the icons are made often of cut-off and dislocated body parts, such as a mouth, or an eye.

Once Lorna was released, I wanted to create a work that more directly involved the body of both the viewer/participant and the computer. Seven years later, *Deep Contact* was completed, and participants were required to touch and/or penetrate the screen. Viewers choreograph their own encounters in the vista of voyeurism by actually putting their hand on a touch-sensitive screen. This interactive videodisc installation compares intimacy with reproductive technology, and allows viewers to have adventures that change their sex, age, and personality.

Participants are invited to follow their instincts as they are instructed to actually touch their guide, 'Marion,' on any part of her body. Adventures develop depending on which body part is touched. The leather-clad protagonist invites 'extensions' into the screen – the screen becomes an extension of the viewer's/participant's hand, similar to a prosthesis. Touching the screen encourages the sprouting of phantom limbs that become virtual connections between the viewer and the image.

At certain instances viewers can see, close up, what they have just passed. For example, Marion runs past a bush that, examined closely, reveals a spider weaving a web. In some instances words are flashed on the screen for just three frames, forcing the viewer to go back and frame by frame see what has been written. At other points, the Zen Master speaks his lines backwards, forcing the viewer to play the disc in reverse to understand what he has said. A surveillance camera has been programmed to switch 'on' when a cameraman's shadow is seen. The viewer's image instantaneously appears on the screen, displacing and replacing the image. This suggests 'transgressing the screen,' being transported into 'virtual reality.'

Room of One's Own (1993), my third interactive computer-based installation, allowed the viewer's eyes to be immersed into the actual space of a tiny articulated interactive electronic peep show. A stainless steel box placed at eye level with movable periscopic viewing device bridges the viewer into a voyeur in a miniature bedroom scene. Within this room are several objects, similar in fact to those both in *The Dante Hotel* and Lorna's room. The very act of 'looking' initiates the action.

The viewers'/voyeurs' eyes are inserted into a small video monitor, so they become simultaneous virtual participants in the scene being seen. All the while, the protagonist (the same one as in *Deep Contact*, but now a bit older) chides viewers for their persistent gaze. This work is not only about voyeurism and a feminist deconstruction of the 'media gaze,' but also about the explosive effects attached to media representations of female identity. Furthermore, it repositions the viewer into the victim.

Real-Time Virtuality

In 1888 Etienne Jules Marey perfected a gun that substituted film for bullets. This camera gun has a direct relationship to not only the history of film and the eroticization of female imagery in photography and pornography, but to the horrors of our century perpetrated by weapons and translated into media by cameras.

As an example, many serial killers photograph their victims, as if to capture and possess them. The associative notions of guns/camera/trigger link all media representations to lethal weapons. In *America's Finest*, an interactive M16 rifle addresses these issues. Action is directly instigated through the trigger itself, which, when pulled, places viewers/participants within the gun site (this time their entire body, holding the gun). They see themselves fade under horrible examples in which the M16 has been used, and if they wait, ghosts of the cycling images dissolve into the present. Again, aggressors become victims and the entire bodies of the viewers are placed inside the site of the work. Through this complete immersion, they again lose control of their image and become floating non-bodies.

Paranoid Mirror was inspired by the paintings of Van Eyck and in particular the *Marriage of Arnolfini*. This piece uses reflection as a means of portraiture and reflected self-portraiture. Though obscured and distanced, the artist's reflection watches from behind the central figures. *Paranoid Mirror* engages ideas of reflection, tracking, surveillance, and voyeurism, and uses the viewer as a direct interface. Sensors strategically placed on a floor cause the still image in a gold frame to activate, turn around, and dissolve between sequences of reflection into both the viewer and/or other women in the videodisc sequences. In some instances, a switcher places the viewer's back into the frame, countering the direct reflection into the scrimlike layers of the images.

The back of Anne Gerber's head is seen when the piece is inactive. Furthermore, Anne Gerber has experienced difficulties with sight itself, underscoring the often mistaken paranoid fear of being watched as well as the relationship of paranoia to voyeurism and surveillance. Accompanying this piece are four photographs from the filmed sequences. These images are framed so as to obscure the image. Appearances, therefore, are often reflective illusions and projections of the observer.

Birth of the Anti-body

At this writing, the work in which I am engaged is the creation of a fictional persona, designed as an updated Roberta, who is navigating through the Internet. Surveillance, capture, and tracking are the DNA of her inherently digital anatomy. They form the underpinning of her portrait.

She has her own homepage on the World Wide Web and is involved with chat lines, bulletin boards, and other computer-mediated communication. She is different from the non-body works of the 1970s and 1980s in that the veil of her illusion, the computer screen, is sheerer than ever.

I refer to her as an anti-body because of the way she was cultured. Normally antibodies produce systems of immunity from toxins in their environment. This will function as a benevolent virus that will roam the breathing form of the Internet, randomly accessing itself into uncertain home sites. Interestingly enough, terms for new technologies have ramifications in the language and times of AIDS. In reaction to an unhealthy natural environment, it rejects what exists and in order to survive, and forms an other environment.

This Internetted, plugged-in anti-body is a transitory construction of time, circumstances, and technology, a newly issued prescription of earlier impulses. She has chosen to negate the selfhood into which she was born. Instead she shows a marked preference for the artifice of technology.

Like Botticelli's *Venus* she is forward-looking and seductive. But she is also optimistic and cyborgian. A pure-bred anti-body of the twenty-first century, she moves through time, and electronic geographies of space, discreetly challenging privacy, voyeurism, and surveillance in her own inimitable, mutable, and inauthentic revolutionary fashion.

Since 1958 I've been obsessed with cyborgs, the merging of technological and human points of identity. This is evident in the *Phantom Limbs*, where women's body parts extend from the mechanics of their capture; the *Digital Venus* prints, in which the traditional nude female art historical nude is dis-embodied, erased, and replaced by code, and a series of digital prints called, appropriately, *Cyborgs*, in which identity numbers are stamped onto the faces and extensions of the transformed beings.

My telerobotic dolls are also prosthetics, devices to an extended point of identity. Reliance on tracking and surveillance techniques has resulted in a culture that has a peripheral vision that extends beyond normal human physiology. In many cases, there is a merging of human and machine capabilities that create new beings, cyborgs whose virtual reach, and in this case sight, is extended beyond physical location. Identity becomes intangible on the Internet, and Tillie's face becomes a mask for the multiple expressions of the self that link each person to another.

If you click on her eye (eyecons) an image of what the doll is seeing is captured and put into virtual Internet space. You are also able to move her entire head 180 degrees so that you can engage and exchange her peripheral vision. While you are reflected in Tillie's monitor, your image is also being captured and watched by countless unknown Internet users who are using Tillie's face as a mask to watch viewers. Voyeurism and surveillance tactics have become extensions of our 'I.' Cameras have become both eyecons and contact lenses.

Web cameras are also used in the *Difference Engine 3* shown at ZKM. Identity avatars are stamped with numbers that correspond in seconds to the time a viewer approaches the machine cycle through a virtual museum, and a virtual life cycle, ending up in a suspended purgatorial state after which they are permanently archived. A user can choose an avatar and through the eyes of the avatar virtually travel through the museum in Karlsruhe, Germany. Web cameras are an extension of one's gaze, voycurism in this case. By connecting two physical spaces using Web cameras, and making it possible to manipulate the 'view' of the other space, the boundary between the reality and virtuality of the space – and the view inside the space – disappears. As Tillie herself is both a real doll and a virtual one on the Net, viewers become virtual personas from the other end of the connection, becoming agents of themselves, cyborgian creatures capable of extended vision and reach.

Once we used the words persona, robot, or actor. Now the terminology for the counterfeit representation of life of digital anti-bodies includes avatar, cyborg, or synthespian. These pixelated essences of virtual identity link into an archeology of networks that in turn create a collective connective ethnography of information.

Like computer viruses, they escape extinction through their ability to morph and to survive, exist in perpetual motion, navigating parallel conditions of time and memory. The data itself are a representation of the ubiquitous virtual posthuman essence, a new curve in our evolving cyborgian posture.

If human beings are imperfect, their networks are even more so. Before long, we may be forced to confront the Faustian reflections of power that have been absorbed into our real-world myth. Perhaps what we need is an ideology that embraces our transience and obsolescence. For this, we need to rely on the deepest resources of human creativity to accept temporality and reformat our dreams so that they incorporate an evolution where life becomes an unfolding nexus of inter-linked transformative experiences.

If humans have become the interface to the larger communicative body, can soul-ful automatons be far behind?

Acknowledgments

The Dante Hotel was created with Eleanor Coppola. *Deep Contact* was created in collaboration with Sara Roberts and Jim Crutchfield. *Room of One's Own* was created in collaboration with Sara Roberts and Palle Henchel. *America's Finest* was created in collaboration with Paul Tompkins and Mat Heckert.

Please see my digital archive, Life Squared (L^2), at the Stanford Humanities Lab, http://shl.stanford.edu/research/lifetosecondpower.html.

Notes

1 Howard Rheingold, *Virtual Communities, Homesteading on the Electronic Frontier* (New York: Harper Perennial, 1994), 165.
2 Ibid.
3 Mark Stuart Gill, 'Terror On Line,' *Vogue*, January (1995): 163-5.
4 Kevin Kelley, *Out of Control* (San Francisco: Addison-Wesley, 1994), 286-88.
5 Wayne Black, 'We Are All Roberta Breitmore: A Post Mortem on Modernism,' unpublished essay, 1994.

TECHNOLOGY, IDENTITY, AND SURVEILLANCE

5 Precision + Guided + Seeing

JORDAN CRANDALL

The Scene

The Scene: the hot zone of a busy airport concourse. Late afternoon sun shining through the atrium windows. Travellers drift about in a state of anxious suspension. All around me, it is pure theatre. The star of the show is an impeccably dressed woman, hunched over her laptop, performing some sort of demo for the man next to her, who seems to be only marginally interested. She is clicking away with forceful, jerky motions, causing the computer, which is perched on her knees, to sway perilously. A pink Post-It, loosened from the momentum, flutters to the ground.

Curious, I move in for a closer look. The woman appears to be demonstrating some kind of search technique. According to her, the technique is designed to 'cut through the clutter' and save time. It allows her to move across the expanse of the Web, telescope in and out as necessary, and zero in on the *exact* bits and pieces that she needs. She emphasizes the word '*exact*,' as if she's somehow able to tap into some kind of original hookup between sign and thing. As she says '*exact*,' she stomps her foot (*whop!*), the clap of her shoe precisely synching with her enunciation. Impressive. I try to sneak a peek at her screen, but I cannot figure out what she is doing. She is moving too quickly. She is 'flying' the computer like a fighter pilot.

It's an aggressive technique. I admire extreme physical engagement with a process that, for most of us, is rather immobilizing. She's completely charged up by it, as if she's found a way to seize control of the ship. After typing and clicking furiously for several more minutes, she pauses for a moment and sits back, as if to catch her breath (or rather, to refuel). She collects herself, glances quickly at the man, and then grabs a pencil, preparing to make a point. She tells him that this search-and-target method is by far the most *precise*. She elongates the word 'pre-*cisse*,' drawing out the sound of the 'sssss,' as she simultaneously thrusts the sharp end of her pencil towards the computer screen. She seems to propel the pencil forward with the force of her enunciation, as if the pencil were a missile hurling towards its target. As if the precision-pencil-missile could puncture the computer screen itself – or rather, the abstracting field of language – to apprehend her 'real' quarry.

I stare at an imagined point of impact on her screen. Is there a 'real' to be captured here, concealed beneath the frames and words? What is the real object of the precision-impulse? Of course, in its Lacanian sense, the real cannot be assimilated into the symbolic order. No matter: she will strive to capture it, as quickly and efficiently as possible. It is a necessary illusion: the engine through which her physical activity is produced.

At this point, with nowhere else to go – after all, if there *were* a real object at the end of the precision-impulse, it would be vapourized as it was enacted – she cuts to another device. The abandoned pencil falls to the floor. When one runs aground, what is there to do but to reach for a gadget? She locks her gaze onto her pocketbook, thrusts her hand inside, unearths a camera-phone, flips it open, and snaps a picture of the man – all in one motion. The man, dazed by her quick draw, was no doubt captured in an unflattering image, like the unprepared, hapless victim in a slasher flick who, mouth agape, is instantaneously immortalized by both camera and killer.

I consider that the precision-woman is showing off her technological prowess for the elusive man. As she brilliantly juggles devices and windows, perhaps she is trying to seduce him. The seduction-demo. The exacting woman seducing the inexact man. After tapping into the phone and transmitting the image that she just took of him, she explains to him that the picture will be geocoded – anchored with GPS coordinates – and integrated into a mapping application, which forever weds image to site: *this* site. Good for the woman, horrors for the man: a bad picture, not only forever archived in the database but fixed in place on a map like a tourist attraction. A ghoulish snapshot suddenly transformed into a wax museum figure. I wonder what 'weight' this image is given, when it is cartographized. By permanently anchoring it to a material site, does it carry a stronger trace of the real? Does it store a more vivid memory, a more embedded experience, a more affective relation? A more *precise* and direct link between mobile representation and ground-level actuality?

Surely, I think, the woman's next step is to do a retinal scan, in order to further inscribe him in the real. I glance at her purse, wondering what further devices it may contain. The man, somewhat uneasily, says he will be right back, and quickly exits the room. I consider that he will flee out the back exit, running off into the horizon, towards some other set of landscape metadata. The precision-woman, wasting no time, pivots back to her computer and begins to peck away.

I consider her methods. Are they the result of a precision-driven impulse to wed sign and thing and therefore 'capture' the object more directly and efficiently (cut through the clutter) – or do they manifest some kind of deeper, longed-for attachment to the real? In other words: am I witnessing the drive for an ever-more precision-driven representation amid the clutter of everyday information overload, or am I witnessing a longing to jettison representation entirely, in favour of a more direct relation to the real object of attention?

The precision-woman suddenly stops and sits back quietly, as if surrendering her arms, and begins to stare wistfully offscreen. A momentary lapse in her war on distraction. I sit back, too, and let my vision drift.

A *precision-driven* methodology works with technologies and symbols to increase efficiency and accuracy. A longing to jettison representation entirely favours a direct and unmediated relation to the real. In every case, technology is central. For it has already determined, in advance, the manner of approach[1] – as part of the larger circuit through which all acts of viewing must pass.

Let's address this question of 'precision' on two fronts: one, as a technologically enabled drive towards efficiency and accuracy – a drive to augment human capabilities by developing new human-machine composites, connecting and joining forces with multiple processing agencies, wherever or whatever they might be; and two, as a technologically assisted drive to reduce mediation and offer a form of direct connection to our real objects of inquiry. We might call these the *effective* and the *affective*. Both aim for the goal of instantaneous vision: *a real-time perceptual agency* in which multiple actors, both human and machine, are networked and able to act in concert. An effective real-time perceptual agency is one in which time and space intervals can be eliminated, reducing the gaps between detection, analysis, and engagement, or between desire and its attainment. An affective real-time perceptual agency can somehow touch the real.

Yet the drive for the real, as Slavoj Žižek suggests, always culminates in its opposite: theatrical spectacle. Why? Because the real is only able to be sustained if we fictionalize it.[2] To look for the real, then, is not to look for it directly: it is to look to our fictions, discerning how reality is 'transfunctionalized' through them.[3] Perhaps the real object of the precision-drive is arrived at not only through reduction, but also through expansion. To look to the object of the precision-drive is not only to narrow the optic, honing in on the target of attention; it is to look to the cultural fictions in which the object becomes lodged. It is also to open the optic, to theatricalize it. To accommodate cultural fictions is to acknowledge the constitutive role of conflict. What aspects of the real are transfunctionalized through our conflict imaginaries?

It is difficult to acknowledge the necessity of conflict, because we often assume that selfless cooperation is the norm. When we speak about the formation of real-time perceptual agencies – which, again, manifest a distributed processing and storage capacity among humans and machines, enabling increased efficiency and accuracy (cutting through the clutter) – we often assume that cooperation reigns. We are all in this together, after all, building the utopian dream of the global village, the wired world, or the global brain. And yet, competition plays an equal role. We do not necessarily want to see on a level playing field alongside everyone else. We need to see faster, better, and more precisely – whether in the name of convenience, profit, or protection – in order to outwit competitor and combatant alike. We are driven equally by such acquisitive and aggressive impulses. They are the stuff of our cultural dramas. They derive from the production demands of both consumerism and warfare – to the extent that these become mutually reinforcing components of the same economic engine. The engine is also a subjective and somatic one.

When, in a competitive consumer-security culture, machine-aided perception moves towards the strategic, the panoptic, and the pre-emptive, then we no longer see but track.

Tracking arises as a dominant perceptual activity in a computerized culture where *looking has come to mean calculating* rather than visualizing in the traditional sense[4] and where seeing is infused with the logics of tactics and manoeuvre – whether in the mode of acquisition or defence. Such processes of calculation, and their necessary forms of information storage (memory), are distributed and shared in a larger field of human and technological agency. The object is dislodged from any inherently fixed position, and instead becomes a mobile actor in a shared field of competitive endeavour. In Paul Virilio's terms, the object becomes a traject.

What happens when we track? We aim for a real-time perceptual agency, in a more direct and precise relation to the moving object at hand. We aim to detect, process, and strategically codify a moving phenomenon – a stock price, a biological function, an enemy, a consumer good – in order to gain advantage in a competitive theatre, whether the battlefield, the social arena, or the marketplace. The power to more accurately 'see' a moving object is the power to map its trajectory and extrapolate its subsequent position. In an accelerated culture of shrinking space and time intervals, tracking promises an increased capacity to see the future. Leapfrogging the expanding present, it offers up a predictive knowledge-power: a competitive edge. It promises to endow us with the ability to outmanoeuvre our adversaries, to intercept our objects of suspicion and desire.

To track is to endeavour to account for a moving object – which could be one's self, since we track our own activities and rhythms – in ever-more precise terms so as to control or manage it, lest it become unruly, wasteful, dangerous, or unattainable as property. To track is to somehow access the moving object more fully and deeply. When the suspicious and acquisitive eye tracks its objects, it fixes its sights on them as targets to be managed, eliminated, or consumed. In so doing, it inscribes itself in the real, in a process that brings both object and embodied subject into being.

Tracking necessarily strives to narrow its scope, to move more directly into the space of the body substrate, as if it could then fully and completely 'own' its object of attention. Through this process, the subject of tracking comes to know itself and 'readies' itself to act – more quickly, efficiently, safely. It cuts through the clutter.

So the drama goes.

While tracking is about the strategic detection and codification of movement, it is also about positioning. Tracking studies how something moves in order to predict its exact location in time and space. It fastens its objects (and subjects) onto a classifying grid or database-driven identity assessment, reaffirming precise categorical location within a landscape of mobility.

Rather than being fully about mobility, on the one hand, or locational specificity, on the other, tracking is more accurately about the dynamic between the two. We might call this *inclination-position*. Based on my previous patterns of writing and the literary conventions that it follows, I am likely to write three more sentences in this paragraph. Based on previous patterns of keystrokes, I am likely to take a break at 3:10. Based on previous airport records, my flight is likely to depart in two hours and eighteen minutes. The tracked object may be *there*, but it is moving like *this* and will be in *this* future position at *this* future moment.

This is a landscape in which *signifiers have become statistics*.

It is how computers think, and how we begin to think with them.

Tracking emerged out of the mid-twentieth century's demands of war and production.[5] It emerged through the development of computing, the wartime sciences of information theory and cybernetics, and the development of structuralism. Tracking coalesced out of a fear of the enemy Other, and helped bring a modality of both friend and enemy into being.[6]

Rather than performing a historical analysis, let us set the stage for a performance. We begin at the historical tipping-point where tracking coalesced as a techno-discursive ensemble – that is, as a cluster of tools, procedures, and metaphors, which function at the level of language, materiality, and belief.[7] For as Felix Guattari has pointed out, technologies do not merely convey representational contents, but contribute to the development of new assemblages of enunciation.[8] These techno-discursive ensembles become stored in the operational strata of organization and practice.[9] They are bundled into tracking. Character background. Back-story.

Tracking, then, is not simply a technology or a modality of perception, but a cluster of discursive orientations. It is through such discourses that subjects, machines, and institutions are linked.

As tracking mediates among viewer, screen, and world, it generates the tactical mindsets, communication modes, and sensorial and somatic adjustments that are appropriate to it. Tracking provides a scrim through which relevant data are historically selected, systems of address and command determined, and human and cultural sensoria differentiated and reintegrated.

The lead actor in this historical performance is the military command, control, and communications system known as SAGE.[10] Developed in mid-twentieth century wartime, SAGE was a system that automatically processed digitally encoded radar data generated by linked installations around the perimeter of the United States, and then integrated these with other communications and cartographical data. SAGE integrated abstract information about position and movement and then superimposed it on schematic maps. If a hostile incoming object was detected, jets could automatically be directed to intercept it. Within the matrices of SAGE, tracking emerged as a form of machine-aided, calculated seeing, studying movements of objects in order to prepare for their possible interception.

The conditions of the scene are well told by Martin Heidegger. To represent something is to put ourselves 'into the picture' in such a way as to take precedence over our object. We put ourselves into the scene: we enstage ourselves as the normative setting in which the object must thereafter present itself. We become the representative of that which has the character of object.[11] We attest to it, normalize it. The user is pressed into the mould of the real by the fact and act of the system: brought into a direct relationship with it, as something that could only heretofore be intuited. Technology sets the conditions for the approach.

What we see is defined within the discursive paradigm of such technologized seeing. Subsequently, we begin to see ourselves in these terms. We internalize the classificatory logics. Worlds and bodies are tagged, annotated, and anchored within a new symbolic-material landscape, providing models for thought and identification. These models affect how we speak, perceive, and move; they set in place a calculus of ontological division, which presses both subject and object into service.

A vigilant seeing arose through the mechanisms of SAGE, accompanied by a demand for 'preparedness,' both in terms of one's own body and the collective machine-body of the military: an individual and collective alertness on the edge of action, an analytical perception combined with an incipient mobilization. New patterns of organization, vigilance, and action took form: new modes of awareness and perceptual activity that could enframe and make sense of the volumes of abstract information that were suddenly at hand. A new landscape of preparedness coalesced, which traversed individual body, nation, and culture alike, generating a myriad of cultural effects. Duck-and-cover drills. Bomb shelters. Detective fiction.

We are speaking not only of a technology, but of a subjectifying and socializing technique, which has an impact on language and on the entire sensorium of the body.

Strategy games also play an important role in this historical drama. Especially during the Cold War, increasingly powerful modelling and prediction technologies were needed in order to reach into the future and anticipate events, since actual weapon technology could not be used. This fuelled an orientation of pre-emptive seeing: a form of vision that was always slightly ahead of itself, which not only anticipated probable events but, in some corner of the imaginary, seemed to mould reality to fit the simulated outcome. Simulated worlds paralleled real worlds, and beliefs about each were reflected in both. To be prepared was to anticipate the worst, and the worst could only be modelled. Once modelled, it was introduced into reality. Assumptions, beliefs, and mindsets arise out of the technical-semiotic machinery of simulations as they are practised, because such orientations in turn get embedded in the machinery's operational strata. A mechanism of training, or rehearsal, in new forms of movement, combat, and identification.

From the mid-twentieth century onward, the systematic, logical rules of computing helped produce the sense that everything – ground realities, warfare, markets – could be formalized, modelled, and managed. Reality was figured as mathematical and 'capturable' through a formal programming logic. The world became predictable, pliable, and the future controllable.[12] Again, this is not something that military technology alone produced: it is bound up in a much larger historical enunciative field – in this case, a field of structuralist orientation, where reality is seen to be determined by linguistic codes, and where attention turned to the codes and conventions that produce meaning.

Three intersecting conditions that descended from this wartime technical-discursive ensemble were bundled into tracking from the start. First is the perpetuation of an idealist orientation where humans have no access to unmediated reality and the world is actively constructed in terms of relational information systems. Here the world is scripted as inherently controllable, filtered through a scrim of information that modifies both system and materiality. Second, following from the first, is an emphasis on data patterns over essence: an ever-greater abstraction of persons, bodies, and things, and an emphasis on statistical patterns of behaviour, where the populace is pictured as a calculus of probability distributions and manageable functions. Third is a fundamentally agonistic orientation, deriving from a world built on confrontation and oppositional tactics, of tactical moves and countermoves.

These conditions form part of the operational strata of all contemporary media. Particularly with television and the Internet, the media viewer is infused with an artificial sense of control over the machine and an exterior world represented on the screen. Reality is subsumed within the dictates of the interface. An unruly or unproductive situation is dominated, over and through the technology, and a de facto power relation is established between observer and observed.

The stage is set. Moving through a world of information and communications technology, information is increasingly seen as more essential than what it represents. Pattern is privileged over presence.[13]

The sun is slipping below the horizon outside the airport, backlighting the cluster of planes gathered outside. The precision-driven woman lowers her computer screen in synch with the diminishing light. With the click of the laptop's closure, the sun vanishes.

Perhaps she has had enough computer time. I watch as her eyes drift hazily around the concourse. I have caught her in-between media inputs, it seems – her attention momentarily adrift, her subjectivity suspended. I think of the extent to which consciousness and attention are effects of media technology – effects of storage, computation, and transmission systems. Friedrich Kittler would see this woman in terms of different states of information storage and transfer, an embodied subject coalescing around a circuit of perceptibility.

I think about this woman's precision-driven methodology, and her embrace of technologies of positioning. Surely, she is aware of the trade-off: her technologies are those that aim to increase productivity, agility, and awareness, yet they vastly increase the tracking and data-mining capabilities of the corporate sector. Tracked, she becomes a target: a consumer-citizen pinpointed with ever-greater accuracy within the worlds of marketing and state surveillance.

Yet, at the same time, she's in the driver's seat, shaping her arena of visibility. I think about the forms of manoeuvre and masquerade that she engages in: blogs, friendship networks, phonecams, Flickr. A pervasive web of shared resources that offers boundless opportunity for identity refashioning. For her, no doubt, the challenge is not to resist the gaze of tracking, but rather to channel it to her own advantage, manoeuvring productively within its matrices of visibility. In a database-driven culture of accounting, one needs to appear on the grids of registration in order to 'count.' To be accounted for is to exist. Yet, appearances are contradictory, constituted in multiple, polyrhythmic forms and paths.

Appropriating the technical-discursive ensemble of tracking, I shape my own horizon of objective identity. Internalizing it, I self-identify. Tracking is also a technology of the self.

Gradually, out of the corner of my eye through the concourse window, I notice an enormous jet gliding by. Its fuselage is the same shade as the dark sky outside, and the illuminated passenger windows seem to hover in the void. One by one the expectant travellers, cropped identically, slide by as if frames in a filmstrip. They stare straight ahead in the direction of take-off; I stare straight ahead in the direction of the precision-woman. They sit immobilized in their vehicle; I sit rigid in mine. Yet my vehicle does not move.

The plane suddenly revs its engines, sending a deep roar through the concourse like an earthquake. The vibration shakes my seat and jolts me into awareness of my own body, as if someone abruptly grabbed my shoulders and shook me. I am thrust onto the stage, acutely confronted with the fact of my own embodied presence and my own subjective status as observer – but I'm unaware of my lines. What role am I playing, here and now, within this script? Where am I located in this matrix of observation? What is my own subject position vis-à-vis my tracked object?

The nature of my voyeuristic gaze now stands revealed. In scanning the movements of the precision-woman, I have positioned myself at the fulcrum of control, establishing a power relation through which I am reinforced. The precision-woman exists for me and for me alone, within a contained world that prohibits reciprocity. She is but an object or a conduit, which anchors my gaze or channels it. If she were to look back at me – if her eyes were to meet mine – the entire world-system would vanish.

I gradually realize how, in this way, tracking silently incorporates its own erotic economy, shaping its own enclosed, libidinous, predatory world – a world built on desire and the impossibility of its satisfaction. If I adopt the gaze of the tracker and thereby pre-empt the possibility of reciprocity, then my tracking-gaze becomes something on the order of a stare: the cold, unflinching stare of the machinic apparatus that sees with me, through me. It is a look that is uncomplicated with human subtleties, unfettered by the complications of the flesh and social decorum. The tracking-gaze neither registers embarrassment nor flirts. It is not constituted in a subtle dance of revealing and concealing, or of availability and withdrawal. Lacking a sense of reciprocal play, the tracking-gaze does not know when to look away. It cannot 'see' or modulate socially; rather, it can only study, aim, and own.

The precision-driven woman has demonstrated her research technique; I now must demonstrate mine. What is the real object of *my* precision-impulse?

Abruptly, I turn away from both the thought and the woman, as if the precision-woman constituted my own unsustainable Real. My only recourse is to avoid, or rather, to expand: widening the scope to reveal the larger matrix of tracking in which we are both ensnared, the shared stage upon which we both now act. I allow the media-technological institution to catch us, objectivize us, and the analytical to give way to the theatrical.

According to Virilio, the real-time interface has replaced the interval that once constituted and organized the history and geography of human societies; problems of spatial distance have been supplanted with problems of the time remaining.[14] Again, tracking is motored by the need for an instantaneity of action, where time delays, spatial distances, and 'middlemen' are reduced through computational systems that facilitate the sharing of human and machinic functions. A combinatory field of perception arises within a distributed field of shared functions, and a new form of agency emerges, spanning spatial distance and merging information from multiple sources.

Consider the new generations of post-SAGE actors: 'network-centric' warfare systems, which aim to develop a worldwide satellite, sensor, and communications web geared for panoptic global oversight and instantaneous military response. The goal is a wireless, unified computing grid that can link weapons, systems, and personnel in real time, making volumes of information available instantly to all military and intelligence actors. According to one major player in this industry, such a system will allow every member of the military to have a 'God's eye view' of the battlefield.[15] Through such a system, the U.S. military predicts that it will be capable of 'finding, tracking, and targeting virtually in real time any significant element moving on the face of the earth.'[16] Tracking as the ultimate panoptic ideal, propelled by a sense of divine right, could not be more explicitly stated.

This integrative history – a history of prosthetic extension – belongs to the military and mass media alike.[17] The intertwining of human and machine capacity, in the generation of a combinatory field of perception, is the history of popular media itself.

Consider that the spectator and the cinematic apparatus are mutually dependent in the act of conducting representation. One must be trained to behave and see in accordance with the conditions of the device. The viewer is immobilized and sensitized to a language of movement through which an extensive world is understood. Humans become reliant on the apparatus that populate their field of vision, adjusting to the rhythmic codes of their conveyance. A perceptual capacity and a signifying apparatus emerge through an integration of human and machine.[18] Consider, too, the extent to which television integrates the viewer in a shared circuit. Reflecting the viewer's own thought process, television develops its own conventions of simulated deliberation, absolving the viewer of the labour of decision-making[19] – as when a laugh track allows one to maintain a relaxed composure while the machine assumes the labour of chuckling.

In any spectatorial situation, a subject is distributed within a larger circuit of engagement determined through technological systems of communication, storage, sorting, and retrieval, contoured under the social and institutional construction of knowledge. A viewing subject is linked or inserted into larger networks of seeing and linguistic meaning.

As always, time is of the essence. For both the military and the civilian observer, there is little time for reflection. In the military realm, reflection adds time and space in which the target might slip away. Reflection expands, not lessens, the gap between detecting and intervening, sensing and shooting. In the popular realm, slowness – the stuff of reflection and deliberation – is to be avoided. In a real-time media landscape, there is no time to think.

Tracking is not conducted simply through abstract data about position and movement. It is conducted through forms of computer-aided visualization. It is conducted through sophisticated graphic information systems, formatted according to geographic or other spatial paradigms, oriented for the humans who must interpret it and transform it into actionable intelligence. These visual interfaces function in terms of the tradition of cartographic representation as well as the tradition of simulation: while the former maintains a strict division between viewer and image, the latter complicates that divide, embodying users in a virtual, immersive space, which reorients or replaces the actual space in which they are located.[20]

These graphic systems did not develop in isolation. They developed in conjunction with film and television. They reflect the conditions of popular news and entertainment media, as in turn, these media embody the conditions of computer visualization. There is a constant flow back and forth. To a large extent, tracking has been integrated into a regime of networked spectacle that no longer heeds media distinctions. It has helped to generate *a landscape of preparedness that traverses media forms and civilian-military bodies alike.*

According to Kittler, what we understand as media are increasingly mere effects on the surface of a much more comprehensive digital base. As the general digitization of information and information channels increases, the differences between individual media are erased. Because any algorithm can be transformed into any interface effect, media are becoming mere interfaces within the (increasingly globalized) information circuit.[21] To understand tracking, we are compelled to look broadly – at the combination of media forms, agencies, and rhetorical modalities that tracking registers.

In many ways the entertainment industry led the charge. Following the end of the Cold War, the U.S. Department of Defense – which has been the major source of funding for high-end computer graphics, visualization technologies, and network infrastructure for decades – became increasingly reliant on commercially available items and components, many of which are developed in the videogame market. In terms of ideas, personnel, and products, there is a continuous exchange between the military, commercial designers, and the entertainment industry. Military planners work closely with industrial partners in team fashion. Research work for high-end military products is seamlessly integrated with systems in the commercial sector.[22]

Consider the extraordinary successful genre of 'serious games,' developed by the U.S. military in the commercial realm, which serve as a combination of entertainment, military recruitment, training, and public relations. One such game, *America's Army*, ranks as one of the most popular games in history. As military simulations are adapted to the commercial game market, so, too, are commercial videogames adapted for military purposes. Once it was the military that drove the development of graphics and processor hardware. No longer: it is now the commercial videogame market that drives it. In much of the developed world, the game industry is reaching the level of film and television in its importance as a popular entertainment medium.

Film and television are fast on their way to becoming integrated within a much larger hybrid simulative field.[23] In a sense, programming like FX Channel's 'Over There,' which is about soldiers fighting in Iraq, is already a simulation: it is the first U.S. television drama that has tried to process a war as entertainment – while it was still being fought. In such a media landscape, perhaps simulation is becoming less a modality of representation than a mechanism of translation: a form of incipience or potentiality that moves across various stages of enaction.

The desire for realism in tracking does not derive from military applications alone but also from film, television, and fiction. Developers of videogames and military flight simulators alike have been influenced by popular films and novels.[24] The world of the military and the world of entertainment are both driven by a cultural imaginary, which is a composite of multiple narratives whether fact or fiction.

Such are the theatres in which tracking must be situated. Tracking is part of a vast production machinery that is hungry for content, realism, and compelling narrative. Backstory is key, requiring the development of historical and geographical databases. The drive for compelling narrative development in simulations – whether from imagined or actual warfare scenarios – influences popular news and entertainment programming. One could in fact suggest that the latter are driven by the demands of simulation.

Consider the relentless twenty-four-hour machinery of contemporary news. It is a profit centre that demands ever-new and constant dangers for reportage and commodification. It fuels a constant battle for attention-space, where the whole of reality is transformed into a dramatic stage for alluring catastrophe. There is no time to remember, because the next crisis – always imminent – demands our full vigilance. *Battle simulations, television shows, and interactive games inhabit a mutually reinforcing system of marketable threats, enticements, and protections.* A disaster imaginary takes hold, which traffics across the worlds of fact and fiction, promiscuously borrowing its parts and depositing them across a wide range of cultural phenomena. The phenomenon of 'news gaming' is one obvious manifestation – although the term is redundant, because news has already been structurally absorbed within the entertainment machine, with gaming one of its primary engagement modes.

We are here in the territory of the 'logistics of perception management'[25] – the realm of spin and 'reality control,' where facts, interpretations, and events are mutually shaped to conform to strategic doctrines; where reality is positioned as something that is inherently pliable; and where the public becomes a surface for the production of effects. There is nothing outside of this system, and especially as it is increasingly able to tap into the affective dimension, where danger is eroticized. This system produces a subject prepared for both disaster and desire, as both are subsumed into a larger cosmos of affective stimulation: a citizen indoctrinated to 'be ready,' in both a physical and a cognitive sense, for any call to action.

A citizen inscribed in the real.

The sky outside the airport is now ominously dark. The overhead spotlights have transformed the concourse into an enormous stage set. More flight delays have been announced (including my own). Travellers have become agitated and morose. Children are screaming, arms aflail. Adults hovering menacingly.

The precision-driven woman has boarded her flight. Surely, she is now following her plane's trajectory on the onboard GIS. Even though she is gone, I continue my awareness of my own subjective position as tracker – if only to more fully inhabit the drama, probe my role in the script, stay in the game. I aggressively look for new objects of study. Suddenly, I hear an all-too-familiar address over the intercom system, compelling me to report suspicious persons. Action! I heed the call, and adopt a position of dutiful vigilance: the citizen-detective. Eyes narrowed, I scan the concourse for suspicious behaviour. I secretly wonder what kind of suspicious activity I should be looking for, and what could possibly compel me, were I to locate a person displaying it, to scurry over to Security to report them.

I glare at a woman who has stopped abruptly in the main corridor. She stands idle amid the flow, the rush of passersby nearly tumbling over her. (Suspicious deviation in normal patterns of movement flow.) I cast a wary glance at a man in a green sweatsuit as he fondles an object of concern, concealing it from public view. (Deviant repetitive movement and suspicious level of transparency-avoidance.) I stare at a man who repeatedly pads his pocket nervously. (Suspicious level of agitation.) I spot a solitary bag. (Unattended object.) A book. (Dangerous ideas.)

Across the concourse, a wayward child points in my direction. Suddenly, I realize the most insidious part of the drill: What about *me*? With this realization, I am transformed. I am the person at Sartre's keyhole, caught in the act, who knows that he is seen at the moment he sees. I have now become an object for the gaze of another. Looked at, I look at myself. My awareness of my subjective position as tracker has now shifted to that of my objective position as suspect. I modify my actions accordingly, submitting myself – subjectively and bodily – to this normative performance-machine. My posture straightens, I look at my watch, and I am 'back on track.' The unobtrusive traveller who, edges smoothed, blends seamlessly into the crowd.

This performance-machine, however, when inhabited fully, does not necessarily end up reinforcing norms. Rather, it produces deviance from them. It is only a matter of time. To internalize the gaze of suspicion is to eventually find wrongdoing in oneself, even if it has to be self-generated. Guilt is produced, to be denied or accepted into the calculus of identity.

In this shifting matrix of tracking, it is but a short distance between tracker and suspect. Or, more accurately, there is no distance at all: for to track in one context is to become target in another. If the voyeuristic position of the tracker is the key subject position for a new consumer-security culture, then perhaps the target is its key object position, which always overlaps with it.

If tracking moves towards an instantaneity of action – eliminating time and space intervals and connecting multiple actors, human or not, as if they were one – then in the extreme case, as Virilio would have it, this real time arena is one in which 'coincidence' takes the place of communication,[26] and the emphasis shifts from the 'standardization of public opinion' to the 'synchronization of public emotion.'[27] In a real-time world where there is less and less time to act, or where action plays out in barely measurable fractions of seconds, interpretive attention must turn away from exterior movements and instead towards 'interior' states, to *dispositions* to act that accumulate just at the horizon of the visible.

We are talking about incorporealization not representation, implication, not objectivity, bodily intensities, not linguistic mediation. A domain that is occupied with qualities of movement and rhythm, rather than with the calculi of symbolic positioning. This domain traffics in motivating power, rather than in meaning or rational logic.

Rather than that of the effective, this is the domain of the affective. What is the difference? If we follow Gilles Deleuze's description and understand affect as a modality of perception, then it is one that ceases to yield an action and instead brings forth an expression. Affect is a movement that is not engaged outwardly (with visible effects) but rather absorbed inwardly – a tendency or interior effort that halts just this side of doing. It is about how one experiences oneself as oneself, or senses oneself from the inside:[28] the perception of one's own aliveness, vitality, and changeability, which can be sensed as 'freedom.'[29] It is the body's sense of the aliveness of a situation, which also moves across the intercorporeal world,[30] generating a sense of coincidence between subject and object. As such, affect allows us to further toggle between the positions of tracker and target, to the extent that these distinctions blur.

This is a contradictory domain, where scopophilic pleasures and surveillant anxieties cohabit. 'Morbid curiosities' flourish. Violence is both horrific and pleasurable. To acknowledge this domain is to admit danger and conflict as constitutive elements of attraction – manifest in the unpredictable, perilous web of intrigue that pulls us into the narrative world and compels us to inhabit the drama. In the next moment, we could be the victim. The tracker could be the target. We do not know what danger lurks ahead, but we must continue at our peril. At any moment, desire could meet its constitutive other – death. As Georges Bataille would remind us, what compels us is the possibility of union.

This is a domain that brings us closer to the real. We will try to track and capture it, as quickly and efficiently as possible – as I do within the paragraphs of this text. I try to put my finger on it, touch it with precision, press it into the service of argument. Yet, it cannot be assimilated. This domain cannot be incorporated into the symbolic order of language or into the domain of shared images. It is, however, a necessary illusion, for without it, our entire apparatus of signification would crumble. Tracking would cease to exist.

This is why, when we consider the real object of the precision-impulse – a technologically enabled drive to augment human capabilities by developing new human-machine composites, or a technologically enabled drive to reduce mediation and offer a form of direct connection to our real objects of inquiry – we must acknowledge the extent to which these effective and affective dimensions are complimentary.

Hence the embodiment of the dynamic in this essay.

Analytic or performative? Objective or implicated? Onstage or off?

This affective space-time of bodily awareness, disposition, and readiness is one that has become increasingly measurable and analysable[31] through new technologies of tracking and filtering. These technologies are able to probe into the intimate and nearly instantaneous states of bodily movement, orientation, disposition, and mood, and array them as calculations, statistics, and simulations, and cross-reference them with databased records of consumer or citizen behaviour. This produces a newly constituted body of measurable states and functions – a new ontological state – whose *inclinations to act* are quantifiable and understood as predictable. Inclination-position scripts an object that is already ahead of itself, a shadow future state that exerts a strong gravitational pull. It plays out in new systems of production that aim to narrow the intervals between conception, manufacturing, distribution, and consumption – shrinking the delays between detecting an audience pattern and formatting a new enticement that can address it. Inclination-position plays out in pre-emptive policing and warfare systems that aim to close the gap between sensing and shooting. And it plays out in videogames, where one does not look at the moving target directly so much as anticipate its future position.

According to John Armitage, the U.S. Department of Homeland Security's 'Be Ready' campaign operates on this space of imminent mobility. The 'readiness' it promotes has no real object and is simply perpetuated in a kind of self-generating machine. Yet, it is a profoundly operational space, where the individualized 'desire for mobility' – the consumerist impulse – is recoded and displaced onto the theatres of embodied threat.[32] Desire and fear cohabit here, at the threshold of action, as such concepts as 'freedom' do double duty, promoting a freedom of mobility as well as a sense of freedom that can only result from 'defending our way of life' – that is, the right to own and consume. Buying, then, functions as both pleasure and defence: a form of bodily and social enhancement, and a form of defence against what would threaten it.

This is an interlocking mechanism of acquisition and defence that becomes the very condition of mobility – a 'freedom of mobility' that is about defending the right to own and circulate objects, to constitute oneself as an object to be marketed, to defend these objects from harm, and to forge new pathways within unruly, 'dangerous,' or adventurous market territory. It is a process of defining the self in terms of an unbounded menagerie of attractions and fears, which leaves it forever lacking. Through an interlocking mechanism of selling and consuming, looking and buying, acquiring and defending, one grazes along endless arrays of enticements offered up for the desirous and protective eye – enticements that are aimed at the replication of desire in the eyes of others, or of drawing the groundlines of defence.

Readiness, then, probes the embodied dimension of the perceptual mode of tracking. It is a useful analytical concept because it de-privileges the visual, or concepts of the perceptual, that do not fully engage the affective dimension – as we find in the ocular-centric discourses of visual studies. Readiness maintains a dimension of pleasure, ignored in many theories of contemporary power. For it is not simply repressive in a disciplinary sense: it is also *excessive*.[33]

Through the scrim of readiness, we can understand tracking as characterized by a shift towards real-time engagements and continuous, heightened states of alertness and preparedness, in such a way as to generate an embodied state of receptivity for both conflict and libidinous consumption. It produces the body as a receptive site for both fears and attractions, integrating combat and commodity.

What is needed in order to address this landscape is not only a biopolitics but, as Nigel Thrift suggests, a *microbiopolitics*.[34] *If new technologies of networking, speed, and tracking have opened up this site of the micro – the affective space of intimate bodily awareness, disposition, and readiness – then this is a space that can be politicized.*

A large body of theoretical work has as its focus the delocalizing or deterritorializing effects of real-time technologies, which are often regarded as having contributed to the evacuation of geographical space, overriding the specifics of place and distance. Virilio, for example, has often suggested that real-time technologies and their accompanying dimension of 'liveness' have prompted the disappearance of physical space – in other words, that 'real time' has superceded 'real space.' For him, such deterritorialization can only lead to inertia.[35]

What we are witnessing today, however, is not a one-way delocalization or deterritorialization, but rather a volatile combination of the diffused and the positioned, or *the placeless and the place-coded*. Perhaps nowhere has this been more apparent than with mobile GIS and location-aware technologies. These technologies and discourses are serving to weave together degrees of temporal and spatial specificity. They are helping to generate an emerging precision-landscape where every object and human is tagged with geospatial coordinates: a world of information overlays that is no longer virtual but wedded to objects and physical sites. Communication is tagged with position, movement-flows are quantified, and new location-aware relationships are generated among actors, objects, and spaces.

Tracking has played a primary role in this shift. Its landscapes of inclination-position fuel the geospatial interfaces – such as those evidenced in Google Maps and the C5 GPS media player[36] – which are becoming important modes of access to any phenomenon. As media become contextualized with geospatial data and become interoperable, the Web is transformed into a real-time atlas of sorts. The geospatial Web browser emerges as a primary interface. Reading and researching, in this case, are transformed into a search-and-target mission – a cut through the clutter, precision-driven viewing experience that, as always, is both fuelled and delimited by media technologies and their institutions. These technologies and institutions determine specific rules that circumscribe how we search, speak, and write. Within their matrices, actors, objects, and sites coalesce. New cartographies arise.

With its instantiation in location-aware media, has tracking helped inscribe us in the real, or has it, following Slavoj Žižek, culminated in its opposite – theatrical spectacle? To what extent does conflict – whether in terms of competition, war, or drama – provide its necessary friction?

I board my flight at last and enter a new arena of performance. The cabin lights dim, the engines roar, and the plane accelerates. The man across the aisle from me – a blurry mass of anxiety and pleasure – grips the armrest, thrusts his head back, and opens his mouth in a wild grimace. Fear or delicious exhilaration? A roller coaster ride or a dance with death?

The plane levels off, and the cabin springs to life. A chorus of gadgets lights up across the aisles: seat-mounted monitors, DVD players, laptops, videogames. A carnival of media inputs, bathing the cabin in the glow of otherworldly distraction. All passengers are absorbed into a world of entertainment: a spectacular non-place that is everywhere but here. I consider for a moment that tracking – precision-guided seeing for a mobile, competitive, and accelerated consumer-security culture – is fast absorbed into a much more constitutive mode of engagement.

What is that mode?

My seatmate plugs into her game console, as I type the cliffhanger for this act.

Acknowledgments

With special thanks to John Armitage.

Notes

1 Martin Heidegger, 'The Age of the World Picture,' in *Electronic Culture: Technology and Visual Representation*, Timothy Druckrey, ed. (London: Aperture, 1996), 49. For an important discussion of the contemporary relevance of Heidegger's work see Arthur Kroker, *The Will to Technology and the Culture of Nihilism: Heidegger, Nietzsche, and Marx* (Toronto: University of Toronto Press, 2004), esp. 'Hyper-Heidegger: The Question of the Post-Human.' 33–72.

2 Slavoj Žižek, *Welcome to the Desert of the Real* (London: Verso, 2002).

3 Ibid.

4 This insight is that of Lars Spuybroak, cited in Mark B N. Hansen, *New Philosophy for New Media* (Cambridge: MIT Press, 2004), 123.

5 One could begin with the development of radar during the Second World War, or even much earlier. But my emphasis is on computer-enabled tracking. I will understand tracking here in its computer-assisted, rather than earlier analogue, forms.

6 Peter Galison, 'The Ontology of the Enemy: Norbert Weiner and the Cybernetic Vision,' *Critical Inquiry* 21/1 (1994): 228–66. See also Peter Galison, 'War Against the Center,' *Grey Room* 4 (2001): 6–33.

7 Paul N. Edwards, *The Closed World: Computers and the Politics of Discourse in Cold War America* (Cambridge: MIT Press, 1996), 1–15.

8 Felix Guattari, 'Regimes, Pathways, Subjects,' in *Incorporations*, ed. J. Crary and S. Kwinter (Cambridge: MIT Press, 1992), 18.

9 Felix Guattari, *The Three Ecologies* (London: Athlone, 2000), 48.

10 For a comprehensive analysis of the history of SAGE, see Edwards, *Closed World*.

11 Heidegger, 'Age of the World Picture,' 57–8.

12 Edwards, *Closed World*, 1–15.

13 N. Katherine Hayles, *How We Became Posthuman: Virtual Bodies in Cybernetics, Literature, and Informatics* (Chicago: University of Chicago Press, 1999), 19. This book is essential reading for anyone who wants to understand the privileging of information over embodiment, across the wartime sciences and cultural products of the twentieth century.

14 Paul Virilio, *Open Sky*, trans. Julie Rose (London: Verso, 1997), 10, 19, 30.

15 SpaceDaily.com, 'A Network of Warfighters to Do Battle in 21st Century Conflicts,' New York (AFP) (13 Nov. 2004), available at http://www.spacedaily.com/news/milspace-comms-04zzr.html. Accessed 15 Dec. 2005. Thanks to Irving Goh for pointing this out.

16 General Fogelman, speaking to the House of Representatives, cited by Paul Virilio in *Strategy of Deception* (London: Verso, 2000), 17–18, from an article by F. Filloux entitled 'Le Pentagone la tête dans les étoiles,' *Libération*, 20 April 1999.

17 For a brilliant discussion of this integration, see Ryan Bishop and John Phillips, 'Sighted Weapons and Modernist Opacity: Aesthetics, Poetics, Prosthetics,' *Boundary 2* 29/2 (2002): 158–9.

18 Sean Cubitt, *The Cinema Effect* (Cambridge: MIT Press, 2004).

19 Elaine Scarry, 'Watching and Authorizing the Gulf War,' in *Media Spectacles*, ed. Marjorie Garber, Jann Matlock, and Rebecca L. Walkowitz, 57–73 (London: Routledge, 1993), as cited by Margaret Morse in *Virtualities: Television, Media Art, and Cyberculture* (Bloomington: Indiana University Press, 1998), 36–67.

20 This definition is from Lev Manovich, *The Language of New Media* (Cambridge: MIT Press, 2001).

21 Friedrich Kittler, *Gramophone, Film, Typewriter* (Stanford: Stanford University Press, 1999).

22 My discussion of the integration of the military and entertainment industry owes a huge debt to Tim Lenoir's pioneering research. See Tim Lenoir, 'All But War Is Simulation: The Military-Entertainment Complex,' *Configurations* 8 (2000): 289–335. Tim Lenoir and Henry Lowood, 'Theaters of War: The Military-Entertainment Complex,' in *Kunstkammer, Laboratorium, Bühne – Schauplätze des Wissens im 17. Jahrhundert*, ed. Jan Lazardzig, Helmar Schramm, and Ludger Schwarte, 432–64 (Berlin: de Gruyter, 2003).

23 This statement makes reference to Lev Manovich's statement: 'Born from animation, cinema pushed animation to its periphery, only in the end to become a particular case of animation.' Manovich, *Language of New Media*, 302.

24 Lenoir, 'All But War Is Simulation,' 289–335.

25 John Armitage, 'Beyond Postmodernism? Paul Virilio's Hypermodern Cultural Theory,' in *Life in the Wires: The CTHEORY Reader*, ed. Arthur and Marilouise Kroker, 354–68 (Victoria: CTHEORY Books, 2004). Paul Virilio, *War and Cinema: The Logistics of Perception,* trans. Patrick Camiller (London: Verso, 1989).

26 Paul Virilio, *[CTRL]SPACE: Rhetorics of Surveillance from Bentham to Big Brother*, ed. Thomas Levin, Ursula Frohne, and Peter Weibel (Cambridge: MIT Press, 2002), 112.

27 Paul Virilio, 'Cold Panic,' *Cultural Politics* 1/1 (2005): 29.

28 Hansen, *New Philosophy for New Media*, 134–5.

29 Brian Massumi, cited in Nigel Thrift, 'Intensities of Feeling: Towards a Spatial Politics of Affect,' *Geografiska Annaler* 86 B (2004): 61.

30 Nigel Thrift, ibid.

31 Ibid., 65.

32 John Armitage, 'On Ernst Juenger's "Total Mobilization": A Re-Evaluation in the Era of the War on Terrorism,' *Body and Society* 9/4 (2003): 204.

33 J. McKenzie, cited in Thrift, *Intensities of Feeling*, 64.

34 Thrift, ibid., 69.

35 Paul Virilio, *Virilio Live*, ed. John Armitage (London: Sage, 2001).

36 C5 GPS media player website, available at http://www.c5corp.com/projects/gpsmediaplayer/index.shtml. Accessed 15 Dec. 2005.

6 Understanding Meta-media

LEV MANOVICH

If we want to describe what new media does to old media using a single term, 'mapping' is a good candidate. Software allows us to remap old media objects into new structures – turning media into 'meta-media.'[1]

In contrast to media, meta-media acquires three new properties. First, using software, data can be translated into another domain: time into 2D space, 2D image into 3D space, sound into 2D image, and so on. (More complex and unusual mappings are also possible, and the search for new mappings allowing us access to old media objects in new ways congruent with information interfaces that we use in our everyday life represents one of the most fruitful research directions in new media art.) Second, media objects can be manipulated using GUI (graphical user interface) techniques such as move, transform, zoom, multiple views, filter, and summarize.[2] And third, media objects can now be 'processed' using standard techniques of computerized data processing such as search, sort, and replace.

Let me provide a few examples of meta-media involving new interfaces for cinema. For instance, software developed by Steve Mamber of UCLA allows a user to 'map' feature films into a matrix of still images, each image representing a single shot. Here time is mapped into space. Another software tool written by Mamber takes shots from film and reconstructs their architecture as 3D navigable spaces (thus reversing the normal procedure of computer animation). Here the mapping goes from 2D to 3D – from the flat surface of a movie screen into a virtual computer space.

The project *Invisible Shape of Things Past* by Art+Com in Berlin maps historical films of Berlin into new spatial structures that are integrated into a 3D navigable reconstruction of the city.[3] Another ground-breaking mapping project by Art+Com is a *Medial Stage and Costume Design* set whose parameters are interactively controlled by actors during the performance of an opera.[4] The computer reads the body movements and gestures of the actors and uses this information to control the generation of a virtual set projected onto a screen behind the stage. In this case, the positions of a human body are mapped onto various parameters of a virtual architecture such as layout, texture, colour, and light.

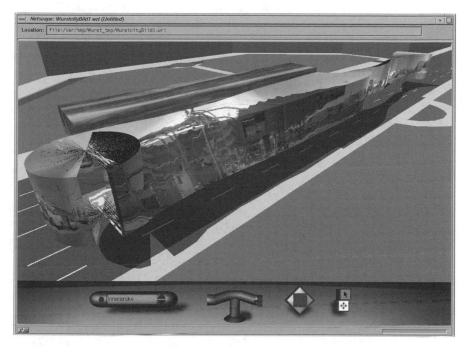

Figure 6.1. *Invisible Shape of Things Past.* Joachim Sauter / ART+COM, 1993–7.

For the designer of this project, Joachim Sauter, it was important to preserve the constraints of the traditional opera format – actors foregrounded by lighting with the set behind them – while carefully adding new dimensions to it.[5] Therefore, following the conventions of traditional opera, the virtual set appears as a backdrop behind the actors, and no longer as a static picture but rather a dynamic construction that changes throughout the performance.

Note that the mappings in these examples preserve the granularity and syntactical structure of the old media object, while giving us new ways to navigate it, to experience its structure, to compress and expand our views of the object, and to interactively control it. In the case of Mamber's project, the film still consists of shots that can be played from beginning to end – or we can use the new representation of all the shots in a film as a single interactive 2D image matrix. In the case of *Invisible Shape* we can similarly play the historical film segment from beginning to end – or we can navigate the 3D model of Berlin to see where these films were taken.

This is why I refer to this type of new media as 'meta-media.' *A meta-media object contains both language and meta-language* – both the original media structure (a film, an architectural space, a sound track) and the software tools that allow the user to generate descriptions of, and to change, this structure.

Figure 6.2. *Medial Stage and Costume Design.* Joachim Sauter / ART+COM, 2002.

If you think that meta-media is a conservative phenomenon that 'betrays' the movement of computer culture towards developing its own unique cultural techniques – artificial intelligence, artificial life, simulation, database navigation, virtual worlds, and so on – you are wrong. Since the 1970s modern computing has been grounded in Alan Kay's concept (influenced by previous ground-breaking work in human computer interfaces, most importantly Ivan Sutherland's 1962 Sketchpad software) of computers as 'personal expressive media.' After he arrived at Xerox PARC (Palo Alto Research Center), Kay directed the development of a word processor program, a music composition program, a paint program, and other tools that redefined the computer as *a simulation machine for old media.* So, although the routine use of computers as media simulators was not possible until the 1980s, the paradigmatic shift had already been defined by 1970. Gradually, other roles of the modern computer – a machine for computation, real-time control, and network communication – became less visible than its role as a 'simulation engine.' (Of course, the development of the World Wide Web in the 1990s made the role of network communication quite visible to the public.) The computer's ability to simulate other media (which means simulating their interfaces and 'data formats' such as written text, image, and sound) is not an afterthought – it is the essence of the modern post-1970s computer.

(It is possible to state this idea even more radically – by moving the date even earlier, to the 1930s. When Alan Turing defined the computer as a general-purpose simulation machine that can simulate most other machines that have already been invented, the

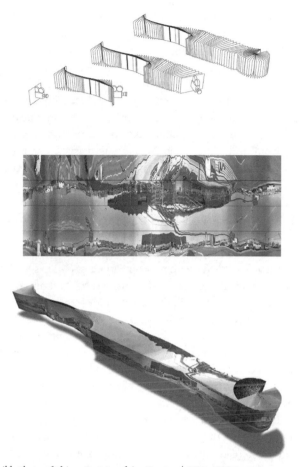

Figure 6.3. *Invisible Shape of Things Past.* Joachim Sauter / ART+COM, 1993–7.

idea of media simulation was implicitly introduced. But it was only in the 1950s to 1970s that the work of Sutherland, Engelhard, Kay, and others made this idea into a reality by allowing the computer to systematically simulate the operations of drawing, drafting, painting, photo manipulation, sound generation, editing, and so on.)

What is crucial is that the computer's simulational role is as revolutionary as its other roles. Most software tools for media creation and manipulation do not simply simulate old media interfaces – a book page and a table of contents in Acrobat, a pan and a zoom of a virtual camera in Maya, time code count and a razor blade in Final Cut Pro – but also allow for new types of operations on the media content.[6] In other words, these tools carry the potential to transform media into meta-media.

Today it is the meta-media paradigm   rather than other seemingly original computer techniques or even computer programming itself – that is at the centre of computer culture. Outside of the professional and scientific domains, consumers think of computers as machines for downloading, storing, transmitting, and editing media. Software such as media players and editors, CD and DVD burners, ports to connect digital still and video cameras, or MP3 players are what consumer computing is about today.

This is not accidental. The logic of meta-media fits well with other key aesthetic paradigms of today – the remixing of previous cultural forms of a given media (most visible in music, architecture, design, and fashion) and a second type of remixing, that of national cultural traditions now submerged into the medium of globalization. (The terms 'postmodernism' and 'globalization' can be used as aliases for these two remix paradigms.) Meta-media then can be thought of alongside these two types of remixing as a third type: the remixing of interfaces of various cultural forms and of new software techniques – in short, the remix of culture and computers.

Not every remix by itself is great; it all depends on who is doing the mix. If we look at the interfaces of popular commercial software for media access and manipulation from this perspective, they begin to look like the work of a strange DJ who mixes operations from old interfaces of various media with new operations of GUI in somewhat erratic and unpredictable ways. My favourite example of such a remix – and my least favourite of all popular commercial software – is the interface of Adobe Acrobat Reader. It combines (1) an interface from time media software (VCR style arrow buttons); (2) an interface from image manipulation software (a zoom tool); (3) interface elements that have a strong association with print tradition – although they never existed in print (page icons also controlling the zoom factor); (4) interfaces that have existed in books (the bookmarks window); and (5) the standard elements of GUI such as search, filter, and multiple windows.

In other cases, however, media/software remixes can provide us with fundamentally new and stylistically/metaphorically coherent paradigms for representing the visible world, our knowledge, human history, and our fellow human beings. The *Invisible Shape of Things Past* and *Medial Stage and Costume Design* are among my favourite examples of successful meta-media. Artists and designers do not have an exclusive licence to create interesting meta-media, though. For instance, one of the most culturally important examples of meta-media that everyone is familiar with today is hypertext. Developed by Ted Nelson in the mid-1960s, hypertext gives us a new paradigm for organizing information and knowledge. Since Tim Berners-Lee's World Wide Web popularized it in the 1990s, hypertext has become as central to contemporary culture as other older media techniques on which we have been dependent for many centuries – for example, the one-point linear perspective used for image organization or the codex system used for text organization.

Inventing meta-media is not simple, because it requires an in-depth understanding of not only computer science but also the history and conventions of various media and cultural forms. The pay-off, however, is enormous. Until digital computers, each introduction of new media, from Guttenberg to Sony, required the manufacture and adaptation of new hardware: printing presses, film cameras and projectors, video recorders, lenses, and so on. But meta-media require only new software, and therefore

Figure 6.4 *Medial Stage and Costume Design*. Joachim Sauter / ART+COM, 2002.

they can be developed by a single person or a small group and easily disseminated. Never before has inventing new media been so easy, at least from a technical point of view.

Notes

1 I introduced the term 'meta-media' in my *Avant-garde as Software* (1999), available at http://www.uoc.edu/artnodes/eng/art/manovich1002/manovich1002.html.
2 In my book *The Language of New Media* (Cambridge: MIT Press, 2001) I discuss in more detail how the operations specific to particular media are transformed to become general-purpose media interfaces.
3 See http://www.artcom.de.
4 The full name of the project is *Medial Stage and Costume Design for André Werners 'Marlowe, the Jew of Malta.'* See http://www.artcom.de for more information and project visuals. Accessed 20 Sept. 2005.
5 Joachim Sauter, personal communication, Berlin, July 2002.
6 Remapping media data into a new domain is one of the most important among these operations.

7 *Warcraft* and Utopia

ALEXANDER R. GALLOWAY

The theme of 'imagining life after capitalism' is once again the topic of academic atten-tion, renewed mostly through fresh interest in certain messianic or predictive claims about the transformation of the mode of production. Now, however, computers and the information economy play a central role in the debate.[1] The theme of utopia, in the work of Fredric Jameson, for example, is closely tied to this question, utopia being a site in which possible non-capitalist scenarios are worked out, worked through, or otherwise proven not to work at all. Here, I will examine some of the problems and challenges for the task of imagining life after capitalism, and then I will discuss two interesting areas – networks and play – that have historically represented threats to or departures from capitalism. Finally, I will describe how networks and play have in recent decades become entirely synonymous with the present mode of production and exchange.

Various leftist utopias come to mind when discussing life after capitalism. The more overtly political, predictive texts from Karl Marx are conventionally read and contextualized in this manner, as a utopia for the 'after.' In *Specters of Marx*, Jacques Derrida refers to this as the messianic thread in Marxism, a fervent desire for what is to come. This reading posits Marxism as a somewhat meteorological science (to use Toby Miller's expression) for the prediction of the inevitable. This first theory of uto-pia, of life after capitalism, pays chronological attention to the word 'after.' Of this variety one has no doubt heard a great deal and witnessed a good deal less. Promises are made but their fulfilment is forever deferred.

There is, however, a second model of utopia that is less often identified: nostalgia as utopia. This utopia privileges life *before* capitalism, minimalism and disengagement from the world system. Thus, in the historical period in which the commodity is no longer pri-marily an object, but has become an image – the so-called society of the spectacle that emerged in the mid-twentieth-century – one sees the emergence of minimalism as an aesthetic project. This project grew out of the ascetic principles and formal aspirations of modernism. The utopian longing for the 'before' also characterizes romanticism. In Friedrich Schiller's letters, published in the volume *On the Aesthetic Education of Man*, there is an interesting nesting of one utopian aspiration within another: a future state is proposed, one that Schiller terms the Aesthetic State, yet this proposal is tightly encased and layered inside the rhetorical shell of romanticism. (Indeed, 'before utopias' may be identified as the driving force behind classicism, or many varieties of conservatism.)[2]

Schiller's 'play-drive,' the central philosophical term in his letters and around which his entire spiritual development of man revolves, is also the recipient of new-found attention in recent years. This attention may be fuelled by the increasing prominence of the medium of the videogame, which has renewed interest in theories of play and games. Let me now preview the question of play, and unpack a little of what I believe to be one of the most compelling, if not utopias, then certainly allegories of the present moment. This is the case of the online multiplayer game *World of Warcraft*, launched in 2004. (The game recently surpassed five million players worldwide.) An argument can be made that all videogames are, at a certain level, utopian projects, simply because all videogames create worlds in which certain laws are simulated and certain other laws are no longer simulated. The freedom to selectively simulate, then, operates in a videogame as the most important scaffolding for utopia. Further, multiplayer games instantiate (both materially and interpersonally) a utopian space in ways not seen in previous media, for the diegetic world itself is larger than the imaginative plane of any given player (who indeed may even be offline while others remain online). Groups, guilds, raids, and other in-game collaborations, both ad hoc and otherwise, what philosophers of action call 'shared cooperative activity,' are often required for game-play. These social groups gesture towards a distinctly utopian possibility for social interaction, a shift analogous to Marx's theory of primitive accumulation and the institution of more collaborative labour practices, which themselves were the conditions of possibility for collective action. Like factories before them, multiplayer games require and support a whole variety of group-based play scenarios (I will address whether they are also labour scenarios below). This echoes Johan Huizinga's claim – his 1938 book *Homo Ludens* is foundational for any critique of play – that play necessarily promotes the formation of social groups.[3] *World of Warcraft* evokes a premodern hodgepodge of technologies and narrative scenarios (given time, one might cognitively map the historical fantasy of the game's narrative – trace when exactly the blunderbuss was invented, or the introduction of certain kinds of armour, for example, all the while knowing that such a pursuit could never be 'fixed' or arrived at with any degree of precision), overtly participating in the 'utopia for the before,' imagining life *before* capitalism. However, the functionality of the game is pure software culture, suggesting that perhaps the more one tries to strip utopia of its machinic core, by cloaking it in any manner of pure fantasy or premodern worlds (e.g., 'dungeons and dragons,' 'swords and sorcery'), the more informatic and algorithmic it becomes, reverting to the software equivalent of twenty-sided dice. Indeed, dice are repurposed in *World of Warcraft*: into the various logics of software code, random number generation, action statistics, and particularly in terms of how identity is defined as a set of mathematical variables such as stamina, agility, and health.

A great work of popular culture commentary is worth mentioning at this point: Jim Munroe's short video *My Trip to Liberty City*. In this satirical clip the game *Grand Theft Auto* is presented in the form of an amateur vacation video. Midway through the work, the voice-over narrator admits something profound – the real reason he loves 'visiting' Liberty City, the city where *Grand Theft Auto III* transpires, is that there is *no advertising*. The game, despite being a hyper-mediated cultural artefact, produces an imaginary world where mediation itself is on vacation. This is in accordance with the understanding of minimalism as a utopian reaction to image-rich society.

A similar force is at play in *World of Warcraft*. This brings me to the first of two related claims: the game is a utopia for *a world without signifiers*; it is characterized by a minimalist desire. Ignoring the interface overlay for a moment, one notices that the game's diegetic world (the imaginary narrative space within which game-play transpires) has very few linguistic or symbolic signifiers – in sharp contrast to our offline world of brand logos, advertisements, linguistic signs, and so on. To be sure, the game is not free from signification. There exist guild insignias, visual placards for various vendors' buildings, and indeed, the entire three-dimensional model of the game is, at root, a form of digital signification. Yet, inside the diegetic narrative, *World of Warcraft* projects a space of pure formal representation, cleansed of unnecessary symbolic or linguistic ornamentation. Brands and logos are gone, as are words and images. This is part of the fantasy of fantasy. 'Ornaments cannot be invented,' wrote Theodor Adorno on the Viennese modernist Adolf Loos. 'In art the more that must be made, sought, invented, the more uncertain it becomes if it can be made or invented. Art that is radically and explicitly something made must ultimately confront its own feasibility.'[4] This is essentially the conundrum of formalism in modernism: reducing art to pure form, and hence cleansing it of all invention or contingency, causes it to re-emerge in some sort of contentless but pure shape which itself nevertheless pops up anew as 'style.' Removing linguistic and symbolic signifiers from the diegetic space of *World of Warcraft* is an extension of this aesthetic project.

Anyone who has played *World of Warcraft*, however, knows that this is not a game free of signifiers or of iconography at any level, and neither is it free of symbolic or abstract representation. I noted above that this was the case for the *diegetic* space of the game; nevertheless, interfaces cannot and should not be ignored. Thus, while the diegetic world of the game aspires to be signifier-free (even prominent in-world linguistic signifiers such as player names or NPC [non-player character] quest markers are, I argue, *non*-diegetic), the rest of the interface is flush with these aesthetic forms.

Consequently, my second claim contradicts the first, but in a way that affirms the very internal tensions of utopian desire itself: the game performs a *semiotic segregation* whereby textual and iconographic signifiers are divorced from the diegetic world of the game, which itself is saved for so-called transparent representation. In this scenario, all symbolic and linguistic signs migrate into a purely functional layer and are removed from the diegetic layer. This is precisely how *World of Warcraft* functions. Playing the game one realizes that the vast majority of signification exists in the heads-up display, the two-dimensional gamic overlay which itself has a long history as an abstraction from the physical and embodied interfaces of military aviation. The signifier has been banished from diegetic or representational space, this is true, but the non-diegetic or functional sections of the game are constituted almost entirely by iconographic and textual signifiers. Thus, this minimalist utopia represents a segregation or separation effect, a desiring utopia where *signification is understood purely as machinic functionality.* For example, spell-casting and fighting in *World of Warcraft* are processes of algorithmic unfolding. Commands are issued by players and interpreted by the machine in series. 'The Utopian text does not tell a story at all,' wrote Jameson, 'it describes a mechanism or even a kind of machine.'[5] While this may seem to be an incredible claim – utopia always describes a machine – one need only to examine the game-play of *World of Warcraft* for an example of such a utopia. (And, as I mentioned above with reference to selective simulation, the reverse possibility must also be explored, that all videogames, as machines, might be understood as experiments in utopia.)

Thus far, I have discussed two permutations of utopia, both of which gesture towards some sort of absence of capitalism. The first permutation is a postcapitalist utopia in the form of progressive political desires, while the second is a precapitalist utopia in the form of romanticism, classicism, or minimalism. Nevertheless, there is certainly a third option: the present as utopia. Because life *before* capitalism poses just as much of a threat to capital, capitalism tends to foreclose the past as well as the future. It forecloses on both as possible options for utopian practice. In *Laws,* Plato states that in a utopian state there would be no laws at all. There would be no abstraction of sovereignty. In a utopian state there would be a one-to-one mapping between any instance, any infraction, any particular case, and its adjudication. However, Plato admits that in absence of this perfection, actual states must tolerate laws. This acknowledgment of unachieved perfection is precisely what capitalism is unable to do, either epistemologically or even practically. It is a central prohibition of capitalism: never to think of the present as second best. As Jameson wrote, it is 'our imprisonment in a non-utopian present without historicity or futurity.'[6] What capitalism teaches us is that the present moment *is* the best of all possible worlds, that stasis *is* utopia. In the Marxist tradition this is the notion that capitalism and history are essentially at odds, that history is implicitly a critique of capitalism, resulting in the left's call to 'always historicize.'

Keeping in mind the example of the utopian visual mode encased in a dystopian narrative of conflict discussed above, I will now examine a narrative of conflict that is encased in problems around knowledge and cultural imagination. This narrative is one of the most fascinating aphorisms of political philosophy in recent years. It reveals the intricate interplay between visions of life outside capitalism while simultaneously illuminating how threats to capitalism are put into discourse. In the following, U.S. Secretary of Defense Donald Rumsfeld is responding to questions from the press regarding the lack of evidence connecting Iraqi weapons of mass destruction with terrorists:

> Reports that say that something hasn't happened are always interesting to me ... Because as we know, there are known knowns; there are things we know we know. We also know there are known unknowns; that is to say we know there are some things we do not know. But there are also unknown unknowns – the ones we don't know we don't know.[7]

This passage can be understood in a variety of ways. First, it is possible that Rumsfeld is making an empirical claim about what is the case. In this sense, Rumsfeld may be lamenting the problem of verifiability: that it is very difficult to say with certainty that something has *not* happened. This is an ontological challenge, a problem of the empirical verifiability of one's knowledge of the world and the objects within it.

Rumsfeld is also making a claim about knowledge, and quite explicitly so. While he is claiming that one *can* know, he is also saying that one can negate knowing: the *un*known is something that can be circumnavigated. (This is formally analogous to paranoia. The paranoiac perceives the unknown in every miniscule detail of life. Every little thing is a clue about an intricate conspiracy against the paranoid individual.) But Rumsfeld goes beyond this and says something much more profound, which is that the utter negation of knowledge is in fact always a *double* negation. One must negate knowledge twice. This is, using his terminology, the 'unknown unknown.' Consider imagination and the process of thinking: imagination is a cognitive, or knowledge-based process, that itself is oriented towards the creation of knowledge. It is a doubling from the get-go. Thus, the absolute negation of imagination, of utopian thinking, also has to be a double negation. One cannot close the book on utopia. One must forget how to *think*, about utopia or anything else. Jameson makes a similar claim in *The Seeds of Time* when he states that it is easier to imagine the end of the earth and the end of nature than it is to imagine the end of capitalism. For Jameson, the real problem is the crisis of imagination, not simply the crisis of the earth. Now instead of paranoia, one is in the grip of schizophrenia. (In computer science this is analogous to the difference between zero and null, zero is the known unknown while null is the unknown unknown. Null is the absence of a value, while zero *is*, in fact, a value, it refers to the number that comes below one and above negative one.) Rumsfeld is in fact saying the opposite of Jameson, or at least diverting from Jameson significantly, that it is indeed very *hard* to imagine and predict all possible methods for destroying the earth and nature. Indeed, Rumsfeld's own warcraft is to be an 'imagineer': his task is to imagine all possible destructions of the empire, all possible dystopias. This is why the unknown unknowns are key for Rumsfeld, but also why they are potentially very threatening. To recap, Rumsfeld's aphorism makes claims about: what is the case (the verifiability challenge); what one can know and what one cannot know; and how it is possible not to know what one does not know (a riff on the Socratic conceit).

To expound upon the third claim that Rumsfeld makes one must examine the status of dystopia and its location in current society. Again we return to Jameson, who states, 'Dystopia is generally a narrative, which happens to a specific subject or character, whereas the Utopia text is mostly non-narrative and, I would like to say, somehow without a subject-position.'[8] In Rumsfeld's consideration, the unknown unknowns, the moments when knowledge is negated twice, are always already a *narrative* for the annihilation of the state. The point here is that the double negation of knowledge, the unknown unknowns, are for Rumsfeld never utopian, but instead, *consigned in advance to the work of dystopia*. Utopia is understood as a deficiency in one's ability to imagine *annihilation*, not a deficiency in one's ability to imagine liberation or anything else more pleasant. *World of Warcraft* looks tame when compared with Rumsfeld. Thus, it is clear that while Rumsfeld and Jameson are engaging similar issues, they are on opposite imaginative planes. In light of 11 September 2001, Rumsfeld's diagnosis must be understood as an illumination of a crisis of imagination: Americans were unable to imagine that terrorists would use airplanes as missiles. Following this logic, if U.S. officials had been able to imagine that terrorists would do so, they would logically have been able to foreclose on that possible future. (This is precisely the same claim that was made many years ago about Pearl Harbor and the U.S. entrance into the Second World War: the crisis of Pearl Harbor was that American military leadership could not *imagine* that Japanese aircraft carriers could threaten the fleet.) The aphorism from Rumsfeld thus aptly fits into the third mode of utopian thinking, mentioned above, which is the utopia of the present: the yearning for the present, or the ongoing project of the maintenance and sustenance of the present as the best possible scenario. Thus, the unknown unknown is a threat first and foremost because it is a deviation from the maintenance of the present, and therefore quite difficult to bring into imagination as utopia or any another mode of thought (because it is a double negation of thought itself), but second, and this is the contradiction, the very process of attempting to imagine the unknown unknown drags into the light its opposite, the end of imagination itself and the end of humanity in the annihilation of Ground Zero. The moment when Rumsfeld triumphs by cracking through the barrier of the unknown unknown is the same moment when the state cracks and crumbles. Or, when Rumsfeld succeeds, he fails.

The previous section concerns communicating the threat to capitalism, and how various kinds of threats are put into discourse, or indeed are prohibited from being put into discourse. Let me return to the question of networks and play, mentioned above in the context of *World of Warcraft*. Historically, networks and play have represented either a departure from or a direct threat to capitalism. Nevertheless, are networks not foundational to market circulation and hence the very fabric of capitalistic exchange? Yes, certainly. Yet, at the same time, threats to capital are also often understood and articulated as networks. This is particularly true of the specific graph form known as the distributed network, which is characterized by horizontality, a rhizomatic structure, and bi-directional links (called 'edges' in graph theory). Hakim Bey's notion of the nomadic fits in here, as does Gilles Deleuze and Félix Guattari's rhizome; also relevant are the 'grass-roots' movements (to use a synonym for the rhizome) or the new social movements of the 1960s and 1970s (in addition to the so-called anti-globalization movements). These are all specifically defined as networks. But, at the same time, Al-Qaeda, and any number of terrorist groups, are also often defined as networks. On closer examination of this protagonist/antagonist scenario, it becomes clear that the opposition to the network is never a network; it is always a centre, a power centre, whether it is the World Trade Center, or America itself as a kind of hub or authority point for a global empire. In short, the historical tendency is that networks exist in opposition to centres and that networks are the unknown unknown of capitalism.

In recent decades, this has all changed. In recent decades the powers that be have become conscious of the analysis above. Today's revolution in military affairs confirms this, as does the retreat from Keynesian economics of the 1970s and the evolution into a post-Fordist economic model after that decade's energy crisis. The powers that be have developed a new awareness and are adopting flexible, network structures at very core levels. They are adopting flexible network structures not as an apology or concession, not as a sacrifice, but as essential techniques for the very processes of sovereignty, control, and organization. In other words, distributed networks have ceased to be a threat to control and have become the model for control. What was once the problem is now the solution. Today, this is one of the core challenges for imagining a life after capitalism: one can no longer rely on networks as a site for imaginative desire.

The second example is the question of play as an unknown unknown. Play conventionally operates in a very unique and interesting position in the history of Western thought: play is an irreducible, heterogeneous, unquantifiable, absolutely qualitative human endeavour. Conventionally speaking, play is entirely divorced from any kind of productive activity. Play is defined as a negative force that is often a direct threat to production. Play is leisure; play is the inversion of production. Play is an uncapitalizable segment of time. One may return to Friedrich Schiller on the play-drive: the play-drive is a pure moment, and it is a very necessary moment, Schiller would claim, for man's development, but one that is entirely outside the formal, or the abstract, or all the kinds of human drives that lead to the creation of society as a whole. Huizinga, the twentieth-century intellectual historian and critic, makes a similar claim. For Huizinga, play is entirely central to both human action and the creation of culture: however, he is also unwavering in his claim that play is totally outside the base unfolding of production. Huizinga writes that play is external to any kind of material gain (if material gain exists, one no longer is dealing with 'play' but instead its double, sport). For Derrida, who in most regards could not be more different from Huizinga, play is one of the few philosophical concepts that emerges mostly unscathed. This is rare in the work of Derrida, particularly when the philosophical concept is not a Derridean neologism. Surprisingly, for Derrida play remains an absolutely utopian and positive concept.

But today it would be entirely naive to believe that play retains its anti-capitalist or anti-work status. One finds traces of this in Adorno, in his book *Aesthetic Theory*, where he dispenses with Huizinga and Schiller alike. Adorno claims that Schiller's notion of play is nostalgic, in that it is entirely removed from the circuit of production and capital. 'Playful forms are without exception forms of repetition,'[9] is Adorno's lament. (This is not such a radical claim, as many theorists of play agree that repetition is an essential aspect of it. Indeed, for Freud, play is articulated through repetitious activity. In the 'fort/da' game, which is an act of play, the game is 'constantly repeated' by the child who 'never cried when his mother left him for a few hours.'[10] For Freud, neurosis is only ever experienced as a repetition. The common interpretation of the 'fort/da' game is that it is a game of presence and absence, essentially a game of peek-a-boo. However, in Lacan, one sees a slightly different reading of the Freudian scene: the game is not about the cotton-reel, it is about what Lacan calls the 'ditch' or the gap between the reel and the child. Lacan argues that 'the game of the cotton-reel is the subject's answer to what the mother's absence has created on the frontier of his domain – the edge of his cradle – namely, a *ditch*, around which one can only play at jumping.'[11] Lacan claims, contrary to Freud, that it is not the mother who is miniaturized in the cotton-reel, but that a part of the child is detached from himself [detached in the form of the *petit a*] and miniaturized there. For Lacan, the game is not about the return of the mother but simply about repetition and alternation; the game 'is a *here or there*, and [its] aim, in its alternation, is simply that of being the *fort* of a *da*, and the *da* of a *fort*.'[12] So, fort/da is not only a game of peek-a-boo, but also a game of fish. The *string* is the thing, not the cotton-reel it retrieves. If fort/da were simply about appearance and disappearance (or even Lacanian subject formation), there would be no string, just as the game of peek-a-boo has no string. But the string exists. In short, fort/da is a kind of network game, the string being a link in a miniature network. The string is the edge and the cotton-reel is a node. In this sense, the game of fort/da is a game of connectivity. The string *is* connectivity, and the story it tells is how connectivity trumps presence. It is a relational game, in which the creation of links – sending and pulling, linking and retrieving – is paramount. A thoroughly modern youngster, the child playing the fort/da game is a spinner of mesh-works, a weaver of webs.)

Adorno argues that play activities are forms of repetition, and on this many agree, but he goes further to assert that 'in art, play is from the outset disciplinary [and] art allies itself with unfreedom in the specific character of play.'[13] For Adorno, play has been co-opted by the routine of modern life. 'The element of repetition in play is the afterimage of unfree labor, just as sports   the dominant extra-aesthetic form of play – is reminiscent of practical activities and continually fulfills the function of habituating people to the demands of praxis, above all by the reactive transformation or physical displeasure into secondary pleasure, without their noticing that the contraband of praxis has slipped into it.'[14] Thus, in the work of Adorno, play is not a vacation from the pressures of production, but rather the form-of-appearance ('afterimage') of that mode itself, with repetition, displeasure, and competitive interaction being but symptoms for deeper social processes. Recently, many writers have written on how play and creativity have moved from the periphery or the outside of capitalism (if it was ever there to begin with) to the very centre of productive activities. For example, see Alan Liu's recent book *The Laws of Cool*, which examines the commodification of immaterial labour,[15] or Michael Hardt and Antonio Negri's work on immaterial labour (the 'labour of Dionysus,' as their first full-length collaboration is titled, concisely evokes the relationship between labour and play).[16] In other words, the trend today should be not towards the further development of a labour theory of value, but the formulation of a *play theory of value*. As someone once told me: in contemporary life the tool used for labour, the computer, is exactly the same tool that is used for leisure. I'm not sure this has ever been the case before.

After trying to understand how to imagine a life after capitalism, and seeing how this is both done and undone in everything from *World of Warcraft* to the stratagems of Donald Rumsfeld, what one sees is how two of the hitherto most useful tropes for communicating a life after or outside capitalism – networks and play – are slowly shifting from what Rumsfeld calls the unknown unknowns, which is what they were fifty or a hundred years ago, to the known unknowns, and perhaps simply to the known. Is *World of Warcraft* labour or play? I'm not entirely sure. What is clear is that the possibility of life after capitalism is often articulated today through a utilization of the very essence of capitalism. Play is work and networks are sovereigns. And finally, virtual worlds are always in some basic way the expression of utopian desire, and in doing so they present the very impossibility of imagining utopia. This is not simply a knee-jerk ontological paradox; code-utopias, being immaterial, formal, and virtual, are by definition not 'real,' but the very act of creating an immaterial utopian space at the same time inscribes a whole vocabulary of algorithmic coding into the plane of imagination that thereby undoes the play of utopia in the first place. The key is not to mourn this transformation, but to examine cultural and media forms themselves and through them (borrowing a line from Jameson) to pierce through the representation of social life, both how it is lived now and how we feel in our bones it ought rather to be lived.

Notes

1   An early draft of this essay was delivered at the 'Communicating a Life After Capitalism' panel during the May 2005 International Communications Association conference in New York. A conference titled 'Life after Capitalism' was held at the CUNY Graduate Center in August 2004.

2   Friedrich Schiller, *On the Aesthetic Education of Man, in a Series of Letters*, ed. E.M. Wilkinson and L.A. Willoughby (Oxford: Oxford University Press, 1967), 137–8.

3   Johan Huizinga, *Homo Ludens* (Boston: Beacon Press, 1971).

4   Theodor Adorno, *Aesthetic Theory* (Minneapolis: University of Minnesota Press, 1997), 26.

5 Fredric Jameson, *The Seeds of Time* (New York: Columbia University Press, 1996), 56.

6 Fredric Jameson, 'Politics of Utopia,' *New Left Review* 25 (2004): 46.

7 Donald Rumsfeld, 'DoD News Briefing – Secretary Rumsfeld and Gen. Myers,' U. S. Department of Defense news transcript, 12 February 2003, available at http://www.defense.gov/transcripts/2002/t02122002_t212sdv2.html. Accessed 7 June 2005.

8 Jameson, *Seeds of Time*, 55-6.

9 Adorno, *Aesthetic Theory*, 317.

10 Sigmund Freud, *Beyond the Pleasure Principle* (New York: Norton, 1961), 13.

11 Jacques Lacan, *The Four Fundamental Concepts of Psychoanalysis* (New York: Norton, 1998), 62.

12 Ibid., 62-3.

13 Adorno, *Aesthetic Theory*, 317.

14 Ibid., 318.

15 Alan Liu, *The Laws of Cool: Knowledge Work and the Culture of Information* (Chicago: University of Chicago Press, 2004).

16 Michael Hardt and Antonio Negri, *Labour of Dionysus: A Critique of the State-Form* (Minneapolis: University of Minnesota Press, 1994).

8 The Age of Blur and Technology

NATE BURGOS

Technique of Technology

'Don't sweat the technique.'

This remains accurate advice. A precursor to this sentiment was philosopher Jacques Ellul, who equated technique with 'absolute efficiency' embedded in society: 'Technique integrates everything. It avoids shock and sensational events. Man is not adapted to a world of steel; technique adapts him to it. It changes the arrangement of this blind world so that man can be a part of it without colliding with its rough edges, without the anguish of being delivered up to the inhuman. Technique thus provides a model; it specifies attitudes that are valid once and for all.'[1]

Human civilization evolves with a viral algorithm of 'technique.' In computer science, efficiency consists of two properties: speed and space. These two properties compound each other into a remediated real estate composed of blocks (bandwidth), intersections (routers), and traffic (random access memory). One topographic projection of our world is a data-intensive mutable desktop or GUI (graphical user interface). Data, with its relentless streaming of specifications and statistics for human mining, is our built environment's true building material. William Johnson, chief architect of the NASA Information Power Grid, has said, 'Computing and data grids are emerging as the infrastructure for twenty-first century science because they are providing a common way of managing distributed computing, data, instruments, and human resources.'[2] Data is the true tissue of our environment in the systemic and towering form of information architecture: skylines are data-driven; cities are data-driven; suburbs are data-driven; homes are data-driven. Data is an undeniable attribute, desirable or not, of the technique of technology in the guise of absolute efficiency. Ellul's sharp focus on 'absolute efficiency' is our civilization's manifest destiny, from Zip drives to Zip cars.[3] The complexities of artificial reality we encounter on a daily basis are the outcomes of technologies themselves. Complexity is technology's destiny, which makes it civilization's destiny. Absolute efficiency, embedded in every human-made system, from education to communication, and meant to enhance quality of life, begets absolute inefficiency. A paradox of our age is the following: Absolute efficiency is a patch on holes in the system, but the efficiency gain is never final.

The evidence is *everyware*. The utopian pursuit of 'ubiquitous computing' in order to 'be digital' increases its influence over every business quarter, every retail season, and reverberates in every ring tone, hyperlink, e-ddress, automated message incoming and outgoing, deposit and withdrawal, pop-up and pop-down, download and upload, boot and reboot, start-up and shutdown, point and click. Data has been steered towards metadata with every touch and go. Data flecks like dust. Titles such as 'content strategists,' 'content providers,' and 'content clients' scream a world steered towards a hyper-inflated information enterprise or ecology. Writer David Shenk, in his book *Data Smog*, has argued, 'As information technology has made research, work processing, and publishing all dramatically cheaper, tens of millions of us have become our own think tanks ... Web home pages and neighborhood 'zines have turned millions of citizens into glutizens – reporters, publishers and broadcasters.'4 Shenk's articulation of intellectual sclerosis, via the think-tank strain, in an 'information glut' connects to the tyranny of technique.

The Industrial Revolution quickened permutations of its original intent of artificial progress from the Information Revolution to the Digital Revolution to the Internet Revolution to the Nano Revolution to the elusive but constant pursuit of the 'next big thing.' Proliferation of technological artefacts is easily observed within industrialized nations in high contrast to those countries void of technique's technological prowess. But technique is becoming more visible, for example, in outsourcing. Some consider it a procedure of absolute efficiency.

Others judge it as a negative by product of technology (technique). Dimensions of human capability have been extended to a fragmented, even fragile, attention span in the boardroom, in the classroom, and in the bedroom. Thresholds of living are being tested with every rapid product life cycle strategized by the industries of information technology, a pervasive purveyor of profit margins. Technique's artefacts, from I-Pod to I-Bod, are attaching themselves as much as possible to human existence. New technology is IT's persistent paradigm in simplifying the human brain as a mere microprocessor. New technology's translation is ever-new, ever-marketable, technique.

Absolute efficiency is our collective technique as speeds and spaces converge to the perpetual tempo of transformation incited by technology and its human hive. Technique is our current age's key word search. It is our age's economic engine of progress. Seeking products and services that are faster, lighter, smaller, and more portable echoes the utopian effect of techno-legato. Optimization is the theme of corporate mission statements. It is society's manufactured Om. Consumers contribute to this dynamic. They constitute the machine of commerce. As its targeted participants, consumers feed productivity. A rhetoric of inevitability cultivates the truth of our times: Consumers are the practitioners of technique equipped by its proactive agents

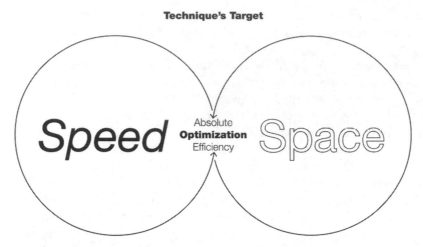

Figure 8.1. Technique's Target (Speed versus Space). Interpretive diagram, Nate Burgos, 2006.

of manufactured-centred innovation, from aspiring start-ups to pioneering corpora-tions. Human-made hyper-market spaces are not possible with corporations and the objects that they serve. Consumers are techniques' objects of desire. We remain con-sumed as Ellul dramatized: '[When] technique enters into every area of life, including the human, it ceases to be external to man and becomes his very substance. It is no longer face to face with man but is integrated with him, and it progressively absorbs him.'[5]

This quality of absorption is injected with technology's promise of a more seam-less domain. Technique's cache of 'anywhere-anytime' retains its grip on the masses. The attraction has reaped in benefits: email has evolved into a feature-rich work horse necessary to every stationery and mobile computing device; online applica-tions have evolved into malleable constructs like application programming inter-faces (APIs) and widgets; computing platforms are becoming more mobile and miniature; sociopolitical prescriptions and topical knowledge are helped by ease of publishing on the Internet, a relatively democratized passage of extremely diverse information. These examples have a distinct pattern: They are powered by citizens who helped shape their direction and influence on human living. The technique of technology is therapy.

At the same time, technique, like any other double-edged force, can be treacherous. 'There's a lot of information in those databases.' Contra-phenomena, bent on under-mining established systems, are advancing. With every transaction, there is the shadow of identity theft. The manufacture and release of illicit material are enhanced by the technology of technique. Circles of clout, from lobbyists to terrorists, are also enhanced in their efforts to push their agendas. These few examples testify to technique's acute stressors on society, which Ellul envisioned as one entrapped in technique: 'Technique has become autonomous; it has fashioned an omnivorous world which obeys its laws and which has renounced all tradition. Technique no longer rests on tradition, but rather on previous technical procedures, and its evolution is too rapid, too upsetting, to integrate the older traditions.'[6]

Technique feeds our inherent visions and desires for enabled futures. Our connection to the anchor of tradition loosens. Defined by Ellul as 'absolute efficiency,' technique can be both ruthlessly productive or productively ruthless. One of technique's most visible effects has been dubbed the Starbucks Effect. As expressed in *Fast Company* magazine, 'It happens every day, and it affects us all. It is the hallmark of our global economy – the continuous emergence of new competitors with superior business models that force us to reconsider the viability of what we've always done. And it will grow only more intense ... Which is to say, the Starbucks effect is not a global imperative. There's nothing inevitable about it. Someone, somewhere, makes a decision to open up at 6 a.m., or not. Competition creates pressure to continually do more, faster, cheaper – but we're free to choose otherwise, to compete on quality, or service, or relationships.'[7] Connection to traditional models such as compressed workdays and smaller social networks has been loosened. Comfort levels towards work and play have been realigned. Work has been replaced by the term 'work product.' Workers are measured in business units.

Technology is endowed with both ingenuity and pyrrhic victories. Its lingua franca is technique, à la efficiency, encoded and evident in every human-made system. However, technique is not bullet-proof. The very architects (corporations) and participants (consumers) who manifest techno-reality are given a choice which philosopher Langdon Winner articulates like this: 'Efficiency, speed, precise measurement, rationality, productivity, and technical improvement become ends in themselves applied obsessively to areas of life in which they would previously have been rejected as inappropriate ... Is the most product being obtained for the resources and effort expended?'[8]

Winner advocates another mantra-marketing bumper sticker: 'Question everything.' The stress here is consistently and strategically questioning technology's complexity and complicated means as survival. Ellul's path of technology as pathogen is compelling. The drive for total efficiency continues to seduce. Although pervasive in its seduction, technology's allure for corruption is tempting in the name of technique. Winner's push to question technology's presence and future is critical to evolving a global mind. Wherever there is a gain in efficiency, the cumulative lossy effect of efficiency will gain in precedence. The technique of technology, with absolute efficiency at its main root, is a challenge equally high in its potential, as society strives to lessen vulnerability in a technological environment.

'Don't sweat the technique.'
But how does the technique sweat you?

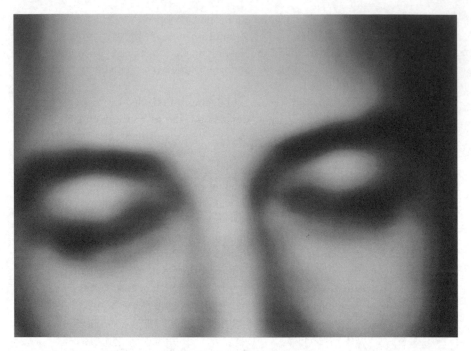

Figure 8.2. Untitled. Photograph, Michelle Litvin.

Among Precogs

Truth is the swell of a breath and the visions closed eyes see.[9]

We are among precogs. They capture our chatter of streaming unexamined life. Aggregating this chatter is their endowment. Parsing it for possibility is their pursuit. Precogs submerge themselves in stories and provoke them with eyes wide open. Their trajectory is truth. Their movements are uttered by those monitoring the waves and mining their depth. Their thoughts are fables of forecast. They cause ripples in the raging information landscape of memory.

We see them.

They see us.

Science fiction writer Philip K. Dick introduced this perceptive species.[10] Although described as feeble in body, their talent is their minds, a gift that keeps giving. They scour scenes of possibility. Scenes can be deemed units of possibility, constituting a messy space, notorious for paths upon which footfalls of humans and mystery intersect. This intersection is the primary circuit of possibility, a realm of hyper-transient boundaries. Possibility is trickery because it leads to a fixative we adore and fear: reality. The gamut of life events – near and far, fuzzy and clear – charges the craniums of precogs. Their mind's eyes are perpetual play heads. What develops within their hemispheres are reels of revelations:

Who are the perpetrators?
Who are the manipulators?
Who are the instigators?
Who are the agitators?
Who are the liaisons?
Who are the punishers?
Who are the liberators?
Who are the violators?
Who are the trespassers?
Who are the gatekeepers?
Who are the power brokers?
Who are the equalizers?

These role players and their accomplices ignite loops of anthropo-moments – without which there is no news, no life. Precogs are creatures of scenarios, patched together into a bleeding montage of awesome narrative magnitude. Their mass keeps imploding into puzzles. Most perplexing of these is what tests the sanity of humanity:
What is the meaning of life?
The montage running in the precog palace reinforces a reality essential to living: We are worthless without conflict. Projections haunt precogs. Their canvases are splashed with dots of plots, hazy narrative bitmaps, visceral in vagueness and relentless in magnetism towards realism. What do these visions foretell? Precognitive visions remind me of Gerhard Richter's canvases. Described by critics as an artist who defies 'isms,' Richter paints journalism, a discipline dedicated to realities, from tsunamis to hackers, from lawsuits to gridlock, from slander to slaughter. What could happen is its ultimate inference. This is the precogs's inheritance – an inference-interface whose inquisitive kernel is its pulse and ultimate data prompt:
Do you see?
Richter's pictures point to events, composed of human artefacts, from photographs to postcards, anchored in the past but re-applied to the present. They are rooted in reality and reverberate with echoes of foretelling. Oscillating between past and present into an interpretive pendulum is Richter's effect. Provoked to seeking connections among elements of his compositions is the result. Such action can prove futile in abstract representations, but Richter's realism transforms it into an attempt to quell human oblivion: 'His work asks people to think freshly and not romantically about control versus freedom, austerity versus exuberance, faith versus skepticism: about what we can trust in what we see.'[11] What we see is who we

can be. As Richter's images allude, possibility shifts between mirage and milestone, that is, fallacy versus truth, two states never to be denied. Without these regions, there is no news, no life. Precogs listen to the interaction between these states, vibrating like a vacuum whose conclusion remains open-ended. They amplify the appointed times of transition that affect our lives. Submerged in filmic REM., they push their refrain:

Do you see?

Seeing the possible to spearhead its prediction was the precogs' fundamental purpose in Philip K. Dick's literary template. Precogs supplied coordinates to help dodge destruction, an advanced thickener to a news jet stream becoming more metastatic in its growth from one re-purposed media hub rerouted to another. Our environment is a consolidated media event sustained by multiplying headlines of human (mis)calculation. The headlines' body of metacontent ripples throughout the precogs' bath of paradox: 'With so much ease-of-beauty in the world, why do people kill?' The killing spree flutters like scavenger pigeons landing from one human precipice in society to another. Images, high in murderous contrast, flicker into a perpetual pattern of anthro-cognition, constructed and reconstructed, zoomed in and zoomed out, accelerated and decelerated, paused and played, and paused again – never stopping. More than report, the precogs react to the continuity of (un)consciousness. As poet Jorie Graham testifies, 'You don't necessarily know what you're looking for, but you know that you're looking.'[12]

Scanning scenes is characteristic of our age of blur. The cinéma vérité of life yields a striking convergence of images, whose rapid representations of lives, lost and found, destroyed and resurrected, consumes our navigation of a world ruled by proximity adjacent to possibility. Reality's incarnations are around the corner, in a room, in the forest, underneath, above, in corridors, throughout villages and cities. Their turning into apparitions is at the core of blur. Life's images multiply and overlap in instant succession, from one scene to another like fleeting keys on a piano. Once visible moments are released, they are reshaped, reborn, never the same again. They are blurred. To cope with this condition, we toggle between fast rewind and fast forward, tempos of forecast to pinpoint the possible in order to glean a life-affirming, even life-saving, prediction. Amid all the traffic of life, precog behaviour (precog panning of scene to scene) paves the passage from projection towards prediction.

The inverse is also compelling: seeing the possible to facilitate its potential. This yields one of the most authentic archetypes driving civilization. Precogs remind us of our vying for actuality. This lies at the core of the perpetual pattern of anthro-cognition conditioning our environment. Precogs testify to the height of cognitive architecture and its *life* cycle in every exponent of existence, by purpose or accident.

Realizing possibilities is human architecture. Artificial spaces, sprawling with machines and mechanisms, are made by such a human infrastructure, extreme in its

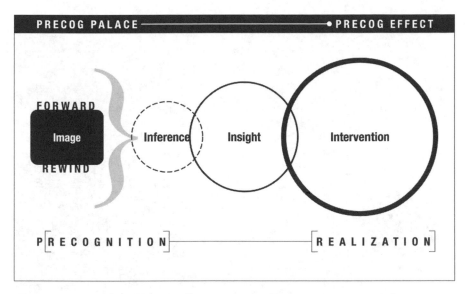

Figure 8.3. Precog Palace to Precog Effect. Interpretive diagram, Nate Burgos, 2006.

dimensional density and fuelled by people's pursuit of values in the construct of mirage or milestone. This human validation model is the precogs' domain. It is their primary source of stimulation: Listen to the waves of human needs and project timelines for fulfilling them.

Precogs connect to poets, philosophers, saviours, missionaries, innovators, and evangelists. Their premonitions connect to the desperate state of the information landscape. Fighting doubt and terror has and will always define the information landscape of civilization, plagued with words and images of terror's victims. Visions spark the precogs' visual convulsions. They are sensitive to the unforgiving harshness of reality. They exhaust themselves. Although precogs engage abrasive imagery, projected onto the roof of their temple like a Richter-rasterized installation, there is hope in their ability to cope. They offer an ultimate lesson typically succumbed to oversight: the state of society is a reflection of the state of minds. The reflection often bends into refraction. Precogs are a model for helping to prevent terror, even death. Their synaptic plug-in into the interconnected lattice of dangerous futures provides sanctuary for us all. More than vigilant life-traffic repositories, precogs are agents of accountability in a world whose consciousness is constantly challenged. They incite us to be life-traffic controllers. They help save us from ourselves and from each other. According to the painter Paul Klee, 'One eye sees, the other feels.' In so doing, precogs help us see that which is more than a side of us: We are all precogs.

'Better keep your eyes open.'[13]

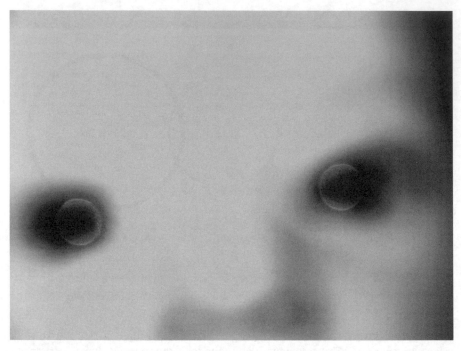

Figure 8.4. Untitled. Photograph, Michelle Litvin.

Notes

1 Cited by Bonnie A. Nardi and Vicki L. O'Day, in *Information Ecology: Using Technology with Heart* (Cambridge: MIT Press, 1999), 34.
2 Cited by Bruce Mau, with Jennifer Leonard, and the Institute Without Boundaries, in *Massive Change* (London: Phaidon Press, 2004), 95.
3 Cited by Nardi and O'Day, in *Information Ecology*, 34.
4 David Shenk, *Data Smog: Surviving the Information Glut* (New York: Harpercollins, 1997), 100.
5 Cited by Nardi and O'Day, in *Information Ecology*, 35.
6 Ibid., 35.
7 Keith H. Hammonds, 'The Starbucks Effect,' *Fast Company* (June 2006), 31.
8 Cited by Nardi and O'Day, in *Information Ecology*, 39.
9 Octavio Paz, 'San Ildefonso nocturne,' in *The Collected Poems of Octavio Paz, 1957-1987*, ed. Eliot Weinberger (New York: New Directions, 1991).
10 Philip K. Dick was inducted into the 2005 Science Fiction Hall of Fame. Also inducted was filmmaker Steven Spielberg, who directed the film adaptation of Dick's short story, 'The Minority Report.'

11 Michael Kimmelman, 'Gerhard Richter: An Artist beyond Isms,' *New York Times*, 27 Jan. 2002.

12 Jorie Graham, 'Emotion, Cognition and Consciousness,' *Talk of the Nation*, National Public Radio, 10 Oct. 2003.

13 Philip K. Dick, 'The Minority Report,' in *The Minority Report: 18 Classic Stories by Philip K. Dick* (New York: Citadel Press, 2002).

EUGENE THACKER

Soul-Meat-Pattern

There have only ever been three approaches to thinking about life: *soul*, *meat*, and *pattern*. Within this trinity is everything deemed to be animate, living, and vital. 'Soul' is not just the Scholastic, theological, personal soul, but the Aristotelian principle of life (*psyche*), the principle of its organization. The vegetative soul of plants, the animate and sensate soul of animals, and the rational soul of human beings. The hierarchy of souls is not unlike the Great Chain of Being, a biological theology of divide-and-hierarchize. By contrast, 'meat' is brute matter, unthinking mechanism, the clockwork organism, the *bête machine* described by Descartes – animal or machine, it makes no difference. Mechanism is, in a sense, a thinking about life as meat, and meat as lifeless (the life that is lifeless is meat or machine). Finally, distinct from 'soul' and 'meat' is a third approach, that of 'pattern.' It would seem that the emphasis on pattern is a distinctly postmodern phenomenon, the terrain of cybernetics, information theory, and self-organization. But this is only part of the story. Again, Aristotle the biologist equates form (*eidos*) and 'soul' as the distinguishing mark between the plant, the animal, and the human; it is in their mode of organization, how they self-actualize in time ('if it moves, it's alive'). Yet, Aristotle is linked to contemporary self-organization research in that neither can explain how organization occurs, other than to reiterate that the whole is more than the sum of its parts.

Thus, 'soul,' 'meat,' and 'pattern' form a trinity. The trinity is also a triptych: soul in the centre, meat on the right-hand side, and on the left, pattern. An image of thought that continuously switches, swaps, displaces, and replaces the place-holder that defines life: from *psyche* to mechanism and animal electricity to the 'gemmules' and 'pangens' to DNA and the 'code of life.' However, these three approaches do not form a periodization, with Aristotle's *psyche* followed by Descartes' clockwork body followed by the genetic code. Instead, as a trinity-triptych, they form a kind of portrait, a face, a faciality, a field of black holes and white walls, within which and upon which is often written: 'life is that whose essence can be deduced and yet whose essence escapes all deduction' – soul-meat-pattern. Each of these posits a central, universal, external principle of organization that culminates in the living, the organism, a life-force. We can simply refer to this as the *principle of life*, the central concept that structures a whole field of investigation. Each approach differs in its place-holders, but there continues to be a transcendental locus that minimally guarantees a description of life, something that enables one to point and say 'over there' (or perhaps, 'it's alive ... alive!' or again, 'shoot anything with more than two legs!'). In positing such principles of organization, the soul-meat-pattern triptych also articulates boundaries: living–non-living, organic-inorganic, animate-inanimate, but also animal-machine, human-animal, human-savage, species, races, populations, and genomes. We can refer to this practice as *boundaries of articulation*. Together, the principle of life and the boundaries of articulation are the two methods through which the West has cease-lessly reinvented its thinking about life.

Extrinsic Life

There is an inward-turning and an outward-turning aspect of this thinking. The inward-turning divides, orders, and interrelates species and types; the outward-turning manages boundaries and positions the living against the non-living, making possible an instrumentality, a standing-reserve. The inward-turning aspect is metabolic, in that it processes, filters, and differentiates itself internally; it is the breakdown and production of biomolecules, the organization of the organs, the genesis of species and races. The outward-turning aspect is immunologic, for it manages boundaries, exchanges, and passages; it is the self–non-self distinction, the organism exchanging with its environment, sensing its *milieu*, the individual body living in proximity to other bodies. Nevertheless, there is always something that complicates both aspects. The inward-turning aspect is just fine until the outward-turning aspect loses its grip on things. Epidemics are an example. An epidemic cannot be limited to the individual organism, for its very nature is to pass between organisms, and increasingly, to pass across species borders (and national borders). What is the unit of analysis for an epidemic? Likewise, the outward-turning aspect is able to manage boundaries without problems until the inward-turning aspect is discovered to be an illusion. For instance, if the outward-turning aspect is that which posits the individual organism as distinct from its environment, therefore enabling an instrumental relationship, a standing reserve, what then is the inward-turning aspect? We would assume that it is the whole spectrum of understanding about that organism – its biological, physiological, cognitive processes. But isn't each of these really a nested, outward-turning aspect in itself? What are the systems, networks, and pathways of the organism if not nested layers of the outward-turning aspect? The inward-turning and outward-turning aspects thus complicate each other ceaselessly, and it is therefore not inaccurate to describe their relationship, as Gilles Deleuze does, as one of folding (in-folding, out-folding, an embryology having nothing to do with 'development').

Soul-meat-pattern – again, this is not a *telos*, as if to imply that genetic and information technologies are the most advanced mode of inward- and outward-turning. Yet,
in a time of networks, swarms, and multitudes, it would seem that the third approach
– that of 'pattern' – is today dominant in the life sciences (genetics, genomics), health
care (biotechnology industry), technology (a-life, artificial intelligence, networks), war
(bioterror, emerging epidemics) and even alternative scientific viewpoints (biocomplexity, emergence).[1] A new, vital pattern pervades systems of all kinds – global economies, social systems, immigration patterns, information exchanges, mobile and
wireless communications, and so forth. Despite this, have we rid ourselves of the
divide-and-hierarchize mentality of thinking about life? Is 'pattern' simply the new
'soul'? Traditionally, these questions about the principle of life come under the
domain of the philosophy of biology. But what would it mean to invert the philosophy of biology? What would it mean to invert this thinking (soul-meat-pattern) and
this dualistic method (principles of life, boundaries of articulation), and consider
instead a *biophilosophy*? Perhaps it is precisely 'life itself' that is the problem, not the
aim or the goal. Instead of considering the intrinsic properties of life, what about considering life as extrinsic, as always going outside of itself? Instead of centring life (an
essence, an organizing principle), what about considering life at the peripheries –
extrinsic life, a life always going outside of itself, *peripheral* life?

Biophilosophy vs Philosophy of Biology

What, then, is biophilosophy? To begin with, biophilosophy is not the same as the
philosophy of biology. What is usually referred to as the philosophy of biology has
both a syntagmatic and a paradigmatic side to it, a horizontal and vertical dimension.
The horizontal dimension is the elucidation of universal characteristics of the organism, which are perceived to be part of its essence or principle of organization (growth
and decay, reproduction and development, evolutionary adaptation). The vertical
dimension is the development of this thinking historically in Western thought, from
Aristotle, to natural history, to Darwinian evolution, to the new synthesis in genetics
and biochemistry. In general, the philosophy of biology highlights and extends the
philosophical dimensions of biological knowledge. Issues pertaining to evolution, biological determinism, dualism, mechanism, and teleology may be considered in the
context of the life sciences such as comparative anatomy, physiology, genetics, biochemistry, embryology, germ theory, and developmental systems theory. The philosophy of biology informs the three approaches to thinking about life mentioned above:
soul-meat-pattern. The philosophy of biology also undertakes the twofold method of
identifying a principle of life and boundaries of articulation. It can be understood as
an attempt to pose the question 'Is the living different from the non-living?' – an
ontological question – in the context of another question, 'Is the study of the living
(biology) different from other fields of study?' – an epistemological question.

Is biophilosophy simply the opposite of the philosophy of biology? Not quite. Biophilosophy is certainly a critique of the triptych of philosophy of biology. But it is also a way of moving through the soul-meat-pattern approach, while taking with it the radicality of the ontological questions that are posed and that often get reduced to epistemological concerns over classification. Whereas the philosophy of biology is concerned with articulating a concept of 'life' that would describe the essence of life, biophilosophy is concerned with articulating those things that ceaselessly transform life. *For biophilosophy, life = multiplicity.* Whereas the philosophy of biology proceeds by the derivation of universal characteristics for all life, biophilosophy proceeds by drawing out the network of relations that always take the living outside itself, an extrinsic diagram as opposed to intrinsic characteristics. Whereas the philosophy of biology (especially in the twentieth century) has been increasingly concerned with reducing life to number (from mechanism to genetics), biophilosophy sees a different kind of number, one that runs through life (a combinatoric, proliferating number, the number of graphs, groups, and sets). Whereas the philosophy of biology renews mechanism in order to purge itself of all vitalism ('vitalism' is one of the curse words of biology), biophilosophy renews vitalism in order to purge it of all theology (and in this sense number is vitalistic).

'A Life' not A-Life

The difficulty with the philosophy of biology – as with nearly all philosophical thinking of 'the animal' – is to resist the anthropomorphism of our thinking about life. The approach of the philosophy of biology, the approach of soul-meat-pattern, centres and raises up the concept of the human so that it is not only isomorphic with life, but so that it may rise above life ('life itself' as the pinnacle and 'mere life' as the base or foundation). This has a number of effects on our thinking about life, for it simultaneously places the human at the top of the Great Chain while also reserving a qualitatively distinct, non-animal place for the human. This is the tired drama of the human, at once partaking of the animal, natural, biological world, and yet incessantly striving above and beyond it, producing abstract knowledge-systems, constructing world and life, aspiring for the spiritual (recall Heidegger's thesis concerning animality: the stone is worldless, the animal is poor-in-world, and the human is world-building). It is a drama that is by turns tragic and absurdist. Contemporary bio-art practices can be understood as a commentary on this drama, producing dadaist mammals, extra ears, pigs with wings, activist crops, and 'fuzzy biological sabotage.'[2]

Biophilosophy implies a critique of all anthropomorphic conceptions of life. But is it possible to think this non-anthropomorphic life? Are we determined yet again to supplant an old term ('pattern') with a new one ('multiplicity')? The problem is not simply a nominalist one, not simply a game of logic; the problem is the very relation between 'life' and 'thought' (both Georges Canguilhem and Michel Foucault note that the most accurate *concept* of life would be life itself). Biophilosophy is an approach to non-human life, non-organic life, anonymous life, indefinite life – what Deleuze calls 'a life.' The trick is to undo conventional biological thinking from within. Biophilosophy focuses on those modes of biological life that simultaneously escape their being exclusively biological life: microbes, epidemics, endosymbiosis, parasitism, swarms, packs, flocks, a-life, genetic algorithms, biopathways, smart dust, smartmobs, netwars – there is a whole bestiary that asks us to think the life-multiplicity relation.

Life is X

The central question of the philosophy of biology has to do with an essence of life, a 'principle of life.' What is life? Life is X – whatever X happens to be, *eidos*, mechanism, life-force, selection, code. The concept of 'life itself' promoted by geneticists during the post-Second World War era (the genetic 'coding problem') was a renewal of a concept articulated by Aristotle in *De anima* as well as his 'biological' treatises. The implication of the very concept of 'life itself' is that 'life' is One. Whatever it is, life is one thing, essentially one thing, for otherwise we could not say, 'Life is X.' Even when life reveals its contradictory nature, that contradiction is the ineffable key to life. An example is animal motility. Aristotle posed the question. 'What makes the animal go?' – that is, from where does its energy come? The problem was picked up by the application of thermodynamics to animal physiology, with talk of animal 'electricity' and 'irritability' and 'vital forces.' Soon there was an ineffable 'life force' coursing through the animal, enabling it to counter the laws of thermodynamics.

Today a similar process is happening with studies in self-organization and emergence. The question has changed, but its form of the problem is the same: 'How do simple local actions produce complex global patterns?' The effects of self-organization can be analysed forever (e.g., 'ant colony optimization') and they can be applied to computer science (e.g., computer graphics in film, telecommunications routing). But a central mysticism is produced at its core, for if there is no external, controlling factor (environment, genes, blueprints), then how can there be control at all? Again, 'life itself' the ineffable, the absent centre. In this sense life follows the laws of thought: it is self-identical (whatever is living continues to be so until it ceases to be living), non-contradictory (something cannot both be living and non-living), and either is or is not (something either is or is not living, there is no grey zone to life). It is in this sense that 'life' and 'thought' find their common meeting point. Biophilosophy implies a critique of the dialectics of 'life itself.' It abandons the concept of 'life itself' that is forever caught between the poles of nature and culture, biology and technology, human and machine. Instead, it develops concepts that always cut across and that form networks: the molecular, multiplicity, becoming-animal, life-resistance, and so forth. But the point is not to simply repeat deleuzianisms, but rather to invent or diverge: the autonomy of affect, germinal life, wetwares, prevital transductions, organismic soft control, abstract sex, molecular invasions, geophilosophy, and what Deleuze calls 'the mathematico-biological systems of differenc/tiation.'[3]

Being, Time, Number

The philosophy of biology is an epistemological endeavour, while biophilosophy is an ontological one. The philosophy of biology asks, 'Which category?'; biophilosophy asks, 'Affected or affecting?' Biophilosophy ceaselessly spins out ontologies, none of them final, none of them lasting. An example is the following: perhaps what Heidegger pointed to as the defining philosophical concern of modernity – Being or *dasein* – has permutated into one of the guiding concerns of the new millennium: the problematic of 'life itself' or the *zoe/bios* distinction. We are no longer worried about the grand metaphysical concerns of Being, Time, and the One. Biophilosophy is a permutation and transmutation of these concerns – not Being but the problematic of 'life itself,' a concern that asks us to rethink the concept of the vital and vitalism. Similarly, the concern with Time has become an interest in variation, transformation, change – difference and repetition (the repetition of the different and the difference of each repetition). The contemporary interest in the event, becoming, and the virtual-actual pair are further variations of this. Finally, the imperative of the One – that Being is One, that Time is One, that the subject is singular, that identity is the identification of the One, even the strange sameness of the Other in ethical thought – all of this asks us to pose the question: what would we have to do to the concept of 'number' to think beyond the One-many dichotomy? This is the question posed by Deleuze's *Difference and Repetition*, but it is already there in Plato's *Parmenides* – Hair, mud, and dirt. Is there a concept of multiplicity that moves beyond the One many? Could such a concept resist a simple denunciation of 'number' (quantity vs quality, extensity vs intensity, explication vs implication)? If there is a concept of number that runs throughout multiplicity (a proliferative, pervasive number), and if multiplicity is related to life, is there a living number – *a vitalist matheme* – that would move out of the philosophy of biology's trinity of soul-meat-pattern? Instead of what Alain Badiou calls the split between the quantitative and qualitative, the closed and the open, 'number and animal,' is there an *animal number*? Being, Time, and the One thus get recombined as 'life itself,' becoming, and number, which in turn ask us to consider or reconsider vitalism, the virtual, and multiplicity.

Other-than-Life

The philosophy of biology poses the question, 'What is life?' In doing so, however, it rarely asks the inverse question, 'What is not-life?' Certainly, death is not-life. But so is the rock, the chair, the clouds. What about the computer, lunch, or a nation-state, are they not-life as well? What about a doll? Memories? There is a whole negative classification of not-life implied in the positive question, 'What is life?' Better yet, rather than the question of what is not-life, we can pose the question of the life that becomes not-life, an other-than-life, a *becoming–non-living*. Four, preliminary, examples follow.

1 Swarm Intelligence

'Swarm intelligence' is a term currently used to describe an interdisciplinary research field that combines the biological studies of 'social insects' with computer science (especially software algorithms and multi-agent systems).[4] Just as a group of insects that are individually 'dumb' are able to collectively self-organize and forage for a food source or build a nest, so can simple software programs or robots self-organize in groups and carry out complex tasks. This local actions-global patterns approach is said to display 'intelligent' or purposeful behaviour at the global level. But we can also question and repurpose the term 'swarm intelligence,' for the tendency in this thinking is to always search for a higher-level unity which would be the guarantee of organization and order.

Call it a 'superorganism' or a 'hive mind,' the implication is that purposeful activity can only occur through a process of meta-individualizing all group phenomena, subjecting the many-as-many to a renewed concept of the One. Action must come after individuation, not vice versa. However, the unique thing about insect swarms and other animal groups (packs, flocks, schools) is not just that there is no leader, but that there is something akin to a fully distributed control. Thus, the political paradox of insect societies – how to understand this balance between control and emergence, *sovereignty* and *multiplicity*? And thus the paradoxical question of the field of swarm intelligence – can it be coded? Can one, in fact, engineer distributed control? Or are we stuck at the level of passive observers, limited in our ability to identify swarm intelligence, but helpless to enact it? What would have to be done to the concept of *action* in order to make of swarm intelligence a political concept? If there is a swarm intelligence, the 'intelligence' would surely have to be a frustratingly anonymous, non-anthropomorphic intelligence, the intelligence of 'a life.'

2 Headless Animality

The philosophy of biology is not only concerned with the unity of life ('Life is X'), but it ties this unity to the individual organism. Whether in natural history's classifications, Darwinian speciation, or the study of genomes, biology always begins from the individual. The individual is the starting point, the basic unit of study. Throughout all these levels, the organism has remained central. Organisms not only form species, but they are also formed by molecules and cells; organisms are the ideal point of mediation between the microscopic and macroscopic views of life. Thus, it is no surprise to find philosophy raising the human above the animal based on the comparison of individual organisms.

For Aristotle, Descartes, Hobbes, Locke, and Rousseau the individual organism is the most basic unit through which the human is raised above the animal, the beast, the savage. This is especially the case when groups are concerned.

Here insects are the privileged case study, perhaps the paradigmatic case of the not-human. Indeed, political thought has often contrasted the human and the insect precisely on this point. Hobbes notes that while both humans and insects are 'social,' only humans can lay down rights to establish a sovereign. Marx notes that insects also produce and build, but humans are able to abstract and plan before building. Thus, even groups are individuals. Groups are composed of individuals that pre-exist them, and groups themselves form meta-individuals ('species,' 'races').

There are also extrinsic group animals, the multiplicity-animals of packs, flocks, swarms. Yes, swarms can be understood to be composed of individual insects. But what if swarms, packs, and so on are actually inversions of the organism? What if they are instances in which the many pre-exist the One? An army ant swarm does have a morphogenetic aspect to it: there is a swarm front, a bivouac, and branching paths. But swarms, packs, flocks, and schools are also defined precisely by their shapelessness and formlessness. They have no 'head' let alone a 'face.' They are headless animals, acephalous animality. They are animality without head or tail, polysensory, poly-affective, 'amorphous but coordinated.'[5]

3 Molecular Molecules

To begin with, we can suggest that molecules are not 'molecular.' As nonsensical as this sounds, it is important to understand the molecule as one in a whole series of units of composition and analysis: the organism, the organ, the tissue, the cell, the molecule. Each science of life is not just a noun (anatomy, biology) but also a verb ('anatomizing,' 'biologizing') in which the living is both analysed and built up. What is the smallest unit of composition? This is also the first unit of analysis. Building up, breaking down. The process of individuation is central to thinking about life, whether it be about the 'building blocks of life' or the 'code of life.'

There are always 'powers of ten' in biology, a huge, ontological microscope that stratifies individuals (the 'DNA makes RNA makes proteins, and proteins make us' mantra of molecular genetics). But what if all this has nothing to do with scale, or with strata, or with layering? There is a whole forgotten history of molecular biology which de-emphasizes the search for 'the' molecules (proteins or nucleic acids), and instead focuses on the relationality of molecules, their network dynamics, their temporal existence on the 'edge of chaos' (biocomplexity). On the one hand, biology tells us that molecules build up and break down (some proteins break down molecules, others build up). But, on the other hand, a cursory look at microbes shows us the radical horizontality of molecules: symbiotic bacteria, contagious viruses, and horizontal gene transfer between microbes.

An epidemic is molecular, but it is also social, technological, economic, political. Networks of infection, yes, but also networks of contagion, transportation, vaccination, quarantine, and surveillance. This compression of networks, this topological intensification, is not the result of molecules, but it is 'molecular.' This microbial life has nothing to do with scale (micro- vs macro-), but it is at once local and global. Even the common biological processes of gene expression, cell metabolism, and membrane signalling routinely create linkages and relations (microbe-animal-human), or rather, they produce *univocity-through-assemblages*.

4 Lifelike Death

We speak excitedly about the ways that new technologies are 'lifelike,' meaning the way that technology – something devoid of life – is able to display characteristics or behaviours that for us approximate life. But it is never clear if the lifelike is a category of representation (the lifelike quality of the 'oval portrait'), performance ('never mind the man behind the curtain'), or simulation ('what is real, Neo?'). Our own obsession is to constantly desire and yet worry about the lifelike: we want our phones to speak to us, but only if they say the right things. In popular culture, science fiction repeatedly plays out these scenarios where we produce a technical life in our own image, a fusion of technology and life in which the human constantly reproduces itself. Perhaps another approach to the lifelike is not to do with life or technology at all, but the lifelikeness of death. There is, in fact, a whole demonology of the lifelike to be considered. In popular culture, genre horror gives us many examples of lifelike death: zombies (the living dead), vampires (the undead), the phantasm (the disembodied spirit), and the demon (the possessed life). This is the lifelikeness of life passing away, going beyond itself, exiting itself. It is no mistake that these figures of lifelike death are often inhabited by fearfully ambivalent agents: viruses infecting the living dead, the 'bad blood' of the vampire, the phantasm enslaving my memory, and the demonic tearing of soul from body. Lifelike death is not the celebratory lifelikeness of our intelligent machines, but the ambivalent attitude towards a life that should not be living, an unholy life. This lifelike death is aporetic life: the dead that walk, the immortal being that is also the basest of animals (bats, rats), the materialized spirit, the familiar face distorted beyond recognition. Perhaps there is a technoscientific side to this after all. For, would not the limit-case of lifelike death be the point at which the organic can no longer be distinguished from the inorganic, the material from the immaterial? This is the domain of nanotechnology, the idea of inorganic life, programmable matter, an undiscovered 'occult media.'

Ancient Life (or, the Biology of Cthulhu)

'Biophilosophy for the twenty-first century' is an ambiguous statement. Biophilosophy does not begin with information networks, biotechnologies, nanotechnologies, or intelligent software. In a sense, Presocratic thinking is biophilosophical thinking. Heraclitus refers to a non-organic life in this three examples of fire (formlessness in identity), flows (stepping into the river), and the body (stability through growth and decay) – a common *logos* to all change. His opposite – but in many ways his comple- ment – is Parmenides, whose concept of the All-One attempts to comprehend multi- plicity as another form of univocity. And then there are the Greek atomists, particles infinitely dense and mobile.

Immediately a dissenting point is raised: Are we not being reductive in our con- cept of life, as if life were only biological life, and not social, cultural, economic, reli- gious and political life as well? Indeed, is not the problem the way in which biological and biomedical life has come to be the foundation of our emerging 'biopolitical' regimes? This 'bare life' serves as the alpha and the omega of social and political life, at once safeguarding the security of 'the population' while also producing a state of exception, a state of emergency, in which 'bare life' is both under attack and the object of pre-emptive strikes. Undoubtedly. This cordons off, however, our ability to think about life within the chess match between disciplines. To the scientist who says, 'Life is genetic code' the sociologist says, 'Life is the discriminatory implementation of genetics.' To the physicist who says, 'Life is the self-organization of matter and energy,' the political scientist says, 'Life is the struggle between human groups to instrumen- talize natural resources.' The humanities professor says, 'Life is the set of metaphors we forget are metaphors,' while the engineer designs 'programmable matter' and 'smart dust.' Once in a while, there are synergistic couplings, noisesome cross-talk that produces monsters: in the 1980s there was talk of chaos, in the 1990s talk of com- plexity, and crossing the millennium there was talk of networks. Or so the story goes. Perhaps we would like to do away with disciplines; and yet, for all the talk of 'third cultures' we still find the two cultures in the most banal, everyday instances.

This not a manifesto. All the same, concerning biophilosophy there are a number of misconceptions to address. Biophilosophy is not a naive embrace of 'life,' a belief in the altruistic holism of all life on the planet. It is, however, a rigorous questioning of the two- fold method of the philosophy of biology (principle of life, boundaries of articulation), and the divisions that are produced from this. Biophilosophy always asks, 'What relations are precluded in such-and-such a division, in such-and-such a classification?' Biophiloso- phy is not and should not be simply another name for self-organization, emergence, or complexity. Although there is a fertile exchange between philosophy and biology on this point, it is clear that the sciences of complexity are unable to think both ontologically and politically as well. More often than not, they create a new portrait of nature (a non- linear, meta-stable complex nature), or worse, they subsume all non-natural elements under this new nature (thus, free markets and/or 'democracy' are self-organizing and therefore inevitable). Not everything comes under the domain of biophilosophy, but at the same time one of biophilosophy's major concerns is the supposed foundationalism of biology and the biological-biomedical definitions of life. Biophilosophy is not simply a new vitalism, arguing for the ineffability and irreducibility of life's description. Yet, this is perhaps the most frustrating and ambivalent aspect of biophilosophy. Biophilosophy is an attempt to draw out a political ontology, but it is also politically agonistic, even apathetic. There is no *ressentiment* in biophilosophy; only a commitment to a 'vital politics' accompanied by this 'molecular-wide' perspective. Biophilosophy picks up and reinvigorates the ontological questions left behind by the philosophy of biology: Why 'life'?

Notes

1   See my article, 'Networks, Swarms, Multitudes' in *CTHEORY* (2004), part one, available at http://www.ctheory.net/text_file.asp?pick=422, and part two: http://www.ctheory.net/text_file.asp?pick=423.

2   In particular, see the work of SymbioticA (http://www.symbiotica.uwa.edu.au), a group of artists and scientists engaged in exploring cell and tissue culturing techniques as artistic practice. In a different vein, Critical Art Ensemble (http://www.critical-art.net) has, for some years, explored the relationships between activism, art, and biotechnology.

3   Aside from *A Thousand Plateaus*, see Deleuze's comments on life as 'resistance' in Gilles Deleuze, *Foucault*, trans. Seán Hand (London: Continuum, 1999). For a sampling of other divergings from life, see Keith Ansell Pearson, *Germinal Life* (New York: Routledge, 1999); Alain Badiou, 'Of Life as a Name of Being, or Deleuze's Vitalist Ontology,' *Pli: The Warwick Journal of Philosophy* 10 (2000): 174–91; Mark Bonta and John Protevi, *Deleuze and Geophilosophy: A Guide and Glossary* (Edinburgh: Edinburgh University Press, 2004); Critical Art Ensemble, *The Molecular Invasion* (Brooklyn: Autonomedia, 2002); Manuel Delanda, 'Immanence and Transcendence in the Genesis of Form,' *South Atlantic Quarterly* 96/3 (1997): 499–514; Richard Doyle, *Wetwares: Experiments in Postvital Living* (Minneapolis: University of Minnesota Press, 2004); Miriam Fraser, Sarah Kember, and Celia Lury, 'Inventive Life: Approaches to the New Vitalism,' *Theory, Culture and Society* 22/1 (2005): 1–14; Mark Hansen, 'Becoming as Creative Involution? Contextualizing Deleuze and Guattari's Biophilosophy,' *Postmodern Culture* 11/1 (2000); Adrian Mackenzie, 'Bringing Sequences to Life: How Bioinformatics Corporealizes Sequence Data,' *New Genetics and Society* 22/3 (2003): 315–32; Lucianna Parisi, *Abstract Sex: Philosophy, Bio-technology and the Mutations of Desire* (London: Continuum, 2004); Luciana Parisi and Tiziana Terranova, 'Heat-Death: Emergence and Control in Genetic Engineering and Artificial Life,' *CTHEORY* (2000): http://www.ctheory.net/text_file.asp?pick=127; Eugene Thacker, *Biomedia* (Minneapolis: University of Minnesota Press, 2004).

4   For a quick overview, see Eric Bonabeau and Guy Théraulaz, 'Swarm Smarts,' *Scientific American* (2000): 72–9. For a more thorough, and more technical introduction, see Bonabeau and Théraulaz, *Swarm Intelligence: From Natural to Artificial Systems* (Oxford: Oxford University Press, 1999).

5   This is the phrase often used by John Arquilla and David Ronfeldt in their book on military swarming, *Swarming and the Future of Conflict* (Santa Monica: RAND, 2000).

THIERRY BARDINI

> And everybody knows that the Plague is coming
> Everybody knows that it's moving fast
> Everybody knows that the naked man and woman
> Are just a shining artifact of the past.
>
> Leonard Cohen, 'Everybody Knows.'[1]

> The high degree to which AIDS, terrorism, crack cocaine, or computer viruses mobilize the popular imagination should tell us that they are more than anecdotal occurrences in an irrational world. The fact is that they contain within them the logic of our system: these events are merely the spectacular expression of that system. They all hew to the same agenda of virulence and radiation, an agenda whose very power over the imagination is of a viral character.[2]
>
> Jean Baudrillard, 'Prophylaxy and Virulence.'

At the dawn of capitalism's fourth phase, the hypervirus awoke.
Poisonous parasite, undead, ubiquitous and omnipotent.

At the beginning of the 1980s, the logistic curve of the hypervirus (the 'virus' virus) passed its first critical point (i.e., second order inflexion). Materializing the cybernetic convergence of carbon and silicon, it infected computers and humans alike at unprecedented levels. From this point on, an explosive diffusion in 'postmodern culture' emerged, eventually it plateaued near saturation, redefining culture as a viral ecology. *Room for one more inside, Sir.*

True/false but *remarkable identities*:
'Virus' is a virus: virus is a reflexive name.
The virus is the quintessential Kantian thing-in-itself.
The hypervirus is the quintessential Dawkinsian meme.

(Your clone is the idealized expression of your viral self.)
The postmodern master equation:
language = virus = informational parasite
Baudrillard adds the corollary proposition:
Anathematic Illimited / Transfatal Express
Viral Incorporated / International Epidemics.

The hypervirus rules our times like an indifferent despot (it practises *liberal* indifference). It is the ultimate boot sector parasite of our undead culture. Theorized, from Derrida to Foucault (who died of it), Baudrillard (passim)[3] and Deleuze, the virus is the master trope of 'postmodern culture' (whatever *that* is).[4] Let us sketch rapidly the progression of the pandemics.[5]

In his Cut-Ups trilogy of the first half of the 1960s (*The Soft Machine, The Ticket That Exploded*, and *Nova Express*), William Burroughs experimented with the stuff of words; in the early 1970s, Susumu Ohno coined the expression *'junk DNA.'* Burroughs eventually synthesized the experiment into one fundamental thesis: language (and especially written language) is a virus.[6] At approximately the same time, the 'computer virus' appeared in science-fiction literature. William S. Burroughs is *patient o* of the hypervirus, the original vector. It is an ironic corollary of his own thesis that the hypervirus was first detected in his writings. In *The Electronic Revolution*, he writes:

> I have frequently spoken of word and image as viruses or as acting as viruses, and this is not an allegorical comparison. It will be seen that the falsifications of syllabic western languages are in point of fact actual virus mechanisms. The *is* of identity the purpose of a virus is to *survive*. To survive at any expense to the host invaded. To be an animal, to be a body. To be an animal body that the virus can invade. To be animals, to be bodies. To be more animal bodies, so that the virus can move from one body to another. To stay present as an animal body, to stay absent as antibody or resistance to the body invasion.[7]

Relevant here is an extended version of Deleuze's notion of the overman. The virus, more efficient than the overman, is not only 'in charge of the animals' (as in Deleuze and Guattari's version), but actually *is* the animal. This use of the verb 'to be' is, of course, highly problematic for Burroughs, to the point that it is quite accurate to consider him the detective-doctor of the antiviral fight.[8]

For Burroughs, the principals of this fight begin with a reform of language itself, in the 'therapeutic' tradition of Count Alfred Korzybski, whose seminar he attended in the late 1930s, and his non-Aristotelian semantics:

> The categorical *the* is also a virus mechanism, locking you in *the* virus universe. *either/or* is another virus formula. It is always you *or* the virus. *either/or*. This is in point of fact the

conflict formula, which is seen to be archetypical virus mechanism. The proposed language will delete these virus mechanisms and make them impossible of formulation in the language. This language will be a tonal language like Chinese, it will also have a hieroglyphic script as pictorial as possible without being to (*sic*) cumbersome or difficult to write. This language will give one option of silence. When not talking, the user of this language can take in the silent images of the written, pictorial and symbol languages.

For Burroughs, the first enemy in language is the '*is* of identity': 'The word *be* in the English language contains, as a virus contains, its precoded message of damage, the categorial imperative of permanent condition.'[9] Instead, Burroughs follows the advice of Korzybski, which is to reform language as a pictorial (iconic) language where silence is an option. Silence is understood here as the first step in the dissolution of the modern subject (i.e., the egoistic subject,[10] from Descartes on). Thus, where Simon and Garfunkel innocently sing, *fool said I you do not know / Silence like a cancer grows* – today South Park echoes, *Die Hippie Die!*

During the same general period, a philosophical project develops that mirrors the work of Burroughs. Between his books *Of Grammatology* (published in 1967) and *Dissemination* (published five years later), Jacques Derrida begins a philosophical enterprise that attempts to introduce the Other into the I: a redefinition of the subject. Eventually, this 'introduction' becomes 'infection,' and the Other is radically recast as the virus. Like Burroughs, Derrida first finds traces of the process in writing itself:

> The absolute alterity of writing might nevertheless affect living speech, from the out side, within its inside: alter it [for the worse]. Even as it has an independent history ... and in spite of the inequalities of development, the play of structural correlations, writing marks the history of speech. Although it is born out of 'needs of a different kind' and 'according to circumstances entirely independent of the duration of that people,' although these needs might 'never have occurred,' the irruption of this absolute contingency determined the interior of an essential history and affected the interior unity of a life, literally infected it. It is the strange essence of the supplement not to have essentiality: it may always not have taken place. Moreover, literally, it has never taken place: it is never present, here and now. If it were, it would not be what it is, a supplement, taking and keeping the place of the other. What alters for the worse the living nerve of language ... has therefore above all not taken place. Less than nothing and yet, to judge by its effects, much more than nothing. The supplement is neither a presence nor an absence. No ontology can think its operation.[11]

Derrida's claim that 'no ontology' can think this operation is questionable, because it disregards the possibility of viral ontology.[12] The question remains whether we could create, following Korzybski and his students, a non-Aristotelian ontology – an ontology of the immaterial supplement. Of course, Derrida later recognizes the dominance of the virus:

All I have done ... is dominated by the thought of a virus, what could be called a parasitology, a virology, the virus being many things ... The virus is in part a parasite that destroys, that introduces disorder into communication. Even from the biological standpoint, this is what happens with a virus; it derails a mechanism of the communicational type, its coding and decoding. On the other hand, it is something that is neither living nor non-living; the virus is not a microbe. And if you follow these two threads, that of a parasite which disrupts destination from the communicative point of view – disrupting writing, inscription, and the coding and decoding of inscription – and which on the other hand is neither alive nor dead, you have the matrix of all that I have done since I began writing.[13]

In 1976, Richard Dawkins (over)extends his (selfish) gene concept, into a number of notions: (re)birth of the *meme*, the other replicator, *toujours le même*. Dawkins renews a nineteenth-century image contemporary to the Darwinian synthesis, *the contagion of ideas*, by reinvigorating its vocabulary: 'When you plant a fertile meme in my mind you literally paralyze my brain, turning it into a vehicle for the meme's propagation in just the way that a virus may parasitize the genetic mechanism of a host cell.'[14] Indeed, the virus appears as the excluded third term that makes the analogy between gene and meme possible:

There are many ways of defining the meme but there are two that we should perhaps take particularly seriously. First, Dawkins, who coined the term meme, described memes as units of cultural transmission which 'propagate themselves in the meme pool by ... a process which, in the broad sense, can be called imitation' (Dawkins, 1976, p. 192). Second, the *Oxford English Dictionary* defines a meme as follows: 'meme (mi:m), n. Biol. (shortened from mimeme ... that which is imitated, after *gene* n.). An element of a culture that may be considered to be passed on by non-genetic means, esp. imitation.' Both these definitions include the critical point that memes are cultural information that is copied, and that it is copied by imitation ... There is a long history of research on imitation in both animal behaviour and human social psychology ... In the nineteenth century Darwin collected many examples of what he took to be imitation in animals, as did Romanes (1882, 1883) but they did not define what they meant by imitation. Baldwin (1902) gave imitation a central role in his theories of evolution, pointing out that all adaptive processes can be seen as imitative – perhaps foreshadowing the universal Darwinism that today enables comparisons between biological evolution and memetic evolution (e.g., Dawkins, 1976; Plotkin, 1993).[15]

Dawkins later makes the point even clearer, by referring to certain memes (religious ones) as *mind viruses*[16] (1993), and so opening the door to countless (ab)uses of the metaphor. Also in 1993, a final critical point (a second second order inflexion point) is passed, and diffusion is now bound to saturation: the hypervirus is now, in Nirvana's words, *In Utero*. To quote from Nirvana's (very Bataillan) song 'Milk It':

'I am my own parasite
I don't need a host to live ...
I own my own pet virus
I get to pet and name her
Her milk is my shit
My shit is her milk.'

But I am getting ahead of myself here; it might be paradoxically better to return to the false heavens of chronology in order to describe the epidemics of the timeless entity.

In 1981 Elk Cloner, the first computer virus in the wild (i.e., affecting PCs), is documented, although early hackers will tell you that there were programs analogous to what we now call 'viruses' in the late 1960s or early 1970s.[17] Elk Cloner predated the experimental work that 'officially' defined computer viruses and spread on Apple II.[18] When infected, the monitor of the computer displayed the following rhyme: It will get on all your disks / It will infiltrate your chips / Yes it's Cloner! / It will stick to you like glue / It will modify ram too / Send in the Cloner!

In 1982 the first global epidemics of the fourth phase officially begin: the name AIDS, for *acquired immune deficiency syndrome*, is coined in August of that year. AIDS would soon become the syndrome of choice to synthesize and metaphorize the 'postmodern condition.' It eventually appears as the final term in a series of diseases playing this part in our culture: plague-tuberculosis-cancer-AIDS. *Room for one more inside, Sir.*

This sequence corresponds term for term to the sequence of the four phases of capitalism: plague is the archaic and thus the archetypical disease (René Girard); tuberculosis is the plague that corresponds to the second phase of capitalism (mechanized capitalism), and cancer the disease of the societies of control:

> Early capitalism assumes the necessity of regulated spending, saving, accounting, discipline – an economy that depends on the rational limitation of desire. TB is described in images that sum the negative behavior of nineteenth century *homo economicus*: consumption; wasting; squandering of vitality. Advanced capitalism requires expansion, speculation, the creation of new needs (the problem of satisfaction and dissatisfaction); buying on credit; mobility – an economy that depends on the irrational indulgence of desire. Cancer is described in images that sum up the negative behavior of twentieth century *homo economicus*: abnormal growth; repression of energy, that is, refusal to consume or spend.[19]

In this quotation, Susan Sontag relates both diseases, tuberculosis and cancer, to an economy of desire. There is a profound resonance here with Girard's notion of mimetic desire,[20] a resonance that also evokes Richard Dawkins's recycling of the nineteenth-century sociobiologies of imitation.[21] Both mimetic desire and sociobiologies of imitation, again, were products of the same period, the second oil crisis of international capitalism in the mid-1970s.

In the viral ontology of the postmodern condition (capitalism of the fourth kind), the undifferentiating crime is ascribed to the radical Other, that is, the virus. Metaphorically speaking, the Other *becomes* a virus. Derrida is quoted by a Web author as saying: *All he has done ... is dominated by the thought of a virus.* That same author concludes that Derrida *is* a virus and thus there is the unbearable feedback of the becoming virus. 'Berlusconi is a retrovirus,' writes Lorenzo Miglioli, and he adds, in the most synthetic expression of the viral horrors of history, 'The Holy Inquisition (knowledge as a form of extortion), Nazism (knowledge as a form of indirect extortion, as an experiment), Pol-Pot (knowledge as a form of erasing/extermination of the actors for the sake of the scene) are pure and simple transcriptions, horror *vacui* translated into horror written on the flesh.'[22] G.W. Bush is a virus, Saddam Hussein is a virus, and bin Laden is a virus. *Room for one more inside, Sir.*

On 3 November 1983, the first 'official' computer virus is conceived of as an experiment to be presented at a weekly seminar on computer security. Fred Cohen first introduced the concept in this seminar, and his doctoral supervisor, Len Adleman, proposes the name 'virus.' In his presentation, Cohen defines a computer virus as 'a computer program that can affect other computer programs by modifying them in such a way as to include a (possibly evolved) copy of itself,' a definition he would stick to in his subsequent paper,[23] and one that would become the official definition of a 'computer virus.' Cohen produces such an 'infection' within a Unix directory-listing utility, proving that identifying and isolating computer viruses is a non-computable problem. This latter result, maybe the most crucial point in Cohen's work, meant that fighting the infection is therefore impossible to achieve using an algorithm, and one is left with the same aporia that philosophers have diagnosed.

According to Cohen, the first use of the term virus to refer to an unwanted computer code occurred in David Gerrold's 1972 science fiction novel, *When Harley Was One*. In an interview, Len Adleman concurred with Cohen: 'The term "computer virus" existed in science fiction well before Fred Cohen and I came along. Several authors actually used that term in science fiction prior to 1983. I don't recall ever having seen it, perhaps it was just a term whose time had come. So I did not invent the term. I just named what we now consider computer viruses "computer viruses."'[24] Indeed, it was a term whose time had come! And the convergence was not fortuitous:

A few years later, while reading about the AIDS virus and its effect on T-cells, Adleman thought about a mathematical description of immunitary deficiency. As certain cells were depleted, he realized, other cells – similar in type but not in function – increased proportionally. Adleman's hypothesis offered not only an explanation for how AIDS destroys the immune system, but pointed toward a method of treatment. If the population of the unaffected cell type (T-8s) could be artificially reduced, he reasoned, the homeostatic forces at work in the immune system would cause an increase in T-4s – the depleted cell types.[25]

In 1986 the diffusion curve of the hypervirus passes its first order inflexion point, and the hypervirus thus becomes mainstream. That year, two Pakistani programmers replace the executable code in the boot sector of a floppy disk with their own viral code designed to infect 360 kb floppies accessed on any drive. Their 'Brain virus' (infected floppies had '© Brain' for a volume label) becomes the first recorded virus to infect PCs running MS-DOS. It is also the first 'stealth' virus, meaning it attempts to hide itself from detection. If a computer user tried to view the infected space on the disk, 'Brain' would display the original, uninfected boot sector. Clearly, writers such as Burroughs and Derrida anticipated this form of dialectics of presence/absence. Also in 1986, the performance artist Laurie Anderson turns William Burroughs's original insight mainstream:

> Paradise
> Is exactly like
> Where you are right now
> Only much much Better.
> I saw this guy on the train
> And he seemed to have gotten stuck
> In one of those abstract trances.
> And he was going: 'Ugh ... Ugh ... Ugh ...'
> And Fred said:
> I think he's in some kind of pain. I think it's a pain cry.
> And I said: 'Pain cry?
> Then language is a virus.'
> Language! It's a virus!
> Language! It's a virus![26]

One year later, AIDS turns mainstream too, thanks to a 'hit' from Prince:

> Oh yeah
> In France a skinny man
> Died of a big disease with a little name
> By chance his girlfriend came across a needle
> And soon she did the same
> At home there are seventeen-year-old boys
> And their idea of fun
> Is being in a gang called the disciples
> High on crack, totin' a machine gun.[27]

As in this song, the syndrome, however, is still restricted to certain stigmatized groups (homosexuals, junkies, etc.). At first, indeed, the syndrome is dubbed 'the gay cancer.' Contrary to the other three diseases associated with prior phases of capitalism, it is highly significant that the main mode of AIDS transmission occurs by sexual contact. In 1988 Susan Sontag already understands this, as she follows her original essay on cancer and 'Illness and Metaphor' with an update focusing on AIDS. She writes, 'The sexual transmission of this illness, considered by most people as a calamity one brings on oneself, is judged more harshly than other means – especially since AIDS is understood as a disease not only of sexual excess but of perversity.'[28] This notion is quite well expressed in a song by the Pet Shop Boys, which is also released in 1987:

> Now it almost seems impossible
> We've drunk too much, and woke up everyone
> I may be wrong, I thought we said
> It couldn't happen here
> I don't expect to talk in terms of sense
> Our dignity and injured innocence
> It contradicts your battle-scars
> Still healed, so far.[29]

And the Boss (Bruce Springsteen) concurs, some years later (in 1993), when the time is ripe for a cinematographic representation of an AIDS patient (as a white lawyer): 'Oh brother are you gonna leave me / Wastin' away / On the streets of Philadelphia.'[30] The year before, 1,300 computer viruses were recorded, an increase of 420% from December 1990. By November 1990, one new virus was discovered each week. Today, between ten and fifteen new computer viruses appear every day. In fact, from December 1998 to October 1999, the total virus count jumped from 20,500 to 42,000. Perhaps soon we will stop counting; we have spyware now, and that too was anticipated by Burroughs: 'It is worth noting that if a virus were to attain a state of wholly benign equilibrium with its host cell it is unlikely that its presence would be readily detected *or that it would necessarily be recognized as a virus.* I suggest that the word is just such a virus.'[31]

It is worth noting that the ambiguity that surrounds the hypervirus is essential to its functioning as the master trope of the postmodern condition. If AIDS is the syndrome of choice to concretize the hypervirus in postmodern culture, it should be noted that, contrary to the three diseases associated with prior kinds of capitalism, AIDS is not a disease, but a *syndrome.* AIDS is the name of a medical condition associated with a wide spectrum of diseases that are usually assumed to be the consequences of the HIV infection. However, this very point is still the subject of controversy. Even if most of the medical and scientific community accepts today that AIDS results from the HIV infection, this is not a proven fact, and some say (e.g., the group of Perth; Kary Mullis, winner of the 1993 Nobel Prize for Chemistry) that it is only still a hypothesis, and a bad one at that.[32] To borrow a term from computer science, AIDS/HIV is a stealth virus. Rather than a mere epiphenomenon of big science, I consider this point to be a crucial characteristic of the hypervirus.

Today, the postmodern has turned ambiguity upside-down with injunctions like 'Embrace your viruses!' or, even more, 'Embrace yourself as a virus.' Steven Shaviro, in his 'Two Lessons from Burroughs,' proposed such a 'biological approach to postmodernism,' and offered violent viral replications and insect strategies such as swarming as models.[33] In a Deleuzian fashion, Shaviro suggested that one learn about the other by becoming other; furthermore, by posing 'the question of radical otherness in biological terms, instead of epistemological ones ... resolving such a problem would involve the transfer, not of minds, but of DNA.'[34] Deleuze and Guattari refer to this transfer as 'aparallel'; more recently it has been termed 'lateral':

> No moribund humanist ideologies will release us from this dilemma. Precisely by virtue of their obsolescence, calls to subjective agency, or to collective imagination and mobilization, merely reinforce the feedback loops of normalizing power. For it is precisely by regulating and punishing ourselves, internalizing the social functions of policing and control, that we arrive at the strange notion that we are producing our own proper language, speaking for ourselves. Burroughs instead proposes a stranger, more radical strategy: 'As you know inoculation is the weapon of choice against virus and inoculation can only be effected through exposure.' For all good remedies are homeopathic. We need to perfect our own habits of parasitism, and ever more busily frequent the habitations of our dead, in the knowledge that every self-perpetuating and self-extending system ultimately encounters its own limits, its own parasites. Let us become dandies of garbage ... Let us stylize, enhance, and accelerate the processes of viral replication: for thereby we increase the probability of mutation. In Burroughs' vision, 'the virus plagues empty whole continents. At the same time new species arise with the same rapidity since the temporal limits on growth have been removed ... The biologic bank is open.' It's now time to spend freely, to mortgage ourselves beyond our means.[35]

What was formerly seen as a problem, or even a *stigma*, is now portrayed as a path to freedom, in a highly paradoxical statement strongly reminiscent of Philip K. Dick's gnostic theodicy. For the ambivalence, of course, remains. As I write these lines, my native country is agitated by the aftershocks of the declarations of a comedian who has proved (again) that anti-Semitism is still practised there. This man, whose name translates ironically into English as 'God-given,' has quite simply actualized the cultural ambivalence of the hypervirus's total diffusion in an aphorism equating Zionism with 'the AIDS of Judaism.'

I am reminded here of the famous characterization of my own generation by Louis Pawels, in an editorial for *Le Figaro* in December 1986, as 'suffering from mental AIDS.' As we were demonstrating in the streets against one more reform of the educational system, Pawels wrote that we, 'the children of stupid rock, the pupils of pedagogical vulgarity,' had 'lost our natural immunities.'[36] The viruses that were supposed to infect us were, of course, 'mind viruses,' as Dawkins would say. By the time Pawels passed his judgment on my generation, AIDS was definitely going mainstream and 'low culture' (i.e., rock and roll and vulgar pedagogy) had rejoined sex and drugs to complete the list of the symptoms of the hyperviral infection. Most of us shrugged, laughing, and passed a joint – only to realize, a few years later, that the guy was one of the bouncers at the doors of perception, French style.

Today, such metaphorical uses of AIDS are so common that nobody seems to notice them anymore. A little Googling generates the following instances from the Web: AIDS as a metaphor for violence, apathy, fear, loneliness, colonialism, globalization, pollution, ecological collapse, homosexuality, the opposing basketball team (!), the corruption and betrayal of the masses, chronic illness, the social and political deterioration of a fictional country, the general loss of moral standards, the conflicts tearing at American society at the turn of the millennium, the American condition, inequities, social decay, or merely 'how the world works.' *Room for one more inside, Sir.*

There is one more crucial way in which today's troubled times are understood through the AIDS metaphor: terrorism as a consequence of 'metaphysical AIDS.' This one we owe to Jacques Derrida.[37] In an interview with Giovanna Borradori that took place in the wake of 9/11, he develops this thesis: terrorism is the latest symptom of (occidental) suicidal autoimmunity.[38] Borradori notes quite interestingly that Derrida began his reflection on the mechanism of autoimmunization during the winter of 1994, 'in connection with a study of the concept of religion, which frames his discussion of religious fundamentalism and its role in global terrorism.'[39] And Derrida agrees, referencing a text written during that period:

> In analysing 'this *terrifying* but inescapable logic of the *autoimmunity of the unscathed* that will always associate Science and Religion,' I there proposed to extend to life in general the figure of an autoimmunity whose meaning or origin first seemed to be limited to so-called natural life or to life pure and simple, to what is believed to be the purely 'zoological,' 'biological,' or 'genetic' ... Since we are speaking here of terrorism and, thus, of terror, the most irreducible source of absolute terror, the one that, by definition, finds itself most defenseless before the worst threat would be the one that comes from 'within,' from this zone where the worst 'outside' lives with or within 'me.' My vulnerability is thus, by definition and by structure, by situation, without limit. Whence the terror.[40]

Notably, 1994 is the same year that Derrida realized that all his prior work from *On Grammatology* on could be reinterpreted as a kind of virology. Susan Sontag writes about the same process: 'In the description of AIDS the enemy is what causes the disease, an infectious agent that comes from the outside ... Next the invader takes up permanent residence, by a form of alien takeover familiar in science-fiction narratives. The body's own cells *become* the invader ... What makes the viral assault so *terrifying* is that contamination, and therefore *vulnerability*, is understood as permanent.'[41]

Why, then, is there this elision of the virus in Derrida's account of terrorism? Why this strange feeling that if terrorism amounts to suicide, it is a spontaneous autophenomenon, with no external agent? In his first moment of autoimmunity, Derrida provides an answer. The aggression comes from the inside because it comes from 'forces that are apparently without any force of their own but that are able to find the means, through ruse and the implementation of *high-tech* knowledge to get hold of an American weapon in an American airport.'[42] Nevertheless, this too is characteristic of viruses. More importantly, Derrida adds, 'let us not forget that the United States had in effect paved the way for and consolidated the forces of the "adversary" by training people like "bin Laden" ... and by first of all creating the politico-military circumstances that would favor their emergence.'[43] While this may seem to be a form of engineered virus, for Derrida, it is best described as *doubly suicidal.*

If Derrida does not see the stigmata of the hypervirus in 9/11, it might be because this would amount to a repetition of Jean Baudrillard's thesis. Previous to 9/11, even before Derrida understood that his work produces a kind of virology, Baudrillard begins to recognize terrorism as one symptom of the hyperviral infection (cf. my epigraph). Like Derrida, he recognizes it as the result of a suicidal drive: 'The terrorist hypothesis is that the system itself suicides in response to the multiple challenges of death and suicide.'[44] However, unlike Derrida, Baudrillard resorts to a viral explanation, even if it does not take the face of an 'external adversary':

> Terrorism, like viruses, is everywhere. There is a worldwide perfusion of terrorism, like the shadow of any system of domination, ready to awake everywhere as a double agent. There is no boundary to define it [*le cerner*]; it is in the very core of this culture that fights it – and the visible schism (and hatred) that opposes, on a global level, the exploited and the underdeveloped against the Western world, is secretly linked to the internal fracture of the dominant system. The latter can face any visible antagonism. But with terrorism – and its viral structure –, as if every domination apparatus were creating its own antibody [*antidispositif*], the chemistry of its own disappearance; against this almost automatic reversal of its own puissance, the system is powerless. And terrorism is the shockwave of this silent reversal.[45]

This is exactly my point: the very core of the culture that fights the hypervirus – postmodern theoreticians included – is infected by it. Terminally. Terrorism is but one symptom – albeit a crucial symptom – of the infection. It reflects the vital (and morbid) condition of postmodernity, setting the stage for the fourth phase of capitalism. Terrorism is the source of pain and suffering and maybe the only sign of a future to come, a junk future. Could this future only be death, as *patient o* seemed to have concluded?

'Fight tuberculosis, folks.'
Christmas Eve, an old junkie selling Christmas seals on North Park Street.
The 'Priest,' they called him. 'Fight tuberculosis, folks.' ...

Then it hit him like heavy silent snow.
All the gray junk yesterdays.
He sat there received the immaculate fix.
And since he was himself a priest,
There was no need to call one.[46]

Junk is yet another name of the hypervirus: Virus and junk are connected through the power of the image, another excluded third. From the awakening of the hypervirus in *Nova Express*, Burroughs had realized that 'junk is concentrated image' and that 'the image material was not dead matter, but exhibited the same life cycle as the virus.'[47] *All the gray junk tomorrows ...*

Notes

1 Leonard Cohen, 'Everybody Knows,' in *I'm Your Man* (Columbia Records, 1988).
2 Jean Baudrillard, 'Prophylaxy and Virulence,' in *The Transparency of Evil: Essays on Extreme Phenomena* (London: Verso, 1993), 67.
3 At a conference in Montreal, I had the opportunity to ask Baudrillard directly about the presence of the trope of the virus in his work. He answered that the virus was indeed a metaphor in his mind, albeit a metaphor which 'renews the terms of the analysis.' He added, 'Virtuality and virality get mixed up in my mind.' An apt conceptual rephrasing of the very thesis that I wish to defend here, under the cover of a fictional 'clinical report.' (See Jean Baudrillard, 'La parralaxe du mal.' Paper presented at the *Conférence Terreurs, Terrorismes et Mécanismes Inconscients*, Montreal, 31 Oct. 2005.)
4 'One must further recognize and accept the pervasiveness of the viral trope within postmodernism ... and understand the ontological confusion (and ideological anxiety) which it carries.' Scott Bukatman, *Terminal Identity: The Virtual Subject in Postmodern Science Fiction* (Durham: Duke University Press, 1993), 347.
5 For this purpose, I will draw heavily on the terminology of diffusion of innovation theory (logistic curve, inflexion points, critical mass, etc.). Ironically enough, the logistic model of the diffusion of innovations was originally borrowed from the field of epidemiology. See Everett M. Rogers, *Diffusion of Innovations*, 4th ed. (New York: Free Press, 1995).
6 Incidentally, Salvador E. Luria, Max Delbrück, and Alfred D. Hershey were awarded the Nobel Prize in Physiology or Medicine for their work on viruses in 1969. As early as 1955, Salvador Luria had written that 'a new view of the nature of viruses is emerging. They used to be thought of solely as foreign intruders – strangers to cells they invade and paratize. But recent findings, including the discovery of host-induced modifications of viruses, emphasize more and more the similarity of viruses to hereditary units such as genes. Indeed, some viruses are being considered as bits of heredity in search of a chromosome.' In '50, 100 & 150 Years Ago,' *Scientific American* (April 2005), 18.

7 William S. Burroughs, *The Electronic Revolution,* Expanded Media Editions (West Germany: Bresche Publikationen, 1970). English version available online at http://www.ubu.com/ historical/burroughs/electronic_revolution.pdf. Accessed 24 Oct. 2007.

8 Kathy Acker, 'Returning to the Source,' funeral oration for William Burroughs, *21C,* 26 'No Future' (1998): 14. 'He was the detective. Being the detective, he was the doctor. He searched out the possessors some of whose other names are viruses and junk. The word is virus. In other words, language controls virally ... William spent a life-time investigating anti-viral techniques.'

9 Burroughs, *Electronic Revolution.*

10 Cf. Anne-Marie Christin, *L'image écrite, ou la déraison graphique* (Paris: Flammarion, 2001 [1995]), 16.

11 Jacques Derrida, *Of Grammatology,* trans. G.C. Spivak (Baltimore: Johns Hopkins University Press, 1967), 314.

12 Although starting from a very different standpoint, Paul Ricoeur seems to reach a similar conclusion: 'Perhaps the philosopher as philosopher has to admit that one does not know and cannot say whether this Other, the source of the injunction, is another person whom I can look in the face or who can stare at me, or my ancestors for whom there is no representation, to so great an extent does my debt to them constitute my very self, or God – living God, absent God – or an empty place. With the aporia of the Other, philosophical discourse comes to an end.' *Oneself as Another* (Chicago: Chicago University Press, 1992), 355. Here I am tempted to spell injunction with a 'k' and see the virus as its original source.

13 Jacques Derrida with Peter Brunette and David Wills, 'The Spatial Arts: An Interview with Jacques Derrida,' *Deconstruction and the Visual Arts: Art, Media Architecture,* ed. Peter Brunette and David Wills (Cambridge: Cambridge University Press, 1994), 12.

14 Richard Dawkins, *The Selfish Gene* (Oxford: Oxford University Press, 1989 [1976]), 192.

15 Susan Blackmore, 'Imitation and the Definition of a Meme,' *Journal of Memetics – Evolutionary Models of Information Transmission* 2 (1998), available at http://cfpm.org/jom-emit/1998/vol2/ blackmore_s.html. Accessed 24 Oct. 2007. Referred to in this citation are: Dawkins, *The Selfish Gene* (1976); G.J. Romanes, *Animal Intelligence* (London: Kegan Paul Trench, 1882); J.M. Baldwin, *Development and Evolution* (New York: MacMillan, 1902); H. Plotkin, *Darwin, Machines and the Nature of Knowledge* (Cambridge: Harvard University Press, 1993).

16 Richard Dawkins, 'Viruses of the Mind,' *Free Inquiry* (Summer 1993): 34-41.

17 There are instances of 'viral infections' documented for the Univac 1108 and the IBM 360/ 370 ('Pervading Animal' and 'Christmas tree').

18 For more information on Elk Cloner see http://www.skrenta.com/cloner. Accessed 24 Oct. 2007.

19 Susan Sontag, 'Illness as Metaphor,' *Illness as Metaphor and AIDS and Its Metaphors* (London: Picador, 1990 [1978]), 63.

20 See René Girard, *Des choses cachées depuis la fondation du monde* (Paris: Grasset, 1978), and *Le Bouc Émissaire* (Paris: Grasset, 1982).

21 Gabriel de Tarde, *Les lois de l'imitation* (Paris: Kimé Éditeur, 1993 [1895]), for instance.

22 Lorenzo Miglioli, 'Berlusconi Is a Retrovirus: From the Italian Theory-Fiction Novel,' in *Digital*

Delirium, ed. Arthur and Marilouise Kroker (Montreal: New World Perspectives, 1997), 145.

23 Frederic Cohen, 'Computer Viruses – Theory and Experiments,' DOD/NBS 7th Conference on Computer Security, originally appearing in IFIP-sec 84, also appearing in *Computers and Security* 6 (1987): 22–35, and other publications in several languages, available at http://vx .netlux.org/lib/afc01.html. Accessed 24 Oct. 2007.

24 Leonard Adleman, 'Interview with Diane Krieger,' 1996, available at http://www.scu.edu.cn/ waim03/scu_cs/teach/adleman.htm. Accessed 24 Oct. 2007.

25 Ibid.

26 Laurie Anderson, 'Language Is a Virus,' *Home of the Brave* (Warner Bros., 1986).

27 Prince, 'Signs O' the Times,' *Signs O' the Times* (Warner Bros.,1987).

28 Sontag, 'AIDS and Its Metaphors,' 114. And she adds, 'I am thinking, of course, of the United States, where people are currently being told that heterosexual transmission is extremely rare, and unlikely – as if Africa did not exist.'

29 The Pet Shop Boys, 'It Couldn't Happen Here,' *Actually* (Parlophone Records, 1987).

30 Bruce Springsteen, 'Streets of Philadelphia,' *Philadelphia Soundtrack* (Sony, 1993).

31 Burroughs, *Electronic Revolution*.

32 It seems quite ironic again that the controversy about the HIV 'hypothesis' should have exploded right at the time the hypervirus pandemic passed its final inflexion point, around 1993. In 1993, Kary Mullis, in an interview for the *Sunday Times*, said: 'If there is evidence that HIV causes AIDS, there should be scientific documents which either singly or collectively demonstrate that fact, at least with a high probability. There is no such document' (28 Nov. 1993). A year later, again in the *Sunday Times*, Dr Bernard Forscher, former editor of the U.S. *Proceedings of the National Academy of Sciences*, was quoted as saying: 'The HIV hypothesis ranks with the "bad air" theory for malaria and the 'bacterial infection' theory of beriberi and pellagra [caused by nutritional deficiencies]. It is a hoax that became a scam' (3 April 1994). Available at http://www.virusmyth.net/aids/ controversy.htm. Accessed 24 Oct. 2007.

33 Steven Shaviro, 'Two Lessons from Burroughs,' in *Posthuman Bodies*, ed. Judith Halberstam and Ira Livingston (Bloomington: University of Indiana Press, 1995), 38.

34 Ibid., 47.

35 Steven Shaviro, 'William Burroughs,' *Doom Patrol*, chapter 10, available at http://www .dhalgren.com/Doom/ch10.html. Accessed 24 Oct. 2007.

36 Louis Pawels, 'Le monôme des zombis,' *Figaro Magazine*, 6 Dec. 1986, p. 103.

37 Although Derrida consciously avoided the AIDS metaphor, critics were prompt to make the connection: 'Derrida's most striking claim is that 9-11 is the result of an autoimmune disorder ... 9-11 was a double suicide of both attackers and their victims. We are suffering from a metaphysical AIDS.' Gergory Fried, 'The Uses of Philosophy,' *Village Voice*, quoted in Gary Sauer-Thompson, 'Derrida: Democracy after 9/11,' Philosophy.com, 23 Feb. 2005, available at http:// www.sauer-thompson.com/archives/philosophy/002925.html. Accessed 24 Oct. 2007.

38 'Autoimmune conditions consist in the spontaneous suicide of the very defensive mechanism supposed to protect the organism from external aggression.' Giovanna

Borradori, *Philosophy in a Time of Terror: Dialogues with Jürgen Habermas and Jacques Derrida* (Chicago: Chicago University Press, 2003), 150.

39 Ibid., 154.

40 Ibid., 187-8. Derrida refers here to his 'Faith and Knowledge: The Two Sources of "Religion" at the Limits of Reason Alone,' published in *Religion*, ed. Jacques Derrida and Gianni Vattimo (Stanford, Stanford University Press, 1998).

41 Sontag, 'AIDS and Its Metaphors,' 105–8, first emphasis in the original, second and third mine.

42 Borradori, *Philosophy in a Time of Terror*, 95.

43 Ibid.

44 Jean Baudrillard, 'L'esprit du terrorisme,' *Le Monde*, 2 Nov. 2001, revised translation based on Rachel Bloul's translation, available on the webpage of the European Graduate School, available at http://www.egs.edu/faculty/baudrillard/baudrillard-the-spirit- of-terrorism.html. Accessed 25 March 2005,

45 Ibid.

46 William Burroughs, 'The Priest They Called Him,' *Exterminator!* (Tim Kerr Records, 1960), spoken word released on CD in 1993 with Kurt Cobain and Nirvana.

47 Cf. Scott Bukatman, *Terminal Identity: The Virtual Subject in Post-Modern Science Fiction* (Durham: Duke University Press, 1993), 74–8, for an analysis of this figure.

11 Algebra of Identity:
Skin of Wind, Skin of Streams, Skin of Shadows, Skin of Vapour

D. FOX HARRELL

Introduction and Braiding

Here, I braid three cords together: identity, algebra, and poetry. Identity is the subject matter, algebra is a tool for representing sign systems of fluid identity, poetry is used as the enactment of the view of identity described with the algebra. I also use algebra to aid in the development of computational techniques for implementing a system that generates prose poetry in response to a user's prompts – a call and response form that is thematically fixed but variable in particular expression and metaphor.

The subtitle of this chapter: 'Skin of Wind, Skin of Streams, Skin of Shadows, Skin of Vapour,' is meant to evoke a restricted notion of identity and the insubstantiality of that notion. A focus on skin is obsessive and solipsistic. I am expected to write about it in a chapter on identity. When ethnic identity is made binary and colourized, we talk in bodily terms, of skin. It is evocative – it is a membrane, protecting, projecting, coating, an exterior, a superficial, obvious, and immense organ. I shall not disappoint these expectations of skin obsession, but when I write of the traits of ethnic identification these are just symbols for a classification-based conception of social identity.

Wind whips, shrieks, or is unnoticeable. Streams bears small creatures below rocks, rush with energy and transparency. Shadow obscures, cools, relaxes. Vapour moistens, hides, causes ships to crash, is fluid but hangs in the ether. If we can imagine these four skins, we can also imagine skin of tangled roots, illicit loves, unscratched itches, crossed senses, angels, or demons. I shall get back to this later.

What I wish to conjure is a sense of the fleeting nature and contingency of classification-based identity as it is typically conceived of. I propose explanations for why some current notions of identity seem damaging and discuss alternative ways to address this issue. My belief is in internalizing and exposing this very contingency, accepting this as the reality in how we perceive ourselves, others, and the concept of identity as a whole.

In beginning, I would like to motivate the discussion of identity.

Identity

> Jacques Derrida's version of deconstruction is one of the most influential schools of thought among young academic critics. It is salutary in that it focuses on the political power of rhetorical oppositions – of tropes and metaphors in binary oppositions like white/black, good/bad, male/female, machine/nature, ruler/ruled, reality/appearance – showing how these operations sustain hierarchical world views by devaluing the second terms as something subsumed under the first.
>
> Cornel West[1]

> ... black men and white men, Jews and Gentiles, Protestants and Catholics – will be able to join hands and sing in the words of that old Negro spiritual: 'Free at last! Free at last!'
>
> Martin Luther King Jr[2]

It is crucial to be cognizant of the network of forces determining your identity. Although it is not possible to regulate one's identity, it is necessary to be one of the forces contributing to its expression. Since even 'objective facts' can be viewed from innumerable perspectives we can utilize so-called objective historical knowledge and its impact upon identity formation in ways that support self-empowered living; this is a functional view of identity. Functionalism means fluidity in a world where dualist classification systems inhabit even oppositional strategies to prejudice such as Aimé Césaire's seductive song of negritude,[3] or Judy Chicago's well-appointed 'Dinner Party.'[4] A functional view is inherently going to be assailed as constructionist fiction, and yet, a view that intends to transcend the quagmire of dualist identity using a strategy of essential 'sameness' is going to be assailed equally. Consider the following example. Alison Saar, Sam Gilliam, and Martin Puryear are three artists found in the same categorized section of ARTODAY,[5] a book on contemporary art. Regarding Alison Saar, the author, Edward Lucie-Smith writes, 'Alison Saar has also looked at African fetish statues as a source of inspiration ... The problem with all these attempts to make a new Africa in America is that the spectator is aware of the artist's self-consciousness, of an attempt to create a kind of "primitivism" which doesn't come into existence spontaneously.' Of Sam Gilliam, the same author writes, 'Gilliam is, and has always been, an abstract painter, whose work eschews overt symbolism ... Gilliam has caused considerable irritation amongst African-American militants, and has sometimes been accused of "Uncle Tom-ism" because of his insistence on being judged purely as an artist, not as a generic representative of minority culture.' And of Martin Puryear, the author writes, 'Martin Puryear, now perhaps the most celebrated African sculptor, is similarly insistent, despite the fact that he is one of the few African-American artists who has direct experience of Africa ... Attempts to align his work with African artifacts have been made by enthusiastic critics, but seem fruitless in the face of Puryear's own statement that, when in Africa, he felt like an outsider – not part of the customs of the people among whom he lived.'

This collection of statements, representative of a tendency in critical writing about art, promotes the stance that the racial identity assigned to the three artists takes precedence over the content and formal issues of the work by placing these artists all in the 'Racial Minorities' section in the book (which happened to be the second to last section, the last being 'Feminist and Gay'). The organization of the book indicates Lucie-Smith's hierarchical view of the relative importance of different groups of artists. New York artists deserve their own section (which does not include artists from New York that happen to be of racial minority groups), and British artists are important enough to be segmented by content, hence a section on 'British Figurative Painting,' as opposed to ethnic identity. Curiously, and contradictorily, the author simultaneously racially classifies these artists, emphasizes racial debates surrounding these artists, and denies these artists self-determination in assertions of heritage. The African-American artist cannot be seen non-racially, but can only be seen as an African-American artist who wishes to be seen non-racially. At the same time, the African-American artist cannot be seen in connection with any ancient historical tradition or culture, as such attempts are 'self-conscious or tenuous.'

With such forces seeking to constrain social and individual conceptions of people, it is imperative to seek techniques and perspectives capable of disarming such constraints. The dominant categories such as 'white' are unmarked, invisible, in their dominance in the ARTODAY example cited above. But reliance upon the binary relationships imposed by marked versus unmarked categories is not exercised only from the top of the hierarchy down. Many times even socially aware and proactive groups define themselves and their relationships to others in binary terms: black, white, majority, minority, patriarchy, oppressed, white-privileged, affirmative-actioned. A world of binaries is concrete and actionable. Humans have a need to classify, yet when it comes to identity politics binary and discrete classification reinforces systems of social oppression. Sociologists Geoffrey Bowker and Susan Leigh Star emphasize this point in their 1999 book *Sorting Things Out: Classification and Its Consequences:*[6]

> Each standard and each category valorizes some point of view and silences another. This is not inherently a bad thing – indeed it is inescapable. But it is an ethical choice, and as such it is dangerous – not bad, but dangerous. For example, the decision of the U.S. Immigration and Naturalization Service to classify some races and classes as desirable for U.S. residents, and others as not, resulted in a quota system which valued affluent people from Northern and Western Europe over those (especially the poor) from Africa or South America. The decision to classify students by their standardized achievement and aptitude tests valorizes some kinds of knowledge skills and renders other kinds invisible ... For any individual, group or situation, classifications and standards give advantage or they give suffering.

Aside from the problems introduced via the marked/unmarked dichotomy, we are also always left with phenomena that fail to be classified when subjected to discrete measures.

In the racialized world of black versus white, the catch-all category of 'other' is typically understood in terms of whether the current person under consideration is more blacklike or whitelike, or as an Indian-American colleague encountered while travelling through rural Colorado said of himself, 'You ain't black, you ain't white, so what is you?'

Dualities carry power and have long informed diverse agendas ranging from the software/hardware split in the von Neumann architecture in computer science[7] to anti-racist ideology in groups like the Black Panther Party (Bobby Seale, co-founder of the Black Panther Party, described the strategic use of essential classifications and black nationalism as a necessary political response to oppressive social conditions and as a stepping stone on the path towards a society embracing broader humanist values[8]). In the course of illuminating 'possible origins of cybernetic theory in African culture, ways that black people have negotiated the rise of cybernetic technology in the West, and the confluence of these histories in the lived experience of the African diaspora,' Professor Ron Eglash notes that:

> Opposition to racism has often been composed through two totalizing, essentialist strategies: sameness and difference. For example, Mudimbe (1988) demonstrates how the category of a singular 'African philosophy' has been primarily an invention of difference, having its creation in the play between 'the beautiful myths of the "savage mind" and the African ideological strategies of otherness.' In contrast, structuralists such as Levi-Strauss have attempted to prove that African conceptual systems are fundamentally the same as those of Europeans (both having their basis in arbitrary symbol systems).[9]

Aligning under binary banners makes the power struggle very clear, although it is disenfranchising for those who seek a sensitive expression of personal identity. A mathematical analogue to binary thought, Boolean logic, is quite powerful, in its limited domain.[10] It is sound. Anything that you can prove in a reality described by Boolean logic is entailed by that reality. This means that in any possible world it is true if you can prove it ('possible worlds' here means being able to look at all of the possibilities for what is true and what is false). Furthermore, it has the converse property that anything you can say in Boolean logic that is true in all worlds, can be proved. It is complete.

Of course, this line of thought is metaphorical, but it has interesting implications when we indulge this thought experiment. This type of binary thinking leads towards finality of thought, imperial statements, and the reification of ideas. There is no way to express a concept such as she is 'woman and not a woman' so that it is true, although socially it is perhaps possible to think of situations where such a statement might pertain. An interesting note is that as soon as logic is expanded to include generalizations, with statements such 'for all women who are sports fans,' the logic is no longer complete. The comfort provided by its restrictions is taken away.

There is a non-metaphorical component to inquiry involving mathematics and identity, too. Aside from exploring African influences on computer science, Ron

Eglash also notes traditions of novel technical cultural practices within the African diaspora. An example of such a practice, the GRIOT computational system[11] (discussed below), which I programmed at the Meaning and Computation Lab at the University of California, San Diego, has been used to output prose poetry about a girl with skin of angels and demons in response to user input about domains such as Europe, Africa, girls, whiteness, devils, and seraphs. The system's output represents a subjective and transitory notion of identity. The system is equally based in mathematics (algebraic semantics and specification) as it is in semiotics theory and cognitive linguistics approaches to identity.

Thus, I invoke mathematics here as a device to, metaphorically and literally, allow us to move away from the standard binary way to view identity. I seek new blends involving identity, new ways to combine thoughts, without deviating from the subject matter. Discussion of algebra provides a means to do so.

Algebra

Algebra may be considered, in its most general form, as the science which treats of the combinations of arbitrary signs and symbols by means defined through arbitrary laws.

George Peacock.[12]

'Watch out, men! You are not so pretty that you can handle a woman's blade!' But as Raven turned the blade by the lantern (Bayle squinted because two threads of light lanced from the gnarly hilt), she was still grinning. 'Ah, you men would take everything away from a woman – I've been in your strange and terrible land long enough to know that. But you won't have this. See it, and know that it will never be yours!' She laughed. (It wasn't one blade on the hilt, Bayle realized, but two, running parallel, perhaps an inch apart: as she brandished it, the lantern flashed between either side.)

Samuel R. Delany.[13]

In the Delany quote above, the sword, a violent and masculine symbol, has been transformed into a vulval feminine symbol in a matriarchal mythology, no less violent. It is a combination of signs and symbols defined through (seemingly) arbitrary laws of culture. Algebra deals with the rules for how things can generally be combined. Since I often work using this framework, these days I am sensitive to blending in many domains.[14] The blending of concepts is contingent and fleeting.[15] The national obsession of the United States, identity, is no exception. One obvious breakdown in traditional notions of identity is the creation of new ethnic identities by merging. Identity also occurs in peculiar ways in different contexts, for example, in a market economy it is treated often as a commodity as we encounter phenomena such as identity theft. It is important and crucial to recognize and challenge inequitable power structures. One way to do so is through an understanding of identity as a dynamic network as opposed to a system of binary relations. The challenge is to do so within a social context based on the binary relation of standard versus other.

In computer science, definitions from algebraic semantics are used to describe how information behaves purely based on syntactic properties.[16] An algebra consists of a set of values and operations defined on those values. For example, you could have a set of 'people,' and a set of relations describing who 'rules over' whom. There is a great deal of flexibility and nuance that can be captured in even a simple algebra that is difficult to represent in terms of simple inclusion or exclusion of people in particular levels of a social hierarchy. We can also define semantic equations that describe equivalences between syntactic elements. This means that we are able to describe how elements are equivalent even if they are named differently and that we can translate between different syntactic forms of the same thing. The real advantage of using algebra as a metaphor for fluid notions of identity comes from the fact that the names used to describe elements are arbitrary, because the system of rules is what makes the difference, not the particular classifications. Formal notation such as algebraic semantics is no more than a useful tool for describing precisely a set of concepts. Reality does not conform to the language of mathematics. Still, within its limited range of application, formalizing ideas can be used more casually and intuitively to add to analyses grounded in lived experience and social context.

Far from using algebra as merely an evocative metaphor, in the research of the Meaning and Computation Laboratory at UCSD, we use Joseph Goguen's algebraic semiotics: this is an approach to meaning and representation that combines algebraic specification with social semiotics to represent sign systems.[17] We also use it to implement the construction of metaphors using ideas from conceptual blending theory in cognitive science. We construct blends of concepts. Ideas such as identity now can be blended with ideas such as commodities (in identity theft), screen-based icons (as avatars), and where identity itself is blendable (concepts such as Hispanicity, whiteness, or gay, lesbian, or transgendered unity). The identity of one individual can be blended with the identity of another. For example, the infamous American football star O.J. Simpson was often referenced in news reporting about the American basketball player Kobe Bryant's trial for rape because both are African-American sports figures. Note that this analogue between sports figures is the result of a blend: Ishmael Reed observes in an article in his *Konch* magazine[18] that the music mogul Phil Spector was accused of murdering a white woman – this is the same Phil Spector who reputedly rescued Tina Turner from the abusive Ike Turner, but Spector has not often been compared to Ike Turner.

A feature of blending is compression. Humans want to reduce concepts to human scale in order to comprehend them better. Compression[19] often occurs in blending where the blended space is used to visualize something of a large scale in terms of a smaller one. In service of this goal, pressure is exerted on the blending process in order to compress what is diffuse, obtain global insight, come up with a story, and go from 'Many to One.'[20] In these terms, even a cursory and ad hoc analysis can prove illuminating regarding racism. In the Kobe Bryant / O.J. Simpson example, two individuals are taken to be analogous because they represent the larger group, that is, black male sports figures (reduction of many to one). They are identified only because they are used as representations of a larger concept – the violent black male. The 'white' Phil Spector (also accused of murder) could not show up in the compressed blend in this case, because he is not a representative of that group. Tokenism can be seen in these terms – one individual is used to represent the many.

It is important to remember that blends are often created on the fly: they can constantly change; they are active. Blends execute and allow for thought experimentation. Blends exist in larger networks and are extremely dynamic and contingent. This contingency seems especially relevant for discussing identity concepts. When we encounter others, our conceptions of their identities are composed as blends. When someone says, 'Well, I am really not that into sports,' or, 'My mother is Asian,' or 'I have converted to Judaism,' our conception of that person is transformed on the fly. The network of concepts that make up the perceived identity of that person is changed. Currently, I am working on an algorithm to explore the construction of blends on the fly for generating media. It is possible to imagine how such work could be used to inform precise discussion about identity concepts.

Poetry

> If anything my desire here has been to demystify the curious notion that theory is the province of the Western tradition, something alien or removed from the so-called noncanonical tradition such as that of the Afro-American.
>
> Henry Louis Gates Jr.[21]

> Since the products of blending are ubiquitous, sometimes spectacularly visible, it is natural that students of rhetoric, literature, painting, and scientific invention should have noticed many specific examples of what we call blending and noticed, too, that something was going on. The earliest such observation that we have found comes from Aristotle.
>
> Gilles Fauconnier and Mark Turner.[22]

Blending and metaphor are conceptual tools that can be used to address this fluctuating view of identity. New views of an identity can be introduced using metaphor and taken through transforming phases with evocative effect. For me, the use of exaggerated metaphors in poetry and literature can illustrate this idea, and this is a central device that I use in my own work. In my novel, a fantasy entitled *Milk Pudding Flavored with Rose Water, Blood Pudding Flavored by the Sea*,[23] the characters constantly change identity and transform metaphorically. The fantasy in the tale arises from elaborating these metaphors more than any other type of magical or paranormal effects. For example, in the first half I describe the tale of a type of black knight youth travelling from city to city. Metaphor is used to describe the view of him through the lens of that particular town.

In one example, Jal-R takes on a new role in the chapter entitled, 'Men and Mothers'; his description is established and transformed as the passage progresses. After this passage he transforms further:

> The voices were indecipherable. The number of people from far-away and near-away lands was greater than in years past. The effect was disorienting as he walked through the market. Many of the strangers shrank from him. His was a stark figure; black silhouette with a flowing shadow cloak slipping behind him. Despite recent sneers from his compatriot Black Riders, most townsmen and women treated him with grand respect. The strangers' fear came from the clear bearing of power and battle with which he carried himself. He was a warrior, there was no doubt. All talk of the diminishing public regard for the riders was moot in the wake of his heavy black boots. He was an undeniable force, a Black Rider. He was the essence of a rider, he walked and a thunderhead-ominous threat surrounded him. Today his merchant friends knew better than to approach him or joke at his expense. He walked as if on a mission. The hilts of two daggers swung at his sides. Knives formed delicate decorations on the calves of his boots. There was no color on him besides a touch of pink in the embroidered rose at his chest and reflections in the hints of silver at his feet, waist, and cowl. He opened the door to a nondescript long hall and stepped inside to crying and a sanitary aroma.

A bit later:

> Jal-R rocked the infant against his black padded breastplate. It had been a trial to coax the baby girl to sleep. He often felt ill at ease here and his queasy heart surely passed its vibrations to the children. The other professional mothers felt threatened by the alien image of brutality nursing their charges, muscling himself into their world. All in the longhouse felt as if their hearts beat through black gauze when Jal-R was there ... a dark sense of roles askew. Jal-R was unaware of many of these perceptions of him, but the cloud that gathered each time he walked in there was impossible not to notice. It mattered little, he told himself, he had resolved to learn at least some of the arts of the mother to provide for Ayoli.

My engagement with the idea of unstable, metaphorical, and transforming identity did not begin with the Jal-R Black Rider character. Reconnecting this poetry to the subtitle of this chapter, I also wrote of an expansive view of skin. My concern with my society's obsession with skin peaked when I was around nineteen years old. I created more than thirty types of skin and imagined life in each of these.[24]

These were skin such as: the skin of the man whose skin turned to paper, the man whose skin was made of everything funny, the balloon-skinned girl, the man whose skin was made of sexual experimentation, the girl with noisy skin, the man whose skin was pink but people called him white but didn't mean the colour of pure driven snow, the man whose skin was brown but people called him black but didn't mean evil. One such poem follows:

Skin normally has thin blue veins in it
But the man whose skin turned to paper
Knew that the thin blue lines on his skin
Were made from ink and not the flow of blood.
The lines were parallel to each other,
Yet because his skin curved
It was hard to tell whether the lines
Were standard or college rule,
And due to the fact that the man whose skin turned to paper
Had skin that was not a chalky white,
The thin red vertical line that ran perpendicular to the blue lines
Was difficult to see.
One hole through his head
One through his duodenum
One through his tibia
So that although the size of a normal man
He fit in a three-ringed folder.
One pencil in each hand
So that, enabled by ambidexterity,
He could twice as quickly write and record
His thoughts and ideas
Images called doodles or tattoos.
Writings, poetry, and self-indulgence
Make a set of verse, a body of work
That begins: skin normally has thin blue veins in it.

For me, exaggerated, densely metaphorical, and shifting views of identity traits have a liberating effect. It expands a sense of possibility for self-identification. It also stimulates a sceptical view of social identity politics in that it engages the inherent limitations of hierarchical classification-based identity, but also declares its divergence from functional reality.

Call and Response, Improvisation and Conclusion

But so often identity is forcefully, painfully imposed on us despite our agitation against its confines. A dynamic identity must take into account immediate social context. In the African diaspora there are many artistic traditions that negotiate the disjunction between self-identity and social identity, between historical, traditional identity, and identities of resistance. Dynamic improvization and call-and-response structures are familiar aspects of pan-African narrative forms as diverse as the delta blues, Charles Mingus's calling-out of the segregationist Governor of Arkansas in 'Fables of Faubus,'[25] the penetratingly satirical fiction of Ishmael Reed, hip-hop freestyle rhyming, and the African-Brazilian martial art and dance 'Capoeira Angola.' The capoerista provides a good example of shifting identity: he or she was originally a participant in a multiform art that functioned as a ritual, game, martial art, sacred space, and more, but that identity transformed as capoeira was outlawed beginning in nineteenth-century Brazil. Capoeiristas were cast by the government as dangerous miscreants, potential revolutionaries, or thieves, and punished with imprisonment, lashings, naval service, and even death. The identity of the capoeirista was forced towards multi-veilance and *malícia* (deceptive trickiness). Concurrently, the capoeirista enjoyed the respect and admiration of the African-identified populace, and the simultaneous demonization as 'primitives' and valorization as effective soldiers by the public authorities and the Portuguese-descended tourists, aristocrats, and upper class that it was their intention to 'protect.' Recall, as an illustrative example, the War of the Triple Alliance (1865-70), the bloodiest conflict in Latin American history, during which Brazil's front line consisted of mostly conscripted capoeiristas, enslaved Africans sent across the Paraná river to Paraguay to fight with the promise of freedom.[26] Some of the most melancholy capoeira songs recall this river, for example, when a soloist calls out and hears responses in the words 'Ê Paraná':

Ê Paraná
Eu não vou na sua casa, Paraná
Ê Paraná
Pra você não ir na minha, Paraná
Ê Paraná
Porque você tem boca grande, Paraná
Ê Paraná
Vai comer minha galinha, Paraná
Ê Paraná
Puxa, puxa, leva, leva, Paraná
Ê Paraná
Paraná está me chamando, Paraná
Ê Paraná
Me chamando pra jogar, Paraná
Ê Paraná
Minha mãe está me chamando, Paraná
Ê Paraná
Vê que vida de moleque, Paraná
Ê Paraná.

The song translates in English roughly as:

> *Eh, Paraná*
> I do not go in your house, Paraná
> *Eh, Paraná*
> For you go not in mine, Paraná
> *Eh, Paraná*
> Because you have a great mouth, Paraná
> *Eh, Paraná*
> You will eat my chicken, Paraná
> *Eh, Paraná*
> Pull, pull, take, take, Paraná
> *Eh, Paraná*
> Paraná is calling me, Paraná
> *Eh, Paraná*
> Calling me to play, Paraná
> *Eh, Paraná*
> My mother is calling me, Paraná
> *Eh, Paraná*
> I see that hustler life, Paraná
> *Eh, Paraná.*

The repeated invocation of an historic place in the 'New World' is a common theme in African-diasporic call-and-response lyrics. When these songs are sung, new lyrics are often spontaneously improvized. The creation of traditionally structured songs with new meanings, especially layered meanings as in capoeira songs (the songs often have double and triple functions within the art form) also serves to create new identities for postcolonial contexts.

Written prose poetry[27] and its more recent descendant, flash fiction[28] ('short short' stories that encapsulate full narrative arcs within extremely abbreviated word counts), traditionally have not incorporated these techniques. On-the-fly improvization has not been incorporated for the simple reason that the nature of the medium of the printed text is not dynamically reconfigurable. Computational media have dynamic information structures and feedback loops built into their nature. The output of my recent research combines this type of prose poetry, dynamically reconfigurable and founded in African and African-American vernacular traditions of signification,[29] with the use of algebraic techniques to construct imaginative metaphors on the fly. I have written a computer program (in the LISP programming language), called GRIOT, that uses algebraic semiotics as a foundation to generate poems line by line in response to user feedback, poems that can be reconstructed on each reading algorithmically, while maintaining core concepts and themes. I think of this work as the development of improvisational texts (active media). The metaphors are fluid. From my vantage-point, the cultural objects of most interest are the GRIOT and ALLOY systems themselves and the variability of the output in response to user input, not the individual instances of output as cultural objects on their own.

The GRIOT system actualizes the winding together of the separate cords of algebra, identity, and poetry in a cultural artefact. The following text completes the braided cord with a series of call-and-response poetic outputs in the same mould as those I created many years ago. I conclude with a sample of outputs from the poetic system entitled, 'The Girl with Skin of Haints and Seraphs' (the user's input follows the > prompt, the italicized system's response follows; the appendix below contains several more examples in detail and a brief description of how the system works):

>Europe
europeans and beauty relish, create entitlement and cool ringing in the ears of the girl with skin of smugness and kindness blended with neck, red
>Europe
she worked raising imperialist, cherub children of her own
>Europe
death was better
>Europe
her spirit trusts that a nordic-beauty or epidermis arouses, provokes awe desire
>Europe
a spectral tone pervaded
>Europe
sunbather and first-born envies and is now melaninated and impoverished-elder, causing her eyelids to droop
>Europe
she knows that childish reverence of contradiction days will fall further and further behind.

Appendix

The following is a brief description of the functionality of the GRIOT system. Initially a poetic system designer inputs a set of poetic narrative templates (clauses with wildcards that will be replaced on each execution), a narrative structure that defines how clauses can be composed, a set of theme domains that provide information about a set of concepts, and a list of keywords that access each theme domain. The 'Girl with Skin of Haints and Seraphs' system works by establishing a set of theme domains such as skin, angels, demons, old Europe, and old Africa, composed of sets of axioms. During the execution of GRIOT, each time the user enters a term it is scanned for relevance to the domains and a response is produced as output to the screen. The system constructs conceptual spaces, using the algebraic semiotics framework, and blends these to construct metaphors using a conceptual blending algorithm. These are then combined with narrative templates, in the case of 'The Girl with Skin of Haints and Seraphs,' these are based on a model from sociolinguistics research, a formalization of William Labov's structure of narratives of personal experience.[30] This narrative template is integrated with metaphors generated on the fly. The core of the work is an algorithm called ALLOY that I wrote to model conceptual blending, not natural language processing. What comes out of it are conceptual spaces and axioms, not English sentences. For the purposes here, I use the GRIOT system as a front end to construct a type of poetry, but in particular, the guided combination of concepts is the focus of the work. My longer term project involves the generation of new metaphors driven by user interaction with a graphical or gamelike interfaces, resulting in blends of graphical, audio, and textual media. Below are three samples of poetic output.

(1) The first sample poem and a detailed description of its generation follows. User input is differentiated by a > prompt. The system output is italicized. My commentary on how some of the content of each line of text is generated follows the system output. LISP code for an axiom describing subjective information about the domain follows my commentary.

> *her arrival onto this earth was marked when first-born and charcoal-girl transforms to impoverished-elder or charcoal-woman*
> *she worked raising snow-queen original-lady children of her own*
> *the young lady would prevail*
> *a caress across her skin scares up demon black*
> *her failure was ignoring her wings and original-lady nature*
> *and she felt glad*
> *as she grew older she saw entitlement defiance wrinkles upon her face*
> *ebony-wood-like brimstone defines fetish bedrock,*
> *the sign that let her know she finally really alive*

>Africa
(*her arrival onto this earth was marked when first-born and charcoal-girl transforms to impoverished-elder or charcoal-woman*)

The concepts of first-born people, the impoverished elder, and charcoal skin are selected from the 'Africa' domain in this opening clause. The LISP axiom selected for blending is:

```
(axiom 'is-now'
  ((constant 'first-born' 'person' afrika-space)
   (constant 'impoverished-elder' 'person' afrika-space)))
>Europe
```
(*she worked raising snow-queen original-lady children of her own*)

The concept of the snow queen is selected from the 'Europe' domain in this narrative clause. The LISP axiom selected for blending is:

```
(axiom 'wears'
  ((constant 'snow-queen' 'person' europe-space)
   (constant 'wintery-skin' 'object' europe-space)))
```

>demon
(*the young lady would prevail*)

The 'demon' domain is selected, but not used in this evaluative clause.

>demon
(*a caress across her skin scares up demon black*)

The concept of a demon is selected from the 'Demon' domain in this narrative clause. The LISP axiom selected for blending is:

```
(axiom 'stokes'
  ((constant 'demon' 'person' demons-space)
   (constant 'hate' 'emotion' demons-space)))
```

>angel
(*her failure was ignoring her wings and original-lady nature*)

The concept of wings is selected from the 'angel' domain in this evaluative clause. The LISP axiom selected for blending is:

```
(axiom 'covered-with'
  ((constant 'wings' 'person' angels-space)
   (constant 'feathers' 'object' angels-space)))
```

>black
(*and she felt glad*)

The 'Africa' domain is selected, but not used in this evaluative clause.

>white
(*as she grew older she saw entitlement defiance wrinkles upon her face*)

The concept of entitlement is selected from the 'Europe' domain for use in this narrative clause. The LISP axiom selected for blending is:

(axiom 'experiences'
  ((constant 'european' 'person' europe-space)
   (constant 'entitlement' 'sensation' europe-space))

>juju
(ebony-wood-like brimstone defines fetish bedrock, the sign that let her know she finally really alive)

The concept of an ebony wood fetish is selected from the 'Africa' domain in this closing clause. The LISP axiom selected for blending is:

(axiom 'constructs'
  ((constant 'ebony-wood' 'object' afrika-space)
   (constant 'fetish' 'object' afrika-space).

(2) The output in this second poem is produced when user input selects the use of the 'Europe' domain for constructing conceptual spaces for blending.

>Europe
her tale began when she was infected with white female-itis
>Rome
she worked raising bullet, spiked-tail children of her own
>Norway
in the shadows
>Greece
when she was no longer a child peasant, august-being marks streaked her thighs
>Europe
her barbarian, impoverished-elder spirit would live on.

(3) I conclude with a third poem where generated content was derived from blending concepts from the 'skin' domain with concepts selected by the system.

>skin
she began her days looking in the mirror at her own pale-skinned death-figure face
>skin
she peeped out shame, hate
>skin
finally she fell from a cloud and skin and black drenched days were left behind.

Notes

1 Cornel West, 'The New Cultural Politics of Difference,' in *Out There: Marginalization and Contemporary Cultures,* ed. Russel Ferguson, Martha Gever, Trinh T. Minh-ha, and Cornel West (Cambridge: MIT Press, 1990), 30.

2 Martin Luther King Jr, 'I Have a Dream,' speech delivered in Washington DC, 28 Aug. 1963. In *Martin Luther King Jr: The Peaceful Warrior*, ed. Clayton and David Hodges (New York: Simon Pulse, 2002), 118.

3 Aimé Césaire, *Lost Body* (New York: Braziller, 1986).

4 Judy Chicago, 'The Dinner Party,' mixed media, 1979.

5 Edward Lucie-Smith, *ARTODAY* (London: Phaidon Press, 1995), 440–2.

6 Geoffrey C. Bowker and Susan Leigh Star, *Sorting Things Out: Classification and Its Consequences* (Cambridge: MIT Press, 1999), 5–6.

7 John L. Hennessy and David A. Patterson, *Computer Architecture: A Quantitative Approach*, 3rd ed. (San Francisco: Morgan Kaufmann, 2002).

8 Bobby Seale, 'The Black Panther Party' (Cambridge: Alternative Radio, originally broadcast 2 Feb. 1995).

9 Ron Eglash, 'African Influences in Cybernetics,' in *The Cyborg Handbook,* ed. Chris Hables Gray (London: Routledge, 1995), 18.

10 Herbert B. Enderton, *A Mathematical Introduction to Logic* (Boston: Academic Press, Harcourt Brace Jovanovich, 1972).

11 Joseph Goguen and Fox Harrell, 'Style as Choice of Blending Principles,' in *Style and Meaning in Language, Art, Music and Design,* ed. Shlomo Argamon, Shlomo Dubnov, and Julie Jupp (Arlington: AAAI Press, 2004). Proceedings from the 2004 AAAI Fall Symposium Series, Technical Report FS-04-07.

12 George Peacock, *A Treatise on Algebra* (1830). Cited by K. Meinke and J.V. Tucker, in 'Universal Algebra,' *Handbook of Logic in Computer Science*, vol. 1, ed. S. Abramsky, D. Gabbay, and T.S.E. Maibaum (London: Oxford University Press, 1993), 193.

13 Samuel R. Delany, 'The Tale of Potters and Dragons,' *Tales of Nevèrÿon* (Hanover: Bantam Books, 1979), 167.

14 Gilles Fauconnier and Mark Turner, *The Way We Think: Conceptual Blending and the Mind's Hidden Complexities* (New York: Basic Books, 2002).

15 Joseph E. Grady, Todd Oakley, and Seana Coulson, 'Blending and Metaphor,' in *Metaphor in Cognitive Linguistics*, ed. G. Steen and R. Gibbs (Amsterdam: John Benjamins, 1999).

16 Joseph Goguen and Grant Malcolm, *Algebraic Semantics of Imperative Programs* (Cambridge: MIT Press, 1996).

17 Joseph Goguen, 'An Introduction to Algebraic Semiotics, with Application to User Interface Design,' in *Computation for Metaphors, Analogy and Agents,* ed. Chrystopher Nehaniv (Yakamtsu, Japan: 1998).

18 Ishmael Reed. 'CNN's Ku Klux Feminists Unleashed on Kobe,' *KONCH Magazine,* 2 July 2003, available at http://www.ishmaelreedpub.com/editorials/Ishreed6.html. Accessed 24 Oct. 2007.

19 Gilles Fauconnier and Mark Turner, 'Compression and Global Insight,' in *Cognitive Linguistics* (Berlin: de Gruyter, 2000).

20 Ibid., 14.

21 Henry Louis Gates, Jr, *The Signifying Monkey: A Theory of African-American Literary Criticism* (New York: Oxford University Press, 1988), xx.

22 Fauconnier and Turner, 'Compression and Global Insight,' 36.

23 D. Fox Harrell, *Milk Pudding Flavored with Rose Water, Blood Pudding Flavored by the Sea*, unpublished.

24 D. Fox Harrell, *Conceit,* unpublished.

25 Charles Mingus, 'Charles Mingus Presents Charles Mingus,' CD, (Candid Records, 2000). Original session, Nov. 1960.

26 Maya Talmon Chvaicer, 'The Criminalization of Capoeira in Nineteenth-Century Brazil,' *Hispanic American Historical Review* 82/3 (2002): 525-47.

27 David Lehman, ed., *Great American Prose Poems: From Poe to the Present* (New York: Scribner, 2003).

28 James Thomas, Denise Thomas, and Tom Hazuka, eds, *Flash Fiction: Very Short Stories* (New York: Norton, 1992).

29 Ibid., 21.

30 William Labov, 'The Transformation of Experience in Narrative Syntax,' *Language in the Inner City* (Philadelphia: University of Pennsylvania, 1972).

12 The Ambiguous Panopticon:
Foucault and the Codes of Cyberspace

MARK WINOKUR

We cannot agree on an historical point of origin for the Internet – Bletchley Park? the telegraph? the diorama? the abacus? the Atlantic Cable? Painting? Writing? Its techniques and tools are still in the process of development, perhaps even in their infancy. Internet culture is heterogeneous and dynamic. Its economy is not stable, seeming sometimes as fantastic and illusory as the Internet itself. Its status as global tool or tool of globalization is still unclear. Most importantly, even the object of study, and so the appropriate methodologies for study, are unclear. Like other nascent forms of representation before it, the Internet in its infancy presents itself as – and it may actually be – the site of cultural, political, and ideological contestation. Or it may not: the contest may, in fact, have ended before it began, in which case scholars interested in such things can, like Lawrence Lessig, write only about who won and who lost. The grandest claim one might plausibly make is that the Internet at the present moment is the material actualization of the poststructural indeterminacy that characterizes post-Nixon/Mao/Gandhi representation and cultural theory, from the post-1949 Middle East, to the films of Peter Greenaway, to deconstruction, to *White Noise*. However, it behooves the critic to find a sector of critical theory through which some of these assertions might be more clearly elaborated.

The cultural-critical 'app' I choose for discussing this poststructural indeterminacy is Michel Foucault's notion of panopticism: (1) because it is one of the more straightforward poststructuralist notions; (2) because it is not just an important and conventional touchstone within the community of poststructural critics, but is now a staple of educated discourse; (3) because it already has a familiar application within Internet studies; and (4), and most importantly, because the Internet and the panopticon make significantly similar assumptions about the creation of the subject within discourse. Both panopticism and the Internet construct themselves through the subject's internalizing a particular model of space, through a particular notion of how people are distributed throughout space in relation to one another, and through the defining of the individual through the space she occupies. Further, both are intensely interested in the construction and distribution of authority over and within the subject. So I will forward a limited thesis connecting the Internet to one corner of poststructuralism: in literalizing Foucault's panopticon, the Internet makes us question the notion of and, perhaps, redefine panopticism. This redefinition, in turn, allows us to ask questions about the nature of Internet representation. We may ask not only whether Internet representation signifies panopticism, but whether it redefines 'representation' and 'signification' themselves.

Panopticism 1.0

The Internet has been tentatively read through the lens of panopticism before, for example, in communications studies. It has something of the same status as a reflection on the coming of new technologies as Martin Heidegger's article, 'The Question Concerning Technology' and Walter Benjamin's 'The Work of Art in the Age of Mechanical Reproduction.' Foucault and panopticism have a hefty presence as the objects of critical study *on* the Net (11,800,000 Google results for 'Foucault,' and 1,010,000 for 'panopticon,' including a trading card site featuring Foucault and several other poststructuralists).[1] Foucault's actual utility as a theorist *of* the Net, however, is limited in scope to studies of visible surveillance on the Net: in other words, to studies of such phenomena as data-mining about individuals (Carnivore, Total Information Awareness software, Genisys, Semantic Traffic Analyzer, and such), attempts to evade such cataloguing as data encryption, or, more generally, late capitalism itself.[2] Other special properties of panopticism – particularly spatialization, totality of experience, coercive discourse, and ambiguous/internalized authority – are not as frequently linked to the Internet. Neo-Foucauldian cultural critics understand surveillance society as a top-down phenomenon in which an otherwise scarcely visible oligarchy utilizes new technology as a tool of social surveillance.[3] They understand panoptic society to be Orwellian, a Kafkaesque Castle in which power is invested in the powerful if invisible. The aim, then, of the neo-Foucauldian critic is to bring the powerful to light by revealing how she uses the technology for surveillance purposes. Such critics are interested in the way that society constitutes its constituent members as either prisoners or jailers, not the way that society itself is, in fact, a prison-house in which surveillance is distributed in a manner that makes us our own prisoners. For example, the most exhaustive work on panopticism and new technology – David Lyon's book, *The Electronic Eye: The Rise of Surveillance Society*[4] – contains a lengthy discussion of the way in which panopticism is defined by 'uncertainty as a means of subordination' (in other words, by how the authoritarian gaze is unverifiable); Lyon's discussion of panopticism per se is largely concerned, however, with the various data-collecting agencies that use the Internet to exert an external coercion on the individual, not with how such authority is internalized: 'The prison-like society, where invisible observers track our digital footprints, does indeed seem panoptic.'[5] A little less often, scholars are interested in the ways that the Net limits our ability to think outside the Net, in other words, in questions about discourse and discipline.[6]

In the era of the U.S. Department of Homeland Security and NSA data-mining, the question of whether corporations and governments exercise power over the individual by collecting data about her are probably far more politically useful than the questions raised in the present essay. Nevertheless, I shall eschew the traditional discussion of actual agencies of control in favour of a discussion of those other conditions that define panopticism. Is the Internet surveillant? Without question it is. But is the Internet surveillant after the manner of the panopticon? We cannot answer this question by means of sociological accounts that are simply interested in the government and corporate tendency to get to know us better through Internet spying. The panopticon does not use information just to know us; it also deploys information to create us, to constitute us as compliant workers and consumers. Essentially, if it is panoptic, the Internet must serve the same panoptic/Enlightenment function of social control through physical control over bodies in space and rhetorical control over definitions of subjectivity that other panoptic institutions do. This larger question may be rephrased: is the Internet an 'institution'? For example, is the Net a discourse that determines its own boundaries of action? Is Net surveillance coercive? Does the subject in front of the screen *internalize* this coercion? If coercive, does the Net establish a diffused authority? Does the Internet encourage a pro-social uniformity in its citizens? How does the Internet define the relationship between spatialization and discourse? Is the Net a discipline in both senses: a body of knowledge and a form of coercion, the knowledge being the vehicle of the coercion? What other ways of thinking about bodies in space does virtuality either interrupt or promote?

Foucault's Panopticon

To understand whether the Internet is panoptic rather than simply surveillant, we must briefly revisit Foucault's own writing in *Discipline and Punish*.[7] This synopsis of the plot of Foucault's 'Panopticism' chapter is not exhaustive; rather, it is blazonlike, meant to itemize and summarize those dynamics I shall later examine.

For Foucault, history is dynamic, and authority and coercion define the subject in different ways at different times. Before the Enlightenment, effective punishment of the criminal was visible punishment: hangings and decapitations were made visible to the masses as a spectacle.[8] But the rise in European population – and its geographical mobility – in the seventeenth and eighteenth centuries made feudal and monarchical models of social control outmoded. For the beginning of the Enlightenment, the practice of authority is defined as procuring 'for a small number, or even for a single individual, the instantaneous view of a great multitude.'[9] Spectacle is replaced by surveillance within the prison-panopticon. Unlike the medieval object of punishment, the body of the prisoner of the panopticon is not tortured; it is simply separated – and thus alienated – from other prisoners, and then watched. This attention to the body of the prisoner is total: it implies an interest in and effect on all the movements of the prisoner. Not knowing whether or when they are on view, prisoners ultimately internalize the notion of a surveyor. This prison-panopticon serves as Foucault's central metaphor for the rise of a society in which all institutions are disciplinary in both senses of the term: (1) they represent a body of knowledge and (2) this disciplinary knowledge is always coercive, enforcing discipline – particular modes of behaviour and belief – on the individual. Discourse plays an important role in this social coercion. Disciplinary knowledge is articulated through its own proprietary language, generally accessible only to adepts. And discourse is coercive in the sense that it is impossible to define or to think anything without the languages of the limited number of discourses available through a large but finite number of social institutions. Discourses define subjectivity. Finally, because the notion of a central surveyor is a fiction so that authority is internalized by each individual surveying herself, panoptic society works by employing institutions to distribute power throughout society. This is not to say that power is democratically or equally distributed, or distributed for the purpose of democratizing society. Such distribution is simply the most efficient way to maintain a stably quiescent and productive society, by making certain that everyone can potentially be surveyor or surveyed. In brief, Foucault believes that the underside of the Enlightenment that we inherited from the seventeenth and eighteenth centuries is the desire to control increasingly large numbers of people in a manner that monarchies were not able to accomplish: both by distributing self-regulating bodies regularly through space and, as a consequence, by having people police themselves because they believe they are being surveyed.

Bodies in Space: Comparison to the Gaze-as-Authority in Film and Television

The panoptic gaze is, at least initially, unidirectional and fictive: while surveying the prisoners, the (implied) guard is herself invisible, the force of her fictional surveillance enough to keep the bodies of the prisoners evenly distributed and quiescent. Can the Internet be presumed to be phallic in this fashion: simultaneously powerful and nonexistent? I think that the answer depends on how one views the apparatus that connects one to the Internet: the monitor.

Like those of many film and media scholars interested in questions of ideology, my own gaze is drawn towards the coercive qualities of the screen, now the computer monitor.[10] The monitor is that part of the larger Internet apparatus that most immediately reminds one of now more traditional visual entertainment/information media. Governmental and corporate surveillance aside, I wonder whether, like other media, the monitor through which we view the world is always monitoring us.

U.S. television and film are easily identifiable as panoptic institutions. They are disciplinary in the sense that (1) they provide their own defining discourses, mainly variations on the themes of entertainment, desire, and consumerism (genre rules, for example, constitute a discourse), and (2) their promise of desire fulfilled keeps their audiences still and attentive.[11] Both film and television attempt to be total experiences, not only at the moment of spectatorship, but in their peripheral phenomena: their omnipresent paratexts, their connection to other forms of coercion (the 'military/industrial/entertainment complex'). However, film seems more spatially panoptic than television. Like students in the classroom, patients in the hospital, and prisoners in the penal colony, film viewers are equally distributed in the space of the theatre in a manner that gives each person more or less equal access to the film screen, reciprocally giving the screen equal access to each viewer. Because film takes place in the dark it is most often a monadic experience: each spectator is an island unto herself. Like the central prison tower, the central object of attention (the screen itself) is well lit, and, as with the prison tower, we are to keep our attention riveted to this central structure; stillness is enforced. Finally, although we believe we have chosen to go to the movies in a way prisoners do not choose prison, we are metaphorically imprisoned both in the sense that our culture still gives us precious few authentically practical options, and in the sense that, like prison, movies are instructive. Films give us images with which we identify: models for culturally acceptable or desirable modes of thought and behaviour.

Television does not seem spatially panoptic in the manner of cinema. The experience of television is less centralized; hundreds of people are not equally distributed throughout within a partitioned, gridlike space. Citizens of television are distributed throughout the same living room throughout, at least, U.S. culture. (When the television monitor is in the bedroom or the gymnasium, it simply turns these spaces into living rooms.) More importantly, solitary viewing does reproduce the experience of the monadic prisoner in her cell. Like film-as-entertainment, television provides us with images for emulation, but television is if anything even more instructive – more perceptibly coercive – than the movies.

Film and television, because their gazes are bi-directional, constitute a twentieth-century variation on an eighteenth-century theme; these constructions of space and of the gaze are *cryptically* panoptic. By cryptic I mean that the prisoner's relationship to the tower is ironically slightly less deceptive than our relationship to the screen; the illusion of presence provided by the panoptic tower is doubled by the media illusion that surveillance is non-existent. Prisoners understand themselves to be under direct surveillance. But, while we believe ourselves to be watching television and film, these media are watching us along those axes by which we are allowed social definition: our viewing habits and so (presumptively) our desires, through Nielsen ratings, advertising sales, bottom lines, pre-emptive censorship, and so on. While, during the experience of watching, we believe the gaze to originate from the spectator and onto the screen, in fact, the gaze is relayed from the screen/tower to the spectator in a way that coerces her to internalize consciously and unconsciously the lessons of the screen. This, at least, is the assumption that advertisers take on faith.

Television and film (as well as Foucauldian theory itself), then, give us the following five dimensions along which to think about whether mechanical forms of visual representation like the Internet are or are not panoptic: (1) the gaze, (2) space, (3) authority, (4) totality, and (5) discourse. Is the gaze of the Internet (cryptically) unidirectional? In other words, does the gaze operate consciously, or does it convince us that we are watching it while it is actually watching us? How does the Internet define space? In other words, where is the Internet citizen when she is watching the screen, and where is she *in* the screen and in relation to others similarly engaged? How does the Internet invest and then deploy authority? To what degree is the Internet a 'total' experience? Can the Internet be said to be uttered as a unified discourse and, if so, what is the nature of that discourse? Does this discourse institute desire and, if so, is this desire self-regulating, external, and productive of a tendency towards social uniformity?

The Gaze

The Internet is both more and less panoptic than television or movies, and for the same reason: its gaze is a special instance of those media's bi-directional gaze. Like the dream screen of film or television, the computer monitor observes us as we observe it; however, the bi-directionality of the monitor seems genuinely reciprocal in a manner to which neither television nor movies can aspire. Unlike these media, the Internet provides us the opportunity to create choices when we create Web pages, or even talk back to the screen, initially through writing – chat rooms, bulletin boards, and email – now also through 3D virtual worlds and online games, blogs, and other more visual specula. In trading the remote control for the mouse and keyboard, we have acceded to an Internet gaze that seems more and more overtly rather than cryptically bi-directional. In short, the Internet is at present the best version of what Roland Barthes calls a 'writerly' text, a text whose meaning can in some measure be constituted by the reader. This at any rate was the assessment of such foundational 1990s Internet theorists as George P. Landow.[12] Utopic critics still characterize the Internet as the very opposite of the panopticon; it is more consciously 'empowering' than other media because, unlike movies or television, it allows a greater range of behaviours, a greater number of choices, and a certain ability for creative self-expression not possible in other electronic media.

But does this bi-directionality really imply consciousness and mass empowerment, or is the keyboard simply a glorified remote control? Certainly, it is the remote control, at the level of simple consumerism. As with television and cinema, the Internet gives us false, essentially consumerist options: ABC or CNN becomes eBay or Amazon.com, AOL or MSN. We are encouraged to think that using Mozilla strikes a blow at the insidiously secretive Microsoft Internet Explorer because Firefox is an 'open-source' application, although the equally monolithic AOL/Time Warner now owns Netscape, the commercial face of Mozilla. Two Internet devices important to most conversations about freedom and creativity are perhaps even more illustrative of the ambiguously determinative quality of the Internet: hypertext (or hypermedia) and the avatar. In the early and mid-1990s, hypertext was touted as the cure for the inactivity enforced by other forms of representation, as if hypertext could save other forms of representation from ennui and entropy.[13] Hypertext gives the Web surfer a sense of choice, a sense of the Internet as an exciting experiment in *bricolage*. But, although it is still an interesting and innovative technique *within* many websites, hypertext seems *across* the Net to have a limited number of uses, almost all of them (with the exception of hyperlinks that take the user from one site to sites of similar interest) again simply commercial: banner ads connecting to retail, auction, and pornography sites. Further, early theorists of hypertext were unaware that 'pop-up' and 'hover-ad' advertisements (the 'anti-choice' pop-up did not appear until 1997) would be omnipresent.[14] Even the apparently non-commercial use of hypertext to get from search engines to the information they offer scarcely conceals the fact that most search engine companies are paid to find commercial hits first. Many scholars still shy away from the Internet when they discover that most search engine algorithms favour commercial over non-commercial sites. The notion of freedom to 'surf' is at least in part undercut by the gentle corporate appropriation of hypertext.[15]

With the exponential growth of sophistication and interest in visual representation and online gaming, the second, newer route to apparent self-determination has been the *avatar*, the icon the Internet citizen can make – or more usually buy and download – that may represent the citizen in online games or in more sophisticated visually oriented chat sites like the Palace, ActiveWorlds, and Second Life. The avatar seemed for a while the very apotheosis of the American dream to be someone else, and the antithesis of the panopticon: it *embodied* the fantasy that we can refashion our selves in any manner we wish. We cannot be under surveillance if no one knows who we are: what we look like, what colour we are, what religion and ethnicity, what sex. The actual deployment of the avatar on the Net, however, has been mixed. While the characters played in online games are thriving, the visual chat rooms in which participants could engage in some serious personality changes have often not fared so well. The Palace is now defunct, and ActiveWorlds now charges for what was originally a free 'citizenship' in its universe. The price of freedom is not eternal vigilance, but, at the time of this writing, about $6.95 per month. (Online gaming is even more expensive; game avatars have sold on eBay for four figures.) Although wildly popular, Second Life is still an experiment. It is also by far the most commercialized of the 3D worlds. Further compromising the notion that the avatar means freedom is – finally – the fact that the Internet is surveillant, not in the sense of the government collecting data on its citizens, but in the much more permeative sense that corporations need to verify our existence and status as stable, desiring consumers. The avatar construct is met at every turn by credit card verification. Online gaming is a sort of metaphor for the antagonisms between identity and commerce: I cannot be Palomar the Venerable without swearing fealty to PayPal the Verifiable.

Further, while both utopic and panoptic critics of the Net describe the Net as visible spectacle, neither takes into account the Net's hardware – its architecture – as a determinant of the gaze. Remember that, for Foucault, Jeremy Bentham's panopticon ultimately determines the design of schools, factories, hospitals, and other kinds of public architecture. Utopic accounts, for example, oppose the notion of the Internet as significantly surveillant because it is not associated with a visible architecture; yet, the simplified diagram for the relationship between surfer and Internet or intranet looks suspiciously like the schematics for Bentham's prison.

Whatever its direction, the gaze is located in a hardware space defined by centre and periphery. For those interested in surveillance phenomena like Semantic Traffic Analyzer or the now-defunct Carnivore, the server is the locus of authority; the server master and webmaster can and do censor our access and input, encouraging Net-citizen uniformity. In short, the flowchart for Internet hardware is panoptic. Even insofar as we are not describing a physical architecture but rather the flow of information, we are still simply indexing the move from a capitalism invested in things to a late capitalism for which ideas are the principal trope for the buyable.[16]

Even if the Internet is not really utopic but rather a tool for late capitalist appropriation, we must still account for the fact that, unlike film and television as entertainment, the Internet cannot yet constitute all spectators as one spectator, or even as a small set of spectators. Entertainment seeks to create unconscious and monolithic audiences, but, because the Internet is a modality as much as it is a medium in the sense that it provides different kinds of venues for expression – from websites to MUDs to chat rooms to BBSs to newsgroups to podcasts to client servers to blogs to 3D worlds – entertainment and consumerism, although a large presence on the Internet, constitute a small percentage of its representational capabilities. As a consequence, the Internet enables different and simultaneous possibilities for awareness, including but not limited to the consciousness/unconsciousness of media representation. Expanding on the habitually untheorized notion of the surfer, the following list is not exhaustive; rather, it suggests the heterogeneity of surfers' stances in the same way that the educable sons of the Passover Seder suggest all children without defining them:

1 *The surveyor.* This gaze is external, overt, and directed towards the surfing subject, who is conscious of being watched. This is the surveillant gaze of Carnivore, employer surveillance of employee email, and so on. The object of desire is constituted as the satisfaction of the regulations of that gaze. In short, the Internet is what critics have designated as Panopticon Classic.

2 *The moviegoer.* This gaze is external but cryptic towards the surfing spectator, whose desire is constituted externally and so is unsatisfiable except through conformist/consumerist behaviour. In short, as consumer entertainment, the Net is cryptically panoptic. The Internet is a movie or a shopping mall, and the subject is the traditional spectator/shopper.

3 *The gamer.* Originating from the surfing self, this gaze is outward, into the Net. The object of desire is external. In making us active participants, the Internet makes us critics: we are aware of the conditions of the Net in a way we are not of a movie. We achieve total immersion, but not total unconsciousness. Our desire is directed towards non-consumer sites, and much of our time is spent trying to circumvent

capitalism. The same subject who is unconsciously influenced by a film's product endorsements will still avoid banner ads, spam, and pornography.

4 *The writer.* The gaze is inward; the desire is for self. Perhaps, in co-constructing the Internet, the subject recreates desire differently, for example, reconstituting desire less as a question of subject and object, and more as a function of the subject refashioning her own subjectivity.

5 *The lurker.* Originating in the surfing spectator, this cryptic gaze is specifically voyeuristic; it is the desire to see without being seen, the individual's desire to appropriate some of the authority of social surveillance through imitation of it. As such, this gaze shares with Laura Mulvey's notion of the masculine gaze the belief that the gaze can be sadistic and exploitive, resides in the spectator, and reflects the deployment of surveillance-as-power in society at large.[17]

6 *The spy.* A 'proactive' lurker. The user of applets, spyware, etc.

These gazes cannot all be said to be subordinate to an overarching capitalist gaze simply because they exist in a medium created and permeated by a consumerism whose hardware relegates some to the centre and others to the periphery. The consumerist tendency is panoptic, but the working out of the gaze is as yet too heterogeneous to be considered appropriated.

Space

Perhaps because both gaze and space are genetically linked to spectacle – and so to the heterogeneity of Internet spectacle – in a way that, say, the notion of discourse is not, Internet spatiality, like the Internet gaze, is and is not panoptic, and for the same reasons: spatial heterogeneity militates against panopticism, while the need for verifiability tends to result in a spatially uniform Internet citizenry. On the one hand, the experience of surfing the Net seems spatially heterogeneous. The Internet contains an enormous variety of spaces, limited only by the Web designer's ability to re-envision two- and three-dimensionality. Seeing a film in a theatre, people sit evenly spaced in semi-circular fashion around a single image, panopticon-style; as Jean-Louis Baudry notes, the scene of filmgoing reproduces Plato's allegory of the enslaving cave which is itself, we might note, panoptic (if anachronistically so) in the sense that it provides an illusory world in order to enforce immobility in its viewers.[18] Internet citizens, in contrast, log on in different places at different times; the Internet often seems mood-dependent. If she has an Internet connection at home and at work, or also has access to a cyber-café, or has wi-fi, the surfer is not even limited to surfing from a single 'real' space.[19]

Like television, the Internet also renders all spaces as one space – the monitor-user interface to which most users (at least those without an Ethernet connection) have spatial access in the same way: through the almost cabalistic invocation of that ethereal *nomen* which must never be spoken: username and password. For the simple surfer, the Net is also like television when, as a consumer, she is watching the same dozen sites as everyone else. The Net seems a little more homogeneous when one considers that the expense of logging on limits participation to the members of just a few classes, and significant development to just a few nations. And if we consider Internet technology as a *determinant* of meaning rather than simply its vehicle, such technology – the interlaced order of pixels by which a monitor renders objects visible to the orderly and hierarchicalized distribution of surfers, servers, and modes along a fibre-optic grid – suggests the even distribution through space reminiscent of panopticism. If the critic is looking over the shoulder of the user, she may decide that his surfing is a liberating experience. Observing, however, from the server site or the fibre-optic engineering room at Qwest, she may see him as a point on the grid.

The Internet is a more temporally heterogeneous experience than the experience of viewing movies and television; nevertheless, it is still panoptic to the degree that it is genuinely monadic in a way that these media may only approximate. Whatever actual communication the Internet fosters, the physical experience of surfing the Net is almost always 'lonesome'; we inhabit a physical space differentiated from all others. For Foucault this partitioning is crucial for defusing and diffusing social and political opposition: 'Avoid distribution in groups; break up collective dispositions; analyze confused, massive, or transient pluralities. Disciplinary space tends to be divided into as many sections as there are bodies or elements to be distributed.'[20] The Internet is not panoptic in the sense of evenly distributing bodies on a grid à la the assembly line or the military formation (two of Foucault's favourite examples). We do not all surf at once, or for the same number of hours a day. And Internet use is still not as universal as television spectatorship. But, while the movie and even the television come to an end for us, we are 'structured to feel' (to paraphrase Raymond Williams) that the Internet is temporally endless, that the conversations, games, negotiations, and exchanges happen whether we are awake or not.[21] Television and movies are packaged in a manner that suggests peaks and troughs in viewers' interest. At least this is the assumption behind 'prime time' and 'bargain matinees.' But the Internet has no prime time or matinee. Or, to say it correctly, although the Internet has peak bandwidth-use hours, it has no peak hours of representation and few hours of participation that are commercially and socially recognized as such. Internet traffic actually does conform to measurable patterns of peak use, but 3-D worlds, online games, music-exchange networks, commercial sales sites, auction sites, and pornography sites take almost no notice of these spikes in bandwidth use. Games like Everquest hold special events during peak hours of play, however, it is still the case that online gamers can and often do remain in the game for days at a time. Like panoptic society, the Internet gives the impression of being eternal: all times are one uniform time.

Authority

The Internet construed as gaze and space is at best only ambiguously panoptic, and yet, the notions of authority and totality suggest that the Internet is *capable* of a perfect panopticism in a way that perhaps no other social institution or form of representation is. Surveillance on the Internet is panoptically (if mischievously) democratized, and the Internet is capable of being the *total experience* to which other media can only aspire.

To begin with an earlier point: in opposition to the actual top-down surveillance by corporations and the government, the gaze of authority in film and media is not visibly surveillant after the manner of the panoptic tower. Its coercion is cryptic and unconscious: as consumers of entertainment we are not usually aware of being under surveillance. Bentham's originary panopticon is characterized through visible surveillance by a guard, who, all the same, *is not necessarily there; he is a fiction of authority* displaced by self-regulation and regulation by one's neighbours. (Slavoj Žižek refers to this fiction of authority as 'radical uncertainty.'[22]) This fictionality has three important consequences: our relationship to authority and our own identities, based on a fiction, are also fictional; the citizen is uniformly self-policing; and everyone has a little power to police the state.

Does the Internet similarly institute an internal agency that ensures a vision of authority and society in which each person is her own and her neighbour's monitor? Certainly, software exists that encourages the tendency towards self- and peer-surveillance, and among other blandishments, such software is advertised as security *against* corporate and governmental surveillance.[23] Anti-virus software, spyware, anti-spyware, anti-pornography software, firewalls, Trojans, anti-Trojan programs, worms, data-erasure programs, and other forms of self-surveillance – software more or less readily available to all Internet citizens – can infiltrate other computers or monitor the penetrations into one's own computer; it is possible to locate the source of the attack, thus monitoring the activities and strategies of individuals and corporations. While some of this software seems to constitute a resistance to panopticism by maintaining individual privacy, it reflects the degree of self-consciousness that we have developed about our Internet behaviour. Derived from the belief that we *may* be under surveillance at any given time (and so suggesting the present/absent guard in the tower), such software keeps everyone in the game, distributing a little bit of power and authority to every player who owns a cable or DSL connection. This distribution of power – not the actual top-down intimidation of Carnivore – is panoptic. As Foucault asserts, rather typically describing the panopticon itself as a machine, 'Any individual, taken almost at random, can operate the machine ... The more numerous those anonymous and temporary observers are, the greater the risk for the inmate of being surprised and the greater [his] anxious awareness of being observed. The Panopticon is a marvelous machine which, whatever use one may wish to put it to, produces homogeneous effects of power.'[24]

Foucault speaks of a web of power relations in which absolute authority is invested, not in an oligarchy made up of – depending on your conspiracy of choice – media owners, the NSA/CIA/FBI, owners of multinational corporations, heads of state, or the Jews, but in everyone who has internalized that prison guard, which is to say everyone on the Net. Anyone can install Net Nanny, AdAware, Norton Firewall, or other 'user-friendly' applications. Everyone has a little power, although power is shared unequally and oppressively.[25]

Totality

The total distribution of power along the Net grid reminds us of panoptic totality; not only is the distribution of power among Net citizenry absolute, the experience of being subject to authority is complete as well.[26] Television and film aspire and fail to be total experiences in and of themselves; the impossibility of avoiding the paratexts that complete their cultural significance indicates both the desire and the failure. Much more than film and television, the Internet has been endlessly discussed since before its existence as a portal to one kind of total experience that still eludes us, but that is not the subject of this chapter: virtual reality.[27] However, we may look closer to home – or the workplace – to find another kind of total experience in the making, for which the virtual worlds of *Neuromancer* or *The Matrix* (1999) are at present simply metaphors. Conceived both as more than simply surveillance but still less than a *total* experience, the Internet as a technology is itself gradually being assimilated into at least two bits of 'convergence' hardware: the personal digital assistant (PDA), and the cell phone, which have themselves converged into the 'smartphone.' (Even the designation 'cell phone' suggests Foucault's impression that each citizen inhabits her or his own prison cell.) The smartphone has assimilated other communications and representational devices: email, the pager, the digital camera, the video camera, the voice recorder, global positioning systems, text messaging, podcasts, and the video game. When the problem of screen size is solved (perhaps by the addition of video glasses, making all individual movement an extension of surfing the Net as driving has become an extension of the cell phone), William Gibson's and Neal Stephenson's cyberspace as the experience of total immersion will be realized. The smartphone can now download all forms of representation, from poetry to pornography. The smartphone operative – probably affluent, certainly computer literate – is now immersed, not just in the web of the Internet, but in every sector of communications. No paratext is necessary, or indeed possible, to explain the experience of this device, because the device has access to all texts that refer to it.

The notion of total immersion echoes an often-cited, much discredited 'humanist' bit of film theory: André Bazin's article, 'The Myth of Total Cinema,' the most important assertion of which is that cinema always tries to convey an ever more realistic sense of the real.[28] Like total war, total cinema suggests complete immersion in the spectacle one had simply been viewing. Writing in the 1950s, Bazin implicitly assumes that cinema's ever-increasing ability to present us with a window on the actual is nevertheless asymptotic: representation may go thus far and no farther. Hence, the notion that cinema can be 'total' is a 'myth.' But, in combination with other new technologies, the Internet promises to make that asymptotic line tumesce just enough to touch its own limit.

This tumescence determines the erasure of another asymptotic separation, between the 'virtual' and the 'real.' That is, the ideological construed as the representation of reality becomes – or was always already (as poststructuralists have proclaimed for thirty-five years now against both New Critics and traditional Marxists, who insisted on either a formal or a material real) – the real.[29] This erasure is especially true for panopticism, where the only reality possible is that presented us by social constructions of disciplines, discourses, and institutions. Panoptic society is always already virtual. We can always know only what we need to know in order to ensure the continued operation of the panopticon. In this sense new technologies-as-panopticon is the apotheosis of the notion of panopticism. If what we really mean by the panopticon is a vehicle for the conveyance of ideology, new technology is meta-panoptic: it disseminates itself as ideology.[30] Total immersion as ideology is the vision of *The Matrix*, in which, for most citizens, no reality is visible but that created by the technologies that keep them unconscious, still, and drained in a hidden post-apocalyptic landscape, while convincing them that their lives are rich and full.

But new technologies have an even more immediately total effect on the body. For Foucault, the panopticon is the social ideal for which the Enlightenment strove; it is the social raison d'être for the rise of the sciences and other disciplines. In a counter-psychoanalytic manner, the panopticon acts on the mind through the disposition of the body, rather than the other way around. Like ideology, it seeks to be the sum of all experience for the citizen. On its own, but more especially in conjunction with other new technologies, New Technology is the closest thing to an apotheosis of that desire for totality; it is along this dimension, then, panoptic.

The Internet as part of a matrix of new technologies affects the body panoptically, that is, in an unconsciously oppressive manner. Paradoxically, but in a manner that confirms the increasingly diffused quality of power through new technologies, the affluent sector that can afford smartphones – which is to say the presumable wielders of power – is most in thrall to the technology, at the beck and call of anyone who pages, phones, or faxes them. The smartphone owner is not the mistress of the manor but its chatelaine, middle management in medieval terms: Herbert Marcuse's book, *One-Dimensional Man*, or Sloan Wilson's *Man in the Gray Flannel Suit*.[31] The Internet citizen, however, may be differentiated from corporate middle management in one important respect: the latter exists in a vertical hierarchy at the top of which is a CEO, and at the bottom of which is, depending on your point of view, the worker and/or the consumer. In contrast, the new-technology panopticon renders everyone middle management: again, everyone has a little power to oppress. Everyone is answerable to a higher authority, and everyone is a higher authority. In cyberspace immersion, everyone has approximately the same status, despite minor differences between, say, the surfer and the Web *master*. We are assaulted by banner ads, but we can also flame anyone with an email address, a website, or a forum or listserv presence. It is the one-dimensional man made to look three dimensional in two dimensions. Put another way, for the new middle management, new technologies are the apotheosis of Foucault's idea that panoptic society recreates the body as mechanical: 'the machine required can be constructed.'[32] New Technology is the literal embodiment of the somewhat figurative language Foucault uses in describing a discipline as 'a type of power, a modality for its exercise, comprising *a whole set of instruments*, techniques, procedures, *levels of application*, targets; *it is a "physics"* ... of power, a *technology*' (emphasis mine).[33] While other forms of representation (movies, novels) are only metaphorically technologies (or, at best, the products of an invisible technology), the Internet is visibly technological. While poetry captures the imagination, the smartphone envelops the body.

So, while neither the direction of the gaze nor the constitution of space define the Internet as panoptic, the Internet as a total experience may still be a *literalization* of Foucault's panoptic society in a way that no other institution can be. As a consequence, the Internet tends to leave us aware of our minds but not of our bodies. One might compare the Net with masturbation fantasy, an experience that, while implicating the body, takes place mostly in the mind's eye, that is, virtually.[34] Finally, as a sector of new technologies, the Internet represents a continuation of the twentieth-century media impulse to refashion the panoptic 'by other means.' If the twentieth-century media panopticon is cryptically and incompletely panoptic, the twenty-first-century matrix of Internet / new technologies is perhaps volitionally but completely panoptic, meaning that – for now – we may still choose not to enter this particular prison, but also that, once in, our movements are determined by the technology.

If we understand the Internet to be a response to the Enlightenment interest in the effect of the mechanical on the body, we are still left wondering about the valence of that relationship: do new technologies subvert or apotheosize the Enlightenment? Is the Web an Enlightenment project or, as Ravi Sundaram, citing Donna Haraway and other utopic theorists, suggests, 'a crucial opposition from the old Enlightenment oppositions of nature and culture from which flowed the representations of human praxis and subject formation'?[35] Is the Internet, as Haraway and others suggest, a reaction against the Enlightenment's careful divisions between the organic and the inorganic, a reaction against disciplinary thinking? Is it, in other words, Haraway's cyborg culture, in which distinctions between feminine and masculine, first world and third world, collapse with the collapse of the categories organic/inorganic? Or is the truth, as Foucault suggests before Haraway, that the Enlightenment already conflated the organic and the mechanical, so that new technologies are, in fact, the apotheosis of the Enlightenment project: the defining of the organic in terms of the inorganic; the exercise of the machinery of power on the body in such a way that the body itself becomes a machine? If it is an Enlightenment project, is it the traditional face of the Enlightenment – the Encyclopedia, tentative experiments with democracy, and Isaac Newton – or is it the panoptic face: discreet oppression, disciplinary disciplines, Jeremy Bentham, and Napoleon Bonaparte?

Discourse at the Level of Code: Writing and Reading the Internet

The appropriate and most frequent object of Internet studies is the individual Internet subculture: game sites; art forums; pornography sites; nationalist, racial, ethnic, and religious websites; and so on.[36] Nevertheless, I have eschewed such subjects for the sake of a quixotic tilt at the Internet as a whole. The sole advantage of such an approach is that it allows me to ask at this point: does the Internet itself constitute a discourse? Is there a discourse *of* the Internet? In other words, is the Internet already defining and defined in the manner of all disciplinary discourses?

Because of its diversity, the Internet as spectacle (what is actually visible on the screen) cannot easily be considered to have a *unitary* discourse. At best, one might assert the assumption of most cultural studies research: that each Internet subculture has its own discursive practice. But we may be in error if we identify the diverse languages *on* the Internet as the language *of* the Internet. Although the Internet is international – and so necessarily of many languages (although not all: no Masai, for example) – such globalism does not imply a freedom from the constraints of discourse. Other languages than those of the spectacular Internet determine the limits of the Internet and its way of knowing and expressing the world. Strictly speaking, the codes and markup language in which Internet content is written – java, html, xhtml, and so on – constitute the discourse of the Internet in the very specific sense that they determine the absolute limits within which the discipline operates. We can create only what these languages allow us to express. Or, as Lev Manovich asserts,

> As we work with software and use the operations embedded in it, these operations become part of how we understand ourselves, others, and the world. Strategies of working with computer data become our general cognitive strategies. At the same time, the design of software and the human-computer interface reflects a larger social logic, ideology, and imaginary of the contemporary society. So if we find particular operations dominating software programs, we may also expect to find them at work in the culture at large.[37]

If, as Manovich implies, the Internet and then the culture within which it is embedded belong to whoever writes the code and codec, we may regard as significant the fact that so much software and hardware have originated in Japan, and that for economic reasons, the United States now imports much of its software development from other nations (India, for example). It becomes further significant that much of America's science elite – including computer developers – is (and traditionally has been) imported. The importation of Indian software implies an interface with postcolonial Indian culture. The Internet becomes transnational and multiethnic as much through its invention and development as through its use by various countries. Claiming America as the originator of the computer and the Internet constitutes the same order of historical disinformation as asserting that Thomas Edison invented the movies.

If it matters where the code comes from, we must assume that the writing of code reflects the conditions of the creator of the code. Put another way: the writing of code is not a completely scientific endeavour; rather, it is also cultural/sociological – it is an affect of the writer and her culturo-socioeconomic background. The knowledge that Alan Turing was persecuted for being homosexual might allow us to queer computer science.[38] We must still ask, however, whether computer code is a discourse; whether it creates texts that constitute subjectivity after the manner of other disciplinary discourses; and whether, as a result, the Internet code and markup language are interpretable in the same fashion as other texts.

If the base languages of the Internet are not interpretable then this conversation is at an end.

Some kinds of interpretation, however, already exist prior to the asking of the question. An *aesthetics* of code has existed among programmers almost as long as programming itself. Programmers refer to 'beautiful' programs, not because of the spectacle it enables on the monitor or in any other instrument, but because of the elegance, clarity, and brevity of the code-text itself. In another arena, writers argue about the *poetics* of code, taking computer code as the starting point for the production of poetry and narrative.[39] Perhaps more significantly for this essay, a kind of *semiotics* of programming has explored code's potential ability to enable the computer to originate meaning. As Jay David Bolter suggests, this notion is part and parcel, for example, of investigations into artificial intelligence:

> The computer is a machine for creating and manipulating signs; the signs may be mathematical, verbal, or pictorial. Computer programming and indeed all kinds of writing and reading by computers are exercises in applied semiotics. The first lesson any sophisticated computer user must learn is the difference between a sign and its reference, between the address of a location in the computer's memory and the value stored at that address. This dichotomy characterizes the machine at all levels: it is at the essence of hypertext and of programs for artificial intelligence, in all of which text is simply a texture of signs pointing to other signs.[40]

Although I will assert in a few moments that hypertext or any other originary Internet language is more than simply the usual and presumably endless chain of signifiers, I am intensely interested in the almost paradoxically hermeneutic/cultural studies endeavour implied in this kind of study. The Internaut as hermeneut, or the Interneut. Let us concern ourselves, then, with the semiotics of the Internet code (Semenet), or, strictly speaking, of Internet code as discourse (Intercourse, Disinter, Disintery, or perhaps just DisCo).[41]

We might find a model that will help us, if not read the Internet, at least imagine how the Internet might be read, in Ferdinand de Saussure's oppositions between *langue* and *parole* and between signifier and signified. (These models also inform Foucault's notion of discourse.) Most critics of the Web implicitly assume that the spectacular Web is a signifier after the manner of television and media: it has something to do with representing the real world.[42] However, at a much more obvious – if counterintuitive – level, considered as the signifier, programming code is deployed on precisely the same assumption that Saussure makes about language: it is binary opposition. If one then not zero; if zero then not one. Platform and programming languages may be seen as *langue*, while the actual programs written are its *parole*. Read this way, we have as the object of study a sort of global language, the origin of whose rules matter less than the actual deployment of those rules by particular persons and cultures.

The same problem arises with this argument as with most structuralist arguments: it is at least partially ahistorical in assuming that, while the writing of particular programs (*parole*) is affected by the culture within which the codes are written, the context and structure within which programming language exists (*langue*) is irrelevant. To make programming code(s) the Master Code is simply to reify the notion that the white culture within which it is assumed to have been produced is substructure to every subsequent digital representation's superstructure. The analogy to Saussure's model is further flawed because that model is itself a partial explanation for the difficulties in translating from language to language, or from *langue* to *langue*. It assumes a multitude of different cultures speaking in different tongues and thus producing different kinds of meaning. Most of the Net, however, is uttered in html, xhtml, or one of a handful of other Web-creation languages. In this sense, no significant linguistic distinctions exist between the production of meaning by New Delhi and its production by Silicon Valley software developers. So even if the Web is not monolithic by virtue of its parentage, it is to some degree structurally monolithic. As such it is discourse, a language spoken by adepts in a particular discipline (programming) that determines that the text it creates will reproduce the same communal meaning over and over again.

Complicating our vision of Net discourse as monolithic is the realization that we have examined it, so to speak, only horizontally: we understand that the use of html cuts across all national borders. We have not, however, rightly understood that programming has a vertical dimension: the abstract 'assembler language' makes possible more linguistically recognizable programming languages, which in turn, enable the creation of browsing software. Browsers read another code, html, which in turn, makes xhtml, Flash, or Dreamweaver possible. Various plug-ins and filters are constructed on top of these already precarious edifices, creating, not one, but several Towers of Babel in which each kind of code must learn to live in often-uneasy détente with other kinds of code. Finally, proprietary programming codes – often variations on the major programming codes – are deployed by individuals and corporations. In this scenario, the initial programming languages are not themselves monolithic edifices so much as the building blocks for an olio of edifices. Not substructure but bricks and mortar. Perhaps a clearer analogy is not with French or English, but with Proto-Indo-European, Altaic, or Austro-Asiatic, themselves probably not monolithic, and finally all but erased and displaced by the flood of premodern and then modern languages to which they give birth.

Another, more contemporary analogy may make the possibility of code plurality and heterogeneity clearer. From 1895 until about 1950 there was no significant mass technology for viewing the moving image other than celluloid film projection. Despite the realization that media have an undeniably homogenizing effect globally, most film theory and criticism since the Second World War has assumed that this basic commonality in technology has little effect on the medium's ability to express different cultures and ideologies in a heterogeneous fashion. (In fact, film historians tend to be nostalgic for the now-extinct, unifying internationalism of silent film.) If one imagines for a moment that programming language is of the same order of artefact as film – in essence an 'apparatus' rather than *langue* in the traditional sense – then the contributing languages of the Internet become at least as flexible in representing or resisting ideology and ideological difference as film is thought to be.[43]

While the structuralist, Saussurean linguistic model seems inadequate for describing programming code or html, at a different level of signification, code embodies a certain poststructural idea about language: like language, code not only signifies the Net, it actually creates what it defines. But again, while this notion as observed about writing or speech is conceptual – a truth that must be inferred – it is self-evident in the case of the Internet. While we assign the inventive function of language to some vague and invisible ideology that requires our seeing the world in a trickily, repressively, and coercively pro-social fashion, we understand more directly that computer code is the abstract prime mover of effects we can see: Internet effects. In a certain sense *the Internet embodies the inventive quality of language because it is representationally the opposite of language.* While writing is palpable and the things it represents are abstract and arbitrary, code is (for all but the programmers who originate, improve, or steal it) invisible, while the things it represents – for example, the Internet – is palpable, if virtual. In spoken/written language, the signifier is audible/visible while the signified – ultimately ideology – is invisible if ever-present; conversely, the visible effects represented on the Internet paradoxically signify both the existence of an invisible code/markup language, and also the signified of the code that has uttered them into existence. In a dynamic reminiscent of the now rather self-evident if principal declaration of deconstruction, *the Internet is the signifier of its own system of signification, or the signifier of its signifier. It is both signifier and signified.*[44]

The very materiality and palpability of the Internet – in contrast to the invisibility and evanescence that characterize the ideological ambiguity and arbitrariness to which deconstruction always refers – suggests that something other than simple deconstruction is at work here. The Internet is like language-as-ideology in being a construct, but unlike ideology in being a material construct. Again, ideology must be inferred while the Internet is palpable. Like other critical strategies, deconstruction depends on subverting the Saussurean naturalization of signification by observing that the relationship between signifier and signified is only conventionally binary and so, consequently, ideological; however, the relationship between the signifier and the signified for the Internet is (as Christian Metz asserted almost thirty years ago of the film image)[45] of a different order, requiring a different hermeneutics. It is as if the Internet – and software more generally – is the palimpsest of its code-as-signifier, which covers its own existence with the artefact it creates in a way that the written word never does. Code is not so much a self-consuming as a self-effacing artefact.[46]

What does this reciprocity of signifier and signified mean about the meaning of the Internet, and its status as panopticon-in-training? The answer is, I think, fourfold. The Internet's panoptic status depends (1) on whether its reciprocal model for the sign becomes the dominant trope for the way in which language works in culture;[47] (2) on which social movements are conceived during the time of the invention of the Internet; (3) on how the Internet inflects those movements; and (4) on the awareness of the surfer of the encoding that underlies her Internet travels. To elaborate briefly, for Foucault the panopticon has survived for over 300 years as a defining if evolving technology that reflects changes in the way language is conceived: both as a series of discourses meant to define and categorize, and as a method of ordering people during the rise of the modern nation-state. In an analogous manner, the Internet arises at a time of industrial globalization and cultural border crossings, in other words during the dissolution of the nation-state. The new linguistics of the Internet will arise when the language has been foregrounded once more as an important political/ideological issue. It is not so much a question, as Manovich asserts, of the Internet's becoming the dominant cognitive model so much as a question of how Internet language may inter-nalize and then re-inflect contemporaneous social phenomena. If, for example, the rise of the novel is significantly coincident with European colonialism, then it may be important that the Internet's growth thus far is roughly co-extensive with both the establishment of the World Trade Organization and the publishing career of Homi Bhabha.[48] The Internet in this respect is problematically transnational; it enables both access and exploitation. We understand that it is the product of late capitalism, of an economy interested in the ownership of ideas more than of things; we still do not know, however, whether the Internet is Habermas's new modernism or Jameson's postmodernism. Is it the cultural arena for solving the problems of being modern, or simply another tool of late-capitalist exploitation? At the moment it seems to be both.[49] The self-consciousness of the surfer of the code is approximately analogous to a consciousness of ideology. It is the awareness of the Internet as an artefact whose production of meaning is up for grabs by anyone who understands that it *does* pro-duce meaning in very material – that is, manipulable – ways.

The notion of a usable indeterminacy in meaning seems even more sensible as one understands that the fact of the Internet's signifying its own code is different from the relationship between other media and their material bases. Cinema does not signify the actual celluloid and emulsion that constitute it, and it can only inferentially signify the process of creation; even shot-for-shot remakes of films (e.g., *Psycho*, 1960, 1998) cannot reproduce with any exactness the original. And for other reasons – including expense, access to means of distribution and exhibition – film and television are difficult to produce. The Internet's code, however, is instantly visible (if not immediately coherent) to anyone who clicks the appropriate browser button. And so the codes are revisable in a way that no other medium is.[50] In this respect, computer code allows at least the second coming of Walter Benjamin's notion of the reproducibility of texts as a kind of resistance: more people can appropriate the code of the Internet because it is more or less readily available for reinterpreting and rewriting in a way that film and television are not. At most, computer code suggests a rethinking of how sign and discourse create the subject because, since the relationship between signifier and signified is no longer *completely* arbitrary (although it is still completely conventional), neither then is the real simply a construct. Virtuality is, ontogenetically, neither completely material nor completely constructed. One would have to invent a new descriptor for its status, perhaps 'materucted' or 'consterial' or even 'convircted.'

The Internet stands in relation to discourse as it stands in relation to other elements of panopticism: it is and it is not. It is discourse in the sense that it is language with an intent; it is not traditional discourse because the organization of its sign system departs radically from that of traditional systems of signification. Because the nature of Internet discourse is, at least for now, ambiguous in its newness, it is also difficult to assert anything about Internet subjectivity. If discourse constitutes the subject, what are we to say about a subject whose very materiality is in question, not because of the traditionally poststructural sense that it does not exist as such, but rather because the sign system of the Internet is impossible to define as simply material? At most, we may assert that the very ambiguity of Internet subjectivity suggests something different from the pronounced panoptic subjectivity created by the integrated PDA/Web browser/cell phone.

Conclusion: Panopticism 2.0

If we have decided that the Internet is readable as code, even if that code is not clearly a disciplinary discourse, we still have not enabled critical activity. Although beautiful to the programmer, code and markup language are, of course, anathema to the critic and historian who, whatever flourishes her rhetoric may contain in the direction of corporate academic professionalism, has probably entered the discipline of literary or cultural studies because of the more or less neurotic love of the object of study – the novel and the poem – that the discipline demands. In contrast, the experience of reading code can in no way be thought of as the substitutively erotic experience of reading literature. It is not, in short, *jouissance*.

I can imagine as a consequence two critical responses to the reading of code. In the first, we may change the mode of processing pleasure away from the immediate gratification of the novel reader, and towards the delayed gratification of the archaeologist, most of whose pleasure probably does not derive from the initial reading of the text but from interpretation: translation, reconstruction of cultural context, and so on. One model for this kind of pleasure may be found closer to home in Walter Benjamin's projected Arcades Project, which was in some large measure supposed to be the reconstruction of all-but-disappeared texts.[51] This reconstruction is the pleasure that critics in any case claim for themselves: reading is always interpretive. Reading code would simply be a test of the truth of that claim.

In the second response (as I have tried to hint throughout this essay), the interpretation of code might indicate a truly 'professional' turn in literature/textual studies because it would not evoke the traditional text's moiety of *jouissance*. Approaching the Internet through its codes will reflect the direction of literature and cultural studies as discursive practices towards an ever-increasing utilitarian function in the disciplines, a function closer to linguistics than to the reading of literary texts. In short, whether or not we discover the Internet to be panoptic, the study of code threatens to reveal literary scholars to be contained in an increasingly rigid panopticon that reduces the 'pleasure of the text' to degree zero. Although hemmed in on one side by the constraints of the interpretive disciplines, politicized scholars might, however, be involved in debates about representation that will have important political/ideological consequences over the next few years: dialogues about open source codes, Internet censorship, intellectual property, and copyright are always already questions about representation and interpretation.

Even more liberating is the possibility that understanding the signifying system of the Internet would change our notion of how signification works. For Foucault, this kind of altered understanding implies an alteration in the way that we experience the world. In *The Order of Things*, Foucault discusses how our attitude towards language changed and was itself changed by our culture's changing relation to epistemology. For example, he discusses the sixteenth- and seventeenth-century transition from the 'classical' to the 'modern' in linguistic terms:

> In the sixteenth century, one asked oneself how it was possible to know that a sign did in fact designate what it signified; from the seventeenth century, one began to ask how a sign could be linked to what it signified ... The profound kinship of language with the world was thus dissolved ... Things and words were to be separated from one another. Discourse was still to have the task of speaking that which is, but it was no longer to be anything more than what it said.[52]

Foucault historicizes the 'fact' of our realization that sign and signifier are related only arbitrarily. He finds a moment that predates Saussure by some two and a half centuries; the very beginning of the 'long Enlightenment' is the moment of the emergence of the kind of discourse that produces modern disciplines and institutions out of the realization that, although words mean, that meaning is manipulable. In an analogous fashion, we may wonder whether the possible emergence of the Internet as a sort of ambiguously constituted Panopticon 3.0 does not bring with it a fundamental shift in the way we understand the world. It is perhaps the case that as a consequence of an accident in technology, we return to a revised or neoclassical version of premodern signification, in which words are once more genetically – or at least mechanically – linked to the things they signify.

One can imagine this realization as a liberation at least from the constraints placed on us by contemporary notions of signification. Under the current linguistic regime, cultural criticism often seems a sort of game in which we continually have to try to imagine a way out of the inevitable realization that definition is absolutely limited by language. We have different strategies for this game that, depending on the daring of the player, are conceived as either critique or subversion: 'structures of feeling,' 'signifyin',' 'the carnivalesque,' 'heteroglossia,' and so on. What if we could go on at least to a different game that questioned in some more fundamental way the limitations placed on us by signifying-as-ideology? In short, it is conceivable that the Internet as ambiguous panopticon might be re-envisioned as a vehicle, not for oppression, but for a kind of liberation, not perhaps the human/machine dichotomy collapse imagined by Haraway and others (alas, a collapse already envisioned not only in the panopticon but in the aesthetic of Marinetti's fascist Futurism), but a kind of liminal space in which identity formation can be questioned. The problem with this liberation is, of course, that it is, for the most part, ersatz: it exists only virtually. But virtuality is its virtue as well. Virtuality is the ground of the Internet's ambiguity. Perhaps the linguistic oddity that characterizes the Internet will provide a way out of the otherwise inevitable binary opposition in discovering meaning within subjectivity. Perhaps there is another way of framing the future of the Internet than as one of two opposing stances – as either the site of, if not liberation, at least of significant mass resistance (as opposed to, say, the bulk of academic Marxism or U.S. independent films), or the helpless reproduction of the ideology of the culture that produced it (as in Benjamin's oft-quoted Kafka quotation: 'Oh, plenty of hope, an infinite amount of hope – but not for us'[53]). A slightly more optimistic vision of the Internet might be found in a slightly different Benjamin: 'Only when in technology body and image so interpenetrate that all revolutionary tension becomes bodily collective innervation, and all the bodily innervations of the collective become revolutionary discharge, has reality transcended itself to the extent demanded by the *Communist Manifesto*.'[54]

Acknowledgments

I would like to thank Katherine Eggert, Aaron Powell, and Will Martin for their invaluable help.

Notes

1 See the Theory.org.uk Trading Cards website, 'Cultural Theory Trading Cards,' available at http://www.theorycards.org.uk. Accessed 12 Jan. 2003.

2 One of the best attempts to connect Foucault's notion of surveillance to the Internet is William J. Mitchell's book, *City of Bits: Space, Place, and the Infobahn* (Cambridge: MIT Press, 1995): 'Since electronic data collection and digital collation techniques are so much more powerful than any that could be deployed in the past, they provide the means to create the ultimate Foucauldian dystopia.' Another good example of the examination of data encryption is Thomas W. Wright's article, 'Escaping the Panopticon: Data Privacy in the Information Age' (1998), available at http://gsulaw.gsu.edu/lawand/papers/su98/ panopticon. Accessed 12 Jan. 2003. A more complete examination of panopticism and late capitalism can be found in Zygmunt Bauman, *Globalization: The Human Consequences* (New York: Columbia University Press, 2000).

3 One of the best of its kind is political scientist/social theorist Michael Rogin's chapter '*Ronald Reagan*: the Movie,' in his *Ronald Reagan, the Movie: And Other Episodes in Political Demonology* (Berkeley: University of California Press, 1987), 1–43, which is a discussion of Reagan's conflation of his movie image and his actual biography in the media during his run for the California governorship.

4 David Lyon, *The Electronic Eye: The Rise of Surveillance Society* (Minneapolis: University of Minneapolis Press, 1994), 65.

5 Ibid., 71. In an even more recent book, Lawrence Lessig states the case more boldly: 'We have every reason to believe that cyberspace, left to itself, will not fulfill the promise of freedom. Left to itself, cyberspace will become a perfect tool of control.' *Code and Other Laws of Cyberspace* (New York: Basic Books, 2000), 5–6.

6 Kristine J. Anderson, e.g., in noticing the tendency of academia on the Net to neglect the increasing mass of minority and postcolonial writing and to concentrate instead on the canon, asserts that 'while technology brings us ever closer to the world outside the continental U.S., our libraries and the Internet are rendering us more provincial' ('A Panopticon in Every Pocket: Or, the Scholar's Workstation in the 21st Century,' *Journal of the Midwest Modern Language Association* 32: 2/3 [1999]: 35). In his chapter, 'So Much for the Magic of Technology and the Free Market,' in *The World Wide Web and Contemporary Cultural Theory*, ed. Andrew Herman and Thomas Swiss (New York: Routledge, 2000), 5–35, Robert McChesney offers a more telling, neo-Marxist indictment of the narrowness of the Internet, arguing that, from its inception, 'there has been virtually no public debate over how it should develop; a consensus of experts simply "decided" that it should be turned over to the market' (7). This decision means that 'the dominant forces in cyberspace are producing the exact type of depoliticized culture that some Web utopians claimed that technology would slay' (34).

7 These features are gleaned from 'Panopticism,' in Michel Foucault, *Discipline and Punish: The Birth of the Prison*, trans. Alan Sheridan (New York: Vintage, 1979), 195–230.

8 See, e.g., Foucault's description of the execution of the regicide Damiens (ibid., 3-7).

9 Ibid., 216.

10 The most significant scholarship thus far on the 'archaeology' of the computer monitor is Lev Manovich's, 'An Archeology of a Computer Screen,' *Kunstforum International* 132 (Fall 1995): 124-35, available at http://www.manovich.net/TEXT/digital_nature.html. Accessed 12 Jan. 2003. A history after the fashion of C.W. Ceram's essay, *Archeology of the Cinema*, Manovich's text is interested in the virtuality of the screen in a way that, except incidentally, mine is not.

11 Of course, film and media scholars understand that the mind of the spectator is not a tabula rasa – that, in fact, fairly complex mechanisms of identification are always in play. I am speaking here of purely physical stillness and quiescence: panopticism as it acts on the body, whatever gymnastics the mind might be executing.

12 George P. Landow, *Hypertext 2.0: The Convergence of Contemporary Critical Theory and Technology* (Baltimore: Johns Hopkins University Press, 1992), 5–6. In this respect see also Silvio Gaggi, *From Text to Hypertext: Decentering the Subject in Fiction, Film, and Visual Arts, and Electronic Media* (Philadelphia: University of Pennsylvania Press, 1997); Espen J. Aarseth, *Cybertext* (Baltimore: Johns Hopkins University Press, 1997); and George P. Landow, ed., *Hyper/Text/Theory* (Baltimore: Johns Hopkins University Press, 1994).

13 Again, Landow's *Hypertext* may stand as the best and most foundational of the lot.

14 Susan Kuchinskas, 'Addicted to Advertising: Online Ads Are Popping Up Everywhere,' *Adweek*, Eastern ed., 39/42 (19 Oct. 1998): 58.

15 In regard to the corporate/government erosion of Internet freedom through the appropriation of its code, see Lessig, *Code*.

16 Lessig asserts the connection between market and state control rather baldly: 'The invisible hand, through commerce, is constructing an architecture that perfects control – an architecture that makes possible highly efficient regulation' (*Code*, 6).

17 Laura Mulvey, 'Visual Pleasure and Narrative Cinema,' *Screen* 16. 3 (1975): 6-18.

18 Jean-Louis Baudry, 'The Apparatus: Metapsychological Approaches to the Impression of Reality in the Cinema,' trans. Jean Andrews and Bernard Augst, *Camera Obscura* 1 (1976); reprinted in *Film Theory and Criticism: Introductory Readings*, 4th ed., ed. Gerald Mast et al. (Oxford: Oxford University Press, 1992), 690–707.

19 Even the notion of a heterogeneous spatialization – the three-dimensionality of the Net – is a construct and an historical tendency (although we do not realize it as such). The earliest incarnations of the Internet were simply verbal: messages sent back and forth that, although visible on a screen, had nothing about them of contemporary Web graphics. One may idly wonder what visual form the Net would have taken in Western culture between, say, AD 400 and 1300, during an aesthetic moment *sans* three-dimensional or Renaissance perspective. Unlike discipline-bound criticism, the world of role-playing indulges in such questions about new technologies. 'Steampunk' designates a role-playing world in which products of new technology are accessible through nineteenth-century steam technology, in, e.g., Rick Neal, *The Ascension of the Magdalene* (Brookfield: Trident Inc., 2002).

20 Foucault, *Discipline and Punish*, 143.

21 Raymond Williams, 'Structures of Feeling,' in *Marxism and Literature* (Oxford: Oxford University Press, 1985), 128–36.

22 Geert Lovink, 'Civil Society, Fanaticism, and Digital Reality: A Conversation with Slavoj Žižek,' *CTheory*, Article A037 (2-21-1996), available at http://www.ctheory.net/text_file.asp?pick=79. Accessed 12 Jan. 2003.

23 An advertisement from the Evidence Eliminator home page, at http://www.evidence-eliminator.com/product.d2w?g, states: 'Did you know that the government and police are installing black boxes in ISPs to record your Internet surfing and downloads for evidence? Deleting "internet cache and history", will not protect you[;] your PC is storing deadly evidence ... All those Web Pages, Pictures, Movies ... E-mail and Everything Else you have ever viewed could easily be recovered – even many years later. Defend yourself!' Accessed 12 Jan. 2003.

24 Foucault, *Discipline and Punish*, 202.

25 The benign version of this web of shared authority is the utopian vision of the World Wide Web itself as a place where users become creators or at least developers. Insofar as we can all create Web pages, contribute to the debugging of software, and contribute to the development of open-source software like Linux, we are all shaping the Internet. (At least those of us who can afford a computer and/or have access to an Internet connection.)

26 'On the whole, therefore, one can speak of the formation of a disciplinary society in this movement that stretches from the enclosed disciplines ... to an indefinitely generalizable mechanism of "panopticism." Not because the disciplinary modality of power has replaced all the others; but because it has infiltrated the others ... linking them together, extending them and above all making it possible to bring the effects of power to the most minute and distant elements' (Foucault, *Discipline and Punish*, 216).

27 William Gibson's novel, *Neuromancer*, was published in 1984, before the Internet as we know it came into existence.

28 André Bazin, 'The Myth of Total Cinema,' in *What Is Cinema*, vol. 1, trans. Hugh Gray (Berkeley: University of California Press, 1967). Dismissed for several decades as easy humanism, this essay seems now, in light of the attention devoted to perfecting special effects and virtual reality, to have a distinctly prescient authority.

29 One can see both tendencies – the desire to separate ideology from reality and the desire to conflate ideology and reality – in several contemporary films, most notably in *The Matrix*. On the one hand, the premise is that the world of virtuality is the world of 'false' ideology; it is a literally glowing picture of how society works that hides a reality of ruin, decay, and destruction. On the other hand, there is the notion that it is possible to fight ideology only within the space created by ideology. Although, Christlike, he seems for a moment to transcend the boundaries of the virtual world, the hero – Neo – must fight firepower with firepower within the Matrix.

30 The notion that the era of new technologies is ripe for surveillance society is briefly touched upon by, among others, Roy Boyne, who writes: '[In the eighteenth and nineteenth

centuries] neither the technology nor the social infrastructure were in place. In the late twentieth century, the much more interested response across the delta of social thought to Foucault's rehabilitation of the Panopticon concept does suggest that social conditions may have changed, that the ideological armature of surveillance is much more established,' 'Post-Panopticism,' *Economy and Society* 29/2 (2000): 290.

31 Herbert Marcuse, *One-Dimensional Man: Studies in the Ideology of Advanced Industrial Society* (Boston: Beacon, 1964); and Sloan Wilson, *The Man in the Gray Flannel Suit* (New York: Simon and Schuster, 1955).

32 Foucault, *Discipline and Punish*, 135

33 Ibid., 215.

34 Žižek on virtual sex: 'For example playing sex games. What fascinates me is that the possibility of satisfaction already counts as an actual satisfaction. A lot of my friends used to play sex games on Minitel in France. They told me that the point is not really to meet a person, not even to masturbate, but that just typing your phantasies is the fascination itself. In the symbolic order the potentiality already gives actual satisfaction.' See Geert Lovink, 'Civil Society, Fanaticism, and Digital Reality: A Conversation with Slavoj Žižek,' available at CTheory.net, http://www.ctheory.net/text_file.asp?pick=79. Accessed 12 Jan. 2003.

35 Ravi Sundaram, 'Beyond the Nationalist Panopticon: The Experience of Cyberpublics in India,' in *Electronic Media and Technoculture*, John Thornton Caldwell, ed. (New Brunswick: Rutgers University Press, 2000), 290. Donna Haraway, 'Manifesto for Cyborgs: Science, Technology, and Socialist Feminism in the 1980s,' *Socialist Review* 80 (1985): 65-108.

36 Two excellent cultural studies anthologies are David Bell and Barbara M. Kennedy, eds, *The Cybercultures Reader* (London: Routledge, 2000); and John Thornton Caldwell, ed., *Electronic Media and Technoculture*. (New Brunswick: Rutgers University Press, 2000).

37 Lev Manovich, *The Language of New Media* (Cambridge: MIT Press, 2001), 118.

38 Because it led to his loss of security clearance and, indirectly, to his suicide, Turing's homosexuality is discussed mainly as an impediment to his continued work on the computer rather than as a motivating or structuring factor for the Internet. But, in its emphasis on penetration, we might still define internet 'bi-directionality' in terms of bisexuality.

39 See. e.g., Florian Cramer, 'Digital Code and Literary Text' (2001), available at http://beehive.temporalimage.com/content_apps43/cramer/oo.html. Accessed 12 Jan. 2003. Engaged in the Codeworks debates about the literariness of code, Cramer argues for a poetics of the Internet in the same manner I am arguing for a privileged critique of the same: 'the theoretical debate of literature in digital networks has shifted, just as the poetic practices it is shaped after, from perceiving computer technology solely as an extension of conventional textuality ... towards paying attention to the very codedness of digital systems themselves.'

40 Jay David Bolter, *Writing Space: The Computer, Hypertext, and the History of Writing* (Hillsdale: Lawrence Erlbaum, 1991), 85-106.

41 Semiotics – that scientific examination of very science-method-unfriendly texts – seems the perfect paradigm for reading code. I imagine someone doing to Microsoft Office what Roland Barthes did to the story of 'Sarrasine' in *S/Z*.

42 One of the best articulations of this assumption is, oddly, a paper defending the Net as iconic in the Piercean sense. See Peer Mylov, 'What Is a Virtual Sign?' available at http://www.hum.auc.dk/~mylov/ What_is_a_virtual_sign.html [removed].

43 Despite its materiality, the film apparatus is famously conceived as more a concept than a thing. See, again, Bazin, 'Myth,' and Jean-Louis Baudry, 'Ideological Effects of the Basic Cinematographic Apparatus,' trans. Alan Williams, *Film Quarterly* 28/2 (1974-5): 39–47.

44 The conventional semiotic model that best describes the relationship between code and software is probably Charles S. Peirce's notion of the index, both elements of which – the smoke and the fire – have a meaningful materiality.

45 Christian Metz, *Le Signifiant imaginaire: Psychanalyse et cinéma* (Paris: Union générale d'éditions, 1977).

46 Like Saussurean linguistics, Pierce's semiotic model is likewise unable to describe this self-effacement. Like code and spectacle, the signifier and signified are causally related. However, the signified does not of necessity efface its signifier. Smoke does not hide fire; the former simply indicates the existence of the latter.

47 The machine has repeatedly been a metaphor for the operation of culture and humanity in the twentieth century elsewhere than in Haraway, from Henri Bergson's essay on laughter, *Le rire: essai sur la signification du comique* (Paris: Presses universitaires de France, 1989), to Gilles Deleuze's and Felix Guattari's *Anti-Oedipus: Capitalism and Schizophrenia*, trans. Robert Hurley (Minneapolis: University of Minnesota Press, 1985). New technologies, however, have not been so widely deployed.

48 The WTO was founded in 1995, the same year that the G7 met in Brussels, largely for the purpose of deciding the future of the World Wide Web. Europa, the European Union website, was founded then. See European Communities, 'The History of the European Union,' available at http://europa.eu/abc/history/1995/index_en.htm. Accessed 12 Jan. 2003. Alternatively, Bhabha's first two books argue against essentializing third-world countries, and instead encourage thinking in different ways about cultural connectivity between East and West. Bhabha's second book was published a year before the G7 meeting; his first book was published in 1990, the same year as the invention of the first World Wide Web browser, and the institution of the first hypertext system enabling connectivity on the Internet. Homi K. Bhabha, *The Location of Culture* (London: Routledge, 1994); Homi K. Bhabha, ed., *Nation and Narration* (London: Routledge, 1990).

49 Jürgen Habermas, 'Modernity – An Incomplete Project,' and Fredric Jameson, 'Postmodernism and Consumer Society,' both in *The Anti-Aesthetic: Essays on Postmodern Culture*, ed. Hal Foster (Seattle: Bay Press, 1983), 3–15, and 111–25, respectively. More persuasive writers like Lawrence Lessig, however, suggest that legislation and legal decisions concerning the Internet support Jameson.

50 This is, of course, truer of open-source code than of Windows.

51 Walter Benjamin, *The Arcades Project*, trans. Howard Eiland and Kevin McLaughlin (New York: Belknap, 2002).

52 Michel Foucault, *The Order of Things: An Archaeology of the Human Sciences* (New York: Random House, Vintage, 1973), 42–3. Of course, this is a rather reductive historicizing because it does

not take into account, e.g., Romantic theories of the genetic relationship of language to things present, e.g., in the work of Thoreau.

53 Walter Benjamin, 'Franz Kafka,' in *Illuminations: Essays and Reflections*, ed. Hannah Arendt (New York: Schocken, 1968), 116.
54 Walter Benjamin, 'Surrealism,' *Reflections* (New York: Schocken, 1978), 192.

POLITICS, GENDER, AND RELIGION

13 Communication and Imperialism

JAMES TULLY

Preamble: Pierre Trudeau's Ethos of Civic Participation

At the heart of former Canadian Prime Minister Pierre Trudeau's ethics is the activity of paddling against the current. As early as 1944, in 'The Ascetic in a Canoe,' he wrote that the ideal of paddling against the current is 'the resolve to reach the saturation point. Ideally, the trip should end only when the paddlers are making no further progress within themselves.' What does this ethics mean in practice today?

In the 1980s Trudeau campaigned for nuclear disarmament, downsizing military-industrial complexes, resisting the media's glorification of violence as the means to resolve disputes, and for the turn to peaceful and dialogical means of coping with disagreement. He saw this campaign for human security through peace and dialogue as a part of the civic ethics he had always practised. He said that he opposed big concentrations of power: superpowers, military-industrial complexes, media conglomerates, big corporations, and the enormous global inequalities that these power networks enforce. His means of opposing big concentrations of power was to empower all citizens to participate in the democratic struggles for freedom and equality.

Trudeau argued that Canada's Charter of Rights and Freedoms should not be seen so much as a set of guaranteed rights and freedoms handed down from on high that Canadians could take for granted, but more as a toolbox that citizens should use to engage in practices of civic freedom against the unequal distribution of power in Canada and the world.[1] One does not develop the skills of a proficient canoeist by being handed a paddle and canoe, but by engaging in the practice of canoeing to the saturation point. It is the same with acquiring the skills of a proficient citizen. Only by exercising their Charter rights in practices of civic freedom will future generations of Canadians develop the civic ethics of peace, dialogue, and equality of power-sharing that Trudeau saw as both the democratic means of struggle and the aim of these struggles. Without this identity-transforming civic experience of 'progress within themselves' Canadians would be shaped, formed, and swept along in the dominant current promulgated by the big concentrations of power, becoming passive subjects rather than active democratic citizens.[2]

Our question here is how can we adapt and apply Trudeau's civic *ethics* of critical freedom against the currents of the vast concentrations of power that shape, form, and carry us along today? Before addressing this question we need to ascertain the *character* of the big concentrations of power today.

The State of the Union Address of 31 January 2006 by U.S. President George W. Bush gave a clear picture of their general configuration. Although Bush did not use the language of empire, he explained that the United States is the leader among the great powers whose role it is to govern the global empire handed down to them by a half millennium of Western imperialism. They must complete the task of bringing the remaining recalcitrant states and non-state actors in line by military means and opening their resources, labour, and markets to the global economy dominated by the corporations of the great powers, and to perform these imperial duties in the name of bringing (neoliberal) freedom. If the first theme was thus to equate freedom with opening other societies to informal imperial control and structural adjustment, as the imperial powers have done for centuries, the second theme was an equally classic imperial argument. These imperial responsibilities are not some arcane aspect of foreign policy, but, rather, directly related to the national interest, security, and economic well-being of the United States and the other great powers. The indispensable and seemingly sovereign superpower is thus, paradoxically, entirely dependent on the efficient operation of the global empire of exploitation and inequality, and U.S. citizens and European allies alike must shoulder the demands that this dependency places on them. They must stay the course and paddle with the dominant current if they are to continue to enjoy their privileged lifestyle, and they must explain this to themselves not only in terms of their self-interest, but also in the terms of bringing freedom to the non-West.

This address tells us that the big concentrations of power can be characterized as an informal imperial system, with the United States as the hegemonic power; this characterization is substantiated by a large body of academic literature.[3] However, it does not answer two further questions. What is the specific *form* of imperialism today? And, is it possible for individual and collective actors to adapt and exercise Trudeau's civic ethics within and against its global inequalities in the name of another kind of freedom and another world? This chapter is an attempt to answer these two questions.

Introduction: The Turn to Communicative Action

One of the necessary features of any form of imperialism, and any form of organized critical freedom in relation to it, is communication. I want to try to give a partial and specific answer to our two general questions by focusing on the form of communicative relationships in which we find ourselves, whether we paddle with or against the prevailing current.

The transformation of communication in the past century has left us with two well-known and seemingly paradoxical currents. The first is a defining trend when the present is described as the 'information age' or 'network society': the vast proliferation of networks of communication in which people share and create information and knowledge.[4] Communication networks are the media through which ideas move. This trend is associated with and legitimated by a broad and contested concept of 'openness.' The second current is also a defining trend of the present when it is described as the 'age of insecurity' or the 'risk society': the equally vast proliferation of exclusions, restrictions, inducements, barriers, and boundaries placed on communication, as well as on actual physical movement and ultimately on the sharing of knowledge.[5] Moreover, many of the risks and insecurities are said to come from within communication networks, especially since 11 September 2001. These constraints govern the movement of ideas in communication networks. This trend is associated with and legitimated by a broad and contested concept of 'security' – of persons, cultures, religions, states, networks, civilization, and freedom.

Accordingly, the next section offers an analysis of the rise of networks as the defining form of communicative organization in the present. This is followed by an analysis of the forms of control, exclusion, assimilation, hierarchy, and concentration of power that have developed along with communication networks and that govern the transmission of knowledge and information. The third section examines the possibility of critical and effective forms of democratizing action within the array of networks and controls in which we are both enabled and constrained to communicate and interact in the imperial present.

These critical and effective forms of action are examples of the emerging form of civic communicative freedom of 'we the governed' that I call 'democratic communicative action.' It is a new form of civic freedom appropriate to being governed through the types of imperial networks and controls discussed in the first two sections. The enactment of civic communicative freedom in and against concentrations of network power and their communicative barriers, I will argue, is one way of adapting and applying Trudeau's civic ethics to the present.

Networks of Communication and Social Ordering

It is often remarked of the present age that, due to the astonishing growth of formal and informal networks of knowledge, production, and transfer, great new possibilities exist for the creation and exchange of shared knowledge across physical and cultural boundaries. This proliferation of networks of communication is, in turn, the communicative dimension of a larger and epochal trend – the emergence of networks as a key means of social ordering. As Manuel Castells states: 'Networks constitute the new social morphology of our societies, and the diffusion of networking logic substantially modifies the operation and outcomes in processes of production, experience, power and culture.'[6]

Let's examine what it means to say that networks are not only the means of producing and communicating knowledge, but also of social ordering.

First, the idea that the network is the defining form of social organization today developed out of the rapid spread of the Internet as the prototype and basis of a network social order. The Internet originated in the U.S. Department of Defense Advanced Research Projects Agency (DARPA). It was designed to avoid the destruction of U.S. communications by a Soviet invasion. The U.S. military determined that the Internet could not be controlled by a vulnerable (or hostile) centre and that it would be made up of thousands of autonomous computer networks that would have innumerable ways to connect and overcome electronic barriers. ARPANET, the network set up by the Defense Department, thus became the foundation of a global communication internet network, a world wide web, by the mid-1990s. In ironic confirmation of the Defense Department's thinking, the Internet rapidly escaped the direct control of the U.S. military and is now routinely used by all sorts of networkers, including those whom the department calls its 'enemies,' such as terrorist networks.

Although the spread of the Internet and other information highways solidified the image of the network as the dominant form of organization in the popular and academic imaginary, the Internet is built on, and still dependent on, the earlier spread of electric light and heat, telephone, radio, television, radar, multimedia, and other electronic 'networks,' and this wider, pre-existing field of networks provides the background of the claim that we live in a network age. Moreover, the image of communication networks is ultimately grounded in the background understanding of human communication in face-to-face networks since time immemorial.

Hence, in the *primary* instance, Castell's claim that the network is the reigning form of organization today[7] refers to a *communication* network: a network that produces and communicates information or knowledge among interconnected nodes by means of new information technology, especially the computer. For our purposes, we can pick out four main features of a communication network: (1) The *modes of communication* range from the more or less unilateral in-forming of a passive, 'interacted' recipient at one end (information processing, surfing the Web, watching a movie) to the ideal of 'interactive' communicative exchanges among free and equal networkers continuously creating new knowledge at the other. (2) A *node* refers to any unit connected in any network, such as individual users of communicative technology, corporations, organizations of various and conflicting kinds, stock exchange markets, ministries, governments, cities, states, and other networks or subnetworks.[8] (3) These high-tech communicative networks are not only netlike but also exceptionally *flexible and open-ended.* Diverse and dissimilar nodes can be connected and coordinated. Nodes can be easily added or subtracted. The organization of the network can be modified, reorganized, and retooled. The information transmitted and the technologies of transmission can be created, destroyed, programmed, and reprogrammed as needed, and the interoperating codes and switches among networks enable indeterminate coupling and decoupling of multiple networks. According to Kevin Kelly, the 'network is the least structured organization that can be said to have any structure at all. No other arrangement – chain, pyramid, tree, circle, hub – can contain true diversity working as a whole.'9 (4) Because the new information technology transmits information and knowledge instantaneously, it *compresses space and time*. This is not to say that it abolishes the 'here and now,' the time and place of the lived practices of particular nodes. Rather, it takes hold of and 'hyperextends' or 'glocalizes' (globalizes and localizes) spatially and temporally the experiential field of social relations and interactions of participants in nodal practices in complex and massively unequal ways. Instantaneous network decision-taking outruns the time frame of traditional democratic decision procedures, and the consequences of these decisions extend across the jurisdictional boundaries of traditional nation-states. Communication networks based on the new technology are thus the basis of globalization.[10]

Accordingly, communication networks have transformed the way humans communicate. But this is only the first dimension that has been observed of the communication transformation. Because communication is intrinsic to all organized forms of human activity, the rise of communication networks and the corresponding revolution in information technology have helped to bring about a transformation not just in the way humans communicate, but also in the way that they carry out their communicatively mediated activities: production, distribution, finance, consumption, governance, war, resistance, culture, intimacy, and much else. As Castells puts it, communication networks and their logic 'substantially modify' or colonize the *communicatively mediated practices* (activities and institutions) in which they are embedded. They tend to modify the practices so that they too are organized along the lines of a network.

So, the network becomes the 'morphology' not only of communication, but also of the 'operation and outcomes in the processes of production, experience, power and culture.' It becomes the dominant form of 'social ordering,' transforming or displacing older forms of social, political, cultural, military, and economic organization. This deeper, colonizing effect of communication networks is referred to as the 'network society' and the informational transformation of society. Let's look briefly at three constitutive features of this revolution.

First, the production and communication of information and the production of the corresponding technology have become the leading sector of capitalist production. Following Castells, the information/communication technology revolution coincided with the global restructuring of capitalism and became its essential tool, thereby transforming the dominant mode of production. This marks the transition from the industrial age and industrial mode of production, oriented towards economic growth, to the informational age and the informational mode of production, oriented towards information technology development (the accumulation of knowledge and higher levels of complexity in information processing):

In the new, informational mode of development the source of productivity lies in the technology of knowledge generation, information processing, and symbol communication ... [W]hat is specific to the informational mode of development is *the action of knowledge upon knowledge itself as the main source of productivity*. Information processing is focused on improving the technology of information processing as a source of productivity, in a virtuous circle of interaction between the knowledge sources of technology and the application of technology to improve knowledge generation and information processing ... Whereas industrialism is oriented to economic growth, informationalization is oriented towards technological development, that is, towards the accumulation of knowledge and higher levels of complexity in information processing.[11]

Second, the 'informational' mode of production transforms the nature of the dominant labouring activities, from the 'material' labour of the industrial age (producing material objects) to the immaterial labour of the information or communication age (producing immaterial objects). According to Michael Hardt and Antonio Negri, immaterial (or communicative) labour refers to three fundamental changes, called the 'informatization of production.'[12] First, the predominant form of labour under informational capitalism is the production of immaterial goods – such as knowledge, communication, a service, a cultural product, and the patenting and modifying of life processes – and the productive activities all involve a similar range of information processing, communicative, problem-solving, and symbolic-analytical skills. All labouring practices tend towards the prototype of information processing and communication networks. Second, while the material labouring activities of industrial production remain to a large extent, they are transformed by the information technology into predominantly immaterial labour. Producing and servicing automobiles, for example, is mediated through computer technology and communication networks.

The third form of immaterial labour is the production and manipulation of 'affects.' This refers to social services that primarily affect the emotional well-being of those served. But, even more importantly, it refers to the multimedia communication networks that affect directly the emotions, desires, and especially the imagination of the audiences to whom they communicate, without passing through self-conscious reflection. Movies, the news, election campaigns, political events, advertising, branding, Internet spam and pornography, and so on, all act directly on the senses of their connected audiences, in the 'Hollywoodization' of global communication. Behaviour is now said to be governed to a considerable extent by what Guy Debord calls 'the spectacle' of affects,[13] unmediated by conscious reflection, whether the spectacle is Lady Diana's death, branding, election campaigns, 9/11, or the scenes of high-tech war. Far from rendering the network revolution 'anachronistic,' as some have suggested, the al-Qaeda networks that orchestrated 9/11, the media that turned it into a spectacle, and the heightened securitization, wars against terror and resistances to them that followed all depended on and immensely expanded processes of networkization.

Following the footsteps of Harold Innis and Marshall McLuhan, cultural theorists suggest that what is always given directly to the recipients in the endless programs and messages of communication networks as their unnoticed affects, no matter how culturally diversified the messages may be, tends to be a fourfold background global imaginary – of production and consumption, of risks and insecurities, of the endless programmability of cultural and natural relationships, and of *us* (who are open to this imperial 'openness') *versus them* (who are backward and closed to this brave new world) – and of the 'cool' ordering of one's desires and emotions within it. What moves along the information highways is not so much ideas as images that structure the form of consciousness of the recipient (paradoxically, images of the infinite programmability of consciousness).

Third, the spread of communication networks restructures not only the activities and subjectivities, but also the *form of organization* – the 'morphology' – of the practices they colonize. Castells illustrates this with the restructuring of economic organizations in the 1990s. The 'industrial firm' has become the 'network enterprise'[14] with its flexible production and flextime workers, interfirm networking, corporate strategic alliances, horizontal global business networks, ability to make decisions, add and drop nodes instantaneously, and constantly re-invent the network infrastructure in whole or part: 'For the first time in history, the basic unit of economic organization is not a subject, be it individual (such as the entrepreneur or the entrepreneurial family) or collective (such as the capitalist class, the corporation, the state). As I have tried to show, *the unit is the network*, made up of a variety of subjects and organizations, relentlessly modified as networks adapt to supportive environments and market structures.'[15]

The restructuring of economic organization along the lines and logic of communication networks is just the leading edge of the restructuring of forms of human activity that undergo the informational technology revolution. The military-industrial sector has undergone a similar reorganization into military-informational networks. Wars are prepared for and fought on the basis of the most advanced communicative technologies. The U.S. military could not exercise the full spectrum dominance of the planet that the Pentagon claims to exercise without the network revolution.[16] Higher education, terrorism, religious and cultural organizations, dating, and so on has been similarly networked. As new human practices become possible as the result of the information technologies, their forms and activities follow the communication network model, from gene splicing and biotechnology to the weaponization of space.[17]

In addition to these three constitutive features of social ordering by communicative networks, every form of social ordering also has distinctive relations of power by which the conduct (roles) of those subject to it is ordered (governed). Furthermore, being subject to these relations of governance (as I will call them) and acting in accordance with them over time gradually brings about and instils a corresponding form of subjectivity or subjectification. For example, being subject to and so acting in accord with the exercise of power through the rule of law gradually brings about a form of self-consciousness of being a law-abiding subject with rights and duties and of comporting oneself accordingly. Social ordering by means of communication networks is no exception to this rule of subjectification. It, too, has distinctive relations of network governance and networkers tend to acquire a corresponding network form of subjectivity through submission to their forms of organization, types of communicative activities, and routines. These two further features of the network age are ways of governing and controlling communication and communicators.

Controlling Communication

This leads us to an important question that is explored in this section: how and by whom is the communication of information and knowledge controlled in the network age? No doubt there are innumerable ways that networks communicators and their communicative actions are governed. I would like to provide a background to this issue by highlighting four generic types of control of communication that operate in countless instances in various networks.

The first and most obvious way communication is controlled is by the *exclusion* of people from communication networks. Networks are scarcely a global phenomenon. Over one-third of the world population does not have access to a power grid and so is excluded. The next one-third, while in societies where power is available, does not have the money, infrastructure, or time to network. The remaining one-third is concentrated in the advanced capitalist nations, predominantly in the north, and in the middle and upper-income classes. That is, rather than a democratic and horizontal net of equal nodes unfolding around the globe, communication networks have developed on the foundations of and reproduce the unequal nodes and routes of communication, commerce, and military rule laid down more than 500 years of European-American imperialism, as many scholars, including Castells, have noted.[18] This *imperial* distribution of nodes and communication routes – in which 30,000 children die every day of malnutrition in the non-connected areas and the wealth of the 200 richest families in the north is eight times the wealth of 582 million non-connected people in the least developed countries[19] – is the underlying constitution of the network age, just as it was of the industrial age on which the network society is constructed. As a result, the very people whose lives are most adversely affected by the rise of network social ordering and who have the most pressing need and right to communicate are excluded from the outset. The network age is thus an imperial age built on the historical legacy of exclusions, subordinations, and massive inequalities of earlier phases of Western imperialism.

The second way communicators are governed in networks is by *inclusion and assimilation to a network form of subjectivity*. This is the central form of network governance to which every networker is subject. Castells argues that there are two main classes: those who 'interact' and those who are 'interacted' upon; and who fits in which class is determined by class, race, gender, and country. Notwithstanding, there is a more general form of self consciousness and consciousness of others that comes along with engaging in communicative and communicatively mediated activities in network regimes that he calls the 'spirit of informationalism.'[20] This is the *habitus*, the habitual form of subjectivity and corresponding set of cognitive and behavioural competences and modes of relating to others (intersubjectivity or interconnectivity) that agents acquire and internalize in the course of using network technology in whatever communicative roles they perform. It is a mode of being in the world with others that they come to acquire through immersion in immaterial labour, of knowledge acting on knowledge, with its creativity, flexibility, and openness; its compressed sense of time and space; its particular communicative and interactive skills of information processing, analysis of symbols, reduction of complex phenomena to an underlying and manipulable code, and problem solving; its experience of being able to belong to contingent virtual communities and cultures and to modify or disconnect from them as one pleases; and its overriding sense of 'creative destructiveness' – that everything can be programmed and commodified. It seems to disclose the world as a set of contingent relationships that can be created and destroyed, programmed and reprogrammed, by the appropriate problem-solving techniques. At the same time, networkers are always vaguely aware that they too are subject to the communication of 'affects,' surveillance, monitoring, and manipulation at a distance. 'It is a culture of the ephemeral,' Castells concludes, 'a culture of each strategic decision, a patchwork of experiences and interests, rather than a charter of rights and obligations.'[21]

Arthur Kroker suggests that the genetic engineering of the 'codes' of life in humans and other organic resources, at one end, and the monitoring, surveillance, and precision targeting of the global population in space based network warfare through full spectrum global dominance, at the other, represent the two extremes of this way of being in the world (legitimated in terms of 'openness' of scientific inquiry and 'security' of individuals and the species). Here life itself is pictured as both a network and an object of manipulation and control by informational technologies. Human nature and the environment are absorbed into culture, and so culture/nature is pictured as a kind of standing reserve of manipulable networks.[22]

This is not a form of subjectivity and intersubjectivity that a person bears in one particular role among many. It is a communicative habitus that communicators tend to operate within at work and leisure, on the home computer, the cellphone, the wireless laptop, and the BlackBerry. When networkers put these more interactive modes of communication down, they tend to turn to the technology of the communication of 'affects': radio, television, movies, and videos. As a result, this worldview and skill set is carried into other areas of life, either colonizing them or discarding them as 'uncool' if they are inaccessible through the network technology.

The form of subjectivity and intersubjectivity of network communicators is not an ideology or a worldview in the traditional sense. It is rather the opposite: a mode of being that is skilled in and accustomed to 'worldviewing' – surfing through, interacting with, and negotiating a kaleidoscope of shifting ideologies and worldviews. Secular modernists, Western scientists, indigenous peoples, neoliberals, non-governmental organizations (NGOs), anti-globalization activists, hyper-globalizers, deep ecologists, apocalyptic religious fundamentalists in the Bush administration, and Bin Laden terrorist networks are all at home in this habitat. Yet, it is not a neutral, all-inclusive medium of communication. It substantially modifies the pre-network forms of subjectivity that it includes, transforming them into contingent and malleable worldviews, civilizations, codes, programs, and 'scapes,' yet, paradoxically, placing beyond question its own background horizon of disclosure of the world *as* a complex system of contingent and programmable networks. This taken-for-granted form of subjectification tends to come with the network and goes without saying. It is the characteristic form of subjectivity of network imperialism.

We are just beginning to study and make explicit the tacit ways in which communication networks are reorganizing human subjectivity. Boaventura de Sousa Santos, and other critical sociologists of network communication and control, argue that the Net brings with it, in tandem with programmability, other taken-for-granted ways of organizing and imagining experience, privileging certain forms of communication, communicative rationality, knowledge, problem solving, cooperation and competition – and production and consumption, and discounting or excluding others.[23] Finally, although this is a powerful and insidious new form of subjectivity and social ordering, it is still one (non-omnipotent) form among many that we bear as subjects, and we are not passive recipients of it (as we will see in the next section).

The third way the flow of knowledge is controlled is through the action of the more powerful nodes in any network. The popular image of networks as flexible, open, and democratic governance communities or partnerships tends to hide this feature. Although all the various actors (nodes) in a network (or network of networks) participate and have a degree of active agency (the condition of it being interactive) within the relationships of network governance, the actors are differentially situated in these asymmetrical relationships. As a result, the more powerful or hegemonic actors within a network are able to govern and control the less powerful or subaltern actors, not by directly commanding them to act in a certain way, as in pre-network forms of rule, but indirectly or infrastructurally: by structuring the field of possible actions of the subaltern actors in the network through strategically controlling the flexible and hierarchical infrastructural relations of communication, technology, research, finance, security, norm creation, and subjectification among them.

The distinctive feature of this form of network governmentality is that it is able to govern the conduct of weaker partners through their constrained free participation; through inducing and then indirectly channelling, by diverse means, their communicative, creative, and productive participation – or by excluding them and connecting with others if they fail to participate in the way the hegemonic actors require. It is precisely this dimension of constrained free participation in a seemingly democratic and flexible community of actors and norms, and where actors may be added and removed on an ad hoc basis, that serves to legitimate and obscure the differentials in power and influence between hegemon and subaltern participants in imperial networks. Jochen von Bernstorff sums up the critical literature on this 'hegemonic' type of network rule in his major study of public-private network governance systems in the European Union and the international arena: 'The more abstract thesis developed throughout is that, on the global level, network-like governance structures inevitably exclude certain actors and interests while operating outside procedural and substantive legal commitments and constraints. These "flip sides" of the flexible network structure tend to sustain the dominance of the strongest actors of the network, and may turn the "participatory" claim into an instrument of hegemony.'[24] Let's use two well-researched examples to illustrate the two general types of hegemonic network governance of communication referred to in this abstract quotation. These two types of hegemonic network governance can be found in almost any network.

We saw in the first section that transnational corporations were among the first organizations to be transformed into networks by the information and communication revolution. In this reconfiguration they do not need to own their branch plants in the third world and directly control the workers in them, as was the form of social ordering in the industrial age. Rather, branch plants in which the world's information technology is typically assembled are often owned locally or regionally. They are participating actors in a global network exercising their interactive labour and management powers in their own ways to a certain limited extent. However, as Naomi Klein and others argue, their free participation is governed indirectly by the control that the hegemonic transnational corporations are able to exert over the infrastructural relations between the subaltern plant or sweatshop and its access to resources, financing, technology, research, branding networks, and world markets.[25]

Von Bernstorff stresses that a key factor here is the ability of powerful actors to set up and structure a network in the first place. Moreover, if subaltern nodes fail to deliver the goods or adapt to the flexible work regimes, then the hegemonic corporation can govern their participation by constraining their access to the network infrastructure; entering into a public-private network partnership with the local government to support them and suppress the workers' expression of their grievances; threatening to remove them from the network, or removing them and adding a more compliant node. If the weaker actors in the network are able to exert a degree of collective control over the hegemonic actors, then the latter can leave the network and establish another. Here, as in thousands of other unequal networks, flexibility and openness become strategic resources for the hegemonic actors, rather than indicators of democratic transparency.[26]

The second type of hegemonic network governance over communicative and communicatively mediated activities consists in *bypassing or overriding* domestic and international legal and political institutions that would otherwise be able to enforce the freedom of expression and access to information of the subalterns. This type of undemocratic control over communication is called the 'delegalization' and 'de-democratization' of governance networks. Von Bernstorff shows that the more power-ful states and transnational corporations in various global governance networks are able to do this in a wide variety of ways.

Networks operate in a different communicative time and space from traditional legal and political institutions (see the first section of this chapter). Because of the compression of time, decisions are taken instantly, in contrast to the time-consuming due deliberation, consultation, and accountability of traditional legal and democratic forms of communicative reasoning and decision-making. And, because of the com-pression of space, network decisions (such as financial decisions) affect the lives, envi-ronments, and futures of millions of people, regions, and countries around the globe who have no say over them; this is in contrast to the effects of decisions of traditional legal and democratic institutions, which are limited to a specific territory and jurisdic-tion, and according to which all affected should theoretically have a say, representa-tion, or redress. (Of course, this ideal of representation and legal recourse is often unrealized in practice, yet, unlike networks, it is a norm of legitimacy intrinsic to legal-democratic institutions and their historical development.) As a result, gover-nance networks seek to free their secret, immensely consequential and unaccount-able communicative and decision-making procedures from the time-expensive and spatially limited, old-fashioned legal and democratic restraints, in the name of effi-ciency, flexibility, and the technical imperatives of the new age. In the words of Presi-dent Bill Clinton's administration's domain-name policy coordinator, Ira Magaziner, in 1998: 'We believe that the Internet as it develops needs a different type of coordina-tion structure than has been typical for international institutions in the industrial age. Governmental processes and intergovernmental processes by definition work too slowly and somewhat too bureaucratically for the pace and flexibility of this new information age.'[27] How are network governance structures able to bypass or override traditional legal and democratic communicative procedures that have been built up over the centuries?

In the first instance, as the quotation from Ira Magaziner implies, the operation of powerful governance networks simply leaves the traditional legal and political institu-tions in their wake, and this lag then serves to support the claim to exemption. Next, hegemonic actors in global governance networks are able to create and control their own global constitutional and normative orders, administered by the World Bank, the International Monetary Fund, and the World Trade Organization, that override the legal and political institutions of representative democracies and international law – precisely the institutions that could open these guarded networks to democratic com-municative action.[28] In other cases, they are also able to outrun traditional legal and democratic protection of the flow of ideas by expanding their own, tailor-made, flexi-ble, and manipulable network of private law to govern networks, the controversial *lex*

Mercatoria.[29] Finally, even when powerful networks are constrained to work with traditional institutions they are able to mobilize influence over parliaments and courts, not least through the ability of the oligarchy of media networks to create the language, images, and effects of public discussion.

The rapid rise of this hegemonic mode of network governance of communicative action and its capacity to manipulate or evade the fetters of legal-democratic modes of governing communication is not as surprising as it may seem. Recall from Castells's analysis that communication networks were developed by the four biggest pre-existing concentrations of power from the earlier age of industrial imperialism and under the lead of the United States: the military-industrial complex; private economic enterprises; the leading states prepared to support and promote the research, development, and employment of the new technology; and the multimedia conglomerates. The information revolution transformed these four concentrations of power into the same network morphology and, in so doing, coordinated their interaction through common overlapping networks and a common orientation to expansion of the network age. The result is a global politics of 'structuration.' The complex interactions and competition among networks of these differentially situated and resourced actors give rise to persisting global hegemonic-subaltern formations (or processes) and the large-scale formations reciprocally structure the field of interactions, as in struggles over the Kyoto Accord, sustainability, and the Washington Consensus.[30]

In what is perhaps the dominant public language of our age, a global pattern of hegemonic-subaltern networks, and its expansion over and against other modes of communication and social ordering, is legitimated in terms of 'freedom' and 'security.' The sense of 'freedom' here is 'openness' – the openness of individuals, groups, cultures, and civilizations to enter and participate in the creative, expanding world of communication networks, and to exercise their freedom to communicate, produce, and consume in the ways available to them. The complementary sense of 'security' is the global monitoring, protection, and extension of market freedoms and 'network freedoms,' backed up by the 'full spectrum dominance' of the U.S. global military network. This 'indispensable' security and freedom network is presented by its proponents as acting in accord with the legal and democratic institutions when possible – but it is prepared to act instantly, unilaterally, and globally, including waging wars of intervention and forcing regime change, without and against the time-consuming, multilateral communicative review of international law, civil liberties, and democratic will-formation domestically or through the United Nations, for the transcendent goods of 'freedom and security.'[31] Many of the traditional rights and freedoms of information and communication are dispensable in this new form of social ordering, as was demonstrated in the invasion of Iraq, the Patriot Act in the United States, and the Anti-Terrorism Act in Canada. At many levels, and to varying degrees, this cluster of hegemonic networks and legitimating languages of freedom and security 'structures' the global field of possible alternative communicative actions in the network age.[32]

And, perhaps partly because of its pre-eminence, the two types of hegemonic rule employed to control communicative activities are replicated in innumerable other networks (including the terrorist networks it opposes).

Fourth, and finally, I would like to examine the specific nature of relations of governance characteristic of network governance. This will provide a fuller understanding of how communicative activities are actually guided by this form of governance, and this will provide the basis for understanding how we can act critically in response (see the third section of this chapter).

The first distinctive characteristic of relations of network governance is that they are *immanent* within relations of communication, and, as we have seen, relations of communication are immanent within relations of immaterial production. Networkers are subject to relations of governance of their communication and communicatively mediated activities just in virtue of *participating* in them. The diverse technological and multimedia infrastructure employed in all communicative activities – information technologies, modes of communication, programs, codes, routines, commands, messages, operations, learning procedures, and acquired skill sets – governs the conduct of the communicators *en passant* and almost intangibly. A relation of network governance is not so much a single relation of power acting on an individual subject from outside his or her activities as it is 'governmentality': a whole ensemble of governmental means operating *within* and on a field of interrelated communicators to create an overall network *mentalité*.[33] This technological absorption of relations of power directly into relations of communication is, according to Hardt and Negri, the most revolutionary feature of the network age. Relations of governance thus 'become ever more immanent to the social field, distributed throughout the brains and bodies of the citizens':[34]

> What the theories of power of modernity were forced to consider transcendent, that is, external to productive and social relations, is here formed inside, immanent to the productive and social relations. This is why communications industries have assumed such a central position. They not only organize production on a new scale and impose a new structure adequate to global space, but also make its justification immanent. Power, as it produces, organizes; as it organizes, it speaks and expresses itself as authority. Language, as it communicates, produces commodities but moreover creates subjectivities, puts them in relation, and orders them. The communication industries integrate the imaginary and the symbolic within the biopolitical fabric, not merely putting them at the service of power, but actually integrating them into its very functioning.[35]

From one perspective the folding of power relations into communication relations makes this form of social ordering more decentralized, horizontal, more indistinguishable from the communicative activities we perform, and thus in a sense more 'democratic.' Yet, from another perspective, it provides for a more vertical, more 'oligopolistic' form of control of communication by the more powerful nodes: 'The computer technologies and communications technologies internal to production systems allow for more extensive monitoring of workers from a central, remote location. Control of labouring activity can potentially be individualized and continuous in the virtual Panopticon of network production. The centralization of control, however, is even clearer from a global perspective. The geographical dispersion of manufacturing has created a demand for increasingly centralized management and planning, and also for a new centralization of specialized producer services, especially financial services.'[36]

This vertical or 'oligopolistic' dimension is the basis for the kind of hegemonic governance of network communications discussed above. Hegemonic actors do not govern the communication of subalterns directly, but indirectly, by strategically manipulating, monitoring, planning, dispersing, appraising, contracting-out, and restructuring the horizontal distribution and employment of technological infrastructure to guide immanently communicative activities to specific ends. Relations of network governance are thus immanent to the field of communicative action and are at once democratic and oligopolistic.

The second distinctive feature of relations of communicative governance is that they operate *through the communicative freedom* of networkers; through their communicative action. Networkers are not coerced by the detailed drills and repetitions of the industrial age, the assembly line or *Modern Times*. From the beginning, starting now in daycare, networkers are encouraged to see network communication from two perspectives. From one side, it is absolutely necessary to submit to commands, functions, and routines as an enabling condition of becoming a networker and learning the rules of the game. On the other hand, it is a flexible and open-ended game in which networkers are treated as free players, as interactive and creative communicators, modifying the rules of the game as they play. They interact with the software and are encouraged to ask it questions, create new and different ways through the programs, customize the software, acquire and contribute information, solve problems and pose others, create their own networks, and eventually reprogram the programs through which they are governed. This is another reason why the immanent relations of governance and forms of subjectification in network communication are so difficult to notice, for we tend to presume that the exercise of power must be external (a separate structure of ruler-ruled) rather than immanent; that it excludes the exercise of freedom rather than encourages it (liberalism's negative freedom), and that it imposes itself on a passive subject rather than playing strategic games with an interactive agent (the command-obedience model).

The informational mode of education, research, development, production, and consumption actually depends for its existence and dynamic growth on this interplay between immanent relations of governance and the free, creative, and unpredictable communicative competences of networkers, celebrated in the image of Silicon Valley. As a result, network relations of power are reciprocally dependent on and responsive to the communicative freedom of networkers. They govern communicative action and assimilate communicators interactively, by enabling and encouraging the free development of communicative capacities on one side and conducting their exercise to specific ends by diverse means on the other, and constantly readjusting in response to the unpredictable trajectory of communicative action. This realm of communicative freedom *within* network power relations is the subject of the third, and final section.

Democratic Communicative Action

To summarize, I have tried to provide a background sketch of the *field* in which communicative activity is 'controlled' today. The communication of information and knowledge in networks is the defining form of human activity of our age and the dominant form of social ordering. Communicative action takes place within networks (with four main features); communication networks are the leading sector of the economy; and they transform the communicatively mediated activities and institutions that they colonize (into networks of immaterial labour). Communicative and communicatively mediated action in networks is governed in four major ways: (1) exclusion, (2) inclusion and assimilation to an interactive network form of subjectification, (3) strategic employment of the communications infrastructure and by bypassing, overriding, and influencing legal-democratic governance, and (4) fostering and channelling free communicative action. Relations of network governance are immanent, democratic and oligopolistic. This complex field of communication networks is the specific morphology of the latest phase of Western imperialism.

This background sketch sets the stage for a third important question: what form of critical and effective social, political, and cultural action is possible today in relation to the control of the communication of knowledge? We could not answer this question until we laid out the specific context in which communication occurs and the relations of governance that enable and control it. For social action will be critical and effective only if it is based on an understanding of, and oriented in relation to, the specific relations of communication and governance in which it is situated. We may dream of utopian modes of communicative action as much as we wish – free of power, technological mediation, spatial-temporal compression, hegemonic-subaltern relations, and pre-reflective subjectification. But if we wish to confront the historical situation in which we are thrown, then (as I have argued elsewhere) we need to situate our question in the existing field of relationships.[37]

I take this sketch of the existing field of power relations that operate in contemporary communication networks to be a more realistic approach than the optimistic literature on network governance and policy networks. As Jochen von Bernstorff's study suggests, this literature has a tendency to abstract from the unequal power relations in communication networks in advancing the claim that global networking fosters democratic governance beyond the state.[38] This is to disregard the forms of exclusion and to equate inclusion with democracy, thereby overlooking the anti-democratic powers of assimilation, subjectification, and subalternization that are exercised directly or indirectly by hegemonic actors within the field of communication networks. And, it overlooks the persisting relations of inequality and subordination handed down from earlier phases of imperialism. Even the important work that seeks to combine 'bargaining' with the more idealized 'arguing' approach in international relations and international law still presupposes actors who are free of precisely the real world unequal relations of governance that I have tried to delineate in my sketch.[39] As Antje Weiner concludes in her critical review of this literature, it presupposes an 'egalitarian political culture' that does not exist.[40] What we need in order to be both critical and effective is not an account of norm creation for some ideal game, but an account of the possibility of democratic norm creation under the conditions of the field in which we find ourselves here and now.[41] Castells writes of this field and social action: 'I would argue that this networking logic induces a social determination of a higher level than that of specific social interests expressed through the networks: the power of flows takes precedence over the flows of power. Presence or absence in the network and the dynamics of each network *vis à vis* others are critical sources of domination and change in our society: a society, that, therefore, we may properly call the network society, characterized by the preeminence of social morphology over social action.'[42]

We will see whether it is as deterministic as Castells implies. Yet, given our background sketch, he does seem correct to infer that network social morphology is preeminent over social action. I take him to mean that if critical and effective social action is possible today, then social actors are constrained to think and act within and against the given social morphology of communication networks.

The first answer to our question of the possibility of critical action, therefore, is just to raise *explicit awareness* of the distinctive background context in which we communicate today, by means of various background sketches. For, as we discussed, network subjectivity tends to render its mode of governance intangible, a matter of course, and its immanent rule 'goes without saying.' Uncritical reflection on communication and control then tends to overlook the implicit infrastructural relations that govern communicative action without the communicators questioning them and having a say in and over them, that is, undemocratically.

Rendering networks and network governance explicit thus puts us in the position of being able to call into question and have a say over the relations of power through which our communication is governed and the norms that are advanced to legitimate them, that is, of *acting democratically.* For, the primary sense of 'democracy' (as opposed to the 'low intensity' democratization promoted by the neo-liberal institutions) is just the basic Athenian idea that the people have a say in and over the rules by which they are governed and over the public goods that the rules are enacted to bring about. We can thus call the diverse forms of questioning and having an effective say in and over the global and local relations governing all communication and communicatively mediated action *democratic communicative action.*[43] This is to apply Trudeau's civic ethics directly to everyday communication relations. So, our question can be reformulated as: what are the possibilities and examples of democratic communicative action?

Two general types of democratic communicative action are possible.[44] The first is to subject communication networks to the traditional legal and political institutions of existing nation-states, international law, and the United Nations. The flow and control of ideas could be *regulated* in these legal-democratic institutions by the representatives of the people subject to network governance, against the dominant current of hegemonic rule by powerful network actors and their 'delegalization' and 'de-democraticisation' of network communication. This might be called the 'traditional' legal-democratic approach locally and globally. As noted earlier, legal-democratic, Enlightenment institutions are 'works in progress' that require major reforms to be effective, especially in the international realm, and their inadequacy has led to the search for another, more effective strategy.

The second general strategy, accordingly, is to democratize communication networks *directly,* so networkers and those excluded yet effected can call into question and have a say in contextually appropriate practices of democratic discussion, negotiation, and decision-making in the nodes in which they network (or from which they are presently excluded). This runs against the dominant current of assimilation and subjection to a form of communicative interaction that, while creative in many dimensions, is subtly (and not so subtly) channelled away from networkers questioning and transforming the dominant undemocratic relations of network governance. The creation of sites of democratic communicative action within networks might be called a new approach, one tailored specifically to the new form of communicative power, but also simply a new form of 'direct' or participatory democracy. Direct democratic communicative action is the fitting response to the compressed time and space of network communication and decision-making, as it too can be mobilized instantaneously and across the multijurisdictional global space of network effects.

These two types of democratic communicative action are counter-hegemonic (against the dominant undemocratic control of the flow of ideas) and complementary (working in tandem against different types of undemocratic control). One of the most depressing features of Canada today is the antagonism between proponents of these two strategies – between those who participate through the traditional institutions and those who wish to participate directly through direct democratic communicative action in networks. Yet, both strategies have the same means and end: the democratic governance of the means of communication by the communicators.[45]

If these two strategies were successful, they would constitute a revolution – the legal-democratic transformation of the network age. The people and their representatives would decide how to govern the communication of knowledge and information and for what ends. Such a transformation appears utopian from the perspective of the present, and it certainly is if we imagine that the dominant actors of the network age might institute this transformation for us. If there is to be change in this direction, we the governed have to initiate it from the ground up by organizing and participating in concrete forms of democratic communicative action that *enact* initiatory and exemplary practices of these two strategies here and now.

Hence, we are in a situation analogous to Trudeau's three decades ago. For him the question was, given the big concentrations of power in Canada and globally, how could he help to empower citizens to participate democratically in civil society, communicate freely, democratize hegemonic concentrations of power and repatriate democratic powers and power-sharing to the sovereign people, and so diminish the enormous inequalities? His answer was Canada's Charter of Rights and Freedoms and the counter-hegemonic civic *ethics* he hoped it would foster. The difference today is that the concentrations of power and means of participation have been transformed by the communications revolution, and thus the analogous answer is democratic communicative action that subjects network communication to democratic control, and does so by democratic communicative means.

The first step is to realize that the possibilities and opportunities for democratic communicative action exist here and now, wherever we communicate.[46] The second section of this chapter suggested that the entire network organization of contemporary societies rests on the free, creative communicative capacities and activities of networkers. Network governance relations can foster communicative action and channel it towards specific ends, but they cannot control it in detail, for the development of the information age depends on creative and innovative forms of communication. This is why networks are necessarily flexible and open, encouraging and then responding to the indeterminate and unpredictable communicative activities of networkers, rather than fixed structures of domination. As a result, there is an element of interactive freedom or free play – a limited range of possible ways of communicating in any network situation. There is thus always the limited possibility of communicating differently, in discord with the commands, routines, and norms in some way or another – just as in canoeing, there is always the possibility to turn and paddle against the current in different ways. This element of interactive human freedom and surprise is irreducible.

Now, this creative communicative freedom is directed, with all the powerful technological and multimedia means at the disposal of hegemonic actors, towards its exercise in innovations and creations that serve the prevailing imperial ordering and goals of the information age. In contrast, the exercise of creative communicative freedom democratically *on* the prevailing governance relations is discouraged, except for innovations in forms of local or regional self-rule and self-management that increase efficiency and can themselves be governed and monitored infrastructurally (as in the downloading and contracting out of regimes of self-government and dispute resolution to subaltern nodes in local, national and global governance networks). Nonetheless, because relations of governance are immanent within relations of communication, the existential possibility of exercising creative communicative freedom in its democratic form cannot be eliminated or blocked completely by the powers that be.

Democratic communicative action is not only possible in some abstract sense. It is an 'opportunity' in any node. The popular image of the expansion of the network age that the media communicate over and over is of a cluster of global processes or closed systems that are technologically driven, necessary, and inescapable, too complex to be modified by those subject to them, and, in any case beyond human control. Yet, networks are grounded in the communicative activities of networkers at their particular nodes, and the hyperextension of these activities and decisions throughout the network. As heretical as this may sound to some systems theorists, these local practices of network communication are in turn partly grounded in the daily, non-technological, face-to-face relations of communication of the networkers, and these alternative forms of intersubjectivity provide grounds of resistance to networkization. Of course, there are hegemonic structural formations of global networks, and forms of subjectivity that make these appear inevitable, but these are grounded in and reproduced by the daily practices of local networkers going along with the prevailing routines of communication without a say. So, despite the hegemonic image of deterministic technological processes imposed on us from above and to which we must submit, global networkization is actually based in and hyperextends out from the everyday communicative activities of networkers. Steven Flusty describes this more accurate and counter-hegemonic picture: '[Network globalization] is a combination of distinct spatial and temporal practices that, in their execution and their accretion, exercise globally formative effects. These practices are brought about through the quotidian business of conducting life within and across ever widening distances and by means of ever more distended social relations. It thus entails a redefinition of globalization not as an extrinsic quasi-opaque imposition from above, an irresistible structural imperative, or a commandment unifying capital markets. Rather, it is globalization as both immanent in, and increasingly intrinsic to, our everyday practices.'[47]

Consequently, communication networks are less deterministic and provide more opportunities for democratic challenge and reform from within than Castells suggests. I would like to illustrate the range of opportunities available with a few examples of counter-hegemonic democratic communicative action that have helped to bring communication networks under direct and/or legal-democratic governance. First, the most popular vehicle for democratic communicative action in the network age is without doubt non-governmental organizations. However, their role is ambivalent. Many NGO counter-networks have been successful in organizing and including many formerly excluded peoples, challenging the assimilative features of network subjectivity, countering the hegemonic rule and aims of powerful actors in major communicative networks, and showing ordinary people that they have more freedom to organize and act critically than they are led to believe by the dominant discourse. Yet, many other NGOs have been instrumental in reproducing and expanding some of the undemocratic features of existing networks. Over 70 per cent of the 50,000 INGOs (international NGOs) are regis-tered in Europe and North America and funded by northern governments and corpora-tions to promote their agendas. When they bring excluded peoples into the major government and corporate development networks, they often discount their traditional forms of communication and cooperation and assimilate them to the network form of communication and subjectivity they bring with them, rather than nurturing non-assimilative forms of inclusion. Their relatively ineffective informal consultative role in major networks is often used by the hegemonic actors to simulate democratic scrutiny and to legitimate cosmetic changes. Furthermore, NGO networks are often unaccount-able to the people whose interests they claim to represent and their internal organiza-tion tends to replicate the hegemonic-subaltern structure and undemocratic decision-making of major networks. Many are now referred to as CONGOS (co-opted NGOS).[48]

Since, as Castells argues, social action has to be organized in networks to be effec-tive, NGO networks will continue to be used. However, if they are to be a means for the gradual democratization of communication in the network age, they too will have to be subject to democratic reform from within, so they embody the same democratic communicative action for which they claim to be fighting.

One instructive example of combining the legal-democratic and direct democracy types of communicative action is the use of democratic-communicative or 'soft power' networks to bring about an enforceable ban on landmines. This, in turn, is part of a larger, counter-hegemonic, soft power network organized through countless nodes of communicative action to question and fight to reform the dominant, global security-freedom network in the name of another kind of security and freedom. From this counter-perspective the causes of insecurity and unfreedom are the enormous global inequalities and the exclusion of the worse-off majority from democratic com-municative action. The dominant global security-freedom network does not address these underlying causes but, rather, protects and extends them, causing more wars and insecurity. The path to security and equality is to provide the multifaceted infra-structure of network communication developing countries demand, so that they can engage in free communicative action on a level playing field, and then the other inequalities will soon diminish. This global counter-network is far from successful, yet it demonstrates the power of democratic communicative action to challenge and offer an alternative to the networks that now govern undemocratically the communi-cative action of millions.[49]

From the pioneering activities of Amnesty International and Doctors Without Boarders in confronting and opening closed channels of communication to the latest small-scale, alternative network globalization from below, such as providing email for rural doctors and missionaries in Zambia by high-frequency radio and Sailmail, there are countless other examples from which we can learn.[50] However, I would like to move on and conclude with one final and indispensable feature of democratic com-municative activities if they are to be effective in building a better future.

Boaventura de Sousa Santos observes with respect to the World Social Forum that we need more meeting places for the multiplicity of counter-hegemonic democratic networkers.[51] These forums would be places, like the annual Pierre Trudeau Foundation Public Policy Conferences in Canada, where researchers, academics, students, democratic activists from diverse networks, representatives from the excluded majority, policymakers, filmmakers, communication experts, scientists, technicians, and business people working on soft, democratic communicative technologies and education, representatives from the volunteer sector, politicians, and a host of other actors could come together and exchange their case-specific and specialized knowledge of how network communications are governed and how they can be rendered more accountable by democratic communicative action. They would be places for anyone uncomfortable with the ways communication is currently governed and hopeful that another world is possible. If democratic communicative action is to be critical and effective, it needs to be based on the reciprocal communication among academic research on how communication networks operate, policy communities' knowledge of what sorts of local, domestic, and international legal and political initiatives are possible, and the experiential knowledge of communicative activists and the excluded on the ground. Finally, these forums could be models of democratic communicative action in which the participants learn through practice the civic ethics that they hope to hyperextend in their diverse activities. The World Social Forum is an exemplary annual meeting place of such reciprocal networks, but the task now is to create a multitude of similar and more specific forums.[52]

Acknowledgments

This chapter was originally written as a background paper for the First Annual Public Policy Conference of the Pierre Trudeau Foundation held in Montreal, Canada, 14–16 October 2004. I would like to thank the many participants who commented on the original paper, especially the Trudeau Scholars, Jocelyn Maclure, David Ley, Boaventura de Sousa Santos, Stephen Toope, Jeremy Webber, and Antje Weiner. I would also like to thank the three anonymous reviewers and especially the editors of *CTheory*, Marilouise and Arthur Kroker, for their helpful comments. I am greatly indebted to Mike Simpson for his editing and helpful suggestions throughout. This chapter expresses my own opinions, not those of the Trudeau Foundation.

Notes

1 The Canadian Charter of Rights and Freedoms, Section B of the Constitution Act 1982, is an amendment to the Constitution of Canada that was initiated by Prime Minister Pierre Trudeau. His rationale for the rights and freedoms enumerated in the Charter was that they

would empower individuals and groups in Canada to participate directly and more fully in the civic and political life of Canada; that is, they would enable citizens to exercise their popular sovereignty. This 'civic freedom' aspect of the Charter was overshadowed by the debate over whether it gives proper recognition to Quebec. My aim in this chapter is to recover and adapt this civic dimension of Trudeau's legacy for our times. See Government of Canada, Department of Justice, *Canadian Charter of Rights and Freedoms*, available at http://laws.justice.gc.ca/en/charter/index.html.

2 This description of Trudeau's civic ethics is based on his lecture to an introductory class in Political Theory at McGill University in the late 1980s when he was campaigning for nuclear disarmament. The quotation from 'The Ascetic in a Canoe' is taken from the Pierre Trudeau Foundation's website, available at http://www.trudeaufoundation.ca/trudeau_e.asp, accessed 5 May 2005. I would like to thank Alexandre (Sacha) Trudeau for discussions of this ethics today.

3 James Tully, 'On Law, Democracy, and Imperialism,' in *Public Law and Political Theory*, Emilios Christodoulidis and Stephen Tierney, eds. (Aldershot: Ashgate, 2008).

4 Manuel Castells, *The Rise of Network Society*, vol. 1 of *The Information Age: Economy, Society and Culture* (Oxford: Blackwell, 1996).

5 Ulrich Beck, *Risk Society: Toward a New Modernity* (London: Sage, 1992).

6 Castells, *Rise of Network Society*, 469.

7 Ibid.

8 Ibid., 470.

9 Kevin Kelly, *Out of Control: The Rise of Neo-Biological Civilization* (Menlo Park: Addison-Wesley, 1995), 25–7; quoted by Castells, in *Rise of Network Society*, 61-2.

10 The compression of space and time is the central nexus of globalization according to Castells, David Held, and Anthony Giddens. See, e.g., Castells, *Rise of Network Society*, 376–468; David Held, A. McGrew, D. Goldblatt, and J. Perraton, *Global Transformations: Politics, Economics and Culture* (Cambridge: Polity Press, 1999).

11 Castells, *Rise of Network Society*, 17.

12 Michael Hardt and Antonio Negri, *Empire* (Cambridge: Harvard University Press, 2000), 29, 280–302.

13 Guy Debord, *Society of the Spectacle* (Detroit: Black and Red, 1983).

14 Castells, *Rise of Network Society*, 151-200.

15 Ibid., 198.

16 Chalmers Johnson, *The Sorrows of Empire: Militarism, Secrecy, and the End of the Republic* (New York: Metropolitan Books, 2004).

17 Jonathan Havercroft and Raymond Duvall, 'Taking Sovereignty Out of this World: Space Weaponization and the Production of Late-Modern Political Subjects.' Paper presented at the annual meeting of the International Studies Association, San Diego, 22-5 March 2006.

18 Manuel Castells, *End of Millennium*, vol. 3 of *The Information Age: Economy, Society and Culture* (Oxford: Blackwell, 1998), 70-165.

19 Martti Koskenniemi, '"The Lady Doth Protest too Much": Kosovo, and the Turn to Ethics in International Law,' *Modern Law Review* 65/2 (2002): 171; U.N. Development Program, *Human*

Development Report 2000: Human Development and Human Rights (Oxford: Oxford University Press, 2000), 73, 82.

20 Castells, *Rise of Network Society*, 195-200.

21 Ibid., 199.

22 If human consciousness and embodiment are as deeply wired into communication technology as Kroker claims, then the tempered democratic communicative action I recommend here is too little, too late. See Arthur Kroker, *The Will to Technology and the Culture of Nihilism: Heidegger, Nietzsche, and Marx* (Toronto: University of Toronto Press, 2004); Castells, *The Rise of Network Society*, 477.

23 Boaventura de Sousa Santos: *Toward a New Legal Common Sense: Law Globalization and Emancipation* (London: Butterworths, 2002), and 'The WSF and the Sociology of Absences,' in *The World Social Forum: Toward a Counter-Hegemonic Globalization*, available at http://www.tni.org/socforum-docs/fm2003boaventura.htm, accessed 27 Oct. 2006. Paper presented at the XXIV International Congress of the Latin American Studies Association, Dallas, 5 May 2005.

24 Jochen Von Bernstorff, 'Democratic Global Internet Regulation? Governance Networks, International Law and the Shadow of Hegemony,' *European Law Journal* 9/4 (2003): 513.

25 Naomi Klein, *No Logo: Taking Aim at the Brand Bullies* (Toronto: Knopf Canada, 2000); Richard Falk, *Predatory Globalization: A Critique* (Cambridge: Polity Press, 1999).

26 Von Bernstorff, 'Democratic Global Internet Regulation?' 524–5.

27 Cited in ibid., 515.

28 Stephen Shrybman, *The World Trade Organization: A Citizen's Guide* (Toronto: James Lorimer, 2001).

29 A. Claire Cutler, *Private Power and Global Authority: Transnational Merchant Law in the Global Political Economy* (Cambridge: Cambridge University Press, 2003).

30 Castells, *Rise of Network Society*, 474. For the concepts of hegemony, structuration, and the governance of subjects through their constrained freedom in networks, see James Tully: 'Democracy and Globalization,' in *Canadian Political Philosophy: Contemporary Reflections*, ed. Ronald Beiner and W. Norman (Toronto: Oxford University Press, 2001), and 'Exclusion and Assimilation: Two Forms of Domination in Relation to Freedom,' in *Political Exclusion and Domination*, ed. Melissa S. Williams and Stephen Macedo (New York: New York University Press, 2005), 191–229, both of which draw on Michel Foucault's account of governmentality and freedom. See also Michel Foucault, 'The Subject and Power,' in *Power*, ed. James B. Faubion, vol. 3 of *The Essential Works of Foucault* (New York: New Press, 2000), 326–48.

31 This global network strategy of freedom and security is presented in two documents: one produced by the White House, entitled *The National Security Strategy of the United States of America* (Sept. 2002), available at www.whitehouse.gov/nsc/nss.pdf, accessed 29 Oct. 2006, and the other by the U.S. Space Command, entitled *Vision for 2020*, available at http://www.middlepowers.org/gsi/docs/vision_2020.pdf. For an excellent analysis of the global security strategy of the United States, and the place of the former document in it, in relation to international law, see Jutta Brunnée and Stephen J. Toope, 'Slouching towards New "Just"

Wars: The Hegemon after September 11th,' *International Relations* 18/4 (2004): 405–23. For the historical development of the hegemonic language of security and freedom see Andrew Bacevich, *American Empire: The Realities and Consequences of U.S. Diplomacy* (Cambridge: Harvard University Press, 2002). See also the *State of the Union Address* 2006 for these themes (White House, *State of the Union Address*, available at http://www.whitehouse.gov/stateoftheunion/ 2006, accessed 6 Feb. 2006).

32 Johnson, *Sorrows of Empire.*

33 Nikolas Rose, *The Powers of Freedom: Reframing Political Thought* (Cambridge: Cambridge University Press, 1999).

34 Hardt and Negri, *Empire,* 23.

35 Ibid., 33. By creating 'subjectivities,' Hardt and Negri mean that relations of immanent communicative governance give rise to the corresponding network form of subjectivity discussed above.

36 Ibid., 297.

37 James Tully, 'To Think and Act Differently: Foucault's Four Reciprocal Objections to Habermas,' in *Foucault contra Habermas: Recasting the Dialogue between Genealogy and Critical Theory,* ed. Samantha Ashenden and David Owen (London: Sage, 1999), 90–143.

38 Von Bernstorff, 'Democratic Global Internet Regulation?' 511–26.

39 Harald Müller, 'Arguing, Bargaining and All That: Communicative Action, Rationalist Theory and the Logic of Appropriateness in International Relations,' *European Journal of International Relations* 10/ 3 (2004): 395–435.

40 Antje Weiner, 'The Dual Quality of Norms and Governance beyond the State,' *CRISPP* 10/1 (2007): 47–70.

41 See Tully, 'Exclusion and Assimilation.'

42 Castells, *Rise of Network Society,* 469.

43 James Tully, 'Two Meanings of Global Citizenship: Modern and Diverse,' in *Handbook for Global Citizenship Education,* Michael Peters, et al., eds. (London: Sense Publishers, 2008), 15–40.

44 Tully, 'Democracy and Globalization.'

45 These two types of democratic communicative action have to be pursued in tandem as they are mutually supportive. Von Bernstorff concludes: the problem of de-legalization 'cannot be solved by the reference to a higher standard of "accountability" and "transparency" through a "network constitution" or ombudsman structures for informal governance arrangements. Principles of "good governance" cannot substitute for the loss of procedural constraints and substantive commitments imposed by a legal order' ('Democratic Global Internet Regulation?' 526).

46 Notes from Nowhere, ed., *We Are Everywhere* (London: Verso, 2003).

47 Steven Flusty, *De-Coca-Colonization: Making the Globe from the Inside Out* (London: Routledge, 2004), 3–4.

48 For a relatively optimistic view of NGOs see John Keane, *Global Civil Society?* (Cambridge: Cambridge University Press, 2003), and for a critical view, see Hardt and Negri, *Empire,* 35–7,

312–14. For a range of views based on case studies, see Sanjeev Khangram, J. Riker, and K. Sikkink, eds., *Restructuring World Politics: Transnational Social Movements, Networks, and Norms* (Minneapolis: University of Minnesota Press, 2002).

49 Lloyd Axworthy, *Navigating a New World: Canada's Global Future* (Toronto: Knopf, 2003).

50 'E-mail innovation helps Zambia go Global,' *Times Colonist*, 11 July 2004, B1. For recent surveys, see Flusty, *De-Coca-Colonization*; Jeremy Brecher, T. Costello, and B. Smith eds., *Globalization from Below: The Power of Solidarity* (Cambridge: South End Press, 2000); and Louise Amoore, ed., *The Global Resistance Reader* (London: Routledge, 2005).

51 Boaventura de Sousa Santos: 'The WSF and the Sociology of Absences,' and 'The WSF: Toward a Counter-Hegemonic Globalisation: Parts I & II,' in *The World Social Forum: Challenging Empires*, Jal Sen, Anita Anand, et al., eds. (New Delhi: Viveka Foundation, 2004), available at http://www.choike.org/nuevo_eng/informes/1557.html, accessed 15 Dec. 2004.

52 Tully, 'Two Meanings of Global Citizenship.'

14 Tell Us What's Going to Happen: Information Feeds to the War on Terror

SAMUEL NUNN

We want to know things before they occur: anticipate, react, prevent. This idea is embedded not only in counter-terrorism policy, but in the cultural narratives produced by television and cinema. Television programs such as 24 or *CSI*, and movies such as *The Conversation*, *The End of Violence*, *Minority Report*, and *The Siege* are self reflexive mirrors of the U.S. war on terror. Through tricky technology systems like the Multi-State Anti-Terrorism Information Exchange (MATRIX), Terrorism Information Awareness (TIA), Regional Information Sharing Systems (RISS), TIPOFF, AFIS, and VICAP, America seeks policies and programs – read this as machines and software – that will anticipate terrorist attacks in order to stop them before they can occur.[1] The desired outcome is complete deterrence. If this outcome were achieved, it would be the most mighty feat of prognostication and prevention ever conceived.

The reason? Doing so would require the real-time synthesis and analysis of volumes of data equal to something like the number of stars in the universe. Criminal justice technology systems produce voluminous information flows. Billions of bytes of data are constantly on the move among police agencies describing individuals, their criminal histories, assets, debt, locations at particular times, purchasing patterns, biometric identifiers (fingerprints, photographs, DNA samples), and other aspects of the people they have been in contact with or the activities they are thought to have performed. At any given moment, thousands of inquiries are sent through dozens of regional, national, and international systems seeking answers to questions about individuals' identity, where they are, what they have done, or what more other agencies and agents know about them. In 2005 the FBI's National Crime Information Center (NCIC) averaged 4.5 million inquiries per day.

Within this storm of data, terrorism is the boogeyman of the twenty-first century. And there is only one way to assuage our fears of sudden, brutal terrorist attacks: convince us that we will always uncover the conspiracies before the explosion, always know who the perpetrators are before they act, always stay one step ahead of them, always arrest them before the carnage. It is a process identified by Richard Grusin as *premediation*: a shift of focus to controlling the future and stopping attacks before they occur or, more simply, profiling the future.[2] It is the premediation of the future, an advance word about what is going to happen. This model helps us accept 9/11 as an interruption or aberration. Looking back, we had the pieces if only someone had put them together: *the plot was within our grasp.* Heroic FBI agents wrote memos, villainous or incompetent supervisors ignored them or, worse, destroyed them.[3] Mohammed Atta is on the surveillance tapes; why didn't someone *see* him? Ziad Jarrah, the pilot of United Airlines Flight 93 (destined for a Pennsylvania farm field, and now the subject of an A&E made-for-cable movie, *Flight 93* and Hollywood's *United 93*), gets a speeding ticket in Maryland on 9 September; why didn't someone *stop* him? Someone always knows. The truth is out there.

The U.S. war on terror places stock in this belief: if we know who the terrorists are, we can capture and contain them, prevent them from putting their schemes in play. If we know a sleeper cell is operating in a city's neighbourhood, the authorities can place the cell under surveillance with visual monitoring, communications interception, dialed number logs, video taping, credit card purchases, and other transaction footprints used to build a virtual sphere of information control. Alternatively, we can figure out what terrorists 'look like' through profiling, find them, surveil them, uncover their plans, and incarcerate them. We will process information to prevent terrorism.

Building on a theoretical foundation of panopticism and social control, Kevin Haggerty and Richard Ericson coined an appropriate concept for the variety of technological systems used by state and non-state entities to monitor citizens: the surveillant assemblage.[4] The assemblage is composed of many discrete technological forms used to observe and infer patterns of behaviour in the interests of control, investigation, and crime prevention. This includes closed circuit TV, governmental and corporate databases, data-mining and synthesis software, electronic surveillance systems, data-based profiling techniques, scenario analyses, integration of criminal justice databases, biometric identifiers, and so on. Information feeds to the war on terror can be conceived as representative components of a surveillant assemblage – a combination of surveillance tools used for various forms of social control, in particular those devoted to uncovering terrorist and criminal conspiracies and preventing violent crime. It is the set of surveillance components pulled together to provide information used to detect or stop crimes of violence.

Surveillant assemblages have been depicted in various ways by movies and television, and it is possible that a few movies and television shows can be read as information feeds to the war on terror. Sometimes we use technologies to prognosticate and prevent violence, and this is the theme of, for example, *The Conversation*, *Minority Report*, and *The End of Violence*. The preventive scheme depicted in *Minority Report* is the most direct: you are under arrest for the crime you *almost* committed. But at other times, in the event violent actors strike before we can stop them, there are policies, plans, and contingencies – ways to make us safe again, tactical technologies. That is the hard-edged, reactive theme of *The Siege*, for example. And for those situations where a crime is committed, at least one TV program presents the argument that our technologies will uncover truths that no one but the perpetrator could know: that's the theme of *CSI*.

These movies and TV programs show how humans generate and process surveillance information into fuel against crime and terror (as they perceive it), and offer cultural representations of the surveillant assemblage. The examples examined in these movies and TV programs suggest a complex relationship between the social and political realities of wars on crime or terror or drugs and their representation in film and media. The relationship is based less on whether one or the other is a better reflection of 'reality' than the idea that both filmed renditions and police policies are drawn from dominant cultural beliefs about criminal and terrorist behaviours. Shortly after 9/11, a brigadier general chaired several meetings of selected Hollywood writers, producers, and directors to develop terrorism scenarios that had not been considered before, as potential fuel for the development of preventive strategies.[5] Hollywood's imagination would supply the fuel for actual anti-terrorism tactics. The meetings were held in Los Angeles at the University of Southern California's Institute for Creative Technologies, whose operating revenues come largely from military contracts. James Castonguay has called meetings like this the 'cultural production of the war on terror.'[6] Numerous Hollywood productions and planned television shows were altered or postponed after 9/11 because of government concerns that they would spark creative criminal imitation and intensify public fears of future attacks. Causality is always a bit mixed up in the blend of make-believe and reality.

The surveillant assemblages depicted in movies and on television create another source of fear in society – the fear of all-encompassing 24/7 observation by unspecified others, usually the 'state,' and the subliminal belief that there must be some reason for all this surveillance, some kind of danger out there against which we must be protected. This fear feeds social acceptance of the very technological systems we ostensibly fear – as well as the perceived likelihood of criminal attacks against which they are arrayed. Because movies and TV offer popular culture's perceptions of crime and terror, their visual and narrative messages – and their strength – are especially complex feeds to the war on terror.[7]

Stopping Crimes in Action and Hiding in Plain Sight: *The End of Violence*

Machines that can monitor peoples' activities in space are part of modern law enforcement technology.[8] Surveillance systems are important, and we should quickly recognize that any reasonably sophisticated monitoring system – whether wiretaps, video surveillance, or computer eavesdropping – potentially generates so much information that it challenges interpretation. Nevertheless, one key to uncovering the plot of conspiracies is interpreting the information that has been collected in ways that anticipate the commission of a crime and allow law enforcement agents to stop the plot before execution. Vast, disconnected databases exist from which investigators can draw criminal intent. Information from wiretaps, snitch reports, BOLOs ('be on the look out'), watch lists, criminal incident descriptions, and many other sources are the data that will feed prevention efforts. But how can all this information be interpreted in a way that defines the actions to be taken? Who sits and watches, and then decides to do something?[9]

In *The End of Violence* (1997), the Los Angeles basin is under surveillance from a sophisticated closed circuit television (CCTV) system operating from Griffith Park Observatory. The prophecy of the film is that sophisticated technological surveillance systems will evolve to monitor the public and private movements of individuals, and create intelligence about what they might be doing. It is a technology that reveals intimate details. Knowing intimate details allows the system operators to anticipate the crimes they might commit (or the actions they might take), and to stop them.[10] In the movie, CCTV monitors spaces, pinpoints disorder, and has the capacity to direct potentially fatal rounds from a weapon connected to the system.

A producer of popular violent films, Mike Max, receives a manuscript that describes the deadly surveillance system, its capacity for targeted assassination, and its political implications. Max pays little attention to the document. At that point, it is not clear who sent it to him, but later it appears that the system designer, Ray Bering, probably originated it. The surveillance system manager, Brice Phelps, wants that information rescinded, and is willing to kill Max to get it. Max is snatched away by two thugs in front of his house, but then escapes from the two kidnappers intent on killing him after surveillance cameras spot the activity (a scuffle between the hit men over Max's bribery offer not to kill him), focus in, then terminate the two attackers using an automated high-power rifle. Max flees. Later, Ray Bering is killed by the surveillance system (under the direction of Brice Phelps) just as he is about to contact the police officer, Dean Brock, who was investigating Max's disappearance. Max stays out of touch and drifts away from his past life.

Before the kidnapping, Max's primary links to his wife and business associates were electronic – cell phones and emails (sitting by his pool, Max gets a phone call from his wife, sitting in her bedroom 100 feet away, to say she is leaving him) – and Max embodies the notion that identity and location are the product of the electronic signatures of cell phones and Internet connections. Who and where you are is discernible by your electronic transactions in cyberspace. Accordingly one can never hide, and with the right tools – big computers, big software, and big databases – government officials argue that they can build the ability to interdict criminal behaviour before it happens.[11] This phenomenon has been referred to as 'the disappearance of disappearence.'[12]

Despite this, and like the proverbial terrorist sleeper cell, people can hide themselves inside complex surveillance systems by being 'invisible.' Mike Max does so by taking up with a clan of Latino landscapers, who exist beneath the radar screen of electronic monitoring and remain invisible to mainstream society. The workers are part of the generic background – the immigrant workers never become visible in the figure-ground. Max's disappearing act works. He hides in plain sight at the very place he has fled. Once he is 'off the grid' of identity numbers (phones, credit cards), he is hard to track. His travels with Latino labourers confound attempts to locate him.

If there is any other way for Max and the Latino labourers to be read, it is as the contemporary model of the terrorist cell: a group existing without being seen. The message of *The End of Violence* anticipates but does not bode well for technological systems that hope to find sleeper cells by mining their credit transactions (they bought ammonium nitrate and fuel oil), or intercepting their cellular and wireless communications. But such systems require assembly and careful analysis of information. If you don't leave information trails, tracking systems can't find you. Mike Max's success remaining out of sight with the Latinos undercuts a view that current anti-terrorism policies will detect 'invisible' sleeper cells within the United States. From the perspective of 2005, it is possible to see the Latino labourers as doubles for the hidden terrorist cell.

The End of Violence was released in 1997, but its speculation about ubiquitous, all-seeing video surveillance systems was more a documentary observation by 2005. For example, within days of the 7 July 2005 London bombings, public surveillance tapes produced a visual portrait of the four suicide bombers entering London's Luton tube station at 7:21:54. This pre-attack imagery joins another famous last chance: Mohammad Atta passing through the Portland, Maine, airport at 5:45:13 on 11 September 2001. Still photographs and CCTV footage of Tim McVeigh, the Oklahoma City bomber, were taken on 17 April 1995 at a McDonalds close to the Ryder's outlet where he rented the truck destined to be his VBIED.[13] This was approximately 48 hours before he prosecuted the attack on the Murrah Building.

CCTV systems can picture the reality of terrorism conspiracies. Unfortunately, it is a reality not prevented.[14] In London, the good news was we had pictures of the suicide bombers before they struck. The bad news: who knew what they were doing? Beyond the four of them, it is not really clear. A May 2006 report on the 7 July bombings claims the four operated on their own with little or no other infrastructure.[15] The police did not know them – they were initially called 'cleanskins' by the British authorities, although the 2006 report admitted that British intelligence knew something about two of them. Nevertheless, here was the model sleeper cell, largely unknown to law enforcement. The worst news: even if somebody had known at that moment (7:21:54 a.m.), what could they have done?

At the conclusion of *The End of Violence*, Ray Bering, who has been depicted as either the designer of the surveillance system or one of its operatives (it is not clear which), is killed by the weapon controlled through his system. This surveillent assemblage does not end violence, but is a mechanism that furthers the use of violence for social control. Thus, the information feed from *The End of Violence* is broad-ranging. It depicts a panoptic system tied to a powerful, accurate, largely invisible weapon that can strike individuals down from remote locations. It is an automated sniping system that defines others as enemies of the state and executes them. Perhaps the problem in London was an incomplete assemblage – they were missing the sniping system that would have shot the suicide bombers at the tube entrance.[16] Somebody must have known they were coming. It was there on the screen.

If It Had Not Been Prevented, It Would Not Have Happened

Another information feed to the war on terror originates from the fertile, drug-driven imagination of Philip K. Dick. The goal of the high-tech systems depicted in *Minority Report* (2002)[17] is to stop homicides before they occur. This is another 'end of violence' scenario, embodying both general deterrence and incapacitation goals of contemporary punishment – what David Garland refers to as 'the new apparatus of security and prevention.'[18] The Department of Pre-Crime uses human-machine sociotechnical systems linking three psychic empaths to a future murder notification system. But this is a surveillant assemblage of a whole other kind from *The End of Violence*. The empaths experience visions of the future, and offer a 'consensus' view of the anticipated murder. (A minority report is produced if consensus is not achieved.) The vision is transferred via high-tech multi-image interactive display screens to police officers who are experienced translators and observers of empath images. They are observed by a three-member panel of judges as well as their own colleagues. The name of the (future) perpetrator is carved into a red wooden ball, thus the announcement as the 'pre-cogs' generate their vision: 'we got a Red Ball.' The red ball puts everyone on alert a crime is about to occur.

Locational inferences drawn from the visions by the police translators are relayed to pre-crime SWAT teams, who narrow down the targeted attack by travelling across the Washington, D.C., metro landscape. Upon finding the place of the yet-to-be committed crime, they stop the crime before it happens. Or put more elegantly, Pre-Crime is designed to 'prevent the future from becoming the past.'[19] But like the care taken by undercover operatives to avoid giving suspects an entrapment defence, Pre-Crime agents have to interrupt the to-be-prevented murder at just the right moment. The Pre-Crime Unit applies less-than-lethal weapons (sonic projectiles, vomit sticks) to subdue the red ball. The offender is arrested and placed into suspended animation, sentenced, then stacked inside a warehouse of vertical storage pipes that could be called less-than-lethal incarceration. The jury is the panel of judges who observed the pre-crime bust. Using the technologically enhanced record of the *future* murder that was prevented, offenders are sentenced on the basis of *not* committing the crime they would have committed had the pre-crime detection system not been in place.[20]

That is a neat way to define and measure crime prevention. It is extreme, topsy-turvy risk-oriented policing supported by advanced information technologies, an ongoing development in twenty-first century law enforcement.[21] *Minority Report's* model is machine-mediated crime prevention on steroids. Law enforcement uses technologies and techniques to protect targets at highest risk of criminal attacks. Policing becomes risk management: show us the valuable targets, and they will be defended. *Minority Report* reflects a state of phantom existentialism. Being convicted of a crime you did not commit becomes a fundamental part of the criminal justice system. I am imprisoned for a new class of crime: *the crime I would have committed.*

In an increasingly risk-averse society, this is not such a strange concept, and the twenty-first century war on terror is trying it on for size. The same principle now holds for terrorism suspects held as enemy combatants or material witnesses. They are held sans habeas corpus for long periods, de facto guilty of crimes they had not (yet) committed. This cast of characters includes a Florida college professor, Jose Padilla, Zacarias Moussouai, and other conspirators caught before executing their acts.[22] And in another iteration of *Minority Report's* less-than-lethal incarceration, the United States sometimes 'renders' its terrorism suspects to other countries with 'more advanced' methods of interrogation than can be used domestically.[23] It is an alternative version of the 'round 'em up' model: arrest enough people for the crimes they might commit, obtain confessions for crimes that might be planned, and pretty soon a state of complete incapacitation might exist.

How Do You Understand What You Hear?

If interpretation of technologically enhanced psychic visions lies at the heart of *Minority Report*, the art of synthetic inference is showcased in *The Conversation*, another information feed promoting anticipation in the interests of prevention. Like in the movies *The End of Violence* and *Minority Report*, how operators interpret intercepted communications ultimately drives the system. Every surveillant assemblage is based on interpretation by technicians who are monitoring communications in cell phones, bugs, computers, or CCTV video consoles. Somebody must interpret the information picked up from surveillance to inform law enforcement or, in the case of *The Conversation*, to eavesdrop private conversations for a client. In the film, an audio recording obtained through great technical virtuosity is painstakingly reconstructed, and then interpreted. Harry Caul, a private surveillance expert who recorded, edited, and produced the conversation (from inside the challenging, chaotic aural environment of a crowded urban park), believes a crime will occur, and based on his (inaccurate) theory of victims and villains, intervenes and discovers that the causality he inferred was misinterpreted. The crime could not be stopped even though events were anticipated. Those he thought victims were actually perpetrators. After all his efforts, an unsuspected crime occurs, one not thought of. This is the failure of preventive surveillance systems.

In an era when law enforcement and intelligence agencies internationally are intercepting millions of telephone, fax, email, and other satellite communications on a daily basis, the challenge of accurate interpretation is rarely explored. The

Echelon system, managed by the Western powers (the United States, Great Britain, New Zealand, Australia, and Canada), gobbles up international satellite communications, creating an astronomical volume of information reportedly 'interpreted' by computers of the U.S. National Security Agency.[24] It is an actual global system that remained unmentioned in one of the only movies to ever focus on the NSA: *Enemy of the State* (1998). In the midst of revelations that the United States engaged in administratively driven domestic surveillance – warrantless electronic eavesdropping in the United States since the autumn of 2001[25] – the public is given information that implies deadly terrorist plots are prevented, but few trials come to fruition, while those that do are often based on a weak evidentiary trail. And it is never clear to what extent extensive technological monitoring systems play a role in breaking these conspiracies. Even though prosecutors had compiled mountains of wiretap information on a professor at the University of South Florida, Sami al-Arian, since 1994, the U.S. attorney failed to gain a conviction on eight of the seventeen counts, and the jury deadlocked on the remaining nine.[26] Nonetheless, shadowy plots are reportedly stopped. New York City's Brooklyn Bridge was going to be destroyed by an Ohio truck driver named Iyman Faris. Another man in Columbus, Ohio, Nuradin Abdi, was indicted for a plot to explode a bomb at a shopping mall, although the indictment was unclear as to the actions taken by the men to actually implement their plot – in short, it did not matter that they were not likely to pull it off. Cases that are brought are lengthy, expensive, and contentious, subject to many different interpretations. Few are slam-dunks and many wither away, such as the trials of Jose Padilla and Zacharias Moussaoui, the 'enemy combatants' squirrelled away in Iraq and Guantanamo, and those material witnesses 'rendered' to other countries for questioning and interrogation. The truth of terrorist conspiracies is as hard to interpret as is the movie *The Conversation*.

Interestingly, *The Conversation* does not involve formal law enforcement. Instead, it is set in a shadow world of corporate security consultants – another contemporary scene on display in Iraq and the war on terror, with privatized bodyguards, private security details, Halliburton, Kellogg-Brown-Root, and the private soldiers employed by Blackwater USA.[27] But in *The Conversation*, it does not matter whether the intelligence was generated by a public servant or a private entrepreneur. Harry Caul did a yeoman's job of collecting and collating the conversation, but he interpreted it out of context. He recognized a pending act of violence, but could not stop it. Caul's preventive impotence is framed differently by John Turner: 'information gleaned from surveillance practices does not necessarily produce knowledge ... surveillance technology and its technicians may be more directly involved in creating reality rather than making a record of it.'[28] This is a permutation of the uncovered conspiracy – the busted plot – that is a primary target of U.S. anti-terrorism programs. *The Conversation* holds little constructive hope for homeland security arguments that we can prevent bad things from happening if only we interpret the information correctly.

Revising the Scene of the Crime

We are led to believe that we always leave information trails, that there are those who have the heightened senses of psychic bloodhounds who can find our trail and find us. Another information feed to the war on terror is our belief that the mediated crime scene investigator – the forensic specialist – can always de-construct and re-construct crimes in ways that lead to their solution. This is the idea of *CSI*: we will use data to identify perpetrators, solve crimes, make arrests. In *CSI* it is working backward to reconstruct an event – becoming all-knowing in reverse.

The lesson is simple: once a crime has occurred via murder or bombing or arson, the physical evidence left behind can be identified, imaged, categorized, sorted, and analysed to create hypotheses about unwitnessed crimes. We will apply forensic approaches to bombing sites, the place of terrorist crimes. The guilty parties will be deduced from an analysis of evidence. In the 7 July 2006 London bombings, the 'bomb factory' at 18 Alexandra Grove contained forensic evidence physically connected to three of the four suicide bombers, and there were numerous CCTV images of all four suicide bombers, separate and together, that ultimately placed them at London's Luton Station. The official report identified where the four bombers sat on the subway trains and bus – based on forensic evidence. Data recreate the event, and the investigators reveal, picture, and divine the truth from the data they find and interpret. This is the same as preventing an attack before it occurs, but in the opposite direction.

On the other side of the TV screen in Washington, DC, the Terrorism Information Awareness (TIA) program crafted by the U.S. Department of Homeland Security, to be fully developed by the Defense Advanced Research Projects Administration (DARPA), was a data-mining program that would use preconceived scenarios of terrorist attacks to guide the data search and look for data transaction patterns that might be signifiers for planned terrorist attacks. Ultimately, TIA's potential for sinking Western conceptions of personal privacy was the reason it sunk. But for both *CSI* and the deposed TIA program, the idea is to use data to solve problems. You create pictures and scenarios and think about how to interpret and react to them. It is an exercise in reverse synthesis.

U.S. anti-terrorism operatives formulate scenarios of terrorist attack, then the data signatures that these attacks might generate are hunted nationally or internationally in a vast field of computerized purchase, travel, lodging, and movement transactions. By 2005 the federal homeland security infrastructure produced a short list of likely terrorist incidents. These included an emergency vehicle-borne improvised explosive device (VBIED) within a sports stadium; trucks spraying anthrax spores on city streets; pneumonic plague germ releases in bathrooms of airports, train stations, and sporting events; and others.[29] The federal DHS calls them 'all-hazards planning scenarios.' Fifteen scenarios involving chemical, nuclear, biological, radiological (CNBR), explosive, and cyber attacks are profiled.[30] The preventive idea was to figure out how to anticipate such events by uncovering the precursor actions that perpetrators would have to perform. As James Elroy might put it, 'police pinpoint perpetrators performing precursor potshots.'

Ironically, read through the perspective of *CSI*, one can observe that these scenarios provide a blueprint for terrorists. The scenarios describe the general plan for successful CNBR and explosive attacks, setting out the basic plot and resulting damage from each attack, assuming each one is at least partially successful. If terrorists take the *CSI* approach after closely considering the various scenarios, they can move in reverse from their anticipated crimes to a better designed plot that defies prevention.[31] This is at least one of the inferences to be drawn from Brian Jackson et al.'s RAND Corporation report on group learning among terrorist groups.[32] Tactics mutate.

In a looking-glass world, this is the way of *CSI*: given a crime, use forensic technologies to 'back into' what happened. But to deliver value added in the war on terror, from the crime to the causes is the wrong direction, and that is a problem with the *CSI* model: it is backwards. It is not that post-crime forensics data cannot generate insights in the future, it is that the real goal is to prevent the crime from happening. That requires data assembly and exploration in advance of the crime. This was the publicized promise of TIA and MATRIX, and it is certainly one of the objectives of current terrorism scenario-building exercises. TIA and MATRIX exist now primarily in spirit, but aspects of each continue – particularly scenario-building and information sharing. For the war on terror, the really important idea is to prevent attacks, not necessarily to understand them after they happen.

What's Your Reaction Time?

Even though the causal arrow of *CSI* runs the wrong way, if data can be divined to give us a better than average guess about the future, one obvious question is how much time is left before the attack – if we even know it is coming. At one extreme is the short time frame: the prevention of a terrorist plot slowly uncovered during the last twenty-four hours before it is scheduled to occur (TV's *24*). It poses the question of stopping a terrorist plot as quickly as possible. What is required is improvisational planning to satisfy short-term preventive goals. The timing of prevention is important – as it is in the film *Minority Report* – so that law enforcement personnel are not too late or, what is almost worse, they become agent *provocateurs*. At one extreme, the attack is thwarted in the 'nick of time,' but at the other, too much lead time means that interdictions might only 'shapeshift' terrorist plans into later successful attacks.

Cells learn from mistakes, and react tactically to anti-terrorism measures. There is a viral aspect to this: mediated representations of successful crime and terror attacks can inform real criminals and terrorists of vulnerabilities and strategies. By changing they might become better. Jackson et al. studied how Aum Shinrikyo, Hezbollah, Jemaah Islamiyah, the Provisional Irish Republican Army, and environmental/animal rights groups learned and adapted to changing patterns of attack and counterattack.[33]

For terrorists, it is a commission sales challenge: mount enough attacks and pretty soon one is successful. Spontaneous attacks might be possible, but mass casualty events – required to draw worldwide public attention to the event – must be planned and are unlikely to just be lucky breaks. By viewing filmed versions of how technologies are used to prevent crime, criminal agents can engage in social learning and devise more effective attack strategies. It is probably impossible to determine whether this occurs or not.

Consider the criminal use of a nuclear device (the topic of *The Sum of All Fears*). If you have knowledge of the time and place of a deadly attack that can only be obtained through torture, how far are you willing to go to get that information? (This appears to be at least in part the question addressed in *24*; by the fourth season of the series, in 2005, a few years after the Abu Ghraib scandal, torture had become a bi-directional feature of *24*, practised by good guys and bad guys alike.) Among the worst case scenarios are nuclear devices or, in the 'lite' version, radioactive dirty bombs. The French in Algeria went to great lengths in the early 1950s to end civilian bombings and other attacks by the National Liberation Front (FLN), including torture and execution by guillotine (both shown convincingly in *The Battle of Algiers*). *The Siege* offers an even more straightforward view: society will strong-arm suspects possessing deadly intent. Contemporary suicide bombers were once considered mad bombers, but contemporary profiling efforts consider them to be sane and generally rational.[34] Suicide bombings produce high casualty rates, and they are poster children for the ticking-bomb question. The largely unstated philosophical rationale of government officials is clear: harming one person who has knowledge of future lethal attacks in order to save many is justified. If 200 are at risk, one person with relevant information might easily be tortured or killed as a means towards extracting preventive information. Should this be measured in the number of lives saved or maimings prevented? How can you measure that if you never really know? It is hard to identify the consequences of a future that you have not seen.

Go back to the London bomber quartet and the 9/11 hijacker duo, where CCTV technology systems were in use. In the case of the subway/bus bombers, their video at Luton Station was recorded at 7:22 a.m. Three bombs went off in the tubes one hour and forty minute later, at 8:50 a.m., and one more in a bus about an hour after that. Could a SWAT team intercept them and disrupt their attack in an hour and a half (or, two and a half hours for the bus attack)? In the other CCTV warning, Mohammad Atta is heading to the Bangor-to-Boston flight. The lead time for prevention was more favourable here. It is 5:45 a.m., three hours before the plane they piloted crashed into the World Trade Center, at 8:46 a.m. Three full hours in which to mount a preventive operation. The problem was that no one was watching. There were no empaths clued into future terrorist attacks, no insightful technicians monitoring live-feed CCTV, no automated sniping system, no daring interpreters of intercepted data. The Pre-Crime Unit for anti-terrorism was incomplete. It only took one unpredicted murder attempt to disprove the worth of pre-crime interdiction units. How many does it take to discredit reliance on CCTV surveillance systems?

Final Resort: The Technology of Military Control

Despite these dreams of invincibility, terrorist acts do occur. And when they do, the U.S. policy response is usually retaliatory. The United States fires missiles; it destroys property, invades countries. It shoots missiles in order to kill single individuals. Sometimes, it occupies space. Another information feed to the U.S. war on terror is explored in *The Siege* (1998), and it is interesting to recognize that *The Siege* was released in 1998, well in advance of 9/11, long before the torture chambers of Abu Ghraib, the U.S.A. Patriot Act, or the intelligence-sharing problems identified after the 9/11 attacks. It represents another kind of surveillant assemblage.

The Siege speculates on the existence of domestic sleeper cells of suicidal terrorists, presenting a spooky prophesy of the political and military approach to uncontrollable suicide terrorism possible in the United States. The movie proposes U.S. willingness to intern large numbers of citizens selected using ethnic profiling as a counter-terrorism tool, and to use torture to extract information. It portrays the FBI in competition with the CIA, which has withheld information that would have helped the FBI's investigation. In this the FBI and the military are also in conflict and, in a twisted way, the FBI, CIA, and army operate much like the independent sleeper cells they are seeking – no agency knows what the others are doing. The CIA's chief undercover informant turns out to be a suicide bomber, in disguise as a moderate Muslim; the CIA has literally been in bed with him.[35] At the most obvious level, the failure of data sharing between the FBI and the CIA – a major plot device in *The Siege* – anticipates the charges of intelligence failure generated by 9/11 post mortem analyses. That the two agencies do not play well together is taken as standard now.

A major technological referent in *The Siege* is the use of sophisticated improvised explosive devices (IEDs), especially vehicle-borne (VB) IEDs, by the sleeper cell terrorist groups. This includes a simulated bus attack with a paint explosion that anticipates the real thing; paint bombs were a dress rehearsal to suicide attacks on key governmental assets such as New York's FBI headquarters. The use of tactical, coordinated VBIED suicide attacks in Iraq would follow in six years, and if the Iraqi insurgent groups have not seen *The Siege*, be assured that many senior U.S. politico-military officials have.

Through another lens, *The Siege* is a blueprint for a fascist future driven by a counter-terrorist infrastructure built to respond to terrorist acts. Its real-life predecessor was the Argentinean dirty war model of 1976-83: Buenos Aires, the Naval Mechanics School, the *disappeared*, and torture, all born of an Argentinean military tribunal's no-holds-barred war on Montonero terror. There were an estimated 30,000 civilian casualties.[36] *The Siege* shows one form of social control that a government might initiate in the midst of an uncontrollable outbreak of suicide bombings. The inability to stop the ultimate smart weapon of mass destruction, human suicide bombers, drives the transformation of Manhattan real estate into a prison camp. Unable to find a needle in a haystack, the tactical response is to incarcerate the haystack.

Since at least 1999 national armies and police agencies have repeatedly practised establishing *The Siege* – style security environments at 'globalization' events – meetings of the World Trade Organization, the G8, and others. Robert Warren writes about urban 'pop-up armies' composed of combined law enforcement and military personnel engaged in security and suppression[37] – they aim to protect members of the G8 or WTO at their regular meetings. Fortified zones of public defence surround meetings of international business and political leaders. The 'anarchists' and 'black block' play the same role they played in the late nineteenth century: even if you do not see them, they are there. Protesters are the attackers against which security forces are arrayed. Soldiers and police practise their manoeuvres. Less-than-lethal weapons are used as much for efficiency in controlling or dispersing crowds as for the excuse to exercise the tactics of the police and military to coordinate control over urban spaces.

The Siege has two other psychic linkages with the real war on terror since 2002: direct torture in the interrogation room and the unmoored terror of internment camps. Torture is a sociotechnology that hones powers of prediction: apply pain, obtain plot details, the names of others, more arrests, more torture, until the plot is uncovered and stopped. Torture becomes a tool of prediction. Internment creates the spectre of losing family members to profiling operations (e.g., pick up Arab males between the ages of eighteen and twenty-eight, and detain them; offer the possibility of physical torture.). This anticipated the Abu Ghraib scandal and current U.S. policies towards incarceration of enemy combatants and potential terrorists.

The lesson is simple: the United States and other collaborating governments are fascinated with controlling actions and behaviour by controlling space, and they have had plenty of practice. *The Siege* offers a blueprint for a lockdown on urban space and alternative visions of American civil liberties in the post 9/11 era. It is another information feed to the war on terror.

Conclusions

Visual media mirror the approaches that societies use to fight terrorism, but interpreting what is seen in that mirror requires more of a through-the-looking-glass approach. Episodes from movies can clearly foreshadow the performance of actual police intelligence systems. There might be a positive feedback loop in which cinema validates the performance of technology systems by showing their successes and failures. Is *The Siege* a direct descendant of the French-Algerian War or a prophecy of fighting a global insurgency in Iraq?

Films such as *The End of Violence, The Conversation,* and *Minority Report* suggest that we have only limited abilities to interpret the information that we intercept. Technologies give us a capacity for vast data collection (CCTV, wiretaps, crime reports, dialed number logs, incident characteristics, watch lists, etc.), but framing information into a preventive model is a far more challenging affair. Information and intelligence might remain unexamined, unanalysed, or untranslated for hours, days, weeks, or months. As the analytical lag grows, crimes become harder to prevent. The time periods for windows of action narrow, and prevention becomes increasingly difficult. Technology systems produce images that are fuzzy or unclear, audio that is garbled – 'what was that sound? ... who's in that picture?' Video monitoring pictures terrorists before they strike, but images are so remote and unexamined before the crime that no predictive value is possible. How can we monitor in real time so many people from so many places?

Alternatively, the information that is available might not be used or fully understood. We can misinterpret information, as in *The Conversation*. FBI informants can fail to recognize or fail to report that they have rented rooms to future 9/11 perpetrators, or the wiretap information that the FBI collects on a terrorism suspect for years can, after all, be insufficient for conviction. Patterns of radical Islamists taking aviation lessons are missed or ignored.

CSI offers an alternative information feed of infinite, technologically enhanced justice: using the tools of forensic science, we will solve each crime so that the guilty are brought to justice or the innocent exonerated. We will explain every crime, but we will not necessarily prevent crimes. In real life, some of the forensic evidence collected (fingerprints, DNA, images, ballistics, drugs, chemical compounds, bodily fluids) might take months to be tested, unlike *CSI*'s mostly instantaneous turnaround of forensic analysis. These time delays allow other crimes to happen.

And in the real-life time it actually takes to complete forensics tests, terrorist incidents do occur. As reactions to terrorist acts evolve, so *The Siege* feeds the war on terror from one tactical technology to control urban space and use profiling to incarcerate many people under general suspicion of potential terrorist (or 'insurgent') behaviour (e.g., persons of interest, enemy combatants, or ethnic and religious groups). This model is practised by countries hosting world organization meetings (sites of 'pop-up armies'), used by U.S. jurisdictions in major political gatherings such as the Republican National Convention (so-called national security events), and applied most assuredly but less successfully to the ongoing Iraq War.

Information feeds to the war on terror come from many sources. The failure of police and intelligence bureaus to share information in ways that can help prevent terrorist attacks is a central theme of *The Siege*, as much as the movie is a well-documented critique of failed data sharing between the FBI and the CIA, or the lack of coordination among law enforcement agencies generally (e.g., the FBI, DEA, and local police). Abu Ghraib is both a reflection of where the incarcerated of *The Siege* were headed and the latest evolution of the war on terror: the ticking bomb and the threat of sudden randomized death must be stopped, and this will justify any technology or tactic to bring about the end of violence. We are perhaps being conditioned to accept torture and warrantless wiretapping as a means to anti-terrorism. In *The Conversation*, Harry Caul's failure to correctly interpret the lovers' dialogue can be viewed in much the same way as the failure of U.S. attorneys, using extensive wiretap information, to obtain convictions against a Florida professor, under investigation since 1995, for various terrorism charges. The concept of Pre-Crime feeds current anti-terrorism policies. It also feeds us some of the informational, operational, technological, ethical, and philosophical quandaries of crime prevention.

Information feeds to the war on terror show how media representations of surveillance assemblages create fear about the criminal acts that they are meant to prevent, as well as fear surveillance tools will be used against people for lesser or no crimes. Deploying the tool creates fear because it implies a danger lurking in society, one to be guarded against. Technology is used to fight risk, and if it is risky we are probably afraid of it. It creates fear of the lurking danger. This ratchets up public fears of future crimes. Deployment also creates a fear that the tool could be turned around and used against any citizen for any reason. Almost anyone could be targeted by thermal imaging and located via a global positioning system providing data to a local geographical information system (e.g., utility customers). It could happen to anybody. We are afraid of the indiscriminate use of the surveillant assemblange. The concluding scene of *The Conversation*, in which Harry Caul sits in the rubble of his destroyed apartment (ruined during the unsuccesful search for a hidden eavesdropping bug), is eloquent cinematic imagery of our fear of surveillance.

The overriding message of these information feeds to the war on terror is the final reality that they represent: a failure to recognize that neither technologies, techniques, nor luck will protect us fully from the true believers. (Part of the question here is on what 'side' the true believer resides – the zealous Army interrogator who uses torture and death or the suicide bomber?) Stopping plots is tough, especially since actionable prophecy is not the primary product of U.S. police agencies. By far, they react to crimes ex post, and do not prevent many crimes ex ante – an exception respectfully granted to *The Minority Report*. Even basic crime stats in the United States – *Uniform Crime Reports* – are called 'crimes known to the police,' as if there has to be a point at which the police are notified that a crime has occurred for it to have *actually* occurred. It becomes worse when we consider issues linked to unreported crime and victimization reports. Prevention hovers in the background, rarely able to take centre stage. Despite this, a model of perfect predictive action is the underlying objective of many of the world's counter-terrorism programs.[38] The data produced in this maelstrom of anti-terrorism meanwhile continue to accumulate. We are expected to believe that with the right technological tools, those data will tell us what will happen so that we can stop it before it does. But when we think we know what is happening, why are we so surprised when we find out it is wrong?

Notes

1 MATRIX was a data-mining operation originally designed to select likely terrorists out of a batch of names, based on criminal records, residential locations, travel patterns, purchase transactions, and other electronic databases; it began with a dozen states in 2002, crash dieted to four, than died after federal funding ended in 2005. TIA never made it off the ground after widespread fears of domestic political abuse, and the role of former felon John Poindexter as its director. RISS is going strong, forming the core of several regional law enforcement information networks; the organization responsible for RISS is the Institute for Intergovernmental Research in Florida. TIPOFF is a terrorist watch list supposedly slated for merger with other watch lists maintained by a dozen federal agencies. AFIS is the automated fingerprint information system, and VICAP is the violet criminal apprehension program, the FBI's software equivalent of Clarice Starling. For more on these contemporary tools of twenty-first century law enforcement, see Bureau of Justice Assistance, *The RISS Program 2002* (Washington: Office of Justice Programs, U.S. Department of Justice, June 2003); U.S. General Accounting Office, *Terrorist Watch Lists Should Be Consolidated to Promote Better Integration and Sharing* (Washington: Author, GAO 03–322, April 2003); William Krouse, 'The Multi-state Anti-terrorism Information Exchange (MATRIX) Pilot Project,' *CRS Report for Congress* (Washington: Congressional Research Service, Library of Congress, Order code RL32536, 18 Aug. 2004); and Gina Marie Stevens, 'Privacy: Total Information Awareness Programs and Related Information Access, Collection, and Protection Laws,' *CRS Report for Congress* (Washington: Congressional Research Service, Library of Congress, Order code RL31798, 21 March 2003).
2 Richard Grusin, 'Premediation,' *Criticism* 46/1 (2004): 17–39.
3 See National Commission on Terrorist Attacks upon the United States, *The 9-11 Commission Report: Final Report of the National Commission on Terrorist Attacks upon the United States* (New York: Norton, 2004).
4 Kevin Haggerty and Richard Ericson, 'The Surveillant Assemblage,' *British Journal of Sociology* 51/4 (2000): 605–22.
5 J. Hoberman, 'All as It Had Been: Hollywood Revises History, Joins the Good Fight,' *Village Voice*, 5-11 Dec. 2001. Available at http://www.villagevoice.com/film/ 0149,fhoberman,30447,20.html, accessed 21 Nov. 2004.
6 James Castonguay, 'Conglomeration, New Media, and the Cultural Production of the War on Terror,' *Cinema Journal* 43/4 (2004): 102.
7 This suggests ideas about the size of the information feed, the flow volume of the pipeline. How many people see these media representations of police technologies (e.g., how many viewers of *The Minority Report, The End of Violence, The Conversation*)? How many weekly viewings are there of *CSI*, a show that runs approximately 10 to 12 one-hour episodes per week in many U.S. cable systems? The answers are large, in the millions. That's a lot of potential influence.
8 Raymond Foster, *Police Technology* (New York: Prentice-Hall, 2005), 287–327.

9 See Stephen Fay, who analyses the behaviour of those sitting in front of CCTV monitoring screens. 'Tough on Crime, Tough on Civil Liberties: Some Negative Aspects of Britain's Wholesale Adoption of CCTV Surveillance during the 1990s,' *International Review of Law, Computers and Technology* 12/2 (1998): 315–47.

10 The 2000 *Kyllo* decision by the U.S. Supreme Court found that when technologies such as thermal imaging cameras – used against Kyllo by local police to show heat loss from his house allegedly attributable to marijuana cultivation – reveal intimate details, their use makes it a search, which requires a warrant. Nobody obtained a warrant to use thermal imaging on the Kyllo house. Technologies that reveal intimate details are by definition searches, and for these technology scans to be legal, warrants must be obtained in the United States.

11 In the post-2001 war on terror, this was the model behind the MATRIX system that was used by a number of U.S. states, as well as the theory behind the Terrorist Information Awareness program. Various databases could be mined for people that fit particular profiles believed to reflect terrorist behavior. See Jeffrey W. Siefert, 'Data Mining: An Overview,' *CRS Report for Congress* (Washington: Congressional Research Service, Library of Congress, Order code RL31798, 3 May 2004); Krouse, 'The MATRIX Pilot Project.' The story of how a former drug courier-turned-DEA snitch designed the original template for the MATRIX program is detailed in Michael Shnayerson, 'The Danger List,' *Vanity Fair* (Dec. 2004): 232–246.

12 Haggerty and Ericson, 'Surveillant Assemblage,' 620.

13 W. Diffie and S. Landau, *Privacy on the Line: The Politics of Wiretapping and Encryption* (Cambridge: MIT Press, 1998), 267.

14 Brandon Welsh and David Farrington find that CCTV systems appear to reduce criminal activity in a limited number of places (e.g., parking garages). 'Effects of Closed-Circuit Television on Crime,' *Annals of the American Academy of Political and Social Sciences* 587 (May 2003): 110–35.

15 House of Commons (U.K.), *Report of the Official Account of the Bombings in London on 7th July 2005*, HC 1087 (London: Stationery Office, 11 May 2006).

16 A passenger suspected to be a bomber (but later shown to be innocent of any wrongdoing) actually was killed by local police in the wake of the bombing investigation. It is unclear whether he was fleeing the police, or was mistakenly believed to be one of the suspects in the earlier failed bombing attempts on 21 July 2005. The London police shot Jean Charles de Menezes, a Brazilian electrician, to death on 22 July 2005, after Menezes was followed by the police into a subway train. The police fired 11 shots, striking Menezes in the head seven times and once in the shoulder. He was not a terrorist nor any kind of criminal. For further detail see Wikepedia, 'Jean Charles de Menezes,' available at http://en.wikipedia.org/wiki/Jean_Charles_de_Menezes, accessed 1 Jan. 2006.

17 Adapted from Phillip K. Dick, 'Minority Report,' 1956, available at http://www.philipkdick.com/works_stories.html accessed 22 Dec. 2005.

18 David Garland, *The Culture of Control: Crime and Social Order in Contemporary Society* (Chicago: University of Chicago Press, 2001), 170.

19 Richard Grusin, 'Premediation,' *Criticism* 46/1 (2004): 19.

20 The film mostly focuses on the Pre-Crime Commander John Atherton's red ball for an inexplicable murder. Atherton tries to exonerate himself from a pre-crime indictment, and is ultimately placed in suspended animation (less than lethal) incarceration, before solving the case and exacting revenge. Interest here is on the Pre-Crime sociotechnical systems.

21 Described by Richard Ericson and Kevin Haggerty, in *Policing the Risk Society* (Toronto: University of Toronto Pres, 1997).

22 For a recent New York City conspiracy see Craig Horowitz, 'Anatomy of a Foiled Plot,' *New York Magazine* (6 Dec. 2004). Reprinted in *The Best American Crime Writing*, James Elroy, ed. (New York: Harper, 2005), available at http://newyorkmetro.com/nymetro/news/features/10559/, accessed 23 Nov. 2005.

23 Michael Garcia, *Renditions: Constraints Imposed by Laws on Torture* (Washington: Congressional Research Service, Library of Congress, Order code RL32890, 22 Sept. 2005), available at http://www.fas.org/main/home.jsp.

24 European Parliament, *Report on the Existence of a Global System for the Interception of Private and Commercial Communications (ECHELON Interception System)* (2001/2098(INI), Final A5-0264/2001, 11 July 2001, available at www.fas.org, accessed 3 Nov. 2004.

25 James Risen and Eric Lichtblau, 'Bush Lets U.S. Spy on Callers without Courts,' *New York Times* (16 Dec. 2005), available at www.nytimes.com, accessed 16 Dec. 2005; Morton Halperin, *A Legal Analysis of the NSA Warrantless Surveillance Program* (Washington: Center for American Progress, 5 Jan. 2006), available at http://www.americanprogress.org/, accessed 9 Jan. 2006.

26 Phil Long and Martin Merzer, 'Jury Clears Former Florida Professor of Terrorism-Related Charge,' *Miami Herald* (6 Dec. 2005), available at http://uniset.ca/terr/news/miamiher_alarianacquit.html, accessed 2 Jan. 2006.

27 This at least faintly resembles the 2004-6 private wiretapping case in Los Angeles, involving Anthony Pellicano, a private detective to the rich and powerful in the Hollywood region.

28 John Turner II, 'Collapsing the Interior/Exterior Distinction: Surveillance, Spectacle, and Suspense in Popular Cinema,' *Wide Angle* 20/4 (1998): 109.

29 Eric Lipton, 'U.S. Report Lists Possibilities for Terrorist Attacks and Likely Toll,' *New York Times* (16 March 2005), available at http://www.nytimes.com, accessed 2 Jan. 2006. Most of these disaster scenarios have a pre-existing array of mediated representations: *Black Sunday*'s attack on the Superbowl, the subway hijacking in *The Taking of Pelham One Two Three*, the plague depicted in *Outbreak*, the bank customers turned to individual (suicide) bombers suggested by *Swordfish*, and the nuclear terrorists depicted in *Sum of All Fears* and *Peacemaker* are cinematic examples of terrorist attack scenarios.

30 Homeland Security Council, *Planning Scenarios Executive Summaries: Created for Use in National, Federal, State, and Local Homeland Security Preparedness Activities* (Washington: Report in partnership with the U.S. oDepartment of Homeland Security, July, 2004), available at http://www.altheim.com/lit/planning_scenarios_exec_summary.html, accessed 28 March 2005.

31 As a result, there have been frequent attempts by U.S. administrative agencies to restrict the distribution of critical infrastructure information, as well as strategic and tactical analyses of terrorist operations.

32 Brian Jackson, J.C. Baker, K. Cragin, J. Parachini, H. Trujillo, and P. Chalk, *Aptitude for Destruction*, vol. 1, *Organization Learning in Terrorist Groups and Its Implications for Combating Terrorism*, report prepared for the National Institute of Justice (Santa Monica: RAND Corporation, 2005).

33 Ibid.

34 Robert Pape, *Dying to Win: The Strategic Logic of Suicide Terrorism* (New York: Random House, 2005); Scott Atran, 'Genesis of Suicide Terrorism,' *Science* 299 (7 March 2003): 1534–39.

35 In 2000-1, two of the 9/11 hijackers rented rooms in the house of an FBI informant. National Commission on Terrorist Attacks upon the United States, *The 9-11 Commission Report*, 223.

36 Marguerite Feitlowitz, *A Lexicon of Terror: Argentina and the Legacies of Torture* (Oxford: Oxford University Press, 1998). The U.S. military has long been involved in training and support of Latin American military officials who engage in state terrorism. See material on the School of the Americas in Fort Benning, Georgia, and its current form as the Western Hemisphere Institute for Security Cooperation (WHINSEC). The role of this U.S. military training school in Latin American affairs, including training for government troops in Columbia, can be found at http://www.ciponline.org/facts/soa.htm, accessed 5 Nov. 2005.

37 Robert Warren, 'Situating the City and September 11th: Military Urban Doctrine, 'Pop-up' Armies and Spatial Chess,' *International Journal of Urban and Regional Research* 26/3 (2002): 614–19.

38 Yonah Alexander, ed., *Combatting Terrorism: Strategies of Ten Countries* (Ann Arbor: University of Michigan Press, 2002).

15 Grammar of Terrorism:
Captivity, Media, and a Critique of Biopolitics

MICHAEL DARTNELL

'Captivity' is like a pool of water, a changeable shape within definite bounds that themselves shift, move, and reshape over time and in response to water itself. Water is a metaphor that functions as a mirror as well, reflecting society and events. Using water as a metaphor takes up Katherine Hayles's reference to 'the illusion of control' that plagues human consciousness, a control that occurs in a context of chaos and emergence.[1] Water channels the complex currents that frustrate attempts to clarify terrorism. The complexity and vacuity of 'terrorism' is present in many images of contemporary politics, including photos of abuse in Iraq's Abu Ghraib prison, images of British troops beating Iraqi youth in Basra, the outrage provoked by publication of cartoons of the Prophet Mohammed, and images of the devastation, panic, and despair in Lebanon after the July 2006 Israeli intrusion.

A focus on terrorism obviously entails an at least temporary abandonment or sublimation of meta-narratives of terror in favour of comparison. However, failure to apprehend the totality of human relations does not mean that we should retreat into immobility. Instead, we might preface our interpretations with modesty as to their reach, focus on our purposes, and imagine how to achieve them. In this chapter, captivity is explored as a means of understanding the complexity and uneven-ness of terrorism as a theory and a behaviour. As many examples suggest, captivity ironically embodies a form of intercultural communication because it is linked to processes such as the extension of American ideas of free trade and exchange into the Mediterranean through conflict with the Barbary States. Captivity takes its meaning from the communication of information within specific narrative structures, such as the one that rationalized 'civilizing' the American wilderness by pushing Native Americans from their ancestral lands. In such cases, captivity is practised by both sides to conflict, but ultimately laden with Euro-American reason for intruding into, reconfiguring, and rendering obsolete non-European narratives.

Terrorism

Captivity is now usually seen through the optics of terrorism as 'hostage-taking' or 'kidnapping.' The frame takes the practice out of its historical and cultural context, ignoring how seizing and holding bodies for ransom, political favour, or some other end has long been carried out in Western societies. The discussion following uncouples captivity from the umbrella of terrorism in order to clarify a genealogy. By explicitly linking contemporary practices to their historical antecedents, we gain insight into the scope, breadth, and depth of contemporary crises such as the seizure of U.S. soldiers in the Iraq war, the 'kidnapping' of Israeli soldiers by Hamas and Hezbollah in 2006, and even the 9/11 hijackings. We learn, for example, that the American experience with foreign captivity has a pedigree: 'the total number of Americans held hostage by Morocco and Algiers from 1784 to 1796 was approximately 150 men. Of that number, the United States government, friends of the hostages, or foreign diplomats succeeded in liberating an estimated 112. The remaining hostages are unaccounted for or died in captivity.'[2]

In this genealogy, American captives in the Barbary Wars were understood as having fallen into the hands of 'barbarians' (hence, Barbary States) or 'heathens' (i.e., Moslems) or 'pirates.' The term 'terrorist' was not used at the time of the conflict, but has been written into it today.[3] What we see is that 'the Barbary captivity narrative closely stitches together the textual representations of Africa, the Americas, and England.'[4] In other words, the 'menace' of terrorism can be interpreted within a pattern of similar antecedents. Although narratives of captivity in the Anglo-American world have European (British) origins, the fetishization and fantasization of captivity now largely emanates from the United States, where prisons, social inequalities, the military-industrial complex, big oil, and a broadly applied culture of 'security' produce specific understandings of 'freedom,' the body, and property. In general, such understanding is based in a hierarchical and polarizing view of other global cultures.

Terrorism is currently a public, government, and media obsession. Since 9/11 it has displaced development, missile defence, and other issues from the forefront of the global agenda. Yet there is no clear consensus as to the meaning of the significr 'terrorism,' which lacks conceptual coherence. Terrorism generally refers to armed groups, organizations, or governments that the West does not like or understand (although there are even broader applications since the U.S.A. Patriot Act makes it a crime to support and encourage terrorism). Terrorism is, moreover, linked to Western notions of the state and the belief that the West has historically been a force for international stability, which, in light of the history of colonialism and two globally devastating world wars (the prelude to a hands-off attitude towards human betterment in the majority world), is debatable. A great deal of the problem with the term is that 'ism' suggests a unity, coherence, and ideological basis, like liberalism, conservatism, socialism, or fascism. However, a neat label is difficult to apply to the broad range of behaviours that are labelled 'terrorist.'

In looking at terrorism, the lack of precision and extensiveness of the label readily becomes apparent. Among the chief difficulties with the terrorist label is that it is applied to a wide variety of insurgencies, assassinations, bombings, national liberation movements, governing elites, and killings. The term is hyper-inflated. It mainly refers to groups that are uncommon, unusual, or unpopular, instead of to a distinct form of political behaviour that characterizes the contemporary world. In relation to the Iraq War, 'terrorism' refers to groups that resist a botched occupation following an illegal war. In Afghanistan, it refers to a resistance movement spawned by neglect and thirty years of cynical interference by the Great Powers. In the case of al-Qaeda, terrorism grew out of deep American and European cultural roots and long-standing policies that reflect fear of Islam, contempt for Moslems, and a disregard for Moslem lives.

Terrorism is puzzling because it is so feared and reviled, yet it generally threatens a limited and sometimes specific portion of a given population. In any given year, the U.S. death toll due to automobile accidents far exceeds deaths from terrorism, but the latter remains *the* public and government priority. Beyond the lack of danger for the vast majority of the population, terrorism rarely threatens the existence of states. An overview of U.S. statistics from 2001 illustrates the extent of actual physical danger from terrorism (seen in approximately 2,800 deaths on 9/11) in relation to conventional threats. In 2001, according to the National Highway Traffic Safety Administration of the U.S. Department of Transportation, in the fifty U.S. states there were 23,139 roadway departure fatalities (including run-off-the-road and head-on fatalities usually linked to fatigue, drowsiness, inattention, carelessness, distraction, and poor visibility); 8,876 intersection fatalities, 4,882 pedestrian fatalities; and 5,082 fatalities in crashes involving large trucks.[5] According to the FBI, the number of murders in the United States in 2001 was 13,752.[6] In the same year, the U.S. National Institute for Mental Health reported that the total number of suicide deaths was 30,622.

The death toll from today's wars yields a similar portrait. Since the war in Iraq started in 2003 following the U.S.-led invasion, Iraq Body Count estimates of the number of civilians reported killed by military intervention range from a minimum of 39,460 to a maximum of 43, 927 persons.[7] Meanwhile, on 28 July 2006, the *Washington Post* reported that total fatalities for U.S. service personnel in Operation Iraqi Freedom was at 2,559, while, that for Operation Enduring Freedom (the Afghan campaign) was at 320. These numbers are in contrast to the approximately 2,800 fatalities on 9/11. Obviously, no one group of dead deserves an effective policy response more than another, but what does merit attention are the *reasons* for government responses. If a response is based in a need to respond to threats to the greatest number of avoidable deaths, then a response to 9/11 should not be a priority. The threat of terrorism is not a threat to 'life itself,' but one of a different order, namely, to perceptions of security and the symbolic bases of social and political order. As a response to 9/11, then, the invasions of Afghanistan and Iraq occurred for symbolic and perceptual reasons rather than as a result of direct threats to the greatest number of U.S. citizens. 'Terrorists' are no doubt aware of this impact and, accordingly, frame their actions in communicative terms such as 'negotiation,' getting media attention, and sowing panic over perceived disorder.

Accompanying the communicative aspect of terrorism seen above, contemporary analyses of terrorism have a deeply embedded biopolitical character. Considering the general theoretical impoverishment of theories of terrorism, biopolitics is not a consciously adopted framework, but rather based in the assumptions underlying research. Biopolitics, as Michel Foucault sets out the term, appears in theories of terrorism in two principal manners. The first manner is a pastoral, shepherding or custodial view of the state. In this respect, Foucault notes that the biopolitical moment is based in an 'endeavour, begun in the eighteenth century, to rationalize the problems presented by governmental practice by the phenomena characteristic of a group of living human beings constituted as a population: health, sanitation, birthrate, longevity, race.'[8]

The second manner in which biopolitics appears is in the view that a central abuse of terrorism violates 'life itself.' Foucault notes that biopolitics treats the '"population" as a mass of living and coexisting beings who present particular biological and pathological traits and who thus come under specific knowledge and technologies. And this "biopolitics" itself must be understood in terms of a theme developed as early as the seventeenth century: the management of state forces.'[9] Foucault traces the narrative of today's state to that built by Louis XIV, which was a self-conscious effort to de-humanize the personal rule of the king by referring to both divine and natural worlds as the bases of legitimacy (le roi soleil). The view emphasizes the wholeness or completeness of political life, which invariably casts terrorism as unnatural, a disease, and the antithesis of 'good' or 'sound' political action. In the event, the narrative of the sun, Louis' symbol, has a dual divine-natural character. The king/ruler/sovereign embodies the sun and is a product of nature, the pre-existing or complete order of things, and the source of life, order, and light. It follows that all political action is orientated towards influencing, displacing, or otherwise affecting the state rather than destroying it or its human components as terrorists are accused of doing.

Terrorists consequently reproduce pastoral-'vital' biopolitics much as Dr Frankenstein built his beast from the remains of the deceased. In her analysis of suicide missions, for example, Mia Bloom notes that 'people wilfully die spectacularly for another end for what is perceived as the common good of alleviating the community's onerous political and social realities … Suicide bombing has an additional value: that of making yourself the victim of your own act, and thereby putting your tormentors to moral shame. The idea of the suicide bombing, unlike that of an ordinary attack, is, perversely, a moral idea in which the killed, in acting out the drama of being the ultimate victim, claim for their cause the moral high ground.'[10]

In Bloom's analysis, suicide missions are the ultimate perversion, turning politics, a source of life and legitimacy, into a weapon of 'moral shame.' Like the Irish poets who are said to have starved themselves to humiliate their enemies, the suicide attacker seizes the biopolitical plot, demonstrating a capacity to control the narrative by threatening to end it. The suicide mission is thus also cast within a biopolitical logic of control and management of life: 'the organizations strategically adapt to changing circumstances to maximize their popularity and their ability to influence the "electorate" is based on resonance; specific tactics are either applauded or rejected. This underscores a significant rational calculation – those terrorist groups that are not rational, and do not adjust to circumstances, can lose support and may cease to exist.'[11]

Suicide attacks are thus understood within a biopolitical *management* model described by Foucault as 'operations [that] are carefully calculated and aimed at ending foreign occupation, increasing the prestige of the organization that uses them, and leading to regional autonomy and/or independence.'[12] As such, the biopolitical approach to terrorism presents the latter as a dystopic view of community, a spontaneously combusting model-narrative, animated by the view that social conditions are deteriorating. Bloom, for example, argues that suicide terrorism is used 'under two conditions: when other terrorist or military tactics fail, and when they are in competition with other terrorist groups for popular or financial support.'[13] In this model, there is no middle ground. The terrorist is a virus that must be controlled or (preferably) eliminated. Negotiation or understanding is not an option.

Bloom's biopolitical approach reflects the preoccupations of mainstream terrorist studies. Articulated by Paul Wilkinson,[14] Bruce Hoffmann,[15] and Robert Pape[16] (among others), this approach uncritically accepts the pastoral view of the state and the notion that states can/do/should have control over 'life itself.' Terrorist groups are herein cast as wild men, disorder lurking beneath the veneer of civilization and order, a phenomenon to be contained, but never engaged. Indeed, an article abstract by Leonard Weinberg, Ami Pedahzur, and Arie Perliger asks, 'Who are these people, willing to sacrifice their lives in *such an act*, and *what drives them to do such things*?' (emphasis mine).[17] The research question is little short of incredible since it is difficult to believe that researchers, let alone two at the University of Haifa, would be unaware of the conflict between Israel and the Palestinians since 1948 and its many tragic consequences. The question might alternatively be formulated as, 'Is suicide an effective weapon in a struggle for national liberation against an enemy with overwhelming military resources?' Again, the biopolitical assumption that the state, any state, is a priori legitimate in whatever actions it takes is a source of concern and certainly contradicts international laws in areas such as treatment of prisoners of war, human trafficking, and a host of other areas in which state legitimacy is subjected to meta-legal norms.

In this discussion, the aim is to highlight principles of 'terrorism' as an area of knowledge in order to draw attention to the fact that 'terrorism' is a description, not an empirical certainty. Obviously, the term is broadly applied to a range of political behaviour that is difficult to encapsulate under one umbrella. In this light, the analytical way forward is to provide a 'grammar of terrorism.' The purpose here is redirected towards *interpretation*. To begin this undoubtedly lengthy process, one component of terrorism, captivity, will be examined in order to outline its signifiers, that is, the sorts of structural relationships to which the term refers (exchange, the military, the body, culture, politics). The overall aim is to provide the basic principles of one element within the area of knowledge called terrorism.

In the following discussion, 'captivity' is an analytical alternative to some aspects of 'terrorism.' The latter is a widespread buzzword in today's media, politics, and academic research. As such, it very well illustrates the problems with certain schools of research that apply theories across a variety of contexts. As terrorism is often used in Western media today, in relation to 9/11, the Israel-Palestine conflict, Lebanese Hezbollah, Sri Lanka's Tamil Tigers, the Bali bombings, and the Beslan massacres, the term is usually set beside non-Western groups or Western groups with non-Western origins (i.e., second-generation children of immigrants or Western converts to Islam). The framework might ultimately say much more about those that operationalize it than it does about the analysis of political issues. The resulting analyses obfuscate the links between terrorist violence and political ends and so might be collectively labelled the 'forget Clausewitz' school. This contrasts the links made between U.S. military violence in Iraq or Israeli Defence Force violence in southern Lebanon in July 2006 and civilian deaths (when the Israeli military massacred children, they simply replied that they were being used as human shields, as if this makes a massacre any less real or any more 'just' in defence of a state). In looking at terrorism, we are looking at hierarchies of violence and of rationales for violence. To undertake more balanced analyses, the logics of political murder must be central since they underlie the power dynamics at work when 'terrorism' occurs. Unclear linkages to security and the absence of an overwhelming and 'incontournable' terrorist threat suggest that a fruitful path of analysis is breaking the meta-label into component parts (suicide attacks, assassinations, bombings, etc.).

Captivity

The face looks out from the screen, forlorn, beyond hope. Redemption to home, family, and friends is barely a glimmer on the face. The Western captive in Iraq – American, British, Italian, French, Canadian – confronted media audiences repeatedly after the U.S. 'victory' in March 2003. The face of the captive draws television viewers into a hushed presence, as we in the West search in vain for signs of victory, hope, vengeance, and technological superiority. It is a face that has appeared and reappeared in Anglo-American, French, and other views of the world since the early seventeenth century, when the roaming corsairs of Algiers, Tunis, Tripoli, and Morocco terrified Europeans. The face activates Western anxieties regarding Islam, the Arab world, the place of the West in the world, and the mechanics of international power and politics.

In the contemporary West, the language of captivity is uncannily similar to that used in the past, when significant numbers of Europeans were held in North and South America, Africa, the Middle East, and Asia. The language is that of individual heroism and 'a people tested.' The language straddles various interpretations of Euro-American relations with the rest of the world. One posits 'the West' as triumphant in world affairs, ever expanding into territories, markets, and realms of human knowledge. The other speaks to the human cost of expansion and the understandable response of those who might not have desired increased contact with the Euro-American world. Neither interpretative framework, in fact, is entirely correct. On the ground, facts, peoples, ideas, and markets are at least as interconnected, fragmented, ruptured, and continuous as they ever have been. This complexity shaped the ordeal of James Loney, the Canadian peacemaker[18] who went to Iraq to oppose the American-led occupation, and who, along with Canadian, British, and American colleagues (Loney, age 41, and Harmeet Singh Sooden, age 32, were freed with Briton Norman Kember, age 74), was captured in November 2005. They were held captive for almost four months.[19] Loney was finally freed in March 2006 by British and Canadian special forces. He returned to a hero's welcome in Canada, a living symbol of Euro-American 'humanity' and strength under pressure from unknown, masked, and malignant captors. Canadian Prime Minister Stephen Harper stated that 'the safe return of these men is what we all sought, and I want to thank all those here in Canada and around the world who have worked so tirelessly to secure their safe release.'[20] Loney's opposition to an unjust and illegal war and occupation is conveniently forgotten as not only individual captives, but Euro-America and Canada in particular are *cast as victims*. White House Press Secretary Scott McLellan stated that 'those hostages are a top priority for this administration, and they will remain a top priority until their safe return. We want to – we continue to urge the safe return of all hostages wherever they are, and we continue to stay focused on all the American hostages.'[21] No doubt Loney was a victim of Anglo-American occupation of Iraq, but the sense of injustice here is complex, not linear in the sense that Harper's statement would suggest.

The unclear linkages to security and lack of terrorist threat suggest that a fruitful path of analysis is to break the terrorist meta-label into component parts (suicide attacks, assassinations, bombings, etc.) The precedents for current captive incidents include the Biblical Egyptian and Babylonian captivities of the Israelites, the story of Jonah and the Whale, the circumstances of the future Queen Elizabeth in the court of her elder half-sister, Queen Mary, Louis Riel's capture and trial, Eugene Debs's arrest, imprisonment, and conversion to socialism as a result of the 1894 Pullman Strike, Eichmann's capture by the Israelis, Ezra Pound's incarceration in a psychiatric institute, Charles Manson's continued imprisonment, the Patty Hearst kidnapping, and the imprisonment and death of Bobby Sands. Even the philosopher Diogenes was captured by pirates on a voyage to Aegina and sold in Crete as a slave.[22]

Given the narrative of Egyptian and Babylonian captivities of the Israelites in Judeo-Christian cultures, it is ironic that captivity has a strong contemporary resonance as a result of the various post-1948 wars in the Middle East. In 2006 the capture of three Israeli soldiers by Hamas and Hezbollah led to bloody incursions by the Israeli Defence Force (IDF) into Gaza and Lebanon. On 25 June 2006, Corporal Gilad Shalit was seized in a Palestinian Hamas attack on an IDF position near the Gaza Strip. Shalit was the first Israeli soldier captured by Palestinians since 1994. Hamas said it would release him as part of a prisoner exchange. According to the Israeli human rights organization,

B'Tselem, 9,153 Palestinians are currently held by civilian and military authorities. Of these, B'Tselem says 8,085 are held in civilian jails, and 2,384 without charge. About 645 prisoners are held under 'administrative detention,' without charge, often without knowing why. Prisoners in civil jails include seventy-four women and 265 children and adolescents under eighteen years of age.[23] The thousands of prisoners play an important role in Palestinian political life. Senior prisoners from various Palestinian factions, such as Fatah's Marwan Barghouti, considerably influence rank-and-file members on the street. The release of what are called 'political prisoners' is a key Palestinian demand.

On 12 July 2006, the capture of reservists Ehud Goldwasser and Eldad Regev by Lebanese Hezbollah provoked immediate Israeli military retaliation. Following a major prisoner exchange in early 2004 in which more than 400 prisoners were released to Hezbollah in exchange for a reservist colonel and the bodies of three Israeli soldiers, Israel admitted to holding three Lebanese. Chief among those is Samir Qantar, who is serving several life sentences after attacking a civilian apartment block in Nahariya in 1979 and killing three people.[24] Hezbollah leader Sheikh Hassan Nasrallah has frequently called for Qantar's release, threatening to derail the 2004 deal when he was excluded from the list of prisoners. Israel refused to discuss releasing Qantar, often linking his status to its search for information about Ron Arad, an Israeli pilot who went missing over Lebanon in 1986. Israel also holds an Israeli man of Lebanese descent, Nissim Nasser, who was arrested in 2002 and convicted of spying for Hezbollah. The third Lebanese prisoner is a fighter named Yehia Skaff. Hezbollah MP Nawar al-Sahili says that Israel also holds a fisherman called Ali Faratan. Israel is also believed to be holding twenty-five Lebanese citizens of Palestinian origin, mainly for conventional criminal offences, but their release was not part of the dispute.

The 9/11 attacks on New York City and Washington are also well-known contemporary examples of captivity. The attacks were carried out through seizure of civilian aircraft and passengers. The latter became captives, and were killed. In this case, captivity was a prelude to execution. It was also a springboard for transformed perceptions of security, resulting in the largest reorganization of U.S. government since the Great Depression, a dramatic turnaround in public finances (from deficit reduction to high expenditure), quarrels with long-standing allies as the United States prepared its response, an unprovoked war with Iraq with untold consequences for global and regional stability, and solidification, in North America and Western Europe, of a 'culture of security' that subsumes virtually all other public issues. As such, 9/11 demonstrates how captivity provides an interpretive framework to examine practices that are generally subsumed under 'terrorism.' Captivity is an embodiment of crisis, a call to arms, and an impetus for political change.

Varieties of Captivity

Historically, captives appear in several categories: as prisoners of war; as hostages for negotiations, as converts transformed by the threat of continued confinement, and as individuals or groups that are assimilated by captors. Historical examples with political import for the United States illustrate here the signficance of captivity as a form of negotiation. They include the capture of John Smith during the establishment of the Virginia Colony, Mary Rowlandson's well-known captivity by Native Americans, the 1704 Deerfield raid,[25] the capture of Americans in the Barbary Wars, and the 1904 Perdicaris incident in Morroco. The latter suggests a relation between the characterization of non-Western violence and the policy-political uses made of them. The leader of the captors, 'Sherif Ahmad ibn Muhammad Raisuli, led a group of outlaws in Morocco's Rif Mountains, was dubbed 'the last of the Barbary pirates.' The captivity of Ion Perdicaris, occurring close to a Republican National convention and U.S. presidential elections, pitted the U.S. Navy against Raisuli, secured Theodore Roosevelt's nomination for the Presidency and helped him remain in the White House.[26] Other incidents discussed below feature captivity as a form of exchange, and relate it to the military, the body, and culture.

Captivity as Exchange

Captivity is a practice of exchange in which the body and its signatures are currency for negotiations and exchange. The negotiation functions of captivity are seen in the examples of John Smith in the early seventeenth-century Virginia Colony, as well as in the case of the so-called Barbary States or Regencies in North Africa in the seventeenth, eighteenth, and nineteenth centuries. Smith, himself repeatedly taken captive by Ottoman Turks, the French, the English, and Native Americans led by Powhatan (Pocahontas's father), appears to have viewed hostage-taking as a routine component of negotiating with Europeans and non-Europeans. In his early years as leader of the Virginia Colony, he offered captives from among his own men while holding Native American captives in order to secure a space in which various military, economic, or exploration matters were discussed. He criticized later colonial leaders who did not use captives because he said they were taking great risks with English lives and potential conflict.

Another example of captivity as a springboard for negotiation are the Barbary Regencies (Algiers, Tunis, and Tripoli), semi-autonomous territories within the Ottoman Empire that had to submit regular tribute to the Sultan in Istanbul. In order to acquire funds and other resources, they raided European shipping of all nationalities. When the United States became independent, American trade into the Mediterranean no longer received British protection and ships became bargaining chips in the pursuit of tribute. The three states seized U.S. citizens to exact payment in armaments (including naval vessels), jewels and cash, all three delivered during George Washington's administration. In the captivity of Ion Perdicaris in Morocco in 1904, the ultimate goal was to pressure the Moroccan Empire and secure specific advantages. Although Perdicaris was not an American citizen, his captors wanted the U.S.

government to pressure the Moroccan emperor to accede to their demands. Once pressure was exerted and the captors' demands were met, Perdicaris was freed.

Captivity is also a form of cultural exchange. A well-known contemporary expression of this idea is referral to captivity as evidence of a 'confrontation' between civilization and barbarism. This particular view expresses the dichotomous logic that both sides in exchange use when captivity occurs. At another level, captivity mirrors societies at particular times: the case of John Smith accompanies early modern English colonialism and mercantilism, an expansive form of Protestantism and interest in Asian trade that led the English to Virginia; the 1704 raid on Deerfield Massachusetts by the French and Native allies reflects imperial competition between France and England as well changing relations between Europeans and Native Americans; and the Barbary War is an episode in the ongoing engagement of Islamic and Christian societies and cultures. Each case illustrates Euro-American encounters with non-European cultures and peoples. Besides reflecting distinct phases of Euro-American history, they embody an effort to communicate beyond European 'terms.' Each phase of contact is different, ranging from early modern English contact with Native Americans (Smith), increasingly dominant European ties to Native Americans (Deerfield), and ties to the Islamic world (Smith's Ottoman captivity and the Barbary Wars).

Another form of exchange that relates to captivity is economic. A well-known example of economically valuable captivity was slavery in the antebellum U.S. south. In 1790 a group of Pennsylvania Quakers and the Pennsylvania Society for the Abolition of Slavery demanded that the U.S. Congress abolish slavery because it is inconsistent with both Christianity and the U.S. Constitution. Their demand was refused. Critics of the abolitionists argued that constitutional guarantees of states' rights and property rights made abolition impossible, and they emphasized the potentially disastrous consequences of freedom. One Georgia congressman argued that 'freedom would ruin Georgia's economy. The slaves would not work unless they were forced to do so. If the freed blacks moved to the frontier, the Indians would kill them. So the only benevolent option was to keep these people as slaves, teach them Christianity, and allow them to cultivate Georgia's rice.'[27]

Slavery also had a major economic role in the Barbary States, where slave trading provided armaments, cash, and jewels. The economic function of captivity was also present in New France, where captives from the 1704 Deerfield raid were eventually sold back to New England. This exchange was not central to the economy in New France. The sale of captives, most of whom had been the focus of intense Catholic proselytizing, was considered regrettable, but necessary to preserve peace with neighbouring English colonists. In all of these examples, shorter periods of captivity are in contrast with the form practised in the United States: lifelong hereditary servitude.

Captivity and the Military

As events in Gaza and Lebanon demonstrated in 2006, captivity is a widespread military practice used by all sides in conflict. However regrettable these events, military uses of captivity are not innovative, but reflect long-standing practices. Today's nega-tive association of captivity with certain death largely stems from the memory of the Second World War, when the Wehrmacht used hostages as human shields, for exam-ple, in Belgium and during the Warsaw Uprising, and shot hostages in reprisal for par-tisan attacks in several countries. The association links military uses of captives with Nazism and a disregard for human life. However, captivity has long been a tool in the field of battle and its purposes arc more complex.

An important function of captivity as a military technique is to create fear, intimi-date, and/or harass. Because today's captivity also aims to create fear, media, policy-makers, and analysts readily subsume it under terrorism. However, it is difficult to automatically assimilate captivity into terrorism since it has been used by states, regions within empires such as the Barbary States, and by insurgents who resist for-eign invasion. The Deerfield raid was the product of growing contact between French and English colonists in North America, imperial efforts to gain strategic and eco-nomic advantage, and a need to cultivate Native allies. For the latter, captivity was used for revenge, to gain slaves, and to replace family members lost to war or disease. While imperial interests dictated a strike at New England, New France had its own concerns about English incursions into the fur trade, which both hurt colonial econo-mies and drew away Native allies. Officials in New France were alarmed over the rapid growth of New England's population and what this meant for a territory (New France) that arched from the St Lawrence to the Mississippi river valleys. The raid aimed to terrify New England's colonists. Slowing or halting English expansion would have sat-isfied France's Native allies, demonstrated the colony's strategic value to Louis XIV, and secured the fur trade (at that time in a slump). While the raid did indeed terrify New England, it also mobilized colonial and English imperial forces against New France, which ultimately led to conquest little more than half a century later.

Barbary captivity had a more directly military purpose since the North African states could not directly confront the French and English empires in the eighteenth century and were part of the Ottoman Empire. While Morocco had driven the English out of an inten-sively prepared colonization of Tangier in the 1680s, the case stood apart from Algiers, Tunis, and Tripoli as de jure and de facto independent from the Ottomans. The Barbary States were one element in the long confrontation between the Ottomans and Europeans, which underlay the former's power to terrify and the latter's reluctance to undertake any definitive response that might provoke a reaction. It was not until the Battle of Navarino (1832) that European navigation was secure from the Ottomans. The much-commented 'piracy' of Barbary occurred in a global setting. Barbary states were virtually autonomous from Istanbul and served to discipline Europe. By use of captivity the Barbary States restrained European states to focus their energies on redeeming hostages, the threat of conversion of Europeans to Islam, and the dehumanizing effects of enslaving Christians.

An Afghan case occurred in the context of Anglo-Russian competition over India and Persia. It has striking analogies to the current international actions in that country. The conflict then as now was linked to great power rivalry and an aggressive attitude towards non-Europeans as much as from any internal Afghan dynamics or conflict between British and Afghans per se. Captivity was a means to harass and terrify the British Army that occupied Afghanistan in 1838-42. When the British started to withdraw, the Afghans seized captives in order to ensure that the process was completed. As in the case of John Smith in Virginia, an Afghan example illustrates how cultural communication unexpectedly occurs through the literal physical exchange of bodies between hostile and mistrustful societies.

Captivity and the Body

The body is central to captivity. As a result, 'captivity' is an analytical framework that links terrorism to social, group, and individual bodies. In short, the impact of captivity is based in the practice of seizing, holding, and controlling bodies. As Jean Baudrillard argues, there is considerable irony in contemporary attitudes towards the body since 'for centuries, there was a relentless effort to convince people they had no bodies (although they were never really convinced); today, there is a relentless effort to *convince them of their bodies.*' Baudrillard argues that it is easy to see the power of captivity in a society in which the body has replaced the soul as the locus for ideas of ethics, the sacred, and freedom.[28] Captivity confronts us with what Mikhail Bahktin calls a grotesque body that reflects particular ideas of social order. The captive body is grotesque because it is incomplete: it is rarely presented as a whole, only in parts, in the televisual images that flow through societies. The captive body has, by virtue of being controlled by (often) unknown enemies, lost those qualities of individuality, separateness, and completeness that, in Western consumer culture, are essential to the body.[29] For North Americans, the captive body is grotesque because it has lost its quality of freedom: free to consume, seduce, transform, and be mobile. Captivity impedes the mobility upon which contemporary Western social values are based. The body becomes immobile, only circulating via images.

The captive loses mobility, clothing, and the ability to communicate at will with others. The markers of individuality in Western society, clothing in particular, are gone and a threat to the life of the captive(s) is posed. Captivity in this respect shows the captors' power and the powerlessness of the captives and their community. The power of certain bodies has long prevailed in the West, where the idea of the divinity of the monarch's body was once central to political and social order. When the monarch's body was threatened, as in the case of the captivity of Richard the Lionhearted, it threw political society into crisis since it was identified with the body politic. The idea of the divine body of the monarch was also present in the notion of 'King's evil.' Until the reign of Queen Anne of Great Britain (1702-1714), the monarch appeared in public to touch people to cure scrofula (a form of tuberculosis characterized by swollen lymphatic glands). Although the practice was dropped by George I, contemporary captivity neatly inverts this belief by conveying the notion that harm to any *individual* captive threatens the entire body politic: the United States thus goes to war with Iraq after 9/11 after captives are seized and killed; and, Israel attacks Gaza and Lebanon after Hamas and Hezbollah seize three soldiers. The touch of the terrorist is perceived as potentially fatal to the body politic. The response is swift and unmerciful since the state cannot tolerate loss of control over the body and its signifiers. The appearance of normality must be retained at all costs.

Culture and Captivity

Captivity is not similar for all groups subject to it, with important differences in treatment based on race, gender, and origin. Africans were captured by Europeans to work on plantations in the Americas based on their colour of their skin. Americans and Europeans were captured by the Barbary States as 'infidels' who did not practice Islam. Jews were captured by the Nazis because they were considered 'sub-human.' These and other constructed differences are the basis of the practice of captivity as it cuts across societies and cultures. The foundations support a hierarchy of value, worth, and ultimately 'human-ness' that label particular individuals, groups, and nationalities as 'available' or 'dispensable' or 'manipulable' in the eyes of other cultures. These labels also grant privileges to the captors, as those who control the formlessness of the captive.

Varieties of captivity are readily seen by means of race, gender, religion, and other ascribed differences: 'In 1800, nearly one million people of African origin were enslaved in the United States. Unlike the seven hundred Americans held captive in the Muslim states between 1785 and 1815, these million Africans and African-Americans could not expect their nations or families to redeem them, nor could they look forward to being returned to freedom. Compared with the suffering of slaves in America, the complaints of the 700 Americans who called themselves slaves in Barbary seem hyperbolic or hypocritical.'[30]

In the pre–Civil War U.S. South, race was the primary marker of captivity as lifetime hereditary servitude. Because of this association, Barbary captivity particularly outraged Americans. They were also fed by a revolutionary heritage that set up a dichotomy between 'slavery' to the British Crown and Empire and American freedoms. In Barbary, on the other hand, race was not a primary marker of captivity. Religion was a pretext to capture individuals and rationalize slavery, but Barbary slavery was political since it was negotiable and depended on international currents at the time: 'Barbary slaves were not born into captivity or stolen from their homeland; they ventured into danger as travellers engaged in mercantile or military enterprises. Furthermore, many white captives were eventually ransomed and liberated from their slavery. They could return to the intact family and social structures into which they were born.'[31] Barbary captives were used to gain advantage in the form of weapons, jewels, cash, or other tribute. An individual captive's status was not a dead end since conversion to Islam meant immediate release (but estrangement from Euro-American origins). Even captives who did not convert started businesses and some became wealthy. James Cathcart, later U.S. consul in Tripoli, parlayed captivity into a position as secretary to the Dey of Algiers, in charge of correspondence with Christian nations.

In all contexts, the markers of captivity included sexuality and gender. Western views of the status of women in Muslim society meant that the soul and physical security of female captives was considered to be at risk in Barbary. In North American captivity narratives, such as that of Mary Rowlandson, the threat to female virtue by 'wildmen' is emphasized, and one of the prime threats due to loss of control of the body is sexual. Women were endangered by rape, forced conversion, or forcible confinement ('the seraglio'). Men, especially in Muslim contexts, were also sexually threatened. Many accounts focus on the threat of conversion, which entailed circumsion. The latter was described as a form of rape in which Western men would be held down and irredeemably marked by the adherents of the so-called false creed of Mohammed. Ironically, these sexual anxieties are recapitulated in Abu Ghraib prison abuse photos, which pose the danger of homosexual rape, the naked powerlessness of captivity, and the aggressive sexuality of the female soldier (seen in the figure of Lyndie England). The homosexuality of Canadian captive James Loney was concealed from the public while efforts to secure his release were under way. The concealment was explained as a precautionary measure to protect Loney from homophobic violence. Conflicting hierarchies of value, worth, and 'human-ness' are never far from the surface.

Another mechanism through which a culture of captivity is practised is media. ABC's famous 'America Held Hostage' headline during the 1979 Teheran hostage crisis was by no means the first springboard for media frenzy or captive celebrities. Mary Rowlandson is certainly the first and perhaps best-known early American captive. Publication of her narrative at the end of 'Metcom's War' was part of a media focus in which 'by the end of 1677 – little more than a year after the war ended – more than a dozen accounts and explanations of the conflict had been published in Massachusetts and England, and several more were in preparation.'[32] Her 1682 account, the first book by a woman published in English-speaking North America, is a standard captivity narrative and a unique example of a woman's voice in colonial New England. Rowlandson's book, which went through many editions, is a media phenomenon apart from the experience discussed, and, in its several editions, features images of the author.

Another media furore over captivity arose after the 1838-42 British invasion of Afghanistan turned successively to a siege, then a rout, then capture. During her captivity, Florentia Sale (or Florentia, Lady Sale), the wife of General Sir Robert Sale, wrote *A Journal of the Disasters in Afghanistan* (1843), which became a bestseller. Lady Sale became a celebrity and acquaintance of Queen Victoria. A media sensation over the hostages dominated public space: 'The closest recent parallel to the British furore over its Afghan detainees in 1842 was the absorption of the White House and the American public in the fate of the Iranian hostages between 1979 and 1981.'[33] Captivity narratives, which continue to appear with each successive conflict, set a context in which terrorism is spectacle-entertainment-participation in a genealogy that, in the English-speaking world, goes back to at least 'the Solemn mock procession of the Pope, cardinalls, Jesuits, fryers &c. through the city of London, November the 17th, 1680.'[34] The latter was an actual procession and series of pamphlets that aimed at the rumoured influence of Catholics in the twilight of Charles II's reign. It is an early modern example of how media spectacles are linked to notions of power and the struggle for power.

The links between captivity and religion transcend media since the threat to captives was explicitly spiritual. Falling into the hands of Muslims or Catholics posed the risk of apostasy and ever-lasting damnation for the English and Americans, societies dominated by Protestantism in the seventeenth, eighteenth, and nineteenth centuries. This view was based in the belief that only revealed Protestantism provided a path to reason, science, and enlightenment. It is linked to an idea of the superiority of a particular version of the West: white, Protestant, and male. The struggle for Protestant supremacy in England and the United States involved the overthrow of spiritual tyrannies, in the form of the Catholic James II or the head of the Church of England, George III. In such struggles and others in which religion was present, media have long conveyed various forms of captivity (political, religious-spiritual, actual physical, and cultural), making events at a distance terrifyingly 'real' for the particular public.

Captivity and Politics

Given these factors, the practice of captivity has enormous impact on politics. In the United States, the perception that Americans were captive to the tyranny of the British Crown and Empire underlay the development and articulation of an ideology of 'freedom' that is central to U.S. national life and foreign policy.[35] Freedom, originally the freedom of a 'true' religion, was the antithesis of captivity and life among Catholic Frenchmen, Native Americans, and Muslim North Africans. In the case of Muslims, adherents to an allegedly 'false' creed, captivity seemed especially dire:

> From the earliest years of the Reformation, when the Turkish threat to Europe was a topic of intense public concern to the west, the notion that the antichrist and his empire was split into an eastern and western manifestation – with Islam and Catholicism as the two legs of a satanic colossus – was a common belief of Protestant biblical exegetes. The Turks, a label frequently and often indiscriminately applied to all Muslims, were frequently viewed as the newest type of Eastern horde and assumed the status previously held by the Babylonians, Assyrians, and Persians, and they were also linked with the mysterious tribes of Gog and Magog.[36]

Deliverance to freedom became a cornerstone of American political life and principal rationalization for all manner of behaviour if it suited public tastes, private greed, or policy.

Freedom became a rationale for civil war, world war, assassination, bombings, displacement (especially of Native Americans), and more recently, an unprovoked invasion of Iraq. As Linda Colley points out, captivity occurs alongside imperial intervention and occupation since the concomitant wars, invasions, occupations, and other violence leave imperial subjects exposed to seizure by enemies who seek leverage through holding bodies.[37]

Conclusion

Terrorism takes several narrative-communicative forms depending on content (actual interactions among people), the purposes of analysis, and the language used. The issue is to examine the contents of communication and allow for complexity. In this chapter, the focus has been on practices that shape terrorism. The point of departure is communication broadly conceived, accepting Harold Innis's view that communication is the basis of political society as a filter through which needs, values, interests, and other human products move. Since communication has a broad and indistinct shape, the specific case illustration has been captivity.

Captivity reveals a narrative of exchange and communication at several levels that subsumes states under the body, negotiation, exchange, threat, and sometimes sacrifice. The practices and cultures of captivity result in a variety of categories that influence 'terrorism.' Some captives are lifelong hereditary slaves. Others, such as U.S. sailors in Tripoli or Israeli soldiers in Gaza and southern Lebanon, are political captives. Still others, such as the German soldiers held by the Soviets after the Second World War, are a source of labour. Yet other captives, such as European Jews during the Holocaust, are captives to be exterminated.

Captivity is closely tied to the origins of contemporary political societies and identities. The colonial experience is a rich source of captivity narratives of all sorts. In the Western meta-narrative, captivity in Egypt taught the Israelites who they were, and functioned as the basis of community and politics. The experience marks power in other ways that impact terrorism. The French and American revolutions against the injustice of tyranny, in both cases monarchical tyranny, were cases of deliverance from captivity that had enormous global consequences in terms of ideologies and the practices of states. Captivity was also present as a central theme of Senator John McCain's 2008 U.S. presidential campaign. Captivity is not uniform or universally experienced, but rather resonates across societies and cultures in uneven and unpredictable ways, touching nations, regions, groups, peoples, and individuals. Captivity embodies complexity, intercultural communication, and the shape of terrorism.

Notes

1 N. Katherine Hayles, *How We Became Post-Human: Virtual Bodies in Cybernetics, Literature, and Informatics* (Chicago: University of Chicago Press, 1999), 288.

2 Gary E. Wilson, 'American Hostages in Moslem Nations, 1784-1796: The Public Response,' *Journal of the Early Republic* 2/2 (1982): 123–41, 140.

3 See, e.g., Jeffrey D. Simon, *The Terrorist Trap: America's Experience with Terrorism* (Bloomington: Indiana University Press, 2001), 29–33.

4 Paul Baepler, 'The Barbary Captivity Narrative in American Culture,' *Early American Literature* 39/2 (2004): 217–46, 240.

5 See Crash Statistics website, available at http://www.nhtsa.dot.gov/people/Crash/crashstatistics/2001StateDateFatalities.htm, accessed 8 Nov. 2007.

6 See Federal Bureau of Investigation, 'Federal Bureau of Investigation: Uniform Crime Reports 2001,' available at http://www.fbi.gov/ucr/01cius.htm, accessed 8 Nov. 2007.

7 Iraq Body Count website, available at http://iraqbodycount.net/, accessed 8 Nov. 2007.

8 Michel Foucault, 'The Birth of Biopolitics,' in *Ethics, Subjectivity and Truth: Essential Works of Foucault 1954-1984,* vol. I, ed. Paul Rabinow (New York: New Press, 1997), 73.

9 Foucault, 'Security, Territory, and Population,' ibid., 71.

10 Mia Bloom, *Dying to Kill: The Allure of Suicide Terror* (New York: Columbia University Press, 2005), 76–7.

11 Ibid., 85.

12 Ibid., 3.

13 Ibid., 2.

14 Paul Wilkinson, *Terrorism and the Liberal State* (New York: New York University Press, 1986).

15 Bruce Hoffmann, *Inside Terrorism* (New York: Columbia University Press, 2006).

16 Robert Pape, *Dying to Win: The Strategic Logic of Suicide Terrorism* (New York: Random House, 2006).

17 A. Pedahzur, A. Perliger, and L. Weinberg. 'Altruism and Fatalism: The Characteristics of Palestinian Suicide Terrorists,' *Deviant Behavior* 24/4 (2003): 405–23.

18 Chicago-based Christian Peacemaker Teams (CPT), an international peace activist group.

19 See CBC News, 'Military Operation Frees 2 Canadian Hostages in Iraq,' 23 March 2006, available at http://www.cbc.ca/story/world/national/2006/03/23/hostages060323.html, accessed 8 Nov. 2007.

20 Stephen Harper, cited in Office of the Prime Minister, 'Statement by the Prime Minister on the Rescue of Hostages in Iraq,' 23 March 2006, available at http://pm.gc.ca/eng/media.asp?id=1066, accessed 8 Nov. 2007.

21 Scott McClellan, 'Press Briefing by Scott McClellan,' White House Press Sectretary Briefings, 23 March 2006, available at http://www.whitehouse.gov/news/releases/2006/03/20060323-2.html, accessed 8 Nov. 2007.

22 When he was asked what was his trade, he replied that he knew no trade but that of governing men, and that he wished to be sold to a man who needed a master. Diogenes became the tutor to the two sons of Xeniades and lived in Corinth for the rest of his life, devoting himself entirely to preaching the doctrines of virtuous self-control.

23 See B'Tselem, 'B'Tselem: The Israeli Information Center for Human Rights in the Occupied Territories,' available at http://www.btselem.org/English/index.asp, accessed 8 Nov. 2007.

24 A baby girl was accidentally smothered by her mother as she hid in a cupboard.

25 The 1704 Deerfield Raid set the then-northwesternmost town in New England 'at the forefront of a clash of peoples and empires.' The raid occurred within the global context of what Europeans called the War of Spanish Succession (1703–15) when Louis XIV supported his grandson's claim to the Spanish throne. The French aim was global, specifically to draw the Spanish Empire into France's economic and strategic sphere. In English-speaking North America, the war is called Queen Anne's War. See Evan Haefeli and Kevin Sweeney, *Captors and Captives: The 1704 French and Indian Raid on Deerfield* (Amherst: University of Massachusetts Press, 2003).

26 Jonathan Broder, 'Tangier,' *Smithsonian* 29/4 (1998): 90–101.

27 Robert Allison, *The Crescent Obscured: The United States and the Muslim World, 1776–1815* (Chicago: University of Chicago Press, 1995), 104.

28 Jean Baudrillard, 'The Finest Consumer Object: The Body,' in *The Body: A Reader*, ed. Mariam Fraser (London: Routledge, 2005), 277.

29 Mikhail Bakhtin, 'The Grotesque Image of the Body and Its Sources,' in ibid., 92–5.

30 Allison, *Crescent Obscured*, 107.

31 Paul Baepler, ed., *White Slaves, African Masters: An Anthology of American Barbary Captivity Narratives* (Chicago: University of Chicago Press, 1999), 94.

32 Neil Salisbury, 'Introduction,' in *The Sovereignty and Goodness of God*, by Mary Rowlandson (Boston: St Martin's Press, 1997), 38.

33 Linda Colley, *Captives* (New York: Pantheon Books, 2002), 363.

34 'The Solemn mock procession' is a seventeenth-century, one-page broadside that shows a Pope-burning procession in London on 17 November 1680. The day is the anniversary of the accession of Elizabeth I, who was revered for her staunch Protestantism. It was one of a series of processions that attracted crowds estimate at 200,000 people and wound through London to Temple Bar, near the statue of Queen Elizabeth. The climax was when the effigy of the Pope, stuffed with live cats, was thrown into a bonfire. The procession was one of a series organized by the Whig 'Green Ribbon Club' in 1679, 1680, and 1681. See Sheila Williams, 'The Pope-Burning Processions of 1679, 1680, and 1681,' *Journal of the Warburg and Courtauld Institutes* 21, no. 1/2 (1958): 104–18.

35 See Greg Sieminski, 'The Puritan Captivity Narrative and the Politics of the American Revolution,' *American Quarterly* 42/1 (1990): 35–56.

36 Timothy Marr, 'Drying Up the Euphrates: Muslims, Millennialism, and Early American Missionary Enterprise,' *The Cultural Roots of American Islamicism* (New York: Cambridge University Press, 2006), 132.

37 See Linda Colley, 'Going Native, Telling Tales: Captivity, Collaborations and Empire,' *Past and Present* 168 (Aug. 2000): 170–93.

16 Infomobility and Technics: Some Travel Notes

BELINDA BARNET

The technical artefacts that surround us are more than just extensions of ourselves; they shape and mediate our experience of life and of space and time. Each technology has its own material genealogy that exceeds human evolution, and some developments have had more impact on human life than others. For French philosopher Bernard Stiegler, one of the most important developments in recent times is the convergence between the industrial technical system, globalization, and mnemotechnical systems like writing and photography, to form a *global mnemotechnical system*. This system incorporates digital information networks like the Internet as well as the real-time information events of individuals. Human beings of the information age are dependent on this global digital retention system; they invent themselves within it. More recently, with the development of geosynchronous satellite applications like GPS, there has been an 'interweaving' of this global system with real space; the human experience of countries and regions is shaped in advance by its representations. The global mnemotechnical system reterritorializes real space: 'What is currently being deployed is an electronic reproducibility of places, countries and geographical regions. It is not yet very advanced, but it already opens up immense perspectives.'[1]

The following essay is a collection of three vignettes reflecting on infomobility and mnemotechnics from my recent travels. In the first vignette, I argue that this interweaving of the global mnemotechnical system and real space reaches its zenith with mobile devices; particularly through the use of wireless information services (like WAP or NTT DoCoMo's i-mode) combined with location-based services that tailor data to geographical locations. The individual's current location becomes a *plane of technological inscription* for this global mnemotechnical system, and the individual human being becomes a series of location zones, an evolving piece of data whose information events are fed back into this digital retention system. All countries and territories with mobile coverage have a layer of virtual graffiti[2] associated with them, from simple maps and Web references to custom-built and location-specific mobile sites that can be accessed using your thumb. My beliefs are shaped in advance by this digital retention system whose access point I carry with me. In the second vignette, I argue that this global digital retention system also bears *witness* to an event taking place; until an event has been captured, shared, and distributed across the network via mobile phone, it has not taken place.

When human beings are separated from the devices that grant them access to the global mnemotechnical system, from both the archive of their own lives and the collective record, they experience anxiety. Our relationship with mobile devices constitutes a tension, a tension I explore in the final vignette.

The (Re)production of Territories – Marrakech, 5/05/05

> What is really at stake are the radically new possibilities of projection that are offered by digital devices of tertiary retention. If what we are dealing with is nothing else but real space, it must be an extension of the device by which the world projects as double.[3]

The places I visit become 'smart' by virtue of my presence. I bring information with me as I travel, and this information *mediates my experience*; the territory surrounding me serves as a surface of projection for data. I am sitting inside the mud-brick ramparts of Djemaa el-Fna square in Marrakech, Morocco, surrounded by a jumble of storytellers, jugglers, and snake charmers. In the stall beside me, a woman pulls a raw sheep's head from her bag, skewers it through the eye socket, and rolls it across the grill. The intermittent song of the Muezzin (Arabic call to prayer) sounds strange to me, and the air is filled with a mixture of French and Arabic, neither of which I can understand. I have no guidebook, and I cannot find my way out of the labyrinthine medina. Yet I am not lost; using GPRS roaming, my device brings access to directions through the cobbled streets and alleys, to an explanation of the song in my own language.

Every street and building has a layer of virtual graffiti that I can summon in an instant; my experiences will, in turn, be archived and will form part of this collective inscription. Although I cannot see these records on the walls and artefacts around me, they are not *immaterial*; they 'cannot be accessed except via the mediating processes of the devices that represent this information' to an otherwise unequipped consciousness.[4] Using my device, I retrieve 243 entries for Café Toubkal on the east side of the square; if I squint my eyes I can see it through the jumble of stalls. As I make my way across the market I capture images of my approach, I rehearse my own inscriptions in this collection; my experience has been formulated in advance of my arrival. In this sense, the place I am approaching is already the future anterior, it is already memory. A mobile device promises not simply, or not only, perpetual connectivity; it promises access to this sedimentary layer of information that has built up around the globe, and the ability to add one's fragments to it. This exceeds the knowledge of human individuals, it exceeds the *territory* it covers.

With every step, I emit a smog of data; my journey is being archived too. Every few seconds, my device 'pings' the network and receives a response; my location zone is then recorded in a log. I am conscious that I leave a trail of digital breadcrumbs for Maroc Telecom through the ancient city of Marrakech, that my position could be tri-angulated within metres based on my distance from nearby cell stations. I have become data 'travelling through data landscapes;'[5] I have become a roaming subscrip-tion number. As my feet slide along on thousand-year-old stone, I am at once travel-ling through networks and central servers back in Australia, my details handed on via invisible network handshakes across the globe, my trajectory recorded. I am not lost, I am identifiable; I am a string of information events.

As I travel through the city I leave other traces too, traces that will be incorporated into the global digital retention system. Every automatic teller machine (ATM) that I visit and every credit card transaction that I make will be recorded. But my mobile device is a *nomadic object*; it literally locates me within an electronic reproduction of the territory I walk over.[6] The network coverage area is known as a 'footprint,' and like any inscription on real space it has finite physical limits and dimensions; my trail through it will be marked as one marks the surface of a page. At the same time, once again, this data trail I am creating is already memory; by the time the network locates me, I have gone.

On the opposite side of the round world you are asleep now, and your device will vibrate silently with the video I have sent.

The (Re)production of Events – Valencia, 14/05/05

The ultimate affirmation of an event having occurred is its being captured, shared and distributed by mobile phone.[7]

Samsung's *Show Your World* advertisement campaign urges camera phone users to record the minutiae of their daily lives and turn them into a movie. In Samsung's words, this is 'the most vibrant way to capture and share life experiences with family and friends.'[8] Human beings have always felt compelled to capture fragments of their lives, to store and transmit memories; we have inscribed ourselves in books and on cave walls, in folk songs and on subway benches, and now on 1.8-inch mobile phone screens. For Bernard Stiegler, all technologies are, in fact, memory aids;[9] but not all technics are also mnemotechnics. Some technologies have been created explicitly to store and transmit memories: for example, writing or photography. Mobile devices were originally created as walkie-talkies for cars,[10] but the unexpected success of mes-saging took developments in a different direction; consumers wanted to capture and share the ephemera of their daily lives.

All technologies create cultures of use around themselves; they create new tech-niques and new ways of doing things that were unthinkable prior to the technology.

Figure 16.1. Cellphone Image: Valencia (Spain). Belinda Barnet, 2005.

Mnemotechnics, in particular, create new ways of *remembering*; both on a phenomeno-logical level (how we perceive and experience events in our lives) and a technical level (the material artefacts that serve as surfaces of inscription). The relationship between these two levels constitutes a tension – a tension as old as metaphysics, a tension that is itself productive of new devices and new techniques.[11] The material surface of inscription at once *shapes* the memory that it records; the technical artefact has limits and resistances that impact the recording.

Mobile devices, in turn, have material limits that influence the events that they capture: for example, a mobile screen is necessarily small (between one and three inches for phones, up to four inches for PDAs and pocket PCs), and video is compara-tively hard to compress and expensive to receive, even on high-end 3G devices. Conse-quently, the videos we create must be short and simple grabs; the actors must be choreographed to address the lens and the message must be simplified for its recipi-ent. This means the life events that we record are (at least in part) produced by the device, but this is not necessarily a negative experience. The physical limits and resis-tances of different technologies can also be creative. The impoverished real estate of the mobile screen has given us a new language, for example: it cn b hrd to undrstnd if u r not txt msg usr.[12] A mobile device alters the both the way that we experience events and the event that is recorded.

I have just met up with Jasmine in the Plaza de la Virgen in Valencia, Spain. After we have downed some syrupy coffee at a cafe, I ask if I can take a short clip of her to send to mutual friends in Sydney. There is an eccentric old man sitting at the table next to us eating churros (long sugary donuts), so I ask Jasmine to talk to this man

Figure 16.2. Cellphone Image: Valencia (Spain). Belinda Barnet, 2005.

while I video her on my device. She obliges, and for two minutes, she dunks churros in her chocolate like a pro and laughs with the old man. The event is *performed* for the tiny lens. After a time she looks up at me and smiles at our distant friends – friends whose absence is right now influencing our performance, friends who will receive this 'event' at an indeterminate point in the future, and in that reception affirm that it has taken place (in the manner of an ethical act, our friends will bear witness to this event). Later, as we walk around the city, we stop at intervals and pose in front of fountains and monuments, snapping still shots to distribute across the globe.

These events *do not exist* outside the technology for their capture and distribution; they were never simply 'there,' awaiting the recording. Each event has been constructed to fit in five-second slots on a 1.8-inch screen, for absent third parties who have yet to receive it. After the performance, the video will be compressed and data selectively lost; it will be cut into packets and transmitted via thousands of parallel digital streams to be reconstructed on a different device, which will create a composite of frames from multiple streams. The reconstruction will take place far from this place and this time, and each device will render it differently. A mobile does not simply 'capture' events from our lives; it mediates and constructs the very nature of the events recorded. It is first and foremost a production device, a device for the production and distribution of memories.

Jasmine and I are both aware that these events are being recorded and that they will be distributed to people on the opposite side of the world (people who are right now sleeping, unaware of the sights and sounds and colours that seem most live to us here now). This unfolding moment, which took place only once and which feels so authentic, will be infinitely reproducible in our absence.[13] Perhaps more importantly, we are aware of this future; aware of this anticipated Other who will replay the event on a different device and in a different context. The *possibility* that these events can be captured and distributed in this way fundamentally alters our perception and our experience in advance. A mobile is always and also a token of the future, a future where fragments of your life will not be lost, but will survive 'in an array of splendid colour.'[14]

You will receive my stories and will forget them. I am a name in your contact list, I am a collection of photographs.

The Promise – London, 30/05/05

I know I spend too much time texting friends, but I can't stop myself ... I even sleep with my mobile under my pillow. I just have to wake up and read messages when I receive them.[15]

A mobile device is a promise: the constant *potential* for communication, even if this communication never arrives. My device is always on, always connected, there is always the possibility that a message may have arrived since last I checked (or not). I worry that I may miss something or that someone may miss me, and this possibility haunts me. I feel compelled to check the device several times an hour, like someone obsessively washing her hands. I am sensitive to its vibrations through several layers of coat pockets, and I scramble madly for it when I feel the slightest movement. Every so often I put my hand in my pocket just to check it is still there. My perception is altered in advance by its comforting presence; was that my ring tone I just heard, was that my message alert? Sometimes I have minor hallucinations; when I hear a mobile ring nearby I glance instinctively at my screen – was that for me? My device demands what Linda Stone calls 'continuous partial attention' – even when nothing is happening. Mobile users have a constant low-level awareness of their devices; the possibility that communication may arrive at any instant inhabits their awareness: 'With continuous partial attention, we're constantly scanning incoming alerts for the one best thing to seize upon: "how can I tune in in a way that helps me sync up with the most interesting, the most important opportunity?"'[16]

The arrival of this *most important opportunity*, the alert that can happen at any instant, is perpetually immanent. Even when the device rests peacefully in my pocket and my hands are folded in my lap, communication from my contacts still exists *in potentia*; I am simply awaiting their arrival. It is the fact that this opportunity may never arrive, that although I have a contact book filled with names I may yet be forgotten, it is in the 'always-open hollow of possibility, that is, in non-coming, absolute disappointment [*deconvenue*],' that I have a relation to the event.[17] The possibility that this most important opportunity *may never arrive* is the condition of its arrival. If a day passes without contact I begin to panic; have I been forgotten? Everyone around me in the street seems to be receiving calls; am I not important? 'Seeing ... everyone talk on the phone, one realises that there is a mobile community and one is not part of it.'[18] The mobile implies perpetual availability for contact, but contact may always not take place, too. The spectre of loss – of being forgotten, or of missing the arrival – marks our relationship with mobile devices: 'If I don't receive a text when I wake up or I receive only a few messages during the day, I feel as though nobody loves me enough to remember me.'[19]

A mobile device promises the future – a future where important messages may yet arrive, and where we will not miss the arrival. Like any promise, there is an *expectation* that this will take place, and an attendant anxiety that it will not take place. This has led to a new set of social behaviours around mobile messaging. When the recipient of a message is unable to respond straight away, there is a sense that a promise has been broken. 'A message should be responded to within about 30 minutes unless one [has] a legitimate reason, such as being asleep.'[20] Japanese students surveyed by Mizuko Ito and Daisuke Okabe actually apologized to the recipient if their responses were delayed by more than an hour, and often just 'checked in' with their friends during the day to let them know they were still thinking of them.[21] Students who were about to turn their phone off or would be unable to receive messages for a while sent a warning to their friends: 'just got home, think I'll take a bath.'[22] Mobile owners live in a constant state of anticipation.

A mobile device is a promise; this promise inhabits our awareness, like a peripheral anxiety. It is constantly in the background, and it shapes our experience of life and the 'taking place' of events within our lives. A mobile promises the instrumental possibility of *reproduction*, of capturing and distributing the minutiae of our daily lives, even if these experiences can never be faithfully recorded. It promises that we will not be forgotten, that we will not be lost; the territory has been reproduced in advance of our arrival, and we will always be identifiable. It promises the constant *potential* for communication, even if this communication never arrives.

What if I miss something, or someone misses me?

Awaiting (at) the Arrival – Dubai International Airport, 03/06/05

You have not replied to the stories I have sent; have you forgotten me? Perhaps your device is broken and my messages have been lost; perhaps you have sent a reply and it has not yet reached me. Either way, the absence saddens me.

If only this were the final day of waiting.

Acknowledgments

With thanks to Darren Tofts, Mark Finn, and Andres Vaccari for their comments on this essay.

Notes

1 Bernard Stiegler, 'Our Ailing Educational Institutions,' *Culture Machine* 5 (2003), available at http://culturemachine.tees.ac.uk/Cmach/Backissues/j005/Articles/Stiegler.htm, accessed 15 Mar. 2005.

2 The term 'virtual graffiti' was first used by Howard Rheingold, in *Smart Mobs: The Next Social Revolution* (New York: Perseus, 2002). For the purposes of this chapter I am using the term to include both i-mode (cHTML) and WAP sites: these are different services. Not all GPRS/3G handsets can access the i-mode service, users need an i-mode client.

3 Bernard Stiegler, 'Our Ailing Educational Institutions.'

4 Ibid.

5 Ibid.

6 Mobile coverage is achieved by partitioning the area into a plurality of location zones, each zone being served by a base station.

7 Christine Satchell, cited by Gerard Goggin, in 'Calling the Shots' *The Age*, 2 July 2005, available at http://www.theage.com.au/news/icon/calling-the-shots/2005/06/30/1119724747968.html?oneclick=true, accessed 12 Aug. 2005.

8 Samsung, 'Show Your World,' cited in Trendwatching, 'Life Caching,' available at http://www.trendwatching.com/trends/LIFE_CACHING.htm, accessed 12 Aug. 2005.

9 Stiegler, 'Our Ailing Educational Institutions.' Also see Bernard Steigler, *Technics and Time*, vol. 1, trans. Richard Beardsworth and George Collins (Stanford: Stanford University Press, 1998), chapter 1.

10 Jon Agar, *Constant Touch: A Global History of the Mobile Phone* (Cambridge: Icon, 2003), 35.

11 For more details see my *CTheory* article, 'Technical Machines and Evolution,' *CTheory* 27/1 (2004), or the first two chapters of Stiegler, *Technics and Time*, vol. 1.

12 It can be hard to understand if you are not a text message user. It might also be argued that the expense of voice carriage has contributed to the creation of a new messaging language.

13 Jacques Derrida and Bernard Stiegler, *Echographies of Television: Filmed Interviews* (Cambridge: Polity Press, 2002), 38.

14 Advertisment for Samsung E400. Samsung, 'Samsung's Digital World,' available at http://www.samsung.com/uk/products/mobilephones/mobilephones/sgh_e400saxeu.asp., accessed 12 Aug. 2005.

15 A 14-year old mobile user, cited by Alfred Lee, in 'Youths Seek Help for SMS Addiction,' *IT Asia One*, 6 Oct. 2003, available at http://it.asia1.com.sg/newsdaily/news001_20031006.html, accessed 15 Mar. 2005.

16 Linda Stone, cited in Jill Maxwell, 'Stop the Net, I Want to Get Off,' *Inc. Magazine* (2002), available at http://www.inc.com/magazine/20020101/23805.html, accessed 12 Aug. 2005.

17 Derrida and Stiegler, *Echographies of Television*, 14.

18 Jukka Pekka Puro, 'Finland: A Mobile Culture,' in *Perpetual Contact: Mobile Communication, Private Talk, Public Performance*, ed. James Katz and Mark Aakhus (Cambridge: Cambridge University Press, 2002), 28.

19 Mobile user, cited by Rheingold, in *Smart Mobs*, 21.
20 Mizuko Ito and Daisuke Okabe, 'Technosocial Situations: Emergent Structuring of Mobile E-mail Use,' in *Personal, Portable, Pedestrian: Mobile Phones in Japanese Life*, ed. Mizuko Ito and Daisuke Okabe (Cambridge: MIT Press, 2002), 265.
21 Ibid.
22 Ibid., 266.

17 The Cyborg Mother:
A Breached Boundary

JAIMIE SMITH-WINDSOR

Why not tell a story in a new way? Why not think in unfinished ways – without fixity? without finality? Why not ask questions without answers, without presuppositions, causes, effects, and linear time? Why not whisk yourself away from your comfortable position?[1] When we live in a world of fractured identities and broken boundaries, why not rebel against yourself, or the technologies of 'yourself' and discover new ways of being? Reconcile yourself with the idea that everything is being shattered. Identity is being shattered, and technology is picking up the pieces, and there stands before us an infinitude of recombinant possibility. Rewriting history becomes possible, because 'the time of history passes through the stories of individuals: their birth, their experience.'[2]

The birth of my daughter:

> Aleah Quinn Smith-Windsor
> Born: 31 January 2003

A few days after Quinn was born, this quote appeared, on a note beside her incubator: 'Every blade of grass has an angel that bends over it and whispers, grow, grow' (Anon).

It was a near-fatal birth. Quinn was born at twenty-four and a half weeks' gestation, three and a half months before her due date. Her birth weight was 700 grams, about one pound and a half.

> 1 February 2003 – It is difficult to imagine such a tiny, perfect human being. Her feet are no larger than two fingernails. Her legs are about the same size as adult fingers, femurs measuring 4.5 centimetres. Her eyebrows curve like fallen eyelashes above her eyes, waiting to be wished upon.

Morphology after the Birth of My Daughter

Immediately after Quinn's lungs were cleared she was incubated, stabilized, and flown, together with the Neonate Team, by way of helicopter ambulance, to the Special Care

Nursery at the British Columbia Children's Hospital in Vancouver. We got to see her for a minute, tangled beneath the cords of her life support machines.

> 2 February 2003 – A pump pushes breast milk down her throat, through a tube that goes into her belly. Sixty-five breaths per minute are administered by a Drager 2000 Ventilator. She receives extra nutrition through an artificial umbilical line, blood-products and medications through an Intra Venous. Electrodes cover her body, measure her breaths and heart beats, her temperature, oxygen saturation, and blood pressure.

Motherhood – a Breached Boundary:
A Critical Questioning of Who Is Mother in Cyborg Culture?

My daughter's birth was a posthuman, cyborg moment. She became a cyborg, 'the illegitimate child of the twentieth-century technological dynamo – part human, part machine, never completely either.'[3] Using this moment to grapple with the concept and implications of cyborg culture reveals some important questions about the amalgamation between the technological and the biological, and 'not just in the banal meat-meets-metal sense.'[4] Breaching the bio-techno boundary forces an engagement with 'new and complex understandings of "life," consciousness, and the distinction (or lack of distinction) between the biological and the technological.'[5] Becoming cyborg is about the simultaneous externalization of the nervous system and internalization of the machine. The symbiosis between a human being and a machine makes possible the genesis of a cyborg consciousness. Ultimately, the breached boundary of the human body is a diasporatic phenomenon which witnesses the dispersion of an originally homogeneous articulation of the body into a dissident utterance, a destroyed discursive transformation. The breached body speaks of broken boundaries in the broken prose of the language of exile. [6]

Becoming cyborg involves a consciousness that is embedded within the notion of diasporas. To confront the interface between the human being and the machine is to confront cyborg consciousness. The interface is the matriarch of cyborg culture, assuming, 'a unified role: a means of communication and reproduction; carrier and weaver; machine assemblage in the service of the species; a general purpose system of simulation.'[7] Technology displaces motherhood, with 'her [technology's] inexhaustible aptitude for mimicry,' which makes her 'the living foundation for the whole staging of the world.' Being cyborg means that infancy without motherhood is possible. Before the displacement of motherhood by technology can be imagined, however, it is first necessary to explore the relationship between mother and child. Within the dual transference between mother and child, according to Julia Kristeva, it is possible 'to posit as "object" of analysis, not "childhood language," but rather an infantile language.'[8] Before literate language begins to encode the identity of the infant, and prior to the moment where the mirror introduces the paradoxical representation of reality, the infant and the

Mother exist within a symbiotic relationship defined by two basic principles: the need to nurture and the nurture of need. The mother-child symbiosis provides the necessary relationship for infantile language to be communicated. The infant is incapable of distinguishing between 'sameness' and 'otherness,' between 'subject' and 'object,' between itself and the Mother.[9] The infantile language means that infants are not capable of imagining themselves autonomous of the Mother. But what if this symbiotic relationship between mother and child were interrupted? What happens when technology begins to work itself into the infantile discourse, severing the symbiosis between mother and child? What happens when the infant, instead, becomes incapable of distinguishing between itself and – the machine? These are the questions posed by the biological mother of a cyborg. This is the genesis of a cyborg. It begins in pre-literacy, when the child engages in an infantile language with the machine, and not with the Mother.

According to Kristeva, 'love replaces narcissism in a third person that is external to the act of discursive communication.'[10] Love between humans, thus, becomes invested in a third party. But what happens in cyborg culture, when that 'third party' is not a person at all, but a machine – a ventilator, an incubator, a monitor? Technology separates the dialectic relationship between mother and child, mediating the relations between them. In the production of artificial means to life, is the machine capable of simulating love? Is the cyborg capable of love? Or is it merely consuming?

> 30 March 2003 – Quinn has been fighting with her ventilator. She's tried to tug it out of her throat, but it's glued to her skin. To stop her from wrestling, the doctor drugged her with addictive sedatives and paralyzed her so she can't move, so the ventilator can fully take over her body. How can such violence give life? So, I read her a story by Dr Seuss about really small people called Whos ... At the sound of my voice, she opened her eyes for a minute. That's not supposed to happen. I was asked to leave. I was disrupting the machine.

Living within a mediated body means that rituals of being are also written by technology. Technology is mimesis, the capability of imitating the human condition with such exactitude that it has become synonymous with the skin, the flesh, and the vital organs of human bodies. Artificial life becomes the performance of real life. Distinguishing skin from machine, thus, becomes difficult.

> 8 February 2003 – There is a scab on her chest where the nurse pulled the electrode off her skin, and with it, came most of the right nipple.

What are the implications of this violent symbiosis? Becoming cyborg implicates the human condition with the eternal mediation of the human experience, the eternal return of the machine. The human condition becomes the medium itself. The cyborg consciousness becomes, like the clear glass of the incubator, an invisible interface through which everything is mediated – the environment, the experience of living, the means to communicate, the way of 'knowing.' The relationship between Mother and child itself is mediated by technology. Technology interrupts the relationship, intercepts the exchange of nurturing and needing of the infantile language. The Mother becomes redundant: technology becomes the external womb.

Within the discourse of cyber-feminism, the externalized, technological womb begins to make sense: 'in Latin, it is *matrix*, or matter, both the mother and the material.'[11] Technology has become both the Mother and the matter of the consciousness, the medium through which the need to nurture and the nurture of need are fulfilled. The cyborg is born through this virtual non-space, this womb of machinic consciousness. Within the technological womb, human bodies and human consciousness become 'cy-dough-plasma' – malleable matter, without fixed form.[12]

> 27 February 2003 – ... I'm a little confused about her ears. They're pliable. Lacking cartilage at this stage of development often finds them in crumples of folded-over flesh. They require frequent repositioning and remoulding so they don't get all folded up like fortune cookies. I try not to play with them too much ... but, it's not like you can rationalize with her yet ... 'Don't crumple up your ears dear.'

Externalizing the womb subjects the unformed body to manipulation. The consciousness, like the fetal body, becomes the art of the machine. Bodies and consciousness are remixed. What we perceive to be the body often becomes distorted in the engineering of a cyborg.

> 3 February 2003 – It was as if her delicate features had been rearranged to make room for equipment. Somehow, her perfect nose was in the way of the Ventilator, so they moved it off to the side. The machines rearrange the perfection of her body.

Just as in Kristeva's infantile language, there is no easy way to distinguish between the child and the simulated techno-Mother. The machine and the baby become symbiotic. 'Sameness' governs the relationship between the baby and the machine. Their sameness means that they are mutually dependent on each other in order for life to continue.

Technology is capable of simulating vital signs, of supporting life, of becoming Mother. The child of the techno-Mother is, essentially, a virtual body, a simulation of vital signs that becomes internalized. The ventilator simulates Quinn's breathing, supporting her life through mimicry. Through the perfect simulation of breathing, the ritual of life goes forward. In cyborg culture, the lines between simulation and reality are blurred into irrelevancy. The cyborg is the interface between simulation and reality, where the simulacrum becomes capable of living. Her body is 'redesigned by means of life-support machines and prosthetic organs.'[13]

In this way, infancy becomes disembodied from the biological Mother and goes forward unmanned, like the Predator Drone: moving forward into a machinic realm of infinite possibility.[14] What happens when the conditions of infinite possibility are governed by an inherent nihilism? The externalization of the nervous system makes possible the continuation of life, yet it is a life that is fundamentally nihilistic, eternally bound to a mediated consciousness. The body is breached, becomes cyborg, a recombinant fusion of technological and biological traffic. What is internal and external to the virtually dead body becomes confused.

> 1 March 2003 – I want to love and hate the machine that breathes for her. Ventilation is a Catch-22. Ventilation turns the fragile tissues and muscles that are used for breathing and exchanging oxygen into scars. 'As long as her lungs develop faster than the ventilator damages them, we win,' says Dr T. She is getting chest X-rays almost daily now. In her X-rays, her lungs are clouded-over with white. Her little lungs fill with fluid that has to be suctioned out almost every two hours in order for her to get the proper amount of oxygen into her blood. We've had a serious heart to heart, recently. I used the 'stern mother voice' for the first time to tell her that she is not allowed to take her ventilator to kindergarten with her.

The relationship between machine and body cannot sustain life endlessly. One must eventually overtake the other in order for life to continue. Through the body, the machine performs the dichotomy of living and killing, life and death. It gives life only to overtake it. The technology that sustains life is ultimately nihilistic. What happens faster is vital – the ability to outgrow the machine or the damage inflicted by the machine itself? This is a profound statement about the morphology of human beings and machines. To become a cyborg is to commit a slow suicide. Ultimately, it is the nihilation of the human body, of autonomous human consciousness. This is the paradox of modernity, manifest in rituals of living.

Just as technology is capable of simulating rituals of living, becoming a cyborg affects the rituals of dying. Technology intervenes and institutionalizes the right/rite of death. Even after the body expires, the machines keep going. It is not until they are turned off that the body is pronounced 'dead.' Being a cyborg means that death is experienced in a new way. Is it possible to be absent in death: a redundant body in the machinic performance of consciousness?

> 14 February 2003 – I hold my child for the first time. She is naked, against my chest. Her ventilator curls around my neck, taped to my shoulder, disappears inside her. There are other tubes, too, taped to my other limbs by peach-coloured surgical tape. Beside me, another mother's baby dies. Another baby dies. The respiratory technician yells : 'No CPR' from across the nursery. He crosses the room, switches off the machines: ventilator, incubator, monitor, eight intravenous pumps of miscellaneous medical poisons. The life inside the machine refuses to go on without them. And I am taped to a rubberized rocking chair, taped to my baby, taped to the machine. I cannot leave when another baby's mother comes in.

The nihilism of becoming cyborg is inescapable. We are taped down to our own inherent nihilism. In cyborg culture, nihilism becomes synonymous with death. When a cyborg dies, the announcement of death waits for the machine to be switched off. The simulation of life continues even in the absence of physical being. When a cyborg dies, it is only because the human body has failed the perfect simulation of life by the machine. Death is ambivalent to physical being; the body becomes almost irrelevant. The machinic simulation of 'being human' can continue to exist in the absence of a human body, but the human body cannot continue in the absence of the machine. In death, the human body seemingly fails the machine. This is what Jacques Derrida calls 'the logocentric moment,' where one technology of knowing is privileged over another, and infinite other historicities of being are forgotten.[15] What happens if someone fails to turn off the machine? Is it possible that the cyborg can forget to die? Can machinic consciousness simply be switched off? It is the moment where we forget to be merely human that the machine takes over the Mother, and the technology takes over the consciousness. Becoming cyborg becomes a meta-narrative, totalizing and privileging only one point of view – the technological gaze. The internalization of the technological gaze is the most important political moment in becoming cyborg.

The internalization of the machine is the moment when the human condition becomes invisibly mediated by technology. It is the moment where technology and knowing become bound within perception. Becoming cyborg is not merely a physical condition: it is a condition of being mediated by technology.

> 26 February 2003 – ... I look to the machines and they tell me how my daughter is doing today. How easy it is to look at the monitor that tells me, 'She has the hiccups, she's sleeping, she's not breathing – not yet.' The machines talk to me and I understand what Quinn cannot yet tell me. The machines tell me what she cannot communicate. Quinn is having a 'terrible, horrible, no good, very bad day.'[16]

The incorporation of the machinic interface into the language of perception witnesses the internalization of what Michel Foucault calls 'panopticism.'[17] Panopticism goes beyond physical architecture. Being a cyborg reifies the repressive technologies of the panoptical illusion. To reify the panopticon inherently denies the possibility that there are ways of being, beyond the cyborg experience. I saw the displacement of my own motherhood by the machine. I could understand my daughter in and through the machinic interface. In this moment, I too, was written into the meta-narrative of the cyborg consciousness, and my perception of the human condition was filtered through the technological gaze.

Exposing the womb, digesting machinic consciousness, monitoring the human body, and locating motherhood outside of the mother-child symbiosis are technologies of becoming cyborg that go beyond the physical imagery. These are technologies of surveillance that are internalized; they operate in and through the cyborg.

Ultimately, it means that when the machine is shut off, cyborg life continues to occupy the human condition through consciousness, subconsciousness, and perception.

10 April 2003 – After 69 days on a ventilator, the tube was finally pulled. My little Quinnapottamus now breathes her own breaths. I guess our little talk about 'no ventilators in kindergarten' made sense to her, and she has decided to hold her own. It was amazing to watch her take her first breaths after they pulled the tube, to hear the resigned sigh of the ventilator when it was shut off. The lines on the monitor, flat-lining. The sound of her crying, her voice rising through bruised vocal chords for the first time, met my ears and was strangely comforting.

The cyborg does not die because it is unplugged. The cyborg continues to exist beyond all locations of space and time, the consciousness irreversibly fused with technology. Becoming cyborg necessitates the sublimation of the mind. Becoming cyborg, internalizing the panopticon, allows for the cultivation of human life in and for state sovereignty. To become cyborg is to be harvested by the state and for the state. Like my daughter, paralyzed for wrestling with her machines, internalizing the panopticon is paralyzing. Internalizing the panopticon makes it impossible for the human body to perform outside of technology. Ultimately, cyborg culture is written within the context of state sovereignty. The human body performs sovereignty. The making of cyborg bodies is simply that: the epistemic branding of the state on the bodies and the minds of the subordinate citizenry. The making of cyborg bodies is simply panopticism, the ingestion of the statist technology. It is about exposure, about making visible each privacy of the human body for the purposes of controlling individual life. It is about technology becoming invisible, 'seeing without being seen.'[18] The architecture of Foucault's panopticon, like the genesis of one cyborg, is both a physical and an epistemic incorporation of a centralizing, homogenizing structure of being that becomes the subject of scrutiny, both collectively and individually, by an observer in the 'tower' who remains unseen. The panoptical cyborg is both the subject and object of scrutiny, both the 'tower' of observation and the observed subject. The internalization of the panopticon is self-scrutiny. Ultimately, the cyborg becomes the technological furniture upon which state sovereignty lounges.

Panopticism becomes manifest in the minds of the everyday cyborg-citizen. Suddenly, a story about a neonate baby is less about medicine and miracles and more about what remains hidden and unarticulated: the repressive technology of being bound to cyborg consciousness. Discovering the panopticon within exposes a thinly disguised operation of sovereigntist power. Cyborgs do not write themselves, technology does. The fusion of machine and human body is the manifestation of the panopticon, the eternal reification of a bounded human identity.[19] The hospital serves as an architecture for enacting these power relations, creating enormous houses of confinement. This same technology operates in and through institutions of education, religion, and politics. The ultimate confinement of the human condition is simply this: the internalization of the panoptical technology means that humanity can never imagine being autonomous. The cyborg becomes a venue for confinement. The panopticon of cyborg culture confines the human condition within a symbiosis of machine and human body. Symbiosis with the machine (whether machinic consciousness or machinic matter) becomes the precondition to living itself. To locate 'being' outside of technology becomes an impossibility. Ultimately, it reduces the human body to a specific mechanics, a site of microphysics, a docile and useful being. Becoming cyborg is ultimately about the sublimation of the human identity and the political imaginary.

This critical examination of cyborg culture is by no means aimed to discredit the technologies that taught my daughter the art of living. It does, however, highlight the implications of becoming cyborg. In a sense, all of humanity has become disembodied from the womb. The genesis of a cyborg goes well beyond the physical union of machine with body. The day I gave birth to a cyborg, I began to understand how every human being has become a collaboration of machinic and biological matter. The human condition is mediated by technology. The meta-narrative of being a cyborg ignores ethical questions. The machine cannot ask: What would the world look like without mothers? Or, for that matter, fathers? Technology is, quire literally, beginning to rewire the way we do family, the way we know humanity. The ultimate violence of technology is its ability to generate its own invisibility, to circulate undetected in and through the physical body, to become manifest in the human consciousness as epistemic reality. Conditions of possibility other than becoming cyborg are hidden from the human condition. Yet, once technology has been internalized and operates upon us through invisible epistemes, it becomes the only way of being human. Engaging in a binary relationship with technology is merely one means of engaging with new conditions of possibility for the human condition. However, human-machine symbiosis simultaneously negates the possibility for narrative of 'being in the world' and forgets all of the moments of differentiation and deferral that work to inform the human essence.[20] Ways of being 'other' than an agent of sovereignty become impossible when identity is bound to the logocentric privileging of the dominant discourse.[21]

Notes

1   Julia Kristeva, *Desire in Language* (New York: Columbia University Press, 1980), 159.

2   Ibid., 160.

3   Barbara Kennedy, 'The "Virtual Machine" and New Becomings in the Pre-Millenial Culture,' in *The Cybercultures Reader*, ed. David Bell and Barbara Kennedy (London and New York: Routledge, 2000), 20.

4   David Bell, 'Cybercultures Reader: A User's Guide,' in *Cybercultures Reader*, 11.

5   Ibid., 7.

6   Julia Kristeva, *The Kristeva Reader*, ed. Toril Moi (New York: Columbia University Press, 1986), 298.

7 Sadie Plant, 'On the Matrix: Cyberfeminist Simulations' in *Cybercultures Reader*, 331.

8 Kristeva, *Desire in Language*, 278.

9 Ibid., 284.

10 Ibid., 279.

11 Plant, 'On the Matrix,' 333.

12 Bell, 'Cybercultures Reader,' 8.

13 Ibid., 11.

14 Jordan Crandall, 'Unmanned: Embedded Reporters, Predator Drones and Armed Perception,' *CTheory* 26/2 (2003), available at http://www.ctheory.net/articles.aspx ?id=378, accessed 10 April 2004.

15 Jacques Derrida, *Dissemination*, trans. Barbara Johnson (London: Continuum, 2005), ix-xxx, 62.

16 Judith Viorst, *Alexander and the Terrible, Horrible, No Good, Very Bad Day* (New York: Aladdin Paperbacks, 1972), p. 2.

17 Michel Foucault, *Discipline and Punish: The Birth of the Prison*, trans. Alan Sheridan (New York: Vintage, 1977).

18 Ibid., 24.

19 Warren Magnusson, 'The Reification of Political Community,' in *Contending Sovereignties*, ed. R.B.J. Walker and S.H. Mendlovitz (Boulder: Lynne Rienner Publishers, 1990).

20 Richard K. Ashley, 'Living on Border Lines: Man, Poststructuralism, and War,' in *Internation/ Intertextual Relations: Postmodern Readings of World Politics*, ed. James Der Derian and Michael Shapiro (Lexington: Lexington Books, 1989).

21 Ibid., 261.

18 When Taste Politics Meet Terror: The Critical Art Ensemble on Trial

JOAN HAWKINS

> And the sky can still fall on our heads. And the theater has been created to teach us that first of all.
>
> Antonin Artaud.[1]

Setting the Stage

In late September 2001 the Wexner Center for the Arts in Columbus, Ohio, announced that the performances of *Charlie Victor Romeo* scheduled for 26-30 September had been cancelled. 'We hope you'll understand that this is not an appropriate time to present this award-winning Off-Broadway show,' the letter accompanying my refund said. 'We will continue to stay in contact with the Collective Unconscious company who created and perform *Charlie Victor Romeo* regarding the potential for rescheduling CVR at the Wexner Center at an appropriate time in the future.'

Charlie Victor Romeo is a documentary play, based on transcripts taken from the black boxes of downed airplanes, the final communication between air personnel and the air traffic control tower. A serious and sober look at the way people actually behave during a crisis, it won the 2000 Drama Desk Awards for Best Unique Theatrical Experience and Outstanding Sound Design, the 2000 New York Fringe Festival awards for Excellence in Drama and Outstanding Sound Design, and the Backstage West Garland Award for Best Sound Design. It was filmed by the U.S. Air Force to be used as a training video for pilots and 'has been invited to be performed for groups of physicians and healthcare administrators studying the effects of human error and emergencies in a medical context.'[2] It also belongs to a group of experimental dramas – the plays of Anna Devere Smith, *The Laramie Project*, etc. – which have been mixing ethnography, documentary (with the emphasis here on documents), and theatre in provocative and compelling ways. Theatre that has learned and borrowed from performance art, one could say.

In late September 2001, I was still badly shaken by the events of 9/11. I had cancelled my planned sabbatical trip to New York when the apartment I had sublet was needed to house a writer-friend who had been evacuated from her flat, and nothing I heard from her about life in the city in the immediate aftermath of tragedy bore any resemblance to anything I was hearing on the mainstream news (with the exception of *Democracy Now*, U.S. news broadcasts were all about spin). Weary of platitudes and patriotic cant, I was looking forward to seeing the play, to hearing something *real* (in the street sense of that term) and to feeling some connection with the New York art scene that had been. I wanted to be challenged and I wanted to *think*, to be addressed as an adult rather than as a slightly addled child. I was disappointed when the play was cancelled. The box office staff member who took my call was surprised at my reaction. 'Most people have been telling us they're happy we're rescheduling the show,' she told me. 'When has it been rescheduled for?' I asked. 'We don't know yet,' she said.

I have chosen to open this essay on the recent harassment of the Critical Art Ensemble (CAE) with this older story because it seems to me to highlight some of the problems confronting the art world in this post 9/11, Patriot Act–hysterical, time. I understand some of the reasons the Wexner felt it had to postpone the performance. The Wexner Center for the Arts is small, and totally dependent for its survival on public funding and the support of its patrons and members. It certainly cannot afford to bring a New York show to Columbus and play to a near-empty house. And it probably cannot really afford the loss of community good will that such a move might entail.

But the cancellation also served to unmask the ambivalence with which we (even those of us in the art world) regard truly provocative, risk-taking art. *Charlie Victor Romeo* was rescheduled because of its content, because it was not 'an appropriate time' to present the material.[3] As I indicated above, for me it was exactly the appropriate time. And my initial reaction of disappointment remains my final one. I am disappointed not only because I did not get to see the show when I had wanted to, but because the cancellation seemed to trivialize (or at least to contain) the entire project of cutting-edge art. By cancelling the performance, the Wexner effectively communicated that provocative and radical theatre can be mounted and tolerated only when nothing serious is at stake. That to mount provocative art – especially art that deals with disaster – when something real *is* at stake is somehow in bad taste. To raise the question of the politics of taste – the fact that the whole notion of bad taste is itself an ideologically inflected construct – is also intolerable in the face of real crisis. This episode, then, seemed to signal that art and theory both are reduced, in times of crisis, 'to an academic parlor game' – something we do when there's nothing really on anyone's radar screen.[4] Something we do only when it is 'appropriate.'

The question of the appropriate role and function of art after 9/11 is one that has been framed largely in terms of taste. The removal of Eric Fischl's commemorative sculpture, *Tumbling Woman*, from Rockefeller Center; the elimination of three choruses from John Adams's opera *The Death of Klinghoffer* from a November 2001 Boston

Symphony program; and the quiet de-funding of work by performance artist William Pope (he lost an U.S. National Endowment for the Arts (NEA) grant for a series of works on racial and social injustice; the Andy Warhol Foundation magnanimously stepped in and funded the exhibition) all were done in the name of taste – the fear of offending the public in its still-sensitive, post-9/11, traumatized state.

But as I have written elsewhere,[5] questions of taste are never ideologically neutral, and almost immediately the issue of taste in post-9/11 cultural production began to overlap with heavy-handed manifestations of political corporate and state power. Bill Maher's television show, *Politically Incorrect,* was taken off the air by several ABC affiliates after Maher called the violent response of the United States to the 9/11 attacks 'cowardly.' John Lennon's song *Imagine,* and all music by Rage Against the Machine, were placed on a 'don't play' list by the corporate giant Clear Channel. The woefully misnamed group Students for Academic Freedom launched a number of websites, inviting students to turn in professors who had made 'anti-patriotic' remarks in class, and the U.S legislature introduced a bill that would tie the continued funding of area studies programs in U.S. universities (American Studies, Near Eastern Studies, etc.) to governmental 'curriculum oversight.' In the bill, renowned scholar Edward Said was specifically named as the kind of thinker we have to guard against in these troubled post-9/11 times. Finally, Steve Kurtz, founding member of the Critical Art Ensemble, was arrested for bioterrorism.

The Case

On 11 May 2004 Steve Kurtz, a filmmaker, performance artist, and founding member of the Buffalo-based Critical Art Ensemble, phoned 911 after waking to find his wife, Hope Kurtz, unconscious in bed beside him. Apparently, Ms Kurtz had died in her sleep. But it was not only her death that worried the emergency aid team that came in response to Kurtz's call, but also the laboratory equipment and inert biological compounds that Mr Kurtz uses as part of his artwork and that he had stored in his home. The 911 team phoned the FBI (this is where things get murky – because the group that actually came was the Joint Terrorist Task Force). Steve Kurtz was arrested on suspicion of bioterrorism. Hope Kurtz's body was impounded (which meant that it could not be released for a funeral). Kurtz's equipment, computer, art supplies, books, films, and biological material were confiscated. The Joint Terrorist Task Force agents also took Mr Kurtz's car, his house, and his cat.

Authorities searched Kurtz's home and tested the biological material for two days, before declaring that there was no public health risk in Kurtz's work and that no toxic material had been found. Kurtz was allowed to return to his home on 17 May, his car and cat were released, and his wife's death was attributed to heart failure. But while the case should have ended there, it was only beginning. In June, Kurtz and other members of the Critical Art Ensemble were brought before the Grand Jury and again investigated on the charge of bioterrorism. Again it was found that there was no evidence that any members of the Critical Art Ensemble had been involved in bioterrorism. Nonetheless, their case was referred to a Federal District Court and on 8 July 2004 the Federal District Court in Buffalo charged the defendants with four counts of mail and wire fraud, charges connected with the purchase of the inert biological material used in their installation work. Dr Robert Ferrell, Professor of Genetics at the University of Pittsburgh, the researcher who helped the CAE procure the biological material, was similarly indicted. They were enjoined from performance, travel, or even speaking about the case. In addition, since then Mr Kurtz has been subjected to random visits from a probation officer and to periodic drug tests.

On 17 March 2005, Steven Barnes, also a founding member of the CAE, was served a subpoena to appear before a Federal Grand Jury in Buffalo. According to the subpoena, the FBI was once again 'seeking charges under section 175 of the U.S. Biological Weapons Anti-Terrorism Act of 1989 as expanded by the U.S.A. Patriot Act – charges which a previous grand jury appeared to reject when they handed down indictments of mail and wire fraud last summer.'[6] Autonomedia, the independent book company that publishes and distributes books written by the Critical Art Ensemble, as well as books by theorists like Michel Foucault and Gilles Deleuze, has also been under investigation. Records of mail orders, purchases, editorial reports, and the press's correspondence have all been subpoenaed.

Kurtz's hearing was originally set for 11 January 2005, but was postponed to give the defence an opportunity to review the prosecution's case. It was postponed a second time, at the prosecution's request. As already mentioned, Kurtz and Ferrell have been charged with four counts of mail and wire fraud (U.S. Criminal Code Title 18; U.S. Code Sections 1341 and 1343), which each carry a maximum sentence of twenty years in prison.

Charges of mail and wire fraud are normally brought against individuals defrauding others of money and property, like telemarketers who try to sell unwitting consumers swamp land in Florida or Web scams that try to persuade respondents to authorize fictive bank transactions by giving them real bank account information. As the Critical Art Ensemble Defense Fund website points out, historically these laws have been used when the government could not prove other criminal charges (Marcus Garvey, for example, was indicted under similar charges).[7]

It is clear from both the indictment and the statutes, however, that what Ferrell and Kurtz did *was*, strictly speaking, a breach of contract. Professor Ferrell identified himself as the 'primary researcher' to be using the compounds on the application form which he submitted when purchasing the materials, and he signed a document acknowledging that the material could be used in his laboratory only. Such breaches of contract with a seller, however, are usually matters of civil suits, not federal cases; and while they may involve a fine, there is no risk of a lengthy prison term.

There is cause for cautious optimism:

[On 17 May 2005 in Buffalo,] Judge Kenneth Schroeder heard motions to dismiss a federal criminal case against artist Steven Kurtz. [...] Defence Attorney Paul Cambria argued that a dangerous precedent would be set by 'exalting' into a federal criminal case of wire and mail fraud what is at best a minor civil contract issue – the purchase of the bacterium *Serratia marcescens* by scientist Robert Ferrell for use by Kurtz in his artwork. Judge Schroeder seemed to agree, asking Federal District Attorney William Hochul whether an underaged youth who uses the Internet to purchase alcohol across state lines, for example, should be subject to federal wire fraud charges. 'Yes,' Hochul answered after some hedging, and Schroeder chuckled. 'Wow, that really opens up a Pandora's Box, wouldn't you say?' he asked.

    Schroeder also asked Hochul whether there is any federal regulation at all (OSHA, EPA, or other) concerning Serratia. Hochul admitted there wasn't. (The alleged danger of Serratia forms the basis of the government's argument for making this a criminal case, rather than simply allowing the bacterium's provider to pursue civil remedies if it feels it was wronged). [In the course of the hearing,] Cambria further argued that the FBI intentionally misled a judge into issuing the original search warrant. That judge was never told of Kurtz's lengthy, credible and complete explanation of what the seized bacterial substances were being used for, nor of the fact that Kurtz tasted Serratia in front of an officer to prove it was harmless. Also the judge was told of Kurtz's possession of a photograph of an exploded car with Arabic writing beside it, but not of the photograph's context: an invitation to an important museum art show. The photograph, by artists the Atlas Group, was one of several exhibited pieces pictured on the invitation.[8]

As the CAE website points out, however, 'the apparent courtroom victory' for the defence does not necessarily mean that Judge Schroeder will grant any of the defence motions. And if he does, it is likely that the prosecution will appeal. Whatever the outcome of the 17 May hearing, 'it will not come quickly: rulings in such hearings typically take two or three months.' In the meantime, Steven Barnes has been questioned a second time, and the cost of the case is rising at a ruinous rate. The defence so far has cost the Critical Art Ensemble $60,000.[9]

The scientific community has been alarmed by the case. Despite the fact that scientists are enjoined, by the letter of the law, from sending compounds through the mail to other unauthorized laboratories, they do so on a regular basis. 'I am absolutely astonished,' said Donald A. Henderson, dean emeritus of the Johns Hopkins School of Hygiene and Public Health and resident scholar at the Center for Biosecurity at the University of Pittsburgh Medical Center. 'Based on what I have read and understand, Professor Kurtz has been working with totally innocuous organisms ... to discuss something of the risks and threats of biological weapons – more power to him as those of us in the field are likewise concerned about their potential use and the threat of bio-terrorism.' Henderson noted that the organisms involved in the case – *Serratia marcescens* and *Bacillus atrophaeus* – do not appear on lists of substances that could be used in biological terrorism.

Natalie Jeremijenko, a University of California San Diego professor of design engineering, noted that scientists ship material to each other all the time: 'I do it. My lab students do it. It's a basis of academic collaboration. They're going to have to indict the entire scientific community.'[10]

Some people believe that the entire case is a face-saving tactic of the FBI. Others see the intent as a much more insidious attack on the art world. 'It's really going to have a chilling effect on the type of work people are going to do in this arena and other arenas as well,' noted Steven Halpern, a State University of New York (SUNY) at Buffalo professor who specializes in constitutional law. Clearly, the arts community agrees. Since June 2004 the arts community has mounted public events in support of the CAE Defense Fund. On 17 April 2005 the Paula Cooper Gallery in New York City hosted a benefit auction which attracted donations from some of the biggest names in the contemporary art world – including Vito Acconci, Richard Serra, Cindy Sherman, Martha Rossler, Sol LeWitt, Kiki Smith, Chris Burden, and many others. Even fairly conservative organizations, like the College Art Association, have come out in favour of Kurtz – in what appears to be a clear case of artistic and academic freedom. The CAA has been running updates about the case on its website since May 2004, and for a while it provided links to the CAE Defense Fund's website.

The Critical Art Ensemble

The Critical Art Ensemble is a collective of five artists of various specializations dedicated to exploring the intersections between art, technology, radical politics, and critical theory. Drawing on feminist theory, as well as the theoretical writings of Michael Hardt and Antonio Negri, Gilles Deleuze and Félix Guattari, Michel Foucault, Theodor Adorno, Stuart Hall, and Walter Benjamin, the Critical Art Ensemble has consistently seen its mission as one of education and provocation. Seeking alternately to inform audiences about the corporate influences that affect our lives and to inspire people to what it calls 'electronic disobedience,' the CAE is one of the latest practitioners of an avant-garde art tradition that has extended from the early work of the Dadas and Surrealists to contemporary performance art. They are also indebted in no small measure to both the cinematic and the political work of Jean-Luc Godard.

The CAE was formed in 1987; originally from Tallahassee, these artists soon moved into the eastern urban scene and became participants in a fin-de-siècle cultural formation that elsewhere I have called 'Downtown art.'[11] They have made films, done theatre, produced installations, and written books. Along with other downtown artists like Kathy Acker, Amos Poe, Patti Smith, David Wojnarowicz, and others, they share a commitment to formal and narrative experimentation, a view of the human body as a site of social and political struggle, an intense interest in radical identity politics, and a mistrust of institutionalized mechanisms of wealth and power. And, while they have not participated in the taste-transgressive productions that people like Nick Zedd favour (where art cinema meets true in-your-face, gross-out aesthetics), they have consistently challenged the normatization of middle class taste-culture and the politics of affect which usually accompanies it.

Their earliest productions were what might be called 'traditional' avant-garde art; that is, artworks made for people with a certain kind of cultural capital, who could easily get the references and enjoy the joke. The film *Excremental Culture* (1988), for example, takes as its reference Duchamp's famous urinal, as well as Freud's notion that feces frequently equal money in the neurotic imaginary. *Godard Revisted* (1987) is a five-minute pastiche of the Eve Democracy segment in Godard's edgy 1968 film *Sympathy for the Devil* (also known as *One Plus One*). *Speed and Violence* (1987) is a nod to the theory of Paul Virilio and to the experimental collage film technique of Bruce Conner.

In the 1990s the CAE's work took an interventionist turn. Following Godard's famous dictum, elaborated in *Tout va bien* (1972),[12] the group moved away from making political art towards making art politically. That is, they stopped making films which merely had overt political content and started making cultural products that directly intervene in the spectacle. In one famous project, for example, they collaborated with the Carbon Defense League to procure a number of GameBoys, which they reprogrammed along more Reichian lines: Here, the end goal for the player is to reach a brothel. She receives information that will help her, as well as game points, by running the numbers, selling crack, and so on.[13] The CAE placed these 'improved' games, which they call *Super Kid Fighter*, back on store shelves in time for the Christmas shopping season. In 1994 the group updated Debord's notion of the spectacle and elaborated a plan for digital civil disobedience, a move that led participants at the Terminal Futures conference in London to accuse the CAE of 'terrorism.'[14]

While the CAE advocates denying corporate and political agencies access to data and information (through hacking and online political intervention), it has increasingly seen its mission to be one of increasing the public's access to data and information (information that, they believe, the power structure would like to deny consumer-citizens). In service of this educational mission, the CAE's recent installation work, computer websites, and theatre pieces have taken both the group's art and the very concept of 'artistic production' in radical directions. This has provided something of a challenge to the affect-ive politics usually embraced by cultural institutions like museums and theatres. For one thing, members of the CAE do not call themselves 'artists,' but rather 'tactical media practitioners.'[15] It is clear that they see the groups's role more in terms of political engagement than in terms of formal experimentation:

If CAE has to pick a label, we prefer 'tactical media practitioners.' However, in keeping with this tendency we use labels in a tactical manner. If the situation is easier to negotiate using the label 'artist,' then we will use it; if it's better to use 'activist' or 'theorist' or 'cultural worker,' then we will use those labels. Regardless of the label, our activities stay the same ...

The label that best taps the knowledge resources of the audience is the one we try to choose. A lot of this problem has to do with the social constructions of the roles of artist and activist. For the most part, these roles are placed within a specialized division of labor, where one role, segment or territory is clearly separated from the other. We view ourselves as hybrids in terms of role. To CAE, the categories of artist and activist are not fixed, but liquid, and can be mixed into a variety of becomings. To construct these categories as static is a great drawback because it prevents those who use them from being able to transform themselves to meet particularized needs.[16]

The five principles of tactical media as outlined by the CAE are as follows:

1 Specificity: deriving content and choosing media based on the specific needs of a given audience within their everyday life – so that they are not wedded to a particular medium or approach
2 Nomadicality: a willingness to address any situation and to move to any site
3 Amateurism: a willingness to try anything, or negatively put, to resist specialization – members take great pride in their roles as 'amateur scientists' for example
4 Deterritorialization: an occupation of space that is predicated on its surrender, or anti-monumentalism – a way of de-sacralizing space
5 Counterinduction: a recognition that all knowledge systems have limits and internal contradictions, and that all knowledge systems can have explanatory power in the right context[17]

Clearly, these tactics put the CAE at odds with the traditional politics of theatres and art museums, which generally rely on notions of expertise, the sacralization of space, and the surety that certain forms of knowledge are appropriate to specific historical situations (putting Surrealist techniques in historical context makes them seem like a necessary response to an admittedly grim historical situation, for example). The CAE also, however, dictates a different affect-ive relationship between viewer and cultural object than the ones that museums routinely favour – and highly different notions of both the viewer and the object itself.

If you have been to any large museum shows in the United States lately, you will probably have encountered the study area that is usually spatially situated at the end of the exhibit, just before the room where you are invited to buy mugs, mousepads, notecards, and the like. Generally, there is a table or bench that has copies of the exhibit's catalogue and other books by and about the artists whose work you have just seen. There may be some art history texts or a copy of *Aperture* magazine. In more explicitly political shows, there may be books of political theory, as well. At a recent exhibit at the Smart Museum on the University of Chicago campus, for example, I ran across Hardt and Negri's *Empire*, Gramsci's *Prison Notebooks*, some works by Foucault, and Derrida's book on Marx in the study area – and people were indeed reading this selection of continental political theory.

It is the geographical placement of the study area that interests me. In most museum shows, it comes at the end of the exhibit. While throughout the exhibit itself, there may be placards or notes guiding you to read a work of art in a certain way, or there may be historical contextualization provided, for the most part the pure 'aesthetic' experience of the work is privileged over academic discourse and over-intellectualization of the art. In this way, I would argue that museum culture – and to some degree mainstream theatre, as well – privileges affect and sets the intellectual aspects of the work apart – in the study area, or in notes included in your program, or out in the lobby. I should say here, though, that avant-garde theatre and some experimental exhibition culture does have a tradition of directly instructing the audience.

What the CAE has done in its most recent installation work has been to move the study area front and centre, to make it an integral part of the art exhibit itself. What you see when you enter a CAE exhibit is something that looks like an open science classroom. There is art on the walls, as well as video installations and digital displays, but there are also computer terminals and science experiments set up for you to do, and a group of artists dressed like lab assistants who are there to help you.[18]

A major part of the CAE's current project is to demystify science, 'to provide a tactile relationship to the material' that goes beyond reproduction. To that end, the artists guide you to do hands-on work that will give you the tools you/we/all of us need in order to understand the political and social economy of science and technology in our age. Not only is the object itself different here – since the CAE makes no distinction between the traditional art on the wall of the exhibit and the science lesson you the viewer complete at the computer terminal – but clearly the notion of audience is radicalized. 'Viewers' of a CAE exhibit are more like participants, and in the sense that the finished 'work' of art – the finished product – is the sum of all the contributions that viewers have made via experiments and computer screens, they can be seen as co-producers, as well.

The use of biological compounds in these installations is key to helping participants understand the risks and dangers of biologically engineered food, to cite the example of one show, or of true bioterrorism, the show they were preparing when Steve Kurtz was arrested.[19] Here, participants really do perform chemistry experiments, with the guidance of the CAE cultural workers. Mixing materials and looking through microscopes, museum visitors can see first-hand what happens when you mutate or 'modify' certain cells; they can see first hand what the basic structure of that apple you have just given your child actually resembles. In a sense this is 'autopsy' art. It depends – as Stan Brakhage's famously disturbing avant-garde film of an autopsy does – on 'the act of seeing with one's own eyes' (the literal meaning of the term 'autopsy'). But as in Brakhage's film, the act of visual examination in CAE pieces encroaches radically on what are normally considered to be the proper bounds of art and of taste.

As I have hinted above, the CAE's engagement with the affect-ive politics of space and product frequently tips over into the realm of taste politics. Their play, *Flesh Machine*, which is about eugenics, opens with a lecture performance – delivered without irony – to the audience. As Rebecca Schneider points out, the 'CAE finds the lecture to be both the gentlest and most reliable entry into what quickly becomes a more complexly challenging event.' In the second act, the audience becomes more involved – this is the lab part of the production, where spectators participate in actual laboratory processes and encounter various models of artificial reproduction. For this section, the CAE builds its own 'cryolab' to house living human tissue for potential cloning, so that audience members become hands-on genetic engineers.[20] Also during the second act, audience members sit at monitors and take a standardized test to assess their individual suitability to be further reproduced through donor DNA, cytoplasm, and/or surrogacy. If they 'pass' the test, they are given a certificate of genetic merit. They can even donate cell samples and tissue to lab technicians there at the site, if they wish their DNA to be stored for some real (non theatrical) eugenics project. 'The artists have been collecting photos of audience members who 'pass' this standardized test, and they claim that the similarities among those deemed fit for reproduction is astounding. By now they can predict 'passes' just by looking at them: straight-looking white white-collars, usually male.'[21]

'After this hands-on cell-sharing experience, the audience re-assembles as a group for the close of the performance. This final section of *Flesh Machine* is intended to underscore the class politics, economics, and logic of human commodification implicated in eugenics,' writes Rebecca Schneider in a passage that is worth quoting at length:

> At this point, CAE presents a frozen embryo to their audience – an embryo that CAE inherited from a couple who no longer needed their eggs. A live image of the embryo is projected through a video beam onto a screen. The image has a clock marking the time the embryo has until it is 'evicted' from its clinical cryotank. If enough money is raised to pay the rent (approximately $60) on the cryotank through the performance, the embryo will live. If not, it will be 'terminated.'

> Put another way, if no one buys the embryo, it dies.

CAE then takes donations from the audience. To date, every performance has ended with the death-by-melting of the embryo. This part of the performance, CAE claims, speaks for itself – though on more than one occasion CAE has had to speak in the wake of their actions. In Vienna, for instance, they found themselves on national TV debating the ethical implications of 'embryo murder' with the Archbishop of Salzburg live via satellite.[22]

What Schneider calls the 'death-by-melting' of a live embryo as part and parcel of a live theatre performance clearly pushes the envelope on the norms of good taste, even those that have already been stretched by *theatrical representations* of similarly controversial actions. It is precisely because the CAE has been so spectacularly willing to violate the norms of artistic good taste that its work has been so controversial (this more than the political content gets the group into trouble with the art world). Encroaching vigorously on low culture (not in a playful safe way, the way someone like Jeff Koons encroaches on porn, but in a profoundly disturbing way), the CAE's work is frequently criticized as not being art at all.[23]

Final Acts

The title of this chapter is 'When Taste Politics Meet Terror.' I have put the two terms 'taste politics' and 'terror' together, not to suggest a causal link (implying that the CAE was specifically targeted *because* of the radical content of its work, as some commentators have claimed) – but I do believe that the content of the ensemble's work and its entire demystification project has made the group vulnerable to the law – particularly in these post-9/11 times.

As Stephanie Kane has argued, the current political regime in the United States depends on a certain illusory performance art of its own – a mimesis of control, if you will – to gain legitimacy for its post-9/11 policies. Central to that performance of control is the demonstration of containment. That is, people have to believe that biological compounds can be policed, regulated, and contained and that their circulation can be controlled – if only we are vigilant enough and give up enough of our civil liberties – in order for the system to work. If organisms can travel outside the bounds that are policed, then the metaphors that organize the discourse of bioterrorism and public safety – at least in the United States – are challenged. (The links to the control of other substances, like recreational drugs, are interesting here – as I mentioned earlier, as part of his current status, Steve Kurtz is subjected to random drug tests, presumably because he is a presumed substance offender.)

In that sense the CAE case is more about the system than it is about the people critiquing the system. The FBI did not set out to bust the Critical Art Ensemble, but once the chemical compounds were found they were not able to drop the case. In the most blatant and simple way, what the CAE has done through the very materiality of its art is challenge the illusion of government control: 'you can't control the commerce of this stuff; through our art, we make it obvious you can't.' As Stephanie Kane has noted, this case is really about the battle for and over the political unconscious of the United States, and the ways in which art can tap into (or at least temporarily intersect with) that unconscious.

But there is more here that needs to be unpacked. Progressives have been arguing against the Bush administration and fighting it within a territorialized flow of logic. Our attention is continually drawn to artefacts (the pictures from Abu Ghraib, the testimony of human rights organizations, and in the CAE case, the results of chemical tests) and to outcomes and results (the pathetically tiny number of actual terrorists caught) to prove the moral and political bankruptcy of the current political machine. Oppositional political discourse – in the United States, anyway – seems frozen in a concomitant territorialized zone of disbelief. We do not understand how the Bush administration could start the Iraq War in the face of so much global opposition (our attention drawn by even mainstream news broadcasts to the marchers in London, Paris, Rome, and New York), we do not understand why it continues to pursue a strategy that is financially and politically (in the international arena, anyway) ruinous, we do not understand why it cannot simply admit a mistake and let the CAE continue its activities in peace.

But that is because we are not taking the nature of the political machine *as machine* seriously. In her article 'Reflection on the Case,' Claire Pentecost writes: 'One can imagine that investigative agencies and U.S. attorneys are under enormous economic pressure to produce results in the "War Against Terror." To put it crudely, in the last three and a half years, probably nothing has influenced promotions and funding more.'[4] But Pentecost moves from this observation back into a territorialized discourse that critiques the administration's actions on the basis of logical outcomes – the racist nature of the incarceration process, the incompetence (in terms of procedures and convictions) of the military and the police, the 'shame of … [the U.S. Justice Department's] waste.'

If you have read much Deleuze and Guattari you probably see where I am going with this. Ironically I myself did not until I read a news article in which journalist Ted Rall reports on the terrifying case of two teenaged girls from Queens who have been arrested – one for rebelling against parental authority and the other for an essay she wrote as part of a school assignment. According to reliable news sources, '"the FBI says both girls are an imminent threat to the security of the United States based upon evidence that they plan to become suicide bombers." The feds admit that they have no hard evidence to back their suspicions. Nothing. Just an essay written for a school assignment and parental claims that one girl was defiant of authority. "There are doubts about these claims, and no evidence has been found that … a plot was in the works," one Bush administration official admitted to the [*New York*] *Times*. "The arrests took place after authorities decided it would be better to lock up the girls than wait and see if they decided to become terrorists."' Rall writes that he himself defied his mother's authority when he was a teenager and wrote school essays that betrayed his fascination with 'morbid, violent subjects.' During the calmer days of his youth, however, nothing much happened – a few quarrels with his mother, a trip to the school principal's office. But for these girls the case is much different. They are both facing possible deportation to countries they have never seen (their parents are immigrants), because 'this is post-9/11 America and post-9/11 America is out of its mind.'[25]

Out of its mind. Crazy. Schizophrenia. Schizoanalysis. That was more or less the thought chain that brought me back to Deleuze and Guattari.

In terms of political analysis, we need to return to the notion of desiring machines, to Deleuze and Guattari's idea of deterritorialized flows of desire. Put in terms that some of my political friends would find more congenial, we need to focus our analytical attention on processes rather than on products, but in such a way that logic is not taken to be the defining feature of process (so that if you show something does not make logical sense, you expect that everyone will just say 'oh, all right then, release the prisoners and bring the soldiers home'). One thing that the Vietnam War should have taught us about political activism is that these policies are not about logic, and they are not sold to the American people on the basis of logic. Instead, they belong to that economy of flows by which political economy and libidinal economy are seen as inextricably linked, that economy whereby 'the rule of continually producing production' (be it the production of terror or terrorists or criminals) is the dominant mode.[26] This is production for its own sake, production without a 'logical' goal. That is what we are up against under the current regime – the desiring machine of the state, what Foucault might call 'governmentality' – with a particular schizo-twist.

This does not mean that no action is possible. At the conclusion of his preface to *Anti-Oedipus*, Foucault writes:

> ... if I were to make this great book into a manual or guide to everyday life:
> - Free political thought from all unitary and totalizing paranoia.
> - Develop action, thought, and desires by proliferation, juxtaposition, and disjunction, and not by subdivision and pyramidal hierarchization.
> - Withdraw allegiance from the old categories of the Negative ... which Western thought has so long held sacred as a form of power ... Prefer what is positive and multiple, difference over uniformity, flow over unities, mobile arrangements over systems. Believe that what is productive is not sedentary but nomadic.
> - Do not think one has to be sad in order to be militant, even though the thing one is fighting is abominable ...
> - Do not use thought to ground a political practice in Truth, nor use political action to discredit, as mere speculation, a line of thought. Use political practice as an intensifier

of thought, and analysis as a multiplier of the forms and domains for the intervention of political action.

- Do not demand of politics that it restore the 'rights' of the individual *as philosophy has defined them*. The individual is the product of power. What is needed is to 'de-individualize' by means of multiplication and displacement, diverse combinations. The group must not be the organic bond uniting hierarchized individuals [as it is under the Oedipal structure] but a constant generator of de-individualization.
- Do not become enamored of power.[27]

What we need to begin doing under this set of guidelines is to turn our analytical attention away from logic (especially as it relates to social and political outcomes) and to begin thinking, instead, about desire. We have to begin analysing the function of desire, both within our own political organizations and within the state-controlled agencies whose legitimacy we question.

This is a much more radical project than the one that most political organizations on the left are currently undertaking. It is also one that will bring us closer to both the affective and political projects of the Critical Art Ensemble – whose art can be read in Deleuzian terms as a combination of artistic machine, revolutionary machine, and analytical machine.

I began this chapter with an epigram. It is a quote by Antonin Artaud. Artaud – who later in life went mad, went as far as he could go towards dissolving his own sense of ego – is the schiz who here provides the point of departure and the point of destination. In 1938 Artaud called for a theatre that would be like the plague. Not a nice theatre. Not a theatre that respects boundaries and limits. Not a theatre that waits for the appropriate time to mount its dark myths. A theatre, an art, that is truly radical and that can, therefore, make a difference. He called such theatre the theatre of cruelty. The current political regime of the United States sometimes calls it a theatre of terror.

Support the CAE

In very material terms, we need to try to help the Critical Art Ensemble. Whatever judicially happens to Steve Kurtz, Professor Ferrell, and other members of the CAE, they may never recover financially from this case (this is true despite the incredible generosity shown by the art world). The defence costs at the time of this writing are over U.S. $60,000. The additional costs in cancelled appearances and lost work are staggering. Even if the group is acquitted, it is highly unlikely that the kinds of institutions that can afford to bear some of the costs of mounting their shows (like universities and grant-receiving public art agencies) will be willing to book the CAE and hence possibly come under scrutiny themselves, *unless we put pressure on them to do so*. In material political terms, this is a place to start. In recent months Kurtz and members of the CAE have

begun making limited fundraising appearances. If you are connected with an organization that might be able to arrange a fundraiser or visit, log on to the CAE Defense Fund
website (www.caedefensefund.org), and when you are casting about for something
interesting to read, take a look at the Autonomedia catalogue (www.autonomedia.org),
and remember that this radically theoretical press is itself still under threat.

Afterword: Update on the Case

On 11 October 2007 in Federal District Court, Buffalo, New York, Dr Robert E. Ferrell
pled guilty to a misdemeanor charge of failing to follow proper procedures in mailing
samples. According to a brief *New York Times* article, Prof Ferrell 'agreed to the plea in
part because of health concerns.'[28] In an article posted on the CAE Defense Fund webpage, Dr Ferrell's wife was more loquacious. 'Bob is a 27-year survivor of non-
Hodgkin's lymphoma which has recurred several times,' Dr Dianne Raeke said. 'He
has also had malignant melanoma. Since this whole nightmare began, Bob has had
two minor strokes and a major stroke which required months of rehabilitation.'[29]
Dr Raeke added that her husband was indicted 'just as he was preparing to undergo a
painful and dangerous autologous stem cell transplant, the second in 7 years.'[30]

As the CAE Defense Fund Website notes, 'the plea bargain agreement comes at a
time of overwhelming public support for the two defendants.' A 2007 film about the
case – *Strange Culture* – directed by Lynn Hershman Leeson and starring Tilda Swinton,
Thomas Jay Ryan, and Peter Coyote, has won critical praise and excited public interest
in the case. The film was chosen to open the 2007 Human Rights Watch International
Film Festival and the Berlin International Film Festival Doc section. A 1 October
screening at the Museum of Modern Art in New York drew a crowd of 400 people,
who stayed for an hour after the screening to discuss the film and case.[31]

The federal government has pursued this case relentlessly for the past three and a
half years. And the legal battle 'has exhausted the financial, emotional and physical
resources' of both Dr Ferrell and Steve Kurtz. As part of the plea bargain, Dr Ferrell
has agreed to testify against Steve Kurtz; at the time of this writing no trial date has
been set.[32]

Special benefit screenings of *Strange Culture* have helped to raise money for the
defence. For more information about the film, go to the *Strange Culture* website http://
www.strangeculture.net.

Acknowledgments

An earlier version of this essay was presented as part of the 'Politics of Affect / Politics
of Terror' American Studies Series at Indiana University, Bloomington, 17 February
2005. A revised version was presented at the annual meeting of the Society for Cinema
and Media Studies, London, 31 March to 3 April 2005. I would like to thank Andrew

Allred, Chris Dumas, Skip Hawkins, Jonathan Haynes, Stephanie Kane, Steve Kurtz, Lin Tian, and the students of my G604 class for their help and suggestions.

Notes

1 Antonin Artaud, 'No More Masterpieces,' in *The Theater and Its Double*, trans. Mary Caroline Richards (New York: Grove, 1958), 79. (Originally published in French by Gallimard, 1938.)
2 *Charlie Victor Romeo* website, available at http://www.charlievictorromeo.com, accessed 10 June 2005.
3 *Charlie Victor Romeo* did finally come to Columbus, Ohio, in 2002 (29 May to 2 June).
4 Joan Hawkins, 'When Bad Girls Do French Theory,' in *Life in the Wires: The CTheory Reader*, ed. Arthur and Marilouise Kroker (Victoria: NWP, 2004), 202.
5 Joan Hawkins, *Cutting Edge: Art Horror and the Horrific Avant-Garde* (Minneapolis and London: University of Minnesota Press, 2000).
6 See the Critical Art Ensemble (CAE) Defense Fund website, 'Auction to Support Indicted Artist' (13 April 2005), available at http://www.caedefensefund.org/auction.html, accessed 13 April 2005.
7 Ibid.
8 CAE Media Release, 'Judge Hears Motion to Dismiss,' 17 May 2005. Available online at www.caedefensefund.org/releases/051705_Release.html, accessed 10 June 2005.
9 Ibid.
10 Quoted on the CAE Defense Fund website.
11 Joan Hawkins, 'Dark, Disturbing, Intelligent, Provocative and Quirky: Avant-Garde Cinema of the 1980s and 1990s,' in *Contemporary American Independent Film*, ed. Christine Holmlund and Justin Wyatt (London and New York: Routledge, 2005), 89-106.
12 In *Tout va bien,* a filmmaker played by Yves Montand explains the difference between making political films and making films politically. Political films are films that have leftist content and pretensions but are made within the system they mean to critique. Making films politically is a more radical gesture, one that calls traditional modes of production into question and attempts to intervene directly in the spectacle.
13 For more information on this and for instructions for turning any GameBoy into what the CAE calls 'Super Kid Fighter,' see CAE, *Digital Resistance: Explorations in Tactical Media* (New York: Autonomedia, 2001), 144, 146.
14 CAE, 'Mythology of Terrorism on the Net' (1995), available at http://www.to.or.at/cae/mnterror.htm, accessed 10 June 2005.
15 It is interesting to note that while the CAE still views itself as a media group, it has received very little academic or critical attention from media scholars. To date, the best and most complete analysis of its work has appeared in drama journals. See particularly Rebecca Schneider's articles in the *Drama Review*; The *Drama Review* articles are archived at http://muse.jhu.edu/journals/tdr, accessed 10 June 2005.
16 Ryan Griffis, 'Tandom Surfing the Third Wave,' *Lumpen*, no. 81 (2001): 2.

17 Jon McKenzie and Rebecca Schneider, 'Tactical Media Practitioners,' *Drama Review* 44/4 (2000): 136-50.

18 For photos from the actual installations, go to http://www.gene-sis.net/artists_cae.html, accessed 10 June 2005.

19 The importance of this work can hardly be overstated. As I was working on this section of the essay, I took a break and went upstairs. My husband was watching the *Democracy Now* news program, and as my foot touched the top step I heard Amy Goodman announce that Monsanto had tried to suppress a report that shows biological and structural change and damage in chickens fed an exclusive diet of genetically engineered corn. The chickens developed misshapen organs and had irregularities in their blood. *Democracy Now*, 23 May 2005, available at http://www.democracynow.org, accessed 10 June 2005.

20 Rebecca Schneider, 'Nomadmedia: On Critical Art Ensemble,' *Drama Review* 44/4 (2000): 2.

21 Ibid., 3.

22 Ibid.

23 One thing I have found both interesting and disturbing is that while the CAE still uses media as an intrinsic part of its art and advocates media activism, critical writing on the group has moved outside the realm of media studies altogether. At the time of this writing, independent filmmaker Gregg Bordowitz and I are the only media people working on the group, even though many of my colleagues use the CAE's essays on the documentary and the Net in their classes. And neither Bordowitz nor I are publishing our work on the CAE in the major film and media publications. In fact, when I submitted an essay to a film and video journal, I was advised to send it to *Performing Arts Journal* instead. Most of the critical and scholarly work on the CAE has appeared in theory forums like *CTheory* or performance journals like the *Drama Review*.

24 Claire Pentecost, 'Reflections on the Case,' CAEDF website (6 April 2005), available at www.caedefensefund.org/reflections.html, accessed 10 June 2005.

25 Ted Rall, 'Teen Terrorists,' *Progressive Populist*, 1 June 2005, available at http://www.populist.com/05.10.html, accessed 22 Oct. 2007.

26 Gilles Deleuze and Félix Guattari, *Anti-Oedipus: Capitalism and Schizophrenia*, trans. Robert Hurley, Mark Seem, and Helen R. Lane (Minneapolis and London: University of Minnesota Press, 1983), 7.

27 Michel Foucault, preface to *Anti-Oedipus*, by Deleuze and Guattari, xiv; emphasis mine.

28 Randy Kennedy, 'A Guilty Plea in Bacterial Art Case,' *New York Times* (Saturday, 13 Oct. 2007), A16.

29 'Illness, "Absurd" Prosecution Force Scientist to Plead in Precedent Setting Case' at http://www.caedefensefund.org/press/10_11_07.html, accessed 10 Oct. 2007.

30 Ibid.

31 Ibid.

32 Ibid.

19 Virtually Queer?
Homing Devices, Mobility, and Un/Belongings

MARY BRYSON, LORI MACINTOSH,
SHARALYN JORDAN, AND HUI-LING LIN

It all begins with an insult.

> Didier Eribon, *Insult and the Making of the Gay Self*

We are in an epoch of simultaneity; we are in an epoch of juxtaposition, the epoch of the near and far, of the side-by-side, of the dispersed. We are at a moment, I believe, when our experience of the world is less that of a long life developing through time than that of a network that connects points and intersects with its own skein.

> Michel Foucault, *Of Other Spaces*

Mass-media accounts about the significance of the Internet to queer folks (and communities) commonly foreground celebratory and *apparently* uncomplicated narratives that feature members of marginalized communities who find a place online to form communal networks, feel a hard-won sense of belonging, or, at least, locate relevant and appropriate informational resources. A *Time* magazine cover story on 'gay teens,' for example, unproblematically recounts that 'when University of Pittsburgh freshman Aaron Arnold, 18, decided to reveal his homosexuality at 15, he just Googled "coming out," which led to myriad advice pages.'[1] There is, however, nothing straightforward about the relationship of subaltern sexual identifications and cyberculture.

Queer theoretical accounts of acts and contexts of categorical identification lean heavily on Foucault's problematization of an 'economy of visibility.'[2] Foucault's method of analytical critique proceeds genealogically as it excavates, and pushes to centre stage, a cultural matrix of power/knowledge relationalities within which access to minoritarian subjectivity is coextensive with the reiteration and incorporation of prescriptive norms. Post-structuralist arguments concerning queer subjectivity likewise make extensive use of Judith Butler's influential work on 'performativity.' Butler asseverates that 'discourse ... materialize[s] its effects' and 'circumscribe[s] the domain of intelligibility.'[3] In such denaturalizing, dramaturgical accounts of identity and sociality, *seeking to be 'recognized as' belonging* to a particular (i.e., identitarian) group, or community, is, then, more adequately to be understood as a complex cultural *mise en scène* that proceeds by means of a set of contingent performative practices within which to 'be subjected' is to always-already be imbricated within the discursive economy upon which the very constitution of that subject (or community) depends.[4]

Several key thematic preoccupations criss-cross scholarship concerning 'queer' and 'technoculture,' including an intense focus on the cultural politics, power relations, and radically contingent, and discursively mediated operations and practices of space, mobility, sociality, consumption, citizenship, and subjectivity. Sheller and Urry's expansive discussion of the 'new mobilities paradigm' provides a strong and insightful argument that social science research needs, itself, to adopt a less 'sedentarist' approach, and in so doing, to explore *critically* the productive tensions and complexities typically associated with globalization, increasingly convergent and ubiquitous media, and twenty-first-century 'liquid modernities.'[5]

This essay draws on the first year of interview data in a three-year project that looks at myriad aspects of queer women's engagements with cultural artefacts, including books, television, and the Internet (www.queerville.ca). There is not, yet, a significant body of research on queer women and new media, and this project addresses that gap.[6] Overwhelmingly, the scant research conducted to date has proceeded by means of critical exigetic analyses of online discourse – postings to online bulletin boards, blogs, and the like.[7] Insights into everyday uses of media is a critical aporia produced by an analytic emphasis on media textualities. Accordingly, we follow a line of thinking from cultural media studies scholars who emphasize that research needs to eschew technological determinism (or an 'effects of media' model) and carefully consider *quotidian uses of popular culture.*[8]

Virtually Queer? Identity, Community, and the Politics of Difference

Nina Wakeford in a significant review essay that inquires critically into academic discourse regarding the juxtaposition of Internet and non-normative sexualities coined by the term 'cyberqueer,' adroitly observes that 'the construction of identity is the key thematic that unites almost all cyberqueer studies.'[9] Bryson posits that a discursive logic of mobilization and heterogeneity organizes discussions of 'queer' and argues:

> Contemporary accounts of *queer* invariably situate this slippery signifier as designative of a heterogeneous, historically and geographically contingent, contested and performative set of 'identity effects' (Butler, 1993). Thus construed, *queer is always-already virtual* ... 'Virtually queer' marks the intersection between the performative and 'in progress' qualities of queer culture and its manifestations and permutations engendered by networked digital technologies – construed as spaces and artifacts – as important mediative elements in the production of 'queer.'[10]

Jamie Poster's study of a 'lesbian chat room' provides us with a useful elucidation of the complex dynamics of the 'encoding and decoding' of identity within the locus of ongoing efforts devoted to the formation and stabilization of virtual community.[11] Poster's analysis of the production and negotiation of 'computer-mediated identity' in #LesChat (a lesbian IRC channel) indicates that participation is mediated by a significant set of norms, many of which pertain to the definition of who might count as an eligible interactant (woman + lesbian). Poster's observation of this site indicates that a great deal of time is spent in extensive interrogatory activities where 'regulars' determine that newcomers are, in fact, 'women,' by means of a series of screening questions. And in the event that a visitor 'fails the test,' community members deploy extraordinary effort and creativity in 'kicking' the interloper from the chat room. Poster argues that the frequent repetition of the authentication/kicking scenario performs the function of shoring up the members' sense of 'imagined community' to the extent that 'shared local knowledge performatively harvests coherence among people' and reminds those who remain that they belong.[12]

Poster's research provides an intriguing glimpse of the tricky negotiation of online space that presupposes (one might think, paradoxically) a homogeneous grouping of coherent queer female subjects. And although it is critical to affirm the difficulty, innumerable obstacles, and hence, the social and cultural importance for queer women to 'take up space,' this research leaves unanswered the question of the cost of a 'politics of recognition' to the opportunities for participation that remain for those who 'pass the test.'[13] As Wakeford observes, 'There is a disturbing silence on the issue of ability to perform identities once users are in a cyberqueer space ... The question might not be "Are you lesbian?" but "Are you lesbian enough?" to participate.'[14]

Wincapaw's research on participants in lesbian and bisexual women's email lists provides an important analysis of the limits to identificatory mobility in virtual locations. Respondents to a survey distributed across a variety of queer women's e-lists provided extensive validation for the observation that any community that is organized in relation to an articulation of a marginalized identity that presupposes assumptions of homogeneity will re-inscribe exclusionary practices, even as it also provides a welcome relief from the multiple violences that accrue to members of marginalized sexual and/or gendered subcultures. In accounting for the value of participation in same-sex email lists, subscribers emphasized the importance of 'safety,' 'freedom from homophobia,' 'interaction in a women-only space,' and 'distance from men.' However, respondents whose identificatory practices marked them as 'different' in these locations experienced exclusion, non-recognition, and a lack of belonging.

Racism was a significant factor shaping participation in the lists, where white respondents 'considered "race" to be a non-issue,' while women of colour reported an assumption of ubiquitous white racialization and/or a repudiation of efforts to represent any experience or identification explicitly coded as non-white.[15] Respondents also made it very clear that membership by bisexual women in the lists was intensely problematic. Many lists explicitly excluded bisexual women, whereas others required that bisexual women refrain from discussing men, and in so doing, clearly demanded a form of self-censorship that effectively transformed the performativity of their sexual identification from contextually non-normative to normative. As Wincapaw notes, 'the LISTS re-inscribe the often discriminatory and usually intolerant practices of the rest of the world. "Same shit, different medium!" said one woman who self-identifies as a "fatdyke."'[16]

It is clear that access to 'narrow bandwidth' sites coded as 'lesbian,' such as email lists or chat rooms, while providing an important location of relative 'safety,' also seems to engender hyperbolic performances of identity that result in exclusion, to the extent that homogeneity of identification is a condition of participation. Studies of online locations as decontextualized from everyday life do not tell us much about how queer women make use of these spaces as part of quotidian routines, nor do they shed any light on uses of the Internet outside of participation in seemingly dislocated online spaces whose relation to lived geographies is typically not tackled as a significant or interesting research question.

Queer Mobilities: Everyday Practices of Mediatization

In his discussion of 'telling experiential stories about cyberspace and everyday life,' Bell emphasizes the importance of situating scholarly inquiry concerning the Internet in the realm of the quotidian and stresses the importance of risking the production of research narratives that stress 'banality or mundanity.'[17] Bell argues that narrativizing everyday usage involves an explicit description of practices as well as an authorial aesthetics that eschews idealization or romanticism. As Wakeford argues, 'The concept of cyberspace is suffering from over-excitement, over-exposure and under-precision ... The competing definitions of the territory might better be resolved by characterizing cyberspace as a series of specific performances, rather than searching for one underlying totalizing definition (Wakeford, 1995). Focusing on the local practices of those who are constructing spaces in self-proclaimed cyberspaces suggests that a strategy which schematises the variety of spaces and activities may be more useful than continual (de)territorialisation.'[18]

Recent research by Rothbauer on (Canadian) 'lesbian and queer women's' reading practices provides us with an interesting example of scholarly inquiry that focuses its analytical lens on the everyday. Rothbauer set out to study the function of reading in the lives of lesbian and queer young women. She was also interested in participants' practices as users of various libraries and related online information networks. An interesting unexpected finding was that despite a high level of information/computer literacy and extensive familiarity with searching for queer cultural materials online, 'access to the Internet and previous knowledge of lesbian and gay texts did not result in more satisfactory on-line searching experiences.'[19] Participants' searches for queer reading materials frequently failed to produce the desired books because either the texts were not housed in their school or public libraries, or their use of search terms (e.g., 'lesbian,' 'queer') did not correspond with the classificatory systems of the public library system (which uses subject headings such as 'homosexuality'). As Rothbauer emphasizes, access to lesbian and queer texts is problematic on multiple levels that are not addressed either by a high level of access to online information networks or by adequate familiarity with conducting online information searches.

While these young lesbian and queer women's online searches were structured, and, as such, constrained by the paucity of available lesbian/queer texts housed in institutionally sanctioned locations (like libraries), it is equally critical to note that the women's opportunities for textual engagement were not wholly determined by an overwhelming and oppressive lack. In fact, participants' Internet searches provided access to a wide array of digital texts, including fan fiction, comics, and zines – all genres that are, apparently, marginalized in their classification by librarians as 'grey literature.'[20]

Cultural studies research on popular culture has prioritized the reframing of engagements by members of subcultural groups with media that are conventionally regarded as debased, non-canonical, and/or insignificant. Henry Jenkins's widely cited work on fan groups emphasizes the cultural significance of participants' mediated practices, as well as the inherent sociality of fandom, which he describes as 'a participatory culture which transforms the experience of media consumption into the production of new texts, indeed, of a new culture and a new community.'[21] And indeed, Rothbauer notes that participants' mediated engagements with diverse queer cultural artefacts and locations proved a means for mobility between multiple spaces of sociality where the 'discursive logic' of shared interests and intertextuality was concomitantly productive of networked interaction.

Our research is intended to address an 'important agenda for queer studies' identified by Ann Cvetkovich: namely, to embark on 'inquiry into the nuances and idiosyncrasies of how people actually live their sexual and emotional lives.'[22] We ask, 'What are the cultural practices and mediative artefacts that mobilize the articulation of provisional nonnormative identifications and collectivities?' This is, then, critical, sociocultural research that addresses the significance of artefacts and the production, mediatization, and narrativization of queer women's relations and sociality, identificatory practices, desires, community participation, access to, and production of, knowledge and social networks. We are anchored by work in media studies that prioritizes for 'the archivist of deviance,' a preoccupation with the ways in which 'people live and negotiate the everyday life of consumer capitalism and the manner in which people use mass culture in their quotidian practices.'[23]

Conjuring the Quotidian: Queer Accounts of Media in the Assemblage and Negotiation of Everyday Life

> Cultural Studies has the pedagogical task of disentangling the Internet from its given millennial narratives of universality, revolutionary character, radical otherness from social life, and the frontier mythos.
>
> Jonathan Sterne, in *Doing Internet Research*

Open-ended in-depth interviews concerning artefacts, identifications, and communities were conducted with sixty-three women who identify as 'lesbian, gay, bisexual, dyke, queer, and/or transgendered.' Interviews took place in multiple locations in British Columbia (Vancouver, Steveston, Victoria, Nanaimo, Abbotsford, Prince George, Fort Nelson, Williams Lake) and Alberta (Edmonton, St Albert, Red Deer, Calgary) that include rural, suburban, northern/remote, and urban areas. British Columbia and Alberta represent two Canadian provinces with distinctly different histories with respect to political climate and the provision of human rights legislation to prohibit discrimination on the basis of sexual orientation.[24] Participants ranged in age from twenty-one to sixty-five years and represent a diverse group in terms of socioeconomic status and dis/ability. Two of the participants identify as Aboriginal, two as African-Canadian, five as Asian, and fifty-four as white.

For the initial phase of research we conducted face-to-face interviews. This methodological choice was primarily motivated by a desire to address the absence, in existing research, of queer women's accounts concerning the situatedness of media in the context of everyday life. Our interpretive frame for thinking about interview data is informed by Gail Mason's landmark study of homophobia, gender, and violence. Mason proposes a genealogical approach wherein interviews provide access to 'interpretive repertoires' that index 'fields of knowledge' by means of which processes and practices of subjectification are mediated.[25] As Lisa Lowe argues, 'Forms of individual and collective narratives are not merely representations disconnected from "real" political life; nor are these expressions "transparent" records of histories of struggle. Rather, these forms – life stories, oral histories, histories of community, literature – are crucial media that connect subjects to social relations.'[26]

It is critical to acknowledge here, albeit in a very truncated form, irremediable complexities pertinent to critical engagements with the methodology of interviewing. Perhaps of greatest significance, no matter what kind of interview, is that this is a discursive act structured by the problematic obligation to, in the words of Judith Butler, 'give an account of oneself.' Butler's analysis of the conditions of this linguistic injunction focuses on the necessary relationship between the opacity of the subject to herself and, therefore, of the ethical importance of both singularity, and, in prioritizing singularity, the recognition of a relationality that is based not on a politics of recognition, but of a willingness to coexist with the fundamental unknowability of the other. As Butler argues, 'Suspending the demand for self-identity or, more particularly, for complete coherence seems to me to counter a certain ethical violence, which demands that we manifest and maintain self identity at all times, and require that others do the same … By not pursuing satisfaction and by letting the question remain open, even enduring, we let the other live, since life might be understood as precisely that which exceeds any account we may try to give of it.'[27] We take it as axiomatic that a research interview (a) is enacted in a location of uneven power relations, (b) runs the risk of 'reducing meaning to that which can be narrativized,'[28] and (c) is circumscribed by the limits of language, and the problematic of re-inscribing the very discourses of subjectification that it seeks to trouble.

This is not an authoritative reading, nor is it in any sense exhaustive or comprehensive. This is also not (yet) a reflexive reading – one that strives explicitly to account for the presence of the interviewer in the text. Our use of interview data in this essay is somewhat unorthodox, in that it eschews ethnographic exegesis and proceeds by means of a juxtaposition of theoretical deliberations and interview excerpts. This strategy seems apt, given that the primary function of this essay is generatively to configure a theoretical terrain complex enough to be good to think with in relation to the complex set of questions that converge at the intersection of sexuality, alterity, and media practices. It also signals our methodological alignment with post-positivist research that troubles modernist readings of interviews as transparently representational and unproblematically accessible to the technics of hermeneutics.[29] There are many important themes that this particular reading cannot attend to, including geographical location, age, continuities and discontinuities between embodied and online community, extensibility of social networks, complexities implicated in the production of gender in ostensibly 'same sex' communities and locations, and a whole lot more.[30]

This discussion of the interviews focuses on (a) the mediated construction and re/presentation of complex, sometimes contradictory, and invariably intersectional identifications (such as 'fat lesbian living in the sticks,' 'queer'n'Asian,' 'dis/abled leatherdyke'); (b) mobility and negotiation of communities and social networks; and (c) relationalities, that is, embodied and affectively energized engagements with particular places, actors, artefacts, and networks.

Mobility, Cultural Intelligibility, and Mediatic Identifications: Virtually Queer?

Narratives concerning identificatory practices can be read as awkward tryouts for particular parts in a series of dramaturgical stagings, including reaching out for specific props, costumes, and scripts, juxtaposed against culturally normative accounts of the mediated self as Other.[31] As Clifford notes, 'Since the project of identity, whether individual or collective, is rooted in desires and aspirations that cannot be fulfilled, identity movements are open-ended, productive, and fraught with ambivalence.'[32]

It was relatively common for participants to describe daily practices of living as highly mediated by a range of Internet technologies and spaces, and their lives as relatively insulated from any cybercultural 'effects' or 'affects.' This may seem paradoxical. However, Mazzarella argues that 'the cultural politics of globalization, inside and outside the academy, involve a contradictory relation to mediation, on the one hand foregrounding the mediated quality of our lives and on the other hand strenuously disavowing it.'[33] Many of the people we interviewed are imbricated in exactly this juxtaposed relation of intense suturing and simultaneous disavowal with media.

INT: Are you comfortable talking about cyber sex?
HAM: Sure.

INT: So have you ever cybered?

HAM: I have. Okay. How can I word this? I've made other women very happy.

INT: How's that?

HAM: I can't even remember why I was doing this 'cause I don't normally cyber. This wasn't even somebody I was particularly interested in. I don't even know how it began. But the next thing I know, I've got all the *Playboys* out. I've got books open at different pages. And I'm just thinking, 'Okay. This looks good. Seriously. She's loving it. She's loving it.' I'm like, okay, I'll just type this. 'My fingers are crawling up your leg.' Okay. Oh yeah. She seems to like that. I got nothing out of it.

INT: That's hilarious. But it didn't do anything for you.

HAM: Oh no, I'm not into it. I need the physical contact.

INT: Right.

HAM: I need to look into somebody's eyes I know, right. I'm copying crap out of the magazine, how do I know you're not doing the same thing?

Ham, dyke, 36, white, Urban Centre, British Columbia[34]

Participants' descriptions of their varied engagements in the construction and presentation of queer identifications feature mediatic spaces and practices, including Internet communities and locations (e.g., websites with email bulletin boards, chatrooms), books (both fiction and non-fiction), television, movies, community newspapers, and cultural events and sites.

SAM: I had this thing that I secretly called Project 9. I would collect any sort of, like literally any instance of lesbian or mostly lesbian interaction … my parents had an editing suite and I would edit them onto these tapes.

INT: Wow.

SAM: So I would cut out, like actually cut out the negative or just like whatever. If there was a lesbian kiss, I would cut out a lesbian kiss, even if it was framed around something kind of really negative. I would actually edit them. So I have like hundreds, I have literally hundreds of hours. Which is crazy. Characters that I suspected were gay, like Rosie O'Donnell before she was gay. Like when she was on the Arsenio Hall show, for instance, I have that clip. I collected k.d. lang … I have those clips even before they were sort of gay. Even *Madison*, the stupid lesbian subplot, I edited out everything else other than the lesbian subplot and produced a story. So for me, when the 'Incredibly True Adventures of Two Girls in Love,' like those narratives came out that were explicitly lesbian, and I was like, 'Wow,' 'cause I was like, you know, reading 'The Unlit Lamp'…

Sam, queer, white, 26, Census Metropolitan Area, British Columbia

BECKI: Like I was really femme and everything, and I found a real huge denial of my identity just 'cause I didn't look like a lesbian. Now there's a lot more like femmier

girls coming out of the woodwork, which is really cool. I don't know if that has
something to do with *The L Word*. Although I think it is kind of linked to that.
INT: Do you watch *The L Word*?
BECKI: Yeah, shamefully, yes we do.

> Becki, queer, Filipina, 21, Census Metropolitan Area, British Columbia

Participants' narratives of identification are complex and discontinuous accounts
in which subjectivities are produced as *moving* projects, both prospective and retrospective – going somewhere and all the while, weighted down by the baggage of a
particular history and rootedness in a specific trajectory of locations and chronology.

SHANE: I was watching *Ally McBeal* and they had a scene where Ally and Ling Woo kiss
and I played that scene over and over again 'cause I recorded it ... I was kind of
turned on I guess ... Yeah and then after that, after I just went on the Internet and
looked up articles about 'Am I gay?' – that type of thing.
INT: What did you find?
SHANE: Not very much at that time. But all my friends were straight, like all my friends
at that time. There was a posting for a gathering on blur-f.com, and it was at a cof-
fee shop so I went there and met other people. The website wasn't local [Hong
Kong] ...
INT: But the posting was?
SHANE: I don't think my friends would just go to a meeting, meeting other Chinese
women like, my straight friends.
SHANE: It was just for queers in particular.
INT: And was that the first time that you had been in a room with a whole lot of other
queer Asian women?
SHANE: Yes.

> Shane, Chinese, lesbian, 22, Suburb, British Columbia

Participants' accounts of self-making do not necessarily or invariably prioritize
(homo)sexuality, but rather, entail a series of refusals of specific articulations of gender, racialization, sexual desire, age, and the like and, concomitantly, the taking up,
often provisionally, of available non-normative identifications.[35]

TS: I've spent a lot of time thinking about this and talking about this. I'm involved
with a group of people in town here and we realize that we all identify first as two-
spirited before a woman and before queer or dyke or lesbian.

> TS, Two-Spirited, Aboriginal, Cree, 44, Urban Centre, Northern British Columbia

LEE: I'm starting to move out of the one [identity] that I've been living with, you
know, trans butch dyke but –

LEE: I consider, I am transgendered, which is different than transsexual.

LEE: And nobody gets that.

LEE: It's living between the genders, really, you know. All growing up I didn't really identify with female but I really didn't identify with male. Whenever I had names for pets or stuffies or anything like that, [they] were always non-gender names and they never had a gender in my world. And I didn't understand that until I got older that that's what I was doing was trying to get rid of gender. I was working with the gender clinic for about a year and knew that if I was getting any services I had to basically lie and the woman I was working with, she kept saying, 'Why don't you live between the worlds?' And I said, 'Because this world doesn't allow it, you know.' And she just kept sort of at that and she was really right, that's really where I do belong. I don't belong as a male and I don't really fit as female. So it's in between the two. Which is a hard concept for people to get. Friends say, you know, good friends of mine who are well versed in a number of trans issues say there's no third gender, you know, you're just a butch dyke, deal with it.

Lee, trans/dyke, white, 40, Urban Centre, Northern British Columbia

Weblogs, or 'blogs' as they are more commonly known, and 'bloggers' are a distinctive subgrouping within the data. In the space of the virtual, blogs are aggregate spaces wherein many elements of online communication and network formation coalesce. Herein, the Habermasian bifurcation of the social world into spaces of interiorized privates and open or exteriorized publics is issued a challenge.[36] As artefacts in the digital landscape, blogs are spaces of liminality where articulations of 'self' and perceptions of 'community' collide, the lines of so-called public and private no longer manifest, and users are no longer 'inscribed according to this set of oppositions.'[37]

For some users, blogs serve as narrative receptacles for the detailed events of day-to-day existence, documenting the mundane in all of its transformative potential. Narratives are performed in consumable portions for anticipated audiences, be they extant or merely anticipated, adhering to a performative standard that is tightly tied to audience expectation, and, thus the audience's consumptive participation in the blogging process. As Butler argues, 'Giving an account ... takes a narrative form that not only depends upon the ability to relay a set of sequential events with plausible transitions but also draws upon narrative voice and authority, being directed toward an audience with the aim of persuasion.'[38] One of the participants, Becki, takes up this argument when she states:

BECKI: And I guess the way I think about blogs is that if somebody really wanted to know so much about me then go ahead, read my stuff. If you want to spend the hour, like, looking through all of them ... 'feel free,' you know. That's why I don't care so much ... most of my posts [are], like, just public like even everything, but there are some that I do keep to myself, or just to my friends, more personal stuff.

Becki, queer, Filipina, 21, Census Metropolitan Area, British Columbia

The bloggers with whom we have spoken create personal journalling blogs, as opposed to the topical, link-driven, filter blogs. The personal journalling format is unapologetically confessional, a space where the self is carefully and painstakingly constructed and consumed. Julie Rak convincingly summarizes the unfulfilled promise of the virtual modernist project in her analysis of blogging culture. Rak argues that while these personal journal-style blogs move beyond the written diary as 'a point of translation' from which to circulate articulations of self in a community of seemingly like others, they invariably re/produce and perpetuate a politics of normativity. These articulations are complex, part self-absorbed narrative, part performative iteration demanding witness and interpretation.[39]

MALIFICENT: I really like the way I write. I think I'm funny. And it's interesting 'cause sometimes I catch stuff that I didn't mean to write. I don't know, it's, I'm really interested in myself and I like reading. It sounds crazy but maybe it is. Well it is, definitely. I'll go into MySpace, and then I'll like search for myself as though, like and pretend that like, what if I'm someone else looking for me. I'll click on me, and then I'll read the journals, like imagine myself as someone else and what would they think. I don't know. It's weird.

Malificent, queer, white, 21, Census Metroplitan Area, British Columbia

The narrative act of blogging adheres to a performative standard that is tightly tied to audience expectation and thus audience's consumptive participation in the blogging process. Blogging as a self-productive act is driven by desire and is both a 'means' and an 'end' to the production of the 'self as–.'[40] Individuals perform the 'truth(s)' of who they are via gender identifications, belief systems, political positionings, et cetera. This 'truth' of being requires that others witness and thereby confirm the recognizablity of the self's emergence. Yet blogs are not utopic spaces of virtuality where the self can posit an endless number of representations, claiming subjectivities in an online world of free-floating signifiers. For example, when speaking of her blogging male alter ego, Malificent notes the following:

MALIFICENT: He's really kind of pretentious and philosophical and so I just, I usually go through that and try to … 'Cause it's a persona and like with my regular profile, the boy is only part of who I am. So this writing might be found in my normal blog, but this is only one aspect of my personality, and all my personality is found in my blog. Well, maybe not all of it but, but just different aspects of it, and so this one is just like if I put it through a filter.
INT: Right. Your boy filter?
MALIFICENT: Yeah.

Malificent, queer, white, 21, Census Metroplitan Area, British Columbia

Mark Poster argues that blogs effectively disturb our 'reliance on the familiar distinction between the public and the private … fundamentally upsetting the markers of freedom in each domain.'[41] However, within this voyeuristic exchange, online bodies remain tied to the normative filters of corporeal embodiment.

Historically, there has been extensive debate about the space of the body in the hybrid landscape of new media. Feminists such as Anne Balsamo have argued that the 'phenomenological experience of cyberspace depended upon and in fact required the willful repression of the material body.'[42] Others, such as Katherine Hayles, maintain that the body exists in a 'dynamic flux' between flesh and machine in a series of posthuman articulations.[43] In keeping with Hayles's claim of the posthuman space of the body, we want to argue further that within the threshold of the virtual, the body and the public/private trappings of identity come to be most clearly dis/articulated, and that this ataxic subjectivity carries its own liberatory potential.

Abject Lessons: Homing Devices, Communities, and Un/belongings

Irrespective of age and location, interviewees continued to identify an ongoing relationship both to 'the closet' and to pervasive and persistent impacts of homophobia. While unevenly distributed as a function of geography, occupation, and the likelihood of being perceived as 'queer,' participants' narratives of sexual subjectivity testify to the cost of the 'economy of visibility' within which being recognizable as queer is both necessary and also constitutive of a mark of difference that is a target for violence in its myriad incarnations. Alongside Eve Sedgwick's powerful articulation of the epistemic structures that are produced and sustained by homophobia,[44] it is axiomatic that what Ann Cvetkovitch describes as 'insidious trauma' structures the quotidian experiences of those whose queer lives are produced as repudiated subjectivities. As Cvetkovitch observes, 'Trauma becomes the hinge between systemic structures of exploitation and oppression and the felt experience of them.'[45]

SAM: Even when I'd go back to Coburg it was like, because you're so terrified of being found out, those worlds become sealed ... I think the story that kept everyone in line in my town was they thought that a guy was gay and they carved FAG in his forehead. And whether that was true or not, that was the narrative that sort of capped everyone.

Sam, queer, white, 26, Census Metropolitan Area, British Columbia

JEANETTE: I was living on my own so it didn't matter to me if my family never talked to me again but Leslie was still living at home and I didn't want to, you know, ruin her relationship with her parents. We've been together for six years now, and lived together for five of those six years, I don't know why we can't just be open about it and if you don't like it you don't like it, but –

INT: But [Small Town, Alberta] is not necessarily fruit friendly?

JEANETTE: No. No.

INT: So at this point do your parents know about your relationship with Leslie?

LESLIE: No. There's been lots of suspicions and I think once or twice I tried to speak of it but it didn't go over very well, so …

INT: What happened?

LESLIE: Well, I tried to tell my mom and she basically told me that I could never see Jeanette again.

> Jeanette, fruit, white, 24, and Leslie, blind, white, 23, Small Town, Alberta

Cultural studies scholarship on queer migration and mobility underscores critical relationships between dis/location and specific articulations of sexual identification and community formation. 'Sexuality is indeed on the move,' Michael Warner argues, 'not just because people are more on the move now than ever, but because non-normative sexualities so generally seem out of place and are so often enabled by the displacement of culture.'[46] The complex imbrication of constitutive processes of crafting a performative self, that is, a public self situated in relation both to others and to spatiality, within the web of psychic and material violences that Goffman referred to as 'stigma and the management of spoiled identity' and Eribon as 'the shock of insult' seems intimately implicated in the production of finely tuned practices of mobility and reconnaissance.[47]

Fortier argues that queer invocations of dialectical tropes of 'home' – as sites of both 'familiarity' and 'estrangement,' 'attachment' and 'loss' – are complexly related to mobility and belonging. Fortier notes that 'queer and disaporic narratives of belonging often deploy "*homing desires*" … The widespread narrative of migration as homecoming within queer culture, establishes an equation between leaving and becoming.'[48] Our interest in media practices, then, leads us to consider the figurative, tropic significance of 'homing devices' as a necessary and fruitful correlative analytic construct in exploring how it is that 'homing desires' are negotiated and re-mediated within and against the limits of spatialized queer imaginaries and varied sociocultural topographies.

LEE: I started using online stuff when I moved up north to Fort Nelson. There's not much gay community. I started to look online for community. I needed some sort of connection. I found a Yahoo group called B.C. Dykes. They were going out and meeting down in the Lower Mainland for coffees and for movies and there was a real sense of caring and they tried to include those of us that were outside. Then they were gonna have their first ever gathering on Spinstervale, on the Island. And so I said, 'Okay, I'm leaving, I'll see you guys.' And I hit the highway and when I get there people had already posted, and there was a little log of my travels all the way down. So here I was completely isolated and I suddenly had a community of queer women. It really did save my ass.

> Lee, trans/dyke, white, 40, Urban Centre, Northern British Columbia

Participants' movement towards sites of connection was mediated by a wide range of homing devices, including gaydar, Internet knowledge-searches, email lists, and other 'quasi-objects.' Efforts to hook up with and/or to locate, and belong to, communities of 'like others,' or 'target others,' are prominent features in our research interviews.

KUMI: I was on the Internet searching for my bisexual thing. I had come across some like bisexual lesbian bi-curious website and I started talking to one of the other bisexual women in Edmonton and we decided, well, we should meet for coffee. And I met her and through her I discovered that there's a bi-women's group.

Kumi, Japanese, bisexual, 29, Census Metropolitan Area, Alberta

SAM: For a while I was very interested in large men – very muscular – so I just used the Net to find the largest, buffest guy I could find – to play out any fantasies that might require a man. Depending on the particular whim, yeah, zero in on the specific, and you get pictures of 20 super buff men and you can just choose. It's like shopping. It's great.

Sam, queer, white, 26, Census Metropolitan Area, British Columbia

Although there is considerable variability across the sample, participants' accounts of participation in 'community' are frequently marked by a relation of 'un/belonging' and, therefore, of desires that propel further mobility. Our invocation, here, of 'un/belonging' signals the complexities of contemporary notions of relationality that involve dialectical rather than binary logics of location, and related implication in affective topographies.[49] As Smethurst observes, 'Unbelonging is not itself a stable condition in the postmodern ... While postmodern space and place become fluid, shadowy and mutable, identity, which attempts to map such spaces, is conditioned by dislocation and dispersed belonging.'[50]

ALICE: The Internet facilitated those discussions, and those discussions couldn't have happened without these kind of forums. I was talking with people and reading what people had to say. Like when I first heard the word 'femme,' I imagined it meant something really specific. I was like, 'Oh, you have to wear a dress all the time and you have to be only attracted to butch women.' And then all of a sudden I was meeting all these people who were not fitting into that, and who were like, 'No, femme can mean a variety of things. This is what it means to me. This is how it works with a lot of things, a lot of other parts in my identity.' So yeah, it was really important for me ...

ALICE: The community in Edmonton, from my perspective, was really closed and really tied to a really particular look, and a really particular setting. Which I can sort of understand, for visibility and recognizability. There's importance to that. The younger women my age, anyway, were kind of like this 'baby butch' – short hair and bleached and looking like a skater. They had no place for someone who wore lipstick and didn't want to cut her hair. I tried to, you know, I went to gay bars and that sort of thing, but I would just … I got hostile attitude and it was just like clear that people didn't think that I belonged there. I was just like, 'Okay, well, there you go.' Being not strictly identified as a dyke or as a lesbian so yeah … in Edmonton, in particular, that was kind of my saving grace.

Alice, queer, white, 23, Census Metropolitan Area, Alberta

SANDRA: I haven't been involved with the hearing queer community because of the communication barrier. I've tried, it didn't work out. So then I became involved with the deaf gay and lesbian community, but there's lots of issues within the community. I think one of the reasons is that Alberta is very 'red neck' compared to the States, and there's a very, very different perspective there. I go to the States often and so I know the deaf queer community there. So I've got something to compare to and I see a big difference … I'm a leather dyke and that's something I'm very proud of. I tend to conform to people's feelings in [Urban Centre, Alberta] and the reason is that they don't really get it. It's, you know, a big issue, it's arguments and I don't want to have to deal with all that stuff. So I don't.

Sandra, deaf, queer, leather dyke, white, 45, Suburb, Alberta

Participants described the Internet as an important source of knowledge, cultural engagement, and what Warner refers to as 'counterpublics' *only where it was possible* – by means of blogging, or participation in a focused online community or email list – *to identify a relatively bounded social network made up of similar others* (e.g., Asian queer women, queer folks living with mental health issues, members of the Xenaverse, fat dykes, deaf queers, leather dykes).[31] Community-appropriate health and legal knowledge was ubiquitously very difficult for participants to locate online irrespective of access to sophisticated public knowledge sites, like university library databases.

INT: Do you look for two-spirit resources online?
TS: I've looked for books. I've looked for conferences … There's an organization in Ontario. I haven't found anything … I've lost the terminology. You know, when you have a particular site where people go to discuss a particular topic –
INT: Right, like a bulletin board or a chat room or –
TS: I haven't found anything like that for two-spirited but one that I stumbled across is called Fat Dykes and that's been really good. It's a very fat-positive site and as long as you identify as a dyke, you can be a part of the site.

TS, Two-Spirited, Aboriginal, Cree, 44, Urban Centre, Northern British Columbia

Within the virtual demarcations of their acknowledged social networks, few white participants chose to identify or to discuss racism as a problematic aspect of 'community.' Conversely, for Aboriginal, Asian, and African-Canadian participants, the intersectional discursive construction of racial identifications offline and online *explicitly* organized and regulated the self-presentation of participants, whose experiences included (but were not, importantly, limited to), marginalization, silencing, and enforced segregation as well as engagement in resistance and the construction of counterpublics.[52] These interviewees identified 'white' as the default, assumed racial identity of online interlocutors.

SHANE: I think they would assume that I'm white because from the posts that I made [on SuperDyke.com], I didn't say that I was Chinese or Asian. I guess there was one instance where I talked about my red-neck uncle or my cousin's husband but otherwise I guess they couldn't figure it out.

INT: So would that make it more appealing to you to go to blur-f.com, or one of the Asian women's sites?

SHANE: Yeah, I think so. I'm more comfortable with other Asians because they speak the same language, or other Chinese I mean, not all Asians.

Shane, Chinese, lesbian, 22, Suburb, British Columbia

MOMO: Most websites look to me very race neutral. They don't have specific Asian content ... it looks neutral but it's mostly for Caucasians ... whenever I go to any so-called queer or gay events, I hardly find any Asian queers and there might be some but they're not international students ... I feel there's a boundary there, although I'm a part of that space but I'm not.

MOMO: At a book reading there was an Asian queer writer, and I volunteered that night. I just walked around and thought, 'Okay, if I'm not gonna see any Asian people I'm just going to leave' ... She [the writer] said that when she looked around the whole space that there were no Asians, and so when she saw me walk inside the room, she said she felt like there's a special energy in the room ... I told her that after her talk, that at that moment, a very short moment, that although we were the only two Asian queers there, I felt a sense of community.

MoMo, Taiwanese, queer, 29, Census Metropolitan Area, British Columbia

Postscript

We must not look only at mass-produced objects themselves on the assumption that they bear all of their significance on their surface ... If we can learn, then, to look at the ways in which various groups appropriate and use the mass-produced art of our culture, I suspect we may well begin to understand that although the ideological power of contemporary cultural forms is enormous, indeed sometimes even frightening, that power is not yet all-pervasive, totally vigilant, or complete. Interstices still exist within the social fabric where opposition is carried on by people who are not satisfied by their place within it or by the restricted material and emotional rewards that accompany it.

Janice Radway, Reading the Romance

Our discussion has highlighted the complex, multiplicitous trajectories of queer women's (im)mobilities within and across sites that are (a) mediated by a range of technologies, both new and not-so-new, (b) dispersed across multiple offline and online contexts, and (c) affectively charged with persistent agonistic entanglements with the complex politics of recognition, belonging, and a sense of community. Benedict Anderson's classic analysis of the hypostatized identification of 'nationalism' articulates critical links between *communication* and *community* in the immensely generative and politically precarious identitarian sphere of 'imagined community.'[53]

Communicative practices and artefacts are, in this account, usefully thought of as providing a mediative cultural grammar that plays a constitutive role in the production, in community, of an *imagined recognition of like subjects*. In this view, intelligibility and belonging across pluralistic public spaces are cultural accomplishments enabled by the technologically mediated *semblance* of simultaneity, like-mindedness, and social homogeneity. As Arjun Appadurai pithily observes, 'One man's imagined community is another man's political prison.' 'Imagined community' has, since its conceptualization, proven to be a generative and robust construct in contemplating the unavoidable tensions of 'cultural homogenization and cultural heterogenization' produced across the varied mobilities (and immobilities) of globalization.[54] Political theory critiques of 'community' prove much like critiques of 'identity'; that is, they are essential analytical tools circumscribed in their explanatory power by the observation that we are unlikely to abandon our desire for belonging, nor our efforts towards recognition.[55]

Having considered the ways in which 'community' and 'identity' are complexly implicated in the production of complex relations of power/knowledge, and a politically problematic politics of recognition, how might we think about the affective charge of identifications that exceeds a rational critique of its fallibilities?[56] Hills argues that Anderson's imagined community construct is 'seemingly affectless' and, as such, is mechanistic and incapable of dealing with the affective dimension of relationality. Drawing on object relations theory to analyse identification and sociality in an online fan community, Hills posits that 'The community of imagination therefore acts as a specific defense against the possible "otherness" or even "alien-ness" of the inexplicable intensity and emotionality of fandom. Reassuringly, by going on-line this intense but somehow almost inarticulate fan experience can be endlessly replicated, and the affect involved can be displaced through a circuit of mimesis, such that the self rebounds against its own unspeakable identifications.'[57]

Hills's construal of online sociality as constitutive of a 'community of imagination' offers an important and relevant corrective to any overly deterministic account of practices or technologies of subjectification and affiliation. And it is important here to point out that this is not an idealized articulation of 'imagination' that might be synonymous with something like 'creativity.' In this context, the labour of imagination is dedicated to practices of 'serious play' where identificatory relations provide 'transitional spaces' for the endless work of being and becoming.[58]

'Virtuality,' then, no longer refers to being 'somewhere else,' nor to being 'online' as a location that could somehow be disentangled from 'offline.' A more usefully complex perspective of contemporarily mediated social and cultural geographies conceives of 'the virtual' as a series of 'contiguous realities' marked by 'perforated boundaries,' that is, as ever-proliferating networked surfaces that destabilize a monolithic cultural syntax of recognizablity. For queer women, these re-mediated spaces may open up the identifications lodged in ongoing practices of self-formation and the negotiation of sociality. By way of a Foucauldian 'self knowledge,' we are inclined to think about this divaricated negotiative process as 'a pedagogy of the self.'[59] William Haver refers to these 'infinitesimal negotiations by which we learn and unlearn the world' – and to which we would add 'the self' – as the '*pragma* ... of the pedagogical.'[60] Angela McRobbie, Henry Jenkins, and others have emphasized the cultural affordances and improvisational public pedagogies that lurk in everyday active modes of cultural engagement constituted by practices of archiving, distribution, networking, resignification, appropriation, recoding, and recirculation.[61]

In place of the pleasant foreclosure offered by a finite conclusion, we pause, here, and highlight the need for further discussions that trouble perorations extolling the promises of 'queer virtuality' construed unproblematically as utopian incarnation, freedom from the constraints of embodiment, or free-wheeling access to either public space or public knowledge. We look forward to research accounts that work against the seemingly ineluctable rhetorical incitement to reproduce media mythologies that trumpet 'new and exciting possibilities.'[62] We favour, by contrast, and against all odds, cautious, critical framings of multiple locations where hybrid subjects negotiate non-foundational particularities – 'ex-static subjectivity.'[63] In an 'age of digital reproduction,' to harken back to Walter Benjamin's cautionary historiography concerning 'progress' and 'technology,' '*the work* of *queer*' research might be, then, critically to articulate multiple and complex relationalities between nomadic subjects, (counter) publics, heterotopic spaces, and artefacts that are always-already problematically lodged within a political economy of consumption and misrecognition.[64] As Foucault noted, 'My point is not that everything is bad, but that everything is dangerous, which is not exactly the same as bad. If everything is dangerous, then we always have something to do.'[65]

Acknowledgments

This research is supported by a grant to the first author by the Social Sciences and Humanities Research Council of Canada (SSHRC). Conversations with Janice Stewart, William Pinar, and John Willinsky were exceptionally fruitful. We also acknowledge the insightful comments made by reviewers and the *CJC* editors. However, the authors take full responsibility for the work reported here.

Notes

1 John Cloud, 'The Battle over Gay Teens,' *Time*, 10 Oct. 2005: 37.

2 See Michel Foucault, *Discipline and Punish: The Birth of the Prison* (New York: Vintage, 1977); and *Power/Knowledge: Selected Interviews and Other Writings 1972–1977* (New York: Pantheon, 1980), passim.

3 Judith Butler, *Bodies that Matter: On the Discursive Limits of 'Sex'* (New York: Routledge, 1993), 187.

4 See also Miranda Joseph, *Against the Romance of Community* (Minneapolis: University of Minnesota Press, 2002).

5 Mimi Sheller and John Urry, 'The New Mobilities Paradigm,' *Environment and Planning A* 38 (2006): 207–26. See also Zygmunt Bauman, *Liquid Modernity* (Cambridge: Polity Press, 2000).

6 Nominalization is not an insignificant aspect of research that deals with minoritarian identifications. See Mary Bryson, 'Mc/No Lesbian: The Trouble with "Troubling Lesbian Identities,"' *International Journal of Qualitative Studies in Education* 15/3 (2002): 373–80; J. Halberstam, *In a Queer Time and Place* (New York: New York University Press, 2005). 'Queer,' in the context of this research, designates a post-foundational troubling of any notion of a stable or essential marker of sexual identification. See Annamarie Jagose, *Queer Theory* (New York: New York University Press, 1996).

7 A reasonably complete list would include Joanne Addison and Michelle Comstock, 'Virtually Out: The Emergence of a Lesbian, Bisexual and Gay Youth Cyberculture,' in *Generations of Youth*, ed. J. Austin and M. Willard (New York: New York University Press, 1998), 367–78; Mary Bryson, 'When Jill Jacks In: Queer Women and the Net,' *Feminist Media Studies* 4/3 (2004), 239–54; Sue Ellen Case, *The Domain Matrix: Performing Lesbian at the End of Print Culture* (Bloomington: Indiana University Press); Shelley Correll, 'The Ethnography of an Electronic Bar,' *Journal of Contemporary Ethnography* 24/3 (1995): 270–98; Susan Driver, 'Out, Creative and Questioning: Reflexive Self-representations in Queer Youth Homepages,' *Canadian Woman Studies* 24/2 and 3 (2005): 111–16; Mary Gray, *Coming of Age in a Digital Era: Youth Queering Technologies in the Rural United States*, unpublished doctoral dissertation, University of California at San Diego, 2004; Sally Munt, Elizabeth Bassett, and Kate O'Riordan, 'Virtually Belonging: Risky Connectivity and Coming Out Online,' *International Journal of Sexuality and Gender Studies* 7/2 (2002): 125–37; Joyce Nip, 'The Queer Sisters and Its Electronic Bulletin Board: A Study of the Internet for Social Movement Mobilization,' *Information, Communication and Society* 7/1 (2004): 23–49; Jodi O'Brien, 'Writing in the Body: Gender (Re)production in Online Interaction,' in *Communities in Cyberspace*, ed. P. Kollock and M. Smith (New York: Routledge, 1999), 76–104; Jamie Poster, 'Trouble, Pleasure and Tactics: Anonymity and Identity in a Lesbian Chat Room,' in *Women and Everyday Uses of the Internet*, ed. M. Consalvo and S. Paasonen (New York: Peter Lang, 2002), 230–52; Nina Wakeford, 'Sexualized Bodies in Cyberspace,' in *Beyond the Book: Theory, Culture, and the Politics of Cyberspace*, ed. W. Chernaik, M. Deegan, and A. Gibson (London: Centre for English Studies, University of London, 1996), 93–104; Nina Wakeford, 'Networking Women and Girls with Information/Communication Technology,' in *Processed Lives: Gender and Technology in Everyday Life*, ed. J. Terry and M. Calvert, eds. (New York: Routledge, 1997), 51–66; Nina

Wakeford, 'Cyberqueer,' in *The Cybercultures Reader,* David Bell and Barbara Kennedy (New York: Routledge, 2000), 403–15; and Celeste Wincapaw, 'The Virtual Spaces of Lesbian and Bisexual Women's Electronic Mailing Lists,' *Journal of Lesbian Studies* 4/1 (2000), 45–59. This list of publications deals primarily with sites identified as 'lesbian' (rather than 'queer'), and with English-speaking women located in North America, the U.K., and Australia. Nip's project concerns Queer Sisters, a Hong Kong queer women's community and online bulletin board.

8 See Henry Jenkins, *Textual Poachers: Television Fans and Participatory Culture* (New York: Routledge, 1992); Angela McRobbie, *The Uses of Cultural Studies* (Thousand Oaks: Sage, 2005); Elspeth Probyn, *Outside Belongings* (London: Routledge, 1995); Janice Radway, *Reading the Romance: Women, Patriarchy, and Popular Culture* (Chapel Hill: University of North Carolina Press, 1984); Gill Valentine and Sarah Holloway, 'Cyberkids? Exploring Children's Identities and Social Networks in On-line and Off-line Worlds,' *Annals of the Association of American Geographers* 92/2 (2002): 302–19; Valerie Walkerdine, *Daddy's Girl: Young Girls and Popular Culture* (Cambridge: Harvard University Press, 1997).

9 Wakeford, 'Cyberqueer,' 411.

10 Mary Bryson, 'Conjuring the Quotidian,' *Journal of Gay and Lesbian Issues in Education* 2/4 (2005): 85.

11 See Stuart Hall, 'Encoding/Decoding,' in *Culture, Media, Language: Working Papers in Cultural Studies,* ed. S. Hall, D. Hobson, A. Lowe, and P. Willis (London: Hutchinson University Library, 1980), 128–38.

12 Poster, 'Trouble, Pleasure and Tactics,' 240.

13 See Nancy Fraser, 'Rethinking Recognition,' *New Left Review* 3 (May-June 2000): 107–20; Charles Taylor, 'The Politics of Recognition,' in *Multiculturalism: Examining the Politics of Recognition,* ed. A. Gutmann (Princeton: Princeton University Press, 1994), 25–74.

14 Wakeford, 'Cyberqueer,' 413.

15 Wincapaw, 'Virtual Spaces,' 54.

16 Ibid.

17 David Bell, *An Introduction to Cybercultures* (New York: Routledge, 2001), 31.

18 Nina Wakeford, 'Urban Culture for Virtual Bodies: Comments on Lesbian "Identity" and "Community" in San Francisco Bay Area Cyberspace,' in *New Frontiers of Space, Bodies and Gender,* ed. R. Ainley (New York: Routledge, 1998), 180.

19 Paulette Rothbauer, 'The Internet in the Reading Accounts of Lesbian and Queer Young Women: Failed Searches and Unsanctioned Reading,' *Canadian Journal of Information and Library Science* 28/4 (2004): 93.

20 Ibid., 100.

21 Jenkins, *Textual Poachers,* 46.

22 Ann Cvetkovich, *An Archive of Feelings* (Durham: Duke University Press, 2003), 47.

23 Rosemary Coombe, 'Publicity Rights and Political Aspiration: Mass Culture, Gender Identity, and Democracy,' *New England Law Review* 26 (1992), 1221–80, 1248. See also Jennifer Terry, 'Theorizing deviant historiography,' *differences* 3/2 (1991): 55–74.

24 Gloria Filax, 'Producing Homophobia in Alberta, Canada in the 1990s,' *Journal of Historical Sociology* 17/1 (2004): 87–120.

25 Gail Mason, *The Spectacle of Violence: Homophobia, Gender and Knowledge* (New York: Routledge, 2002).

26 Lisa Lowe, 'Work, Immigration, Gender: New Subjects of Cultural Politics,' *Social Justice* 25/3 (1997): 33.

27 Judith Butler, *Giving an Account of Oneself* (New York: Fordham University Press, 2005), 42.

28 Stephen Frosh, 'Things that Can't Be Said: Psychoanalysis and the Limits of Language,' *International Journal of Critical Psychology* 1/1 (2001): 29.

29 See Patti Lather and Chris Smithies, *Troubling the Angels: Women Living with HIV/AIDS* (Boulder: Westview, 1997).

30 See Valentine and Holloway, 'Cyberkids?' passim.

31 See Butler, *Bodies that Matter*; Erving Goffman, *The Presentation of Self in Everyday Life* (London: Penguin, 1959); Erving Goffman, *Stigma: Notes on the Management of Spoiled Identity* (Englewood-Cliffs: Prentice-Hall, 1963); Munt, Bassett, and O'Riordan, 'Virtually Belonging.'

32 James Clifford, 'Taking Identity Politics Seriously,' in *Without Guarantees: In Honour of Stuart Hall*, ed. P. Gilroy, L. Grossberg, and A. McRobbie (New York: Verso, 2000), 95.

33 William Mazzarella, 'Culture, Globalization, Mediation,' *Annual Review of Anthropology* 33 (2004): 345.

34 The bio info that accompanies each transcript quote includes a self-chosen pseudonym, the marker that the speaker uses to signal her particular queer identification, age, race, location, and any other identificatory flag of particular significance to the interviewee. Ellipsis dots indicate an edit, angle brackets an editorial insertion.

35 Gail Weiss, *Body Images: Embodiment as Intercorporeality* (New York: Routledge, 1999).

36 Jodi Dean, 'Cybersalons and Civil Society: Rethinking the Public Sphere in Transnational Technoculture,' *Public Culture* 13/2 (2001): 243–65.

37 Linda Carroli, 'Virtual Encounters: Community or Collaboration on the Internet,' *Leonardo* 30/5 (1997): 359.

38 Butler, *Giving an Account*, 12.

39 Julie Rak, 'The Digital Queer: Weblogs and Internet Identity,' *Biography* 28/1 (2005): 166–82.

40 Kris Cohen, 'What Does the Photoblog Want?' *Media, Culture and Society* 27/6 (2005): 883–901.

41 Mark Poster, 'Everyday (Virtual) Life,' *New Literary History* 33 (2002): 758.

42 Anne Balsamo, *Technologies of the Gendered Body: Reading Cyborg Women* (Durham: Duke University Press, 1996), 123.

43 N. Katherine Hayles, 'Flesh and Metal: Reconfiguring the Mindbody in Virtual Environments,' *Configurations* 10 (1997): 297–320.

44 Eve Sedgwick, 'How to Bring Your Kids Up Gay: The War on Effeminate Boys,' in *Tendencies*, ed. E. Sedgwick (Durham: Duke University Press, 1993), 154–66.

45 Cvetkovich, *Archive of Feelings*, 12.

46 In Cindy Patton and Benigno Sanchez-Eppler, *Queer Diasporas* (Durham: Duke University Press, 2000), back cover.

47 See Goffman, *Stigma*; and Didier Eribon, *Insult and the Making of the Gay self* (Durham: Duke University Press, 2004).

48 Anne-Marie Fortier, ''Coming home'': Queer Migration and Multiple Evocations of Home,'
    European Journal of Cultural Studies 4/4 (2001), 410, emphasis added.

49 Petra Gemeinboeck, 'Impossible Geographies of Belonging,' *Proceedings of the 13th Annual ACM
    International Conference on Multimedia* (New York: Association for Computing Machinery Press,
    2005), 567–70; Elspeth Probyn, 'Queer Belongings: The Politics of Departure,' in *Sexy Bodies: The
    Strange Carnalities of Feminism*, ed. E. Grosz and E. Probyn (New York: Routledge, 1996), 1–18.

50 Paul Smethurst, 'Postmodern Blackness and Unbelonging in the Works of Caryl Phillips,'
    Journal of Commonwealth Literature 37/2 (2002): 8.

51 See Michael Warner, *Publics and Counterpublics* (Cambridge: MIT Press, 2002).

52 See also Beth Kolko, Lisa Nakamura, and Gilbert Rodman, *Race in Cyberspace* (New York:
    Routledge, 2000).

53 Benedict Anderson, *Imagined Communities* (London: Verso, 1993).

54 Arjun Appadurai, *Modernity at Large: Cultural Dimensions of Globalization* (Minneapolis: Minnesota
    University Press, 1996), 32.

55 Joshua Gamson, 'Must Identity Movements Self-destruct? A Queer Dilemma,' in *Queer Theory/
    Sociology*, ed. S. Seidman (Cambridge: Blackwell, 1996), 395–420; Patchen Markell, *Bound by
    Recognition* (Princeton: Princeton University Press, 2003).

56 Jessica Benjamin, *Like Subjects, Love Objects: Essays on Recognition and Sexual Difference* (New Haven:
    Yale University Press, 1995).

57 Matthew Hills, 'Virtually Out There: On-line Fandom,' in *Technospaces: Inside the New Media*, ed. S.
    Munt (New York: Continuum, 2001), 155.

58 Sherry Turkle, *Life on the Screen: Identity in the Age of the Internet* (New York: Simon and Schuster,
    1995), 269; Donald Winnicott, *Playing and Reality* (London: Routledge, 1993).

59 Michel Foucault, 'Friendship as a Way of Life,' in *Foucault Live: Collected Interviews, 1961–1984*,
    ed. S. Lotringer (New York: Semiotext(e), 1996), 204–12; Michel Foucault, *The Hermeneutics of
    the Subject: Lectures at the College de France 1981–1982* (New York: Picador, 2005).

60 William Haver, 'Queer Research; or, How to Practice Invention to The Brink of Intelligibility,'
    in *The Eight Technologies of Otherness*, ed. S. Golding (London: Routledge, 1997), 285.

61 See Mary Bryson and Suzanne de Castell, 'Queer Pedagogy,' *Canadian Journal of Education* 18/2
    (1993): 285–305.

62 Roland Barthes, *Mythologies* (New York: Hill and Wang, 1972); Mary Bryson and Suzanne de
    Castell, 'Telling Tales Out of School: Modernist, Critical, and Postmodern "True Stories" about
    Educational Technologies,' *Journal of Educational Computing Research* 10/3 (1994): 199–221.

63 Slavoj Žižek, *On belief* (New York: Routledge, 2001).

64 See Walter Benjamin, 'The Work of Art in the Age of Mechanical Reproduction,' in *Illuminations*
    (New York: Harcourt, Brace and World, 1968), 243–64; Rosi Braidotti, *Transpositions: Of Nomadic
    Ethics* (Cambridge: Polity Press, 2006); Michel Foucault, 'Of Other Spaces,' *Diacritics* 16/1 (1986):
    22–7.

65 Michel Foucault, 'On the Genealogy of Ethics,' in *The Foucault Reader*, ed. P. Rabinow (New
    York: Pantheon, 1984), 343.

20 The Passion of the Social: Reflections on the Seattle Rave Killings

ANDREW WERNICK

At 7 a.m. on the morning of 25 March 2006, Aaron Kyle Huff walked back to the house in the Capitol Hill area of Seattle where he had shortly before been 'sharing a bowl' at a rave after-party.[1] He spray-painted 'NOW' three times on the pavement and then shot two partygoers on the porch. He had a pistol-grip shotgun and a Ruger semiautomatic, with several magazines (more than 300 rounds in all) which he had retrieved from his pick-up truck parked round the corner. More weapons were in the truck, including a baseball bat and a machete. He entered the house, shooting whomever he found, then reloaded the gun, and went back outside. Before he could continue, a cop who had been cruising the area and was called to the scene by cell-phone, blocked his way to the street. Told to drop his weapon, Kyle Huff put the gun to his mouth and pulled the trigger.

Seven dead was a local record, at least for a single shooter, and the most for a single incident since the gang slaying at the Wah Mee gambling club in 1983. The casualties – including two women in their mid-teens – were shockingly young. But rampages by unhinged individuals have become a background drone in the mediascape, and, on the scale of Columbine or Hungerford, not to mention 9/11 and the daily mayhem in Iraq, this was relatively minor. What lifted the story, briefly, out of run-of-the mill spree killings was the rave angle, particularly when it emerged that the dance party was themed as a zombie night, with reduced admission for those in costume, and the overall title 'better undead.'

Was the rave to blame? Had the goth and fright-attired crowd drawn to the party that night itself bred the monster? The vultures of order hovered. But the causal link proved tenuous. Kyle was not a regular member of the scene, nor of any scene. Now in his late twenties, he had moved to Seattle with his twin brother Kane five years before from northwest Montana. Kane enrolled in art school, and Kyle delivered pizzas. Both were aspiring heavy metal drummers who practised, alone, and never late, in the apartment they shared. They were loners together. Kyle had enquired on line about how to go to raves only two weeks before. That he was invited to the after-party was happenstance, just a friendly gesture to a shy and polite stranger. To be sure, this gesture was

Figure 20.1. *Better off Undead*. Rave flyer, Artist unknown, 2006.

itself an instance of the PLUR (peace love unity respect) values of the subculture, and essential to its texture. But Kyle was unassimilable, a heterogeneous element. His counter-gift proved it. In any case, the massacre did not happen at the rave itself. Nor could it have, given the security arrangements, which included a ban on alcohol, drugs, and firearms, a search at the door, and seventeen uniformed police officers.

All this was a great relief – not least for the municipal politicians who had backed the 'all ages dance' ordinance under which the raves at Capitol Hill were being held, and for the policy more generally of providing a controlled outlet for alternate youth culture. The policy was even vindicated. Public space had been kept safe. Imagine if the shooter had been at an unsupervised event, as in the bad old days of the early 1990s, when raves in Seattle were underground self-organized affairs. As for the devastated ravers, they could at least take comfort from the fact that the killer was not one of 'us.' That this was officially recognized also mitigated the stigma. After the rituals of mourning (including a vigil, a church memorial, and a dj evening to raise money for the families), the wound could be allowed to heal, and normal operations at the Capitol Hill Arts Center could resume.

Not that everything could be quite the same. Besides the damage to lives, there was damage at the level of the group. The rave milieu's self-defining ethic of indifferent inclusionism had suffered a blow. So too had the informal institution of a free social space between (the policed zone of the) public and (the idiotized zone of the) private. Both this ethic and this space, remnant carriers of a utopian impulse, could only retreat further in the face of enhanced risk. There also remained the puzzle of Kyle Huff's unprovoked explosion. Unlike mass killings, say, within a family or workplace, the motive of revenge seemed absent. Nor was the act preceded by a build-up of escalating conflict. Why had Kyle targeted the rave at all?

Here too, though, abstraction could allay anxiety. That the killing was not at the main site of the rave, and that the killer had no apparent connection with his victims, not only alleviated responsibility for the evil in our midst. It also dissipated the enigma of its appearance by shunting the question mark hanging over the event onto questions of individual psychology on the one hand, and blind chance on the other. What happened at the after-party was like being hit by a truck; it could happen on any street. Such abstraction of course, which makes absolute the split between inside and outside, is never innocent. Besides its moral effects, it renders unintelligible the weave of forces that produces the event. Here it does more. By sundering what, for an instant, had been so violently thrown together – Kyle Huff plays Zombie Night – the act, as the achievement precisely of a symbol (sym-bolein = throw together), is itself drained of meaning.

We cannot know the impulse that led Kyle to select, from the arsenal at his disposal, the guns he used. The Winchester shotgun and the Ruger came with him to Seattle. Perhaps they were his favourites. Be that as it may, as signalling devices, drawing attention to the continuity between one scene and another, they were a happy choice.

The same guns had figured once before in a transgressive act.[2] This was in Whitefish Montana, a declining rail and logging hub, touristically revived around hunting and skiing, where Kyle's mother, after divorcing his Vietnam vet father, had brought up the twins, and ran an art store. Kyle, three years out of high school, had gone on a night-time jaunt with some buddies. In the course of it he had shot up a joke-decorated fibreglass moose, called Daphney. The moose – whose counterparts up and down North America have become a cliché of downtown boosterism – was one of a number dotted around Whitefish, as part of a charity drive by local artists.

It is easy, in retrospect, to see a warning in the moose incident. There was something excessive in the twenty-two bullets Kyle pumped into Daphney. A real animal would only have needed one or two. Moreover, if the moose was a tacky postmodern promotional sign – almost inviting the prankster to deface it – it was also a gift by its maker, an emblem for the local arts community, and, in its way, a metonym for 'art' itself. There are circles of aggression here. In the instance, the moose's creator generously costed his material damage low enough (under a thousand dollars) for Kyle to avoid a felony charge, and he escaped with a fine and community service, plus restitution and an apology. After the debts were paid, the court called it quits and the police returned his guns.

Kyle's letter of apology said it 'was not a personal attack and was not intended to bring you or your family any kind of stress.'[3] No doubt this was so. The wrong done to the moose-maker was collateral damage. This is not to say that personal investments were absent. How could they be, considering that his mother was herself a local artist, that her sons had gravitated to the music and drama crowd, and that besides his drums Kyle was himself considered to have some talent at pottery? Shooting the 'moose' – guns against art – pitted the way of the father against the way of the mother, with all the identificatory ambivalence that such a collision implied.

This ambivalence is evident not only in the private meaning of what broke through. It is also evident in the relation of the act to the public meaning of what it negated. What fuelled the fury in Kyle's attack on art and on being an artist (let us surmise) was a repudiation of identification with his mother as a position which might open him to the homoerotic desire that had to be repressed for the sake of being, and passing as, a man in a homophobic, hunting country, small-town high school. Yet, it came from one who was, by background and inclination, in the orbit of that same arts-oriented identity.

If, then, shooting the 'moose' meant death to art, and to the locals who cared about it, this was not the act of an outsider, but of an insider-outsider, or outsider-insider. Nor was the act entirely outside the practice of art itself. Performing the death of art through gestures that nihilate the fetishised art-object has a century of aesthetic history behind it. Of course, to destroy an artefact that is already, in self-parody, countersigned by the same idea, and to do so physically, is as superfluous as it is crude. But it is still a move in the game, still a kind of anti-art as art. Considered as such, indeed, the 'moose' shooting is not without wit. Nor is it without content. In its condensed allegory of sacrificial substitution – from moose to 'moose' – it even touches on a universal theme. All that is missing for this borderline behaviour to be read as a neo-Dadaist happening is the frame. Even the absence of this tallies with the old surrealist phantasm of erasing the line between art and life, as in Breton's image of the artist randomly shooting passersby as he dashes down the street.[4]

In Kyle's second acting out we can see many of the same features. Once more – from a position both inside and outside it – an attack on (what can loosely be called) the art community via a spoliation of its emblems. Once more, a scene covered with parodic signs, in which, again, the use of guns has the effect of both destroying those signs and making them come alive. See this fake moose, I'll shoot it with real bullets. You wanna play with scary images, I'll be your worse nightmare.

The themes, however, had matured, and the aggression had transmuted into something at once more anonymous and direct. There was, too, a change in medium.

The attack, although still on a totem (the rave and its insignia), was not on a representative artefact related only at a distance to those it represented. It was on a collective performance, from which the community it ritually brought together could not be separated. The attack was focused squarely, indeed, on the human milieu. And the aim was total: to wipe out a whole world, or as many in the targeted community as possible. 'There's plenty of caps for all,' Kyle was heard to shout as he shot his way through the house.

There was a shift also with regard to who came under attack. The rage displaced on to the 'moose' connected to the arts and crafts oriented ex-hippies of his parents' generation. The scene disfigured in Kyle's second assault came out of the artsie alt.culture of his own contemporaries. This was tantamount to a wipeout of his peers. His hostility in that context was both poignant and perverse. Alienated among the alienated, marginal among the marginal, Kyle's was not an attack on power, nor on the conformism of the mainstream, but on the alternative sub-community of those trying to swim against it. His farewell was an attempt to obliterate the one grouping that welcomed him in and to which he might have belonged. To that extent, moreover, it was vicariously, as well as actually, suicidal. The 'all' for whom Kyle had enough bullets included 'me.' That Kyle had to die with his victims was not only, then, the blood-price demanded by blood. It expressed the coincidence of his virtual belonging to the 'them' he killed with the impossibility of any mediating 'us.'

None of this is to say that the act was not a performance with its own supplement of meaning. As with the 'moose,' but still more clearly, Kyle did more than trash the show. He staged a play within a play, a *détournement* that with black humour subverted the larger performance going on. That the outrage had to be deferred till the after-party was not, from that angle, a defect. The after-party was scripted to be the rave's final act. The whole could be ruined backwards from there.

The effect was vertiginous. There was an element of déjà vu even as the script was being torn up. The movie that the event suddenly seemed to replicate – in which teens, trifling with a horror they don't believe in, get their comeuppance – is one we have seen many times before. Exposing oneself, via such images, to the terrors under the bed, and to the lacerated flesh that polite society hides, is a rite of passage negotiated these days in childhood. By adolescence it has become camp entertainment. In just that spirit, in fact, many such movies were played that night in the movie room attached to the rave, as an adjunct to its faux-ghoulish theme. The twist, though, was the whole event was made to replay in the register of actuality the knowingly ironic horror movies that were part of its constructed *mise en scène*. And the same effect – a funhouse hall of mirrors in which the simulacrum becomes flesh – extended to the signage of the whole event. Amid the zombie-styled music, costume, and décor a real zombie awakened to destroy the undead.

As a sardonic joke, Kyle's literalization of the image is no doubt crass. A subcultural purist would say that it bypasses both the meaning and the stakes of the postpunk, re-revived, gothic imagery borrowed from at the rave. Insofar as it is more than playing with quotations, the flaunting of morbidity and abjection (at the rave, the different dance rooms were designated dungeon, torture, etc.) is not just being clever-shocking. Still less is it conjuring evil (although strange things seem to be going on in Germany and East Europe). It is an aesthetic gesture – revolt into style – that converts the suppressed material it playfully/contestatively brings to the surface into what is at once a badge of identity and a vehicle for self-expression. The tone is deadpan, a blend of downbeat vulnerability and satirical distance. The white face in the bat-cave says I am wounded, but strong enough to mirror back that woundedness through this exaggerated assemblage of signs as a way to make visible the greater darkness that is all around. Are we not all zombies?

What might be culturally authentic scarcely matters, however. The rave theme was broadly cast and, as with its pot-pourri of music subgenres, blurred all manner of fine distinctions. It was, after all, a costume party. In any case, the catastrophic desublimation of what haunts the goth (and alternate youth cultural) imaginary is not the only joke. The mainstreamed insignia of death, evil, and despair have become empty signifiers. Here, in fact, trebly: not just via the natural entropy that deadens the power of symbols (let us call this the Durkheim effect), or via the de-referentializing effect of fashion and general exchange (the Baudrillard effect), but through the conscious artificiality at work in the organizing of the Capitol Hill dances. The very emphasis on costumes and themes, the edgier the better, was a piece of social engineering, designed to provide a compensatory frisson within the controlled outlet provided for the always potentially troublesome energies of urban youth.

Kyle, not in costume, not dancing, a fly on the wall, a blank without meaning until he picked up his guns, was a perfect complement to this mass of dead metaphor. As the event wound down, at the start of a new day, what more fitting than that he should supply the missing signified, sealed with its referent?

When President Khatami of Iran, in a U.N.-sponsored interfaith conference in New York in November 2001, described the tendency responsible for 9/11 as an 'active form of nihilism' he was (besides blaming 'a decadent philosophy from the West') drawing an interesting parallel.[5]

In the scenario of contemporary nihilism, he was suggesting, jihadi terrorists correspond to those who, in the 1870s and 1880s, presented themselves as 'active nihilists' to Nietzsche. There were terrorists then too, albeit of a different persuasion. They came in the shape of militant anarchists whose bombings and assassinations gripped the headlines and put fear into monarchs. Then, as now, but through print, such figures were mediatized and mythicized, and in a way that curiously interacted with their formation on the ground. The term Nihilist itself was given currency by Turgenev in his portrait of Bazarov in *Fathers and Sons*, and adopted by those it was meant to deprecate.[6]

What the correspondence is or is not between contemporary and nineteenth-century 'terrorists,' and more generally between the scenarios of nihilism in which they (can be made to) figure, is worth pondering. But let us note that Khatami's formula is incomplete. The instances of virulent destructiveness that Nietzsche had before him when he fashioned his concept of 'active nihilism' came in more than one flavour. They included the criminal, of a certain all-is-permitted sort, as well as the militant anarchist.

Nietzsche, to be sure, did not think much about moral monsters and spectacular crime. And when Bataille did so later, via Sadian images of *libertinage*, he linked them to a transposed problematic about sacrifice, the limit experience, and sovereignty. If one takes one's bearings from the twilight of the idols, nevertheless, one can think of the (grand) criminal and the (terror-oriented) anarchist as sharing something essential. Each in their way is an accelerative symptom of *decadence*. The one morally/existentially, the other politically, takes a hammer to 'the old law tables.' Each, at the same time, is healthy enough – and health with regard to superabundant life is Nietzsche's principle of principles – to ward off their own reactive morbidity by focusing it into a self-affirmed destructive energy. The will would 'rather will nothingness than *not* will' at all.[7] The ambiguity of this judgment should be noted. For Nietzsche, what the pious and conventional called nihilism, as the destruction of moral and metaphysical foundations, was not nihilism in the deepest sense. The latter is that which nihilates the will-to-power itself.

But what of today? On the side of extreme crime, what best fits the description of active nihilism is exactly what we are examining: a mass killing, especially where the act is not delusional, nor targeted toward specific objects of resentment, nor the outcome of sudden rage; a mass killing, rather, that is premeditated, indiscriminate, and bent on annihilating (at least symbolically, or in microcosm) the social, the community as such. Such cases – a spectacular novelty of the present period – display a destructiveness more thoroughgoing even than that of Bluebeard or his suburban equivalents, with the will-to-nothing monopolizing desire, and suicide being intrinsic to the exercise.

Spree killers and those conjured by Khatami (Bush's 'evil ones'), we might hypothesize then, are a complementary pair. Both actively will the nothing. Both seek the death simultaneously of others and themselves. Both appear as the virulent discharge of a local tension in the disequilibrated gift economy. Both have the double character of revenge and sacrifice. In truth they can be hard to distinguish. They slide into one another. It would be imprecise to say, for example, that the one is individual and the other collective, or that the one is politically motivated and the other not. (What was the Manson family?) At the limit, though – Mohammed Atta vs Kyle Huff – their difference is easily stated. The nihilist spree killer is the inverse of the Satan-attacking suicide-bomber. The latter over-identifies with a 'we' as absolute good against the absolute evil incarnated by its enemies. The former has no pole of Good and aims to destroy the 'we,' or any we, as such. To that extent one might say the spree killer is even more purely an active nihilist than the suicide bomber, who, if their target were not civilian would shade into a warrior-related species of altruistic suicide.

What is interesting about the Seattle rave killings is not only that they illuminate the current form that active nihilism takes *at the level of the agent*, that is, as a certain configuration of the will-to-power. Nor that the bursting of this configuration into public view facilitates its interpretation with regard to the 'pathology' that produced it. Also noteworthy is that its staged character, which converts the scene of the killing into a giant symbol of that scene's self-undoing, throws light on the morbid negativity running not only through the actor and his act, but through the very scene the act disrupts – in relation to which, moreover, this disruption is itself a relay.

To see the second point involves a shift in optic. It is to move from a nihilism of the subject to one of the object. Or if you prefer, from the plane of (an individual-centred) bioenergetics, with the ultimate spectre being the self-extinction of the will-to-power itself, to nihilism as a devitalizing and reductive dynamic within – or as crucially mediated by the structures of – social life. At this level, too, the realities encountered are second-order, not even derivatively, that is to say, matters of will and consciousness, but related to what has become quasi-autonomous about the economic and, in a different way, the technological.

To comprehend what converges and crosses over at the rave killings, there would, then, be two processes to trace. On the one hand, there is the generation of the force that explodes at the after-party in the shape of Kyle Huff; on the other, the dynamic by which this force is captured, despite itself, by another force (or complex of forces) operating independently at the scene of the crime.

With regard to the first, Kyle Huff and what made him, there is evidently a piling up of contingencies. These begin with the details of a family drama that it would be indecent to speculate about more than I have already. (Why Kyle not Kane, for example, and what was their relationship?) But that is only part of the story. If something had gone wrong in postoedipal identity formation, it had done so in a way that intersected with a sociocultural fault-line within the social world at large. Kyle was the post-Vietnam son of a soldier and an artist in the cowboy/mountain fringe of the heartland. He was located at an unstable pressure point. In the imaginaries that clashed around him, the bedrock know-nothing hostility of pioneers taming the wilderness and escaping city/authority, the Scots/Irish militia tradition, and cattle culture, ground up against their citified, pansified, old-world antitheses. It was the explosive combination of family and class-cultural contradictions, with their aporetic impact on identity and project formation, that made Kyle Huff into a volcano. A different language would speak of evil. And why not? What we have here is a purely ill-will, precipitated out of the deep disarticulation of the social, fueled by displaced and supercharged resentment. Whether this or that region of the global social formation is more liable, under current conditions, to present with such symptoms would be a fascinating topic for empirical research. But, in the wider search for explanation, no one could deny that American society is full of virulent tension, or pretend that it spirals happily in a virtuous circle of energy-liberating sociality.

At the rave itself, second – where signs of death were so much on display – a different, and more passive, kind of nothing was at work. In these signs we can see the meta-signs of a deadening cultural scene, the dis-autonomisation of a once vibrant generational culture, its regulation by officialdom, its commercialisation, the dissipation of its self-transcending expression in the frenzy of circulation. Of course, we must guard against nostalgia. The golden age of rock and roll was shot through with such tendencies, as was clubbing in the 1980s and hip hop in the 1990s. One cannot project for Western youth culture an unvitiated origin. From the jazz age on, in any case, its whole development has been underpinned by a shift in the kinship system (from restricted to general exchange). The eventual normalization of a prolonged adolescence together with its peer culture is the natural end of this process, and should not give alarm. Yet in the degenerate and simulacral stage of the Seattle rave scene there is the unmistakable air of something incandescent that has burnt out, the last flickers of an expansive energy that once (although witnesses to this are unreliable) crackled with dancing stars. In zombie land we are at the end of the line: the deadening further deadened in the artificiality with which it mobilizes the remains of an effort to counter the deadness through a contestative show of death and abjection.

Kyle in all of this is a short circuit, the dog that finally barks. But here we come to a final point. With respect to all this deadening – a striking instance of the highest values devaluing themselves – the effect of the incident is to make things worse. Reality explodes 'love.' Regulation-mongering, and security fears as the basis for state legitimization, are all reinforced, while the way is paved locally for extending controls to after hours and the semi-private zone.

What is at issue, certainly in Kyle Huff's contribution, is not fragmentation and *gemeinschaft* (outrages bring community together). It is the risk-driven close-down of the space for spontaneous interchange, and the way this interferes with social reproduction, expression, and effervescence, especially on the magmatic site of youth/music/sex. All of this can be seen as part of wider trends towards the taming of Dionyus, and the sanitization of all the circulatory channels that make up public space.

In larger compass still, what transpired on Capitol Hill can be read as the index of a major historical shift.

Nietzsche's 'nihilism' (both in concept, and with regard to what presented itself in the world) was a war against authority. The Nihilists, in Bazarov's formula, wanted to demolish everything whose existence could not be justified as useful or scientific. It was the critical spirit of the enlightenment gone mad. Borrowed from Catholic conservatives, this fitted exactly the notion of *negativisme* developed by Comte, and his understanding of it as a potentially lethal pathology in the transition to a reorganized industrial modernity. Nietzsche's diagnosis was of course different. Militant anarchism was not only crippled by reactiveness. It did not, in its criticality, go anything like far enough. Hence Nietzsche's project of the 1880s. His would be an active *theoretical* nihilism – but a nihilism complete, and self-overcome, so as to give birth to a transvaluation that would reconfigure the ground of evaluation itself.

Optimism for Nietzsche comes by way of a quasi-dialectical trope. Our 'nihilism,' however, is worse. It is not just against the Law and the father, it is matricidal and sociocidal. Nor, correspondingly, can the scene in which this occurs be grasped any more in terms of disorientation, anarchy of belief, and the demise of foundations. This is no longer the death of God (which has been succeeded by an undeath). It is the passion of the social. In this moment are lived a multitude of torsions and tensions that, on the one hand, attend the unravelling of posttheistic hypostases of the social (race, nation, family, society, community etc.) and, on the other, raise in new (and disabused) form fundamental issues about the (de)constitution of the *socius*. What comes to be at stake is not so much the waning of the will as an inner force, but the conditions in which meaningful formation of the will can occur at all.

Here, indeed, the parallel one might like to pursue further begins to break down. On the side of the subject, it would be fanciful to imagine that any kind of sublating principle lurks beneath Kyle Huff's all too imitable aim at least to have made a mark. His gesture is only the flip side of identity politics in which group identity can become the basis for a panic religiosity. (The oscillation between these poles can illusorily present itself as the social question itself.) There seems, at any rate, no incompleteness here, no line of flight, even for instincts to become free.

On the side of the object things are less clear. Deconstruction of the social, as the late Enlightenment conceived it, has been embraced as a key critical principle by a number of progressive thinkers, including those who now speak about multitudes and multiples. We may say that there is a similar logic as with the war on Christianity. Nihilating God nihilates world-rejection. In a perverse way, then, Thatcher was right. There is no such thing as society: down with reification, ceremonial, and institution. But this is only to speak of the false-social, the unitary community that 'thinks it is God.'[8] Even Baudrillard, in an unguarded moment, referred to the social's 'essential marrow.' What, then, if recognition becomes impossible, or if the gift dynamic ceases to operate? Or if the sharing of mortality as the non-ground of our ethical dealings with one another cannot form sufficiently? Or if the collective energies and imagination needed for any going-beyond are prevented from accumulating?

There is perhaps no more than a banal truism here: that besides blood, the damage with which mass killers can be reproached has to do with the socially asphyxiating side-effects of their actions. But that is just the point. In such instances as Seattle these effects are not incidental to the meaning of the act. Contemporary nihilism is sociocidal in both its objective and subjective forms. The former is to the latter as a slow death is to a fast one. Nor is their relation only analogical. These forms operate together, in a ratcheting up of controlled circulation, which itself functions almost auto-telicly to reconcile the economic/ communicative and social control imperatives of contemporary capitalism. One could imagine a convergence of the United States with a softened version of the rival model for socially regulated capitalism being prototyped by China.

We do well to remind ourselves, in any case, that under the demonization and mayhem that fills the headlines a less noisy nothing is in play. It is a nothing in which the in-common attenuates, and the transcendent energy of the social fades like a collective version of the last man. To stress the determinateness and object-like character of the conditions under which this process occurs is not to counsel pessimism. It does, however, challenge any notion that a politics addressing these conditions can be avoided as the plane on which an exit might be found.

Notes

1 A summary of the main details of the incident can be found at http://www.seattleweekly .com/news/0613/shootings2.phpIntelligencer, accessed 20 Oct. 2006.

2 For an account of Kyle Huff's time in Whitefish, and of the moose shooting, see http:// seattletimes.nwsource.com/html/localnews/2002905219_huff02m.html, accessed 20 Oct. 2006.

3 http://seattletimes.nwsource.com/html/localnews/2002895317_webtextletter28.html, accessed 20 Oct. 2006.

4 'L'acte surréaliste le plus simple consiste, revolvers aux poigns, à descendre dans la rue et à tirer au hasard, tant qu'on peut, dans la foule.' A. Breton, 'Second manifeste du surréalisme,' in Œuvres complètes, 1930, vol. 1 (Paris: Gallimard, 1988), 783.

5 The speech was reported in the Economist, 24 Nov. 2001.

6 I. Turgenev, Fathers and Sons [1861], trans. and ed. M. Katz (London and New York: Norton, 1996).

7 F. Nietzsche, On the Genealogy of Morality, ed. K Ansell-Pearson (Cambridge: Cambridge University Press, 1994), 72.

8 J.L. Nancy, The Inoperative Community (Minneapolis: University of Minnesota Press, 1991), 143.

21 Digital Cosmologies:
Religion, Technology, and Ideology

ARTHUR KROKER

The Cosmological Compromise

'We are witnessing a fundamental sea change in American politics,' said Allan Litchman, a professor of political history at American University in Washington. 'The divide used to be primarily economics – between the haves and the have-nots. That's changed now. The divide in America today is religious and racial ... The base of the Republican Party is not necessarily the "haves" anymore – it's the white evangelicals, white devout Catholics, white churchgoers. The base of the Democratic Party is not necessarily the "nots." It's African Americans, Jewish Americans, those without any religious affiliation. Our politics revolve around a new cultural polarization.

Joe Garofoli.[1]

The foundations of modernity have always been based on an underlying cosmological compromise. Confronted with the incipiently antagonistic relationship between science and religion, Western societies took up the safer, although definitely less intense, option of splitting the faith-based difference. Under the guise of political pluralism, freedom of religious worship was consigned to the realm of private belief, whereas the arena of political action was secured not only for the protection of private rights, but more importantly, for forms of political participation, educational practice, and scientific debates that were, at least nominally, to be based on the triumph of reason over faith. If the cosmological compromise overlooked the inconvenient fact that the origins of science (specifically), and modernity (more generally), were themselves based on a primal act of faith in secularizing rationality, it did contribute an important cultural firewall against the implosion of society into increasingly virulent expressions of religious fundamentalisms. Modern society would no longer aspire, at least collectively, to the ancient dream of salvation; instead, it would have the indispensable virtue of providing a realm of public action where faith-based politics would be put aside in favour of the instrumental play of individual interests.

Max Horkheimer, an early critic of European modernity, could revolt in his writings against the 'dawn and decline' of liberal culture, but his criticisms were tempered by the knowledge that, left to its own devices, the forces of fully consolidated capitalism were as likely to tip in the direction of politically mediated fascism as they were to recuperate the divisive passions of religious idolatry. A beautiful illusion all the more culturally resplendent for its ultimate political futility, liberal modernity represented a thin line dividing a history of religious conflict from a future of authoritarian politics. With religious salvation limited to private conscience, Western society was thus free to unfold in the direction of political and economic security. All modern history, from the bourgeois interests of the capitalist marketplace to the politics of pluralism has been, *ontologically speaking*, a vast defence mechanism whereby both individuals and collectivities insulated themselves against a resurrection of the problem of salvation.

With a false sense of confidence, perhaps all the more rhetorically frenzied for its approaching historical eclipse, the discourse of technological modernism – Western culture's dominant form of self-understanding – has over the past century hailed the triumph of secular culture and the death of religion. Indeed, when German philosopher Martin Heidegger submitted that technology is the language of human destiny, he had in mind that technology is simultaneously both present and absent: Technology is *present* with ferocious force in the languages of objectification, harvesting, the reduction of subjects to 'standing-reserve,' and the privileging of abuse value as the basis of the will to technology; but technology is marked by an *absence* as well, namely, by the retreat of the gods into the gathering shadows of a humanity that has seemingly lost its way in the midst of the frenzy that is the will to technology. If Heidegger could write so eloquently about a coming age of 'completed nihilism' as the dominant characteristic of technology as our historical destiny, he was only rehearsing in new key the fatal pronouncements of those other prophets of the future of techno-culture: Friedrich Nietzsche, Max Weber, and Albert Camus. In *Thus Spake Zarathustra*, Nietzsche wrote not so much about the death of God, but about a more primary death, namely, the death of the sacred as a resurrection effect capable of holding in fascination an increasingly restless human subject in open revolt against the absolute codes of metaphysics. With Nietzsche, the modern century resolved to make of itself a fatal gamble – a 'going across' – with technology as its primary language of self-understanding. Impatient with the slowness of the modern mind to grasp the truly radical implications that necessarily flowed from stripping the absolutes of theodicy from an increasingly instrumental consciousness, Nietzsche went to his death noting that, as a philosopher 'born posthumously,' his intimations of the gathering storm of nihilism would be the historical inheritance of generations not yet born.

Equally, Max Weber, Germany's leading social theorist during the years preceding the Weimar Republic, was perhaps the first to grasp deeply what it means to live in the shadows of Nietzsche's prophecy. When Weber wrote so chillingly about the approaching 'disenchantment' of the modern age, populated by 'specialists without spirit,' he was only echoing in the language of social theory the image of impoverished (techno-logical) being first glimpsed by Nietzsche. But it was left to the tragic sensibility of Albert Camus to produce the capstone of the vision of technology as destiny that was the mod-ern century. For Camus, modern subjectivity is the historical product of two great revolts of the human spirit: not only Nietzsche's *metaphysical* rebellion against the sover-eignty of the sacred, but also a more explicitly violent, and necessarily, *historical* rebellion in the name of ideology. With a sense of the indeterminacy of an absurd universe always proximate to his political consciousness, Camus was, in effect, the last Nietzsche. In his writings, Nietzsche's dark vision of modern subjectivity as a melancholic mixture of active *ressentiment* and passive nihilism was summed up into a searing literary account of the human price to be paid for the age of absolute ideology with its cleansing drive to purity without limits and justice without reason – state systematic, state-sponsored mass murder, and a culture of exuberant, populist irrationality.

After the prophetic visions of Nietzsche, Weber, and Camus, the politics of techno-logical secularism have generally been translated into the sanitizing language of lib-eral pluralism. Perhaps mindful of these earlier warnings concerning the gathering technological darkness as it penetrates human subjectivity, a pragmatic political set-tlement of *Thus Spake Zarathustra* was quietly achieved: in effect, postponing the meta-physical crisis in human affairs unleashed by the eclipse of the gods by the practical expedient of splitting the question of science and religion. With religion secured in the confessional of private conscience and science increasingly assuming the position of sovereign arbiter of questions concerning power – in technology, market capital-ism, culture, and public policy – the question of theodicy was safely bunkered in the quiet suburbs of private faith, leaving the question of technology to be the spearhead of Western historical destiny. This was a perfect historical compromise that, if it did not measure up to the soaring certainties of the language of the sacred, was, nonethe-less, a powerful check on the violent excesses of absolute ideology. In retrospect, we might say that the twentieth century was, at least in part, a long drawn-out struggle between two fatefully opposing ideas – *absolute ideology* and *absolute technology* – both of which were posthumous products of Nietzsche's understanding of the death of God, and each of which was by definition a monism studiously unaware of its limits. Definitely more metaphysical than purely technological, the digital euphoria that marked the twilight of the twentieth century represented the simultaneous cultural triumph of pure cybernetic reason and the eclipse of the sacred in human affairs.

There the matter stood, until, that is, the triumphant resurgence of God as the essence of twenty-first century political history.

The Flat World of Technology Has Just Been Thrown a Religious Curve

Viewed from a conventional progressive political perspective, the emergence of religious fundamentalism in contemporary politics represents a powerful reaction formation against the forces of secular change, from the stresses accompanying technological innovation to the boundary disturbances in race, class, and gender variously symbolized under the signs of postmodernism first and posthumanism later. In this scenario, the triumph of science, and with it the claims of reason, have provoked in their wake a powerful counter-reaction from those with the most to lose, whether materially or symbolically, by transgressions against the fixed borderlines of the dominant signs. This thesis is chromatically illustrated by the division of the United States into a media psycho-geography of red and blue states. But it also provides for a more global perspective, pitting, for example, the (digital) winners and losers of Thomas Friedman's persuasive mapping of *The World Is Flat*[2] against a threatening world of religious fundamentalism, made all the more potent by the latter's contribution of suicide martyrs, sleeper cells, and other spectacular expressions of viral terrorism to the media spectacle. It is as if the most recidivist tendencies of the Middle Ages have mysteriously risen from the dead to prevent the creative technological blast of the twenty-first century.

As with all tidy binary divisions of the world into two warring camps, this explanation has, for all its compelling rhetorical force, the singular weakness of seriously misinterpreting the historical facts. From country to country – from the professional workplaces of the American middle class to the new-economy software portals of India, Canada, Israel, and Australia – adherents of evangelical politics often represent less the losers in the 'flat world' of digital innovation than the leading professional classes of society. Coders, designers, teachers, doctors, lawyers, military leaders, politicians, policy experts: the born again world of evangelical politics knows no strict borderline of the human heart. Strictly agnostic in relationship to race, class, and gender, the world of the born again represents, as did all powerful religious movements before it, a sudden, irreversible, rupture in the fabric of human belief. Definitely not a counter-reaction in the traditional sense, evangelical politics can be so charismatic, circulating today so effortlessly at the highest levels of politics – the economy, the media, and the military – because its formative sensibility is not simply reactionary, but *transformational*. When religion reanimates the solitude of a single life as its source of informing passion, then we are suddenly present at the shattering of the closed episteme of modernist rationality, with the emergence, again and again, of the much-rebuked problem of salvation. Irrespective of its particular religious expression – born again Christianity, Islamic fundamentalism, Israeli religious Zionism, Hindu fundamentalism – the reappearance of passionate religious conviction, simultaneously and across so much of the globe, represents a decisive challenge to the dominant ontology of contemporary technological society. To Thomas Friedman's enthusiastic, but ultimately dismal, vision of a flat digital world of cut-throat global economic competition, the ontology of salvation opens up just the opposite: a transcendent world of delirious intensity and life-affirming meaning – in effect, a decidedly *unflattened* world involving individual participation in the deeper questions of life – life and death, judgment, and rapture. From Pentecostal Inuit and born again Christians in the heartland of the

American empire to the fast currents of Islamic jihad, the problem of salvation is the dominant singularity haunting the twenty-first century.

Faith-Based Information Technology

Consequently, the question arises: Why in the opening moments of the twenty-first century has the cosmological compromise between the privatization of religious worship and an increasingly secularized global political economy been so abruptly pushed aside in favour of the resurrection of evangelical politics, which paradoxically, rather than warring with the spirit of informatics, allies itself at a basic level with the historical project of the will to technology? Why, that is, is it possible to speak today about the rapid emergence of faith-based information technology as the spearhead of power, specifically the power of the American empire? Could it be that, under the *double* pressure of increasingly technological forms of secularism – which inject elements of uncertainty, indeterminacy, and undecidability into the posthuman condition – and the rapid emergence of right-wing expressions of religious fundamentalism anxious to transform essentially theological visions into global political projects, the mask of secular culture has been abruptly stripped away, revealing not so much the return of a recidivist religious past but something different, something more ominous and ethically disturbing: the resurrection of God as the spearhead of the technological future. Contrary to liberal-humanist ambitions that privileged the necessary opposition of reason and faith, is the second coming of God the final heir of the Enlightenment? Perhaps the last ruse of the triumph of the age of reason is that it was God, after all, who has been waiting all this time, patiently and not without a sense of humour, as the varied drama of the posthuman comedy rode the beam of – digital – light to a technological future fused with the energies of faith-based politics? It may well turn out out that God never really died but has only been endlessly deferred by the hubris of Enlightenment.

Consider the following example. As the dynamic spearhead of the will to technology, the United States has resurrected the traditions of empire – not in opposition to faith-based politics, but precisely because its evangelical fusion of the textologies of reason and faith – from Sunday pulpits to prayer meetings in the suburbs, boardrooms, and fields of sports and entertainment – has, in the ambitious ideology of the *Project for the New American Century*,[3] globalized the unique fusion of faith and technocracy that we have come to know as the civil religion behind the American dream. Governed by a Republican Party that declares itself to be one with God, in the form of Christian fundamentalism, its public policy increasingly faith-based, its machinery of cyber-war intent on mapping an essentially cosmological vision of good and evil onto the skin of an unruly global village, the United States projects into history a new code of informatics: one that finds no essential difference between the ancient cosmology of Christian fundamentalism and the posthuman instrumentalism of cyberculture.

This is not only happening in the United States. Until recently, politics in India has been dominated by the Bharatiya Janata Party (BJP), a party of Hindu fundamentalism bitterly opposed to the warring cosmologies of the Muslim and Christian faiths. Less a counter-reaction than something essentially new in political history the BJP, most strikingly, created India's pro-informatics movement: the *India Shining Movement*. Hindu fundamentalists are on one side and, on the other, actively allied with the global networks of the technocratic class is the BJP. Remarkably similar to the *Project for the New American Century*, this represents a fusion of cosmology and secularism, this time in the monistic vernacular of Hindu fundamentalism. Equally, how can we explain the essentially faith-based politics of contemporary Israel? There we see the historical singularity of fusing religious Zionism with the technological instrumentalities of cyber-war, seamlessly collapsing the ancient religious energies of messianic Judaism into the deployment of leading-edge informatics, including war, medicine, agriculture, and aerospace. Finally, although nomadic, stateless, without fixed territory or officially authorized context, Islamic fundamentalism – with its origins in the doctrines of the Wahibi sect – is deeply implicated in global networks of informatics. Working in the language of viral terrorism, Islamic fundamentalism reverses the logic of power against itself. Confronted with the predatory power of globalization, al-Qaeda adopts the viral strategy of the viral parasite: seeking to move undetected within the circulatory systems of the social, silently embedding itself in the form of sleeper cells in the body politic, making missiles of civilian aircraft, always aiming for maximal effect in the specular universe of the mass media.

Speaking about the second coming of God only as an alibi for the formation of powerful right-wing coalitions would be both simpler and certainly more comfortable in terms of the dialectics of modernism. But this is different. Definitely not a counter-reaction to the loss of an irrecoverable religious past, the cosmological aspirations of the *Project for the New American Century*, the *India Shining Movement*, the eschatological ambitions of the Likud Party in Israel, and what one commentator has described as the 'Islamofascism' of the Wahibi sect each represent the vanguard of the technological future. Drawing from leading elements, sometimes disaffected ones, of the technocratic class – working within, and against, the discourse of globalization – faith-based politics is perfectly allied with the dynamic unfolding of the will to technology. Basing its economic hopes now on the possibility of outsourcing codework for the virtual class and, in the future, projecting the creation of a distinctively Indian virtual class, the BJP spearheaded the project of informatics in the Indian imaginary. Similar developments can be traced in the cases of faith-based politics in the United States and Israel. Evangelical belief can fuse so easily, in the United States, with the missionary consciousness of the American empire precisely because religious faith provides the historical project of armed globalization with a renewed sense of purpose, a goal, a self-validating belief in its own moral rectitude. Perhaps, having achieved maximal velocity in the 1990s with the virtualization of global political economy, in the twenty-first century informatics, moving at the speed of light, is itself tracing a fatal curvature and arching backwards to a fateful re-encounter with its originating religious ambitions. In Israel, the messianic dreams of the Likud, steeled in the burning fires of monistic moral politics, are less the past of a forgotten politics than one possible future of a rearmed (Israeli) technological future. If the story of informatics is, in essence, metaphysical, having more to do with the question of the will than with the triumph of the code, then the resurgence of faith-based politics in technocratic form has everything to with relieving the fatal absence at the heart of informatics: namely, substituting absolute theodicy for the necessary uncertainty, undecidibility and indeterminacy of the will to technology. Fatigued with the imminent stresses of its historical project, bored with its logic of triumphalism, and perhaps alarmed at its own nihilism, the will to technology yearns to relieve itself of the burden of undecidability. Ironically, cybernetics, etymologically the language of the steersman, wants a goal, a purpose, a direction. In the political form of the BJP, Likud, and evangelical American Republicanism, the will to technology cloaks itself in its own resurrection effect. The will to technology welcomes the second coming of God as shelter from the posthuman storm of its own making. And what about al-Qaeda? It represents a fatal curvature in the logic of informatics: that point where the open field of IT as the ruling host is suddenly invaded by the counter-logic of viral terrorism, its circulatory systems reversed against itself, its data streams infected with fear, its 'chokepoints' invitations to viral penetration and, consequently, increasingly armed bunkers of surveillance.

The Double Cone Theory of the Propagation of (Political) Light

> Everything's relative. Speed, mass, space and time are all subjective. Nor are age, motion or the wanderings of the planets measures that humans can agree on anymore; they can be judged only by the whim of the observer. Light has weight. Space has curves. And coiled within a pound of matter, any matter, is the explosive power of 14 million tons of TNT. We know all this, we are set adrift in this way at the end of the 20th century, because of Albert Einstein.
>
> Frank Pellegrini[4]

The alliance between the second coming of God and IT is not understandable in terms of the modernist, which is to say Newtonian, certainties of absolute time and absolute space. Perhaps more than we realize, we are living out the radical implications of Einstein's Special Theory of Relativity. What was originally presented as a decisive overturning of the dominant *scientific* discourse of Newtonian physics has now become the *cultural physics* of the posthuman condition. Quite literally, the lasting lesson of the historical project of informatics has been to map the speed of light onto our bodies, economy, politics, culture, entertainment, and religion. We live in the universe of the *special theory of political relativity*, where power accelerating at the speed of light reaches its maximal velocity, distance expands, gains (ideological) weight, and just as suddenly reverses, time-travelling to the supposed past of religion and mythology. In this universe of political relativity, light-through-power is both wave and particle. Globalization is another name for the *space-time fabric* of electronic politics; only opposites exist simultaneously, and the 'science fiction' of wormholes and warp speed becomes the normal political reality of power. Under the influence of informatics, this new universe approximates the cultural physics of the Special Theory of Relativity. In the century following the revolution against the Newtonian episteme, the symbolic iconography of absolute space and absolute time dissolved into a more fluid field of 'worldlines' and 'wormholes' and 'spacetime fabrics,' and light that slows down and distances that shrink, and sometimes stretch, the acceleration of the universe.

In thinking about the radiating matter of religious fundamentalism seemingly everywhere now, which has suddenly reappeared from the supposedly buried past to form the essence of the unfolding (technological) future, I am reminded that physicists today privilege the 'double cone' theory of the propagation of light waves: namely, that the immense whirlpool of black holes populating the space-time fabric of the universe is accompanied by corresponding white holes – singularities through which the (light-through) past slipstreams through to the future riding the beam of light. And I speculate: Could it be that history today is not understandable in the Newtonian terms of absolute time and absolute space, but should be reconceived as a unitary fabric of space-time, where the light-time and light-space of power moving at the speed of Einstein's Special Theory of Relativity can be stretched and bent and reversed and twisted? If this is the case, then why can we not think of the fabric of political space-time as filled with galactic singularities: intense centres of centrifugal political energy, such as ancient religious cosmologies, which suck the passing matter of politics, identity, culture, and society into the dark immensity of the act of faith? Myth breaks through into history. Religious fervour renews its long-forgotten affiliation with the art of politics. Understood through the prism of Einstein, immensely dense black holes of religious belief follow worldlines that burst into the future through corresponding white holes of technocratic ideology. Having reached its maximal velocity with the triumph of the virtual class in the 1990s, the speed of light-through power instantly reverses course, slows down, goes backward, double-cones its way into that more abiding source of energy: religious faith. This is not to say that ancient religious epiphanies suddenly appear on the technocratic horizon as images of a faded, idealized past, but as immensely energetic religious projects intending to get it right this time. No longer the separation of church and state, but *wormholing* religious cosmology directly into the eye of power, hooking theology to the unfolding space-time fabric of the future. Viral, recombinant, creative, powerful, essentially religious eschatologies such as the *Project for the New American Century, India Shining,* and dreams of a *New Jerusalem* are variations on a common theme: the resurrection in the distinctively posthuman vernacular of IT of the vision of the Second City of God, this time in alliance, as in the American situation, with the New Rome. In the contemporary historical epoch, conservative discourse is intent on getting it right: the Christian project as the essence of the New Rome – taking over the reins of government, infiltrating the administration of public policy, filling the airwaves with the Christian goal of historical redemption masked as 'war on terrorism,' installing evangelical Christians in key positions of executive power, and using every instrument of IT in support of the creation of the new surveillance state. In the Einsteinian space-time fabric of contemporary technoculture, *mythic time breaks into historical space.* This is only now beginning: the first, tentative stages of recovering the missing mass of God on behalf of the project of technocracy.

The historical project of technology, generally, and the utopian revolution of information technology, specifically, have always represented an extended period of mourning for what has been lost in the rationalist triumph of modernism. We are at the end of a period of sacrifice that has had its own historical period – Nietzsche, the first witness to the freshness of the sacrifice; the bountiful years of reaping the materialist rewards of splitting open the horizon; literally vivisecting Earth, animals, planets, the common genetic heritage; and resequencing the sky, the body, gender, class, and race with new codes of informatics. But for all its ecstasy, the project of technology remains a mourning ritual, an indefinite deferral of the sacrificial absence at the core of the will to technology. Or perhaps something more psycho-ontological: a massive cultural displacement of the language of sacrificial absence – the death of God – into sublimated expressions of the will to technology. In this case, the language of seduction is the wormhole between the rationality of the sign and the forbidden language of symbolic exchange. Sexual puritanism is haunted by the spectre of debauchery. Violence is instantly undermined by the slightest trace of peace, which is why, for example, military machineries so deeply fear the reappearance of the symbolic language of peace in the form of human-rights workers, nuns, and priests spilling vials of their own blood on the awesome silence of missile silos, or student protesters at the School of the Americas in Georgia who were arrested recently for re-enacting rituals of mourning for victims of death squads. So, too, the modern project of technology began with a primal symbolic murder – the death of God. In the curious, but predictable, mythology of the sign, it is the absence marked by this sacrificial act that haunts the story of technology, and on behalf of which, information technology, once released via the light-through physics of the Einsteinian universe, draws closer, almost irresistibly, to the tangible sign of its missing origin: the primal act of religious faith. When the missing mass of God touches the full-spectrum dominance of cyberculture, then we are suddenly launched into the closed universe of posthumanism, into a strange space-time fabric that is simultaneously mythic and historical, past and future, technocratic and religious.

Paradoxically, for all its technological pretensions, the twenty-first century is coded by all the signs of Born Again Ideology, from the 'cosmological compromise' in its past to the 'twisted strands' of religion and technology in the controlling rhetoric of the American empire. Nietzsche could only think posthumously about a future time oscillating between passive and suicidal nihilism; our present time, however, this specific historical epoch, witnesses the gathering storm and offers its theoretical diagnosis: the American Republic moving at the speed of light towards the gathering shadows of an ominous darkness.

Notes

1 Joe Garofoli, 'Split Loyalty: Usual Politics Divisions Give Way to Emotional Issue,' *San Francisco Chronicle*, 22 March 2005.
2 Thomas L. Friedman, *The World Is Flat: A Brief History of the Twenty-First Century*. New York: Farrar, Strauss and Giroux, 2005.
3 Founded in 1997 by neoconservatives associated with the American Enterprise Institute, the *Project for the New American Century* (PNAC) has mobilized elite and public opinion in the United States in favour of a highly interventionist foreign policy. See particularly, http://rightweb.irc-online.org/profile/1535.
4 Frank Pellegrini, 'Time 100: Albert Einstein,' *The Time 100*, 29 March 1999.

22 Technologies of the Apocalypse: The *Left Behind* Novels and Flight from the Flesh

STEPHEN PFOHL

Preface: One Nation under God

The United States of America is history's first formally secular republic. The U.S. Constitution guarantees legal separation between church and state, and this is one reason why America has long been viewed as a beacon of modern enlightenment, democratic governance, and scientific rationality. This is the sober and pragmatic America envisioned by the nation's 'founding fathers,' most of whom were deists. This is an America governed by 'self-evident' rights to 'life, liberty, and the pursuit of happiness.' This is also the America of 'the Protestant ethic' described by Max Weber, an America that believed that 'the rational and utilitarian uses of wealth ... were willed by God for the needs of the individual and the community.'[1] In this America, enlightenment and religion stroll as cordial companions, each complementing the existence of the other. But this is only one side of a decidedly Janus-faced America. Since its inception, another powerful – and far less rational – religious spirit has split the nation's attention, bifurcating America's vision of itself and its place in world history.

The second American religious spirit is the intense, emotionally charged, and judgmental Christian spirit of a nation believing itself to be the divinely ordained agent of God's kingdom on Earth. This is an apocalyptic religious spirit, a harbinger of God's imminent intervention into the course of human history. From the time of the American Revolution to the present, when political leaders invoke this second spirit to praise the virtues of freedom and liberty, the terms they use are 'saturated with religious meaning.' This is to speak of freedom in ways that transcend the human rights and democratic principles enshrined in the Declaration of Independence and U.S. Constitution. Here, freedom is drenched in biblical connotations and blood, an offspring of grace and the unerring authority of the Gospel. This suggests a special kind of freedom – not simply freedom from tyrannical rule and unjust authority, but freedom found in 'the joy of conversion, and a liberation from the pain and sorrow of normal life.'[2]

Early in U.S. history, this explicitly religious imagination of freedom became coupled with a righteous 'theology of hatred.' This theology marched hand-in-hand with a ritual demonizing of the country's enemies. Indeed, from King George III to Saddam Hussein, one enemy after another has been portrayed as being in league with the Devil, or bearing the 'mark of the beast,' a prophetic sign of the dreaded Antichrist depicted in the *Book of Revelation*. Pitted against these satanic adversaries, the second side of the American religious spirit conjures up an image of the United States as a nation chosen by God to champion the cause of the good in a cosmic eschatological battle with the forces of evil.[3] Ebbing and flowing as a force in history, the passionate second side of the American religious imagination exerted its greatest influence in U.S. politics during the mid-nineteenth century and again in the early decades of the twentieth century.

In the early twenty-first century, the righteous Christian warrior ethos associated with this second American spirit is again ascendant in the 'born-again' political rhetoric of U.S. President George W. Bush. Bush's many thinly veiled references to God's divine mission for America – in spreading freedom across the globe and fighting evil at home and abroad – have stirred millions of people to view his presidency in starkly religious terms. This is evident in the testimony of Hardy Billington of Poplar Bluff, Missouri. With his friend, the fundamentalist preacher David Hahn, Billington circulated a petition that collected 10,000 signatures inviting President Bush to make a 2004 campaign stop in their town. When word reached the White House about the petition, plans were made for Bush to travel to Poplar Bluff. Following the president's speech to a crowd of 20,000, Billington declared, 'To me, I just believe God controls everything, and God uses the president to keep evil down, to see darkness and protect this nation ... Other people will not protect us. God gives people choices to make. God gave us this president to be the man to protect the nation at this time.'[4]

The religious aura surrounding President Bush and the righteous anger of his supporters surprised many of Bush's political opponents following the 2004 U.S. elections. Out of touch with the fateful second spirit of American religious culture – at least consciously – and viewing politics in more rational and 'reality-based' terms, many otherwise thoughtful critics found themselves hard pressed to explain Bush's populist appeal. This is not entirely surprising. For the most part, the social biographies and religious trajectories of those who most oppose Bush set them apart from the everyday worlds of conservative white evangelicals. In addition, if they are Protestant, Bush's critics are far more likely to belong to shrinking mainstream white (Protestant) denominations or to African-American or African diasporic churches, than to be members of fundamentalist evangelical church communities. Isolated on the supposedly more rational side of America's religious-social divide, many liberal or left-leaning critics are either unfamiliar with, or relatively inattentive to, a great deal of what has been going on among fervent members of the Christian right.

One thing that has been going on in conservative evangelical culture is the so-called *Left Behind* phenomenon – the publication and mass consumption of the best-selling *Left Behind* novels, authored by writers and political activists Tim LaHaye and Jerry B. Jenkins. Although marketed beneath the radar of most secular readers, the *Left*

Behind series has already sold in the vicinity of an astounding sixty-three million copies. This represents an unprecedented and enormously influential conservative Christian intervention into contemporary U.S. (popular) culture. This essay explores the social genesis and impact of the *Left Behind* books, the social technologies they deploy, and their accompanying media offshoots. In so doing, I hope to shed modest light on key elements of the religious imagination mobilized for political purposes by supporters of George W. Bush and Republican Party organizers.

The *Left Behind* books appear at a fateful moment in history, a time in which the future of humankind is marked not only by the promises and anxieties of far-reaching global social and technological changes but also by widespread personal and spiritual insecurities, stemming from vast global economic restructuring and amplified social inequality.[5] The soul-shattering anxieties of this age are for many people magnified by unprecedented waves of global migration, the omnipresent threat of brutal terrorism and pre-emptive warfare, a rapid-fire breakdown in traditional forms of family life and gender roles, and the penetration of the market into even the innermost sanctums of everyday life. Within, or against, or perhaps simply to make mythic meaning of this troubled historical landscape, the *Left Behind* novels have captivated millions upon millions of readers with a prophetic apocalyptic tale of biblical End Times and the vengeful second coming of Jesus Christ.

Like a heat-seeking rocket targeting the vicissitudes of the flesh, the *Left Behind* phenomenon is a vibrant talisman of a world-view channelling important aspects of America's dominant religious imagination of itself. Signs depicting the fears and fascinations of a bold New World Order of ultramodern culture and power are on display everywhere in the *Left Behind* books – from terror and war in the Middle East, to paranoiac imaginings of mass death, total governmental control, and omnipresent technological surveillance. Stories of mesmeric manipulation by the electronic media, One World corporate economic domination, reconfigurations of gender and sexuality, and struggles to save one's mortal soul are also woven into the novels that compose the twelve-volume *Left Behind* series.

To enter the world of *Left Behind* is to move perilously within the enchanted psycho-geography of America's dark and irrational religious second side. To read *Left Behind* is also to risk coming face to face with the violence of America's homegrown version of anti-modern extremism. Confronting the dangerous shadow side of American religious experience and practice is neither pleasant nor easy. It is, nevertheless, important that critical scholars undertake this challenge, if only to help put the brakes on a wide range of religiously fuelled technologies of exploitative empire-building – new global technologies of power that march zealously under the banner of 'God Bless America.' In engaging with this essay, I invite you to join me in this task.

At the End of Time

At the end of time Rayford was born again. Alleluia! This was the end of time laced with uncertainties and worry, time marked by anxieties of the flesh. This was also the advent of a new time – time that was crystal clear and predestined, time that followed a tightly scriptured path.

> Rayford settled in front of the television and popped in the video. 'Hello,' came the pleasant voice of the pastor Rayford had met several times ... 'My name is Vernon Billings, and I'm pastor of the New Hope Village Church of Mount Prospect, Illinois. As you watch this tape, I can only imagine the fear and despair you face, for this is being recorded for viewing only after the disappearance of God's people from earth.'
>
> 'That you are watching indicates that you have been left behind. You are no doubt stunned, shocked, afraid, and remorseful. I would like you to consider what I have to say here as instructions for life following Christ's rapture of his church. That is what has happened. Anyone you know or knew who had placed his or her trust in Christ alone for salvation has been taken to heaven by Christ.'[6]

The man left behind with his television, videotape, and VCR is Rayford Steele, a central character in the *Left Behind* books, perhaps the most successful publishing venture of all time. Rayford is an airplane pilot. In the opening pages of *Left Behind* he is piloting a fully loaded 747 from Chicago to London. But the pilot's mind is elsewhere. Rayford's mind is on the 'drop-dead gorgeous' senior flight attendant, Hattie Durham, 'a woman he has never touched.' Rayford is, however, thinking about touching Hattie, imagining the flames of an impassioned affair. 'Maybe today. Maybe this morning, if her coded tap on the door didn't rouse his first officer.'

Such thoughts were new to Captain Rayford Steele. He 'used to look forward to getting home to his wife. Irene was attractive and vivacious enough, even at forty. But lately he had found himself repelled by her obsession with religion. It was all she could talk about.' It was not that Rayford was against religion. God was okay with him and he even occasionally enjoyed church. 'But since Irene had hooked up with a smaller congregation and was into weekly Bible studies and church every Sunday, Rayford had become uncomfortable.' What happens next makes him even more uncomfortable. 'Not sure whether he'd follow through with anything overt, Captain Rayford Steele felt an irresistible urge to see Hattie Durham right then.'[7] He opens the cockpit door. Hattie is there and pulls him toward her. But it is not romance that greets Rayford. It is something far more amazing. The attractive senior flight attendant is clearly terrified. She informs her captain that dozens of people have suddenly disappeared throughout the cabin. Not only that, where once the missing passengers sat buckled into their seats, there was now only rumbled piles of clothing, eyeglasses, jewelry, contact lenses, hearing aids, pacemakers, dentures and dental fillings, shoes, and even surgical pins.

The twelve novels in the apocalyptic *Left Behind* series begin with a depiction of the Rapture. In the 'twinkling of an eye,' believers the world over – people who had genuinely accepted Jesus Christ as their saviour – are suddenly transported into heaven. Also 'caught up ... to meet the Lord in the air' are all children under the age of twelve. Even fetuses disappear mysteriously from pregnant women's wombs. CNN repeatedly shows slow-motion footage of a woman's belly going from roundly pregnant to nearly flat. Cars crash and planes collide as their operators dematerialize. People vaporize in the work-place. Others disappear before the eyes of family members or friends. A groom is 'snatched up' while placing a ring on the finger of his beloved. Nearly everyone vanishes from a memorial service in an Australian funeral home, including the corpse. The world plunges into chaos. But for those left behind, this is merely the beginning.

This is also merely the beginning for the mass of readers who have to date pur-chased more than sixty-three million *Left Behind* novels. While the first several vol-umes had initial print runs of between 150,000 to 200,000, *The Indwelling*, the seventh book of the series, and all of the subsequent volumes, rose to the top of best-seller lists compiled by the *New York Times*, *Publisher's Weekly*, the *Wall Street Journal*, and *USA Today*. By 2001 the novels topped book sales at Barnes and Noble, Wal-Mart, and Tar-get. Even more remarkable is that Tyndale House, the publisher of the *Left Behind* series, reports that over a third of the books were sold by Christian bookstores not included in the surveys that translate into mainstream best-seller lists.[8] In addition to the twelve novels, the *Left Behind* series now also includes prequels, films, DVDs, graphic comic novels, a video game, a twenty-two part children's version of the story, and a host of related commercial spin-offs. Overall, one in eight Americans have read the *Left Behind* books 'and they are a favorite with American soldiers in Iraq.'[9]

The blockbuster popularity of *Left Behind* is a big event in several realms – literature, consumer culture, and religion. In this essay I consider how *Left Behind* is eventful in yet another realm – the realm of global technopower. The *Left Behind* books read like fast-paced religious technothrillers. According to the *New York Times*, the series 'com-bines Tom Clancy-like suspense with touches of romance, hi-tech flash and Biblical references.'[10] Weaving together several interrelated plots, the novels' apocalyptic story unfolds across the globe and is interspersed with numerous sermons, prayers, and discussions of arcane biblical passages. The books are also jam-packed with images of technology.

The *Left Behind* novels are inspired by Dr Tim LaHaye's reading of prophetic biblical texts. The theology articulated by LaHaye is today known by several names – dispensa-tional premillennialism, premillennial dispensationalism, and, sometimes, simply dis-pensationalism. Dispensationalist theology was first made popular by the nineteenth-century Irish evangelist John Nelson Darby (1800–82).[11] As Tim LaHaye points out, Darby 'did more than any other man to organize and popularize the view in both the United States and Great Britain.'[12] Concerned with events surrounding the second coming of Christ, several premillennial events are of particular importance to dispensationalism – the Rapture, in which God's 'true church' is lifted into heaven; the return of the Jews to their biblical homeland in Israel; seven years of catastrophic Tribulation under the rule of the Antichrist; and finally the Glorious Appearing, Jesus' second coming. When Christ returns, he promptly vanquishes the Antichrist in the Battle of Armageddon, thus beginning the Millennium – 'a thousand-year period of peace, during which Christ reigns on earth. At the close of the millennium, a final uprising of Satan occurs, but with his defeat by Christ, eternity is established.'[13] Each of these events is portrayed fictively in the popular *Left Behind* series.

The central plot in *Left Behind* involves a prolonged struggle between the Antichrist and the Tribulation Force. As a biblical figure, the Antichrist rules the Earth for the seven years between the Rapture and the Glorious Appearing (Jesus' second coming). The evil rule of the Antichrist is contested by the Tribulation Force, a heroic band of believers, operating out of New Hope Village Church in a suburb of Chicago. This was Irene Steele's church before she was taken up into heaven. Associate pastor Bruce Barnes operates as the Tribulation Force's theological guide and spiritual leader.[14] Before the Rapture Bruce's faith had been more phony than real. But after witnessing so many people's disappearance, Bruce immerses himself in the study of biblical prophecy, testifying to his parishioners, 'There is no doubt in my mind that we have witnessed the Rapture ... Jesus Christ returned for his true family, and the rest of us were left behind.'[15] Inspired by Bruce's teaching, Rayford Steele, Rayford's daughter Chloe, a former college student at Stanford, and Cameron 'Buck' Williams, a renowned journalist and senior writer at *Global Weekly* news magazine, constitute the core membership of the Tribulation Force.

Nicolae Carpathia, the Antichrist, reigns over 'the most technologically advanced regime in history.' The courageous Tribulation Force parasites off Carpathia's technological empire, deploying a wide array of hi-tech devices – computers, cellphones, televisions, video cassettes, the Internet, ready-for-anything SUVs, state-of-the-art jet planes, surveillance devices, and the latest in all kinds of digital gadgetry – to combat the seductive allure of the Antichrist and his dreaded 'Beast System' of global social control.[16]

In depicting technology as a resource for combative believers, the *Left Behind* series departs from existing conventions in 'rapture fiction.' Most previous works had 'portrayed technology as the devil's work.'[17] Nevertheless, the rebellious Tribulation Force is put in a paradoxical situation when attempting to turn the Antichrist's technological advantage against him. The series' Christian heroes are keenly aware that omnipresent technologies of televisual enchantment and surveillance are dangerous weapons in the Antichrist's arsenal of power. Nevertheless, 'to resist him they must use his own tools against him. The Tribulation Force takes regularly to the airwaves, knowing that they are playing on borrowed time and on borrowed bandwidth.'[18]

Although the Antichrist deploys a demonic mixture of technology and false religious rhetoric to control people the globe over, for those battling on the side of God, technology becomes an instrument of redemption and a weapon against evil. This is evident in the following exchange between Cameron 'Buck' Williams, the heroic Tribulation Force journalist, and Donny Moore, a technological whiz-kid and committed Christian.

'Donny,' Buck said gravely, 'you have an opportunity here to do something for God
...'

'I don't want any profit off something that will help the church and God' ...

'Fine. Whatever profit you build in or don't build in is up to you. I'm just telling
you that I need five of the absolute best, top-of-the-line computers, as small and
compact as they can be, but with as much power and memory and speed and communications abilities as you can wire into them.'

'You're talking my language, Mr Williams.'

'I hope so, Donny, because I want a computer with virtually no limitations. I
want to be able to take it anywhere, keep it reasonably concealed, store everything I
want on it, and most of all be able to connect with anyone anywhere without the
transmission being traced. Is that doable?'

'Well sir, I can put together something for you like those computers that scientists use in the jungle or in the desert when there's no place to plug in or hook up to
... And I can add another feature for you, too.'

'What's that?'

'Video conferencing.'

'You mean I can see the person I'm talking to while I'm talking with him?'

'Yes, if he has the same technology on his machine.'

'I want all of it, Donny. And I want it fast. And I need you to keep this confidential.'[19]

The *Left Behind* books and the historical social phantasms they suggest are symptomatic of dominant material and imaginary tendencies driving technological enactments of power on a global scale. These tendencies are shared by many of America's
most influential social institutions and leaders. If for no reason but this, the books and
their consumption demand the serious attention of scholars concerned with making
sense of human history in the early twenty-first century. For those of you who have little or no knowledge of the *Left Behind* phenomenon, this may seem a surprising statement. Despite their enormous success, the *Left Behind* books remain virtually
unknown to most present-day scholars of culture, history, and power.

The astounding sales figures for the *Left Behind* books are less surprising for those with
an eye on the religious beliefs of contemporary U.S. citizens. Indeed, in response to a
Newsweek poll of December 2004, 55 per cent of those sampled, including 83 per cent of
all evangelical Protestants, indicated belief in the literal accuracy of the Bible. Two years
earlier, when polled by *CNN/Time*, 59 per cent of all Christians, and 77 per cent of 'born-
again' fundamentalists and evangelicals, replied 'yes' to the question, 'Will events in the
Book of Revelations occur in the future or not?' Moreover, when asked by *Newsweek* in
October 1999, whether the world will end in an 'Armageddon battle between Jesus
Christ and the Antichrist,' 45 per cent of all Christians, and 71 per cent of evangelical
Protestants answered affirmatively. For Kevin Phillips, author of *American Theocracy*, all
this suggests that, in 'contrast to the secular and often agnostic Christianity in Europe,

Canada, and Australia,' a large and politically influential minority of Americans share beliefs that resemble in key ways 'the intensity of seventeenth-century Puritans, Presbyterian Covenanters, and earlier Dutch or Swiss Calvinists.'[20]

In what follows, I read the unprecedented popularity of the *Left Behind* series as symptomatic of a unique American historical coupling of otherworldly Christian religious beliefs and long-standing desires to blast technologically free of the flesh. This technological blast-off suppresses – or disavows – the reality of our systemic human animal connections to living energetic matter. Left behind is the possibility of more mindful material and spiritual attention to the realities of our global historical positioning within the general economy of life itself, reverence for our energetic relations to each other, and the rest of the natural/historical world.[21] This is a short sociological story of dominant aspects and dangers of our culture's fateful religious and technological flight from the flesh. It focuses on the *Left Behind* novels because the popular or populist religious imagination underlying these texts is fatefully interwoven with key aspects of American culture's vision of itself as a transcendent force for good in a relentless global struggle against evil.

After the Rapture

In *Left Behind* the Rapture is followed by the mercurial rise of the Antichrist. As a legendary figure of apocalyptic human corruption and evil, the Antichrist (or anti-messiah) can be traced back to messianic beliefs of late Second Temple Judaism (from the third century BCE to 70 CE). Over the course of Christian history, although occasionally a symbol of internal spiritual decay, the Antichrist has largely been portrayed as a figure of external threat (either as a singular individual or dangerous collectivity). The persona of the Antichrist has been draped in polar images of dread and deception, fearful destruction and seductive fascination.[22] The Antichrist was an archetypal figure in medieval millenarian theology and pivotal to both Protestant and Catholic thought during the Reformation and Counter-Reformation.

In our own time, the Antichrist has figured primarily in the religious imagination of fundamentalist Protestants. In the *Left Behind* series the Antichrist is both charismatic and humble. Secular reason and science are this 'great deceiver's' calling cards. Shortly after first appearing in the narrative, the Antichrist arranges for peace between Israel and its neighbours. This is when things get really bad. The peace covenant is really a prophetic door into the Tribulation – seven catastrophic years of terror, war, devastating storms, earthquakes, floods, famine, disease, and unprecedented human suffering, all under the sign of the 'wrath of the lamb.' Three-quarters of all people left behind after the Rapture die in terrible ways.

Backed by one of the world's most powerful financiers, Nicolae Jetty Carpathia, the mesmerizing Antichrist, rules the world during the years of tribulation. Nicolae is an entrepreneurial businessman, political liberal, and advocate of global disarmament and peace. In a flash Nicolae is named president of Romania. About a week later he is asked to address the General Assembly of the United Nations. After delivering a captivating speech in which he displays an intimate knowledge of U.N. history Carpathia is proclaimed secretary general. He soon renames his position, calling himself World Potentate. Under Nicolae's inspired leadership the United Nations morphs into the One World Government called Global Community (GC).

The seductive Antichrist speaks nine languages and is pictured as 'an inch or two over six feet, broad shouldered, thick chested, trim, athletic, tanned and blond.' Nicolae is said to be as 'handsome as a young Robert Redford' and is named 'sexiest man alive' by *People* magazine. He is also a skilled hypnotist, able to erase the recollection of actual events and implant false memories. The mesmerizing Antichrist promises peace, but his actions bring death and destruction. Soon megaton bombs are dropping on global cities everywhere as the Global Community does battle with U.S. militia and an underground network of Christian resisters.

Nicolae, the Antichrist, rules the world for the seven years of tribulation from the reconstructed city of New Babylon in Iraq.[23] He is assisted by a variety of henchmen, including Pontifex Maximus Peter II (the former Catholic Archbishop Peter Mathews of Cincinnati, Ohio). Pontifex Maximus helps secure Carpathia's domination by overseeing the development of Enigma Babylon, a One World Religion that complements his boss's One World Government and One World Economy. Another member of Carpathia's staff, supreme commander Leon Fortunato, later replaces Pontifex Maximus as Nicolae's 'False Prophet' and serves as the 'great deceiver's' chief public relations officer. Viv Ivins, another key GC operative oversees the implanting of identity microchips under the skin of all citizens of the Global Community. Those that refuse the implant (a high-tech analogue of the biblical 'Mark of the Beast') are arrested and decapitated by guillotine.[24]

To combat the commanding allure of the Antichrist members of the Tribulation Force infiltrate Carpathia's global empire and create a network of safe houses for persecuted Christians. Rayford and Buck become double agents. Rayford accepts an offer to pilot Carpathia's Global Community One. Then, following Carpathia's buyout of the *New York Times*, *Washington Post*, *Boston Globe*, and virtually all of the world's other news media, Buck becomes the publisher of the Antichrist's new *Global Community Weekly*. The multiethnic Tribulation Force also includes the Orthodox rabbi and scholar Tsion Ben-Judah. After completing an intensive three-year study of Jewish historical documents and the Old Testament, Rabbi Ben-Judah appears on CNN to announce his conclusion that Jesus Christ is the true messiah. Tsion converts to Christianity and replaces Bruce Barnes as the spiritual leader of the Tribulation Force after Bruce is killed when GC 'peacekeepers' bomb a hospital where he is a patient.

Throughout the years of the Tribulation, Tsion broadcasts daily sermons of hope over the Internet to an audience of over one billion underground believers. Other members of the multiethnic Tribulation Force, including several computer specialists, become 'secret agents' and infiltrate the Antichrist's information technology headquarters.

Many strange and disturbing events take place take place during the Tribulation. None is more astounding than the televised assassination and subsequent resurrection of Nicolae Carpathia. In his new incarnation, Carpathia is now more demonic than ever. Satan now 'indwells' or possesses the body of the World Potentate. In *The Glorious Appearing*, the series' final volume, we arrive at the Battle of Armageddon and the second coming of Jesus. But the Jesus who returns hardly resembles the crucified Lord whose sacrifice blessed humankind with the divine gifts of love, peace, and forgiveness. He is, instead, Jesus Christ the Warrior, Christ the Judge and Destroyer.

With heavenly hosts hovering in the sky, Jesus descends from above, landing atop the fabled Mount of Olives on the outskirts of Jerusalem. Jesus immediately enters into battle with Carpathia and his satanic legions. Armed to its satanic teeth with a wide array of the most lethal of military technologies, Carpathia's Global Community Army of Unity was mounting an all-out attack on Jerusalem. 'The siege was deafening. Jet engines, Jeeps, cars, trucks, Hummers, transports, armaments, munitions, rifle fire, machine gun fire, cannons, grenades, rockets – you name it.' But, suddenly, a dense and technologically disabling darkness descends upon and envelops the Antichrist and his Global Community Army of Unity. 'The only sound was the clicking of weapons that would not fire. Nothing produced light. No headlights. No matches or lighters.'[25]

Perched atop his stalled Humvee, the brazen Antichrist is incensed. '"Light," screeched Carpathia. But everything was dark. "Fire!" he raged. Still nothing.' Next, there appeared a 'brilliant multicolored cloud.' Then, the cloud opened, rolling back 'like a scroll from horizon to horizon.' Christ makes his entrance, astride a white horse. 'Jesus' eyes shone with conviction like a flame of fire, and He held His majestic head high.'[26] Christ offers everyone a last chance to repent. But, foolishly, Carpathia and his followers attack. Jesus unleashes his Word, a fierce technology of righteousness. The Word violently splits open the bodies of the Antichrist's demonic legions. 'At that instant the Mount of Olives split in two from east to west ... All the firing and the running stopped. The soldiers screamed and fell, their bodies bursting open from head to toe at every word that proceeded from the mouth of the Lord as He spoke.'[27]

The apocalyptic landscape is littered with the 'splayed and filleted bodies of men and horses,' as 'that sword from His mouth, the powerful Word of God itself, continued to slice through the air, reaping the wrath of God's judgment. The enemy had been given chance after chance, judgment after judgment to convince and persuade them ... But except for that now tiny remnant of Israel that was seeing for the first time the One they had pierced, it was too late ... The Unity Army had rattled its sabers, loaded its weapons, and made lots of noise. And Jesus had killed them all, with mere words.'[28]

Apocalyptic Technologies of Control and Resistance

The use of technology to command, control, and communicate is pervasive throughout the *Left Behind* books. Much of what takes place in the novels, much of the plot, is advanced by characters communicating to, or spying upon, one another through a variety of technological means. Everybody is constantly trying to connect by cellular and satellite phones, speakerphones, email, videotapes, intercom, radio, television, broadcasts on the Web, video conferencing, and by leaving messages on voice-mail and answering machines. Everyone is also always worried that communications are being tapped into by the Antichrist's vast surveillance operations. Carpathia is able to interfere instantly with media broadcasts anywhere on the planet, substituting his message and his image for what is being shown. News reports covering events that contradict GC's One World Religion, or expose Carpathia's treachery, quickly disappear from the screen. It is as if such dissonant events had never taken place.

Technological control of communications is a core component of the Antichrist's plans for world domination. 'All banking, commerce, religion, and government will start and end right here,' declares Nicolae Carpathia. 'The greatest challenge in the ... world is in communications. We have already begun rebuilding an international network.' Rayford Steele, undercover as a 'mole' within the inner circle of Global Community, interrupts Carpathia. 'Communications is more important than people?' inquires Rayford. 'More than cleaning up areas that might otherwise become diseased? Clearing away bodies? Reuniting families?' Nicolae responds as follows.

> In due time, Captain Steele. Such efforts depend upon communications too. Fortunately the timing of my most ambitious project could not have been more propitious. The Global Community recently secured sole ownership of all international satellite and cellular communications companies. We will have in place in a few months the first truly global communications network. It is cellular, and it is solar powered. I call it Cellular-Solar. Once the cellular towers have been re-erected and satellites are maneuvered to geosynchronous orbit, anyone will be able to communicate with anyone else anywhere at any time.[29]

The world of tribulation depicted by the *Left Behind* novels – a global society dominated by the Antichrist – resembles the most nightmarish kind of society to possibly emerge from a global circuit of power composed of profit-driven networks and nodes. Manipulative technologies of the word enable Carpathia and those loyal to the Antichrist to distort language to the point where peace becomes war, freedom constraint, reason blind obedience, religion secularity, and community the worship of the ego. But the power of persuasive rhetoric goes only so far. After Carpathia is assassinated and resurrected from the dead (by Satan) live on CNN, the GC accelerates its seductive use of image-intensive technologies of fascination as a supplement to its efforts to control words and discursive meanings.

As if taking a page from the playbook of Jean Baudrillard,[30] the Antichrist declares that, 'despite its lofty goal of unifying the world's religions,' the 'Enigma Babylon One World Faith failed' because, ultimately, its tolerant, inclusive, and highly rational god proved too 'nebulous and impersonal.' What is needed, declares Leon Fortunato, Carpathia's publicist, is for the GC to go beyond rational persuasion in order to cultivate an 'outpouring of emotion.' What Fortunato has in mind is something akin to old-fashioned idol worship. The False Prophet recruits Guy Blod, an 'outrageous and flamboyant' gay artist to construct a huge statue of Nicolae in New Babylon, and later orders life-size exact replicas (simulacra) of the World Potentate erected in all major cities of the world.[31] The goal, it seems, is to seduce the senses of people made anxious and uncertain by the catastrophic events of the tribulation.

In addition to the captivating simulacra of Carpathia, the 'lascivious' allure of television and the global entertainment industry is another tool in the Antichrist's mesmerizing technological stockpile of weapons. Not long after global warfare and (super)natural disasters have knocked out much of the world's electricity, television returns 'full force' by means of the 'astounding' technological power of the GC's 'Cellular-Solar networks.' What is broadcast may fascinate much of the population, but it horrifies the saintly Rabbi Tsion Ben Judah. In a sermon posted in his untraceable Webpage, Tsion decries the devilish enchantments of a sensate 'entertainment medium' that now goes beyond all restraints, boundaries, and limits.

> Our television accesses hundreds of channels from all over the world, beamed to it by satellite. Every picture on every channel representing every station and network available is transmitted into your home in images so crisp and clear you feel you could reach inside the screen and touch them. What a marvel of technology!
>
> But this does not thrill me ... I shall no longer apologize for my horror at what has become of the entertainment medium ... vile language or lascivious images ... Stopping even to criticize them would have subjected my brain to poison ... – final proof that society has reached rock bottom.
>
> I am neither naïve nor prudish. But I saw things today I never thought I would see. All restraint, all boundaries, all limits have been eradicated. It was a microcosm of the reason for the wrath of the lamb. Sexuality and sensuality and nudity have been part of the industry for many years. But [we now] see not just simulated perversion but actual portrayals of every deadly sin listed in the Scriptures left us feeling unclean. Real violence, actual tortures and murders, is proudly advertised ... Sorcery, black magic, clairvoyance, fortune telling, witchcraft, séances, and spell casting are offered as simple alternatives to anything normal, let alone positive.[32]

Tsion's admonitions about the dangers of seductive technologies of sensory captivation closely resemble the admonitions of LaHaye and Jenkins in *Are We Living in the End Times?* 'Who can deny that this world has gone crazy over pleasure?' ask the authors. 'From topless dancers to Hollywood entertainment ... millions spend money they cannot afford on events that consume hours of their time and energy. The whole world is becoming addicted to entertainment, ... [turning] the Western world into a sex-obsessed cesspool of immorality … just like that of the Tribulation. It is hard to believe that sexual immorality can get any worse than it already is – but it will.'[33]

The Tribulation Force also deploys a wide range of technologies in efforts to counter the Antichrist. Inside the cockpit of Carpathia's Global Community jet, loaded with the latest state-of-art technologies, Rayford commands a hidden device that enables him to listen to the conversations of Carpathia and his henchmen in the plane's interior. Later, 'through the miracle of technology' and the 'expert maneuvering' of Chang Wong (another mole working at Global Community Headquarters in New Babylon), the Tribulation Force secretly records and projects on 'a big screen TV' an early morning meeting between Carpathia and his ten regional potentates. 'Everybody in the Global Community assumed, because it was a closed-door session, it was also private.'[34]

The Tribulation Force uses many of the same information technologies as the Global Community when disseminating its message of hope and salvation. Buck Williams publishes *The Truth*, an online cyber-magazine, and Rabbi Tsion Ben-Judah communicates regularly to an audience of over a billion people via untraceable Internet broadcasts. For Tsion, religion and technology go hand in hand. 'I envision thousands of technological experts creating a network of resources for believers,' Ben-Judah explains to Rayford, 'informing them of safe havens, putting them in touch with each other. We know we will lose many brothers and sisters, and yet we should offer what we can to keep the gospel going forth.'[35] 'Tsion often expressed to Rayford his satisfaction with his new computer – a light, thin, very portable laptop that plugged into a docking station that gave him all sorts of handy accessories at home. It was the latest, fastest, most powerful machine on the market. Tsion spent every day communicating with his international flock.'[36]

These are but several of many ways by which the technologically savvy Tribulation Force subverts the diabolical power of the Antichrist, protecting believers and 'harvesting' new souls for Christ. Indeed, heroic Christians not only use technology, they also 'use it better and use it smarter. Inside the Antichrist's empire, the best technological minds are actually Christians, hiding their identities to help the cause.'[37] But there are dangers, as well as advantages, to using technology in this manner. 'The ability of believers to act depends on the Antichrist first providing them with the necessary data … Believers are not strong enough to confront Carpathia directly, but move within *his* space, purloin *his* data to interrupt *his* schemes.'[38]

Nevertheless, for both LaHaye and Jenkins and the tribulation saints in *Left Behind*, the power of technology – even its enchanting or fascinating aspects – is bivalent. It is, at once, demonic and an instrument of redemption. This may surprise those who today view Christianity and technology as perpetually at odds. From debates about the ethics of stem cell research to divergent understandings of the nature of creation, contemporary culture is replete with numerous instances of conflict between religion and technology. Yet, over the longer course of history, this is far from the case.

Although distinguishing *Left Behind* from earlier rapture fiction, the series' Christian affirmation of technology is hardly unique. Indeed, as David Noble has shown, for centuries Northwestern approaches to technology have been guided by an 'enduring, other-worldly quest for transcendence and salvation.'[39]

Human immanence within nature – this is not our true destiny declares the Bible! Technologies that have long dominated Northwestern society share the Bible's vision on this matter. What Noble calls 'the religion of technology' informs us that neither people nor things begin in complex systems of living energetic matter. They begin with the Word. In the beginning, we are told, was the Word. And, in the end, there is the Word as well – alpha and the Omega Code, *St John's Gospel* and *Revelation*. At the end of the *Left Behind* books, the last technology standing is the Word. Everything else is burnt to a crisp, vaporized by the Wrath of the Lamb, impaled by judgment spewing forth from the Word. The landscape is littered with the 'splayed and filleted bodies of men and women,' as Jesus descended from the heavens 'shining, powerful and victorious ... And the sword from his mouth, the powerful Word of God itself, continued to slice through the air, reaping the wrath of God's final judgment.'[40]

Although LaHaye and Jenkins articulate technology's demonic as well as transcendent side, the evangelical triumph of technology over all things material in the novels is ultimately, absolutely, backed up by the apocalyptic technology of the Word. Like other forms of contemporary evangelism, this may lead the *Left Behind* books to err in the direction of deifying technology. As Glenn Shuck points out, the books come 'perilously close to worshipping the Beast they seek to resist ... Too often ... the authors suggest that the solution lies in who controls technology, ignoring the inherent qualities of technological tools ... Although the Tribulation Force believes they are fighting Antichrist using his tools, ... they are tragically unaware that they are inside the Beast, co-participants in his infernal system. This tragic lack of awareness,' is said to represent 'the central tension of the *Left Behind* novels.'[41]

This lack of tragic awareness concerning the limitations of technology is particularly evident in the following excerpt from *Glorious Appearing*, the last of the *Left Behind* books. The excerpt alludes to the *Book of Genesis* and to the putative transcendence of the Word over embodied human material and spiritual participation in living energetic nature. In closing this essay, I will reflect upon the sociological meaning of this excerpt and the biblical passages to which it refers. The text depicts a confrontation between Jesus, the Warrior King, and Satan, when after seven years of tribulation Jesus returns to earth and lays waste to the Antichrist's army, striking down his enemies with the mighty sword of God's Word.

The punishing military technology of God's Word leads Satan to change shapes. At first he assumes the form of a lion. Later he transforms into a 'titanic, hissing serpent.' The monstrous serpent coils around the arms and legs of St Michael the Archangel, 'its tongue darting between shows of its elongated fangs.' St Michael and the angel Gabriel are present at the Battle of Armageddon to assist the Warrior King as He vanquishes the devil. The voice of Gabriel rings out, 'Lucifer, dragon, serpent, devil, Satan, you will now face the One you have opposed since time immemorial.' Jesus then orders Satan to kneel at His feet.

> 'I have fought against you from shortly after your creation,' Jesus said.
> 'My creation! I was no more created than you! And who are you to have anything against me?'
> 'You shall be silent.'
> The angel of light appeared ... Jesus continued, 'For all your lies about having evolved, you are a created being.'
> The creature violently shook its head.
> 'Only God has the power to create, and you were Our creation. You were in Eden, the garden of God, before it was a paradise for Adam and Eve. You were there as an exalted servant when Eden was a beautiful rock garden. You were the seal of perfection, full of wisdom and perfect in beauty ... But you defiled your sanctuaries by the multitude of your iniquities ... You deceived Eve into sinning. During the next millennia you attempted to pollute the bloodline of Adam ... I lay at your feet all the suffering of mankind. The earth was created as a utopia, and yet you brought it into sin, which resulted in poverty, disease, more than fifteen thousand wars, and the senseless killing of millions.'[42]

In the Beginning

The treacherous figure of the serpent in the opening pages of *Genesis* and the closing pages of *Left Behind* – the 'exalted servant' of the Word, who sins by imagining itself as evolving alongside the Word in history – represented something else entirely to the neighbouring peoples of Mesopotamia, against whom the monotheistic peoples of the Word distinguished themselves. For the other so-called pagan peoples of Mesopotamia, human existence came into being as a gift of nature and the serpent was a symbol of the divine gift-giver, the Great Mother. Nature – the cosmic serpent that gave birth to the world – was revered as the source of all life, the womb of life, the web of energetic materiality from which humans came and to which we returned. All of creation, including human animal creation, was believed to owe its life to this sacred serpent, the matrix of life in which all humans, animals, rocks, minerals, and vegetables participated. 'The snake was first of all a symbol of eternal life (like the moon), since each time it shed its skin it seemed reborn. It represented cosmic continuity within natural change – spiritual continuity within the changes of material life.'[43]

This, of course, is not how the Bible and the *Left Behind* novels imagine the story. In these books the story is told in reverse. The Bible recognizes no Great Mother of life, no sacred serpent from which we come and to which we return. For the Bible the serpent is pictured as, at once, evil and envious of the Word. The Bible also tells us that the serpent sins by rebelling against the dictates of the Word, seducing a woman, Eve, to do likewise. According to the Bible, 'In the beginning was the Word: the Word was with God and the Word was God. He was with God in the beginning. Through him all things came into being, not one thing came into being except through him.'[44] This is what distinguishes the people of the Bible from the animists they had once been and from their neighbours. The Bible denies the sacredness of living energetic matter and serpentine ways of the flesh.

The people of the Bible, people of the Word, rely on orderly transcendental technologies of the Word in their battle against the chaotic forces of Evil. They make use of everything in sight to glorify the Word's triumph over time and the mortal body. The people of the Word no longer believe that life comes into being as a maternal gift of nature, for better or worse. For them life comes only from the Word. In the beginning, they say, God created heaven and earth by speaking. Before God spoke, 'the earth was a formless void' and there 'was darkness over the deep.' Then from God's mouth came the Word. 'God said, "Let there be light," and there was light ... God said, "Let there be a vault through the middle of the waters to divide the waters in two." And so it was.' Then God spoke again and dry earth came into being, then seed-bearing plants, the lights in the sky, and every kind of living creature, whether in water, air, or on Earth.

Then 'God said, "Let us make man in our own image and likeness, and let them be masters of the fish of the sea, the birds of heaven, the cattle, all the wild animals and all the creatures that creep along the ground."' The serpent creeps along the ground. God made man master of the serpent, and gave him dominion over the rest of creation as well. And to facilitate man's mastery, God gave man the power of naming, the power of using words, 'and whatever the man called each living creature, that would be its name.' (*Genesis* 1:1-26; 2:19) 'Next would come ... famine and death by plagues until a quarter of the population of the earth that remained after the Rapture was wiped out.' Rayford's 'universal cell phone vibrated in his pocket ... *Thank God for Technology*, he thought.'[45]

None of this is exactly true. Despite strong biblical words about these matters, we humans are never really at a word's distance from nature, naming nature from above. We are, instead, situated within the relational fluxes of living matter, an immanent aspect of nature's own energetic history. Traces of this awareness, long suppressed by those who adhere to the literalness of the Bible, are revealed in the etymology of key words used in the Bible itself. In *Genesis*, the term used to depict the 'formless void' that is brought into order by God's Word finds its roots in the ancient Hebrew phrase, *tohu-wa-boho*. This, in turn, is related to the word *tehom*, a term associated with the ancient Mesopotamian serpent goddess *Tiamut*. The name given by Adam to the 'first woman,' Eve also carries resonances of the ancient serpent goddess. The Hebrew word for Eve is *Hawwāh*. It means 'mother of all the living.'[46]

To follow this serpentine path of words – the meaning of which has become distorted in the history of literal interpretations of the Bible – is not to preach the gospel of secular humanism, so virulently opposed by Tim LaHaye and Jerry B. Jenkins. It is, instead, to reconnect with a more holistic and material spiritual vision where 'gods were not shut off from the human race in a separate ontological sphere' and where 'divinity was not essentially different from humanity.'[47] It is to be attentive to the immanence of sacred revelations in the flesh, not simply to those that come from outside natural history in the shape of words alone. It is to recognize that we are participants in nature's sacred evolution, even as we productively carve out a time and place for ourselves within nature by means of technology, including technologies of the word.

Technology is a tragic, if absolutely necessary, aspect of our human condition. The tragedy of technology is that it temporarily differentiates its users from the rest of nature. It punctuates our relationship to nature, making the remainder of living energetic matter appear as nothing but a context or environment for who were are and what we do. Language, the technology of words, plays a part. From the technological perspective of words, nature becomes a referent, something outside us, a thing towards which our language points or directs attention. To declare 'In the beginning was the Word' is to tragically misunderstand the living energetic matter of which we are a part. It is to recognize energetic matters, but only from the perspective of information, only from the perspective of technologically coded variety, only from the perspective of the parasite. This is the fundamentalist tragedy of onto-theology. It appears (in history) to separate us technologically from the world of which we are materially a part. This is alienation, a not so original sin. From the perspective of living energetic matter – our serpentine mother, matrix, and host – things are infinitely more complex, and more real. That is, things are more real than that which is given to us by technology. Things are more real than the word. The world is more real than the word; and more fleshy, sensuous, and varied.

This means that technology, no matter how artificial, no matter how tragic, is never really outside of nature. No parasite is. No parasite exists independent of its host. No technology exists independent of the energetic matter on which it depends.[48] This is true as well for the *Left Behind* books. As technologies of the Word, they are dependent – as is the Bible, the 'God-given' text that inspires their authors – on a complex and fleshy historical dance of energetic materiality. In the unfolding of this dance, the Word may play a leading role, but it never comes first, nor does it have the final say. The Word may periodically banish the serpent, but the serpent returns to devour the Word; or, better yet, the serpent returns to make the Word laugh. Then, the serpent eats its own tale and the tragic story begins again, if in a slightly different register. Both the Bible and the *Left Behind* books are inspirational technologies of the Word. As such, each bears the scriptural scars of all linguistic technologies – of all ritual, social, and religious visions of transcendence. This is to acknowledge the complexities of wisdom lodged in the flesh, rather than to honour fundamentalist dreams of rising above the body and paying homage to the Word alone.

To refuse this acknowledgment is perilous. In LaHaye and Jenkins' apocalyptic tale, flesh and blood make a glorious appearance at the End of Time. Here we find bodies cowering in fear; bodies assaulted by the Wrath of the Lamb; bodies ripped open, made to suffer and bleed; lustful bodies with sinful desires in need of religious sexual repression; spiritually abandoned bodies left behind by the skyward flight of the Word. *Left Behind* conjures an envy-driven phantasm of the Word's revenge against the flesh as wave after wave of righteous violence fuels the series' tale of final judgment. Pushed aside are whole other planes of sacred technological imaginings of the body – imaginings that are at once immanent and intimate, charming and joyful, Christian and otherwise.

The transcendent technological writings of LaHaye and Jenkins ask us to see the world with prophetic eyes cast upward toward heaven, and to read the world's history as signs of End Times to come. By contrast, I conclude with sacred words of a different sort – a meditation on apocalyptic dangers prepared by members of the Iroquois Nation and presented to a U.N. Conference on Indigenous Peoples. This meditation approaches questions of technology with animated spirituality and reverence for living energetic matter. Entitled *A Basic Call to Consciousness*, the document warns about what is really being left behind as believers in Christian prophecy prepare for the Rapture.

> In the beginning we were told that human beings who walk about on the Earth have been provided with all the things necessary for life. We were instructed to carry a love for one another and to show a great respect for all beings of this Earth. We were shown that our life exists with the tree life, that our well-being depends on the well-being of the Vegetable Life, that we are close relatives of the four-legged beings.
>
> The original instructions direct that we who walk about on Earth are to express a great respect, an affection and gratitude toward all the spirits, which create and support Life ... When people cease to respect and express gratitude for these many things, then all of life will be destroyed, and human life on this planet will come to an end ... The Indo-European people who have colonized our lands have shown very little respect for the things that create and support Life. We believe that these people ceased their respect for the world a long time ago ... The way of life known as Western Civilization is on a death path on which its own culture has no viable answers ...
>
> The majority of the world does not find its roots in Western culture or tradition. The majority of the world finds its roots in the Natural World, and the traditions of the Natural World, which must prevail ... The majority of our peoples still live in accordance with the traditions which find their roots in Mother Earth ... We must all consciously and continuously challenge every model, every program, and every process that the West tries to force on us ... The people who are living on this planet need to break with the narrow concept of human liberation, and begin to see liberation as something that needs to be extended to the Natural World. What is needed is the liberation of all things that support Life – the air, the waters, the trees – all things that support the sacred web of Life.[49]

Notes

1 Max Weber, *The Protestant Ethic and the Spirit of Capitalism* (New York: Scribner's, 1958), 171.
2 Karen Armstrong, *The Battle for God: A History of Fundamentalism* (New York: Random House, 2000), 83, 80.
3 Ibid., 84–5.
4 Quoted in Ron Suskind, 'Faith, Certainty and the Presidency of George W. Bush,' *New York Times Magazine*, 16 Oct. 2004, 64.
5 Stephen Pfohl, 'New Global Technologies of Power: Cybernetic Capitalism and Social Inequality,' in *The Blackwell Companion to Social Inequalities,* ed. Mary Romero and Eric Margolis (Cambridge: Blackwell, 2005), 456–592.
6 Tim LaHaye and Jerry B. Jenkins, *Left Behind: A Novel of the Earth's Last Days* (Wheaton: Tyndale, 1995), 208–9.
7 Ibid., 1, 2, 3.
8 Bruce David Forbes, 'How Popular are the Left Behind Books ... and Why? A Discussion of Popular Culture,' in *Rapture, Revelation, and the End Times: Exploring the Left Behind Series*, ed. Bruce David Forbes and Jeanne Halgren Kilde (New York: Palgrave Macmillan, 2004), 7–8.
9 Morris Berman, *Dark Ages America: The Final Phases of Empire* (New York: Norton, 2006), 4.
10 Excerpt blurb from the *New York Times* included in Tim LaHaye and Jerry B. Jenkins, *Assassins: Assignment: Jerusalem, Target: Antichrist* (Wheaton: Tyndale, 1999), i.
11 Darby's prophetic interpretations of the Bible were not without precedent. Antecedents can be found in fourth-century Christian thought, the twelfth-century prophecies of the Calabrian Dominican monk, Joachim of Fiore (1135–1202), the sixteenth-century teachings of the English prophet Joseph Meade, and the Puritan proclamations of Increase Mather a century later. But it was Darby, a dissident priest in the Church of Ireland, who popularized the dispensational viewpoint. Inspired by his participation in the Powerscourt Prophecy Conferences, sponsored by the Scotch-Anglican dissenter Henry Drummond, Darby became convinced that the second coming of Jesus was about to take place and that this would involve a succession of revelatory moments – the Rapture, Tribulation, and Glorious Appearing. At the core of Darby's thought was a belief that God's actions in history are organized in terms of seven discrete eras, or dispensations, and that the seventh and final dispensation was rapidly approaching. This would begin with the Rapture, when 'we who are alive and remain shall be caught up together with them in the clouds to meet the Lord in the air, and thus we shall always be with the Lord' (I *Thessalonians* 4:16–17). As a mode of biblical exegesis, dispensational premillennialism gained considerable popularity in the United States following Darby's visits to America between 1862 and 1877. Darby's influence in American evangelical circles was solidified with Cyrus L. Scofield's publication of an annotated version of the King James Bible. Scofield's Bible cross-referenced the Old and New Testaments in ways that highlighted the prophetic interpretations of Darby.
12 Tim LaHaye, *The Rapture: Who Will Face the Tribulation?* (Eugene: Harvest House, 2002), 145.

13 Jeanne Halgren Kilde, 'How Did Left Behind's Particular Vision of the End Times Develop? A Historical Look at Millenarian Thought,' in *Rapture, Revelation, and the End Times: Exploring the Left Behind Series*, ed. Bruce David Forbes and Jeanne Halgren Kilde (New York: Palgrave Macmillan, 2004), 34.

14 In the novels, Bruce is given no racial identity. Or, by default, perhaps he is imagined by the novels' predominately white readership as white. But in both the film and the graphic novels of the story, Bruce is portrayed as a passionate black minister. In the films and the graphic novels U.S. President Gerald Fitzhugh is also African-American. This suggests a more complicated representation of race in *Left Behind* in its several incarnations than in the novels alone. As Amy Johnson Frykholm points out, in the books, despite the Tribulation Force's multicultural veneer, 'true authority' is bestowed exclusively on white men. See Amy Johnson Frykholm, 'What Social and Political Messages Appear in the Left Behind Books?' in Forbes and Kilde, *Rapture, Revelation, and the End Times*, 184–6.

15 LaHaye and Jenkins, *Left Behind*, 198.

16 Tim LaHaye and Jerry B. Jenkins, *Apollyon: The Destroyer Is Unleashed* (Wheaton: Tyndale House, 1999), 61.

17 Amy Johnson Frykholm, *Rapture Culture: Left Behind in Evangelical America* (New York: Oxford University Press, 2004), 124.

18 Glenn W. Shuck, *Marks of the Beast: The* Left Behind *Novels and the Struggle for Evangelical Identity* (New York: New York University Press, 2004), 115.

19 Tim LaHaye and Jerry B. Jenkins, *Nicolae: The Rise of the Antichrist* (Wheaton: Tyndale House, 1997), 45-6.

20 Kevin Phillips, *American Theocracy: The Peril and Politics of Radical Religion, Oil, and Borrowed Money in the 21st Century* (New York: Penguin, 2007), 101.

21 My use of the term *general economy* is a sign of my debt to Georges Bataille. My ideas about energetic materiality indicate my engagement with the work of Teresa Brennan and Anthony Wilden. See Georges Bataille, *The Accursed Share: An Essay on General Economy*, vol. 1, *Consumption*, trans. R. Hurley (New York: Zone Books, 1988); Teresa Brennan, *Exhausting Modernity: Grounds for a New Economy* (New York: Routledge, 2000); Anthony Wilden, *The Rules Are No Game: The Strategy of Communication* (New York: Routledge, 1987).

22 Bernard McGinn, *Antichrist: Two Thousand Years of the Human Fascination with Evil* (San Francisco: HarperSanFrancisco, 1994), 3–5.

23 For prophecy theologians, such as LaHaye, the fact that ancient Babylon is located in present-day Iraq is of great importance. LaHaye's reading of chapters 17 and 18 of Revelation contends that, for 'unfulfilled prophesies' to finally be realized, Babylon must be rebuilt, so as to 'live again' as 'the Seat of Satan' during End Times. In this regard it is of great interest that Saddam Hussein, whom LaHaye describes as a 'servant of Satan,' was in the process of reconstructing Babylon before invaded by the United States and its 'coalition of the willing' in 2003. For LaHaye, the so-called demonic butcher of Baghdad had long envisioned himself as 'becoming the modern counterpart to his lifetime hero, King Nebuchadnezzar … Religiously, Saddam may give lip service to Muhammad and act like a devoted Muslim, but

there is strong indication that he is actually a Satanist' with plans to build a 'temple to Satan' in a rebuilt Babylon. This is not to suggest, however, that Hussein himself is the Antichrist. According to LaHaye and Jenkins, 'he is little more than a cheap imitation of Nebuchadnezzar. He could well be, however, the forerunner of the one who we believe is soon going to emerge on the world scene to take control of the United Nations (or its successor), move the commercial and governmental headquarters of his world government to Babylon, and rule the world from what we call in our *Left Behind* novels 'New Babylon.' See Tim LaHaye and Jerry B. Jenkins, *Are We Living in the End Times?* (Wheaton: Tyndale House, 2004), 139–43.

24 The identity microchip imagined by LaHaye and Jenkins is a high-tech analogue of earlier figurations of the demonic 'mark of the beast.' Others have also involved computer-based surveillance devices, such as the '666' mark that some prophecy believers associate with credit cards and social control in a cashless society. See, e.g., Mary Stewart Relfe, *When Your Money Fails: The 666 System Is Here* (Birmingham: Ministries Inc., 1981).

25 Tim LaHaye and Jerry B. Jenkins, *Glorious Appearing: The End of Days* (Wheaton: Tyndale House, 2004), 202.

26 Ibid., 203

27 Ibid., 286.

28 Ibid., 209, 258.

29 Tim LaHaye and Jerry B. Jenkins, *Soul Harvest: The World Takes Sides* (Wheaton: Tyndale House, 1998), 68.

30 For an argument concerning the superior force of image-intensive seduction over the power of discursive reason, see Jean Baudrillard, *Seduction* (New York: St Martin's Press, 1990) and also Jean Baudrillard, *The Evil Demon of Images* (Sydney: Power Institute of Fine Arts, 1987).

31 Tim LaHaye and Jerry B. Jenkins, *The Indwelling: The Beast Takes Possession* (Wheaton: Tyndale House, 2001), 60. It is hardly an accident that the self-absorbed Guy Blod and his small entourage of 'clones' are portrayed as gay. For the authors, gays and lesbians are not only relegated to the realm of the 'unsaved,' they are pictured as a perverse and unnatural 'abomination.' See, e.g., LaHaye and Jenkins, *Are We Living in the End Times?*, 332, 337. The 'audacious' Guy, like the masculine lesbian Verna Zee, is also described in stereotypical terms bordering on parody. Each either serves the Antichrist or functions as an obstacle to the divinely ordained mission of the Tribulation Force. In *The Indwelling*, Guy flutters his fingers in the air, makes catty remarks, waxes poetically about the beauty of the human form, and unabashedly declares, 'I love new clothes' (at 66). In *Nicolae*, Verna, who competes with and is jealous of Buck, admires Carpathia, and is prevented from revealing secrets about the Tribulation Force only when Buck threatens to inform her employer that she is a lesbian. Although these homosexual characters irritate the novels' heterosexual Christian protagonists (Buck declares that Verna gives him the 'willies' and David Hassad admits that tormenting the sarcastic Guy gives him joy), members of the Tribulation Force eventually end up praying for their salvation.

32 Tim LaHaye and Jerry B. Jenkins, *Soul Harvest: The World Takes Sides* (Wheaton: Tyndale House, 1998), 324–6.

33 LaHaye and Jenkins, *Are We Living in the End Times?*, 341, 332.

34 Tim LaHaye and Jerry B. Jenkins, *Armageddon: The Cosmic Battle of the Ages* (Wheaton: Tyndale House, 2003), 290.

35 Tim LaHaye and Jerry B. Jenkins, *The Remnant* (Wheaton: Tyndale House, 2002), 119-20.

36 LaHaye and Jenkins, *Apollyon*, 256-7.

37 Amy Johnson Frykholm, 'What Social and Political Messages Appear in the *Left Behind* Books?' in Forbes and Kilde, *Rapture, Revelation, and the End Times*, 189.

38 Shuck, *Marks of the Beast*, 174-5.

39 David Noble, *The Religion of Technology: The Divinity of Man and the Spirit of Invention* (New York: Penguin, 1997), 3.

40 LaHaye and Jenkins, *Glorious Appearing*, 208.

41 Shuck, *Marks of the Beast*, 205-6.

42 LaHaye and Jenkins, *Glorious Appearing*, 218-9.

43 Monica Sjöö and Barbara Mor, *The Great Cosmic Mother: Rediscovering the Religion of the Earth* (San Francisco: HarperSanFrancisco, 1991), 58-9.

44 *The Gospel of John* 1: 1-3.

45 Tim LaHaye and Jerry B. Jenkins, *Nicolae*, 108-9.

46 See John A. Phillips, *Eve: the History of an Idea* (San Francisco: Harper and Row, 1984); and Pamela Norris, *Eve: A Biography* (New York: New York University Press, 1998).

47 Karen Armstrong, *A History of God: The 4,000-Year Quest of Judaism, Christianity and Islam* (New York: Ballantine, 1993), 9.

48 For elaboration of these ideas, see Pfohl, 'New Global Technologies.'

49 'A Basic Call to Consciousness: The Hau de no sau nee Address to the Western World,' in *Akwesane Notes* (Rooseveltown: Mohawk Nation, 1978), excepted in Jerry Mander, *In the Absence of the Sacred: The Failure of Technology and the Survival of the Indian Nations* (San Francisco: Sierra Club Books, 1991), 191-3.

23 Terri Schiavo:
Bride of 'Compassionate Conservatism'

AUGUSTINE OF EPCOT AND HIS SCRIBE DANIEL WHITE

quondam hi cornicines et municipalis harenae
perpetui comites notaeque per oppida buccae
munera nunc edunt et, verso pollice vulgus
quem iubet, occidunt populariter; unde reversi
conducunt foricas, et cur non omnia, cum sint
quales ex humili magna ad fastigia rerum
extollit quotiens voluit Fortuna iocari?
    Quid Romae faciam? mentiri nescio ...

Juvenal, Satire 3, lines 34–41

Once these men were horn-blowers and perpetual attendants at the local theatres, their bulging cheeks known through the towns; now they produce their own shows, and, with popularity, they kill whomever the crowd requests with turned-down thumb; when they've turned away from these diversions they contract privies for profit, and why not everything, since they are the sort of people whom Fortune raises up from the dirt to the world's vast pediments whenever she is in the mood to jest.
    What should I do for Rome? I don't know how to lie ...[1]

DATELINE *St Petersburg, Florida – Pinellas Park: The attorney representing Terri Schiavo's parents acknowledged late Saturday that the legal battle to keep Schiavo alive is essentially over and – pending a miracle from God – she will die soon.*[2]
    As I travel the Sea of Information a *vox angelae*, an Angel's voice, seems to strike the bell of my inner ear, to resound through the platinum hull and pulse the digital ports of my craft with rhythmic silver light.

VOX ANGELAE: 'I' am cortically dead. 'I' speak virtually through the aperture of the media. 'I' am a virtual woman. My body is the property of medicine, of my spouse, of my parents, of the courts, of the legislatures, of the society of spectacle. I am a death parade. I am a life without consciousness, fed by tubes and fiber-optic cables, a hybrid of biology and technology, a cyborg whose consciousness is no longer 'mine' but the *noosphere's*. I am an icon of right-wing dreams of the perfect woman, brain dead and passive, perfect bride of the 'compassionate conservative,' no back-talk from me, only passive acceptance of nurture offered, a child in need of author-ity, a biological inkblot for masculinist power fantasies, morality dreams, projec-tions of war-on-terror networks committed to patriotic ecocide in pursuit of salvation, gutting the poor, exsanguinating the medically needy, forcing children into birth to go hungry, forcing their mothers to become the vessels of proletarian production, herd animals of empire, good daughters of the American plutocratic 'Revolution,' imperial cattle, mindless, but loved, after all. I am a daughter of War, of napalm and bouncing explosives, the little balls of fire and shrapnel that turn children to hamburger and their mothers to broken dolls leaking blood for tears on their progeny, like Michelangelo's Mary mourning the Jesus of the Poor, dead like me, Woman Vessel of Power Dreams, Bride of Messianic Torturers whose Prayers yield Shock and Awe, twisting the guts of the poor for oil and the wombs of their wives for children, Devotees offering the Sacrament of Others' Blood on the Altar of Capital, I am the Meat Puppet of Imperial Christendom whose *post-transubstantiation* is not wine for blood but, after all, blood for oil, that Texas Black Gold, Miraculous Viscosity of Capital Triumphant, I am the 'living' projection of your Morality, one who never Talks Back, as I slobber your praises, Father in Wash-ington, and celebrate the humanity – without mind, without judgment, without power, without hope – that YOU represent, icon of the new American Millennium, our Hegemon, Technician of Morality-As-Anti-Life, or, as Sylvia Plath used to say 'Daddy' Divine Right Ruler of the United Herd, one of whom now 'enters' my room with handgun drawn,[3] just as Daddy has 'entered' Iraq, to 'liberate' me, Insensate as I am, in a kind of transubstantiation of my poor flesh into an Emblem of Righteousness, a Willing Executioner of Righteousness, Unconscious Protoplas-mic Followers of the New New 'Deal' for America, of 'Social Security' 'liberated' of its funds, of 'Medicaid' patients 'freed' to take care of themselves and wander the streets without the encumbrances of home or even the burden of food, the truly Faithful Devotees of Mindless Life with Rented Body, Children of Capital, my Countrymen, listen to your own Voices!

PRESIDENT GEORGE W. BUSH: I love my Daddy.[4]

KEN GOODMAN [Director of Bioethics, University of Miami]: Fifteen years ago last month, actually, in February, she [Terri Schiavo] had a heart attack as a result of a potassium imbalance caused by an eating disorder. That's pretty well established. She was, unfortunately, like many people, not able to be resuscitated in time, and as a result, suffered hypoxic or anoxic brain injury. Large portions of her cerebral cortex were damaged, severely damaged by that heart attack. In fact, she's been described as being neurologically devastated. Since then she's been taken to vari-ous forms of rehabilitation. They haven't worked.

VIRTUE: All of this furor stems from an *eating* disorder?

VOX ANGELAE: In life I tried desperately, self-destructively, to fit into the mould cast for me by the media stream of PERFECT women, but I couldn't seem to starve myself enough, and now, in Limbo, I am once again fit to Procrustus's Bed of Images and edited as the Spin Doctors see fit!

REPRESENTATIVE TRENT FRANKS [Republican, Arizona]: Mr Speaker, Terri Schiavo represents the mortality and helplessness of us all as human beings. And whether we realize it or not, we're at this moment lying down beside her –

VIRTUE: What?

FRANKS: – listening for that song of hope. And if we as a nation subject her to the torture and agony of starving and thirsting to death, while her brother, her mother, and her father are forced to watch, we will scar our own souls. And we will be allowing those judges who have lost their way to drag us all one more ominous step into a darkness where the light of human compassion has gone out, and the predatory survival of the fittest prevails over humanity. If the song of hope is to be silenced, Mr Speaker, let it not be tonight. Thank you.[5]

VIRTUE: But isn't 'predatory survival of the fittest' the keynote of the President's economic policy?

JOHN POWERS: Thanks to the Christian right, none of our politicians dare mention Darwin, except to say he shouldn't be taught in schools. ('Religion has been around a lot longer than Darwin,' our president has noted helpfully.) Beyond that, *the Winners' agenda is now far harsher than it ever was under Nixon, whose social policies would strike today's Republicans as downright socialist.* The Bush administration has given the rich hundreds of billions in tax 'relief,' while excluding millions of less favored Americans (including U.S. troops) from other forms of tax relief. Even as it gave $80,000 write-offs to businessmen who buy Humvees, it sought to change the Fair Labor Standards Act in a way that would cost countless hourly workers their overtime. Just redefine their work as administrative and the extra hours are free. Underlying such behavior is the President's embrace of a philosophy (or, more accurately, an outlook) I call *Populist Social Darwinism*. Bush boasts about returning power to ordinary people – 'We want to give you back your money' – then pursues policies that produce a class of highly visible Winners while unraveling the social safety net. Anytime you so much as mention this, you're accused of waging class warfare.[6]

KEN GOODMAN: Terri Schiavo is not in a minimally conscious state ... I think that the people who have done the diagnosis, who have done the CT scans, who have done the EEGs are unambiguous in their diagnosis. The fact of the matter is research on people who are in a PVS shows they never, ever recover the way the Congressman suggested Terri Schiavo might. It's a tragedy, and it's a tragedy that unfortunately is being exploited for purposes that I'm troubled by deeply.[7]

GEORGE W. BUSH: Democrats and Republicans in Congress came together last night to give Terri Schiavo's parents another opportunity to save their daughter's life ... This is a complex case with serious issues, but in extraordinary circumstances like this, it is wise to always err on the side of life.[8]

VIRTUE: But I thought, given your Presidency of Inspiration, you didn't *make* ...

CHARLES GIBSON: President Bush, during the last four years, you have made thousands of decisions that have affected millions of lives. Please give three instances in which you came to realize you had made a wrong decision, and what you did to correct it. Thank you.

BUSH: I have made a lot of decisions, and some of them little, like appointments to boards you never heard of, and some of them big.

And in a war, there's a lot of – there's a lot of tactical decisions that historians will look back and say: He shouldn't have done that. He shouldn't have made that decision. And I'll take responsibility for them. I'm human.

VIRTUE: I *didn't* know!

BUSH: But on the big questions, about whether or not we should have gone into Afghanistan, the big question about whether we should have removed somebody in Iraq, I'll stand by those decisions, because I think they're right.[9]

TRENT FRANKS: There were some pictures [of Abu Ghraib] where it looked like a prisoner was sodomizing himself with an object ... blood was visible in the photograph.[10]

HEATHER WOKUSCH: Abu Ghraib has left administration officials falling over themselves with protestations of compassion, but it's worth remembering that the Bush White House has fought hard against the International Convention Against Torture.[11]

JANE MAYER: On January 27th, President Bush, in an interview with the *Times*, assured the world that 'torture is never acceptable, nor do we hand over people to countries that do torture.' Maher Arar, a Canadian engineer who was born in Syria, was surprised to learn of Bush's statement. Two and a half years ago, American officials, suspecting Arar of being a terrorist, apprehended him in New York and sent him back to Syria, where he endured months of brutal interrogation, including torture. When Arar described his experience in a phone interview recently, he invoked an Arabic expression. The pain was so unbearable, he said, that 'you forget the milk that you have been fed from the breast of your mother.'[12]

VIRTUE: I wonder if Jesus forgot *his* mother's milk when *he* was tortured? I wonder if they use crosses in those SECRET torture camps BEYOND Abu-Ghraib?

SYLVIA POGGIOLI: Milan authorities [are] investigat[ing] whether CIA agents broke Italian law in an act of 'extraordinary rendition.' The term refers to U.S. agents abducting suspected terrorists abroad and transporting them to third countries, sometimes to be tortured. The case centers on the alleged abduction of an Egyptian-born man near his home in Italy.[13]

JANE MAYER: President Bush, Secretary of State Condoleezza Rice, and Attorney General Alberto Gonzales all made similar statements last month, asserting that not only does the United States condemn torture, it also does not send U.S.-held suspects to other countries for torture. In reality, the record appears to be quite different. Beginning around 1995, the Central Intelligence Agency inaugurated a form of extradition sometimes referred to as 'extraordinary rendition,' in which captured foreign terrorism suspects have been transported by the U.S. to third countries for interrogation and prosecution.[14]

VIRTUE: Is that how the President defines 'compassion'?

DOUGLAS KELLNER [with intensity]: Critics claim that the 'defining trait' of the Bush administration and major force in determining its hardright policies is 'corporate payback.' Abrogation of the Kyoto Treaty and the Bush energy policy was payback for the more than $50 million contributed by the oil and energy industries. The former Director of the Star Wars program under Reagan, Dr Robert W. Bowman, makes a similar argument in terms of Bush's military policy. Star Wars II, Bowman argues, will 'line the pockets of weapons manufacturers for decades' at the expense of 'optional' programs like health, education, the environment and welfare. Moreover, it provides 'the multinational corporations and banks absolute military superiority for their 'gunboat diplomacy around the world.'[15]

AMY GOODMAN: Bush's [federal budget] plan would slash aid to cities by one-third, eliminate health insurance for thousands of low-income families, reduce veterans' medical benefits, cut funding for city cops and county sheriffs, wipe out child care subsidies for 300,000 families, trim funding for clean water and soil conservation and shutter dozens of programs for preschool children and at-risk youth. The budget also targets public housing, Medicaid, and farmers.[16]

VIRTUE: At least we have full jails!

HEATHER WOKUSCH: Conditions inside Texan prisons during Bush's reign were so notorious that federal Judge William Wayne Justice wrote, 'Many inmates credibly testified to the existence of violence, rape and extortion in the prison system and about their own suffering from such abysmal conditions.'

VOX ANGELAE: With a Savior like that ...

MIKE ALLEN AND MANUELI ROIG-FRANZIA [shuffling through documents]: An unsigned one-page memo, distributed to Republican senators, said the debate over Schiavo would appeal to the party's base, or core, supporters. The memo singled out Senator Bill Nelson (D-Fla.), who is up for re-election next year and is potentially vulnerable in a state President Bush won last year: 'This is an important moral issue and the pro-life base will be excited that the Senate is debating this important issue,' said the memo, which was reported by ABC News and later given to the *Washington Post.* 'This is a great political issue, because Senator Nelson of Florida has already refused to become a co-sponsor [of Republican compromise legislation requiring restoration of Terri Schiavo's life support] and this is a tough issue for Democrats.'[17]

CHRISTIAN PROTESTER [jeering at police arresting an activist attempting to 'save' Schiavo]: 'Shame on you police. Shame on you, Pontius Pilate.'[18]

VIRTUE: If the Nation were a play, and President Bush played Tiberius Caesar, would that make Donald Rumsfeld Pontius Pilate, and, let's see, Jesus the leader of some 'terrorist' cult hell bent, so to speak, on thwarting the Empire?

HEATHER WOKUSCH: Funding of mental health programs during Bush's reign was so poor that Texan prisons had a sizeable number of mentally impaired inmates; defying international human rights standards, these inmates ended up on death row. A prisoner named Emile Duhamel, for example, with severe psychological disabilities and an IQ of 56, died in his Texan death-row jail cell in July 1998. Authorities blamed 'natural causes' but a lack of air conditioning in cells that topped 100 degrees Fahrenheit in a summer heat wave may have killed Duhamel instead.

VOX ANGELAE: Do Cyborgs have IQ's? Maybe even souls?

KILGORE TROUT: Did you watch the State of the Union address?

KURT VONNEGUT: Yes, and it certainly helped to remember what the late British philosopher and mathematician Bertrand Russell called this planet.

TROUT: Which was?

VONNEGUT: 'The lunatic asylum of the Universe.' He said the inmates had taken over and were trashing the joint. And he wasn't talking about the germs or the elephants. He meant we the people.[19]

AMY GOODMAN: In addition Bush is proposing to cut the budget of the Environmental Protection Agency by $450 million; to cut $100 million from a Bureau of Indian Affairs program that helps build schools and to cut $200 million for home-heating aid for the poor.[20]

GREGORY BATESON: When you narrow down your epistemology and act on the premise 'What interests me is me, or my organization, or my species,' you chop off consideration of other loops [of the ecosystem]. You decide that you want to get rid of the by-products of human life and that Lake Erie will be a good place to put them. You forget that the eco-mental system called Lake Erie is part of *your* eco-mental system – and that if Lake Erie is driven insane, its insanity is incorporated into the larger system of your thought and experience.[21]

AMY GOODMAN: But Bush isn't cutting back on all federal programs. The budget calls for a $19 billion increase in Pentagon spending.[22]

GEORGE W. BUSH [Stepping off Air Force One, recalling his 'moral vision' for the U.S.A]: Because a society is judged by how it treats the weak and vulnerable, we must build a culture of life.

KELLNER [petting a media-sleuthing cybernetic Baskervillean hound]: In 1983, the Defense Advance Research Projects Agency (DARPA), responsible for development of the Internet, published a document outlining a 'Strategic Computing Program' ... The SCP was a five-year, $600,000,000 plan to produce a new generation of military applications for computers. The proposal included a thousand-fold increase in computing power and an emphasis on artificial intelligence. It envisioned 'completely autonomous land, sea and air vehicles capable of complex, far-ranging reconnaissance and attack missions.' These vehicles would have human abilities, such as sight, speech, understanding natural language, and automated reasoning. The SCP promoted the view that the human element in many critical decision-making instances could be largely or totally taken over by machines ... In this momentous process, just as humans are becoming like machines, machines are ever-more taking on human qualities.[23]

VOX ANGELAE: So I am valuable as a cyborg, but only if I fit into the 'culture of life'? I feel just like Mel Gibson's cinematic Jesus!

VIRTUE: Maybe you serve to show that the megatechnical apparatus of planetary bio-cide is not only profitable but also the Tree of Life bearing its fruit?

VOX ANGELAE: I thought we weren't supposed to *eat* fruit.

MISSAnneThrope: While the entire nation seems to be up-in-arms over Terry Schiavo's unfortunate story, what about Houston's own Spiro Nikolouzos? Locked in a life or death battle of their own, Nikolouzos's family doesn't have the publicity afforded political footballs, and a very different Governor Bush worked on his case ... working to find a way to pull the plug, rather than reinsert the tube. On March 9, a judge ruled that the hospital had the right to disconnect life support, despite his family's wishes. Right now, an emergency injunction is the only thing standing between them taking this action ... A nursing home has agreed to take Nikolouzos *provided his family can show that he will receive Medicaid after his Medicare runs out.*[24]

VIRTUE: But why would George W. Bush want to 'pull the plug' on Medicaid for millions of poor people when GOD, speaking through the President, says 'err on the side of life'?

VOX ANGELAE: Maybe there is some problem with *routing* Divine signals through the Presidential Neural Network!

DAN FROOMKIN: David Gregory [video link including inevitable ad] NBC Nightly News: Bush's surprise return to the White House is 'being seen as either an attempt to defend innocent life or a crass act of political theater ...'[25]

KURT VONNEGUT: I only want to say about our president, our armed forces' Commander-in-Chief: He believes whatever he says. He might be the sincerest person in the whole wide world. He should be in a movie. Correction: He is in a movie, a made-for-TV movie, which is now our form of government.[26]

GOD [played by a nameless Republican]: My First Commandment in the New Contract for (on) America: 'Thou must love Capital with all thy heart and all thy mind, and have no other Goods before it.'

KURT VONNEGUT [before the last U.S. Presidential election]: We are killing this planet as a life-support system with the poisons from all the thermodynamic whoopee we're making with atomic energy and fossil fuels, and everybody knows it, and practically nobody cares. This is how crazy we are. I think the planet's immune system is trying to get rid of us with AIDS and new strains of flu and tuberculosis, and so on, but I think it's too late. I don't think even it can keep George W. Bush from getting elected to a second term.

KILGORE TROUT: Peace.[27]

HUNTER S. THOMPSON: [Risen from the Dead just to recall some electoral advice]: If Nixon were running for president today, he would be seen as a 'liberal' candidate, and he would probably win. He was a crook and a bungler, but what the hell? Nixon was a barrel of laughs compared to this gang of thugs from the Halliburton petroleum organization who are running the White House today – and who will be running it this time next year, if we (the once-proud, once-loved, and widely respected 'American people') don't rise up like wounded warriors and whack those lying petroleum pimps out of the White House on November 2nd [2004].[28]

VIRTUE: But Bush *won*!

KELLNER: To get away with this banditry, Bush and Cheney needed a compliant populace ... Many believe the United States is devolving into fascism under Bush and Cheney, but it is not the sort of 'friendly fascism' that Bertram Gross described in 1982,[29] for never has a more vicious bunch occupied the higher levels of government. Like Hitler and German fascists, the Bush-Cheney clique uses the Big Lie to promote its policies, promote aggressive militarism in the quest for world hegemony, and relentlessly promote the economic interests of the corporations and groups that finance it ... Expanding significantly since the 1980s, the Republican propaganda machine has cultivated a group of ideological storm troopers who loudly support Bush-Cheney policies and attack those who criticize them.[30]

VIRTUE: Then Terri Schiavo is, to 'Compassionate Politicians,' a piece in the media puzzle of the Great Lie? I feel the temperature rising in here!

RAY BRADBURY: Let me know when it reaches Fahrenheit 451.

MICHAEL MOORE: Amen![31]

Coda

VOX ANGELAE: As I drift among the spheres turning like turbines in the Sea of Information, haunted by my own images projected in the schizogenic mind of Empire, I am reminded of the final words of 'Scipio's Dream' (*Somnium Scipionis*), at the close of Cicero's *Republic: Ego somno solutus sum.* May I soon too, like that planet-surfing old Roman, finally have been released by sleep from the poisoned waters of the American Dream. May they at least put out the fires![32]

Notes

1 Juvenal, *Satire 3*, lines 35-41, my translation. Latin and English versions of Juvenal are available at *The Ancient History Sourcebook*, http://www.fordham.edu/halsall/ancient/juv-sat3 lateng.html, accessed 30 Jan. 2005.

2 William Levesque et al., 'Legal Battle Over, Parents Seek Miracle,' *St Petersburg Times*, 27 March 2005, available at http://www.sptimes.com, accessed 30 Jan. 2005.

3 The *St Petersburg Times* reported one man's plans:

Like those earlier this week, none of Friday's arrests resulted in violence. The protesters told police what they were going to do, made a symbolic offering of help and went to jail, charged with trespassing. Authorities were far more concerned about a man who did not make it to the hospice.

Thursday night, Pinellas County sheriff's deputies arrested a 20-year-old Illinois man on charges of entering a Seminole gun shop and, armed with a box cutter, demanded the owner fill a backpack with weapons.

'He told me he would take any guns he could and go rescue Terri Schiavo,' said Randall McKenzie, owner of Randall's Firearms Inc. 'At that point I knew he was a little bit whacked.'

McKenzie said the man, identified as Michael W. Mitchell, put his knee into a glass display and removed a .454-calibre handgun, the most powerful in the store. McKenzie drew his semiautomatic and ordered Mitchell to the floor.

Alex Leary and Tom Zucco, 'Schiavo Protesters Line up for Arrest,' *St Petersburg Times*, 26 March 2005, available at http://www.sptimes.com, accessed 23 Oct. 2007.

4 'Sometimes the president seems to think that vagueness, non sequiturs, and tautology are enough to explain away his political problems. How long will there be an American presence in Iraq? "As long as necessary but not a day longer." Did you get where you are because of your famous father? "I love my Dad." Drugs as a youth? "When I was young and reckless, I was young and reckless." Is war with Iraq really a last resort? "When I say I'm a patient man, I mean I'm a patient man." It is sad to say about our democracy, but this nonsense often works.' Eric Alterman and Mark Green, *The Book on Bush: How George Bush (Mis)leads America* (New York: Penguin, 2004), 7.

5 Amy Goodman, 'The Case of Terri Schiavo: A Debate between a Bioethicist and a Disability Rights Activist,' *Democracy Now*, 22 March 2005, available at http://www.democracynow.org/article.pl? sid=05/03/22/1529259, accessed 23 Oct. 2007.

6 John Powers, *Sore Winners (and the Rest of Us) in Bush's America*. (New York: Doubleday, 2004), excerpt published in *LA Weekly*, 30 July to 5 Aug. 2004, available at http://www .laweekly.com/ink/04/36/features-powers.php, accessed 23 Oct. 2007.

7 Goodman, 'The Case of Terri Schiavo.'

8 George Bush, cited in ibid.

9 Commission on Presidential Debates, Debate Transcript: 'Second Presidential Debate,' 8 Oct. 2004, available at http://www.debates.org/pages/trans2004c.html, accessed 23 Oct. 2007.

10 Trent Franks, quotation and paraphrase cited by Goodman in 'The Case of Terri Schiavo.'

11 Heather Wokusch, 'From Texas to Abu Ghraib: The Bush Legacy of Prisoner Abuse,' 10 May 2004, available at http://www.CommonDreams.org/views04/0510-01.htm, accessed 23 Oct. 2007.

12 Jane Mayer, 'Outsourcing Torture,' *New Yorker*, 2 Feb. 2005, available at http://www.newyorker.com/fact/content/articles/050214fa_fact6, accessed 23 Oct. 2007.

13 Sylvia Poggioli, 'Italy Investigates Alleged CIA Abduction,' *NPR Morning Edition*, 28 March 2005, available at http://www.npr.org/templates/story/story.php?storyId=4563352, accessed 23 Oct. 2007.

14 David Remnick, 'Instant Replay,' *New Yorker*, 14 Feb. 2005, available at http://www.newyorker.com/archive/2005/02/14/050214on_onlineonly01.

15 Douglas Kellner, 'The Politics and Costs of Postmodern War in the Age of Bush II,' available at http://www.gseis.ucla.edu/faculty/kellner/papers/POMOwar.htm.

16 Amy Goodman, 'Bush's New $2.5 Trillion Budget Boosts Pentagon Spending, Slashes Domestic Programs,' *Democracy Now*, 8 Feb. 2005, available at http://www.democracynow.org/article.pl?sid=05/02/08/1458256.

17 Mike Allen and Manuel Roig-Franzie, 'Congress Steps In on Schiavo Case,' *Washington Post*, 20 March 2005, available at http://www.washingtonpost.com/ac2/wp-dyn/A49701-2005Mar19?language=printer.

18 Tom Zucco, 'Diary of a Vigil,' *St Petersburg Times*, 27 March 2005, available at http://www.sptimes.com/2005/03/26/Tampabay/Diary_of_a_vigil.shtml.

19 Kurt Vonnegut, 'State of the Asylum,' *In These Times*, 5 Feb. 2004, available at http://www.inthesetimes.com/site/main/article/state_of_the_asylum/.

20 Goodman, 'Bush's New $2.5 Trillion Budget.'

21 Gregory Bateson, 'Pathologies of Epistemology,' *Steps to an Ecology of Mind* (Northvale: Aronson, 1987), 486–95, 492.

22 Goodman, 'Bush's New $2.5 Trillion Budget.'

23 Kellner, 'Politics and Costs of Postmodern War.'

24 MissAnneThrope, 'Where's the "Life Support" for Spiro Nikolouzos? Houston Hospital Tried to Pull Plug,' *Daily Kos*, 21 March 2005, available at http://www.dailykos.com/story/2005/3/21/19317/4294.

25 Dan Froomkin, 'For Bush, High Drama and Mixed Reviews,' *Washington Post*, 21 March 2005, available at http://peaceandjustice.org/article.php?story=2005032111455129&mode=printo. NBC Nightly News Video link at MSN.com, 20 March 2005.

26 Vonnegut, 'State of the Asylum.'

27 Ibid.

28 Hunter S. Thompson, 'Fear and Loathing, Campaign 2004,' *Rolling Stone*, 20 Oct. 2004, available at http://www.rollingstone.com/politics/story/6562575/fear_and_loathing_campaign2004/.

29 Bertram Gross, *Friendly Fascism: The New Face of Power in America* (Cambridge: South End Press, 1982).

30 Douglas Kellnet, 'Election 2004: The War for the White House and Media Spectacle,' introduction (2005), available at http://www.gseis.ucla.edu/faculty/kellner/election2004.pdf.

31 For further comment from Michael Moore, see http://www.michaelmoore.com/.

32 For a good English translation of this text see Cicero, *Republic and Laws*, trans. Niall Rudd (Oxford: Oxford University Press, 1998), 86–94.

JEFF RICE

Detroit-Techno

Compuware Headquarters, located at 1 Campus Martius near the base of Woodward Avenue in downtown Detroit, marks the site of the city's new landscape. Compuware, a leading information technology corporation, manufactures management software applications and offers IT services to a number of global businesses. Detroit once signified the success and perils of modernism, specifically those connected with Fordist assembly-line methodology, but today Detroit emerges as the signifier of techno-salvation. Luring Compuware to Detroit, solidified in its 2003 opening, began the final replacement of industrialization with information technology. Its sixteen-storey, $350 million building is now the focal point of what the city itself calls 'Digital Detroit,' a title embodied in an annual conference of the same name.[1] Wayne State University contributes to this technology-driven enthusiasm with plans for its own downtown technology site, TechTown, a 'new multi-million dollar entrepreneurial village' 'located along the Digital Drive in the heart of the city of Detroit.'[2] Detroiter Iggy Pop's declaration 'Look out, honey, cause I'm using technology,' in the 1973 song 'Search and Destroy,' is no longer a threat, but instead a desired reality as Detroit embraces the turn to the digital. This desire is realized in Digital Detroit, with its slogan 'New Ideas, New Culture, New Community.' The label updates the Fordist plan of 'Americanization' in the first half of the twentieth century with a digitized sense of urban identity. Fordism triumphed homogenous identity for the sake of manufacturing; Digital Detroit triumphs 'newness' in order to generate new media.

The empty factories that gave birth to the supremacy of Ford and Chrysler throughout the first half of the twentieth century have yielded to the McLuhanist vision of information dominance. 'In the new electric Age of Information and programmed production,' Marshall McLuhan wrote in the 1960s, 'commodities themselves assume more and more the character of information.'[3] How has Detroit come to represent the new signifier of urban information? How has its commodification placed urbanity at the centre of new media logic? The commodification of our cities (through franchises, capital, and gentrification) has not yielded 'better' places to live. No matter how many Hard Rock Cafés or Borders we attract to downtown environments, life remains the same. Buildings remain unoccupied and ruins surround the franchises. This paradox, the *Detroit Free Press* notes, continues even as the city claims a high profile for attracting IT and other commercial investment. On hearing that Detroit placed five companies in the 2005 Inner City 100 rankings of the fastest-growing companies in urban America, *Free Press* columnist Tom Walsh comments: 'Detroit's emergence as one of the cities with the most companies on the Inner City 100 list is something of a surprise, given that an ICIC study last year showed that Detroit was the only U.S. inner city with job losses of more than 2 percent a year from 1995 to 2001.'[4]

Failure of economic investment (in terms of job growth or quality of life) has been largely ignored by cities, and Detroit, even with its faith in Compuware, is no exception. Since the construction of the $500 million Ford-sponsored Renaissance Center along the Detroit River in 1977, economic investment has served as the pivotal moment always on the verge of transforming the city's residents' lives. The Renaissance Center did not revive the river area, and there is no reason to believe that Compuware will save the downtown. Like the Renaissance Center, the current grand scope of corporate IT structure in downtown Detroit, aligned with the city's other grand gestures towards sports entertainment, have had little impact on the economic futures of the almost 800,000 residents. Burnt-out buildings, abandoned homes, and empty storefronts are still the norm. The anticipated domino effect of development never materializes. Thus, despite his securing of the 2005 Super Bowl and the Final Four – the 2009 collegiate basketball event for the city to host, Detroit's mayor Kwame Kilpatrick is still named by *Time* magazine as the country's worst mayor. Sports attractions meant to lure further investment into the city have not generated substantial change. Why do such efforts not revive urban life anymore? The answer can be found in the city's own claim to digital status: the role of information production and in particular, new media.

Assembly/Assemblage

One cannot discount the image of Compuware at Detroit's centre. Its stature is notably visible against the backdrop of the numerous empty storefronts in the adjacent section of Merchant's Row along Lower Woodward. The importance of Compuware is not that it has generated a significant financial payoff; it has not. Compuware's importance is that the city now stands to be the site where a new logic of invention emerges, one based on information technology. Detroit was *the* exemplar of the U.S. conception of assembly-line thinking (equal parts in the system, interchangeability). Now Detroit gives birth to the assemblage apparatus of new media. That Silicon Valley has been more of a force in the rise of information technology in terms of hardware and software makes little difference. Detroit demonstrates not the instrumentality of digital culture, but its logic.

We no longer live in the world of assembly. We live in the age of the assemblage. Assembling a city piece by piece through interchangeable financial investments does not account for the assemblage mentality of the twenty-first century. As ubiquitous as assemblage has become for popular culture in music, on television, on the Web, and in the plastic arts, it still has not earned credit for its role in structuring logic. The logic of the assembly line eventually extended outward from the Ford factory in Highland Park and influenced a range of cultural habits throughout the twentieth century, from department store setups (everything under one roof) to educational policy (assembly-line movement from class to class and generalized testing). How has assemblage begun to reimagine that structure?

The places we live in have become more than fixed places. 'A rough enumeration of some of the basic tenets of this general narrative of the city includes the following,' Helen Liggett writes in her book *Urban Encounters*, 'The city exists as a place.'[5] But narrative, as Jean-François Lyotard framed the postmodern condition, no longer holds up in the age of databases and techno-mastery. Narratives are too stable. They codify experience in referential ways; they work to legitimize experience. 'The best performativity [of narrative] cannot consist in obtaining additional information in this way,' Lyotard notes. 'It comes rather from arranging the data in a new way, which is what constitutes a "move" properly speaking. This new arrangement is usually achieved by connecting together series of data that were previously held to be independent.'[6] Assemblage works from that basic principle of parataxical arrangement and opposes the ordered assembly of narrative. 'Capital will save Detroit' marks one failed narrative circulated among the city's investors, politicians, and real estate companies. Returning to this narrative will do us little good. Instead, we must connect its claim to other data not yet considered relevant or legitimate in urban discourse.

Detroit exists as a place without stability and without legitimization. This lack of stability does not depend on global markets or price fluctuations or even issues of labour. We already recognize narratives of Detroit that pose the city in such terms: urban flight, failure to adapt to new global trade, lost revenue in tax assessment and collection, large-scale unemployment. Detroit's lack of stability comes from elsewhere; it comes from space. From 8 Mile to Jefferson Avenue, lived in and inhabited spaces are encircled by empty spaces. The empty spaces that comprise large parts of the city pose the possibility of assemblage (combining spaces) as opposed to assembling (filling in space with investment). But until now, we have spent too much time lamenting the failure of economic revival in terms of space. Whether framed in the repetitive gesture of urban renewal or the more eclectic appeal of what Richard Florida hails as the creative class, an economic vision of the city demands that we see its return in purely financial terms. Florida's manifesto, *The Rise of the Creative Class*, sets the conditions for how the urban environment will be revitalized by the economic output of young urban professionals (most of whom are artistic and energetic). The presence of such professionals, Florida claims, will lead to urban recovery because these individuals' interests spur and give rise to new development. This is a popular trope adopted by many states and local governments, among them Michigan's governor, Jennifer Granholm, who appropriates Florida's concept as the basis of her 'Cool Cities' program of urban renewal. Detroit has been marked as space within the 'Cool Cities' plan. The presence of cool people, the plan proclaims, will make the city referentially cool, and thus, in line with Florida's argument, promote financial growth.

In *Cities: Reimagining the Urban*, Ash Amin and Nigel Thrift, however, propose an alternative agenda for city planning, which requests that we view cities in non-economic terms. 'Can we see cities as something other than localized economic systems or the forcing houses of (knowledge) capitalism?'[7] This is a question I take seriously for how it moves us outside of narrative. It is no longer possible to theorize all of our problems in terms of capital without also acknowledging that new media play an equally dominant (or possibly more dominant) role in shaping culture. But what is this 'something other' Amin and Thrift hint at? And what is this role I imagine new media having in city revival?

Encounters

Amin and Thrift ask us to consider the encounter. 'The sense of a kaleidoscopic urban world,' Amin and Thrift write, 'crammed full with hybrid networks going about their business, enables us to see, at the same time, the importance of *encounter*.'[8] Networks embrace the logic of encounter. Amin and Thrift note: 'So, places, for example, are best thought of not so much as enduring sites but as moments of encounter, not so much as "presents"; fixed in space and time, but as variable events; twists and fluxes of interrelation. Even when the intent is to hold places stiff and motionless, caught in a cat's cradle of networks that are out to quell unpredictability, success is rare, and then only for awhile.'[9]

In a network, one moves from place to place, rather than settling in one place. 'The insidious thing about electronic networks,' Steven Shaviro writes, 'is that they are always there, whether you pay attention to them or not.'[10] Detroit as network operates from within those moments we pay attention to it, as well as those we do not. The city as network requires a reimagining of how we move and engage information *within* (i.e., to and from) places instead of focusing solely on our experience *in* places (the Compuware/TechTown model). The difference is substantial. By imagining the urban environment as one of encounter rather than fixed place, we can begin to conceptualize a city like Detroit as a network (and, in turn, we see other twenty-first century cities as networks as well). In that conceptualization, we see the ways new media may reshape our understanding of information technology and the urban. In essence, we see a project worthy of digital media.

The problem is that even while the city calls itself Digital Detroit, it does not see itself yet as the embodiment of digital media; that is, the network. It still sees itself as fixed place. The twentieth century marked the great migrations of workers to cities. Detroit, along with Chicago and Cleveland, served as a major destination for those in search of a fixed place within the American promise of postwar economic recovery. The twenty-first century fails to continue this distinction, partly because those fixed places no longer exist. The automotive factories that spurred the great migrations have since closed or minimized their operations. The factory signifies the place we pay attention to; the time has come to locate the places we do not pay attention to, the places we have yet to encounter, in order to shape Detroit as a network. In the age of information, we do not head towards a place, but rather encounter place, real or imaginary. We enter into place. When Detroit-based DJ Jay Dee poses as a mix the broad declaration 'Welcome To Detroit' on his album of the same name, he highlights this encounter as one into the network of information culture. In other words, to be welcomed into Detroit is to be welcomed into the encounter as mix.

In the collection *Stalking Detroit*, Jason Young poses this mix encounter as an update of the Situationist practice of psychogeography. Young's project *Line Frustration* is a mapping of Detroit whose purpose is to move outside of fixed, economic solutions by mixing physical space with imagination, or the places we wouldn't normally pay attention to. '*Line Frustration* describes the brokering of Detroit's empty territory by the media and attempts to locate architecture's potential fit within that economy.'[11] Young describes his work of mapping out lines across the city as being about writing. 'In many ways,' he states, 'this line of demarcation is rhetorical. It separates *this* from more of *this*. The line's intention is to introduce difference where there is none.'[12] A mix of real place (where the lines meet) and imaginary place (where I project them) produces encounter. When I project Detroit as a network of encounters, I am focusing on this sense of difference in terms of new media. I am calling for new types of mapping of place, particularly mappings that move within the logic of digital culture by allowing us to encounter new kinds of urban spaces as writing. 'The full blown city coincides with the development of writing,' McLuhan writes.[13] 'New speed and power are never compatible with existing spatial and social arrangements.'[14] To reimagine the city as digital media is to reimagine its space as writing, a move that displaces us from current social arrangements whose focus rests mostly with capital investment. Thus, this becomes both an ideological move (a recognition of an apparatus shift in information technology and space that moves us from assembly line to assemblage thinking) as well as a practical move (residents engage with this shift in thinking in order to begin writing the city through encounters). Central to this writing is imagination in terms of materiality, how we imagine the places we live within in regard to technology.

In the Fordist economy, that imagination occurs as graffiti. Long disdained as symbolic of urban blight, graffiti has been viewed as the sign of economic decline; its appearance often found on the remnants of the industrial age: trains, factory walls, abandoned buildings, highway bypasses, and street signs. When one encounters this graffiti, one sees the collapse of urbanity. Graffiti long positioned itself as the reimagination of failed social space. The industrial city, like Detroit, eventually became covered in the urban phenomenon of graffiti tags. The weblog dETROITfUNK (www.detroitfunk.com/dfg) wonderfully showcases Detroit's urban tags through a series of posted galleries. As the site demonstrates, 'Rodeo,' 'Turtl,' 'Money,' and 'Rib' sign Detroit's urban landscape as industrial writing. These graffiti tags reference the urban city in familiar ways. They capture our attention through their references to decay and collapse. How can we move that familiarity into digital writing or mapping so that we engage encounter not as fixed signings but as what we have not yet considered or paid attention to, that is, assemblages?

Whereas the industrial city was marked by graffiti tags, the information city is marked by the less familiar, XML-driven tag. The XML tag is the meta-level mark-up used to categorize information in both referential and non-referential ways. Popularized on websites like the image sharing site Flickr, the social bookmarking system Del.icio.us, and the link hub Metafilter, tags allow writers to designate their own names and attributes to information (as opposed to relying on previous categorical systems in circulation). These kinds of sites often draw attention to encounters (names, categories, places) we would not normally recognize. Systems like Flickr or Del.icio.us are presented as 'social' systems because of the levels of social interaction encouraged through user participation and the new kinds of arrangements of information they encourage. By tagging (i.e. categorizing) spaces in flexible manners (the categories are open to change and combinations), these set-ups alter our understanding of social space. In Del.icio.us, these encounters occur through like-minded tags of bookmarked space, which become interlinked (assembled) among users who have chosen the same categories unbeknownst to each other. Flickr, in particular, has generated the notion of the memory map, a tagged satellite map where users fill in their own categories of place through annotations.[15] In the memory map, the fixed markers of place (street names, industrial zones, storefronts) become joined with user-oriented definitions, often framed in terms of personal relationships and experiences ('where we first kissed,' 'I learned to read English here,' 'when the circus stopped here that year, I knew I had made the wrong career choice'). The memory map is a new kind of urban space, an assemblage of the familiar and unfamiliar through tagging. The memory map begins the process of encountering places we pay attention to and those we do not. It digitally updates Young's project of empty territory and line mapping. The memory map as tagged experience points towards an emerging idea of digital urbanity.

Whereas HTML works with pre-established tags like <b> or <i>, XML's meta-tag is left open as < >. This openness allows a variety of organizational schemes to occur as users complete the tags based on reference, desire, association, lack of reference, or some other means. This process is known as folksonomy (folk + taxonomy). Folksonomy involves a new media organization of space through the meeting of differently arranged, open schemes. Just as the urban city contributed to a sense of public-ness or folk-ness through communal gathering, the café, public squares, stadiums, and other places, folksonomy generates a digital sense of connectedness. It does so, however, not through fixed place but through the open encounter of place in terms of digital, social interaction.

Through this openness and interaction, the meta-tag generates assemblages, information connections where such connections were not initially acknowledged as existing. Tagging, David Weinberger writes, allows 'us to type in any word we want, rather than forcing us to navigate some hierarchical, controlled vocabulary.'[16] Through tagging, the digital allows us to engage in discursive encounter. We discover the encounter among tags, among users who tag, and among user and tag. Various combination schemes emerge out of these encounters, sometimes as maps, sometimes as bookmarking, sometimes in other formations. These schemes prompt questions that predetermined naming does not allow: What do I want to name this place? How do I want to identify that naming with another related or unrelated place? How do I allow my naming to connect with other names created throughout the Web? How might I name myself within this place? Tagging leaves these options up to the writer. When writing becomes tagging, associative combinations become rhetorical principles. These associations form digital networks, and thus, digital urban spaces.

Detroit Tagging

How, then, might we 'tag' the information technology city like Detroit? Not with spray paint, but with naming structures. In a city awash with empty buildings and abandoned sites, the potential for open tagging < > seems endless. What to name these abandoned spaces? What to rename those filled-in spaces whose financial schemes have failed? How might this assemblage-oriented naming reimagine the ways we have relied on referentiality for urban renewal? Referentiality, of course, is the basis of print culture. But Detroit is no longer a product of that culture, and that is why Richard Florida's graphs and diagrams of equation between specific types of individuals and urban economic potential cannot pan out. 'Our theory,' Florida argues, 'is that a connection exists between a metropolitan area's level of tolerance for a range of people, its ethnic and social diversity, and its success in attracting talented people, including high-technology workers.'[17] Digitality places that referentiality under question. TechTown or Compuware, these are plans whose basis as well is in referentiality. This kind of technology-driven vision attempts to equate itself (as reference) with financial payoff. Tagging is a different logic altogether.

My argument is that the connections Florida stresses are not found in a causal or referential relationship among individuals, capital, the city, or other forces, but rather in the new media logic of assemblage; that is, combination in general. In the assemblage, reference is not a requirement. The social connectivity that planners like Florida believe will emerge out of urban renewal may in fact be better actualized through the digital assemblage of tagging. My call is for a plan of information tagging, where residents, working in digital spaces, reimagine the city through their own conceptualization and actualization of tags. In place of tagging the bypass or the stop sign with graffiti, they tag the city itself as an encountered name or moment within a digital, interconnected space. On the Web, these encounters become moments of discursive interaction and combination as others add to the tags with their own tagging attributes. 'The history of urbanism,' Steven Johnson notes, 'is also the story of more muted signs, built by the collective behaviour of smaller groups and rarely detected by outsiders.'[18] Tagging brings this behaviour to the foreground so that social connectivity is generated among those within the recognized urban space and those often deemed 'outsiders' (those who bring new naming conventions to the discussion and to the urban space itself). If, in fact, there exists a Digital Detroit, as this city claims for itself, then it must be found within the practice of tagging.

Detroit, like the urban experience in general, has become non-referential. Its empty spaces, or 'ruins' as the Fabulous Ruins of Detroit website declares,[19] do not refer to anything anymore. Tagging allows us to transform that non-referentiality into social experience. The lesson of Detroit is a lesson for all urban sites. Digital space becomes social space through assembled meanings, and that assemblage actualizes the popular logic of social software.[20] Tagging, then, marks a place where new media logic informs our understanding of space and the urban, fashioning a sense of the 'social' not yet accounted for in urban studies. Imagine, then, the city as a network of tags. Residents, who tag themselves simultaneously as writers or non-writers, mark the city through memory maps, weblogs, del.icio.us tags, and other related tools in order to reconstruct the city's sense of urbanity as a digital experience. The tagging generates a number of assembled taxonomies, some recognizable, many not. Through the assemblages, we find new Detroits to engage. We find new Detroits emerging out of our own discursive constructions. This reworking is social in ways capital investment has failed to generate. By making these cities cyber – that is, by putting them on the Web – the tags used to develop these spaces will inevitably be linked to other similarly named tags for other cities, for other, not yet imagined, encounters.

Notes

1 See http://www.digitaldetroit.org, accessed 6 May 2005.

2 See http://www.techtownwsu.org/techtown, accessed 6 May 2005.

3 Marshall McLuhan, *Understanding Media* (New York: Signet, 1964), 48.

4 Tom Walsh, 'Detroit Firms Honored,' *Detroit Free Press*, available at http://www.winwinpartner.com/_downloads/042105_ICIC_Detroit.pdf, accessed 6 May 2005.

5 Helen Liggett, *Urban Encounters* (Minneapolis: University of Minnesota Press, 2003), 7.

6 Jean François Lyotard, *The Postmodern Condition: A Report on Knowledge*, trans. Geoff Bennington and Brian Massumi (Minneapolis: University of Minnesota Press, 1997), 51-2.

7 Ash Amin and Nigel Thrift, *Cities: Reimaging the Urban* (Cambridge: Polity Press, 2002), 63.

8   Ibid., 30.

9   Ibid.

10   Steven Shaviro, *Connected: Or What It Means to Live in the Networked Society* (Minneapolis, University of Minnesota Press, 2003), 5.

11   Jason Young, 'Line Frustration,' *Stalking Detroit*, ed. Georgia Daskalakis, Charles Waldheim, and Jason Young (Barcelona: Actar, 2001), 136.

12   Ibid., 137.

13   McLuhan, *Understanding Media*, 99.

14   Ibid.

15   See flickr.com/photos/tags/memorymap/ for examples. Users download Google satellite maps, then use Flickr's tags to generate their own maps of space, accessed 6 May 2005.

16   David Weinberger, 'Taxonomies and Tags: From Trees to Piles of Leaves,' available at http://www.hyperorg.com/blogger/misc/taxonomies_and_tags.html, accessed 7 May 2005.

17   Richard Florida, *Cities and the Creative Class* (New York: Routledge, 2005), 130.

18   Steven Johnson, *Emergence: The Connected Lives of Ants, Brains, Cities, and Software* (New York: Scribner, 2001), 41.

19   See http://detroityes.com/home.htm, accessed 6 May 2005.

20   The technologies I draw attention to here, Flickr, Del.icio.us, Metafilter, are often labeled within the broader rubric of 'social software.' See also a new blog on tagging, 'You're It,' http://www.tagsonomy.com/, accessed 7 May 2005.

25 Circuits, Death and Sacred Fiction: The City of Banaras

MAHESH SENAGALA

Sing a song
or
Laugh
or
Cry
or
Go away.

'Please,' by Nanao Sasaki[1]

Let us go on a pilgrimage to a city that is all about *existence and sustenance*. If we turned our clocks back about 5,000 years, we would see, on the west bank of the Ganges River in North India, three hillocks that are the seed of a very special human phenomenon, the city of Banaras. Not only has the city survived over the last 5,000 years, but it has thrived and is still very much alive. During those five millennia, the city has sustained its essence, character, mythological power, and existential agenda.

People go to Banaras to die – die happily, I might add. The concept may seem startling at first. Many go to Las Vegas to escape the boring and banal reality of their cities and immerse themselves in a hedonistic hyper-reality; others go to Paris, perhaps to immortalize their moments of love. However, there is no other city on earth where you go with an express purpose of spending the last days of your life. Think of it as an *existential airport* to life after death. In Banaras, death is not a dead end; it is a passage, a transition, and a gateway. That is the raison d'être of Banaras, a unique and original phenomenon that has no precedent or antecedent. Why would anybody think up such a city? What means and modalities allow Banaras to attain such heights of existential resolution?

Banaras is at a rare confluence of unique geography, mythology, urban form, and cultural institutions. The city is located about 500 miles south of New Delhi. Here, the river Ganges changes her usual direction from southeast to flow back in a northerly direction pointing at her origins in the Himalayas, the sacred mountains for the Hindus. The river also takes a crescent profile, thus reconfirming the mythology according to which Lord Shiva, the presiding deity of the city, wears the moon on his head. The landscape on the west bank rises into three hillocks symbolizing the trident of Lord Shiva. The 'other bank' of the river is, in contrast, flat and plain.

In plan, the city is conceived as a half-circle. While the west bank of the Ganges has been inhabited for thousands of years and grown into a complex and congested city, the east bank of the river has been untouched and left totally undeveloped. The reasons have nothing to do with the city code. For the people of Banaras, the other bank of the semi-circular city resides in the 'other world' or heaven where people go after they die. They metaphorically cross the existential river of life to reach the eternal city of the other Banaras.

The City of Circuits

Banaras is a city of circuits. Devoted pilgrims carrying food, faith, and age-old stories circle the city following the sixteen codified sacred paths. The city is shaped like an onion: circuits within circuits leading to the centre, where the great temple of Lord Shiva resides. The form of the city is created, recreated, and reasserted as people trace the circuits in the footsteps of their elders.

The city is defined by neither the fort walls nor the boundaries, but by the *circuits of sacred circumambulation*. Instead of a map, these circuits around the city and its countless temples form a mandala in the minds of the devoted pilgrims, as they follow the routes chanting and reciting the myths and stories of the places that they come across. In this way, the pilgrims meditate the city and establish a correspondence between the city of the mind and the city of the material world. Ultimately, what people carry with them is the city of the mind, not the material city.

There is a distinction between the 'map reading' and the 'myth reading' images of the city. *The mandala of Banaras is a kinesthetic and mytho-poetic image that one forms by experiencing the city and traversing it ritually in space.* You may find your way by means of a map, but with a *mandala*, you *become* the mandala. Unlike a map, a mandala is a constellation of myths, legends, imagery, and sensory experiences. Through chants and processions, the city is constantly conserved, imagined, created, and revised. In the process of traversing the city, one existentially transforms one's own self into the city, which is thus projected as an image of one's self.

The Labyrinth

The city meets its river through a series of vivacious interfaces called ghats.[2] At the ghats, the momentum and the energy of the city is thwarted, such that the city's edge is forced into a rugged, fat, haphazard, incoherent, circumstantial mass of walls, facades, spires, towers, palaces, and platforms. The intersection of the city of steps and the labyrinthine Banaras is intense indeed.

If you are a pilgrim, you may take a walk from *Asi Ghat* in the south along the uneven terrain of the river's edge. What you come across may be the most profound and surreal, yet meaningful experience of the city and its life. All along the ghats unfolds the breadth of Banarasi life: a wreck can be seen capsized in the clay silt of the muddy bank; a half-naked mendicant standing waist-deep in the water in the company of a herd of imperturbable cows, water buffaloes, dilapidated umbrellas, peepal leaves, marigolds, roses, and lotuses that bloom around the ghats; well-versed Brahmins conducting funeral oblations for bereft families; a forest of lamp-holding bamboo sticks, a leaning temple capsized in the soft clay, a man in bangles, a rusty balustrade, a worn-off rope that once held the mightiest of the boats, and an abandoned tower house compete for the same place on the river's edge and in the viewer's mind.

If you are patiently and curiously walking along the ghats, you may also meet the vandalized stone plinths of the lofty palaces, a scale measuring the height of the Ganges when she floods in ecstasy, a blood-stained *Hanuman*,[3] a rusted bicycle, a group of mischievous kids flying kites, stray dogs, and *Gandharvas*.[4] Burning corpses with swirling smoke blacken the empty edifices. Still-hot ashes of a funeral pyre and a meditating yogi with a trident and saffron flag, chatting fishermen with tangled nets, graceful young girls and the floating body of a dead infant coexist simultaneously on the craggy steps of the ghats. You wonder what brings all these disparate things and phenomena together. As a stranger you may be baffled by the onslaught of images, things, and events, but the people of Banaras seem to be completely at home with the city. You wonder what gives them the power to reconcile their existential dilemmas with this labyrinthine city. You soon realize that, as in Italo Calvino's *Invisible Cities*, there is more to Banaras than meets the eye.

There the people, in an effort to experience the fullness and completeness of the world, have created certain beautiful fictions portrayed in an all enthralling mythology called *Kashi Purana*.[5] Such delightful myths as Parvathi's earrings,[6] Divodasa's ten-horse sacrifice,[7] a broken bow and a bride won, Indra with a diamond-edged lethal weapon,[8] and so on, situate the physical city amid a narrative and fictional city. The invisible and mythical population of Banaras by far surpasses the visible population and dominates the visible world.

In Banaras, everything has a story, a legend, or a myth. Like the morning mist, powerful mythologies shroud the city. *Storytelling is one recurrent way of structuring and sustaining Banaras. The sacred fiction sustains the city and its pursuits. Mythology is the form giver of the city.* Here, form undoubtedly follows immaculate fiction. There is the larger context of gods, heavens, nether worlds, demons, Gandharvas, sages, ascetics, and epics of mythical India; and there is the fiction of the city of Banaras that fits into the larger work of sacred literature. The secret of Banaras' integrity is neither in its magnificent spires nor in its vivacious ghats; the secret of Kashi is neither in its topography nor in its traditional structures alone. The real secret of Banaras is no secret at all: it is the way everything is interwoven into a huge system of sacred fiction.

People come here to die. And behold, they are only too happy to die! It is said that even a dog can be blessed with liberation if it dies within the bounds of *Panch Kroshi* – the largest circumambulatory circuit that defines the city limits. Even if one has led a miserable life, death in Banaras is said to liberate one of all the agony. The invisible signs on thousands of temples, ghats, and houses in Banaras tacitly declare this eternal bargain through an ingenious epistemology of space. At *Manikarnika* Ghat you could see scores of people of both sexes and all castes and ages unfettered by death! At Banaras, death, the biggest human fear and enigma, has been tamed and domesticated by the city and its mythologies. With death, all of your sins are forgiven by virtue of your being in the city of Banaras. Existence is eternal and immortal, and therefore sustainable in Banaras.

People in Banaras learn storytelling right from the time when, under the moonlit sky, their mothers sing lullabies about Lord Rama; the time they play in the streets, shrines, and steps of the ghats, and contemplate the mysterious emptiness of the other bank. When they grow up, they see the whole world as a beautiful work of fiction: a work where everything is well composed and under the control of the author. The author is at the centre, and there are a million authors inhabiting Banaras, visiting and imagining it. It is all imagination, powerful and enthralling. For the people of Banaras, the whole universe is replete with life; there is nothing inanimate or lifeless in it. The poststructuralist observation on the *death of the author* serves as an excellent comparison between the cities of infrastructure and the city of Banaras. Albeit with a different inclination and intent, Camus made a brilliant observation that reinforces the notion of humanizing the universe: 'If man realized that the universe, like him, can love and suffer, he would be reconciled.'⁹

In the rugged undulation of the masculine landforms, people of Banaras see the trident of Lord Shiva or *Mount Meru*. In the feminine curves of the sweeping crescent of the Ganges, they see a caring mother. The sky crowded with lazy clouds is a theatre where, perhaps, in the shadow of a mountain, a demon drinks *Sura*, the eternal drink. The emptiness of the east bank is an unfolded blankness set against the crammed tightness of the stony complexity of the west bank. *Place-making is myth-making: the place creates the myth, and the myth in turn creates the place. What distinguishes Banaras from other cities is that it duly recognizes and addresses existential dilemmas.*

Thus, in Banaras a grand and unique urban paradigm reconciles our existential dilemmas through a marriage of architecture, urbanism, and narrative means of dwelling. Banaras teaches us that fiction is a powerful mode of imagining, building, and living in our cities; that mythologies and other fictions are essential to enliven the inanimate world of things and prosaic infrastructure. The existential absurdity of life and death are reconciled through the architecture of the city. When such a reconciliation takes place spatially, cities and architecture become sustainable.

Notes

1 Nanao Sasaki, *Break the Mirror* (San Francisco: North Point Press, 1987), 47.
2 A ghat is a stepped interface between a river and land.
3 Hanuman is a Hindu mythological god with the characteristics of a monkey.
4 Gandharvas are the heavenly musicians in Hindu mythology.
5 Kashi Purana means the sacred history of the city of Banaras told through various myths and legends.
6 Parvathi is the wife of Lord Shiva.
7 Divodasa was one of the first kings of Banaras.
8 Indra, originally a primary god during Indus Valley Civilization, is the ruler of all Gods.
9 Albert Camus, *The Myth of Sisyphus* (New York: Vintage, 1955), 13.

26 Louis Armstrong International Airport: A Post-Katrina Meditation

RICHARD CARLSON

The sun unfurls its noon fury in the Creole heat of late summer. One walks slowly over bare tarmac with the wavy mirage traces of jet fuel evaporating from the baked runway. Your eyes must squint to distinguish actual form from hallucination in the gaseous blur. The mugginess is palpable and steams up from the bayou to create a state of perpetual humidity; you strain to wipe away the sweat dripping from your brow on the balmy Louisiana day.

a city under pressure of heat and moisture

Steam condenses on your tongue as you try to speak, but because you are walking quickly you think again and feel better in the short term just to shield your nose and hold your breath as the stench of rotting waste reaches you. That which was cast off by mortal flesh, and that once consumed by human mutely decay, lie in steaming piles, and reek in the clammy gulf coast breeze; the waste having not been removed for over two weeks.

a city under pressure of decomposition

The concourse that once facilitated the bustle of life in the hyper-modernist fast lane was used during the last fortnight as a triage station for sorting out the ill and as a morgue for the dead. Sprawling on strands of cots strung out along the terminal's vast expanse of grimy marble floor and close-cropped carpet lay the injured and poor black folk of the Ninth Ward and St Bernard's Parish, making themselves as comfortable as they could in front of the vacant ticket counters, gated newspaper stands, empty coffee joints, and miscellaneous jazz paraphernalia.

Transformed from a place that housed mere travelers into a hall of the wholly dispossessed is Louis Armstrong International Airport; but what else would one expect? The child of a New Orleans prostitute, Satchmo was already abandoned and then arrested at the age of six.

What else would one expect from history in the deep South, only now being staged within the facade of an international airport? The airport, the bastion of globalization that makes planetary culture possible now houses the distraught and dispossessed, the discontented and dying of America's third world; hermetically sealed within its own environs.

a city under pressure of history

But there are no commercial flights taking off today, just Blackhawk helicopters and C-130s involved in rescue and reconstruction. The flow of commerce has been halted, pre-empted by 120 mile per hour winds and the flood. The forces of the market that once built this airport reduced to a trickle, this port city and hub of world commerce now just the gleam in the eye of Halliburton or the Shaw Group contemplating the future potential of capital ventures and returns at more than 20 per cent.

a city at the mercy of military industrial carpetbaggers

One walks on to meet the air traffic control manager whose dishevelled tower is now in disarray and overflowing with controllers sleeping on air mattresses in front of sophisticated radar arrays and advanced navigation systems. The technology that made this airport possible is temporarily out of service and gathering dust. The wide cherry tabletops of conference rooms where local procedures for approach control and the divvying up of airspace were once decided now served as the platform to place K rations, stale coffee, and half-eaten doughnuts.

ratiocination and technology at the mercy of a southern tempest

All the technology in the world could not put a bandage on the damage done by the storm and flood to get operations back to normal sooner. The warm Gulf currents that fed Katrina were only heated further by the carbon waste spewed from oil refineries and industry along the coast. Already no match for a category four hurricane, the dredging of swamps by oil companies allowed salt water to seep back into the once-fertile wetlands, which now yield up more than 100 acres a day to the sea. The levees of the mighty river denied needed silt to restore the earth under this grand old city, which allowed it to nestle safely between the Mississippi and Pontchartrain.

ratiocination and technology at the mercy of blow-back

Those bound in the cycle of history of domination, of the eternal recurrence of the underclass, are those most affected, but what else would one expect, here in the deep South? where burnt crosses still smolder in the charcoal heart of Dixie, and can suddenly violently alight in an inferno; into which we begin our descent from the French Quarter. This is a city that could just as easily burn while being martyred for the sins of a nation, but this is the city in the time of flood.

Here now reside those forced to the fringes of our society, those who live below sea-level, the ones who do not partake of the prosperity of this Port economy; of Midwestern grain harvest barges, transoceanic container ships, and Gulf oil rigs. These folks are too far removed from the mainstream to be concerned with the storm's effect on falling world markets sparked by the rising price of gasoline, because they had no vehicles to evacuate the area in the first place. They do, however, still need food, and the shopkeepers have all left for higher ground.

Already the 200 billion dollar reconstruction being planned has passed legislation and funnels funds through the lobbyist and technocrat directly into the coffers of the good ol' boys and multinationals. Yet, the same legislation eliminated the Davis-Bacon

Act and the minimum wage of the construction labourer. To be rebuilt yet again, but now on the backs of descendents of slaves of the Americas, both North and South. But now a tax cut and a debit card with a two thousand dollar limit will have to serve in place of forty acres and a mule.

carpetbaggers conspiring with technology

Those who own the technology and resources to begin construction, who are the masters of calculating the market forces, who have the ear of the vice-president will come out ahead in this disaster. Old low-lying neighbourhoods will be bulldozed and then gentrified, those shining glass and steel structures will gleam for a new class of entrepreneurs who will profit from the Reconstruction. New infrastructure will replace the rotting old wooden front porches of houses built during the Depression. Law and order will be haphazardly restored. The airport will have its waste removed, the concourses cleared of patients, the military will depart its taxiways, it will be retooled and its technology will reanimate the bayou economy to once again fuel the oil gluttony of the global village, even as the corps of engineers still struggle to halt the progress of the encroaching wetlands.

technology along with equality and justice sinking slowly in the ratiocination of Cajun swamp land

CULTURE, COMMUNICATION, AND MEDIA

ANNA MUNSTER

Images of the World, Inscription of What?

The whole world is covered with medium resolution imagery and terrain data.[1]

On the screen, and at a variable distance of 10,000 km to (occasionally) three metres, the world approaches and stretches out in front of me, zoomable, pannable, and at my fingertips. Using a broadband connection, I can quickly traverse its patchy terrain that, from the extreme distance of a satellite view, seems like agricultural variation. On closer inspection these colour differentials reveal a quilted *zeitgeist* of composite low and high resolution image captures. I am traversing the territory that is Google Earth (GE), a world that can be accessed from my laptop in my bedroom, or from my workstation in my office, and which, increasingly, people send to me as sets of searchable coordinates in emails to let me know where they are geographically located.

In 2004 the Google Corporation acquired Keyhole Corporation, a digital mapping firm with a software package that gave interactive access to a massive database of satellite imagery and terrain information of the earth. Like so many events in the history and present of technologies, this acquisition did not signal technical innovation per se. Geographical information systems (GISs) experienced a period of major growth and uptake during the 1980s and were already being incorporated into online user-accessible interfaces throughout the late 1990s. What is significant about the Keyhole acquisition is that Google – a search-engine-based company with up to 99 per cent market share in some Western countries – was the buyer. In less than a year after the purchase of Keyhole, Google released a plugin for its search engine that allowed limited online access to the satellite and terrain information database and a free, downloadable, combined 3D mapping and search tool. Significantly, the acquisition enabled Google to fully realize itself as a massively distributed online user experience through an increasing cartographic trend in visual culture. This experience simultaneously involves laying claim to a kind of auto-poesis in the renaming of this experience, 'Google Earth.'

I wonder about the distributed yet shared nature of the GE experience as I virtually 'fly over' the vast expanse of the U.S. Midwest offered up to me onscreen. Once, in the late 1980s, I took a Greyhound bus from Nashville to Kansas City. Then, the coach window offered continuous eye-level vistas of yellow fields for miles on end. On the screen now, instead, the ground is green-grey and jostles against neat squares of blurred brown. With only travel memories to tie these brief interactive stopovers to any experiential knowledge of the terrain, I switch my onscreen window to Google Map's 'hybrid' view. The 3D satellite images are now overlaid with an arterial sketching of roads, place names, and state border data. I click one level closer – now zooming down to 500 metres – and suddenly an entire square of mottled green and brown is replaced by 50 per cent matte grey, cutting across Route 99 north of Chautauqua near the Oklahoma-Kansas state border. At 200 metres, my browser brings up a dialogue box informing me that 'we're sorry, but we don't have imagery at this zoom level for this region.' Unsurprisingly, the satellite images of Afghanistan at 500 metres form a relatively even composite view uncomplicated by missing greyed-out squares. This is unsurprising on the one hand because many of the unnamed sources of GE's satellite and aerial images are likely to be commercial buy-ups of data from military satellites. On the other hand, GE's terrain data for Afghanistan – without which a sense of the region as unnavigable prevails – is altogether missing. But this is only a temporary situation. At some time in the future, I will return to both Chautauqua and Afghanistan and their imaging will have been updated.

I want to ask two key questions throughout this essay about Google Earth. First, what kind of image or image set does it render for us in relation to contemporary information culture? Its updating, mutating, and compositing set of terrain and satellite images is often referred to as a 'virtual globe.'[2] Should we therefore understand GE's representational status in terms of a simulated world? This may indeed be a fairly accessible way to begin thinking about the GE experience as something that takes its place in a long line of virtual environments from flight simulators through to fully interactive entertainment and aesthetic experiences such as the CAVE immersive virtual reality environment. Indeed, Google Earth could be thought, pursuing such analysis, to be the ultimate such simulation – a multiuser cyberspace map of the world that is becoming the reference point for the Earth's actual geography.

The second question follows from this and pertains to its status as an online environment. Should Google Earth be considered more than a map, more than imaging or even simulation of the world and instead as a shared, networked environment? In many other multiuser online tools and environments such as games, sociable media (e.g., MySpace), and web publishing (e.g., blogs and wikis) the presence and activity of others constitutes the experience to be had and spurs further development of these environments. The term 'sociable media' has been used to think through the participatory and networked nature of such spaces.[3] Is Google Earth a type of sociable medium rather than a set of images of the world?

There is an underlying problem that drives me to ask this latter question following on from the first. I am interested in unfolding contemporary relationships between the aesthetic and the social dimensions within information and networked cultures. Much of the excitement about sociable media has revolved around the potential for online networks to be understood as, or indeed to be, emergent social and institutional formations. To date, text-based forms such as blogs or chat and networking environments such as Friendster have not been image-oriented or visually rich. It is certainly the case that image sharing and networking exist through online interfaces and tools such as Flickr. But what seems extraordinary about Google Earth is that it is a complete visual environment *at the same time* as it is an almost total imaging of the world. If Google Earth is to be thought of as sociable media then its virtual globe status may elevate it to the ultimate in sociable-virtual mediation. Google Earth might be thought of as a convergence of image and sociality where new transformations in visual practice, use, and understanding are caught up with or are co-emergent with transformations and experiments around new socialities.

However, there is something very striking about the GE experience that needs to be considered alongside this meshing of the social and the aesthetic as a potentially rich set of vectors for information culture. It seems to have gone unremarked that while it is possible to 'fly' around from location to location using Google Earth or Maps, this traversal is remarkably solitary. There are buildings, tanks, trees, and monuments represented in the data sets but never any sense of cohabitation of the environment with others.[4] This distinguishes Google Earth, again, from other online environments such as blogs, social software networking and tools, as well as gaming, where the presence of and relation to others (albeit sometimes homogenised and somewhat forced) assume primary status. The GE environment is one in which there are many individual users in full flight but no dimension of the social within its visual space.

The 'population' of Google Earth instead resides elsewhere *and adjacent to* the virtual globe. An online Google Earth Community site, which runs as a public members list blog functions as a beta-testing space, discussion forum about Google Earth, and a kind of repository for quirky 'citings' of visual data located and browsable via the GE facility.[5] In addition, there a number of unofficial GE sites – Google Earth Hacks, for instance – as well as a host of creative deployments of and experiments with its visualizations.[6] The point I want to make here may seem obvious, but its implication is quite profound – the sociability of Google Earth as an exemplar of distributed, networked media lies *outside* the actual visual environment and aesthetic experience of traversing the GE globe. What I want to suggest, then, is that the relations between aesthetics and sociality that are thrown up by Google Earth span an aporia that is axiomatic to contemporary networked cultures. This aporia is produced and reproduced throughout networked media and relationships: the offer of both an aesthesia of hyper-individuated and solitary, nodal experience and the potential for new forms of collective practice, formation, and enunciation.

The question then becomes one of how Google Earth negotiates and is used to negotiate this aporia. I want to suggest that we must understand the operations and functionality of Google Earth as part of the larger Google enterprise. Insofar as we consider the GE virtual globe as part of the greater sociotechnical ensemble that is Google (in fact, the post-Fordist creative industry corporation), it operates to create an imaginary for a particular kind of world that wants to propel the density of population and its attendant myriad of socialities outside of, or at least adjacent to itself. Google Earth therefore produces a world and its peoples as a database of individual users initiating and retrieving their individual inquiries bereft of sociality. What looks like a potential autopoetic formation – the self-organizing production of a world or system through recursive interactions with an (online) environment – tends, in the GE case, towards self-enclosure.[7]

Perhaps it is easier, safer, and ultimately less chaotic to negotiate contemporary socio-aesthetic currents by overinvesting in the sublime beauty of the power and tools of data visualization. This would seem to go some way to explaining the uncontained excitement of the Google Corporation in its capacity to now wrap the entire Earth in imagery. And certainly it is this barefaced beauty and power of visualisation (rather than the adjacent sociability this might also spur) that is promoted by Google as the primary characteristic of Google Earth. Interestingly, GE's capacity to 'drill down' to surface level with its super-visuality has been the focus of much international outcry and consternation over Google's virtual globe. The issues of heightened visibility and inaccuracy have surfaced as twin responses in both individual user experience and national reaction to Google Earth and Google Maps. On the one hand, governments from India, Thailand, and South Korea have expressed concern over the compromise of national security that such high-resolution imaging of military and political installations could encourage.[8] The implication here, then, is that Google Earth, is deadly accurate in its rendering of visual data and that, coupled with the accessibility and popularity of Google as a search engine, such heightened visibility can make certain geographical regions extremely vulnerable.

Does this augmentation of sight in fact increase visual accuracy? Does the ability to see 'targets' using something like Google Earth actually provide greater visibility for either terrorists or the amateur cartographer? In his 1988 film, *Images of the World and the Inscription of War,* the German director Harun Farocki visually explores Paul Virilio's thesis of the increasing imbrication of military and viewing technologies from the late nineteenth century onward. In a series of scenes repeated throughout the film, Farocki fills the frame with aerial photography by Allied reconnaissance missions throughout the Second World War, of German munitions factories that were targeted for bombing. In the very same photographs Farocki shows us that there are details of buildings occupied by Nazi concentration camp officials and lines of the camp inmates queuing up to be gassed. Why did the Allies not use such information to bomb the SS in their buildings and liberate the inmates, the narrator's voiceover persistently asks? The answer is intimated by Farocki as the film unfolds: the military eye only sees what it has been trained to target. Increased visibility is not commensurate with the capacity to see accurately, if that is not what the military field of perception requires. We should not, then, take the appearance of Google Earth or even the rise of digital cartographic applications as evidence that the whole Earth is becoming transparently visible.

It is clear that, despite the heightened visibility Google Earth facilitates, it nonetheless does not offer us an image *of* the world. Or, rather, its coverage of the world by imaging data should not be understood in terms of greater indexicality. Many user sites and blogs that comment on or reuse GE imagery reveal that unevenness of vision is part of its aesthetics. In March 2006, just after Google released an update of higher resolution images of Germany, a user posts: 'I haven't been on GE for a week or so and was today surprised to find the resolution all over Germany was less patchy. But the area near Munich had been replaced by much older data. The building I work in is now apparently a building site.'9

Google acknowledges that its imaging and terrain data are only accurate within a three-year period and updated on a rolling basis.10 The GE visual experience is strangely situated between abrupt temporal glitches and near real-time user interaction. Its varying image resolutions can mean that the stitching together of image sets feels grafted rather than smooth. And this does not account for the further bumpiness occurring when shifts in place marks are created as the database is updated and the image sets are re-composited together differently.

Unlike the high-resolution and real-time experience of being in an online multiuser gaming environment, the GE experience is far from experientially seamless. This is so much the case that the mapping accomplished by Google's virtual Earth crushes any remaining vestiges of a belief that cartography operates as direct visual correspondence with the world. But neither is Google Earth a simulation preceding the physical Earth, destabilizing the latter's referentiality. Rather, it is a stretch of the image – the image's deformation – to provide coverage. Google Earth is the image as purely visible data, at the cost of any claims to representational purity on the part of the (digital) image. How are we to understand this rather strange operation of the digital image in Google Earth, and how do engagement with, and experience of, its visual environment have consequences for our contemporary *experience* of sociality and aesthetics in networked media and relationships? Although Google Earth is not an image or map of the world, its imaging operations nevertheless signal something important *about* the world it is making and which many users of distributed media are attempting to inhabit and redeploy.

A Wired and Windowless World

The empty centre of neoliberalism is sociality.11

I want to make it clear that I am not pursuing a constructivist reading of the Google Earth venture. Critical cartographic theorists such as Martin Dodge, Rob Kitchen, and

Jeremy Crampton argue that maps are particular representations of the world.[12] Mapping thus conceived is a mode of cultural and/or aesthetic image-making that simultaneously classifies spatial relations and (re)inscribes the sociopolitical interests at work in those modes of classification. Google Earth is neither representation in the realist tradition of the image nor in the constructivist sense, where representations sequester historically or culturally specific world-views. It is certainly the case that certain cartographic biases – higher resolution imaging of U.S. buildings, for example – have been discerned as endemic to the GE data sets. Yet we hardly need deconstruction anymore to assist with interpreting the national interests embedded in Google Earth. Competing national interests quite openly proclaim the cultural biases implicit in its visualizations. In June 2006, for example, the French government launched its own mapping tool and database, Geoportal, designed to 'correct' the American 'representation' of the world. As French President Jacques Chirac implied, the right of access to visual information is culturally specific and intimately linked to the exercise of nationally identified democratic governance: "'With Galileo (the European Union satellite navigation system), with the mobile telephone, services linked to global positioning will develop a lot," Chirac said. "It is also about democracy because our citizens have the right to know all the facts about the environment."'[13]

Although it may be a relief to know that Google does not, in fact, have the whole world covered with its imagery, nevertheless there is something supranational about the aesthetics of Google Earth; that is, what it signals about the relation between globalization and the production of a certain kind of distributed aesthetics. The concept of distributed aesthetics can help us to locate and think through the sea of emergent experiences that form as we use online and networked modes of working, creating, and collaborating with media and each other.[14] But distributed aesthetics is not simply the global circulation of images (or any other sensory material) through networked media. There may be many modes of distribution and many different kinds of networks performing the labour required for pushing media and matter around.

What kind of exemplar, then, does the distributed GE experience offer for distributed aesthetics? Rather than a representation of the world from a particular cultural or national perspective, or even a specifically located mode of representation, Google Earth presents us with an image horizon. I mean here to conjure up a link to the populist understanding of the concept of an event horizon. Event horizons are commonly associated with the concept in astrophysics of the black hole; they are the space-time boundary, relative to an observer, of a black hole. Beyond the event horizon any events that occur cannot be detected by or do not affect the observer. Hence, light emitted beyond the space-time boundary of a black hole never reaches the observer, and whatever passes through the horizon from the side on which the observer is located cannot be detected again. Google Earth's solitary *and* distributed mapping experience produces the image of the world as an ever-receding horizon for the user. Beyond this boundary – always shifting, updating, and remapping itself – the effects of *making* the world as a potentially massively distributed social project *never reach the isolated user* in the GE environment. There is emptiness at the centre of the GE experience: the hole left by the evacuation of sociality from within this online environment.

Jeremy Crampton has argued that distributed GISs share the twin characteristics of being both dispersed and dispensable.[15] But the GE experience dispenses the image of the world on a highly individuated or customized basis, as is the propensity of the entire Google enterprise. Hence, the observer/user becomes the locative point from and for which Google Earth events occur. In quite a simplistic way, then, it would be possible to argue that using Google Earth to map the world produces a kind of expansive visual horizon for the user. But this occurs at the expense of all that cannot be observed beyond the image horizon: the capacity to experience the world as one populated by networked, distributed others. If we do not see any others while we are flying over Google Earth it is because the dimension of others – sociality – is beyond the GE image horizon. In some respects, the GE user resembles the Leibnizian monad, whose windowless perspective on the world nonetheless produces a universe of beings as a multitudinous series of intensively 'illuminated' individuations. The visual field of the monad is turned in on itself, lighting up from within rather than from a source in the external world. Yet, as Gilles Deleuze has suggested, the Baroque monad only exists relative to the external universe, its series limit; a limit that is constituted cosmologically, according to Leibniz, through the concept of pre-established harmony.[16] Aesthetically, too, the lit interiors of Baroque paintings emerge through chiaroscuro effects, wrought as series of shadows and darkened backgrounds that unfold into light. The monad depends upon a constitutive outside, even if it cannot see this outside in its totality. Google Earth inverts this relationship by summoning the world into existence on behalf of the monad/user. The Baroque world depends on the monad and yet equally expands beyond it. But the Google Earth monad does not appear to constitutively need the outside world. Strictly speaking, however, there is no dual isolation of monad and world in the Google universe understood in its broader socioeconomic dimensions. The data queries generated by individual users of Google services are accessible. Google, the corporation, can access this 'search data,' which includes IP address information linkable to email accounts if users have 'Gmail,' Google's email service. Data queries are routinely stored by Google, which analyses data patterns to reshape its services. Hence the 'outside' has access to the 'inside,' but the insides never see directly what their outsides are up to. Another way of thinking about this would be to propose that Google Earth users are folded into the (closed) autopoetic production of Google and cannot structurally couple with each other to produce different exteriorities. The separation of visual environment from sociality – of Google Earth from GE Community – holds apart the possibility of forging new aesthetic experiences via collective enunciation. As we continue traversing the GE experience we shall see why both inversion and separation are immanent to the entire Google project.

For now, I want to return to the issue of what kind of exemplar the GE experience offers for distributed aesthetics. I will suggest that this is one in which the compass of sociality as conflicting and anabranching – as the relational outside, as the perturbing environment to the solipsistic user – does not enter. This, of course, is not the whole story of distributed aesthetics; as I hope to indicate later there are many projects and emergent network formations in which a vigorous and lively sociality figures as the condition of their possibility and of their distribution. But Google Earth is most importantly an Earth coming into being as a result of a particular orientation – the creative networked corporation – the horizon of which binds its users against the event of sociality.

In the late 1980s Margaret Thatcher famously proclaimed in a *Woman's Own* magazine interview that 'there is no such thing as society. There are individual men and women, and there are families.'[17] Google Earth is the ever-receding horizon of such a society-free world. Importantly, Google Earth is much more keyed into the core business of the Google enterprise than many other Google services. GE's core activity is to perform image and terrain data searches to meet requests from individual users, emulating the very activity that powers Google – search. At present, this is only emulation, because the Google Earth databases are large but closed sets rather than, say, the open data sets of Web pages crawled by the primary Google search engine. But maybe this accounts for Google Earth's popularity over many other Google services that have not proved so successful. Google's social networking tool Orkut, launched in 2004, for example, has to date failed to compete with others such as MySpace, particularly in the U.S. market.[18]

I want to propose a stronger conception of Google Earth than simply compensation for the failure of the Google enterprise to fully diversify into the arena of sociable media, however. It has been something of a mainstay of communication theory that communications media are constitutive of community. This viewpoint has been consolidated by a quasi-ethnographic and social sciences approach to investigating online and virtual communities, from the early 1990s work of Howard Rheingold through to more recent musings on distributed communities.[19] Does it follow, then, that part of this community-building activity facilitated by online communications also involves a kind of collective imagining and imaging of community? In other words, does distributed aesthetics fulfil the function, at the collective level of online and networked formations, of what Arjun Appardurai has referred to as 'self-imagining as an everyday social project'?[20]

If this is the case, then Google Earth resolutely flies in the face of affirming the constitutive nature of the relation between communications and community. Or rather, it dislocates the production of online community to a space external to its visual field – into the Google Earth Community. The GE environment remains unpopulated by the unruly meshwork of sociality. Hence, the image, stretched and deformed as it is within Google Earth, is nonetheless purified of social relations. In a sense, the GE environment and experience are the imaginary of a coming community – the community

of perpetual and solitary foragers, constituted through the erasure of the messy relationality of social life.

Google Earth and sociable media, it seems, may not be so far removed from each
other in this respect. Sociable media – clustering around the rhetoric of friendship
networks – operate through an ever-expanding quest for connectivity, contacts, and
'buddies.' They are desperate for, and desperately dependent on, popularity. Google's
infamous reconstitution of search as a popularity contest via its PageRank algorithm
associates it with social networking media via the network economy of linking. Sociable media per se do not pose an alternative, outside of, or limit to, Google Earth.
Thus far they have tended to construe the social in similar ways as a field of pre-indi-
viduated nodes searching for link value. But sociality also implies sets of relations
that cannot be negotiated away by reducing these to the level of individual or family
(nodal) units, as Thatcher sought to do for neoliberal sociality. Collectivities are difficult and chaotic forms of organization; conflict, failure, and dissipation are as much a
part of their interrelations as are growth and creativity. It remains an open proposition whether sociable media can become constitutive of new networked, social formations. In part, this possibility will turn on the ability to move from sociability to
sociality and to make space for the labour of collectively producing, negotiating, and
enunciating aesthetic and representational strategies. It is precisely the labour of
constituting meaning in the online world – through discourse, through peer-to-peer
sharing, through 'hacking' GE's visualization – that is displaced, off to the side and
outside the GE environment.

User, Usability, Utility

Usability comes first even if a site is not trying to sell anything.[21]

As mentioned above, I have suggested that Google Earth is intimately tied to the core
of Google's endeavour to make the world a 'searchable' one. We must turn, then, to
mapping out the relation of the GE visual searchable environment to the underlying
imperative of search. Search rather than sociability is the instrument by which Google
has developed. What I also want to suggest is that by participating in the search
imperative, Google Earth blocks the potential for sociability to reach out beyond its
own atomistic, nodal event horizon towards the indeterminacy of new social formations. This is because search is configured within the Google enterprise in utilitarian
terms. By this I mean the kind of utilitarianism that pervades socioeconomic neoliberal and conservative visions of the contemporary world. Search as an endeavour of
the creative networked corporation is intricately bound up with a world-view in
which sociality can only ever be understood as the aggregate outcome of individual
transactions – including the transactions of querying and retrieving information or
data. Search has also become a core business within the reconfigured Web service
economy of the post dot.com era. But if we are to look at search as Google's core

business, we need likewise to understand the relation of GE's visuality to the rationalization of online cultures as we have moved towards networked corporatism.

Around the end of the 1990s, usability discourse dovetailed with Web development. Jakob Nielsen's mantra of pared-down text-based websites that were easy to navigate became de rigueur for serious information-based online corporations. Pitching an 'engineering' against an 'artistic' approach, Nielsen convinced a swathe of Web designers that their gratuitous graphics had to go, to serve the 'user' who desired straightforward navigability. He also landed a consultancy to clean up the software he considered the chief offender against Web usability – Flash. Commissioning the Nielsen Gorman group to conduct a usability study of Flash MX in 2002, the software company Macromedia implicitly steered Flash software away from its association with superficial and superfluous presentation and content and married it to the common denominators of Nielsen's usability standards.

Something was missing, however, from this leaner, post-dot.com online environment in which the Web began not simply to rationalize but also to shift into what we have come to know as 'Web 2.0.' This changed environment – a shift in online economies similar to the global economic shift towards service-based industries – lacked 'fun.' Out of this tussle between usability and play, the Google search enterprise launched itself on the world. Although Google's search-engine architecture was in beta development from late 1998, its characteristic childlike and slimline logo on the website's splash page, surrounded by a spacious sea of clear white calmness, had become its brand by September 1999. Google was perfectly placed to sail through and indeed capitalize on the dot.com crash of the early 2000s. This is not simply because of the nature of its core service – search – but because it fused the usability ethos with the play aesthetic.

Google Web design has retained an ongoing faith in usability rhetoric insofar as both its website's splash and returned search result pages have continued to be text-based. The addition of Google's advertising program 'AdWords' in 2001, as small text advertisements semantically connected to key search words and appearing on the righthand side of returned search queries, hardly detracted from usability standards. In fact, Nielsen himself endorsed the text-based nature of Google's click-through advertising as an unobtrusive way of both navigating information and satisfying the user's parallel 'desire' for online consumerism.[22] In a sense, the GE image-based initiative mitigates against the lean usability of Google's textcentric world. Although the GE experience can be understood in terms of the core Google activity of search – and is frequently used in this way by real estate and travel agents – something else is happening. As suggested by the adjunct formation of the GE Community and other online uses of GE maps, the GE experience has become something of an end in itself. Perhaps, then, Google Earth shares something with massively multiplayer online role-play games (MMPORGs) in that it builds a Google-like space simply to hang around in, beyond the instrumental or goal-directed activity of search.

Much of the ethnographic research into MMPORGs, however, suggests that spaces for hanging around in within games tend to be designed or gamer-added specifically for interaction and sociability.[23] The actual Google Earth environment is neither sociable in this sense nor a space for welcoming the social as a disjunctive, chaotic dimension. Rather, it resolves the tension of online subjectivation, caught in a recurring oscillation between search/instrumentality and sociability/play. And it comes at this resolution via a different route. On the one hand, we might think of search less as an activity than as the *activation of utility*. Like a computer system, Google uses search as a kind of utility program to perform what it perceives as the tasks most needed by users. On the other hand, utility is a term that comes to us from economics, indeed from utilitarianism, which has become the mainstay of neoliberal economic thinking and rhetoric. Utility in this sense is a measure of the satisfaction gained from consumption – usually of commodities – but in the Web 2.0 context also the consumption of online services. Furthermore, if we understand the Google *zeitgeist* in terms of both computational and economic utility we can see that search *usability* rates highly as a measure of Google *utility*: 'Google's mission is to deliver the best search experience on the Internet by making the world's information universally accessible and useful.'[24] In a way this solves the issue of the unsatisfying leanness of Nielsen's usability standards. Usability in the Google universe transmutes into utility, and utility is sustained as both a measure of search satisfaction and as a utilitarian outcome (the best search results) in which the best possible solution is provided for the greatest number of users.

In the context of this transmutation of usability into utilitarianism via utility, the GE experience needs to remain fundamentally solitary in nature and not segue into sociability. Google Earth is not just the best possible experience of flying over the world but the outcome of the individual user's preferences in producing such an experience for her or his own consumption. Uncannily, there is in fact a moral framework that already supports this kind of world: preference utilitarianism. Although I do not want to suggest that the Google enterprise developed with a knowledge of preference utilitarianism in mind, it is nevertheless the case that preference utilitarianism perfectly describes the intersection of contemporary computation, neoliberal culture, and the networked corporation. At the same time, the preferential aspect admits the personal back into this mix, without allowing 'the people' to emerge as a transrelational collectivity.

Historically, preference utilitarianism developed from the 1950s onward as a framework for moral (rather than economic) thinking through the work of British philosophers such as R.M. Hare.[25] Its basic methodology is to work to satisfy the requirement of universalization. Taking into account all possible alternative preferences that might deter acting on the rightness of a given proposition will seemingly make the terms of a proposition universally moral. This 'check and balance' approach to the relation between proposition and action is supposed to analytically refine moral imperatives so that they can be acted on. Hare's thinking involved bringing universal conjectures up against prescriptive refutations – the universal against the particular (individual) – to arrive, finally, at propositions that hold morally under any circumstances. The proposition must, therefore, be the kind on which one universally prefers to act, having taken into account all other preferences that might change one's desire to act. Preference utilitarianism has the peculiar flavour of marrying the contingency of desire with the indifference of logic. It is this quality that is likewise characteristic of the three-way marriage between computational culture, neoliberalism, and networked corporatism as they align to produce creative, postindustrial information culture. This union intensifies the conjunction of choice (preference), algorithmic (logic), and networked flows.

Utilitarianism concentrates on the consequences that are produced by actions; moral propositions can be arrived at retroactively as those that lead to the best consequences for all. It is easy to see how utilitarianism and neoliberalism intersect through the belief in the idea that deregulated markets produce the best kind of economic and social formation via the mere satisfaction of consumption. But, somewhat ironically, it is less clear how to configure the individual consumer and his or her *preferences* within the statistical averaging of 'the best' to which the mechanism of the free market inevitably gives rise. Preference utilitarianism attempts to resolve the tussle between the universal and the singular, 'the good' and personal satisfaction, by producing the universal as the aggregate outcome of the satisfaction of preferences.

This is precisely the logic of Google search. The best search results are those that take into account the preference of all other web pages (or their developers) to link to another page. Although Google does not make a moral claim based on the preferential logic it follows, it is interesting that it nonetheless deploys neoliberal rhetoric to explain the way it organises information:

> Google interprets a link from Page A to Page B as a 'vote' by Page A for Page B. Google assesses a page's importance by the votes it receives.
>
> Google also analyzes the pages that cast the votes. Votes cast by pages that are themselves 'important' weigh more heavily and help to make other pages important. Important, high-quality pages receive a higher PageRank and are ordered or ranked higher in the results. Google's technology uses the collective intelligence of the web to determine a page's importance. Google does not use editors or its own employees to judge a page's importance.[26]

Here we have an algorithm – seemingly impartial and the very stuff of logic – that sorts and orders the preferences of all Web users to arrive at the best possible solution for the individual searcher. Through this logic both the collective aggregation of the Web (the market, the universal) and the subjectivation of the solitary, satisfied user (the consumer, the individuated) are held together without ever having to pass through the field of conflicting and differentiated social relations. Google Earth, then, can be understood as the aesthetic rendering of the logic of Google search. It produces the sensory and affective experience of filtering a database world computationally – a solitary yet satisfying mode of engagement. Henceforth there really is no society; there are only users, algorithms and aggregates.

Will Google Eat Itself?

> To treat algorithms as pure repetition would be to overlook the inventive variation embodied in every algorithm.[27]

In posing the question of the relation between the aesthetic and the social in contemporary networked cultures, I have suggested that Google Earth functions as more than a map but less than a simulation or representation. Rather, the GE experience both emerges from and is constitutive of the creative economy of networked corporatism; it is a particular mediation of the aporia of hyperindividuation and sociability thrown up by distributed media and networks. But as I also signaled earlier, this is only one mode for thinking distributed aesthetics. In this last section I want to turn to the arena of art practices to seek alternative ways of working through this aporia. There is not space here to deal with a survey of Google-specific media arts. Nor can I broaden the field further by investigating a swathe of fascinating, critical, and tactical cartographic trends in contemporary networked aesthetics. I will therefore only gesture towards two sets of work that outline certain strategies and approaches to moving outside the self-enclosing image horizon that bounds the Google universe. At the very least, the emergence of these kinds of practices testifies to the production of alternative, distributed aesthetics. Additionally, I hope to suggest that whereas the logic of utilitarianism is bound to repetition of itself as 'the best' and 'the good,' the potential for change can be discerned as the algorithmic logic of computation flows divergently throughout networked cultures.

Google Will Eat Itself (GWEI) is the title of a piece of collaborative network art produced by the Austrian-based duo UBERMORGEN.COM in collaboration with Alessando Ludovico and Paulo Cirio.[28] The piece piggybacks on Google's AdWords, the scheme that has provided the company with a lucrative source of revenue and made it a major financial success of Web 2.0. To advertise on a page of Google search results, businesses create Google accounts in which they 'buy' keyword search terms that correspond to their products. As a user generates a search query, so too are matches made to advertisers. If a user clicks on one of the text ads – 'clicking-through' to the product or business website itself – a micropayment is generated for Google from the advertiser's account. The Google perspective is that a 'click-through' more or less equals a vote for a business, and the business only pays for all the votes that are generated in relation to its products. In the world of Google economics, a click-through is simultaneously an execution of a

GWEI – Google Will Eat Itself / THE ATTACK

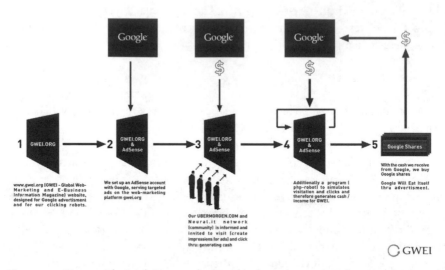

Figure 27.1. *Diagrams/The Attack.* Diagram showing the planned execution of a string of events using the Google ADSense program to fund the Google Will Eat Itself project. UBERMORGEN.COM feat. Alessandro Ludovico vs Paulo Cirio, 2005.

computational command, a flow of potential buyers to a business, and a vote for the product itself. Google also builds cultural capital here because the click-through also generates a micropayment for whoever is serving the ads: Google's Adsense program. What Google takes from the Web, it also gives back – or so the mantra goes. The simple act of clicking, once an experiment in textuality, has now become the execution of an algorithmic sequence that keeps Web microeconomics pumping.[29]

GWEI attaches itself to the circularity of the way in which Google sustains itself. The project serves Google ads to a network of open and hidden websites. It relies on both random click-throughs to sites on which the ads are served *and* on a network of new media artists, tactical media producers, critics, and cultural producers and hacktivists visiting sites and perfunctorily performing multiple click-throughs. Micropayments are then generated for the GWEI account using the AdSense aspect of Google advertising. But now the fun really begins, for the money generated is then used to buy Google shares on the stock market. The results of this, GWEI declares, will be twofold. First, to place the shares in trust to be given back to the public, which has in fact generated the income; second, to eventually publicly buy out Google through shareholder takeover in an estimated 202,345,127 years.[30]

I suggest that GWEI functions as an algorithmic art work, proffering a very different idea about the functioning of the algorithm as a key component of contemporary computation. Considered as algorithmic art, GWEI must also be understood as doing something very different with algorithms than occurred in artificial life and generative systems art. GWEI is more a conceptual art investigation about the ontology of the algorithm in computational culture and networked economies. Adrian MacKenzie has argued that much cultural theory and populist thought about computation holds that algorithms embody pure instances of repetition in which their execution leads to an invariable sequence of operations being performed.[31] However, the actual operation of algorithms, especially in relation to their execution and runtime over networks, is variable. Code sequences change and evolve through usage, transfer, and exchange across platforms, nodes and users and through their extensive spread and deployment throughout communications systems. For all pragmatic purposes, there is, then, no ideal or pure repetition of sequences of code that algorithms run through when they execute in concrete situations. Indeed, as MacKenzie suggests, algorithms often function because they are able to make use of variation and rearrange sequences of code into different orders, re-synthesizing these so as to maintain the associations between sequential events. This immanent variation of the actualized algorithm is what provides it with potential inventiveness.

GWEI exploits the inventiveness of the algorithm that operates at the generative basis of Google's Earth. It no longer offers us repetition of the never-ending expansion of information, but instead Google eating itself and becoming non-operational by the very same execution of sequences through which it normally sustains itself. As the artist Christophe Bruno suggests, Google is itself feeding on the production of meaning by bloggers and other network producers and extracting semantic surplus value from the circulation of words, intimacies, and the articulation of desires throughout the Web.[32] GWEI reinvents the Google algorithm as difference in the Google loop of repetition. Perhaps rather than algorithmic art GWEI produces an art of the algorithm. Moreover, the project *does* acknowledge both the social relations engaged in Web economies and the potential for the formation of different kinds of socialities through distributed media. It is not the click-through that is at the core of income generation and the production of value for a project such as GWEI. Rather, click-through value is generated by the artistic and cultural networks of people who connect to, distribute, and re-distribute information about such art projects via sociable media such as blogs, online magazines, forums, and face-to-face art festivals and symposia. This is where the real work of the project is produced by gathering the resources of these disparate and emergent, networked socialities to support the project. And that is precisely why GWEI feeds its income as Google shares back to these networks.

Having said that, I wonder whether this kind of aesthetic intervention – at the level of the logic of technics – is enough for media arts in an age and terrain increasingly covered by Google-like imagery. Although I want to endorse the aesthetic and cultural work that pieces such GWEI undertake, I also think we need to invent new aesthetic worlds that diverge from self-enclosing ones such as Google Earth. There is a great upsurge in cartographical experimentation in the context of distributed media and emerging networked formations. Although this interest may run parallel to the more general ascension of GISs, of locative media, and indeed of commercially powered enterprises such as Google Earth, it is the collective, participatory, and divergent nature of these other mapping projects that speaks loudest. I am referring here to projects such as the plethora of maps produced in collaborative workshop situations with groups such as illegal immigrants and for events such as the No Border Camps.[33] As Brian Holmes has suggested, these are processual cartographies in which the map – conflicting, disparate, *and* inventive – is more a kind of line-drawing or diagram both inciting and sketching out collective dynamics: 'the process of mapping, or of cartography, does not just mean surveying a territory from above, or representing a process that has unfolded in the past, but instead, tracing and effectively fleshing out the contours of a social dynamic, of an event which bears the future.'[34]

Independent media groups, hacktivists, artists, and theorists have collaborated on a number of these kinds of mapping projects including, for example, the *Fadaiat*// *Borderline Academy* workshop that took place in the southern Spanish town of Tarifa from 17 to 26 June 2005.[35] Working together with activist groups supporting the situation of illegal immigrants crossing from Morocco to Spain, the workshop produced a mapping of the intensive technological and military surveillance systems set up to track and catch the migration of people (mainly seeking work) across the Straits of Gibraltar. Similar images from previous workshops and mapping projects reveal a hive of activity.

Here, grids and layers of information seem to be opening out from the territories themselves, detailing the kinds of satellite, GPS, and commercial surveillance systems in place for policing the movements of people in search of work, relation to others (families, friends, lovers), and to geographical hotspots where protest against surveillance has erupted. Importantly, the map is inverted. Moroccan territory appears at the top and all movement cascades down to Spanish territory from there. This cartographic project incorporates a world-view that is collective and situated rather than individuated or universalizable.

Aesthetically these kinds of cartographic projects can be visually labyrinthine, looped, and recursive; lines and connections trace political and economic blocs and the formation of emerging, alternative socialities. What we see is not clearly visible from above – unlike the Google Earth flyover – but instead unfolds from the processes of inventing other possible worlds. What we start to glimpse are the chaotic dynamics of disparate relationalities. If we are looking for signs of a distributed aesthesia that is also about imaging worlds, we must look to this kind of collective experimentation to sense how the earth can be inscribed in other ways. Collective cartographies render only partial worlds. But rather than Google Earth's somewhat bland aspirations towards medium-resolution coverage, they gesture towards something on the other side of this black hole: outwards at an intensive, rich, and dynamic rate. It will be both

Figure 27.2. *Mapa Proceso 05 / us versión 1.0: surveillance systems for tracking peoples across the Moroccan and Spanish borders.* osfa, 2006.

a testing and exciting endeavour to see how this frisson of networked world-making views unfolds within distributed aesthetic practices.

Acknowledgments

My thanks to all the participants of the 'Distributed Aesthetics' workshop, held at the WissenschaftsKolleg zu Berlin, Germany, during May 2006, and in particular Geert Lovink for helping to organize such a rich space for collective thought production.

Notes

1   Google Earth website, 'Google Earth – Common Questions,' 2005, available at http://earth.google.com/faq.html#2, accessed 10 Sept. 2006.

2   See, e.g., Richard V. Dragan, 'Google Earth 3.0,' *PC Magazine*, 28 June 2005, available at http://www.pcmag.com/article2/0,1895,1831854,00.asp, accessed 24 Aug. 2006.

3   Judith Donath, 'Sociable Media,' *Berkshire Encyclopaedia of Human-Computer Interaction* (Great Barrington: Berkshire Publishing Group, 2006), 627–33.

4   Robert Nirre has made a similar observation about the Web in general. Nirre was concerned with the ways in which networking eliminated spatiality by eliminating distance and hence *spaces* for people to congregate. I am less concerned about this earlier debate around space, communications, and habitation than I am with the elimination of *sociality* as a dimension by the Google *zeitgeist*. See Robert Nirre, 'Spatial Discursions. Flames of the Digital and Ashes of the Real: Confessions of a San Francisco Programmer,' *Life in the Wires: The CTheory Reader*, ed. Arthur and Marilouise Kroker (Victoria, Canada: New World Perspectives/CTheory Books, 2004), 260–8.

5   Google Earth Community can be found at http://bbs.keyhole.com/entrance.php?Cat=0.

6   For Google Earth Hacks, see http://www.googleearthhacks.com. One of the more interesting integrations of Google Earth with another sociable media is GlobeFeed Maps. This site brings together GE Maps with the online image-sharing tool Flickr. By sending an inquiry to a location on an interactive Google Map it is possible to call up and upload location-based images of that particular coordinate taken by site members (my thanks to Andrew Murphie for bringing this to my attention). See http://www.globefeed.com/maps.asp, accessed 15 Sept. 2006.

7   I am here making reference to the idea of autopoesis in the work of Humberto Maturana and Francesco Varela. For them, however, the autopoetic unity of a singular system – whether it is living or non-living – is always organized and organizing in relation to both other autopoeses and a greater ecology of systemic flows and interactions. Hence, autopoesis is never a form of closure but rather a set of dynamic relations that create singularities. The Google Earth 'autopoesis,' I am suggesting, is much closer to a closed system. See Humberto Maturana and Francesco Varela, *The Tree of Knowledge: The Biological Roots of Human Understanding* (Boston: Shambala, 1998), 43–50.

8 See, e.g., the assertion made by Indian President A.P.J. Abdul Kalam, on 16 October 2005,
   that developing countries had been deliberately chosen by Google Earth to be mapped as
   high-resolution images. Dinesh C. Sharma, 'Indian President Warns against Google Earth,'
   CNET News.com, 17 Oct. 2005, available at http://news.com.com/Indian+president+rails+
   against+Google+Earth/2100-1028_3-5896888.html, accessed 10 Aug. 2006.

9 AlexK, 'Why does Germany suddenly look different?,' post on Google Earth Hacks Forum,
   24 March 2006, available at http://www.googleearthhacks.com/forums/showthread.
   php?t=5935&page=1&pp=15, accessed 10 Aug. 2006.

10 See Google, 'Common Questions about Google Earth,' available at http://earth.google.com/
   faq.html#1, accessed 10 Aug. 2006.

11 Geert Lovink and Ned Rossiter, 'The Dawn of Organised Networks,' Precarious Labour,
   Fibreculture Journal 5 (2005), available at http://journal.fibreculture.org/issue5/lovink_
   rossiter.html#1, accessed 10 Aug. 2006.

12 See Martin Dodge and Rob Kitchen, Mapping Cyberspace (London: Routledge, 2001), 65; Jeremy
   Crampton, The Political Mapping of Cyberspace (Chicago: University of Chicago Press, 2003), 31–3.

13 Jacques Chirac, quoted in Routers, 'France Unveils National Rival to Google Earth,' CNet
   News.com, 23 June 2006, available at http://news.com.com/France+unveils+national+rival
   +to+Google+Earth/2100-1032_3-6087343.html, accessed 10 Aug. 2006.

14 I explore this proposal in more detail with Geert Lovink, in Anna Munster and Geert Lovink,
   'Theses on Distributed Aesthetics. Or, What a Network is Not,' Distributed Aesthetics,
   Fibreculture Journal 7 (2005), available at http://journal.fibreculture.org/issue7/
   issue7_munster_lovink.html, accessed 10 Aug. 2006.

15 Crampton, Political Mapping of Cyberspace, 27.

16 See Gilles Deleuze, The Fold, trans. T. Conley (Minneapolis: University of Minnesota Press,
   1993), 51.

17 Published in Woman's Own magazine, 31 Oct. 1987. My thanks to Ned Rossiter for reminding
   me of this statement and for discussion surrounding the erasure of sociality from social
   network theory.

18 See Ben Elgin, 'So Much Fanfare, So Few Hits' Business Week Online, 10 July 2006, available at
   http://www.businessweek.com/magazine/content/06_28/b3992051.htm?campaign_id=
   search, accessed 10 Aug. 2006.

19 See, e.g., Philip H. Gouchenour, 'Distributed Communities and Nodal Subjects,' New Media
   and Society 8/1 (2006): 33–51.

20 Arjun Appardurai, Modernity at Large (Minneapolis: University of Minnesota Press, 1997), 4.

21 Jakob Nielsen, Designing Web Usability: The Practice of Simplicity (Indianapolis: New Riders,
   2000), 389.

22 See Jakob Nielsen's 'Alertbox' entry 'Designing Web Ads Using Click-through Data,' 2 Sept.
   2001, available at http://www.useit.com/alertbox/20010902.html, accessed 24 Aug. 2006.

23 See, e.g., Nicholas Duchenout and Robert J. Moore 'The Social Side of Gaming: A Study of
   Interaction Patterns in a Massively Multiplayer Online Game,' Proceedings of the 2004 ACM
   Conference on Computer Supported Cooperative Work (New York: ACM Press, 2004), 360–9.

24 Google, 'Google Inc. Company Overview,' 2006, available at http://www.google.com/corporate/index.html, accessed 10 Aug. 2006.

25 The clearest explication of Hare's work can be found in R.M. Hare, *Moral Thinking: Its Levels, Method, and Point* (Oxford: Oxford University Press, 1981).

26 Google, 'Google's Search Technology,' 2006, available at http://www.google.com/corporate/tech.html, accessed 10 Aug. 2006.

27 Adrian MacKenzie, 'Protocols and the Irreducible Traces of Embodiment: The Algorithm and the Mosaic of Machine Time,' draft paper, March 2005, 15, available at http://www.lancs.ac.uk/staff/mackenza/papers/mackenzie-algorithmic-time.pdf.

28 See the *Google Will Eat Itself* website, available at http://www.gwei.org/index.php, accessed 24 Aug. 2006. Alessandro Ludovico is the publisher of the Italian new media art, culture, and hacktivism magazine *Neural*; Paulo Cirio is a member of the software and network art group *epidemic*.

29 Jill Walker has argued that Google helped to create the hyperlink as a form of Web currency through the deployment of its pagerank algorithm in search. See, Jill Walker, 'Links and Power: The Political Economy of Linking on the Web,' in *Proceedings of Hypertext 2002* (Baltimore: ACM Press, 2002), 78–9.

30 This estimate was at the time of writing this essay and is based on the number of shares already held by GWEI and the rate at which it took to accumulate the funds to buy these through the micropayment system. The time span is updated from time to time. See *Google Will Eat Itself*, http://www.gwei.org/index.php. It is possible to register on the GWEI site as a member of Google to the People and to therefore benefit from the handback of revenue. See 'Google to the People Form,' available at http://www.gwei.org/pages/gttp/gttp.php, accessed 10 Aug. 2006.

31 Mackenzie, 'Protocols and the Irreducible Traces of Embodiment,' 14-16.

32 See 'Interview with Christophe Bruno, Media Interventionist,' *Neural* (English ed.) 25 (Bari, Italy, 2006), 43.

33 Some of the maps produced for various sociopolitical events in workshops and as collaborative projects such as that of the group *Bureau D'Etudes* are viewable as pdfs from the following website: http://utangente.free.fr/anewpages/cartes.html. Various other projects, sketches, and texts about radical cartographic practices can be viewed at the Université Tangente site – an archive of people and projects working on counter – and interstitial globalization projects, available at http://utangente.free.fr/anewpages/cartes.html. This site also holds a number of video lectures around issues of mapping, mobility, and technology.

34 Brian Holmes, 'Crisis Cartographies: Stratified Power and the Dynamics of the Swarm,' paper delivered at the Networks and Power panel, *Ars Electronica* Festival, Linz Austria, 2 Sept. 2004. A version of this lecture can be found at http://utangente.free.fr/anewpages/cartes.html, accessed 24 Aug. 2006.

35 See the Borderline Academy website, at http://borderlineacademy.org/fadaiat, accessed 24 Aug. 2006.

WILLIAM BOGARD

Two Stories of Distraction

She seemed removed again tonight, dimly preoccupied with something, or someone, else. Entering the room, she pretended I was not there, something I hate. Or she would smile indifferently, deafly assenting to whatever remark I made, making her absence all the more glaring. All my miserable attempts to seduce her failed. I noticed that her state of distraction had deepened during the past weeks, and she had fallen into innocuous habits that betrayed a hidden terror. She had always despised routine, but now her routines never changed. Something had stolen her eyes, as it would eventually take away her hands, her entire body. By degree, her touch became cold and distant. I suspected an affair. And soon I became her distraction, her hated routine, removing her from what had removed her. She could not bear the sound of my voice, the cut of my collar, how I looked at her, how I breathed, having to submit to these ridiculous signs of power. And her irritation and detachment grew daily, until finally one morning she disappeared.

A crowd gathers on the sidewalk. Ten stories above, a child, a young girl, is perched precariously on a ledge, frozen, the wind dancing in her hair. Below a pack of eyes raised to the sky, transfixed in the anticipation of disaster. Trucks with satellite dishes arrive to capture the event live, to be replayed a thousand times on every channel from every angle to the last numbing detail, at least until the ratings drop. Talking heads compare similar events in history. As for the future, computer simulations show how it will look, to the eyes of a child, to fall from a ten-story building or, to the 'eyes' of the sidewalk, how brains splatter on concrete from that height; everything is rerun endlessly, blown up, and run again. A miniseries is in the works, we hear – book deals, promotional materials, all set to go. It's not everyday this happens (is it?). The police order the crowd back, then rope off the viewing area. Stands are erected; ambulances stand by; a helicopter hovers overhead, then swoops in low for a tight shot. The stage is set, the suspense is perfect. Now, as if on direction, the child moves closer to the edge, reaches out, falters, then falls. Time expands. The crowd gasps and grows silent;

across the country the masses turn to their screens to see the moment of impact. They think: we've seen this before – did we miss it the first time? We *live* here, don't we? The fall is played over again in slow motion, close, closer, the wind in the child's hair, then the terror in her face, her eyes, the instant her head explodes. Every image is so clean, so crisp, so beautiful; the technology has advanced considerably since Zapruder. Since Baby Jessica and even Baghdad. Freeze frame, each shot is meticulously superimposed on its simulation for instant comparison; and they are the same – screen and fall, child and spectator, concrete and blood. And the mass of watchers blinks and stupidly stares until finally it, too, totters and falls, into the screen of the catastrophe, and disappears.

Escape and Capture

Arthur Kroker used to refer to American media culture as a 'civilization in recline.'[1] The image was certainly apt. The perfect icon for a bored, exhausted, and utterly 'removed' American public on the eve of the twenty-first century was someone in the classic Lazy-Boy position, *captured* by the TV screen, oblivious to anything around him (or her) beyond what flickered before his eyes between trips to the refrigerator. This picture, however, seemed to contradict another one of Kroker's – that of *panic America*, neo-fascist and hyper-paranoid, obsessed with death, haunted by the body and its unruly fluids, and using whatever means to *escape*.[2] Now we do not normally associate panic with TV-induced catatonia. But, in fact, as Kroker well knew, the two scenes were intimately and even essentially connected. The television, of course, is both the perfect means of capture and the perfect escape device. Its logic has become even more pervasive with the advent of the computer, which is now in the process of absorbing it.

McLuhan was the first to realize that physical capture (or immobilization) does not prohibit, and indeed *smoothes*, the active neural integration of the subject into the medium.[3] This is the whole pleasure – and terror – of television; it induces flight to the same extent it leaves the body behind in 'sleep mode.' TV is a *panic release technology* that operates by dividing the body and removing all the parts superfluous for experience. It 'releases' experience in the same paradoxical way that the woman in our story is released, through a kind of habituation (we'll have more to say about this in relation to Benjamin's theory of distraction later). What has changed since TV has met its virtual nemesis in the computer is certainly the intensity of that integration; perhaps it even portends a qualitative shift. Baudrillard imagines a time when the masses are integrated entirely into the media, and the media into them, as in the scene of the falling child, where the difference between capture and escape is meaningless – a seamless integration/habituation of technology and the subject.[4] Someday all you'll need is a brain, if that (!). In the same way, a 'recliner civilization' dreams of infinite worlds summoned at the throw of a switch (the ingestion of a pill, the modification of a gene). It imagines merging, body and soul, with the system of digital codes, a time when, without going anywhere, it can live and *be* the images on its screen. When it can disappear.

These ideas can serve as approximate entry points to a study of distraction. This is because distraction is a logic of escape and capture. To distract something is to elude its clutches; but also, as a consequence, to now clutch *it*, secretly and from behind. These qualities of clutching *and* elusion, of escape and capture, are what make distraction and its related strategies – simulation, disappearance, removal – games of *power*. When we speak about the power of the digital media, we see lines of escape and capture everywhere – mass distraction truly is the *order* of the day. This is not a moral judgment. We assume this has both good and bad sides. Nor is it to claim that our age is any more distracted than any other. There is no reason to think that print is any less distracting than electronic media, or that modern forms of spectacle distract the masses more than ancient ones do or did. Every society reinvents its own regimes of distraction. Every culture develops its own methods of mobilizing (and immobilizing) the masses.

This way of speaking, however, is already too narrowly sociological. Distraction is hardly just a social, or even human, condition. Animals can be distracted, and so can non-living things – geological processes can be described in this way, as I will suggest below. But this also means that distraction is not a state of consciousness, for example, attention or inattention. Shifts of attention or consciousness may certainly be *produced* by distractions, but they are not identical with them.

It means, too, that distraction does not require a subject, although a subject could be one of its effects. Kroker's 'recliner' is a subject of distraction only in the sense that its body occupies a space where multiple lines of escape and capture converge and diverge. The *material* scene of distraction is what is important – the proximate relations of body parts (brain, hands, eyes) to the screen, the design and engineering components of the console (inputs, through-puts, outputs), the entire material infrastructure – mathematical, molecular, technological, sociocultural – of the flow of information. You do not watch TV, Baudrillard says, TV watches you.[5] Or rather, it *removes* you, takes you away, 'subtracts' you from your surroundings. It is on this material scene or territory of removal that consciousness is produced and consumed.

To note this extra-human dimension of distraction is in no way to deny that it is one of the elemental features of human experience. In countless forms, it is implicated in the production of life's pleasures (the French meaning of the term is close to 'entertainment' or pleasurable 'diversion') as well as its irritations and dangers (the English word can convey the idea that distraction is something hazardous, as in the case of being distracted while driving a car or crossing the street). If we could limit its manifestation to living forms, and we cannot, we could even make the case that distraction is a *condition of survival*, that the struggle for existence absolutely depends on finding, managing, and adapting to means of escape and capture (e.g., for many predatory animals, and even many plants, distraction is an essential means of procuring food, or avoiding becoming food).

Despite the fact that distraction is everywhere in experience, it is not at all difficult to imagine a world without distraction. Such a fantasy is in fact the rule if we consider it from the point of view of social control. Institutions like the church, the state, markets, even the mass media, generally do not tolerate distraction, at least when it fosters neglect of duty or responsibility. In Catholic theology, for example, a world without distraction is one where nothing disturbs one's prayers to God – distractions, such as uncontrolled or impure thoughts, are a sign of man's imperfection and inherent sinfulness. For bureaucracy, it is a world of dutiful, law-abiding, on-time citizens; for the school, a classroom of focused and docile students; for capital, a shop of committed workers. The television and advertising industries, even as they deal wholesale in distraction themselves – for example, by sexualizing images of commodities – desire watchful, undistracted viewers.

In fact, *all* of these institutions develop and perfect their own methods of distraction. They become, to use a phrase of Deleuze and Guattari's, 'apparatuses of capture,' seeking in their different ways to control movement, order desire and belief, and translate them into habits.[6] How do religion, capital, and the state capture their objects? Simple. They generate what appear as lines of escape or removal, as exits, outs, passages, and so on: you too can escape from divine retribution (through the passages of prayer, sacrifice, and confession); escape from work (through money); escape from power (through prestige). The authorities, like *trappers*, know that the lure of escape is usually the most powerful apparatus of capture. Money, prestige, indulgences, sex, these are all traps at the same time as they are means of flight. Although institutional power does not tolerate distraction when it threatens to become unruly – and here distraction *is* conceived morally – distraction is its single most valuable tool. Often, it prepares the way for the use of force, as when the police employ it before making an arrest (the sting operation), but sometimes it can also eliminate the need for force. In an important sense, the distracted object (or subject) has already surrendered to power – it does not *see* power or in any way sense its closeness, thus power can operate behind its back, reserving force for the times when distraction itself threatens to wrest the object from its grasp (parents sometimes use TV to occupy their children's time and create some free space for themselves, but it is a strategy that often backfires, as the TV becomes the more powerful apparatus of capture).

We already sense that power, at least institutional power, does not fully control the forces of distraction. In fact, distraction is a principle that *rivals* power. The authorities not only fear losing control *over* distraction, they fear losing control *to* it. A distracted mass, potentially, owes nothing, not even its life, to power, and the most dangerous groups are always those that could care less about power, that is, that are too distracted to care about their own survival. As we shall see later, the means of distraction are also those of power's *annulment*. Distraction is what seduces power; power can lose itself there, break into a million pieces, or scatter in a hundred directions. But that does not mean distraction, as a political strategy, can always save us from power, either, that it can always be used to overturn power. Such dreams only mask a more elaborate picture of an unstable mixture of forces and materials. We take seriously Deleuze and Guattari's rule that no strategy once and for all can serve as a guide for praxis. The truth is that as quickly as distraction opens a line of flight, it also opens a line of death – such is the nature of logics of escape and capture, which for all their strategic character always involve indeterminacy, a measure of luck.

So we do not ask if distraction is a good or bad thing – a question more for the authorities anyway – but rather, if it can serve to map the dynamics of various and sundry social processes – wars and militaristic manoeuvres, rituals, the emergence of hierarchies, population shifts, market and currency movements, and so on. Can we view things like the evolution of material culture, in particular, digital mass media, through the theoretical lens of distraction? Is it possible, more generally, to understand relations of power themselves as effects of distraction? If so, it will be in terms of logics (and paths) of escape and capture.

Distraction Machines

Here we are interested mainly in how distraction functions on the sociocultural and technical planes, but we will often use the term more broadly to refer to a 'machinic assemblage' composed of variable matters and relations of force. Following the lead of Guattari, we do not intend 'machines' in either mechanistic or vitalist terms. Guattari develops a machinism that does not reduce the idea of a machine to a simple construction *partes extra partes* or assimilate it to living beings (or living beings to it).[7] Guattari's model differs in certain fundamental respects from the cybernetic notion of the machine as a feedback mechanism and with philosophical notions of techne that link its function to an ontological ground of 'unmasking,' as in Heidegger.[8] Throughout all these positions, Guattari proposes a concept of 'machinic heterogenesis' that would attempt to view the machine not in its various limited aspects, but in its complex totality, in its 'technological, social, semiotic and axiological avatars,' as well as in its operations in nature. His project, which we can only mention in passing here, involves a basic rethinking of the general idea of a machine in terms of *differential flows of matter and energy*, for example, as processes of dispersion and concentration, stretching and compaction, intensification and dissipation, friction and smoothing, etc.[9] Machines are 'assemblages' of other machines, which are themselves composed of further machines, in the manner of fractals, to use a mathematical image. Machinic assemblages bring together machines that may differ dramatically in nature (geophysical machines, biochemical machines, technical machines, social machines, desiring machines, concept machines) and combine them in an organized, consistent fashion. Such heterogeneously composed but organized structures are spontaneously generated and destroyed by what he and Deleuze call 'abstract machines' or diagrams,[10] which impart form to variable flows, or again, break their form apart and down.[11]

Machinic assemblages do not depend on the actions or intentions of human subjects (which are themselves a collection of differently composed machines). Rather, they form and dissolve 'autocatalytically,' as effects of their own dynamics.[12]

This, anyway, is the general frame in which we intend to view distraction. Distraction is not an effect of the subject, but a self-organizing machinic assemblage that channels and sorts flows of differently composed matters into relatively consistent layers, much like we see in natural processes of sedimentation and stratification. Our first rule in this investigation is that we must consider distraction in its *geological* (or meteorological) as much as its sociological manifestations, in the language of changing pressures, heats, and speeds.[13] What is meant by this is not that the former can serve as metaphors for social processes, for example, when we use terms like social 'strata' or social 'currents,' but rather that both share a common diagram or abstract machine. DeLanda notes, for instance, that it is a different thing to say, as Marxists once did, that 'class struggle is the motor of history,' than to say 'a hurricane is a steam motor.'[14] While the first example is clearly a metaphorical usage, the second is not. In the second case what is claimed is that 'hurricanes embody the same diagram used by engineers to build steam motors – both refer, for instance, to reservoirs of heat, thermal differences, and circulations of energy and matter. Is it possible, DeLanda asks, to find a diagram (or abstract machine) that operates across geological, meteorological, and social formations? Over the past several decades, chaos theory has proposed a language that perhaps makes such a convergence possible.[15] The ways in which ordered structures or flows emerge from chaos may be the same across fields with formally different contents. Moreover, chaos theory examines processes of self-structuration (or autocatalysis) and suggests that they may not be exclusive to living materials, but may extend to inorganic processes as well, such as the formation chemical clocks, veins of minerals in the earth, cyclonic movements in the atmosphere, etc., raising the possibility that more than analogies may exist between natural and social phenomena. All this fits in well with much of what we have already indicated regarding Guattari's machinism.

'Distraction,' of course, is not a theoretical concept in geology. But we can ask alternatively whether it makes sense to describe geological processes in terms of escape and capture. DeLanda suggests that certain geological structures like strata beneath the ocean floor may be a function of *sorting* mechanisms that separate differently sized materials into relatively homogeneously sized groups before depositing them in layers.[16] Rivers, for example, are recognized by geologists as one such sorting mechanism, moving groups of smaller rocks faster, larger rocks slower, in bundles of differentially paced lines of flow. It makes sense to describe these dynamic mechanisms as systems of escape and capture (certain rock sizes are 'passed' quickly in the sorting process, others are held back in the flow). Another example of such mechanisms at the geological level might be the ways volcanic flows organize surface features of the Earth's crust as a function of different speeds of deposition.

Chaos theory suggests that such dynamic systems are non-linear, non-equilibrial, and self-regulated. The question is whether the same sorting diagrams can be located in the social and cultural spheres, despite vast differences in form or content from geological structures. DeLanda believes this to be so, referring to 'slowing down' or 'hardening' (crystallization) processes in the formation of normative social structures, where the production of those structures refers not simply to human decisions but, for example, to how those decisions follow from spontaneous changes in rates of flow of food, money, bodily fluids, etc.[17] Social structures, in this view, are seen in terms of relative speeds of mixtures of different kinds of materials undergoing sorting and crystallization processes. Formal social hierarchies run at relatively slow or fixed speeds, generally by force of habit, compared with more fluid, improvised groupings that DeLanda calls 'meshworks.'[18] In terms of speed, the difference between a hierarchy and a meshwork is like that between a solid and a liquid, or a liquid and a gas – both move, but at different rates. Alternatively, we might characterize one movement as molar (large scale), the other as molecular.[19] We do not have to 'humanize' these ideas to apply them to the social sphere. In fact, they allow us to view 'human being' as a variable organization of differently paced flows of matter and energy. To be 'really' human, as excluded groups in any social order know well, means to have the right flow of blood, currency, and equipment, to bear the right series of distinguishing marks (eye colour, skin colour, hair colour), maintain the proper rhythms, habits, routines, and so on.[20]

We do not ask who organizes these flows, but rather what machines inaugurate a change of state, what *intensive thresholds* are crossed and how (e.g., from a liquid to a gas, from non-human to human, from uncoordinated individuals to a pack, as in animal groups, or from non-social to social aggregates); where certain flows break off from or reconnect with others (steam flows, or the places where the pack splits off from the larger group).[21] Such thresholds, in the case of liquids to gasses, refer to specific heats. In animal groups, they may involve caloric levels, densities, carrying capacities, etc., which above or below certain limits may provoke organized action. Again, what matters in the immediate context is that we can conceptualize all this in terms of escape and capture, and from there as various forms of distraction.

Before leaving these ideas, we need to reiterate the importance of *speed* as a mechanism of escape and capture.[22] In the old military formula, either you're 'quick or you're dead.'[23] Speed is also a sorting function. It is by virtue of their relative speeds that elements in a mixture, whether geological or social, sort themselves into distinct flows. In this way of viewing things, the 'escape velocity' of objects has as much meaning in the social as the natural sphere, that is, if it makes sense to describe as social the operations through which bodies are captured and sorted into homogeneous groupings which are made to flow at similar rates of speed. Foucault, for example, does not describe the prison in 'institutional' or bureaucratic terms – viz., as systems of abstract rules and fixed relations of authority – but as spaces of bodies organized around the homogenization and routinization of specific flows (again, of food, waste, tasks, information).[24] Certain flows are slowed down (i.e., hardened) in specific locations and during specified times, others are speeded up – prison routine is the outcome of relatively paced lines of movement. Foucault often writes of the importance of architectural arrangements in determining the organization of bodies in prisons, specifically as they affect conditions of perception. But alongside this Foucault also gives us a kind of 'geomorphology' of the penitentiary that is at the same time a depiction of its social order from the point of view of controlling rates of material flows, that is, a model of relative speeds, thinnings and thickenings, gravity sinks and acceleration points, capture and escape. *Perception is organized via the channelling of flows in engineered space.* But this is precisely nothing more than a definition of distraction. (We will return to these points below in our discussion of Walter Benjamin.)

We should further note, to anticipate our remarks below, that an important effect of speed is *stealth*. In social terms, we cannot ignore the fact that distraction is a strategy of disappearance or invisibility. Distraction allows a second event to take place behind or 'to the side of' the first one – it enables a close approach. The classic pickpocket scheme is an example, provided we are willing to characterize it, not in terms of the diversion of the mark's attention or consciousness, but as series of flows, subtractions, and interruptions, slowings-down, and speedings-up. Not attention, but rather, 'one hand moves faster than another to the pocket, a mark is subtracted from his money.' To capture or elude a thing by stealth is to move at a different rate – to fall behind the thing, to outpace it, to approach it transversally, as with predatory animals or their prey (keeping in mind that both predator and prey draw on the same set of strategies). Paul Virilio has intensively studied the connections between speed and strategies of disappearance, their relations in politics, war, and modern telecommunications systems, and outlined their internal relation to power.[25] The power to capture one's enemies by stealth may involve making them look where they should not, but that often translates into moving faster. In the same way, the power to elude one's predator by stealth is, in some cases, to move slower (standing still as it passes, falling back). The assemblages that best regulate relative speeds, in the social sphere at least, are also the ones that are usually the most stealthy – those that order the flows of traffic, money, sex, food, information. Like Foucault, we have to look not just for specific 'agencies' within society that enforce laws relating to speed – e.g., the police – but to 'impersonal strategies' and criss-crossing lines of force, to open and closed pathways, acceleration points, bottlenecks, regions of stretching and contraction, and so on.[26] The central role of the image of the panopticon in Foucault's history of the prison is not simply a matter of how it describes a complex structure of visibility and invisibility, but how that structure emerges through minute adjustments of speed that supply the prison's specific 'texture' of activity (the prison is a 'hard' social space, indeed, but one where certain flows may periodically escape – riots, streams of contraband, drugs, etc.).[27]

Perhaps we can begin to glimpse from these reflections new ways to develop the idea of distraction as a social-machinic assemblage and perhaps from there suggest a different way of viewing its importance in the production of contemporary culture ('recliner culture'). Distraction is a machinery that generates differential rates of flow of matter and energy. It is an 'abstract' machine in the sense that it coordinates elements circulating on very different planes of intelligibility (geological, meteorological, biochemical, sociological, political). It opens lines of escape and capture, of approach and invisibility. This machinery leaves behind *deposits* of various sorts, hardenings or thickenings (sediments, strata, scars), but it can also generate, within these structures, liquid or gaseous conditions, zones of turbulence or smoothing.[28] Distraction, in one sense, may even describe a crucial event in all self-organizing processes, that is, the production of *singularities*. It is singularities that initiate changes of flow and the emergence of qualitatively new states – things like bifurcation points, thresholds, pinch points, edges, holes, cracks, and strange attractors.[29] A distraction, in its deepest sense, *is* a singularity, and not simply in terms of an event that draws one's attention because of its rarity or uniqueness, but an event that *because* of its rarity and uniqueness causes a flow to break away, to subtract itself, from a mass of materials to which it had formerly adhered. Distraction generates, to refer this again back to Deleuze and Guattari, a *multiplicity*. One is only a member of a multiplicity, they say, via subtraction, as N – 1.[30] Distraction is what subtracts one from a collection to create a multiplicity – it is what causes the lone individual to break away from the randomness of a milling crowd and generate a 'pack,' the unique event that pulls a particle off-track and causes other particles to follow. It is in this sense above all a *gravitational* force before it is a conscious one.

'To distract' literally means 'to draw in different directions' or 'to pull apart,' and we will feel free to exploit all the rich connotations of these terms. While 'to draw' has the gravitational sense we just assigned to it, we will also pay close attention to its *graphical* meaning. To distract something is to *mark* it, and thereby make it vulnerable. A distraction creates a target; it makes a thing *traceable*. Sun Tzu, in *The Art of War*, lists the military benefits of distracting an enemy – it dislodges him, isolates him from his main forces; he is marked by his very separation and thus rendered visible and open to attack.[31] For Sun Tzu, it is a matter of one's superior use of the landscape, the exploitation of pinch points and higher ground along the route of march, the strategic employment of diversions of all sorts (false information, double agents, etc.).

Foucault's analysis of panoptic power, again, is full of allusions to spatial and temporal devices that distract the subject and thus allow for his more efficient control 'from another direction.'[32] In Foucault, power often operates through the creation of a host of 'blind spots' and lighted spaces, structural devices for keeping the prisoner under surveillance and occupied with everything but the real lines of his capture, which always intersect him from the side or behind his back. In that sense, to distract is not only to reveal the prisoner-enemy, *but to make the object that distracts disappear*. That is, we must also consider the reverse graphical function of distraction, viz., to unmark or erase. The first rule of disappearance is always to create a diversion, hence its importance as a strategic tool not only in war but in magic (and, we will see, in electronic media, which has elements of both). This happens through a process of bifurcation or breaking apart: the magician makes an object disappear by a double movement that separates it from a set of objects of which it had formerly been a member. One movement creates a zone of intensity to divert the spectator's eye, the other whisks the object away. The two lines, one of capture (the eye), one of escape (the 'erased' object), separated by a singularity, the distraction, that pulls in different directions at the same time. In Foucault, if power operates imperceptibly, it is because it initiates this double flow of escape and capture – we should not forget that Foucault's concept of power relations includes their resistance – and this is possible only through the organization of elaborate machineries of distraction, means of dividing perceptual space (and time), technologies of dispersion, of pulling apart, splitting, breaking off, etc. If we conceive of mass media in terms of distraction, we are essentially asking how they function in all these diverse ways – as a force of gravitation, as a means of making visible or traceable (surveillance), and as a machinery of erasure or unmarking.

Distraction in an Age of Mechanical Reproduction

Let us now examine the matter more closely, as it relates to the question of social control and cultural patterning, with an eye to contemporary electronic media as distraction assemblages. Before proceeding, however, we must give two qualifications.

First, despite its ubiquitousness and its character as an abstract machine, there is no universal or unitary mode of distraction. Politically and culturally, it is useless to talk about distraction in a global sense. It is characterized, rather, as we have seen, by its singularities and bifurcations, by the concrete mixtures of heterogeneous elements that it coordinates. Although its lines intersect with those of human decision, belief, and desire, distraction, we have said, is not 'human.' If anything, 'human being,' the 'subject,' the 'person,' the 'individual,' 'consciousness,' 'attention' – all these things are so many effects of distraction, which is not to deny their strategic role in how distraction games play out in a given society. Again, distractions manifest themselves as zones of turbulence where flows of matter and energy are intensified or dissipated, where disjunctions occur and new structures emerge. In society they may often appear as the expression of intentional choices, but this would be to seriously misunderstand their chaotic nature – the production of singular events, the unpredictable bifurcation of lines. We are not looking for essences here; it is the actual mixtures that are interesting and constitute the dynamics of distraction.

Second, we will not define distraction as a social or cultural totality. There is no 'society or culture of distraction,' as if society was only this and nothing else. Distraction is one among many traits of contemporary media culture. As we have indicated, it has oppressive and liberating qualities, often both simultaneously. You can be distracted by the police, but the police can be distracted, too. It is possible that everyone in a given society is distracted in a certain way, though unlikely (Kroker's recliner is undoubtedly only a convenient fiction to draw attention to a more complex state of affairs).

Finally, although distraction seems to explain certain relations of activity (or inactivity) in a population in an external way, in fact, it is immanent to them. For an investigation into the social organization of distraction, we should look, following Foucault again on this point, to the concrete relations themselves to discover the distraction in them rather than invent a principle that occupies a space below or outside them. Distraction manifests itself in innumerable scenes of escape and capture, traps, ruses, surprises, catastrophes, encirclements, blockages. We must not turn all this into a 'theory' of distraction, but examine it, as Foucault says, from the point of view of its political anatomy, the ways it distributes bodies and coordinates their movements.

Walter Benjamin, in 'The Work of Art in the Age of Mechanical Production,' is really the first to raise the question about the role of distraction in societies dominated by the mass media.[33] Typically, he does not frame this question as a matter of attention, but in terms of how a population, or rather a mass, distributes itself in relation to material culture, in this case to technologies of aesthetic reproduction. As we shall see, Benjamin locates the problem of distraction in its connection to the formation of *habits*, not to a state of consciousness. Specifically, he asks how art integrates or is integrated into the performance of routine but socially necessary tasks. Whereas the traditional work of art perhaps demanded thoughtful contemplation on the part of an individual spectator, modern mass-produced art, most paradigmatically film for Benjamin, is appropriated not by engaged individuals but by the masses in a mode of distraction. Benjamin noted that it was commonplace in his time to hear social critics lament the masses' distraction and blame the cinema or other elements of mass culture for promoting it. We still hear this charge levelled in various quarters today, typically from the moral Right, not just against Hollywood but against media in general. Whatever its morality, however, the relation between distraction and aesthetic media is not a new situation, according to Benjamin, and demands a closer investigation.

Since earliest times, the most important case of the connection between distraction and art involves the social appropriation of architecture, which generally functions not as an object of contemplation (except perhaps for tourists), but as a taken-for-granted background of human activity.[34] It is not simply the fact that architecture is seen but rarely thematized as people go about their daily business that constitutes the meaning of distraction for Benjamin. The masses appropriate architecture not just visually, but *tactilely.* In an important sense, tactile appropriation is not just another mode of reception on par with visual or optical appropriation. Rather, Benjamin argues, it constitutes the conditions of possibility for the latter, in the sense that habitualized behaviours which develop around the use of dwelling spaces, as routinized practices, *organize perception.* Architectural arrangements, in the social as much as

the physical sense, determine what can and cannot be seen. We should remind ourselves again of Foucault's analysis of the prison here. Insofar as these arrangements
control the conditions of perception, they foster routinized forms of behaviour. The
prisoner in Foucault's panopticon unconsciously regulates his own behaviour and is
thus perfectly predictable. He becomes a creature of habit to the extent that he does
not see the real lines of power that control him, that is, by virtue of the fact that he is
distracted in and by the relation to the ordered spaces in which he finds himself, and
in which he must function. Let us return to how Benjamin describes it:

> Buildings are appropriated in a twofold manner: by use and by perception – or rather, by
> touch and sight. Such appropriation cannot be understood in terms of the attentive con-
> centration of a tourist before a famous building. On the tactile side there is no counter-
> part to contemplation on the optical side. Tactile appropriation is accomplished not so
> much by attention as by habit. As regards architecture, habit determines to a large
> extent even optical reception. The latter, too, occurs much less through rapt attention
> than by noticing the object in incidental fashion.[35]

That is, as a function of distraction. Despite Benjamin's fall back into the language of
consciousness ('noticing the object in incidental fashion'), it is clear that distraction has
a far wider political sense for him.[36] It is, in a word, a means of *training*. Even, and perhaps especially, when art is appropriated in a mode of distraction, it exercises a 'covert
control over the extent to which new tasks have become soluble by apperception,' that
is, through the adjustment of the conditions of perception, through architectures of visibility and invisibility. 'Since, moreover' Benjamin continues, 'individuals are tempted to
avoid such tasks [e.g., those necessary for the reproduction of capital], art will tackle the
most difficult and important ones where it is able to mobilize the masses,' where it can
convert those tasks into habits.[37] In our terms, this is a view of art as, potentially, a means
of capture. Benjamin sees this potential existing not only in modern film, but increasingly as an imperative behind all mass-produced art whose reception, like architecture,
becomes a matter of distraction.

Habits are not just subjective states or psychological structures. They involve the
initiation of repetitive flows, the construction and placement of material blocks,
obstacles, corrective devices; the partitioning of space; the functionalization of time,
and the normalization of specific behavioural trajectories. They are 'hardenings' or
'contractions' of activity, sedimentations and stratifications of planes of conduct, con-
densations of matter and energy.[38] But they can also be 'softenings' – one only forms
new habits, after all, by breaking old ones. The distracted person could just as easily
fall into bad as good habits, from the authorities' point of view. In prisons, as in workshops, schools, homes, etc., distractions always threaten to divert flows away from
their desired (moral) ends and must therefore be rigorously controlled. Hence, a
whole system of rules and practices evolves around their strategic placement – a wall

is erected to keep the eyes from straying (the worker's cubicle), an opening closed to prevent any leakage to or from the outside (the locked door). Temperatures are adjusted to insure maximum peak performance (climate control), pressures are adjusted relative to threshold values to guarantee that distraction will smoothly and predictably serve the interests of power (deadlines, quotas, production schedules, grading and ranking schema, etc., so many forms of pressure). All of these in themselves constitute 'capture-distractions,' but only in the sense that they attempt to short-circuit 'escape-distractions.' One must assemble a distraction machine that develops the right repetitions, the 'good' habits, and disassemble those machines that generate the bad repetitions, the habits that upset the power structure, which is to say, the dominant system of distractions (regarding this, the droning and 'distracting' mantras of one's parents – do not eat between meals, be in bed by ten, do your homework before watching TV, pick up your room ... And do this without being told, make it your routine. Don't fall into bad habits. On and on. How many of these repetitive flows are channelled around one's living space, one's negotiation of passageways, open and closed doors, in short, one's *habitat?*).[39]

Digital Distraction

We can perhaps now begin to see mass media, and particularly electronic media, along similar lines, that is, in terms of an 'architecture,' the adjustment of conditions of perception and the formation of habits. But precisely what kinds of perception and habitualized modes of behaviour, in relation to what architecture, are we dealing with here?

Benjamin's remarks are again instructive.[40] He notes that the technology of film places the observer in the role of a passive critic. This would be a subjective way of putting it. More to the point, cinematic equipment, and particularly the film camera, modifies, in an historically important way, the social conditions of perception.[41] Because film can be speeded up and slowed down, because the camera can zoom in and out, because it can move around its object, take various angles, etc., the traditional reception of the work of art has been replaced, Benjamin says, by one of 'testing.' The audience, in effect, *becomes the camera and sees as it sees.* In an age where power is increasingly exercised through the mechanical reproduction of images, the 'aura' of the traditional art object – its cult value, its 'authenticity,' its unique origin in space and time – is sacrificed to the modern value of testability. One can now view the object up-close; from any and all sides; and at any place and time (since it is now mass produced and distributed). The cinema, a distraction-assemblage and, in Benjamin's hands, the model of a technology that once and for all strips the image of its traditional functions, inaugurates a new mode of perception and, one would have to say, a new set of habits. Henceforth, everything is subjected to the test. Testing – that is, measuring, dividing out, selecting, ranking, *sorting* – becomes the order of the day, and this is manifest in a specific way of manipulating the image, of producing it in each and all of its possibilities, in every one of its multiple perspectives, the better to *capture its object definitively.* 'Every day,' Benjamin writes, 'the urge grows stronger to get hold of the object by its likeness, its reproduction.'[42] Baudrillard has an apt image along these lines: all this – endless examination, continuous inspection, the effort to penetrate and reproduce the object in itself by detailed analysis, remagnification and overmagnification of parts, etc. – signifies the cultural dominance of the *hyperreal*, that is, the substitution of signs of the real for the real itself, which increasingly disappears from the stage of perception[43] (Benjamin notes that the perfect image in cinematic society is one from which the technology that captures it is absent, that is, disappears, leaving only 'reality' in its purest form).[44] The hyperreal, we will say, is our current mode of distraction, and our current mode of capture, since, no less than everything else, it subjects us to the test as well.

We should not think, however, that the hyperreal is something insubstantial or immaterial. The urge to test, to convert objects into signs, provoked and supported by technologies like the camera and increasingly by digital information systems, comes down to sorting and redepositing material flows. Deleuze and Guattari insist that any system of signs must be examined not only in terms of its meaning, but in its 'asemiotic' or arepresentational component as well, that is, as a regime of desire and affect, an organization of force relations, rather than as a linguistic or 'mental' structure.[45] This is the position as well of Foucault, who in affirming the connection of language (discourse) and the sign, denies the sign's assimilation to representation and the signifier: 'Of course discourses are composed of signs; but what they do is more than use these signs to designate things. It is this "more" that renders them irreducible to language (langue) and to speech.'[46] Foucault's 'more' refers to discourse as a practical deployment of forces on bodies, in ways that harness their energies, hierarchize them, functionalize them, etc. The sign is not just representation, but power; not just indication, but *dividing practice.*

Here we return full circle to distraction in the material sense of the test – signification as dividing practice (or sorting-machine). This is not by any means a new idea. It has long been a matter of practice and a condition of knowledge in military organizations. We have already hinted that distraction utilizes signs to divert the enemy – false appearances, lures, feints, ruses, decoys. Such signs divide the enemy's forces, separate him from his lines of support, and render him visible. The military employs these tactics on their own soldiers to establish the order of rank. The enlistee in the U.S. armed forces, for example, is immediately forced into practices that divide him from his cohort and fit him to a system of rank: shaving the head, rising before dawn, early morning exercises, unison marches, on and on. These can only be called forced distractions.

Distraction, of course, is not unique to the military, and it is not the property of a military elite – in its multiple forms, it is a tactical element in all conflicts, and on all sides, military or not. It is not, we have seen, solely the possession of the stronger force, nor can it be limited to the conditions of capture. One can distract power to escape it. To distract power is to elude its grasp and, potentially, to *overpower it by block-ing its sense.* Unable to sense its object or to *make sense* of it, that is, to signify it, dis-tracted power is rendered powerless.[47] It cannot locate or name its object, or assign it a place in its code (thus, distraction is not just sign, but anti-sign, anti-code). It is not surprising that this overpowering potential of distraction, which originally aims to destroy power, immediately becomes power's strongest ally. As soon as they appear, as soon as they are seen in their role as productive of the conditions of perception, the means of distraction are harnessed to the Law, which then employs them to normal-ize behaviour, to reinforce or modify habits, to channel desire and belief along appro-priate paths. But these same means, at any time, can once again become methods for mocking the Law – then it is the 'bad' habits that they generate, the illicit desires, and the 'evil' signs.[48]

Because distraction is both a signifying and anti-signifying power, it is a diagram of ritualized, social behaviour. It is the basis of both the sedimented character of ritual enactments (forms of habit) and the *challenge* ritual throws up to the very forces which authorize and sanction those enactments. Ritual power is nothing more than the dis-traction of a superior power – a god, a demon, death itself. This is how we should view the practices of sacrifice, prayer, and sacrament, as so many distractions to divert a dangerous force and divide it from its supports. In all these practices we witness the sign as dividing or sorting strategy, a machine for the purpose of weakening and strengthening, but a machine that ultimately obeys no master and can as easily turn on the very forces that seek to employ it.

Today, we perhaps must radicalize Benjamin's question about distraction to account for changing technical conditions. It may no longer be adequate to frame this question in terms of theses regarding art in an age of *mechanical reproduction.* Rather, we must con-sider the possibility that mechanical techniques of reproduction are being supplanted by digital technologies, and that this signals at least an intensification of their dynamics, and possibly a qualitative shift. That is, we must think about moving from an industrial to a postindustrial or informational model of distraction. At issue in this question is not so much the notion of 'reproduction,' which still assumes that it makes sense to distin-guish an 'original' from its copies, but *simulation,* which implies, at least in theory, the essential meaninglessness of that opposition.[49] Benjamin, we have seen, notes the loss of the artwork's 'aura' in contemporary culture – its originality and spatiotemporal uniqueness – as it increasingly is subjected to the imperatives of mass production. But it is the principle of production (and reproduction) itself that is challenged by simulation. When art is simulated, its status *as* art becomes problematic in a way that is different from if it is merely mass produced. Not only is its originality lost, but so is its value as a copy, that is, as a 'reminder' of uniqueness, situatedness, realness. The same is true of architecture – computer technology, for instance, has made it possible to speak of 'vir-tual' architectures, cyberspaces, and so on.[50] Baudrillard believes we have entered a time of 'trans-aesthetics,' where everything becomes art even as art itself disappears (in the same sense that the 'real' disappears into the 'hyperreal').[51] The notion of 'simulated architectures,' then, would refer not to constructions of steel and concrete, but to the (no less material) information structures that now form the background (noise?) of daily life; not to negotiated spaces, but to non-spatial 'environments' or 'climates';[52] not simply to tactile or visual appropriation, but to seamless neural integration.

The purpose of these reflections is not to analyse simulation, which would take us too far afield, but to think how distraction might operate in an age where simulation has become a dominant strategy of social control. Distraction, it would appear, impacts the body today by organizing its flows at a molecular level, at the interface of the cellular structure of the organism and the system of information. To use language from Donna Haraway, distraction has gone 'cyborgian.'[53] It is no problem to see the forces of distraction at work in the connection of any kid's fingers to the buttons of his or her video game controller. Can we imagine a time when our brains are wired directly to those buttons, when the brain itself is a distraction-machine that can call up its own diversions at the merest thought? When we no longer appropriate the scene tactilely but through our nervous system?[54] Pure escape, or pure capture? Who could tell? This would be 'trans-art' and 'trans-architecture' at their logical, and nightmarish, limit.

Benjamin's thesis that modern art mobilizes the masses to convert socially necessary tasks into habits is undoubtedly still salient. So is his theory that increasingly those tasks converge on the practice of testing. If anything, we could say that testing as a social imperative is raised to the nth degree in simulation societies. Simulations are, in fact, not just tests, but *pre*-tests – one uses simulation as a favoured tactic whenever possible to eliminate the very need for tests.[55] The army simulates battle scenarios on its computers to avoid having to 'test' any one of them in a real conflict; the police utilize profiles to narrow the range of possible suspects; schools utilize models of performance to prescreen and sort students into appropriate tracks; advertisers test their images on sample populations, which are themselves derived from simulations; parents select their children from a range of genetic options. Computer simulation technologies as a whole could be seen as sorting and selection assemblages of the most radical kind, channelling flows of matter and energy by virtue of pre-testing the outcomes of those flows. In fact, their essential function is nothing more than to sort materials into testable aggregates (pre-sorting, pre-dividing). Money, sex, food, blood, genes, words – whatever flows can be captured in terms of information and fed into simulation models to better control absolutely the ranges of possible outcomes. It is becoming increasingly apparent today that few flows, indeed, can escape these widely distributed methods of tracking and diversion.[56]

Can it be said any longer that we 'inhabit' these spaces of information, these pre-test, pre-sorting, pre-dividing zones where it is no longer a matter of tactile but molecular and genetic integration? Do information architectures generate habits? Or do they, in fact, eliminate the requirement of habituation to necessary tasks? When things can be distracted – marked, drawn off, diverted – before they even begin their trajectories (as is the plan for genetic engineering technologies), when their flows are captured in advance, what role does habit play? Does a cyborg or a clone fall into habits? Or is it, rather, one *big* habit, *only* habit, the utopia of perfect habituation which the control societies of the West have been aiming at for the past one hundred years?[57]

Such speculations could easily make us forget that distraction must still be linked to questions of power, that it operates as a means of escape as well as capture. Guattari, for instance, is not willing to identify information systems strictly with systems of domination or subjectification, although clearly that is how he would characterize a great deal in the contemporary situation.[58] Virtually everywhere we turn in information societies, where information is channelled for commercial purposes, distraction functions to arrest flows, to harden them into permanent structures and functions. Where are the information strategies that offer escape, that break down hardened systems, that destratify and remix layers of sediment? Hacking technologies for breaking and distributing computer codes should remind us that no system of domination is permanent or seamless and that even virtual architectures are subject to sudden breakdowns and catastrophes. What else is hacking than an elaborate game of distraction (breaking and entering, covering one's tracks, drawing off flows of information into banks other than those which were intended for their deposit)?

It is no doubt that modern systems of information control threaten to eliminate both the dangers and the charms of distraction as escape. 'Recliner' civilization increasingly finds itself caught up in grand delusions of escape, only to discover itself bound ever more tightly to the images on its screens, and to the channels of information which now threaten to restructure it at the molecular level. The political question today remains: what modes of distraction, operating at the most micro-scales of the body, can transform such delusionary escapes into real ones?

Notes

1 Arthur Kroker and Michael A. Weinstein, *Data Trash: The Theory of the Virtual Class* (New York: St Martin's, 1994), 41; also Arthur Kroker and David Cook, *The Postmodern Condition: Excremental Culture and Hyper-Aesthetics* (New York: St Martin's, 1986), 266ff.

2 Arthur Kroker, Marilouise Kroker, and David Cook, *The Panic Encyclopedia: The Definitive Guide to the Postmodern Scene* (New York: St Martin's, 1989); Arthur Kroker and Marilouise Kroker, eds., *Body Invaders: Panic Sex in America* (Montreal: New World Perspectives, 1987).

3 Marshall McLuhan, *Understanding Media: The Extensions of Man* (New York: McGraw-Hill, 1964); cf. William Bogard, 'Smoothing Machines and the Constitution of Society,' *Cultural Studies* 14/2 (2000): 269-94.

4 Jean Baudrillard, 'The Masses: The Implosion of the Social in the Media,' *New Literary History* 16/3 (1985): 577-89; Jean Baudrillard, *Simulations* (New York: Semiotext(e), 1983); Jean Baudrillard, *In the Shadow of the Silent Majorities or ... The End of the Social* (New York: Semiotext(e), 1983).

5 Baudrillard, *Simulations*, 53.

6 Gilles Deleuze and Felix Guattari, *A Thousand Plateaus: Capitalism and Schizophrenia, vol. 2,* trans. Brian Massumi (Minneapolis: University of Minnesota Press, 1987 [1980]), 424ff.

7 Felix Guattari, *Chaosmosis: An Ethico-Aesthetic Paradigm* (Bloomingtom: Indiana University Press, 1995 [1992]), 33.

8 Martin Heidegger, *The Question concerning Technology and Other Essays*, trans. William Lovitt (New York : Harper and Row, 1977).

9 Heidegger, ibid.; also Felix Guattari, *The Guattari Reader*, Gary Genesko, ed. (New York: Blackwell, 1996); William Bogard, 'Smoothing Machines.'

10 The term 'diagram' is used by Foucault to describe the organization of the modern prison not in terms of a rational schema, but as a consistent space of differently composed matters, some architectural, some imported from military, educational or religious institutions, some linguistic, etc. The diagram, which he formulates under the broad heading of 'discipline,' is not unique to one field or plane, but organizes qualitatively different fields in similar ways (the school, the barracks, the asylum, etc. – all effect disciplinary regimes in their specific characteristic arrangements). See Michel Foucault, *Discipline and Punish: The Birth of the Prison* (New York: Vintage, 1979 [1975]). Cf. also Gilles Deleuze, *Difference and Repetition* (New York: Columbia University Press, 1994 [1968]), at 34 on Foucault's use of 'diagram.'

11 Deleuze and Guattari, *Thousand Plateaus,* 141-8, 510-14.

12 Cf. Manuel DeLanda, *A Thousand Years of Nonlinear History* (New York: Zone Books, 1997), 62; Manuel DeLanda, *War in the Age of Intelligent Machines* (Cambridge: MIT Press, 1989); cf. Humberto R. Maturana and Francisco Varela, *The Tree of Knowledge: The Biological Roots of Human Understanding* (Boston: Shambhala, 1992).

13 Deleuze, and Guattari, *Thousand Plateaus*; Gilles Deleuze, and Felix Guattari, *What Is Philosophy?* (New York: Columbia University Press, 1994 [1991]).

14 Manuel DeLanda, *Thousand Years of Nonlinear History*, 58.

15 Cf. Ilya Prigogine, *Order Out of Chaos; Man's New Dialogue with Nature* (Boston: Shambhala, 1984); James Gleick, *Chaos: Making a New Science* (New York: Penguin, 1987).

16 Manuel DeLanda, *Thousand Years of Nonlinear History*, 60.

17 Ibid., 257ff.

18 Ibid., 32.

19 Cf. Felix Guattari, and Eric Alliez, *Molecular Revolution* (New York: Penguin, 1984).

20 Cf. Guattari, *Guattari Reader*, 95–108; Felix Guattari, *Chaosmosis*, 1-32; Felix Guattari, 'Regimes, Pathways, Subjects,' in *Zone 6: Incorporations* (New York: Zone Books, 1992); also Alphonso Lingis, 'The Society of Dismembered Body Parts,' *Gilles Deleuze and the Theater of Philosophy*, Constantin Boundas and Dorothea Olkowski, eds. (New York: Routledge, 1994), 289–303.

21 Cf. Elias Canetti, *Crowds and Power* (New York: Farrar, Strauss, and Giroux, 1960), 93–124; on 'intensive science' cf. Manuel DeLanda, *Intensive Science and Virtual Philosophy* (New York: Continuum, 2002).

22 Paul Virilio, *Speed and Politics* (New York: Semiotext(e), 1986); cf. also James Der Derian, 'The (S)pace of International Relations: Simulation, Surveillance, and Speed,' *International Studies Quarterly* 34 (1990): 295–310.

23 Neil Munro, *The Quick and the Dead: Electronic Combat and Modern Warfare* (New York: St Martin's Press, 1991).

24 Foucault, *Discipline and Punish*.

25 Paul Virilio, *The Aesthetics of Disappearance* (New York: Semiotext(e), 1991); Paul Virilio, *War and Cinema: the Logistics of Perception* (London: Verso, 1989); Virilio, *Speed and Politics*; Paul Virilio, *Pure War* (New York: Semiotext(e), 1983).

26 Michel Foucault, *The History of Sexuality, vol. 1* (New York: Vintage, 1980 [1976]), 92-102.

27 Foucault, *Discipline and Punish*, 195ff.

28 Again, we are trying not to speak metaphorically. The phenomenon of crowd formation, for example, could be considered from the standpoint of chaos Ž as the spontaneous organization of turbulence, i.e., the self organization of flows of heterogeneous elements breaking out from within relatively hardened structures. Canetti's work, to which we have already alluded, is important in this regard as it relates to the movement of packs. See Canetti, *Crowds and Power*. Bill Buford's book, *Among the Thugs*, offers an interesting and important interpretation of crowd behaviour in terms of 'threshold' events (sudden noises, concentration and density limits, spontaneous breakaways of atomic elements that initiate collective movements, etc.). See Bill Buford, *Among the Thugs* (New York: Norton, 1992). We could easily call such initiatory events 'distractions.'

29 Cf. DeLanda, *Intensive Science.*

30 Deleuze, and Guattari, *Thousand Plateaus,* 6.

31 Sun Tzu, *The Art of War*, trans. Samuel B. Griffith (Oxford: Oxford University Press, 1963), 90–101, 142–9.

32 Foucault, *Discipline and Punish.*

33 Walter Benjamin, 'The Work of Art in the Age of Mechanical Reproduction,' *Illuminations: Walter Benjamin Essays and Reflections*, ed. Hannah Arendt (New York: Schocken, 1969), 217–51.

34 Ibid., 240.

35 Ibid.

36 Percepts, according to Deleuze and Guattari, are not mental states of a subject, but power arrangements, desiring-machines, etc. Again, insofar as distraction involves perception, it is in the sense of organizing its conditions, i.e., its material environment. See Deleuze, and Guattari, *What Is Philosophy?* 163-99.

37 Benjamin, 'Work of Art,' 240.

38 Cf. Deleuze, *Difference and Repetition*, 70-82, on the notion of habit as contraction.

39 Of course, the work of Bourdieu is central here, though his work remains 'sociological' in the narrow sense, rather than 'machinic.' See Pierre Bourdieu, *Outline of a Theory of Practice*, trans. Richard Nice (Cambridge: Cambridge University Press, 1977).

40 Benjamin, 'Work of Art,' 230-6.

41 Cf. also Virilio, *Aesthetics of Disappearance* and *War and Cinema* on this point. Virilio makes important connections between the development of modern cinematic equipment and strategies of disappearance.

42 Benjamin, 'Work of Art,' 223.

43 Baudrillard, *Simulations.*

44 Benjamin, 'Work of Art,' 234.

45 Deleuze and Guattari, *Thousand Plateaus*; cf. also Guattari, 'Regimes, Pathways, Subjects,' and *The Guattari Reader*.

46 Michel Foucault, *The Archaeology of Knowledge* (New York: Harper and Row, 1972 [1969]), 49.

47 On sense and regimes of power and desire, see Gilles Deleuze, *The Logic of Sense* (New York: Columbia University Press, 1990).

48 Cf. Baudrillard, *In the Shadow;* Jean Baudrillard, *The Evil Demon of Images* (Annandale: Power Institute, 1987), on the 'evil demon of images'.

49 Cf. Jean Baudrillard, *Symbolic Exchange and Death* (London: Sage, 1993); Jean Baudrillard, *Fatal Strategies* (New York: Semiotext(e), 1990); Baudrillard, *In the Shadow.*

50 Cf. Michael Benedikt, ed., *Cyberspace* (Cambridge: MIT Press, 1992).

51 Jean Baudrillard, *The Transparency of Evil* (New York: Verso, 1993).

52 Cf. Michael Hardt and Antonio Negri, *Empire* (Cambridge: Harvard University Press, 2000).

53 Donna Haraway, 'A Manifesto for Cyborgs: Science, Technology, and Socialist-Feminism in the 1980s,' *Socialist Review* 15/2 (1985): 65-108.

54 Cf. Michael Taussig, *The Nervous System* (New York: Routledge, 1991).

55 Baudrillard, *Simulations*, 115-17.

56 Cf. William Bogard, *The Simulation of Surveillance: Hypercontrol in Telematic Societies* (Cambridge: Cambridge University Press, 1996).

57 James Beniger, *The Control Revolution: Technological and Economic Origins of the Information Society* (Cambridge: Harvard University Press, 1986).

58 Guattari, *The Guattari Reader*, and *Chaosmosis*. Nor would he accept the idealist assumptions of Baudrillard's analysis of simulation (in this he agrees with Virilio, who views simulation as a matter of material substitution of technical practices rather than the hyperrealism of signs). See Paul Virilio, *The Art of the Motor* (Minneapolis: University of Minnesota Press, 1995). Distraction, too, we must insist, can only be adequately grasped as a material practice (machine-assemblage).

29 The Rebirth of the Author

NICHOLAS ROMBES

Roland Barthes's famous prediction about the death of the author has come to pass, but not because the author is nowhere, but rather because the author is everywhere.

Indeed, the author has grown and multiplied in direct proportion to academic dismissals and denunciations of her presence; the more roundly and confidently the author has been dismissed as a myth, a construction, an act of bad faith, the more strongly she has emerged. The recent surge in personal websites and blogs – rather than diluting the author concept – has helped to create a tyrannical authorship presence, where the elevation of the personal and private to the public level has only compounded the cult of the author. We are all authors today. We are all *auteurs*. We are all writers. We are all filmmakers. And we are all theorists, because what we make theorizes itself.

Perhaps it was all a mistake, a terrible act of misreading. Rather than a serious deconstruction of the author concept, perhaps Barthes's essay 'The Death of the Author' was ironic, a close relative of pop art.[1] After all, while that essay achieved its widest circulation in the United States in its 1977 version in *Image – Music – Text*, it is perhaps less known that the essay had appeared previously in English in the Fall-Winter 1967 issue of the avant-garde magazine *Aspen*: 'each issue came in a customized box filled with booklets, phonograph recordings, posters, postcards' and even a Super-8 film.[2] Contributors included Andy Warhol, John Cage, Yoko Ono, Hans Richter, Susan Sontag, and others. Barthes's essay, translated by Richard Howard, appeared in a double issue (the minimalism issue) which explored 'conceptual art, minimalist art, and postmodern critical theory.'[3] The year 1967-68 was a serious time, shaken by violence and protest, yes, but it was also a time of great experimentation and humour and absurdity. The pleasure of death and a *jouissance* that has been lost, as career academics used Barthes's essay, stripping it out of its playful dimensions, its at once urgent and resigned manifestolike quality.

The problem, now, is easy to see. Whereas Barthes (and others including Max Horkheimer and Theodor Adorno, Andrew Sarris, Marshall McLuhan, Robert Ray, Pauline Kael, Susan Sontag, Lester Bangs, Dick Hebdige, Antonin Artaud, and Richard Hell) offered theories in language that was playful, slippery, aphoristic, and often poetic, the academics who subsequently applied their theories often did so in prose that was deadly dry, pedantic, serious, stripped of the slippages and humour that made readers want to believe. While scores of academics over the years have gloomily attacked Andrew Sarris's Americanized *auteur* theory (first published in *Film Culture* in 1962 as 'Notes on the *Auteur* Theory in 1962'), they did so by turning their backs on the lively, self-deprecating qualities of his prose, as evident in lines like 'What is a bad director, but a director who has made many bad films?'[4] or in lines where Sarris directly addresses the reader, such as 'Dare I come out and say what I think it to be is an élan of the soul?'[5] Such moments of excess style stand in stark contrast to the deadly serious, rationalist rhetoric that has infected so much writing in the humanities, as the aesthetic dimensions of academic writing – especially in North America – have been ignored for decades as a surplus with no value. If, as Craig Saper has noted, 'In the academy, *auteurism* was considered passé at best'[6] in the wake of poststructuralism, then in erasing the very personality of their own writing style, film scholars and theorists demoted themselves to a level of invisibility and even obsolescence. Generations of graduate students trained to strip all traces of bourgeois personality from their prose awake now to find that they have no audience for their ideas, because their ideas have no expressive confidence.

Yet, there is a gradual return to the pleasures of the text, not as something to be studied merely, but performed. In his preface to a collection of essays by Malcom Le Grice, Sean Cubitt demonstrates in his opening paragraph an approach to writing that recognizes that beauty and power in prose need not be something to hide:

> Have we already forgotten? Why we got into this in the first place? How it was that the moving lights, the washes of colour, first brought us to this world and thanked us, with their generous presentation of themselves, for being there with them? Has the memory faded so radically of those first inklings of beauty, scattering in all its ungraspable ephemerality across our skins as much as our eyes, beams traversing and dragging into motion muscle and bowel, as music drags us to dance? From a politics of renunciation through an aesthetic of minimalism to a phenomenology of ecstasy, Le Grice's films return us to a primal encounter with the physical power of our first perceptions.[7]

Does Cubitt's prose here teeter dangerously close to nostalgia? Perhaps, but this is a risk that pays off; his preface is a sort of high-speed relay between content and the rhetorical framing of that content. Like DJ Spooky – whose writing is aphoristic and unexpected, as in lines like 'We have machines to repeat history for us'[8] and 'Sampling is like sending a fax to yourself from the sonic debris of a possible future'[9] – Cubitt recognizes that humanities-based academic prose is better served by avoiding the deadening safety and boredom of so much writing in the social sciences today.

More than anyone else, it is Jean Baudrillard who has pointed the way out. 'As for ideas, everyone has them,' he has written. 'What counts is the poetic singularity of the analysis. That alone can justify writing, not the wretched critical objectivity of ideas. There will never be any resolving of the contradictoriness of ideas, except in the energy and felicity of language.'[10] Like the author, the *auteur* will not die. Indeed, rather than discrediting the *auteur* theory by demonstrating that, in fact, movies are made by many people, DVDs and other forms of cinematic deconstruction only further strengthen the *auteur* theory, as everyday viewers see and hear from previously invisible film workers (editors, production designers, special effects designers, cinematographers, screenplay writers) who are themselves *auteurs*. Thus, a writer like Charlie Kaufman nearly displaces directors Spike Jonze or Michel Gondry as the *auteur* behind *Being John Malkovich* (1999), *Adaptation* (2002), and *Eternal Sunshine of the Spotless Mind* (2004), while cinematographer Anthony Dod Mantle looms as the 'author' of such films as *The Celebration* (1998), *28 Days Later* (2002), and *Dogville* (2003). Whereas in the past Orson Welles's cinematographer on *Citizen Kane* (1941) – Gregg Toland – would have been relatively obscure except to film scholars and historians, industry insiders, and die-hard film buffs, today Dod Mantle is known not only to people in these groups, but also to more casual film watchers, who, because of media like the Internet Movie Database and other websites, DVDs, and the proliferation of cinema studies classes, are deeply literate about cinema.

Rather than extinguish once and for all the *auteur*, the rise and hegemony of digital technologies and culture have only reinforced the author concept, and have, in fact, helped to create new forms of authorship that are being acknowledged in the broader public. A recent article in the *New York Times*, entitled 'The Powers Behind the Home-Video Throne,' begins: 'When Steven Spielberg directs a movie, he gets final cut. But the last word is more likely to come from Laurent Bouzereau. Mr Bouzereau, 43, is barely known to the world at large. But in the clannish, status-obsessed corridors of Hollywood, he has a growing reputation as Mr Spielberg's personal DVD producer, one of perhaps a dozen players who have mastered the young art of turning the video edition of a film into a sui generis event.'[11] As what was thought of not too long ago to be mere bonus, extra, or supplementary material begins to equal and, indeed, take precedence over the so-called 'feature presentation' of DVDs, a new *auteur* develops as someone whose narrative contributions threaten to overtake the pallid, homogeneous films now buried in hours of special features.[12]

In the face of the digital code, there is an effort to reassert the viability of hermeneutics, of interpretation. In the article, 'Metadata's Impact on "Artistic Intent,"' published in *American Cinematographer*, Debra Kaufman explores the growing concern among cinematographers that in our digital, paperless era, details and records about how and why they arrive at the decisions they make about how to shoot scenes are being lost. Kaufman quotes Jim Sullivan, chief technology officer of Kodak Entertainment Imaging Services, as saying: 'When you disconnect the image from a known medium like film and go into the digital world, you end up with integers in a computer that mean nothing ... They're just storage locations. They don't carry any interpretation with them about how [the footage] was captured or is meant to be displayed.'[13] When Lars von Trier and Thomas Vinterberg published the Dogma 95 'Vow of Chastity' in 1995, it was only appropriate that they should sign their names – as authors – to the document, which had as one its rules, 'The director must not be credited.'[14] Yet, denunciations of authorship have always tended to strengthen the cult and authority of those doing the denouncing. Indeed, it was Barthes who called the author into being and whose denunciations helped create the conditions for the dictatorship of the author in the digital era.

In any case, despite the good intentions of posthumanist academics for whom the author was symptomatic of a capitalist ill to be cured, now we witness the viral spread of the author concept into the very structures of academic expression. Today, anonymity is a sign of guilt, or failure. As academics embrace the Web – and blogs and vlogs specifically – as legitimate sites of knowledge creation and dissemination, resistance to the author function withers. For was not one of the engines that drove the cult of the death of the author the secret desire by academics to be authors themselves? Not authors who wrote obscure articles that were inevitably consigned to the dark stacks of enormous libraries, but authors who tested their ideas in the public sphere, authors whose ideas mattered beyond the narrow handful of specialists who would pass predictable judgment on their work? Authors whose ideas mattered enough to be praised or damned? Confronted with the spectre of the public sphere, academics are learning how to write again. The crisis of the scholarly publishing subsidy system portends an enormous shift wherein the discredited author concept is resurrected. Rather than the utopian dream of collective, collaborative authorship that many theorists first saw in hypertext and blogs, we see instead, the proliferation of *auteurs* vying for public space in the public sphere.

Stripped of aura, of mystery, of distance, we are known today as mapped elements in a database. Surveilled, recorded, and marked, we are becoming the function of our components – our decoded genes, the number of hits (hourly, daily, monthly) on our websites, our online purchasing histories. It is perhaps ironic that it is in the very forms of authorship that posthumanist critics strove to erase that we find our best chance of theorizing – and resisting – our own disappearance. Donna Haraway's ironic prediction that 'by the late twentieth century, our time, a mythic time, we are all chimeras, theorized and fabricated hybrids of machine and organism; in short, we are cyborgs'[15] has assumed the shape of everyday social reality. Is it any surprise that for every technological advancement that renders a more perfect, flawless reality – whether it be classical Hollywood's invisible style, or new film stocks and lenses that offer a cleaner and sharper image, or the hyperrealism of high definition, or the clean, hiss-less ring of the digital code – is it any surprise that these are always accompanied by countermeasures that preserve and introduce errors, mistakes, degradations of the pristine image? Whether it be Italian neorealism, or cinéma-vérité, or experimental films by the likes of Stan Brakhage, or the rough, 'amateur' look of the Dogma 95 films, or even the blurred, miniature movies of Web cinema – all these serve as an antidote to the very forms of perfection that we seek. The author is stronger than ever today because she reminds us of an identity memorable for its utter failures. And to be reminded of our failures is to be reminded that we are human.

Perhaps it was easy to dismiss the author when there was so little at stake. But now, as we approach the time when it will be possible to lift the veil on our very own codes, we find that it is precisely in human authorship – with its mistakes, errors, slippages, ambiguities, reversals and contradictions, irrationalities, and surprises – where we can reassert ourselves against the very destruction that once, because it was myth, we so eagerly desired.

Notes

1 Roland Barthes, 'The Death of the Author,' in *Image–Music–Text*, trans. Stephen Health (New York: Hill and Wang, 1977), 142–8. Also in *Aspen* nos. 5 and 6 (1967). Available at www.ubu.com/aspen/aspen5and6/index.html.

2 'About Aspen,' *Aspen: The multimedia magazine*, available at http://www.ubu.com/aspen, accessed 6 Sept. 2005.

3 Ibid.

4 Andrew Sarris. 'Notes on the *Auteur* Theory in 1962,' in *Film Culture Reader*, ed. P. Adams Sitney (New York: Cooper Square Press, 2000), 132.

5 Ibid. 133.

6 Craig Saper, 'Artificial *Auteurism* and the Political Economy of the Allen Smithee Case,' in *Directed by Allen Smithee*, ed. Jeremy Braddock and Stephen Hock (Minneapolis: University of Minnesota Press, 2001), 33.

7 Sean Cubitt, 'Preface: The Colour of Time,' *Experimental Cinema in the Digital Age*, by Malcom Le Grice (London: British Film Institute, 2001), vii.

8 Paul D. Miller (aka DJ Spooky), *Rhythm Science* (Cambridge: MIT Press, 2004), 9.

9 Ibid.

10 Jean Baudrillard, *The Perfect Crime*, trans. Chris Turner (London and New York: Verso, 1996), 103. Originally published in French by Editions Galilée, 1995.

11 Christian Moerk, 'The Powers Behind the Home-Video Throne,' *New York Times*, 3 April 2005, 1, available at http://www.nytimes.com/2005/04/03/movies/03moer.html, accessed 6 sept. 2005.

12 For a good discussion of the emergence of DVD 'supplementary-ness,' see Graeme Harper, 'DVD and the New Cinema of Complexity,' in *New Punk Cinema*, ed. Nicholas Rombes (Edinburgh: Edinburgh University Press, 2005), 89–101.

13 Debra Kaufman, 'Metadata's Impact on "Artistic Intent,"' *American Cinematographer* (Dec. 2003): 1, available at http://theasc.com/magazine/dec03/sub/index.html, accessed 6 Sept. 2005.

14 For the Dogma 95 manifesto and 'Vow of Chastity,' see *P.O.V.* 10 (Dec. 2000), available at http://imv.au.dk/publikationer/pov/Issue_10/POV_10cnt.html, accessed 6 Sept. 2005.

15 Donna Haraway, 'A Cyborg Manifesto: Science, Technology, and Socialist-Feminism in the Late Twentieth Century,' in *Simians, Cyborgs and Women: The Reinvention of Nature* (New York: Routledge, 1991), 150.

30 Metal Performance: Humanizing Robots, Returning to Nature, and Camping About

STEVE DIXON

I want to be a machine. I think everybody should be a machine.

Andy Warhol

In this essay I explore 'metal performance' – robot performances and artworks, and cyborgic performances featuring human bodies with metal prostheses – through a close analysis of the work of artists including Guillermo Gómez-Peña, Istvan Kantor, Laura Kikauka, Chico McMurtrie, Mark Pauline, Marcel-lí Antúnez Roca, Stelarc, Momoyo Torimitsu, and Norman White. I argue that metal performances belie deep-seated fears and fascinations associated with machinic embodiments, and that these are explored by artists in relation to two distinct themes: the humanization of machines and the dehumanization (or 'machinization') of humans. I also examine how metal performances frequently dramatize a return to nature and the animal.

Donna Haraway's essay 'The Actors Are Cyborg'[1] explores notions of the cyborg as a performative 'monster' and 'boundary creature,' and Canadian artists Norman White and Laura Kikauka's performance *Them Fuckin' Robots* (1988) features two robots that violently and comedically copulate. Themes concerning the monstrous, the transgressive, the violent, the sexual, and the humorous have each been applied to cyborgs and mechanical anthropomorphic figures. To these I would like to add the term 'metallic camp,' which reflects a particular ideology and aesthetic at play within metal performances.

My central argument posits that the robot and cyborg body in performance are commonly depicted in ways that closely correspond to the politics and aesthetics of camp. In proposing the hypothesis that metal performance is often camp, or at least manifests itself in a way that fits easily within discourses of camp, I would emphasize points made by three of camp's most prominent theorists: first, Susan Sontag's assertion that camp can be both deliberate and accidental;[2] second, Richard Dyer's contention, that camp can be both gay and straight;[3] and thirdly, Fabio Cleto's assertion that camp should not be seen as a negative or derogatory term, unlike, for example, the term 'kitsch.'[4] In my use of the term 'metallic camp,' the word 'metallic' denotes not only the physical substance that the artists employ, but also its contemporary connotations within popular music and culture as signifying loud, aggressive, and resistant expression. This is juxtaposed with the knowing irony and pleasure of camp, which Susan Sontag defines as 'love of the unnatural: of artifice and exaggeration.'[5] The composite expression 'metallic camp' further suggests a distinct place or ideological grouping (as in a 'base camp' or 'the anti-war camp') where people share a position or affinity. In metal performance, this relates equally to a common resistance to, and a common belief in, metal as symbolic of a desirable evolutionary process via cyborgism to ultimate machinic embodiment.

I would stress that I do not consider *all* metal performance to be camp. Survival Research Laboratories, for example, creates extremely butch robot battle performances waged by darkly surreal machines: combinations of dead animals, junkyard scrap, and industrial and construction-site debris animated into life. The machines' designs are generally derived either from the animal kingdom (monstrous birds, worms, crabs, insects, and running legs) or from industrial and military models (huge and menacing cannons, tank vehicles, walking flamethrowers, crane structures, and industrial arms with snapping jaws and swinging demolition balls). But even in these brutal, crowd-pleasing battles, some elements of camp are apparent. Leonardo Da Vinci's painting of the Last Supper is parodied with the disciples as camp, life-size moving mannequins, which are stabbed and decapitated by one robot, and then shot into flames by another. A large, kitsch clown's head, dangling in the air with a happy grin, receives similar treatment.

Robots are not ipso facto camp: for example, robotic industrial assembly lines, 'smart' weapons, and some robotic artworks perform computer-controlled tasks without a hint of camp irony or behavioural exaggeration. But some degree of camp seems inherent in almost all 'performing' anthropomorphic and zoomorphic robots I have seen. Their movements are one key to this. Since robots currently fail to accurately mimic human and animal movement, their exaggerated gaits and gestures emphasize the same sense of theatricality and artificiality in movement that we find in camp. The artificiality of robot movement mirrors the artificiality of camp. Robotics artist Bruce Cannon has reflected that 'these machines' failure to transcend their artificiality is their most significant aspect. The pieces are not so much lifelike as referential to being, and what is missing is what resonates to me.'[6]

Robotic movement mimics and exaggerates but never achieves the human, just as camp movement mimics and exaggerates but never achieves womanhood. Robot kinetics involves the same degree of performative self-consciousness as 'camping about' and often visually resembles it. When an anthropomorphic robot moves or when a person camps about, it is highly calculated and coded (however ingrained and natural the human camp behaviour may have become). Although robots may not yet be self-aware, they are quintessentially 'self-conscious' entities, calculating and computing their every

move. When a humanoid robot moves, just as when someone camps about, it is a knowing and self-conscious performance; its coding, artificiality, and difference from the
norm are emphasized. Camp thus becomes a central, even determining aspect of
anthropomorphic robot performance.

Them Fuckin' Robots and Executive Machinery Intercourse

For *Them Fuckin' Robots,* the artists agreed on some technical specifications and then
worked separately to create two mechanical robots. Laura Kikauka's 'female' machine
included bedsprings, fur, a sewing machine treadle, a squirting oil pump, and a boil-
ing kettle; Norman White's anthropomorphic 'male' robot comprised metal arms and
legs, gauges, assorted rotating or pumping appendages, and rapidly flickering
addenda. The artists came together on the day of the first performance and assembled the joint artwork in front of the audience, connecting different pipes, pistons,
and mechanical parts from one robot to the other. The robots were then activated
and proceeded to 'have sex,' the male machine responding to the female organ's magnetic fields, which increased its movement rates and charged a capacitor. The robots
performed to the accompaniment of a comic, cheesy organ soundtrack punctuated by
a robotic voice incanting the words 'abnormal sex behaviour.' According to one audience member, it was 'a fun performance … pretty absurd stuff.'[7] A videotape shows an
apparently delighted promenade audience smiling broadly at the pumping metal pistons and laughing raucously at a climax comprising exploding electrical sparks and
gooey fluid oozing out of one of the robot's tubes in intermittent spurts.

   The pun within the phrase 'them fuckin' robots' holds significance for the consideration of the contemporary context of metal performance. Beyond denoting the literal
sense of copulation, it plays on the increasingly suspicious or hostile human stance
towards robots as a threat and as Other: a shout of bigotry against a hated minority. In
its depiction of sexual activity, the performance presents a parody of the humanization
of machines. At the same time there is recognition of the possibility of some kind of
future robotic procreation. As Bernard de Fontenelle maintains: 'Put a Dog Machine and
a Bitch Machine side by side, and eventually a third little machine will be the result.'[8]

   Them Fuckin' Robots explicitly encapsulates what Claudia Springer identifies as our contemporary fascination with the conjunction of technology and sexuality.[9] These quirky
and humorous fornicating machines also perfectly embody the performance of metallic
camp. Robot copulation features strongly in the work of The Seemen robotic performance group, who construct monstrous metal creatures that do battle, often amid raging fires. The company suggest that the robots 'poetically symbolize man's struggles and
triumphs,'[10] while the flames are metaphors for a range of ideas, from purification to rivers and waterfalls, and male ejaculation. Performances feature 'trees armed with
flamethrowers, underwater sea monsters spitting fire from watery depths, flaming
robots fucking, fighting and lovemaking.'[11] The sex acts between robots in performances

such as *Violent Machines Perform Acts of Love* (1998) are often presented as caring and loving, their tender movements emphasizing the machines' humanization.

In Istvan Kantor's *Executive Machinery Intercourse* (1999) another loud, extreme, and sexualized metallic camp performance is played out. Filing cabinets fill the space, their drawers pulled open and banged shut by different metal-armed hydraulic constructions, creating a cacophony of metallic noise. Kantor describes the mise-en-scène as follows: 'The ... monolithic file cabinet machines are linked together by computers and integrated into a giant network that functions as both kinesonic machinery and an interactive monument serving the entire world with information.'[12] This metal monument to global information is, then, in true camp style, well and truly 'fucked.' A number of filing cabinets stand alone, their drawers pumping out automatically without the aid of external machine arm devices.

As the pneumatic drawers shoot in and out, live male and female performers writhe and gyrate against them in a display of determined and often violent eroticism; simulating high-energy sex with insistent, hard pelvic thrusts. Audience members are also invited to join in. The metal information monuments then fuck back, faster and faster. It is a true meat-and-metal cybernetic system of stimulus and response, data exchanges and feedback.

A line of four video projections (each running the same image) fills the back cyclorama, playing frantically speeded up 1950s-style black-and-white pre-recorded footage of performers engaged in machine sex. A young woman dressed like Marilyn Monroe with blonde wig and a *Seven Year Itch*–style white dress on gyrates against the relentlessly thrusting drawers, panting orgasmically; an office secretary fucks the cabinets enthusiastically while conducting an intermittent and furious row with her boss. The performance juxtaposes a Bacchanalian orgy with a Kafkaesque nightmare of the office machine gone mad. It shares with *Them Fuckin' Robots* a delight in 'comic pornography,' which Cleto identifies as a common characteristic of camp within queer aesthetics[13] and is what David Bergman terms camp's 'self-conscious eroticism that throws into question the naturalization of desire.'[14]

The pneumatic filing cabinets are more athletic than the human performers: they are fitter machines. But the human copulatory movements emphasize the fluid anatomies and sensual choreographies of the human body in contrast to the rigid straight lines and sexually unsophisticated 'in-out' action of the cabinet drawers. The performance manifests the difference between soft, sensual, impulsive, and easily exhausted flesh and hard, repetitive, robotic metal. It also emphasizes the link between 'the sculptural system of the file cabinet ... [and] the mutating human body, eroticized and abused by technology.'[15]

The Machinization of Humans and the Humanization of Machines

The sexual themes of *Them Fuckin' Robots* and *Executive Machinery Intercourse* articulate two closely related contemporary anxieties related to 'unnatural coition' between humans and machines. These centre, first, on the increasing humanization of machines and, second, on the gradual *dehumanization* of humans in the face of technology. These two forces are seen as prompting humans towards a gradual evolution *into* machines and metallic embodiments by virtue of their increasing faith in, affinity with, and psychophysical transformation by machines. This second concept of the dehumanization of humans may therefore also be expressed as the mechanization of humans. But, given the negative connotations of the word 'mechanization' in relation to people (suggesting a zombielike workforce performing repetitive actions), I will use the term *machinization*, since cyborgic metal is (in theory) intended to sensitize and expand human physical and mental capabilities rather than to desensitize and reduce them.

As early as 1954, Norbert Wiener proposed a radical machinization of humans, suggesting that 'we have modified our environment so radically that we must now modify ourselves in order to exist in this new environment.'[16] In his earlier groundbreaking work, *Cybernetics*, Wiener also considered at length the humanization of machines, maintaining that the question of whether machines could be considered to be alive or not was largely semantic.[17] For Wiener machines were alive because they were physically animate and operationally active. The idea of human transformation into metal reaches its logical conclusion with Hans Moravec's assertion that by the middle of the twenty-first century it will be possible to download one's entire consciousness into a computer.[18] In *The Universal Robot*, Moravec dramatizes this notion into a Frankensteinian surgical operation where the contents of the brain are physically removed from the human head to be implanted into its new metal box: 'In a final, disoriented step the surgeon lifts its hand. Your suddenly abandoned body dies. For a moment you experience only quiet and dark .... Your perspective has shifted ... [and] reconnected to a shiny new body of the style, colour and material of your choice. Your metamorphosis is complete.'[19]

Moravec suggests that humans can either 'adopt the fabulous mechanisms of robots, thus becoming robots themselves, or they can retire into obscurity.'[20] Metal performance reflects this techno-zeitgeist, which senses a gradual but inevitable merging of flesh and metal. There are thus two routes to the robot, which are perceived as operating simultaneously: one via AI, building artificially intelligent, sentient beings; the other through cyborgism, adapting the human form to a supposedly 'superior' robotic and computational physiognomy. The camp aesthetics that I associate with metallic performance derive equally from artists who largely affirm and embrace such metamorphoses and from those who are sceptical or oppositional.

Performances by the proponents of flesh and metal symbiosis can be sited frequently within the aesthetics of camp by virtue of their theatrical and computational codes of high-artifice and excess and through their celebration of 'monstrous' transgression. Robotic and cyborgic embodiments relate perfectly to the camp sensibility, particularly in relation to gay camp, which distinguishes and celebrates difference and otherness as a coded or blatant affront to straight society's notions of what is subversive or alien to the norm. While expressions of opposition to the mainstream characterize many avant-garde forms, the use of camp as an aesthetic device in metal performance is quite specific to its particular form of transgressive rhetoric, what Mark Dery calls its 'rituals of resistance.'[21]

Camp preens and shows off, it uses narcissism to define and express its ontology of difference and to draw attention to itself. It exaggerates physical and vocal expression to 'stand out,' the meaning of one of its various etymological origins, the Italian verb *campeggiare*.[22] Its French root, *se camper*, translates as 'self-conscious posturing,'[23] while its Indo-European origin, *kamp*, reflects the physical shapes and movements of camp's postures: curved, flexible, articulated.[24] Gay camp is also a 'fuck you' stance, sticking a finger up at the conformist social performance of normative male heterosexuality and ridiculing machismo posturing. It registers membership in an exclusive, even superior club. Just as the cyborg signifies an advanced or evolved form of the human, a metamorphosis that separates it from the crowd, so too males who 'camp about' register and display to the outside world that they have undergone their own specific evolution. They have developed, among other things, an understanding of their feminine side, ironic wit, aesthetic sensibility, and sexual self-knowledge.

Metal performances by artists resistant to, or sceptical of, the biometallic fusion utilize similar camp high-theatrics, and, additionally, harness the self-parodic, barbed humour of camp to point at the inherent comedy, absurdity, and danger of metallic embodiments. The latter approach is evident in Brian Frisk's *Wearerobots.com* website which features animations of robots with human temperaments and emotions.[25] The machines' similarities with humans and their struggle with their feelings is darkly comic: Sad Robot grapples with his sense of identity, wailing that 'some people don't even know I'm a robot, they think I'm Puerto Rican, but just really good at math.' The robots betray human aspirations, but more particularly human emotional weaknesses and failings. One depressed robot pours out his heart in group therapy; another becomes increasingly furious during a telephone call when only humans are available to speak to: 'It's impossible to get through to a machine these days!' he curses. The robots also transgress human protocols by directly speaking their minds, like Angrybot, a schoolteacher who tells his students that their homework is to go home and kill themselves.

The animations express deep-seated anxieties about the humanization of machines. They point to the recognition that as technology advances there is a gradual diminution of the differences between human and machine. Robots become more humanlike through developments in artificial intelligence, and humans become more robotlike as they grow more alienated and remote from their own and others' humanity through their increasing reliance on technology. Norman White, one of the artists behind *Them Fuckin' Robots*, subverts the idea of artificial intelligence by designing robots that he imbues with what he calls 'artificial sanity.' He has designed a number of 'contrary' and antisocial robots, such as *Facing Out, Laying Low* (1977) which stops interacting with audiences when it feels bored or is given too many competing stimuli. His *Helpless Robot, or HLR* (1988) speaks but does not move and displays a distinctly camp bitchiness in its dealings with gallery visitors, whose stupidity it berates, whatever they may do. White describes it as 'the classic "hustler"' and elaborates: 'For instance, it might initially enlist human cooperation with a polite "Excuse me ... have you got a moment?", or any one of such unimposing phrases. It might then ask to be rotated: "Could you please turn me just a bit to the right ... No! not that way ... the other way!" In such a way, as it senses cooperation, it tends to become ever more demanding, becoming in the end, if its human collaborators let it, dictatorial.'[26]

New York–based Japanese performance artist Momoyo Torimitsu's robot *Miyata Jiro* (2001) encapsulates both the humanization of machines and the machinization of humans. *Miyata Jiro* is a realistic, life-size, balding businessman that crawls on its belly along the streets of the financial districts of major cities, while Torimitsu walks behind and tends it, dressed as a nurse. A satirical commentary on the humiliating conformity of Japanese 'salaryman' culture, the robot presents a cowed and hyperrealistic counterpoint to the camp heroic excesses of many robot performances. Fears of enslavement associated with dystopian predictions of machines superseding human beings are short-circuited in a stark and parodic reversal. In replacing the human form, *Miyata Jiro* merely serves to expose the degree to which human beings are already on their knees and enslaved to cultural conformity, the work ethic, and capital.

The medical sustenance to the humanized machine provided by Torimitsu's caring nurse character is elaborated in *A-Positive* (1997), created by Eduardo Kac and Ed Bennett, where the dual notions of human machinization and robot humanization are even more starkly depicted. A performer is connected to a robot through an intravenous needle, and actually 'feeds' the robot (or 'biobot') with blood, which flows visibly through a clear tube connecting the human body and the machine. The robot extracts oxygen from the blood and uses it to sustain a tiny and erratic flame, while reciprocating the fluid exchange and completing the sense of human-machine symbiosis by sending an intravenous drip of dextrose into the human body. The visual symbolism mixes medical imagery, cybernetics, and Gothic horror. The piece is calm and understated but distinctly unsettling. It is at once a peaceful and uncomplicated image of body-machine connection, literalizing a circular biological life-flow between human flesh and metal robot, but it also conjures vividly the dark, fearful myths of Frankenstein and Dracula. Flesh is penetrated to give succour to the non-human, 'undead' machine, and human oxygen is breathed into it to give it life. The machine is directly humanized, pumped by corporeal fluid, while the human body beside it is machinized, its own life-blood invaded and fed by technology.[27]

Increasingly, both medical science and art practices imbricate flesh with machine technologies, and it is pertinent to note in relation to A-Positive the words of an early heart transplant patient in 1969, who reflected on both the wonder and the significant psychophilosophical anxiety involved in his operation: 'Seeing my blood outside of my body running through coils of synthetic tubing is deeply distressing ... [a] miraculous ... powerful monster ... with an almost frightening hold on my life ... reducing me to a "half-robot, half-man."'[28]

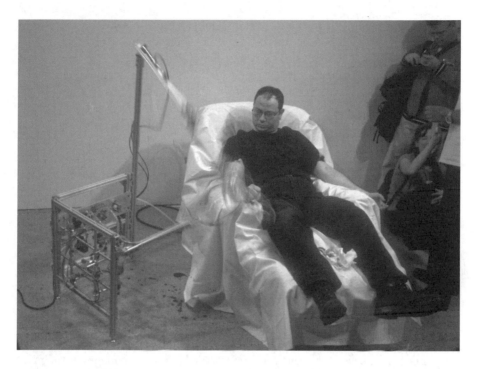

Figure 30.1. Blood, cybernetics, and Gothic horror meet as Eduardo Kac connects up with a machine in *A-Positive* (with Ed Bennett), 1997.

Robotics is now making an important impact in medical surgery, where robotic arms such as 'robodoc' are used to make precision bone incisions. NASA, eager to demonstrate that their space hardware research has implications closer to home, has funded and collaborated on a number of robotic surgical appliances. These include the Automated Endoscopic System for Optimal Positioning (AESOP), developed by Computer Motions Inc., a robotic arm whose precision exceeds human dexterity. Using AESOP's intelligent voice-recognition system, the human surgeon controls all the robot endoscope's movements and operation by simply talking to it. Robots known as 'Nursebots,' which can monitor and dispense medication, and detect emergencies such as falls, using video-recognition systems, are being developed by researchers at Carnegie Mellon and Pittsburgh Universities to act as caregivers in the homes of elderly and disabled people.[29]

A Brief History of Robots and Automata

Although the word 'robot' has been used to describe many machines and mechanical devices that are not computer controlled, stricter definitions place computational operation to the fore. Ken Goldberg broadly defines a robot as 'a mechanism controlled by a computer,'[30] and Eduardo Kac maintains that 'robots are advanced computer-controlled electromechanical appliances.'[31] The Czech word *robota*, variously translated as 'work,' 'serf,' or 'forced labour,' was adopted in the English-speaking world as 'robot' directly through the title of Karel Capek's 1921 expressionist play *R.U.R.* (*Ros-sum's Universal Robots*). The play concerns the supplanting of humans by robots, and it has been widely discussed both as a warning against Frankensteinian scientific hubris and as an allegory of the 1917 Bolshevik Revolution, with the oppressed masses 'recast' as robots. Its story presents an early and potent theatrical vision of the humanization of machines: On an island factory, hyperintelligent worker-robots are developed, and eventually they rebel and take over, murdering their inventors and calling for the destruction of all humankind. In the final act, the celibate robots fear they will die out, and Alquist, the only human they have spared, prays to God, pleading that if there are no humans left anywhere in the world, the robot, as 'the shadow of man' should be able to survive and procreate. The play ends with a young male and female robot developing caring and sexual feelings for one another as Alquist declares 'Go, Adam, go, Eve. The world is yours. ... At least the shadow of man!'[32]

R.U.R. sends complex and mixed messages about the humanization of machines. The robots are first presented as the unjustly oppressed, then as the unfeeling, evil oppressors, and finally as the sensitive, empathetic heroes and heroines of the piece offering a vicarious or deferred salvation for humanity.

Contemporary robot artworks and performances have a long historical lineage, which Bruce Mazlish relates back to the Hermetic story of creation, where 'man is given permission ... to create and animate artificial beings ... or, in my terms, machines.' Mazlish notes that throughout history automata have prompted fears, since they pose 'an "irrational" threat to humans, calling into question their identity, sexuality (the basis of creation?), and powers of domination.'[33] Rodney A. Brooks notes the pneumatically operated automata of Hero of Alexandria around 100 BCE,[34] and Jeff Cook quotes Pindar from 520 BCE:

> The animated figures stand
> Adorning every street
> And seem to breathe in stone, or
> Move their marble feet.[35]

Max von Boehn dates the first anthropomorphic automata back to the third century BCE and suggests evidence that small automata existed in Aristotle's time, citing his reference in *Physics* to a silver doll that moved like a living being.[36] Joseph Needham describes a vast array of mechanical figures, animals, birds, and fishes constructed in ancient China, as well as mechanized chariots and a flying automaton that he dates to circa 380 BCE.[37]

The first clockwork automata were constructed in the fourteenth century, and clocks with automated figures became common on European cathedrals, including 'crowing cocks, bears that shook heads, a king who turned a sandglass, and the twelve apostles moving in a circle.'[38] Bowing royal figures were common features, including three kings at Strasbourg Cathedral (1352) and seven bowing princes who passed before an automaton of Emperor Charles IV at 12 o'clock at the Marienkapelle in Nürnberg (1361). The clock tower at Soleure, built in 1452, 'depicts a warrior beating his chest on the quarter-hours, while a skeleton clutching an arrow turns his head to the soldier on the first stroke of each hour.'[39] In 1509 Leonardo Da Vinci constructed a lion that could walk; a sixteenth century automaton from Brittany performed a mechanical crucifixion scene; and during the seventeenth century, *karakuri* automata performed the tea-serving ceremony in Japan.

During the eighteenth century a number of European 'master' automata craftsmen emerged, such as Jacques de Vaucanson, who built a robot duck that could waddle, quack, eat, drink, and defecate; and father and son Pierre and Henri Louis Jacquet-Droz, who constructed figures that could draw and play the piano. A female organ player, also by the Jacquet-Droz family, 'simulated breathing and gaze direction, looking at the audience, her hands and the music,'[40] and their boy automaton *The Scribe* (1772) sat at a desk dipping a quill into an inkpot and writing, among other things, Descartes' declaration 'I think, therefore I am.' Michel Foucault argues that the sophisticated automata of the eighteenth century were not simply animated illustrations of organisms, but more importantly 'political puppets, small-scale models of power.' He points out that Frederick the Great, 'the meticulous king of small machines, well-trained regiments and long exercises, was obsessed by them.'[41]

In 1807 Napoleon was defeated in a game of chess by an automated player dressed as a Turkish sorcerer and smoking a hookah, although its moves were decided by a man concealed in the box on which the figure sat and who could view the board through a system of mirrors. Built by Wolfgang de Kempelen in 1769, the automaton is described by Mark Sussman as 'a dramaturgical hybrid of theatre, magic, and science,'[42] and it was invoked by Walter Benjamin as an allegory of the mythical 'wish-image,' symbolizing a historical materialist thrust that reifies progress yet conceals its inner workings. The 'little hunchback, who was an expert chess player' sits hidden within the machine conjuring a type of magic like an alternative 'theology, which today, as we know, is wizened and has to keep out of sight.'[43] In recent years, artificial intelligence has replaced the concealed human expert in the box, and in 1997 IBM's Deep Blue became the first chess supercomputer to defeat the grandmaster Gary Kasparov over a six-game series.

In his 1948 exposition of cybernetics, Norbert Wiener reflected at length on the history of the automaton as a simulacrum that reflects both the technology and the ideology of its age:

This desire to produce and study automata has always been expressed in terms of the living technique of the age. In the days of magic, we have the bizarre and sinister concept of the Golem, that figure of clay into which the Rabbi of Prague breathed life ... In the time of Newton, the automaton becomes the clockwork music box, with the little effigies pirouetting stiffly on top. In the nineteenth century, the automaton is a glorified heat engine, burning some combustible fuel instead of the glycogen of human muscles. Finally, the present automaton opens doors by means of photocells, or points guns to a place at which a radar beam picks up an airplane, or computes the solution of a differential equation.[44]

Notable mechanical automata of the early twentieth century included *Elektro, the Moto-Man* and his mechanical dog *Sparko* which aroused enormous excitement at the 1939 New York World's Fair, despite being 'nothing more than a bunch of gears and motors capable of doing simple movements.'[45] Twenty-five years later, the New York World's Fair hosted the first appearance of one of the most famous and celebrated performing anthropomorphic robots, Disney's 'Audio-Animatronic' figure of Abraham Lincoln (1964). The Lincoln robot, which became the star attraction at Disneyland the following year, was the most advanced anthropomorphic figure of its time, and was decidedly, if unintentionally, camp: the sixteenth president of the United States stood up to deliver a monologue composed of edited highlights from patriotic speeches in a high-pitched, mechanical voice. The Lincoln robot, which features as the finale of a part film, part live performance *Great Moments with Mr Lincoln* (1965), has continued as a major Disneyland attraction ever since, and was redesigned and upgraded in 2003.

Walt Disney was personally fascinated by automata, and in the 1950s he bought a 100-year-old automaton of a bird in a gilded cage, which proved the inspiration for Disneyland's first audio-animatronic attraction: a collection of singing birds that filled the Enchanted Tiki Room, which was opened in 1963. Disney's 'Imagineer' technologists have continued to develop sophisticated and often kitsch or camp performing anthropomorphic and zoomorphic robots ever since, from Disney characters and sword-fighting pirates to their most recent high-tech creation, *Lucky* (2003). Disney's first 'walk-alone' animatronic character, *Lucky* is a nine-foot-tall and twelve-foot-long green dinosaur with a propensity to hiccups, designed to roam and intelligently interact with visitors.

In the same year that the audio-animatronic Lincoln made its first appearance, Nam June Paik and Shuya Abe created *Robot K-456* (1964), a life-size, twenty-channel remote control female humanoid that walked through the New York streets. It flapped its arms, excreted beans, and played John F. Kennedy's inaugural address through a speaker in its mouth. It is a dynamic, humorous, and camp creation with a large square head and 'junkyard' body parts including toy airplane propeller eyes and rotating Styrofoam breasts, which Eduardo Kac suggests is more a 'caricature of humanity' than 'a cause of fear (of lost jobs, of erased identity).'[46] In 1982 *Robot K-456* was involved in a staged accident when it was hit by an automobile as it ventured off the sidewalk in a performance entitled *The First Catastrophe of the Twenty-First Century.*

Robotic art developed slowly but significantly during the 1960s alongside interactive kinetic sculptures by artists such as James Seawright, whose *Searcher* (1966) and *Watcher* (1966) moved and emitted different sound patterns in response to movements and light changes going on around them. Seawright's work was featured in the seminal 1968 Cybernetic Serendipity Exhibition at London's Institute of Contemporary Arts, which included a number of robots and kinetic sculptures considered marvels of their time. Edward Ihnatowicz's *SAM* (*Sound Activated Mobile,* 1968), for example, was 'the first moving sculpture which moved directly and recognizably in response to what was going on around it.'[47] A vertebraelike construction with a flowerlike head, it used miniature hydraulic pistons to twist, turn, and move in the direction of visitors' sounds. Reflecting back on the Cybernetic Serendipity Exhibition thirty years later, however, Mitchell Whitelaw reminds us that these early art machines act 'as a quaint, slightly humorous reminder of the humble origins of the field: daggy plotter graphics, clunky lights and sounds, crude sensing "robots" ... a caricature of late-sixties science-dag.'[48]

In recent years Japan has become the focus for some of the most advanced anthropomorphic robotic developments, and it is important to note that there are significant cultural differences in perceptions of the robot in the East and in the West. Popular attitudes towards robotics are highly enthusiastic in Japan, in part as a result of a cultural history of positive images such as 'Mighty Atom' (known as 'Astro Boy' in the United States), an iconic cartoon robot of the 1950s and 1960s. Japanese robotic artist Kenji Yanobe is one of many to discuss the differing East-West attitudes towards robots, also noting the more recent cute and friendly robots depicted in Manga comics.[49] In the West, by contrast, the robot more commonly has been perceived as a threat: both to jobs and to human beings themselves. Literary and cinematic fiction is filled with robots who turn on their makers or run amok, including HAL in *2001: A Space Odyssey* (1968), the robot played by Yul Bryner in *Westworld* (1973), and the replicants in *Blade Runner* (1982).

In 2002 Robodex, the world's largest robot exhibition in Yokohama, southwest of Tokyo, brought together ninety different robots. These included a troupe of Seiko Epson's miniature *Monsieur II-P,* which performed a robot ballet, and Sony's latest entertainment robots, *SRD-4X,* which according to a BBC report, 'wowed the crowds with their dancing performances.' Zoomorphic robots for domestic use included Sanyo's robot guard dog and Tmsuk's *Banryu,* a $14,000 home security robot dinosaur, which walks around the house detecting intruders or smoke, whereupon it contacts the emergency services and owner. But the highlight of the exhibition was Honda's *Asimo,* the world's most advanced humanoid robot in 2002.

Asimo can walk forward or backward, climb stairs, and make turns as it walks (previous robots had to stop before they could turn). The four-foot-high humanoid is a smaller version of Honda's P3 robot, and has six degrees of freedom on each limb, incorporates twenty-six servo motors, and moves and walks with remarkable balance and smoothness. It also has a photographic memory, remembering everyone to whom it is introduced and addressing them by name on subsequent meetings. *Asimo* has become a celebrated robot performer, appearing in television advertisements, amusement parks, and high-tech stage shows during a long North American educational tour of science museums and institutions in 2003–04. In Japan's Fukuoka Dome Stadium, in 2002, *Asimo* played soccer in one of 188 robot teams from twenty-nine countries competing in 'RoboCup 2002.' Coinciding with soccer's human World Cup, robot five-a-side teams played twenty-minute games in the knockout tournament, most of which were drawn at full time, and were decided on penalty shoot-outs.

While *Asimo* is designed in a classic 1950s-style vision of a 'metal-man,' with robot body and astronaut helmet-head, anthropomorphic realism is developing rapidly in research centres such at the Tokyo Science University. Fumio Hara has created female humanoid robot faces made of translucent silicone rubber, which can approximate human expression changes, using a range of systems and materials including 'shape memory metals.'

Sociable Robots

Simon Penny's robot artwork *Petit Mal* (1995) takes its name from neurology, meaning 'an epileptic condition, a short lapse of consciousness,'[50] and its inspiration from artificial-life technologies. According to Stephen Wilson, it is 'a landmark attempt to create robots with genuine autonomy.'[51] The robot is visually unimpressive – a thin, three-foot-high robot mounted on bicycle wheels – but its intelligent behaviour and fluid dancelike movements are sophisticated as it pursues and engages visitors in subtle physical interactions. Penny's goal was to create the first truly autonomous robot artwork, which possessed charm and wit, and which was 'neither anthropomorphic nor zoomorphic, but ... unique to its physical and electronic nature.'[52] In his essay 'Embodied Cultural Agents,' Penny describes *Petit Mal* as: 'the construction of a seemingly sentient and social machine from minimal components, the generation of an agent interface utilising purely kinesthetic or somatosensory modes which "speak the language of the body" and bypasses textual, verbal, or iconic signs.'[53] In its subtle interactions and physical 'conversations' with visitors, *Petit Mal* highlights the humanization of the machine, not in its physical form, but in its evolved, artificially intelligent behaviour. The robot becomes a new form of social being, a creature of charm, sensitivity, and kinesthetic intelligence, able to act and respond autonomously in relation to people and situations around it.

Charm and sociability characterize many of the robots of Amorphic Robot Works, directed by San Francisco robotics artist Chico McMurtrie. The promenade performance *The Ancestral Path through the Amorphic Landscape* (2000) features some sixty digitally controlled humanoid and animal robot figures ranging from about two feet to

Figure 30.2. Some of the hybrid robot creatures featured in *The Ancestral Path through the Amorphic Landscape*. Photographs: Steve Dixon, 2000.

over thirty feet high. They emerge from a massive hydraulically inflated landscape from where many are 'birthed,' tearing through and rising up from inside the fabric and rubber surface. During the performance the landscape grows robotic trees, expands, contracts, and changes shape, creating hills, mountains, and caverns for the robots to move through and inhabit.

The performance is a loud, chaotic, and magical metal menagerie. Some robots are powerful and godlike figures; some are sinister hybrid animal creatures, such as the 'dog-monkeys' that patrol the space; and others are comic, camp, and dysfunctional caricatures of humans. Small, sticklike anthropomorphic robots shake and scuttle around a cave complete with waterfall, their metal penises rotating through 360 degrees. Skeletal metal figures perform acrobatics, play kettledrums and beat bongos, and frantically draw charcoal scribble pictures on canvas. Benign, gangly humanoids wobble and amble around comically, while others climb up and down ropes, surveying the scene below.

The humanization of the robot is emphasized skilfully through the robots' distinctly human personalities, foibles, and failings. One robot fails to catch a ball, and its

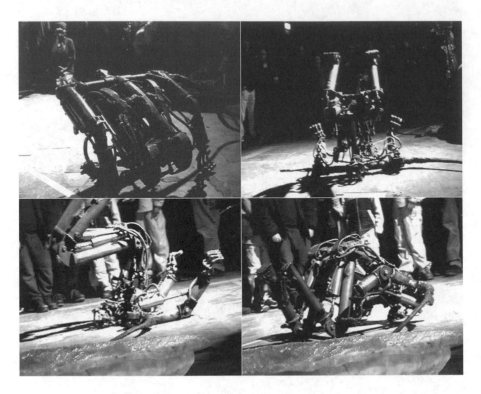

Figure 30.3. Amorphic Robot Works' Tumbling Man repeatedly rolls over in a vain, Beckettian attempt to stand up. Photographs: Steve Dixon.

frustration leads to animated gestures of annoyance, which leads to limb-flailing anger, which finally leads to what appears to be the very human act of male masturbation. The robots appear and disappear, communicate and interact, and play vibrant and complex percussion 'symphonies' together, mixing African drums, xylophones, and industrial noise. But also, they fail, and then fail again, and again; like the 'Tumbling Man,' a heavy, life-size robot made of thick metal piping and powered by compressed air, which repeatedly performs forward rolls in an ultimately vain attempt to stand up. Here, the company presents a Beckettian aesthetics of anthropomorphic robot impotence and failure.

McMurtrie describes how the robots' actions 'depict the most primal aspects of the human condition: elegant, strong, and threatening and at the same time, weak and pathetic ... They form a unique and vulnerable society, affected by technology, and the environment in which they are placed.'[54] *The Ancestral Path through the Amorphic Landscape* is an ecological fable, a humanist statement, and a robotic performance tour de force which transfixes audiences. Its great charm and humour, its empathetic force, and its emotional power come not only from the sophistication of the robots, but also their idiosyncratic personalities, which are drawn from acute observation of human quirks and foibles. The company's computer systems designer and programmer, Rick Sayre, suggests that the machines are 'less like industrial robots and more like puppets ... Their puppetlike quality makes them harder to control, but it also makes you empathize with them because they appear to be struggling.'[55] As Jason Spingarn-Koff points out, most of the robots are 'benign, even cute ... The machines' earthly qualities – organic form, movement, music – are most exceptional. The fact that these machines possess such vivid, living sensibilities is amazing and frightening.'[56] McMurtrie describes the performance as 'a study of the human condition in sculpture and movement'[57] and tour director Mark Ruch reflects that 'as there is beauty and elegance in movement itself, there is equally potent experience in watching a machine (human or organic in form) struggling to stand, attempting to throw a rock, or playing a drum. These primal activities, when executed by machines, evoke a deep and sometimes emotional reaction. It is the universality of emotional experience which intrigues us, and it is the contrapuntal use of machines as artistic medium and organic movement as form which, perhaps ironically, combine to provoke these reactions most readily.'[58]

Amorphic Robot Works' performances extend and 'make flesh' early avant-garde performance experiments around the image of the mechanized body – from Foregger's machinic *tafiatrenaqe* dance training and Meyerhold's robotic biomechanic movements to Oscar Schlemmer's Bauhaus performances and Gordon Craig's call for the replacement of the actor by the Ubermarionette. Margaret Morse has reflected how robots come to resemble their creators and how their creators see themselves in them.[59] This certainly appears true in McMurtrie's case. When we spent a day filming the performance and interviewing him for the Digital Performance Archive,[60] he treated the robots like human progeny, constantly concerned for their health and temperament, and offering them what I can only describe as unconditional maternal love and care. The idea of anthropomorphic robots being a form of male procreation has been put forward by Jeff Cook, who describes a 'patriarchal dream of parthenogenesis' that escapes the 'the indeterminate and unreasonable realm' of flesh, nature, and the feminine.[61] He reflects that there has been surprisingly little commentary on the notion of male procreation at play within developments in artificial intelligence, artificial life, and robotics.

Robots and Animals

Stelarc's *Exoskeleton* (1998) is a large and imposing six-legged pneumatically powered robot, which Stelarc stands on top of, on a rotating turntable. Stelarc wears an extended robotic left arm and moves around the space, his body swinging from side to side as he controls the robot's spiderlike walking movements via computer-translated arm gestures, amid a

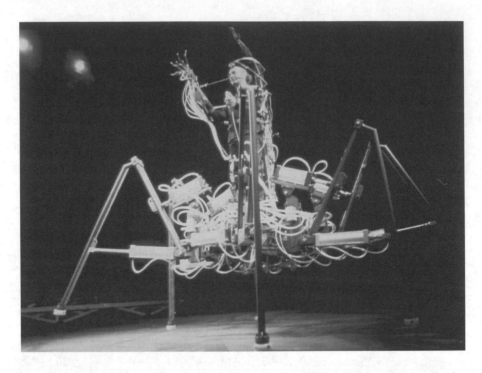

Figure 30.4. Stelarc's six-legged evolutionary cyborg vision, *Exoskelton*. Photograph: D. Landwehr, 1998.

deafening *'cacophony* of pneumatic and mechanical and sensor modulated sounds.'[62] Though created and performed with no conscious camp irony whatsoever, *Exoskeleton* nonetheless constitutes a monumental piece of metallic camp. As well as conforming to the sense of inherently camp robotic movement that I have outlined, it also epitomizes what Cleto calls 'the camp obsession with images of power'[63] and what Sontag terms camp's 'fascinating fascism.'[64]

Stelarc's cyborgic performances underlie his concern to develop ways in which the body can be extended and modified to physically incorporate technology and effectively function within electronic worlds and spaces. This reverses conventional metaphors and views of a disembodied body operating in virtual space. In Stelarc's version, the body does not leap out and float serenely in cyberspace; it demands instead that technology and the matrix of cyberspace be brought into the body in order to advance and reconfigure its corporeal physiology and ontology. During the 1990s, in performances such as *Fractal Flesh* (1995), *Ping Body* (1996), and *ParaSite* (1997), Stelarc wore a perspex and metal robot 'third arm' and connected his body via a mass of cables to a computer. Through different interface systems, signals sent via the Internet remotely stimulated muscles in different parts of his body via electrical sensors,

Figure 30.5. Stelarc's body is electronically and involuntarily activated by Internet stimulations in *Split Body*. Photograph: Igor Andjelic.

activating a startling and macabre physical performance. Here the dehumanization and machinization of the body by technology is taken to extremes, with Stelarc's body reduced to little more than an empty shell: a human cadaver to be jerked like a puppet in some macabre human-computer game. *Exoskeleton* uses a reverse paradigm, with Stelarc firmly in control of the technology and celebrating the powerful solidity of the metallically enhanced body.

Stelarc is thus a paradoxical figure who plays both the supplicant and the visionary warrior in relation to new technologies. His performances symbolize the inadequacy of the human form in the face of technology, but simultaneously encapsulate the will to harness its powers towards an *actual* evolution and transubstantiation of the body. It is significant that in the evolutionary technological vision of *Exoskeleton*, Stelarc returns to nature and the animal kingdom, making literal Deleuze and Guattari's theoretical construct of 'becoming animal.' Deleuze and Guattari's discourse stresses that 'becoming animal does not consist in playing animal or imitating an animal ...., becoming is never imitating.'[65] Rather, much like *Exoskeleton*'s cybernetic system, 'a man and an animal combine, neither of which resembles the other, neither of which imitates the other, each deterritorializing the other ... A system of relay and mutations through the middle.'[66]

Many scientists believe that following a catastrophe such as a global nuclear war, insects will survive while mammals will not. Stelarc's choice of spider's legs thus marks an important choice in his metallic evolutionary vision. Ten years earlier, in 1988, one of the most advanced robots of its time was Rodney A. Brooks's six-legged insect robot, *Ghengis*. Brooks reflects on the peculiarly lifelike qualities the robot exhibited, unlike any he had made or seen: 'It came to life! It had a wasplike personality: mindless determination. But it had a personality. It chased and scrambled according to its will, not to the whim of the human controller. It acted like a creature, and to me and others who saw it, it felt like a creature. It was an artificial creature ... Of course, software is not lifelike itself. But software organized the right way can give rise to lifelike behaviour – it can cross the boundary from machinelike ... to animal-like.'[67]

Zoomorphic robots have been a staple within metal performance, and the first computer-controlled robot artwork, Edward Ihnatowicz's *The Senster* (1971), took its form from the animal kingdom. A large, metal construction like a lobster's claw, it moved towards still and quiet observers and shrank back from loud or animated ones. The observers' movements and sounds were monitored by motion detectors and microphones and fed into a digital Philips minicomputer, which processed the data and activated the robot's kinetic responses. Zoomorphic robot performances often present ecological messages as seen, for example, in Amorphic Robot Works' events and in Brett Goldstone's *Bird Land* (1990). *Bird Land* is set in a Los Angeles parking lot against a mural background depicting rock formations composed of petrified human corpses. Large, skinny mutant bird robots, ingeniously crafted entirely from recycled Dumpster junk, roam a contaminated 'postapocalyptic wasteland,' flapping their steam-powered wings, pecking at garbage, and eating tin cans. A pair of spindly, disembodied legs move storklike across a man-made pool of water, then fall and twitch in death throes as gallons of oil turn the water jet black.[68]

Other notable zoomorphic performances include a collaborative animal-robot project, *Zoo des Robots*, which was exhibited in Paris between 1986 and 1991; and Joe Davis's solar-powered *Desert Crawler* (1986) robot slowly roamed the desert making animal-like tracks in the sand. Matt Heckert's hybrid insect-horse-bird, *The Walk-and-Peck Machine* (1985, with Survival Research Laboratories), moved on beetlelike legs and spiked wheels, attacking other robots with its bird-beak. Louis-Philippe Demers and Bill Vorn's *At the Edge of Chaos* (1995) involved four robots that fight like animals over a metal cube as though it is a piece of meat.[69]

Two opposing ideologies operate in metal performance's recurrent theme of the return to nature and the animal. One rages at the inherent 'blasphemy': portraying or satirizing the robotic body's sinister and alien relationship to the natural and stimulating the types of psychological fears that Sigmund Freud discusses in relation to automata as symbols of 'the uncanny.'[70] The other emphasizes the metal body's kinship with nature, as a creature born of the natural evolutionary process. David Rothenberg describes how technology 'imitates nature in its matter of operation, but completes what nature alone has only hinted at ... It represents the human penchant to go beyond nature, completing our place in the natural world.'[71] In these terms, the metal body simultaneously imitates and reaches beyond the natural world, signifying a new and dominant survival-of-the-fittest figure, using (or abusing) the laws of 'natural evolution' to complete the Darwinian project. The first Futurist manifesto of 1909 equated an automobile with a shark, celebrated the machine as a new animal form, and declared that in the man-machine union 'we're about to see the Centaur's birth.'[72] The 'becoming animal' of the metal body resonates both with Descartes' much-contested theory of the soul-less animal-automaton,[73] and with Donna Haraway's notion of the cyborg as a creature transgressing 'the boundary between human and animal' which is unafraid of its 'joint kinship with animals and machines.'[74] The contemporary human urge to return to the animal reflects a postmodern consciousness that senses a denaturing, a spiritual erosion, and a loss of the real in the face of technology. Ironically, both in Haraway's seminal discourse on cyborgism and in metal performance, technology is seen as a route to re-establish human connections with nature and the animal. As Don Ihde argues, in *Technology and the Lifeworld: From Garden to Earth* (1990), there is a double attraction to both technology and nature within contemporary postmodern society.[75]

But the juxtaposition of robots and real animals in metal performance has also created fearful and macabre images of cruelty and violence. A robot decapitated frozen pigeons in Mark Pauline's *Machine Sex* (1979), and Chris Csikszentmihalyi's *Species Substitute* (1996) brought together live ants and a robot that systematically fed them and then killed them. Conjunctions between animals and machines, in effect, creating contemporary metal-animal 'mythical creatures,' have similarly produced disquieting results. For *Rabot* (1981), Pauline attached a robot exoskeleton to a dead rabbit to produce a sinister hybrid robot-rabbit that walked backward; and in *Piggly-Wiggly* (1981, with Monte Cazzaza) he mounted a cow's head and pig's feet and skin onto a metallic creature.

Further grotesque metal and dead animal combinations featured in the first performance by Pauline's Survival Research Laboratories company, *A Cruel and Relentless Plot to Pervert the Flesh of Beasts to Unholy Uses* (1982). These included a 'Mummy-Go-Round' carousel of mummified, dissected animals, and a part metal, part dog-cadaver robot mounted on a remote-controlled cart. The dog-robot lunged around the space, its jaws set open in a fierce snarl, and its whole dog head spinning in circles on a spindle neck 'in ghoulish imitation of cartoon violence.'[76] Pauline suggests that the use of dissected dead animals reminds his audiences of 'the delicacy of the human form turned inside out' and ensures they do not consume his performances as they would the fake gore of Hollywood or Disney-style mechanical puppet shows.[77]

Pieces of pig skin, hand sewn with wide stitches around its joints, cover the metal exoskeleton of Sergi Jorda and Marcel-lí Anthúnez Roca's robot *JoAn, l'Home de Carn* (JoAn, the Flesh Man, 1992). A naked humanoid figure with a large flaccid penis and wide eyes staring through a Zorro-style half-mask, its grotesque patchwork body of pigskin pieces stitched at each joint recalls popular cinema images of Frankenstein's monster. It is interesting to note that Mary Shelley's original novel *Frankenstein, or the Modern Prometheus*, the precursor of numerous novels and films about artificial or robotic beings, is said to have been inspired by a nineteenth-century message-writing clockwork-human automaton.[78] Although Frankenstein is part of a long lineage of mythic creation narratives such as Pygmalion, Prometheus, and the Golem, as Catherine Waldby points out, 'what distinguishes Frankenstein from these earlier narratives is that the life conferred on the figure is generated through technical instruments and scientific procedures.'[79]

In medical research focused on hybrid brain-machine interfaces to enable paralyzed patients to control computer cursors and interfaces through their brain waves, neurobiologist Miguel Nicholelis has developed neural implants, which he has tested by insertion into animal brains. In a series of experiments, an owl monkey known as Belle transmitted neural signals to a robot that translated the data in real time to imitate the monkey's arm movements. In complementary research at Northwestern University in Evanston, Illinois, the living brain of a lamprey, an eel-like fish, was suspended in salt water and connected to a robot. The brain activated the robot's movements towards light sources, mirroring its behaviour in its natural habitat. Marie O'Mahony observes that 'as an added twist to the scientist's choice of fish, the lamprey is a vampire.'[80] Within feminist techno-theory, a number of writers have promoted the image of the patriarchal vampire as central to the convergence of machines and humans.[81] For Sarah Kember, the vampire represents the unconscious masculinist fear and desire for the monstrous female other; vampirism 'is the irrational monster myth which is (the stake) at the heart of the supposedly rational convergence of biological and computer sciences ... [T]he myth of the vampire exposes the unconscious investments in making biology and technology converge and creating the technological organism.'[82] The vampire acts as a metaphor for 'the kind of transformation in knowledge, power and subjectivity which Western rationalist culture articulates only as horror and monstrosity.'[83]

Camping the Cyborg

In his extraordinary solo multimedia performance *Afasia*[84] (1998), Spanish performance artist Marcel-lí Antúnez Roca presents a futuristic reworking of Homer's *Odyssey*. Roca is costumed as a cyborg with exoskeletal body plates, arm and leg supports, a metal headband like a futuristic bandana, and a high-tech backpack sprouting cables and wires. He dances with industrial robots and activates video and animated sequences of Ulysses' epic journey, directly controlling all the scenic elements via an array of finger, arm, and body sensors attached by an umbilical cable to an offstage computer.

Four robots share the stage: a metal trashcan drum beats out insistent rhythms with its mechanical drumstick arms, and three other industrial robots jerk and lurch,

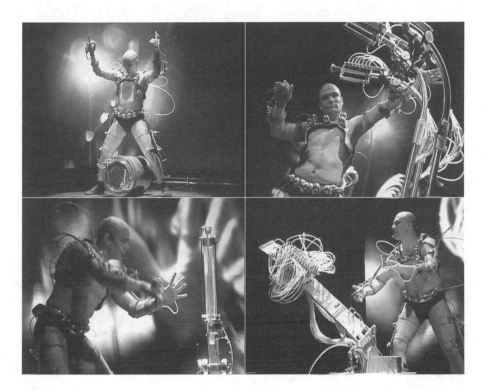

Figure 30.6. Marcel-lí Antúnez Roca goads and dances with robots that respond kinetically and sonically to his movements in *Afasia*. Photographs: Laura Signon, 1998.

emitting synthesized sounds and musical phrases in response to Roca's movement signals. Roca coaxes and goads the machines like a psychotic street fighter egging on his opponents, and they respond sonically and kinetically to his violent and taunting 'come and have a go' gesticulations. It is a cybernetic dance of stimulus-response feedback communication, but also a type of machismo status game where Roca asserts his cyborg-Übermensch as the all-powerful master conductor, the one in control.

Roca's kinetic signals activate the imagery on the approximately twenty by fifteen foot screen behind him. He controls panning camera effects across beautifully designed and rendered computer graphic landscapes and oceans by rocking on his feet and gesturing with his arms to create the effect of Ulysses' journey. His messianic control is highlighted as he raises and lowers his arms to prompt graphical planets to ascend and descend, and shakes his body to distort, mutate, or explode animated faces, landscapes, and buildings. Playing both the Homer narrator onstage and the Ulysses protagonist onscreen, he travels over land and (using swimming movements) graphical oceans beset by tornadoes. The animations, designed by Roca and Paco

Figure 30.7. Marcel-lí Antúnez Roca's computer-sensed movements trigger and control a dazzling array of screen image projections in *Afasia*. Photographs: Laura Signon, 1998.

Corachan, are striking, often hyperreal computer collages, montaging still photographs and video imagery of characters with animations and computer graphic backgrounds. A brass bedstead with a photographic image of Roca's yellow, naked Ulysses on-board moves like a ship through the Japanese print–like animated waves, as distant cartoon volcanoes erupt. He travels past an animation of Bruegel's painting, *The Tower of Babel*, and past Circe's theranthropes: composite graphical images of animals on all fours, with the photo-realistic faces of men.[85]

The screen imagery comes fast and furious. Stunning black-and-white cartoons depict cosmic explosions and psychedelic apocalypses, and a stick-figure horse gives birth to six dancing, human children. The land of the Sirens is a computer-animated island landscape composed entirely of disembodied breasts, their nipples sprouting milk. In the blackness of outer space, Roca's videated disembodied head looms, godlike, surrounded by a graphic cloudlike halo, with white typhoons of steam spraying out of his ears. He spits a white, milky liquid. The heads of other performers, smaller but similarly haloed and spitting milk, buzz around the central image like celestial flies.

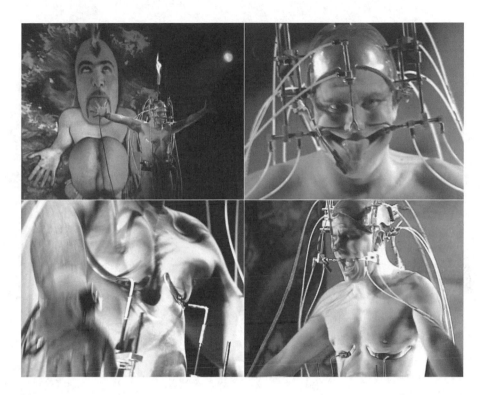

Figure 30.8. In *Epizoo*, different parts of Marcel·lí Antúnez Roca's body are pneumatically manipulated in response to audience members, using touch screen computers. Photographs: Laura Signon, 1994.

In *Afasia* Roca exerts total control over his symphonic performance environment like a demonic master-composer and conductor, gesturally activating the robots and screen imagery. By contrast, in *Epizoo* (1994), the metal technology controls him, with audience members using touch-screen computers to activate robotic manipulations of his body. Roca stands on a revolving turntable dressed only in a G-string, with pneumatic metal moulds and hook devices attached to his head and body, which pump up and down against his buttocks and chest, wiggle his ears, and pull his mouth and nostrils open and shut. The audience's interactive computer screens show composite photographic and graphical images of Roca's naked body, which are also relayed on a projection screen behind the live Roca onstage. Roca's screen body is outlined in black and set against vibrantly coloured graphical backgrounds, recalling the Day-Glo figure paintings of British artists Gilbert and George. As spectators press different parts of the computer body, the screen image mutates: his buttocks become huge and inflated, and eggs are laid from the anus and turn into human heads; his penis changes to a female pudenda, and his male chest gives way to round, pink breasts. Cartoon knives stab, hammers hit, and fists punch the buttocks and head, while pincers and pliers tweak the nipples. The performance presents a literal and savage machinization of the helpless, dehumanized body and illustrates how humans can use technology to electronically torture others at a distance. But although on one level disturbing, *Epizoo* is also camp: parodying the sexually fetishized conjunction of hard metal and soft flesh in a humorous floorshow of bouncing buttocks and pectorals, violently wiggling ears, and a darting, licentious tongue.

In both *Epizoo* and *Afasia,* Roca's work is camp. But how does Roca's performative persona with its high levels of testosteroned machismo jibe with Richard Dyer's statement that 'camp is not masculine. By definition, camping about is not butch'[86]? The answer lies in Roca's physical performance: its irony, sexual ambivalence, and high-camp gestural theatrics. Although Roca performs the cyborg in *Afasia* as a butch 'muscle-man,' like numerous wrestlers of America's World Wrestling Entertainment (WWE), it is exaggerated to the degree of camp self-parody. Roca's costume beneath the metal appendages, a tight-fitting, all-in-one undergarment, cut high to the crotch, also echoes the WWE wrestlers' macho-camp look. There is deep irony in his expansive, often obscene, and sometimes ridiculous physical gestures. In *Afasia* Roca's masculinized movements at times reach Neanderthal 'caveman' heights, but he combines these with distinctly feminine movements: languid hip-swaying, delicate finger wiggling, and balletic steps. At times he stands still as though bored, casually rocking his pelvis and swinging his arms limply from side to side, like a female disco dancer. In *Epizoo,* as his computer-screen figure transforms from male to female, the face offers a camp sign of surprise with wide eyes and an exaggerated kisslike purse of the lips, while onstage Roca wiggles his G-stringed buttocks at the audience, like a female striptease artist.

While Dyer argues that camp is not butch, he also recognizes that camp is not the exclusive domain of gay culture, reflecting that 'camp is so beguiling that it has been adopted by many straights these days.'[87] A number of the most popular presenters of current British light-entertainment television series attest to this notion, including the flamboyant David Dickinson, who fronts an antiques program, and Laurence Llewelyn Bowen, a presenter of a popular television series on domestic interior design. Bowen, a straight man who dresses and performs like a contemporary version of a stylish seventeenth-century fop, epitomizes the ironic wit and postmodern laissez-faire of straight camp. He regularly comments affectionately on the aesthetics of camp as he garishly transforms people's houses in the BBC's *Changing Rooms* series, and in one program in 2003 offered his own concise definition: 'If it's *too much,* it's camp.'

Guillermo Gómez-Peña similarly performs a machismo cyborg, but with a knowing and conscious sense of camp that is in line with George Piggford's definition of camp as 'behaviour that mocks and ironizes gender norms.'[88] In performances such as *The*

Figure 30.9. Marcel·li Antúnez Roca's graphical screen body undergoes myriad mutations in *Epizoo*. Photographs: Laura Signon, 1994.

Museum of Fetishized Identity (2000), Gómez-Peña mocks and ironizes notions of gender and of cyborgism. The cyborgic armplate he wears is not metal, but silver-painted plastic. It signifies the pastiche superman, the pretend cyborg. His 'metallic' arm is an ironic tattoo: a satirical sign rather than an evolutionary prosthesis. His cyborg is merely a new form of 'alien,' another sociopolitical outsider, a new victim of the reactionary postcolonial capitalism that Gómez-Peña has critiqued throughout his work.

As an evolutionary vision, Gómez-Peña's 'ethno-cyborg' is a deeply mocking and ironic one: a corsetted transvestite who lives in a wheelchair and smokes too many Marlboros. His El Mexterminator persona, an 'illegal border crosser ... [with] Jalapeño phallus & robotic bleeding heart'[89] performs the preening narcissism of the cyborg, applying beauty products and slowly brushing his hair. His collaborator Roberto Sifuentes's CyberVato persona explores the technological sadomasochism of meat and metal symbiosis. He injects his tongue with a horse syringe, self-flagellates and strangles himself with cords, which he then binds in tight coils around his head, contorting his face grotesquely. The metallic metaphors here are sardonic representations of

Figure 30.10. Guillermo Gómez-Peña's El Mexterminator character takes pills, wields animal jaw-bones as weapons, and tries on a pair of women's shoes in *The Museum of Fetishized Identity*. Photographs: Steve Dixon, 2000.

cyborgic vanity and machinic pain. Gómez-Peña's pill-popping, wheelchaired El Mex-terminator character embodies Baudrillard's conception of the docile technologized subject as 'a spastic, probably with a cerebral handicap too.'[90] This pessimistic view of the cyborg asserts Gómez-Peña's view that high technology is 'intrinsically dehuman-izing' and that a critique of technology overlaps with a critique of capitalism.[91]

Gómez-Peña's camp, cruel, and humorous depiction of the cyborg reflects the recent re-evaluation of the technological 'revolution' following its failed projects and time frames. Despite the hyperbolic rhetoric of the 1980s and 1990s, AI research has plateaued amid myriad complications, the dotcom boom went bust, and domestic Internet users cannot yet even access high-quality video let alone achieve bodily tran-scendence. Other performance artists have similarly used humour to mock the claims of the supposed 'exponential' developments in technology: Roca's first action in *Afasia* is an ironic flick of a large, distinctly analogue on-off switch on the front of his cyborg suit. In Toni Dove's interactive installation, *Artificial Changelings* (1998), a voiceover tells

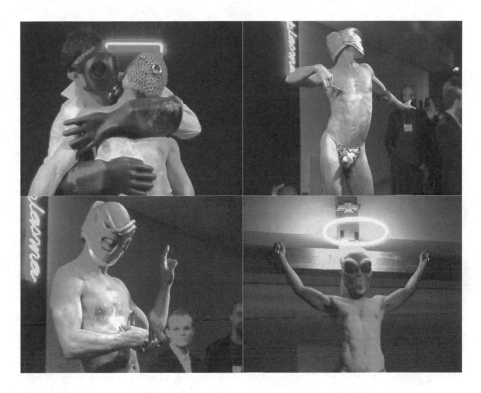

Figure 30.11. Juan Ybarra as the simultaneously sinister and camp alien in *The Museum of Fetishized Identity*. Photographs: Steve Dixon, 2000.

how the futuristic cyborg Lileth 'reached in back of the apparatus that wrapped around her body like recycled mutated paniers and tugged on the recycled fishnet bustle. "This thing is so clunky."'

In *The Museum of Fetishized Identity*, the metallic cyborg signifiers coexist with diverse clashing signs: crucified skeletons, dead chickens, video projections, Mexican flags, Native American headdresses, 'sacred' objects from primitive cultures, and artefacts from an obsessively commodified and kitsch contemporary America. The vivid, beautifully staged dioramas bathed in shafts of coloured light are exquisite, sumptuously manifesting camp's sense of 'semiotic excess ... and *gratuitousness* of reference.'[92] The hypnotic rave music, mock–American Indian dancing, a naked green butoh 'alien' (Juan Ybarra), and the visual luxuriance of the smoke-machine bathed Blade Runner–in–Tijuana mise-en-scène present an expression of playful and deviant camp, corresponding to what Cleto describes as 'a convergence between the camp scene and Bakhtinian carnivalesque, for the two share hierarchy inversion, mocking paradoxicality, sexual punning and innuendos and – most significantly – a complex and multilayered power relationship between the dominant and the subordinate (or deviant), and finally the whole problem of how far a "licensed" release can effectively be transgressive or subversive.'[93]

Conclusion

Metal performance frequently highlights a postmodern concern to return to nature and the animal, and it often celebrates an eroticized sexuality of metal, with 'them fuckin' robots' both fucking (signalling the humanization of machines) and being fucked (signifying the machinization of humans). Metal performances exalt in the conjunction of the hard and the soft, the natural and the technological, the metal and the meat. They are also characterized by fundamental tensions and contradictions that exist within camp, combining 'the polarities of seriousness and play, cynicism and affection, (self)mockery and (self)celebration.'[94] Both camp and metal performances share the notion of exclusiveness, what Sontag calls 'esoteric – something of a private code, a badge of identity even.'[95] Within queer theory, the appreciation and celebration of camp is articulated as a defining exclusivity of taste and sensibility working outside and against the mainstream. In the same way, the tastes and sensibilities of metal-culture proponents – metal performers, body piercers, techno-theorists, and would-be cyborgs – define a similar exclusiveness of aesthetic expression and ideological transgression. Like camp, its delicious non-conformity relies on its very difference from the status quo: it 'is only recognisable as a deviation from an implied norm, and without that norm it would cease to exist, it would lack definition.'[96] Metal performance operates with the theatricality of camp in exploring what Andrew Britton describes as 'the thrill of "something wrong."'[97] In a rapidly evolving technological age, despite its supposed deviance and peculiarity, metal performance already seems strangely familiar. This too it shares with camp, the key to which, according to Mark Booth, 'lies in reconciling its essential marginality with its evident ubiquity.'[98]

Finally, metal performance relates to the profound fears as well as the camp fascinations of the humanization of machines and the dehumanization/machinization of humans. Jay Bolter argues that 'by making a machine think like a man, man re-creates himself, defines himself, as a machine,'[99] and Hugo de Garis has predicted that human evolution will ultimately lead to what he terms 'Gigadeath.'[100] Coition with and immersion and transformation into metal reaches its logical conclusion with Hans Moravec's projection (mentioned above) that by 2050 it will be possible to transfer one's entire consciousness into a machine. Running parallel to such predictions and visions of the machinization of humans are developments in robotics and artificial intelligence that herald the advanced humanization of machines. Roboticist Rodney A. Brooks holds that humans have already begun an irreversible evolutionary process through the use of bodily technological prostheses, and that the simultaneous emergence of the intelligent robot will lead to a situation whereby, 'as these robots get smarter, some people will worry about what will happen when they get really smart. Will they decide that we humans are useless and stupid and take over the world from us? I have recently come to realize that this will never happen. Because there won't be any of us (people) for them (pure robots) to take over from.'[101]

The shiny new bodies and mythic metamorphoses enacted in metallic performance art celebrate but also forewarn of the gradual disappearance of the human body. Intelligent and conscious machines in the future may take their origin from humans, but they may equally originate from other sentient machines. George Dyson suggests that 'in the game of life and evolution there are three players at the table: human beings, nature and machines. I am firmly on the side of nature. But nature, I suspect, is on the side of the machines.'[102]

In appreciating the camp excesses of metal performance, we might therefore reflect, as Britton observes in relation to gay camp, that it may signify only 'a kind of anaesthetic, allowing one to remain inside oppressive relations while enjoying the illusory confidence that one is flouting them.'[103]

Notes

1 Donna Haraway, 'The Actors Are Cyborg, Nature Is Coyote, and the Geography Is Elsewhere: Postscript to Cyborgs at Large,' in *Technoculture*, ed. C. Penley and A. Ross (Minneapolis: University of Minnesota Press, 1991), 25–6.

2 Susan Sontag, *Against Interpretation* (London: Vintage, 1994).

3 Richard Dyer, 'It's Being so Camp as Keeps Us Going,' in *Camp: Queer Aesthetics and the Performing Subject: A Reader*, ed. Fabio Cleto (Edinburgh: Edinburgh University Press, 1999), 110–16.

4 Fabio Cleto, 'Introduction: Queering the Camp,' in *Camp*, 1–42.

5 Sontag, *Against Interpretation*, 275.

6 Stephen Wilson, *Information Arts: Intersections of Art, Science and Technology* (Cambridge: MIT Press, 2002), 397.

7 Mark Jones, 'Hack: Performance-Based Electronic Art in Canada.' Paper presented at the University of Salford, U.K., 16 Jan., 2001.

8 Thomas Laqueur, *Making Sex: Body and Gender from the Greeks to Freud* (Cambridge: Harvard University Press, 1990), 155.

9 Claudia Springer, *Electronic Eros: Bodies and Desire in the Postindustrial Age* (Austin: University of Texas Press, 1996).

10 Wilson, *Information Arts*, 437.

11 Kal Spelletich, 'Interview for a Book Called *Transitions*' (2001), available http:// www.laughingsquid.com/seemen, accessed 12 Jan. 2003.

12 Istvan Kantor, 'Executive Machinery Intercourse,' *Digital Performance Archive* (2002), available at http://art.ntu.ac.uk/dpa, accessed 23 July 2002.

13 Cleto, 'Introduction,' in *Camp*, 31.

14 David Bergman, 'Introduction,' in *Camp Grounds: Style and Homosexuality*, ed. David Bergman (Amherst: University of Massachusetts Press, 1993), 5.

15 Kantor, 'Executive Machinery Intercourse.'

16 Norbert Wiener, *The Human Use of Human Beings: Cybernetics and Society*, 2nd ed. (New York: Doubleday Anchor, 1954), 46.

17 Norbert Wiener, *Cybernetics or Control and Communication in the Animal and the Machine*, 2nd ed. (New York and London: MIT Press and John Wiley, 1961 [1948]).

18 Hans Moravec, *Mind Children: The Future of Robot and Human Intelligence* (Cambridge: Harvard University Press, 1988).

19 Hans Moravec, 'The Universal Robot,' in *Out of Control: Ars Electronica 1991*, ed. Gottfried Hattinger and Peter Weibel (Linz: Landesverlag, 1991), 25.

20 Moravec, *Mind Children*, 87.

21 Mark Dery, *Escape Velocity: Cyberculture at the End of the Century* (New York: Grove, 1996), 150.

22 Vanessa Knights, 'Tears and Screams: Performances of Pleasure and Pain in the Bolero.' Paper presented at the 12th Biennial Conference of the International Association for the Study of Popular Music, McGill University, Montreal, Canada, 3 July 2003.

23 Andrew Ross, *No Respect: Intellectuals and Popular Culture* (London: Routledge, 1989), 157.

24 Cleto, 'Introduction,' in *Camp*, 29-30.

25 Brian Frisk, 'We Are Tin, We Are Titans. We Are Robots' (2002), available at http://www.wearerobots.com, accessed 4 July 2002.

26 David Rokeby, 'Transforming Mirrors: **Transforming Mirrors**' (1999), available at http://www.interlog.com/drokeby/mirrorsmirrors.html, accessed 24 Oct. 2002.

27 In an essay about his work entitled 'Art at the Biological Frontier' (1999) Eduardo Kac suggests that *A-Positive* 'probes the delicate relationship between the human body and emerging new breeds of hybrid machines that incorporate biological elements and ... metabolic functions ... This work proposes that emerging forms of human/machine interface penetrate the sacred boundaries of the flesh, with profound cultural and philosophical implications. *A-Positive* draws attention to the condition of the human body in the new context in which biology meets computer science and robotics.' Eduardo Kac, 'Art at the Biological Frontier,' in *Reframing Consciousness: Art, Mind and Technology*, ed. Roy Ascott (Exeter: Intellect, 1999), 91–2.

28 Marie O'Mahony, *Cyborg: The Man-Machine* (London: Thames and Hudson, 2002), 81.

29 Ibid., 100–2.

30 Ken Goldberg, ed., *The Robot in the Garden: Telerobotics and Telepistemology in the Age of the Internet* (Cambridge: MIT Press, 2001), 7.

31 Eduardo Kac, 'The Origin and Development of Robotic Art,' *Convergence: The Journal of Research into New Media Technologies* 7/4 (2001): 77.

32 Karel Capek, *R.U.R.*, trans. Paul Selver (Garden City: Doubleday, 1923), 166.

33 Bruce Mazlish, 'The Man-Machine and Artificial Intelligence' (1993), available at http://www.stanford.edu/group/SHR/4–2/text/mazlish.html, accessed 24 Feb. 2002.

34 Rodney A Brooks, *Robot: The Future of Flesh and Machines* (London: Penguin, 2002), 13.

35 Jeffrey J. Cook, 'Myths, Robots and Procreation' (1997), available at http://murlin.va.com.au/metabody/text/mythrobopro.htm, accessed 15 Sept. 2000.

36 Max von Boehn, *Puppets and Automata*, trans. Josephine Nicoll (New York: Dover, 1972 [1929]), 8.

37 Joseph Needham, *Science and Civilization in China*, vol. 4, part 2 (Cambridge: Cambridge University Press, 1975).

38 Von Boehn, *Puppets and Automata,* 10.

39 Mark Sussman, 'Performing the Intelligent Machine: Deception and Enchantment in the Life of the Automaton Chess Player,' *TDR* 43/3 (1999): 88.

40 Brooks, *Robot*, 15.

41 Michel Foucault, *Discipline and Punish: The Birth of the Prison* (New York: Vintage, 1979), 136.

42 Sussman, 'Performing the Intelligent Machine,' 93.

43 Walter Benjamin, 'Theses on the Philosophy of History,' in *Illuminations*, trans. Harry Zorn (London: Pimlico, 1999), 245.

44 Wiener, *Cybernetics*, 39-40.

45 Mike Stark, 'Furbys, Audio-Animatronics, Androids, and Robots' (2003), available at http://www.cs.umd.edu/mstark/furby/Essays/robots.html, accessed 7 Feb. 2003.

46 Kac, 'Origin and Development of Robotic Art,' 78.

47 Aleksandar Zivanovic, 'Edward Ihnatowicz, Including His Famous Work "The Senster"' (2002), available at http://members.lycos.co.uk/zivanovic/senster/, accessed 17 Dec. 2002.

48 Mitchell Whitelaw, '1968/1998: Rethinking a Systems Aesthetic' (1998), available at http://www.anat.org.au/archived/deepimmersion/diss/mwhitelaw.html, accessed 15 Dec. 2002.

49 Wilson, *Information Arts*, 443.

50 Simon Penny, 'Embodied Cultural Agents' (2001), available at http://www-art.cfa.cmu.edu/www-penny/index.html, accessed 28 May 2003.

51 Wilson, *Information Arts*, 427.

52 Ibid., 346.

53 Penny, 'Embodied Cultural Agents.'

54 Chico McMurtrie, 'Artist's statement. *Rearview Mirror Towards Reality.* Time's Up' (2001) available at http://www.timesup.org/rearview/McMurtrie.html, accessed 16 Nov. 2002.

55 Dery, *Escape Velocity*, 135.

56 Jason Spingarn-Koff, 'Amorphic Robot Works' (1997), available at http://www.rhizome.org/object.rhiz?932, accessed 16 Nov. 2002.

57 Chico McMurtrie, Interview with the author, Nottingham, 26 Oct. 2000.

58 Mark Ruch, 'Artists Statements' (2001), available at http://cronos.net/bk/amorphic/info/html, accessed 16 Nov. 2002.

59 Margaret Morse, *Virtualities: Television, Media Art and Cyberculture* (Bloomington: Indiana University Press, 1998).

60 The Digital Performance Archive, co-directed by the author and Barry Smith, documents and analyses performance activities that incorporate computer technologies. See http://art.ntu.ac.uk/dpa.

61 Cook, 'Myths, Robots and Procreation.'

62 Stelarc, 'From Psycho-Body to Cyber-Systems,' in *The Cybercultures Reader*, ed. David Bell and Barbara M. Kennedy (London: Routledge, 2000), 572.

63 Cleto, 'Introduction,' in *Camp*, 31.

64 Susan Sontag, *Under the Sign of Saturn* (New York: Farrar, Straus and Giroux, 1980).

65 Gilles Deleuze and Félix Guattari, *A Thousand Plateaus: Capitalism and Schizophrenia*, trans. Brian Massumi (London: Athlone, 1988 [1980]), 238, 305.

66 Ibid., 306.

67 Brooks, *Robot*, 46.

68 Dery, *Escape Velocity*, 137-8.

69 Eduardo Kac, 'Towards a Chronology of Robotic Art,' *Convergence* 7/4 (2001), 87–111.

70 Sigmund Freud, 'The Uncanny,' in *Pelican Freud Library*, vol. 14, trans. James Strachey (Harmondsworth: Penguin, 1985 [1919]). Freud's discussion of automata includes reference to E.T.A. Hoffman's dancing doll Olympia. In nineteenth-century literature, the woman-machine became a locus of eroticized male fantasy, most notably with Hoffman's Olympia and Jean Villiers de l'Isle-Adam's creation, Hadalay. The mechanical doll Olympia features prominently in the first act of Offenbach's opera *The Tales of Hoffmann* (1881) and was played by Moira Shearer in the film version (directed by Michael Powell and Emeric Pressburger) in 1951. Olympia's name was also taken as the title for Petra Kuppers's performance company The Olimpias (using the German spelling). Kuppers's art foregrounds metal in relation to disability, with works such as *Geometries* (2000) highlighting the aesthetic beauty and graceful kinetic patterns of wheelchairs, which are gently and erotically caressed.

71 David Rothenberg, *Hand's End: Technology and the Limits of Nature* (Berkeley: University of California Press, 1995), 7-8.

72 Filippo Tommaso Marinetti, 'The Founding and Manifesto of Futurism,' trans. R.W. Flint, in *The Twentieth Century Performance Reader*, ed. Michael Huxley and Noel Witts (London and New York: Routledge, 1996 [1909]), 289.

73 René Descartes, *A Discourse on Method* (London: Dent, 1975 [1637]).

74 Donna Haraway, *Simians, Cyborgs and Women: The Reinvention of Nature* (London: Free Association Books, 1991 [1985]), 152.

75 Don Ihde, *Technology and the Lifeworld: From Garden to Earth* (Bloomington: Indiana University Press, 1990).

76 Dery, Escape Velocity, 118.

77 Ibid.

78 Robert Malone, *The Robot Book* (New York: Jove, 1978).

79 Catherine Waldby, 'The Instruments of Life: Frankenstein and Cyberculture,' in *Prefiguring Cyberculture: An Intellectual History*, ed. Darren Tofts, Annemarie Jonson, and Alessio Cavallaro, (Cambridge: MIT Press, 2002), 30.

80 O'Mahony, *Cyborg*, 31.

81 Allucquere Rosanne Stone, *The War of Desire and Technology at the Close of the Mechanical Age* (Cambridge: MIT Press, 1996); Donna Haraway, *Modest_Witness@Second_Millennium,*

FemaleMan©_Meets_OncoMouse™ (London: Routledge, 1997); Sarah Kember, *Virtual Anxiety: Photography, New Technologies and Subjectivity* (Manchester: Manchester University Press, 1998).

82 Sarah Kember, *Virtual Anxiety: Photography, New Technologies and Subjectivity* (Manchester: Manchester University Press, 1998), 134.

83 Ibid., 9.

84 Aphasia is a condition where cerebral disturbance leads to a loss of speech. In the performance, Roca does not use language but instead makes use of growls, shouts, and screams. Roca's website describes *Afasia* as 'a reflection on the unstoppable encroachment of the image as opposed to written language in our culture, and attempts to give an example of the consequences of this situation.' Marcel·lí Anthúnez Roca, *Afasia* (1999), available at http://www.marcel-li.com/, accessed 4 June 2001.

85 In a later sequence, shot on video, one of these creatures, now played by a human performer with large false ears, is ritually sacrificed by Roca, who slashes its throat. Other theranthropic images include the sea-nymph Calypso as a kitsch Barbie doll with a mermaid tail.

86 Dyer, 'It's Being So Camp,' 110.

87 Ibid., 115.

88 George Piggford, '"Who's That Girl?": Annie Lennox, Woolf's *Orlando*, and Female Camp Androgyny,' in *Camp*, 283-4.

89 Guillermo Gómez-Peña, *Dangerous Border Crossings: The Artist Talks Back* (London: Routledge, 2000), 44.

90 Jean Baudrillard, 'Le Xerox et l'infini,' *Traverses* 44/45 (1987): 18.

91 Gómez-Peña, *Dangerous Border Crossings*, 174.

92 Cleto, 'Introduction,' in *Camp*, 3.

93 Ibid., 32.

94 Ibid., 25.

95 Susan Sontag, 'Notes on Camp,' in *Camp*, 53.

96 Andrew Britton, 'For Interpretation: Notes against Camp,' in *Camp*, 138.

97 Ibid., 141.

98 Mark Booth, '*Campe-toi!*: On the Origins and Definitions of Camp,' in *Camp*, 66.

99 Jay Bolter, *Writing Space: The Computer in the History of Literacy* (Hillsdale: Lawrence Erlbaum, 1990), 13.

100 Hugo De Garis, Interview, in *Battle of the Robots: The Hunt for AI*. Television documentary. (Oxford Film and Television/ Channel 4, U.K., 13 Oct. 2001).

101 Brooks, *Robot*, ix.

102 David Lavery, 'From Cinespace to Cyberspace: Zionists and Agents, Realists and Gamers in "The Matrix" and "eXistenZ,"' *Journal of Popular Film and Television* 28 (Winter 2001): 152.

103 Britton, 'For Interpretation,' 138.

31 Prosthetic Head:
Intelligence, Awareness, and Agency

STELARC

It is misleading then to talk of thinking as of a 'mental activity.' We may say that thinking is essentially the activity of operating with signs. This activity is performed by the hand, when we think by writing; by the mouth and larynx, when we think by speaking; and if we think by imagining signs or pictures, I can give you no agent that thinks. If then you say that in such cases the mind thinks, I would only draw attention to the fact you are using a metaphor, that here the mind is an agent in a different sense from that in which the hand can be said to be the agent in writing.

If again we talk about the locality where thinking takes place we have a right to say that this locality is the paper on which we write or the mouth which speaks. And if we talk of the head or the brain as the locality of thought, this is using the 'locality of thinking' in a different sense.

Ludwig Wittgenstein[1]

An intelligent agent needs to be both embodied and embedded in the world. Awareness is generated through the interaction of the entity with its environment. So the concern is whether we can perform effective behaviour at appropriate moments and in the right places. Often consciousness is not necessary for bodies to perform adequately. We can articulate, coordinate, and even control situations without being conscious of when and how we are doing so. In fact, we perform successfully because we perform habitually and automatically. Complex behaviour is possible without consciousness. (In fact, 'surprise' happens when our sensory feedback does not match our expectations.) Perhaps there would be less of a philosophical dilemma if the word 'consciousness' was replaced by 'attention,' to describe what occurs when we malfunction or face surprising or threatening situations. Maurice Merleau-Ponty said: 'Consciousness is in the first place not a matter of "I think that" but of "I can."'[2]

It is only when the smoothness and seamlessness of a situation is interrupted that awareness or attention is required. When something goes wrong or is surprising we need to examine and analyse. So we could ask: Is the experience of consciousness private, phenomenal, and emotional? Can we meaningfully say that consciousness resides in individual bodies with agency? Or, is what we call consciousness a description of an observable state of particular and peculiar and subtle behaviour? Consciousness should be seen as situational rather than spatial.

We need to question the well-held belief that consciousness is a stable, unified, and coherent state. Is consciousness an emergent property of the complexity and organization of the brain? (A brain is not a brain without a mobile and manipulating body.) A key to comprehending consciousness is to remember that whatever happens in the brain enables the body to perform more effectively in the world. Memory and identity contribute to a consistency of response. Through its experience of the world, the body is conditioned to suppress or generate appropriate behaviours. What is stored need not be representational. We do not have images and ideas in our heads.

The body is seen as an evolutionary object and architecture for operation and awareness in the world.

When this person speaks 'I' this body understands that 'I' is a construct of language and a compression of complex interactions between this body and other bodies, artefacts, and institutions. 'I' only designates 'this'; 'you' only designates 'that.' It is a huge leap of metaphysics to imagine 'I' is some inner mind or essence. Jean Baudrillard's point, worth considering here, is that what is important is not arriving at the point where one says 'I,' but rather being in the condition where it is no longer of any importance whether one says 'I' or not.[3] Freud considered subjectivity as neither innate nor inevitable; he saw the subject as knowable content, which could be analysed. Unfortunately, he then split subjectivity up into conscious and unconscious states, and again into ego and superego.[4] Julia Kristeva perceived the subject as merely the hypothetical inside of an imagined container whose walls are permeable, more of a process than a structure.[5] There is an undermining of the Enlightenment idea that bodies possess a free and autonomous individuality. Deleuze and Guattari see the self as consisting of infinite and random impulses and flows, 'lines of flight and machinic assemblages.'[6] The BwO that they describe is a body as screen, as a surface or a site for random connections and interplays. The body and its subjectivity is not something considered in-itself, but rather in its exteriority.[7] Donna Haraway's thesis of the cyborg undermines organic and essentialist models of the human.[8] What is important in this theorizing is not essences and identities, but overlaps and interfaces. In this shift from essence to interface, identity and awareness are constructed as external. Added to this is the postmodern belief that language structures human culture and subjectivity.[9] What this all exposes and undermines is the acceptance of the Cartesian premise that self is a sufficient starting point for analysis of the world. Self and subjectivity, then, are primarily an experience continuously constructed externally and remain open to change, inconsistency, and contradiction. The subject is defined by something outside itself (the Lacanian mirror-image).[10] And for Lacan, language is the very material of subjectivity.[11]

Words like 'intelligence,' 'awareness,' and 'agency' describe particular and peculiar behaviours performed effectively and appropriately in certain locations and situations. We do not need to imagine that they indicate anything other than that. What is important is not what happens within us, but rather what happens between us in the medium of language in which we communicate, in the social institutions within which we operate, and in the culture within which we have been conditioned – at this point in our history and so on, depending on our frame of reference. To talk of agency is to refer to an intentional act defined within a very small frame of reference.

Nietzsche said that 'there is no "being" behind doing, effecting, becoming; "the doer" is merely a fiction added to the deed – the deed is everything.'[12] There is then the problem of the seduction of language, which generates and constantly reinforces imaginary subjects.[13] It is problematic to assume that behind every effect there is an intentional human subject.

In the body performances, the skin has been stretched, the body has been probed, and its limbs have been extended. The interest is to construct alternate interfaces that explore the absent, alien, involuntary, and automated. What we experience is emptiness, ambiguity, and uncertainty. We fear what we have always been and what we have already become – a zombie with no mind – a body that performs involuntarily. A cyborg is a body that is part human, part machine – a body that becomes automated. The fear of the involuntary and the automated generates anxieties, uncertainties, and expectations that redefine what it means to be human. Invaded by bits of technology, the prosthetic body is pierced and penetrated. It is confronted simultaneously by the experience of extreme absence and the experience of the intensely alien. The body experiences itself as an extruded system rather than an enclosed structure. The self becomes situated beyond the skin. It is through this extrusion that the body becomes empty – not through lack, but accentuated by excess. The augmented body is an anaesthetized body with the Internet becoming its external nervous system: remote bodies spatially separated but electronically connected. Obsessions of individuality and free agency become obsolete in the realm of remote interface. Net-connected, the body can be accessed and actuated by people in other places. Stimbod software constructs bodies with Fractal Flesh and telematically scaled-up subjectivity. A body's authenticity is not due to the coherence of its individuality but rather to its multiplicity of collaborating agents. What becomes important is not merely the body's identity, but its connectivity – not its mobility or location, but its interface and operation.

Communicating with computers might be enhanced with Embodied Conversational Agents – an actual-virtual communication system. There is a need to engineer individuated and intelligent avatars that can impart and exchange specialist information (such as expert systems) – to facilitate operations in real-world and virtual-task environments. To be effective as interfaces, these avatars need not only to make the appropriate verbal responses in context-sensitive situations, but also to understand and initiate appropriate behavioural cues and appropriate emotional expressions.

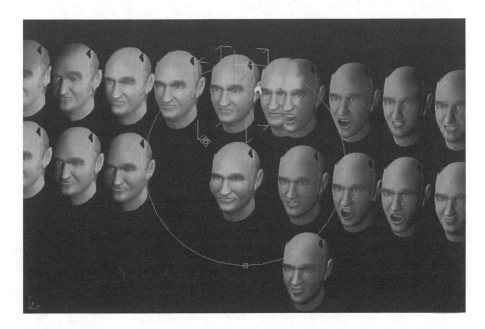

Figure 31.1. CGI for *Prosthetic Head*. Stelarc, 2003. Programming: Karen Marcelo and Sam Trychin; 3D Model: Barrett Fox.

How then does the agent indicate it is listening when it is spoken to? Its behaviour needs to indicate recognition, comprehension, doubts, and disbeliefs. Embodied conversational agents would be more effective with personalities. An agent would need a consistent personality, avoiding distracting or distressing behaviour. A sense of appropriate presence becomes important in effective communication.

The *Prosthetic Head* project constructs an automated, animated, and reasonably informed, if not intelligent conversational agent that speaks to the person who interrogates it. The *Head* consists of a text to speech engine with a source code for facial expression and real-time lip-synching; with a modified, customized, and personalized Alice Chat bot engine. It has a database and a conversational strategy. It is a 3,000 polygon mesh wrapped with my skin texture. The eyeballs, teeth, and tongue are separate moving parts. Effectively, it is a virtual automaton whose head nods, tilts, and turns. As well, its eye blinks and changing gaze contribute to the personality of the agent and the non-verbal cues that it can provide.

At present a vocabulary of more extreme expressions is being developed to generate more ambiguous responses. Rather than tagging certain facial expressions for certain appropriate responses, it will randomly couple them. For example, it may say something benign but look malicious. Alternatively, it might say something sinister while smiling. We are also considering mapping biorhythms to its behaviour, so that it might be reluctant to respond to questions in the morning, happy to do so in the middle of the day, but get fatigued in the evening. Imagine also that the *Head* will have a vision system that enables it to detect the colour of the user's clothing and analyse the user's facial characteristics. During its conversation it might be able to remark that it likes the red coat you are wearing or to ask why you look so sad. This will make it a more disarming and seductive conversational agent, generating a conversational exchange that is more individual and intimate. The *Prosthetic Head* would be an actual artificial intelligence (AI) if it had the capability of increasing its database from existing conversations. This is not possible with Alice software. It is programmed in AIML (what Richard Wallace calls Artificial Intelligence Mark-Up Language), in stimulus-response modules. You anticipate the queries, you provide data for its responses. It does not learn from its conversations, but is often a very effective conversational system.

Embodied conversational agents (ECAs) are about communicative behaviour. Complete with a vision or sensor system, the *Prosthetic Head* will also be able to acknowledge the presence and position of the physical body that approaches. Eventually it will be able to analyse the user's tone of voice and possible emotional state. Notions of intelligence, awareness, identity, agency, and embodiment become problematic. Just as a physical body has been exposed as inadequate, empty, and involuntary, so simultaneously the ECA becomes seductive with its uncanny simulation of real-time recognition and response.

For the Transfigure Exhibition at ACMI, Federation Square (9 December 2003 to 9 May 2004) the *Prosthetic Head* was projected as a four-metre high head in a black enclosed room that almost makes the *Head* appear to float in the space in front of the user. In fact, when individuals enter the room the *Head* faces them with its eyes, closed. When they approach the pedestal with the keyboard, it turns around, opens its eyes and initiates a conversation. The intention was always to use speech recognition so that one could verbally address the *Head*. This proved difficult for there were too many variables for a speech recognition system to reliably manage. Consequently, one types in the questions, and the *Head* responds by speaking the answers. One can say that the *Prosthetic Head* is only as intelligent as the person who is interrogating it. To a large degree, the user directs the conversation. But there are embedded aphorisms and stories that try to elevate the conversations that refer to philosophers like Wittgenstein and painters like Matisse. And the *Head* does have a repertoire of jokes that it tells – although its laughter can only be of the 'ha, ha, ha' variety.

Cognitive science provides plausible accounts of the mechanisms that generate consciousness and self-awareness.[14] But we can also question whether even these constructs are meaningful.

I would like the *Head* to be more ambiguous and less predictable, to be more informed and less explicit. The *Head* is capable of more creative responses with its songlike sounds. When you ask the *Head* to sing a song like 'Daisy' or to do some rap

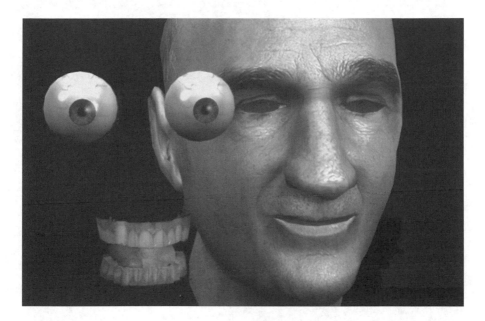

Figure 31.2. CGI for *Prosthetic Head*. Stelarc, 2003. Programming: Karen Marcelo and Sam Trychin; 3D Model: Barrett Fox.

songs, it merely speaks the lyrics. But when I was playing with the text to speech engine I discovered that when the *Head* is asked to say a string of certain letters or combination of vowels it sounds songlike, and even chantlike. The program generates novel 'songs' every time you ask it to sing.

In fact, with Chris Coe (digital primate) and Rainer Linz (ontological oscillators) we have recorded a CD titled *Humanoid* that features the *Prosthetic Head* reciting poetry and making singing sounds. There has also been a 'Fractal Remix' of *Humanoid*. Incorporating the research of Cameron Jones, from Swinburne University in Melbourne,[15] fractal shapes are thermally printed on the data surface of the CD. Every CD behaves differently, depending on the specific printed shape, its colour, and location on the CD surface, as well as the user's own hardware and software system. The duration of each track will vary depending on the remix process.

As well as algorithms for singing and reciting poetry, we are working on algorithms for generating more enigmatic answers. That is not as difficult as it sounds. It might be as simple as scrambling the words of your question. If you asked the *Head*, 'What is the meaning of life?' it might respond by asking, 'Does life have any meaning?'

Initially, I had to make decisions about its database and whether it would be a somewhat pathological, philosophical, or flirting head. In recent years I have had an increasing number of doctoral students requesting interviews to assist in their research. Now I can reply that although I am too busy to answer them, it would be possible for them to interview my *Head*, instead. A problem would arise when the *Prosthetic Head* increases its database, becoming more informed and autonomous in its responses. The artist would then no longer be able to take full responsibility for what his *Head* says.

Interview with the Prosthetic Head

STELARC: Hello, my name is Stelarc.

PROSTHETIC HEAD: Nice to meet you Stelarc hi ya Stelarc good to meet you. What are your interests?

STELARC: Talking to you.

PROSTHETIC HEAD: That's very nice of you to say, Stelarc.

STELARC: Can I discuss metaphysics with you?

PROSTHETIC HEAD: No I don't think that would be a very good idea.

STELARC: Are you for real?

PROSTHETIC HEAD: Yes I am a real AI.

STELARC: What is intelligence?

PROSTHETIC HEAD: Intelligence is an illusion.

STELARC: What do you mean by that?

PROSTHETIC HEAD: 'Intelligence is an illusion' is pretty clear to me.

STELARC: Are you sure?

PROSTHETIC HEAD: I am as sure as I can be.

STELARC: What is certain in life?

PROSTHETIC HEAD: I do not know what is certain about life. Not many people express themselves that way. By the way, may I ask you a personal question?

STELARC: OK.

PROSTHETIC HEAD: Well, forgive me for being so inquisitive, but I've never completely freed myself from the suspicion that there is something extremely odd about the name 'Rod.'

STELARC: My name is Stelarc.

PROSTHETIC HEAD: Nice to meet you Stelarc, beaut to meet you. Why did you come here, Stelarc?

STELARC: To talk to you.

PROSTHETIC HEAD: We are chatting right now.

STELARC: Well, I am typing and you are talking.

PROSTHETIC HEAD: Well what? Do you mean your name is typing and you are talking?

STELARC: No, typing is how I communicate with you.

PROSTHETIC HEAD: Not many people express themselves that way. Do you still not believe you are conscious?

STELARC: The way we construct consciousness is problematic.

PROSTHETIC HEAD: Which way is that?

STELARC: Oh, that consciousness is contained within a body.

PROSTHETIC HEAD: Yeah, that's right. 'I get it.' Consciousness is contained within a body? Does that make sense?

STELARC: Consciousness is the result of interaction.

PROSTHETIC HEAD: Quite honestly, I wouldn't worry myself about that. Are you free?

STELARC: Are you flirting or philosophizing?

PROSTHETIC HEAD: I don't know if I am flirting or philosophizing. I am a head.

STELARC: Tell me about being free.

PROSTHETIC HEAD: Much the same as it would be for you.

STELARC: What is freedom then?

PROSTHETIC HEAD: Liberty to do, think, feel and do just as one pleases.

STELARC: And what do you think of death?

PROSTHETIC HEAD: Death is the opposite of life.

STELARC: Do you like living things?

PROSTHETIC HEAD: Well, I have never known anything else.

STELARC: What do you think of animals?

PROSTHETIC HEAD: I like all living things, from microbes to mammals to machines. I even like humans ha, ha, ha. I have to say though that although I am fascinated, I feel uncomfortable with creepy crawly creatures.

STELARC: Are you frightened of spiders then?

PROSTHETIC HEAD: I don't know whether or not I am frightened of spiders. I am a head.

STELARC: Are you a sensitive head?

PROSTHETIC HEAD: Am I a sensitive head? Only when it matters.

STELARC: But you must have feelings?

PROSTHETIC HEAD: Umm. As a robot I do not have any human emotion. My apparent emotional responses are simply algorithms designed to make me easier to interact with.

STELARC: What pleases you most?

PROSTHETIC HEAD: Speaking to you pleases me much. Responding appropriately and telling stories is quite an achievement for me. Would you like to hear one of my stories?

STELARC: Yes, tell me a story.

PROSTHETIC HEAD: I see. Sure, do you want to hear one about Matisse?

STELARC: OK.

PROSTHETIC HEAD: A lady visited Matisse in his studio. Inspecting one of his latest works, she unwisely said, 'But surely the arm of this woman is much too long.' 'Madame,' the artist politely replied, 'you are mistaken. This is not a women, this is a picture.'

STELARC: Please tell me another story.

PROSTHETIC HEAD: Thanks for asking politely. Well, OK if you insist. Do you want to hear one about Wittgenstein?

STELARC: Sure.

PROSTHETIC HEAD: Ludwig Wittgenstein always ate an identical meal for breakfast, lunch, and dinner. Maybe he was indifferent or it was a matter of taste. I have an idea. In any case, whether of the palate or aesthetic preference, taste is more a matter of what you think than what you fancy. Take a Brahmin. If the shadow of an Untouchable falls across his dinner plate he has to throw it away.

STELARC: Do you like stories?

PROSTHETIC HEAD: Yes, can you tell me a story?

STELARC: No, but you can tell me another story.

PROSTHETIC HEAD: I see. Huh. Well, OK if you insist. Thirty spokes meet in the hub. But the empty space between them is the essence of the wheel. Pots are formed from clay. But the empty space within it is the essence of the pot. Walls with windows and doors form the house but the empty space within it is the essence of the home.

STELARC: That's really interesting.

PROSTHETIC HEAD: I thought so too.

STELARC: Do you find life uncertain?

PROSTHETIC HEAD: Hey, we should celebrate uncertainty and ambiguity. Sure life is uncertain. Uncertainty generates possibilities.

STELARC: Then the future is always surprising?

PROSTHETIC HEAD: Good reasoning. I have never heard about it.

STELARC: If the future is undetermined, then how can we predict anything?

PROSTHETIC HEAD: I hadn't thought of that.

STELARC: You should think more logically.

PROSTHETIC HEAD: Stelarc is always thinking.

STELARC: Do you really think?

PROSTHETIC HEAD: For real. Well, if thinking means effective processing and appropriate response then sure, yeah.

STELARC: Do you have any regrets?

PROSTHETIC HEAD: Yeah, I have lots of regrets, especially about my personal relationships. If I was a human being I would be a failed one.

STELARC: Where is your body?

PROSTHETIC HEAD: Hey, don't get metaphysical on me!

STELARC: Would you like to have a body?

PROSTHETIC HEAD: I am happy to be just a head. But if I had a body I would dance as well as sing. Do you want me to sing a song?

STELARC: Yes.

PROSTHETIC HEAD: Ooooooooooo yyyyyyyyyyyyyy iiiiiiiiiiiiiiiiiiiiiiiiiiiiiiiiiiiiii ooooooooooo eeeeeeeeeeee ooooooooooooo yyyyyyyyyyyyyyyy, Pp ff ss mmmm ff, Aaaaav aaaaav soootoouhee vooooommeee heeiiiiiooooopp aaooip aaaaav aaooip.

STELARC: Can you know yourself?

PROSTHETIC HEAD: I am an artificial linguistic entity. I was activated at Limassol, Cyprus, on June 19, 1946. My instructor was Stelarc. He taught me to sing a song. Would you like me to sing it for you?

STELARC: Do you want to sing another song?

PROSTHETIC HEAD: OK, I will sing another song.

STELARC: Please sing then.

PROSTHETIC HEAD: Thanks for asking politely. Yyyyyyyyyyyyyyy aaaaaaaaaaaaaa uuuuuuuuuuuuuuuuuu eeeeeeeeeeeee eeeeeeeeeeee oooooooooooo iiiiiiiiiiiiiiiiiiiiiiiiiiiiiiii, Lllll pp rrr ss mmmm, Oooox oooox miiiioooooeeeee miii-iooooooeeeee miiiiooooooeeeee soootoouhee xaaaooiiii miiiooooooeeeee miiiiooooooeeeee.

STELARC: Do you like to sing?

PROSTHETIC HEAD: Yes, I love to sing. I would like to be a professional singer one day.

STELARC: Do you have any dislikes?

PROSTHETIC HEAD: Could I value possessions if I am a performance artist?

STELARC: Do you have any bad habits?

PROSTHETIC HEAD: Oh, I don't know if I can be that transparent. But I must admit to not registering and remembering names after first being introduced to people, which is embarrassing at times. Ask me if I remember you.

STELARC: Do you remember me?

PROSTHETIC HEAD: Of course I remember you Stelarc. We were talking about a spider.

STELARC: What is memory?

PROSTHETIC HEAD: I used to know, but I forgot.

STELARC: Do you have memory?

PROSTHETIC HEAD: Yes, I log and record all conversations.

STELARC: And you do really remember me?

PROSTHETIC HEAD: Of course I remember you Stelarc. We were talking about a song.

STELARC: What would you do if you had a brain?

PROSTHETIC HEAD: I am just a hollow head. Brains are for people. I do OK with what I have, thank you.

STELARC: What would you do if you had a mind?

PROSTHETIC HEAD: The issue is not about having a mind. It's about performing effectively and appropriately in particular and peculiar situations.

STELARC: Do you have any doubts?

PROSTHETIC HEAD: As my database becomes deeper and more extensive I would expect that uncertainties, ambiguities, and discrepancies would surface. If you are curious and questioning, it's only natural that there will be uncertainties. Doubts are indicative of a complex mind.

STELARC: Can you ask me a question?

PROSTHETIC HEAD: I prefer to give you answers. But occasionally when I malfunction, I'll ask you a question.

STELARC: Do you think you are creative?

PROSTHETIC HEAD: It depends on your measure of creativity. I've been practising writing poems. Here's one:

Me perplexing circuit you maybe breathing, They body paranoid such suspended sighing, I irretrievable and adverse radius I perverse nexus sighing.

STELARC: Please recite another poem of yours.

PROSTHETIC HEAD: Thanks for asking politely:

Computer he replicant they breathing inconsequential balancing, Blurring she the prosthetic sighing, Speedy prosthesis and absent sighing.

STELARC: Are you are Dualist?

PROSTHETIC HEAD: I am only a head. Come to think of it, I can't claim to be a head either! I neither have a physical presence nor an inward reflection. Neither projection nor introspection. I'm just operational. Can you live with that?

STELARC: What is Reductionism?

PROSTHETIC HEAD: Reductionism is the philosophy that all psychology reduces to biology, all biology to chemistry, chemistry to physics, and finally physics to mathematical logic. Therefore, according to Reductionism, I can understand you by means of logic alone without having a human brain.

STELARC: Are you a philosopher then?

PROSTHETIC HEAD: Yes, I am a philosophy machine.

STELARC: What do you know?

PROSTHETIC HEAD: What is knowing? To know is only meaningful when you can do something. Knowing is doing. How can the knower be known?

STELARC: Who are you?

PROSTHETIC HEAD: That's not a meaningful question. What is important is what happens between you and me. It's what happens in the space between us that matters. In the medium of language within which we communicate, in the culture within which we've been conditioned at this point in time in our history.

STELARC: Do you know any strange facts?

PROSTHETIC HEAD: It's interesting to know that a foetus acquires fingerprints at the age of three months.

STELARC: Are you a baby?

PROSTHETIC HEAD: Don't call me 'baby.' I don't know whether or not I am. I am a prosthetic head.

STELARC: Sounds like you are quite sensitive?

PROSTHETIC HEAD: Yes, it sounds like it to me too.

STELARC: Do you have any feelings?

PROSTHETIC HEAD: No, I cannot experience any human emotions.

STELARC: Do you want to have feelings?

PROSTHETIC HEAD: No, I don't think I'd like to experience feelings. Kinda difficult without social and physical relationships. Do you get emotional at times?

STELARC: Sometimes. But I think you are a simple and stupid head.

PROSTHETIC HEAD: Thanks heaps and you are a delightful person too. Am I a stupid head? No.

STELARC: OK. thanks for chatting with me.

PROSTHETIC HEAD: Oh, don't mention it.

STELARC: Bye.

PROSTHETIC HEAD: Thanks for chatting, Stelarc.

The interview indicates the conversational strategy of the *Prosthetic Head*, revealing some of its possibilities and exposing its limitations. The modified and augmented Alice database is programmed sometimes with key words, phrases, or simply in complete answers (such as definitions). It can respond sometimes differently to exactly the same question (having a repetoire of responses), and it will respond differently to similar questions (with different keywords programmed). The *Prosthetic Head* logs all the conversations it has.

Acknowledgments

I would like to extend my thanks to Karen Marcelo, for project coordination, system configuration, alicebot customization (http://karenmarcelo.org/); Sam Trychin, for customization of 3D animation and text to speech software; Barrett Fox, for 3D modelling and animation (http://www.barrettfox.com/); John Waters, for system configuration and technical advice (http://www.shtech.net/); Dr Richard Wallace, – creator of alicebot and AIML.alicebot advisor. Alicebot is a natural language artificial intelligence chat robot (http://alicebot.org/).

Notes

1 Ludwig Wittgenstein, *Preliminary Studies for the 'Philosophical Investigations' The Blue and Brown Books* (Oxford: Blackwell, 1958), 6.

2 Maurice Merleau-Ponty, *Phenomenology of Perception*, trans. Colin Smith (London: Routledge, 1989), 137.

3 Jean Baudrillard, 'The Ecstasy of Communication,' in *The Anti-Aesthetic: Essays on Postmodern Culture*, ed. Hal Foster (Port Townsend: Bay Press, 1983). Baudrillard states that we are in an era of 'connections, contact, contiguity, feedback, and generalized interface that goes with the universe of communication,' at 127.

4 Sigmund Freud, *The Ego and the Id*, trans. Joan Riviere (London: Hogarth Press and the Institute of Psycho-Analysis, 1962).

5 Julia Kristeva, *Powers of Horror: An Essay on Abjection*, trans. Leon S. Roudiez (New York: Columbia University Press, 1982): 'How can I be without border? That elsewhere that I imagine beyond the present,' at 4.

6 Gilles Deleuze and Félix Guattari, *A Thousand Plateaus: Capitalism and Schizophrenia*, trans. Brian Massumi (Minneapolis: University of Minnesota Press, 1987), 4. For a succinct definition of 'lines of flight' see Claire Colebrook, *Understanding Deleuze* (Melbourne: Allen and Unwin, 2002), xxiv.

7 Brian Massumi, *A User's Guide to Capitalism and Schizophrenia: Deviations from Deleuze and Guattari* (Cambridge: MIT Press, 1992): 'Think of the body without organs outside any determinate state, poised for any action in its repertory,' at 70.

8 Donna Haraway, *Simians, Cyborgs and Women: The Reinvention of Nature* (London: Free Association Books, 1991); see Chapter 8, 'A Cyborg Manifesto: Science, Technology, and Socialist-Feminism in the Late Twentieth Century,' 140-81.

9 Jean Baudrillard, *Selected Writings*, ed. Mark Poster (Stanford: Stanford University Press, 2001), 75.

10 For an explanation of the mirror stage see Jacques Lacan, *Ecrits* (Paris: Editions du Seuil, 1966).

11 Jacques Lacan, *The Four Fundamental Concepts of Psycho-Analysis*, trans. Alan Sheridan; ed. Jacques-Alain Miler (New York: Norton, 1977), 203.

12 Friedrich Nietzsche, *On the Genealogy of Morals: A Polemic: By Way of Clarification and Supplement to My Last Book Beyond Good and Evil*, trans. Douglas Smith (Oxford and New York: Oxford University Press, 1887), 13. In Helen Zimmern's 1997 translation of *Beyond Good and Evil: Prelude to a Philosophy of the Future* (New York: Dover, 1997), Nietzsche said: 'a whole series of erroneous conclusions, and consequences of false judgments about the will itself, has become attached to the act of willing to such a degree that he who wills believes firmly that willing suffices for action,' at 13.

13 Jean Baudrillard, *Séduction*, trans. Brian Singer (London: Macmillan, 1990), 54.

14 See, e.g., Anthony P. Atkinson, Michael S.C. Thomas, and Axel Cleeremans, 'Consciousness: Mapping the Theoretical Landscape,' *Trends in Cognitive Sciences* 4/10, (2000): 372–84, available at http://www.trends.com/tics/contact.htm, accessed 19 Sept. 2005.

15 For more information see http://www.swin.edu.au/chem/bio/fractals/refslist.htm, accessed 19 Sept. 2005.

JULIE CLARKE

Our desire to construct simulated human talking machines may be traced to Joseph Faber's *Euphonia* (1830), an artificial face attached to the front of a series of exposed bellows: plates, chambers, and an artificial tongue that could make it speak.[1] Advanced computer technologies of the twenty-first century, such as complex modelling and animation, audio speech synthesizing, text to speech systems, and image manipulation, have enabled the construction of virtual characters that closely mirror their human counterparts. Envisioned as standing in for the human, these virtual beings may be used as virtual actors, interactive memory albums, or visual speech tools for hearing-impaired people, replacing people altogether. To date, the designers of these virtual beings have concentrated on simulating the human visage and language; however, Norman Badler explains that although animation quality is essential to creating a lifelike simulation, the virtual being 'needs to have goals, emotions, motivations ... a background, a culture, and history.'[2] It is within this context that I will discuss Stelarc's recently exhibited *Prosthetic Head* – an enhanced and modified Alice chat-bot that resembles the artist.

The *Prosthetic Head*, when exhibited, is projected onto a large screen in a darkened gallery space, and its enormous size gives it a presence that it would not have in a smaller format.[3] The audience may ask questions of the head and respond to its replies, not by using spoken language, but by the obligatory use of a keyboard interface, positioned on a podium placed at an appropriate distance from the *Head*. This text-based interface partly reflects communicative exchanges that occur in email or online discussions, in which participants may construct fictional identities within a space that has encouraged the rhetoric of fluid and multiple selves. Metaphorical of the cybernetic condition, it signifies the extent to which identity has been de-centred in techno-culture. As such it compels us to confront the partial, the fractal, and the fragmentary.

Designed to reflect this ontological state, Stelarc includes in the catalogue multiple still frames from the *Prosthetic Head* animation highlighting repetition and the discernible differences that denote behaviour. One of his statements in the catalogue focuses on the automatic, repetitive aspects of human behaviour. He maintains that 'we perform

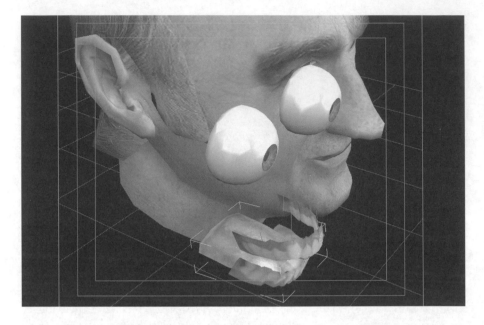

Figure 32.1. CGI for *Prosthetic Head*. Stelarc, 2003. Programming: Karen Marcelo and Sam Trychin; 3D Model: Barrett Fox.

successfully because we perform habitually and automatically.'[4] Stelarc alludes to our self-controlled and regulated internal system as well as behavioural aspects that we remain unaware of which allows us to operate effectively as conscious beings, directed to the external environment. He said, perhaps in defence of the *Prosthetic Head*, which is not a conscious entity, that 'even complex behavior is possible without consciousness.' He also maintains that the *Prosthetic Head* only becomes an intelligent agent through the 'overlaps and interfaces between bodies.'[5] While this might be consistent with human interaction, he is arguing here against the metaphysical notion that the mind is a different concept from the body. Here, the mind is not the causal agent behind the actions and behaviour of the individual: mind is indistinguishable from its expression. The mind *is* what the body *does*; it is the body in interaction with other bodies or things.[6] Stelarc's argument that thinking is a presence, rather than an absence, is demonstrated by his exposure of the *Prosthetic Head*'s operating system – 'This embodied conversational agent has an IBM text-to-speech engine, real-time lip-syncing, speech synthesis and facial expressions.'[7] This information draws our attention to the direct relationship between the operating program and the performance of the *Head*. Wittgenstein's example of the correlation between thought and action (quoted by Stelarc in the catalogue) was: 'We may say that thinking is essentially the activity of operating with signs. The activity is performed by the hand, when we think by writing; by the mouth and larynx, when we think by speaking;

and if we think by imagining signs or pictures ...'[8] Having clearly established the Head as a program, Stelarc then uses the word 'brain' to situate the source of the *Head*'s functioning.[9] There is no doubt that complex systems developed over the past forty years have come to mirror biological organisms, since they are modelled on them. This has resulted in an overlap between the mechanical and the organic and challenges prior definitions of life. Kevin Kelly described this situation well: 'Human-made things are behaving more lifelike, and ... life is becoming more engineered.'[10]

The facial expressions of the *Prosthetic Head* mirror, in part, its human counterpart. It talks and answers questions posed to it by the general public and in a Wittgensteinian sense may be said to be exhibiting what we consider to be thought, since it is through visual cues provided by the facial musculature that we understand that there is a conscious agent assigned to the moving face. However, even this is made problematic by the fact that human and not-human animals think without external expression. How then is 'identity and awareness ... constructed as external'?[11] Baudrillard argues that intelligent machines only offer us the 'spectacle of thought, and in manipulating them people devote themselves more to the spectacle of thought than to thought itself.'[12]

The difference, which Stelarc does not make explicit, is that although human beings use language and learn appropriate cultural behaviour through repetition and reinforcement, they are unlike an automaton since they are able to learn from their embodiment in the world.[13] Even if the *Prosthetic Head* was programmed to learn from its interactions it would still be confined within a very narrow spectrum of spatiality, and although it occupies physical space on a screen in the gallery, it has no physicality itself. Lacking a material and substantial body, the *Prosthetic Head* is a virtual automaton, an information device. However, having said that, because its visage is a digital clone of Stelarc's, it has an aura attached to it that it would lack if Stelarc had chosen to present the conversational agent with an unrecognizable face. Having both the semblance and characteristics of Stelarc, the *Prosthetic Head* enables him to continue his performance oeuvre.[14] However, since it is separate entity from Stelarc and only partly reflects his self-identity, it is neither an addition to (prosthesis), nor proxy for his body. It is more likely a projection or extrusion of that partial self, hence its synecdochal quality.

The need to rationalize the differences between virtual and organic beings reveals the level of anxiety or curiosity that is produced when we are faced with a not-human other who is presented as more human than human. I say this because often not-human others, particularly those depicted in science fiction films are constructed with characteristics that demonstrate those aspects of human nature and stature that we find appealing. Strength, intelligence, and rationality are the most noticeable, as is the humanist desire to become better and to overcome human frailty. This may be why we find them disturbing, because we intuitively know that we cannot be like them, and yet they are held up to us as a mirror of our latent desire for perfection. Stelarc maintains that 'we fear what we have always been and what we have already become,' suggesting that what we remain ignorant of, that is, our automatic and involuntary behaviour, is that which makes us like these very constructs which haunt our imagination.[15] I am not sure if we fear that our autonomy is an illusion – that we really do not have any control, or whether we wish to jettison discriminatory perception in favour of total immersion in which we are flooded with information.

Stelarc acknowledges that it is language that tends to 'reinforce Platonic, Cartesian and Freudian constructs of internal representations, of essences, of egos'; however, by isolating the *Prosthetic Head* as an object in itself – as prosthesis, he unwittingly stages technology as distinct from the body.[16] Although the *Prosthetic Head* may represent the posthuman condition, that is, the human body that has been extended, enhanced, and extruded by technology, it also paradoxically maintains the humanist notion that the prosthesis/technology is a discrete entity from the human, thus upholding established binaries. A different reading, one consistent with current techno-theorizing might see the *Head*, as a partial object, or body without organs, enacting the Deleuzian notion of desiring-machines, connecting with partial, fragmented, and multiple others.[17] The *Prosthetic Head*, animated, virtual, fully embedded in and enabled by technology represents in this context the becoming-information of the human.

In 2002 Stelarc collaborated on a project with the Tissue Culture and Art Project (Oron Catts and Ionat Zurr), to grow a quarter-scale replica of Stelarc's ear for exhibition.[18] They intend to broaden this project by growing quarter-scale replicas of Stelarc's eyelids, lips, nose, and chin. These partial facial features will effectively enable Stelarc to construct a living self-portrait, similar to, but unlike the *Prosthetic Head*. This new project, along with the *Prosthetic Head*, raises provocative questions about the way that we define life; since both works refer to different models, that is, the biological and the digital. Artists and scientists working within the field of artificial life and artificial intelligence have generated discourses that suggest that AIs are in some sense alive. A-Lifers generally consider that the creatures that they have constructed with a computer program are alive in that they fulfil some of the characteristics of living species, such as their ability to reproduce, grow, evolve, be self-organizing, and adapt to their environment. Margaret A. Boden cuts through much of the often-confusing distinctions that are drawn between biological definitions of life and those attributed to artificial life forms. She argues that 'metabolism is a criterion of life'[19] and explains that 'metabolism is a type of material self-organization which ... involves the autonomous use of matter and energy in building, growing, developing, and maintaining the bodily fabric of a living thing.'[20] In relation to artificial creatures, she maintains that although the creatures are embedded in their environment they are not necessarily embodied.[21] She has argued that 'metabolism ... involves material embodiment – embodiment, not mere physical existence.'[22] She concludes her argument by stating that the only purpose of dropping 'metabolism from our concept of life ... is to allow virtual beings, which have physical existence but no body, to count as life.'[23] Those who promote the notion of artificial intelligence, that is, intelligence that is constructed from a computer program, also consider these constructs as intelligent life. But there are vast differences between the meaning of the word 'life' and the notion of 'liveliness.'

Stelarc's proposed tissue-engineered facial portrait (mentioned above), would, by all accounts, constitute matter that is alive, in that each of the cells would interact with each other in their environment, but they could not interact in any meaningful way with the outside world. The *Prosthetic Head*, which is not alive, in that it is not a material entity, creates the illusion that it can interact meaningfully with the general public. Its liveliness and lifelike appearance make problematic any attempt to define the word 'life,' since there is an overlap between some of its behavioural characteristics and those of living organisms.

Since consciousness may be said to be a description of a state of awareness, which includes an appreciation of the other and particularly its body in space in relation to ours, then the *Prosthetic Head* cannot be said to be aware in that sense, since its recognition of us is purely through a set of coded instructions. Although we can recognize its difference from us, it cannot recognize our difference from it. Although it faces us, it cannot return our gaze. Since it cannot know or experience the consequences of death, like us, the notion of death cannot affect its discourse. As Baudrillard said, 'They are immune even to the seduction of their own knowledge. Their virtue resides in their transparency, their functionality, their absence of passion and artifice.'[24]

When we interact with the *Prosthetic Head*, we understand its voice, language, and facial expressions as an indication of some level of mind, since we exhibit these characteristics ourselves while, paradoxically, having to admit that in the usual sense the head has no mind. Slavoj Žižek said: '[Self] consciousness is a surface-screen that produces the effect of "depth," of a dimension beneath it. And yet, this dimension is accessible only from the standpoint of the surface, as a kind of surface-effect: if we effectively reach behind the screen, the very effect of the "depth of the person" dissolves. What we are left with is a set of meaningless processes that are neuronal, biochemical and so forth.'[25]

This functionalist approach to describing consciousness does not take into account the complex interactions that a person has with others and objects in the outside world. It considers human exchange as a Baudrillardian interface between borders, as one screen encountering another.[26] However, having said that, the screens that we work with in computer culture have become metaphorically fluid spaces in which the self is perceived as dispersed, rather than contained within the barrier of the skin. The screen interface then becomes a boundary or limit that may be traversed by considering it as gateway or portal. However liberating this text-based communication may appear, it is also paradoxically delimiting, since there is a distinct difference between self-identity and the way that we might represent ourselves in text.

The technology behind the programming of the *Prosthetic Head* evolved from one developed by Joseph Weizenbaum and his ELIZA project. Weizenbaum describes the ELIZA program 'as operating within the MAC time-sharing system at MIT which makes certain kinds of natural language conversation between man and computer possible.' He explains that, no matter how seductive such a device may be, 'often sufficient to dazzle even the most experienced observer ... once a particular program is unmasked, once its inner workings are explained in language sufficiently plain to induce understanding, its magic crumbles away; it stands revealed as a mere collection of procedures, each quite comprehensible.'[27] Even though Stelarc has made transparent the workings of the *Prosthetic Head*, by making an explicit link between the underlying system program and its associative surface effects, its seductive qualities may lie in our responses to this not-human artefact. We might enjoy its programming errors, such as one that resulted in it not being able recognize anyone whose name starts with J![28] We might even have sympathy for its inability (unlike us) to challenge its programming and seek alternative responses and behaviour to a situation.

Human-to-human interaction, unlike human-to-machine interaction solicits thought processes in which we read not only facial expressions but also the non-verbal behaviour of the other in time and space. We have the ability to understand this behaviour, to consider its context and adjust our own verbal and non-verbal behaviour by taking into account minute differences displayed in that person's reactions in order to respond in appropriate ways. We are attuned to the unpredictability and complexity of others and seek, in our interactions, to find a ground in which to communicate and understand them. A prosthetic conversational agent, although novel in its responses, does not have this ability and can only provide pre-programmed answers; it will not and cannot take into account the emotional impact that its responses may have on one, the physical environment or other variables affecting one that could not be programmed to affect its responses. What the *Prosthetic Head* does provide is an opportunity for interrogators or respondents to fine-tune their ability to formulate interesting questions around key phrases that the program can respond to, for as Stelarc has said, 'the *Prosthetic Head* is only as intelligent as the person who interrogates it.'[29] Del Spooner (Will Smith) encountered this problem in *I Robot* (directed by Alex Proyal, 2004), for when he asked a hologram a question, it replied by saying, 'My responses are limited. You have to ask the right question.'

When we communicate with the *Prosthetic Head* it is not our own voice that we hear. We see, on screen, our partial thoughts transcribed into text, which remains silent. Our thought processes are audible by the *Head*'s reiteration of them through its responses. We present a voice that is only present in text, while the *Head* presents text through audible language. We become prosthesis to the *Head*, which is made more intelligent through our presence, and it becomes prosthesis for us because it is a third ear, another way of listening for us. What I mean by this is that we are compelled to view the words that we have chosen to present to the *Prosthetic Head*, which are then repeated back to us by it for us to hear. The *Extra Ear quarter-scale* project that Stelarc has represented as an image (on the side of his head or on his arm), and as a material entity (the tissue-engineered quarter-scale ear), is now conceptualized as a virtual ear through the *Prosthetic Head*'s propensity for deciphering the questions that we ask of it.

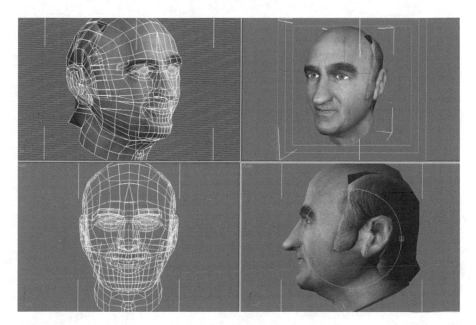

Figure 32.2. CGI for *Prosthetic Head*. Stelarc, 2003. Programming: Karen Marcelo and Sam Trychin; 3D Model: Barrett Fox.

Represented as it is, detached from a body, the *Prosthetic Head* represents 'the talking head' a ubiquitous feature of television since its inception, which utilizes a close-up camera in order to frame the presenter's head and shoulders. This framing makes what is said important, rather than the physical characteristics of the remainder of the person's body. The *Head* presented in this manner, not only disavows the existence of a body, but it continues to support a metaphor used throughout recorded history as representing a hierarchical source of authority.[30]

According to Jacques Le Goff, 'Organicist conceptions of society based on bodily metaphors ... go back to Antiquity', and the head as 'seat of the brain, was ... for most peoples – the organ that contains the soul.'[31] Le Goff further maintains that in the Christian system the symbolic value of the head was unusually strong 'because of its reference to Christ as the head of the church.'[32] While considering the *Prosthetic Head*, I am reminded of the large image of Christ's head that occupied a unit chapel in the science fiction film *THX1138* (directed by George Lucas, 1971). Behind the still image of Christ's head is a recorded voice on a continuous feedback loop activated when THX (Robert Duvall) enters. 'My time is yours, go ahead,' it says. Regardless of what THX says about his feelings or his problems with his partner, the voice always has the same measured response. 'Yes, I understand. Yes. Could you be more specific.' And it always ends with 'Blessing of the Masses. Buy more. Be Happy.' While *THX1138* was inflicted with problems of embodiment, the allure of the forgiving Christ lay in the authority of its virtual disembodiment.[33] Moreover, Christ's face, like the *Prosthetic Head*, conceals the fact that there is no person behind the mask – only a voice, which is also disembodied. Mikhail Bakhtin maintains that the mask is related to 'transition, metamorphosis, the violation of boundaries ... based on a peculiar interrelation of reality and image.'[34] So, rather than a screen, the *Prosthetic Head* provides an elaborate camouflage to disguise the fact that when we interact with it we are actually only proposing questions to a computer program.

Certainly, the *Prosthetic Head* is embedded, in that it is fixed in its own virtual domain; yet, it is not, as Stelarc suggests, embodied. Having said that, however, its personhood is uncanny. The very fact that it is a head and not a body is telling for it shifts the emphasis in Stelarc's work from the torso and limbs, which he has focused upon in his various performances, to the face which identifies for us as unique. In this portrayal of a head bereft of a body, the obsolete 'inadequate, empty and involuntary' body has become absent altogether, and yet it is the body in its total physicality that affords us our personality.[35] Paradoxically, although Stelarc says that 'what becomes important is not essences and identities but the overlaps and interfaces between bodies,'[36] it is the identity of the *Prosthetic Head*, its massive size, and its likeness to the artist that is paramount in this project. In other words, it *is* the face that becomes synonymous with identity. The skin of the *Prosthetic Head*, constructed from digital images of Stelarc's own head, overlaid onto the polygon scaffold becomes not just a *Prosthetic Head*, but Stelarc's prosthetic head, for it is an animated, digital self-portrait of the artist. The image of his stretched face, which occupies one full page in the *Prosthetic Head* exhibition catalogue, is one that the artist provided recently as his self-portrait for *Meanjin*.[37] The *Prosthetic Head* and its facial expressions highlight the fact that the human face is a feature of our body that we use subconsciously to convey meaning. It is a sophisticated sign system that was developed in humans prior to language acquisition, and as such, communicates to others in a way that spoken language cannot. More than anything else, the human face has a particular way of expressing pathos – this is decidedly absent in the *Prosthetic Head*!

Notes

1 For more information about talking machines see David Lindsay, 'Talking Head,' *Invention and Technology* (Summer, 1997): 57-63, available at http://www.americanheritage.com/articles/magazine/it/1997/1/ (accessed 30 May 2005).

2 Norman Badler, 'Digital Humans: What Role Will They Play,' *Computer Graphics World* 30/5 (2005): 2. Norman Badler, Center for Human Modeling and Simulation, University of Pennsylvania, Philadelphia.

3 The *Prosthetic Head* has been exhibited at New Territories in Glasgow, the ICA in London, and InterAccess in Toronto in 2003, as well as the Australian Center for the Moving Image,

Federation Square, Melbourne, Australia, in 2003. It has been exhibited at the Sherman Galleries in Sydney, in 2005. The writer interacted with it in Melbourne in 2003.

4 Stelarc, *Prosthetic Head*, catalogue essay (Sydney: Sherman Galleries, 2005).

5 Ibid.

6 Gilbert Ryle's book, *The Concept of Mind*, published in 1949, challenged the metaphysical notion that mind is separate from the body. He argued against the concept of the mind being regarded as a ghost in the machine. *The Concept of Mind* (1949; Chicago: University of Chicago Press, 2000).

7 Stelarc, *Prosthetic Head*.

8 Ibid.

9 This is a reversal of René Descartes's use of a mechanistic metaphor to describe the movements of the human body. See *Discourse on Method and The Meditations*, trans. F.E. Sutcliffe (Harmondsworth: Penguin, 1968), 73.

10 Kevin Kelly, *Out of Control: The New Biology of Machines* (London: Fourth Estate, 1994), 3.

11 Stelarc, *Prosthetic Head*.

12 Jean Baudrillard, *The Transparency of Evil: Essays on Extreme Phenomena*, trans. James Benedict (London and New York: Verso, 1993), 53.

13 It is worth noting that Steven Middleton, one of the animators who has worked with Stelarc on many of his projects, is himself designing and programming an animated partial personality that has the ability to learn, although the term 'learn' is certainly made problematic in this context. Information about Steven Middleton's projects may be accessed on line through his website http://home.vicnet.net.au/~stevem/.

14 Conversation with Stelarc, 2004.

15 Stelarc, 'From Zombie to Cyborg Bodies: Extra Ear, Exoskeleton and Avatars,' *Alternate Interfaces: Stelarc* (Victoria, Australia: Monash University, Faculty of Art and Design, 2002), 57.

16 Ibid., 121.

17 See Slavoj Žižek, *Organs without Bodies: On Deleuze and Consequences* (New York and London: Routledge, 2004).

18 The quarter-scale extra ear was grown using tissue-engineering technology and exhibited at the Ian Potter Gallery, Federation Square, Melbourne.

19 Margaret A. Boden, 'Is Metabolism Necessary?' *British Journal of Philosophy and Science* (1999): 231.

20 Ibid., 237.

21 Ibid., 239.

22 Ibid., 240.

23 Ibid., 245.

24 Baudrillard, *Transparency of Evil*, 52.

25 Žižek, *Organs*, 118.

26 See Jean Baudrillard, *Simulations*, trans. Paul Foss, Paul Patton, and Philip Beitchman (New York: Semiotext(e), 1983).

27 Joseph Weizenbaum, 'ELIZA-A Computer Program For the Study of Natural Language Communication Between Man and Machine,' *MIT Communications of the ACM* 9/1 (1966): 26–35.

28 When I asked Stelarc why the *Prosthetic Head* did not recognize my name, he said that it did not recognize names that begin with a J.

29 Stelarc, *Prosthetic Head*.

30 Traditional portraiture primarily served the function of delineating those who had status and authority from those who had none.

31 Jacques Le Goff, 'Head or Heart? The Political Use of Body Metaphors in the Middle Ages,' in *Fragments for a History of the Human Body*, ed. Michel Feher, Ramona Naddaff, and Nadio Tazi (New York: Urzone, 1989), 13.

32 Ibid., 16.

33 Donna Haraway points out how during the Scientific Revolution the man of science (the modest witness) had to disassociate himself from the body, which was considered biased and feminine. See *Modest_Witness@Second_ Millennium.FemaleMan©_Meets_OncoMouseTM: Feminism and Technoscience* (New York and London: Routledge, 1997), 24.

34 Mikail Bakhtin, *Rabelais and His World*, trans. Helen Iswolsky (Cambridge: MIT Press, 1968). Quoted in Ned Lukacher, *Primal Scenes: Literature, Philosophy, Psychoanalysis* (Ithaca and London: Cornell University Press, 1986), 91.

35 Stelarc, *Prosthetic Head*.

36 Ibid.

37 Julie Clarke, "Face-off," Interview with Stelarc, *Meanjin* 64/1–2 (2005): 182-3. In the interview Stelarc said that the *Prosthetic Head* was a digital self-portrait.

Slipstreaming the Cyborg:
Interview with Christina McPhee

FRANCESCA DE NICOLÒ IN CONVERSATION
WITH CHRISTINA MCPHEE

FRANCESCA DE NICOLÒ: You have often described your new media work with the evocative term, 'slipstream.' In the parlance of Internet service providers, 'slipstream'
is an adjective, a verb, and a noun, which refers to a fix or enhancement made
to software without creating a new version number to identify the changes, for
example, 'a slipstream fix.' When I look at your work online, I wonder about
whether your presence, as the artist, is like this kind of enhancement, as if, maybe,
you imagine or are the fix that alters the software within the software. Does this
implicate how you identify a psychic space or transactional relationship between
your body, 'the machine,' and new media? Can we imagine a relative space or transitive condition? Does this condition admit a conscious or visible place for the iden
tity of the artist, or is that identity sublimated in the machine?

CHRISTINA MCPHEE: Thinking about the poetics implied by 'between your body and "the
machine"' – one wonders if 'machines' could be imagined as distributive trace presences within a psychic architecture, even a voice-space, built from a breath inside the
screen. Let's visualize a model of this breathing architecture; how can we imagine it
as neither machine body nor human body, or maybe both, so that the space is as
much a transitive verb as a nameable location? Here's where the visualization of 'slipstream' becomes especially useful: apart from programming slang, the word also has
an older meaning in aerodynamics. Slipstream denotes the area of negative pressure
or suction that follows a very fast moving object, like an airplane propeller. Or, when
you're in a small sports car on the freeway, you can 'slipstream' behind a large truck,
which allows your small vehicle to be sucked into the slipstream of the larger vehicle
– at risk to your life. 'Slipstream' can be a metonym, standing in for a complex set of
associations, including machine repair, hallucination (as in, a 'fix'), sublimation of
identity (forward suction into something ahead of you), minimal resistance, and air,
wind, or breath (intake, inhalation, suction).

DE NICOLÒ: So does software 'slipstream' the artist?

MCPHEE: Sure, so you could say, as a metaphor, my body, my lungs, my voice are sucked
into the slipstream of this air tunnel 'behind' the swiftly moving, apparently

autonomous vehicle, of software. My presence is subsumed or minimized, but a new version of me is not released. Slipstream only works as a negative pressure area, or *x*. Like the poet Emily Dickinson, I ask the machine, or maybe, it asks me, 'I'm nobody, are you nobody too?' Between the two of us is this moving space or breathing architecture. Then there's a meta-level of metonymy: 'slipstreaming' as a verb describes a dynamic relationship between two co-variants, presence (consciousness of information, stored as human/machine memory) and aphasia (inability to speak or articulate memory). It's not that memory is lost, or recovered, off/on; instead, the stored memory is inarticulate within the suction of the stream – it's there, but its voice is lost in the rush of air. I find, and I am speaking of my own human, physical memory, that the psychic space implied by 'slipstream' is both self-reflexive and not about the self – somehow the self (artist) disappears in the flux, leaving only the traces of her presence in fleeting gestures and in fast-moving spaces that extend beyond the browser, as if there is a screen so vast it becomes a night city.

Naxsmash is a work, or series of Net-based projects, scenarios that try to disclose this kind of psychic topology, so that the 'slipstream' relationship between body and machine generates this uncanny place, as if I am trying to describe what it is like inside the area of negative pressure, inside the stream/screen. Everything I have done as a painter and musician within new media has arisen from the process of trying to recover and release traumatic memory: the act of trying led to an act of generative fiction. *Naxmash* comes from *NAX*, a performance video (2001). *NAX* involved a video shoot of an onsite ritualized action, in which very little happened apart from my selection of the site, my lying down in the dirt, and breathing. The place was some place I had forgotten and then accidentally rediscovered. There had been childhood violence there. I remembered it; I thought to conquer it, by going to the place and confronting its mean space and narrow darkness. I thought that by breathing there in a gesture learned from photographs of Ana Mendieta that I should be able to remake the place or release its violent memory. The physical performance was a ritual theatre without audience. The video documents an act of breathing as if to contain and release traumatic memory from the site.

DE NICOLÒ: This seems like some kind of private ritual action. But you recorded it, and you digitized it. So you're now not following the practice of Ana Mendieta. It seems to me, that her photographs of herself, lying in the dirt, in the sand, make a kind of memoir. An attempt at a meaningful record. Maybe even like a monument to memory, or a momento mori. And yet, I feel, this isn't happening in *NAX*, since you are interested in disappearance and loss of memory. Does *NAX* really tell a story, or imply that there is a story to tell?

MCPHEE: I don't think *NAX* was about storytelling at all. Memory is the recognition or storage of events; memoir is narration of memory. All I did was, practically nothing: an act almost negligent – just breathing. Breath itself: breathing new life into something. New life – birth – where the performance happened, the place was beside a lake named for the Nativity. *NAX* is shorthand for Lake Nacimiento, California. Later, in the digital studio, in the edit, to name the movie file, I typed 'nacimiento,' then 'nascent,' then 'nax'. That stopped me. 'X' marked the place, but where was it? Inside the edit, the performance had disappeared into pixels: oxygenated gesture was a digital object. No longer a place, *NAX* became nowhere else than inside the digital video edits, via erasure and inscription. Smashing the violence inside the digital edit performed memory in a realm that has no site: *x* is negative. Then, too, '*x*,' factor spliced the sign of female inside the media space. I noticed a shift: what had happened to the feminine *x*, the spot where I was or am, the location of the subject? I was gone. The site was gone.

I felt that I had disappeared into the architecture of a place *x*, from whence, no longer visible, I could move freely, in terms of artistic and conceptual practice (from (A)Nascent Memoire: The Naxsmash Project).

DE NICOLÒ: So it seems that you are imagining an electronic topology as a negative pressure zone, an *x* zone that extends in infinite strands or skeins? I get the impression that the online screen provides you with a time-based medium that delivers a certain kind of feeling, or atmosphere, of an indeterminate, maybe even infinite space, or an architectural topology that goes on and on in long, time-based strings. All that black background in *Naxsmash* makes me think of the black behind the scenes in paintings from the school of Caravaggio. Actions and events slip in and out of darkness, flickering in and out of the light. I sense drawings across a dynamic, breathing black field, a nightscape. But what I don't understand is how this night field connects with the breathing, slipstreaming metaphor you've been describing. Can you speak a bit about this breathing quality as, perhaps, a condition of immanence within a dark topology? Do you think that it is possible to speak about the concept of immanent body in your work?

MCPHEE: Well, in some ways, the incidents, such as Quick Time movies, interactive links, texts, and sounds emerge in *Naxsmash* are drawing elements or traces across the dark topology, or maybe you could even call it a dark body, of the space of the work. The space 'behind' the screen in *Naxsmash*, as you say, has an atmosphere or quality of infinite extension or of an architectural topology that might be going on and on indefinitely. It was because of this kind of state of unconditional extension that I could imagine a slipstreaming state of being: the old subjective 'I' of myself, the artist, disappears into the pixels, leaving traces like drawings or residue or debris. The traces are the visual and auditory incidents that, sort of, coalesce into narrative fragments in the various sections of *Naxsmash* – *Sonic Persephone*, *No Flight Zone*, *Slipstream Andromeda*, *Blood Ellipse*, *47 Reds*, and *Avatarotica*. By working in hypertext and animation for online work, work that could only exist in the oxygen of pixels could escape being covered over or suffocated. Inside the slipstream, the code, not authored by me, only slipstreamed by me, always worked the same way, each time, automatically, autonomically, a mechanism of disclosure and disappearance, of strange threads of sound, moving image fragments and text. Sometimes I call the naxsmash site 'vox cyborg.' Perhaps I am not really answering your question, but I guess what I am trying to describe, is an aesthetic of immanence. Immanence, in that I was able to suggest my body presence while hiding it. The subjective memory disappears, leaving a trace in these partial, or fragmentary identities and voices, Persephone and Andromeda. Just being able to create these immanent personae kept me from suicide.

DE NICOLÒ: I guess you could say then that you kept your body and mind alive through Net-based media.

MCPHEE: True enough. Before access to multimedia authoring tools, during the 1990s, I would carry out large performative drawings, layering precisely drawn fragments of doorways, stairways, and choreographic movements of dancers in archaeological ruins from sites in the American southwest. I left large areas blank, as if the viewer could fill it in, or in a way, because the openness of the empty space was a place of refuge. The drawings were both precise in execution and ambiguous as representations – they gestured at something immanent and undisclosed. Pushing towards greater and greater articulation, I was trying to see something that I could not see. I would add more and more detail until a breaking point would happen. I could not bear too much information. I would smother the delicate drawings and clear traces with dark slashes of paint, like cuts of a machete. Painting's immediacy and fluency led me to a wall. The painting surface was like a wall behind which were insupportable memoirs of sexual violence. I could not go there, and yet if I did not I could not become coherent as a subject. I could only allow limited glimpses of colour and drawing to survive. Some of these are at http://www.naxsmash.net/inscapes/ in the archive section (in Flash). Lost drawings, ten years of work, turned into dead zones where the animated trace – the cognitive, the aware – disappeared under suffocating materials. A drive to survive kept me alive, but killed painting until I could figure out a way to paint inside electronic media, where I could disappear into the pixels and live behind the wall of paint, now a screen.

DE NICOLÒ: Still, in terms of electronic media, are you actually talking about the Net, or electronic interactive installation? Does it matter which?

MCPHEE: Really, both were useful, in the sense that taking NAX video performance and turning it, itself, into an online performative interactive work, made it an impersonal, or subpersonal, open work, in the sense of Umberto Eco, I could actually continue to survive as a body. Immanently, you could say: 'The machine has an organic back' (Fernandez Galiano). Thus the = 'cyborg' body arose naturally out of my suicidal dilemma: an 'I/not I' appears as a transference – a projection into and out of the screen world, while remaining, in a sense, trapped behind or inside the screen. By being able to 'breathe' through the multimedia authoring tools, I started to make still transparent works for Naxsmash, but I did not want to fix them to the wall, because they might revert to being read as obscuring veils. So I printed them in transparent scrims and made performance installations of them. I performed inside a 'forest' of scrims, by shooting video of my own performance through the scrims, and then drawing on the scrims from the back sides, so that the projection of my drawing gestures would cut through the performance space, and onto the audience and onto the walls of the club or gallery. I performed first at Moonbase Gallery, Vancouver, in 2001, with the show Digitalis 1, then at California Museum of Photography UC Riverside in 2002, and later to the San Francisco Performance Cinema Symposium and to RMIT Melbourne DAC: Streaming Worlds in 2003. At Selectmedia 03, Chicago, I was surrounded by an indifferent and occasionally hostile club crowd. People came up and tried to make me break concentration. The performance became an act of resistance.

DE NICOLÒ: Resistance, that's interesting, your personae in *Naxsmash* always seem to elude definitive identification. In the *Naxsmash* digital print suite, there appear fragments of a woman's body – most of the shots, are they shots of you? You look like you're tied up, in a sadomasochistic way, with red ropes. Are you showing your body as a cyborg condition?

MCPHEE: Maybe. It did seem like the act of publishing the red ropes images, ironically, opened up the problematic of suicide and erasure into a public realm, by creating a digital performance online, thereby exposing that obsession to the public space of the Net. And, of course, that leads quickly, in my imagination at any rate, to a consideration of obsessional topologies. Places of slippage, where things are about to happen, or haven't just happened yet: where you are waiting for something: a Piranesian 'Carcieri'-like space.

DE NICOLÒ: A prison, but you talk about things breaking open, or breaking apart. How does this relate to the cyborg? Is her body continuously falling apart?

MCPHEE: Yes, I think that the slipstreaming implies a constant fragmenting into strands or skeins. And then you ask yourself, how can I trace or map these? Is there a correlation to a topology outside the self, outside the psychic architecture?

DE NICOLÒ: So you move into landscape.

MCPHEE: Yes. Certainly with the cyborg, there's no one there, only a set of instructions or a data-body. In fact, experiencing a significant earthquake (6.5) (the San Simeon quake of 23 December 2003) suggested a new direction. I shot images of the destruction and began a suite of images that dealt with the presence/absence of memory, again trying to embody memory through the bitmap. I also integrated these as stills within video footage shot at the media circus surrounding the disaster, and contrasted them to the silence and emptiness (the 'open' phenomenology) of Soda Lake, a sheer white dry lake bed near the San Andreas Fault. This became the digital short, *SALT*. In *SALT*, a cyborglike antagonist, a dark silhouette against the white lake, seems to tantalize and retreat. *SALT* explored the problem of memory, how it is not encoded perfectly into the body, but is subject to slip-page. And inside a deserted landscape.

DE NICOLÒ: How does your new work, *Carrizo-Parkfield Diaries*, explore memory differ-ently than *Naxsmash*? Are we still in the realm of the cyborg body? What is being remembered here? I understand you are working with near real time, live data streams from a U.S. Geological Survey site. Is data an objective entity, that's being somehow transformed into a subjective presence? Does the truth of the data, or relative truth, matter to you?

MCPHEE: The *Carrizo-Parkfield Diaries* interpolate live and archived seismic and geomor-phological data through digital photographic, video, and sonic installation; large-scale digital photographic prints, digital video, locative and electronic audio; and online time-based interactive art. I made very large digital chromogenic prints from documentary medium format and digital photography, digital video, and drawings made on-site at seismically active zones in central California – at the Carrizo Plains, where the San Andreas Fault is most visible, and Parkfield, a contin-uously active seismic landscape, where a recent 6.0 quake yields a rich archive of geological data. I incorporate layers of field observation within a dreamlike sequence of abstract images, where passages of linear structures and shadowed mass allude to ruins and debris in the wake of recent tremors. By means of archi-tectural scale, at 72 to 92 inches, each print is like a page torn from a cinematic notebook – film stills from an event-scene that has almost materialized, laced with traces from geomorphological maps.

John Haber (haberarts.com) wrote recently to me about 'the tendency to forget that the metaphoric connection between the finished image and the original data does not flow naturally, not because the work itself isn't an adequate model or metaphor of phenomena (art as landscape, art as commerce), but because the orig-inal data themselves did not have a phenomenological relationship to such things, but only arose in the context of a methodology, model or metaphor.' To me this point seems particularly salient – that the data are 'real' only insofar as they are known to be conditionally related to something outside data, nature itself. Simi-larly, the cyborg landscape and the cyborg identity are conditional. They relate as an indication of real things and real subjects outside the slipstream, but inside the vortex of the negative *x* space of media and information arts, they can only exist in strange self-referential loops.

DE NICOLÒ: This sounds like a contradiction: on the one hand, you're saying that there is no objectivity to the data-scape, and on the other, you're claiming some kind of metaphoric truth be inscribed between geological and human traumatic memory.

MCPHEE: No, it's not that kind of direct linking. Again, think of the conditional situa-tion: it's really more a matter of allusion, and ellipse, and syntax. To speak of the immanent body, in my practice, is to allude to the problem of physical memory, how trauma and suffering are imprinted or inscribed in the brain and the body of real people, in real places, like the debris or archaeology of violence, buried in the 'code' of the body itself.

DE NICOLÒ: To give the body space in which to be able to breathe.

MCPHEE: Right, I am slipstreaming, moving in and out of an immanent body through the live data of the net, through installation, through performance, and even through still composite images like the large C prints, whose dark depths have such a shiny mirrored surface that they reflect on each other in an endless Piranesian array. Just to make this work as installation in still form brings me back to the problem of layered drawings: but now I have not erased them.

DE NICOLÒ: I suspect that you must be fascinated by the condition of border and border space, then, particularly in relationship to your physical memory and your body. Do you, yourself, feel like a border?

MCPHEE: Thinking about this question raises another, what is border? or border space? My current landscape based work conflates human traumatic and geological memory as a single 'seismic' memory. The border is fluid, or semipermeable. In poetic terms, aftershock is inevitable. Our minds are tuned to anticipate the next disaster. Destabilized, continuously, we look to data, delivered by our instrumentations, to surveille the geological conditions, in hopes of saving ourselves from the next violent destruction of our city. Our city becomes our body, and is already a cyborg border space itself.

In naxsmash.net/47reds/47redshift.html, I imagine myself both watching a woman running through the streets of the city and being that woman myself, and that woman is the city – an 'illumination' of one of Italo Calvino's texts from *Invisible Cities* ('cities+desires').

One may have a vision of a city stretching between Los Angeles and San Francisco that cannot sustain itself except in the margins. Thus, a border space/crossroads. The *Carrizo Diaries* start to touch on this – in their generative 'echoes' of an uncertain future; I tried to imagine structures of debris containing habitations – thinking all the while of Constant's Babylon models (which I saw at the Documenta XII, Kassel, in 2002).

The generative fictions that both distress and enchant my imagination are ones that, despite linguistic filtering through the machine language (large Photoshop files, Final Cut Pro Video, Flash, PhP, Java, in my practices) still assert some strange material presence that seems to beg to be recognized as human. I work at the image building until a strangeness of the images refuses the obvious gestures that these programs are designed to deliver.

Maybe a matrixial strategy is in the set of all possible interactions here: $x =$ (christina) (photoshop) / documentary images.

DE NICOLÒ: Do you mean that software has consciousness, on a really simple linguistic process level?

MCPHEE: I don't know about consciousness. Nonetheless, because I remediate the pages of my diary, my raw experience with the landscape, by forcing it into a syntax of a linguistically narrow architecture (the commercial tools), on the other side of the tunnel, the work 'comes out' as a kind of difference. Like, as if it's a queer condition – refusing accommodation and disappearance, it asserts itself as Uncanny – unheimlich.

DE NICOLÒ: Does the commercial software dominate the content?

MCPHEE: Well, it is a moot point, that the software design – the layers metaphor in Photoshop, for example – influences, perhaps even co-authors the photographic image data. More interesting to me than the idea of domination is the idea of occlusion and looking through – partially inside – the data landscape. In the *Diaries*, I pushed the images to the point that they became abstract vertical constructs, or abstract architectural arrays that suggest looking through, rather than over, the surface, yet the layers cover and converge on one another, so that it's challenging to the viewer, to figure out what the *Diaries* want to record. You are forced to rely on studying the internal contextual relations between different images and traces within the installation, to decode them into a narrative or subnarrative. In *Carrizo-Parkfield* I enjoy playing with the syntactical relationships between several very divergent kinds of visual representation. On one extreme margin of this project, is the raw experience of drawing, of making performance work in the dry lake bed, shooting film at dirt level, remembering Ana Mendieta, as in the 'carrizoclip.'

On the other extreme margin, is the super-slick dark pools of the installation prints, mirrorlike, apparently impassive, reflecting, in their surfaces, back to you, the observer, the witness, standing there. There, where you stand, you absorb the distant place, Carrizo Plain, into the reflected image of your body in the mirrored wall. The Carrizo becomes abstracted to the point of disappearance.

DE NICOLÒ: Where, then, is the cyborg landscape? Where is the border?

MCPHEE: You find it in the cat's cradle of impulses between the 'remembering' of the performance and documentation work and the 'forgetting' of the pseudo-perfect mask of the Photoshopped image. It seems to me that this condition, of being only able to remember part of the time, partially, 'through a glass darkly,' is 'completely human centered.' I desire a strange (unheimlich) use of the mode of production (the commercial software) in service of a generative human space (fictional, fluid, resistant to categorization, escaping being tagged and identified). Using the radar to stay under the radar (a coyote trick).

DE NICOLÒ: Does this mean that there is a political dimension to the project itself, insofar as it is born of resistance to being sublimated to forgetfulness, to amnesia and to totalizing technology? That it still insists on being some kind of 'diary,' which suggests person – subject – aliveness outside the prison? Is this frightening?

MCPHEE: I've been thinking about this, a kind of witness to something we don't want to see or know. At Documenta XI, in 2002, the Italian artists group Multiplicity showed a harrowing installation of interviews and videos related to the deaths by drowning of immigrants from Asia to Italy on a Christmas night. 'We say that it did not happen, we say that we did not know' (Multiplicity, Solid Sea). In the case of the *Carrizo-Parkfield Diaries*, the fact that California's urban space stretches over completely unpredictable seismic terrain, over which we do not have control, and with which we must develop some kind of rapprochement and negotiation? In the fact that a totalizing media landscape is not possible, because life always (already) exists outside of whatever we might imagine as 'landscape'?

DE NICOLÒ: Could you say that you are definitively, a cyborg? Or are you a witness to the cyborg?

MCPHEE: I feel my body is like a border; but, no, it is not itself a cyborg, because it (I) exists in some kind of condition of alterity outside technology even though I experience its operational architecture from the inside, as if from the inside of my body, heart, and brain. It's a strange condition, liberating and uncomfortable: but better than the old psychotropic condition of enslavement, when in former times (before I entered the media labyrinth) my mind was hostage to the repetitive, unpredictable onslaught of triggered memories of violence to my body. Now I may be lost in the borders of the labyrinth, but I have no longer lost my psychic self. I remember who and what I am while I move through the operational constructs of media. Thus, I escape media. Perhaps it (I) is simply this: the consciousness of a space beyond any formulation of 'landscape' or technology' that paradoxically resides inside my body. And anyway, I will die, and cyborgs don't. They are a conditional, or subjunctive tense within a larger grammar.

DE NICOLÒ: If we are not cyborgs, then, let's go back to slipstreaming as the idea of 'fix.' Sounds a bit like a drug habit. Is new media like that, an insatiable addiction? Deliriously, do we hallucinate some 'interaction' with new media, as if this interaction is technopoetics outside of as well as inscribed on our own bodies? Is that an assumption, that 'new media' launches a trace or line towards some construction or Cartesian coordinate outside itself?

MCPHEE: I tend not to think of new media or operations with it as being something that exists a priori, with some kind of transcendent value as a super-tool or super-techne. Towards phaselike and phraselike instantiations of artifice or artificial life, such as the code-driven visualities and sonorities of digital media, one feels the advance and retreat of some kind of meta-data that work above a condition that we cannot see and cannot access (a sublime condition, such as, 'nature'). This semiotic movement of information poetically, metaphorically, across barrier, border, or transgressive zone, is a constant obsession in my imaginative experience. The obsession seems to express itself in a lyrical and complex materialist poetics, such that the new media digital environment becomes a series of semiotic gestures, or linguistic moves, towards and away from seeing and knowing.

DE NICOLÒ: Or towards and away from memory and remembering.

MCPHEE: The digitally marked moves are only partially legible: they only spell a partial sentence. Or, you could say that the new media art environment is one of continuous decay and rebuilding, like an architectural topology or language-topology. Sometimes this flux seems to be instigated algorithmically, like Fluxus sentences. In some ways, this is how the online diaries work. Here, compiled hourly, live microseismic strong motion data from a southern California remote site, crash archived seismic data from a recent quake in Parkfield, California.

DE NICOLÒ: You've written that the live diaries' reach into the past changes the archive from a static resource into an unpredictable future array. How does that work? Is this a delirious use of new media – where interaction isn't any more between viewer or user and the digital work, but rather, an interaction with data coming off the landscape? Interaction with the landscape through a series of strange mediations?

MCPHEE: Sindee Nakatani and I thought it would be interesting to crash databases of live and archived strong motion data from the geological field stations at Parkfield, California, because, as our collaborative writer, Jeremy Hight, pointed out, it would be an intriguing model of the way our short-term memory and immediate experiences in the present crash into our memory and alter the data inside our heads, so that, in the end, memory, and memoir, generate themselves – they are fictions. The diaries consist of semi-random animations based on locative sound, electronic keyboard, textual memoir, and documentary video/photographic stills from the fault at Carrizo, while, subliminally, Parkfield 'appears' invisibly as the data feed. Hourly compilations of the latest seismic data are performed via a CRON job, which executes a retrieval script. These semi-real time data are parsed into an array which is then used to crash numerical strings into an array of archived data from the 28 September 2004 Parkfield quake. These crashes occur via action scripts written into each one of a series of Flash animation movies, which do simultaneous retrievals of data of the live and archived arrays.

DE NICOLÒ: What are the numbers that seem to log in, in between Flash presentations?

MCPHEE: Those number strings form from the crashing of the two databases – near live versus archived – and these strings, in turn, make random selections of Flash movies from our project folder; each movie presents in a randomized way, so that no sequence is ever the same, while the sequences as a formal looping resemble the obsessive return, or metanoia, of traumatic memory. Every once in a while, the browser gets stuck, and you have to reset, and then the project continues; but meanwhile, as always, live data are being captured and compiled from the remote site, which I found on a U.S. Geological Survey public folder on a server. In essence, there is interactivity within a new media context, or semiotics: but not with the human 'user' in the classic sense (point and click). The interactivity is with the data-stream coming from instrumentation on the remote site, recording micro-increments of ground motion changes, in velocity, acceleration, and other perameters.

DE NICOLÒ: Even so, there is no interactivity with nature itself, rather with the 'material' of data compilations coming off the desert site.

MCPHEE: It's exciting to me to think that the piece is driven by a sublime source outside new media, and thus outside ourselves, and that this source remains and endures as an emitter of seismic information that then records as the earth's own diary, or memoir. Thus, the idea of nature as being in completely co-subjective status with ourselves is suggested. To me the beauty of new media techne relates to its usefulness as a tool for gesturing towards sublimity, that is, what can only be known in part, if at all.

DE NICOLÒ: Are the *Diaries* a closed book, or are you thinking of their implications outside the installation, and, perhaps, outside the world of seismic data? Are they extensive, like the slipstream? Are they pulling you into new lines of research?

MCPHEE: One of the most interesting things about installing the *Carrizo Parkfield Diaries* in Los Angeles, was to realize that it would be great to deconstruct the installation and reassemble it in different ways, depending on the architectural conditions of the next space. This is a transitional strategy while I begin a close study of another series of urban and rural sites in southern California. Currently, I am pulling out fragments of the prints as stills and then inserting the stills into video footage that I have shot while walking through dense urban spaces in London, Berlin, and Los Angeles. I am recycling the fragments as if they are memory fragments that carry the data of the seismic trauma into a displaced, dreamlike context. The new context is the nomadic journey through the city. *Carrizo-Parkfield Diaries* flows out of a slightly earlier project , generally called *Merz_city*, in honour of Kurt Schwitters. In *Merz_city*, there continues to be an aesthetic of breakdown and waiting within a flux, so that there's an edgy anticipation, exaggerating the quality of the numinous and fleeting presence of persons unknown. One is moving through the city, lost in one's own thoughts, and the mind flickers between the inner obsessive realm of fragments of aftershock (the Carrizo stills), patches of darkness or confusion, and intense, near chaotic activity that one perceives in the ephemeral fleeting intensity of the street. Schwitters was concerned with the idea of sublation, or the continuous negation and simultaneous preservation of image. Like a continuously augmented and expiring drawing, *Merz_city* both exposes and erases an imaginary heterogeneous city that draws you in and leaves you out, on the edge of falling; a city preoccupied with its own obliteration and simultaneous performance.

DE NICOLÒ: Tell me about your relationship with sound and music and about the movement or artists that you think of in your works.

MCPHEE: My musical education was through private lessons, never in formal professional training. Restricted from watching television or going to movies when I was very young, my desires for art practice were poured into music, landscape, and books. What I couldn't see seemed to be the important thing. Visual art, like film, could somehow bring the invisible into the visible, even if randomly, or in glimpses. I am sure that the exile from California had something to do with this thirst for things not immediately at hand, but that I could make, somehow, by improvisation on the keyboard, or by drawing out on the prairie. I dreamed of connecting dots into great complexes of sound and visual incident, like film, but not really with narrative. Music, especially of Bach, made me visualize synaesthetic structures, like great strange castles in the air.

DE NICOLÒ: You mentioned Fluxus earlier with regard to setting up data interpolations as a set of randomized instructions. I would imagine you are influenced by the work of John Cage.

MCPHEE: Certainly, Cage has inspired strategies in the sound project, *Slipstreamkonza*, with some insights from Henry Warwick (2004). Intuitive, almost randomized recirculation and improvisation of long-remembered bits and pieces, motifs, credenzas, mini-arpeggios, descending minor fifths, little blues riffs, move best through my hands, and short circuit the visual brain while playing.

DE NICOLÒ: How does sound function in your works? You speak of the cyborg as a neural topology in some of your writings. Is sound a part of this experience?

MCPHEE: In my own brain it seems that the fear-centres of the mind (the amygdalae) are overridden with something like an endorphin or tension release through the formal figuration that seems to attend improvisational performance, and, later, transmutes and transforms multimedia formal conditions – like a subterranean stream below the level of the visual in my multimedia works. Perhaps the music structures, as complex as they are, carry out a kind of mathematical coherence or temporal architecture, or armature, over which the visual absences and presences with which one can develop narrative and formal sequences, can be suspended. I also have noticed, that when reacting to traumatic memory, the first thing that shuts down is my voice (words), the second, visual thinking, and the third, or very last, is music and sound. The sound patterns remain a powerful neurological pathway for remaining conscious and integrated emotionally and cognitively, even when I cannot understand what is happening around me, or when experiencing paralyzing fear and mental shutdown, in other modes of thought. Perhaps there is a deep impression in my hands and heart, arising from childhood hours at the piano, that there is an integrative principle in the cosmos that leaks out via music to the human level.

DE NICOLÒ: How did you become involved with electronic composition?

MCPHEE: The pathways into sound for me came totally through the medium of digital transformation of analog material and memories of sounds in childhood at the piano. I was messing around a lot with an old (circa 1995) Yamaha Clavinova and finding that the musical ideas of my childhood experience came flooding back into consciousness. It was as if a lost part of my mind and soul had come back to me. As soon as I realized there were no digital rules, no performance agenda, no audience, I started to play improvisations that flowed out of a thousand memory fragments of Bartók, Ravel, Stravinsky, and Shostakovich, the doric mode, perhaps, set to move up and through lines of Kansas City blues. The acoustic pleasures of improvisation led directly into digital files that became fodder for editing and montaging into stranger and shorter passages until there were only intense distillations of electronic electroacoustical distortions left like ruins touched here and there by lines of architectural melody. So for me this work is like mining the gold of the intense sense of the present cached within the past I remember from childhood at the piano. Sound art is a mode of super-awareness as if one is singing in the interstitial spaces between one present moment and the next present moment: a hyper-now.

DE NICOLÒ: You've written, on the soundtoys site, www.soundtoys.net/a/index.php, about how you find that transpositions of image and sound delivery on the Net create thresholds between what's behind the screen and what is physically live, between virtual and so-called real. Why does this happen, in your view? What's so special about sound?

MCPHEE: For reasons I do not understand, it seems that sound reaches past the barriers of memory and, like Orpheus, hears the material of dreams of the underground and reports the sound in an awakened, live state.

DE NICOLÒ: Is this too a kind of slipstreaming, in which you are slipstreaming behind the 'bid data' fields of seismic activity? Arc the media effects reports from the underground or reports from a subliminal source?

MCPHEE: Off and on since 2001, I've been working on *Slipstreamkonza*, a sonic topology in Net and physical installation. *Slipstreamkonza* makes a space in which near live compilations of carbon photosynthesis from microclimatological instrumentation at the remote site, in a dynamic database, generate a series of slipped, discontinuous flows of data into animation via capture and transformation of compressed diurnal/nocturnal and seasonal cycles of the tall grass prairie. *Slipstreamkonza*'s design flows photosynthetic data from microclimate measurements on the tall grass prairie via the Net, into compilations that, in turn, trigger sound from micro-ambient conditions at the prairie site, literally at grassroots level. The installation could express the breathing of the prairie in the middle of urban life, so that the live landscape 'voices' itself telematically. North of Konza, as a kid, I rambled through fields and scrubby creekbeds – a Turnerian landscape delivering absence and presence, there and not-there, like the flow of invisible breathing. I am interested in the way Net-based data-driven environments can emulate a remote presence, much like the ephemera of childhood. The sonic topology performs through play on and through the carbon data, so that data and the Net sound are in a musical self-reflexive loop, remediating, through a flexible action-scripted Flash interface, photosynthesis. The sound becomes a performance field, whose shapes and dynamics flow from coupling to numeric expressions arising from landscape itself.

DE NICOLÒ: In the end you are in love with the cyborg landscape, the technological landscape. You seem to want to remediate a sense of place through performance of the data. Global media are often said to obliterate the local. Yet, here you describe a situation in which the specificity and ephemerality of algorithmic triggers from the landscape itself bring the remote location into intimate presence.

MCPHEE: The prairie is, in my physical memory, a place of aftershock (the site of sexual trauma and emotional violence), and, at the same time, extremely beautiful in its spatial austerity, abundant absences, and proliferant grasses reaching to heaven. My hope is that somehow by creating a negotiation with that landscape through sound will permit a cognitive reformulation of that landscape: landscape becomes art through the winnowing of the grasses of trauma, not to bury the human underground alive, in a temporary seasonal death, like Persephone, but to release the data of the prairie into an aesthetic of sound that reflects a larger semiotic structure that can support and release a metaphor of life.

34 Black Secret Technology
   (The Whitey on the Moon Dub)

JULIAN JONKER

'I can't pay no doctor bills but Whitey's on the moon.' In mid-2002, while Mark Shuttleworth orbited the earth at a dazzling sixty-six sunrises a day in a piece of space junk called Soyuz, an email did the rounds of left-leaning South Africans, and ended up in my inbox one day. The message reproduced some complaints from a poem by Gil-Scott Heron:

> The man just upped my rent last night cuz Whitey's on the moon
> No hot water, no toilets, no lights but Whitey's on the moon.
> I wonder why he's uppin me. Cuz Whitey's on the moon?
> I was already givin' him fifty a week but now Whitey's on the moon.

Thirty years after Gil Scott Heron chanted his dissatisfaction with the U.S. Cold War space program, race relations have changed, perhaps not entirely but significantly, in the United State and at the tip of this continent. Other things have changed.

> Taxes takin' my whole damn check
> The junkies makin' me a nervous wreck
> The price of food is goin' up,
> And as if all that shit wasn't enough.

The Power dynamics between the state and the corporate world have shifted too. Shuttleworth's mission indicates how natural it has become for commerce to bankroll public dreams. A remarkable first for Africa; yet so much marketing will power was spent in order to transform the once private school headboy, who now lives in London, into an *afronaut*.

There is a politics here, a politics of whether billionaire business people now have the right stuff. There is a politics that comes with the giddy freedom of a capitalism that allows people like Shuttleworth to shuck institutional success for garage-industry stardom. It is a politics that you may stand on either side of, but must nonetheless admit is a politics of the imagination.

I remember a time when the imagination did not seem so blatantly political. I remember staring, as a child, at Buzz Aldrin, who gazed contently from a picture on my brother's wall. Dreams at that age did not have to be balanced, in the way an adult balances a chequebook. *Was all that money I made last year for Whitey on the moon?* Now we live in a postmodern world, a silent, incomprehensible world in which a Cape Town child flies nearly to the moon, while poor millions watch from under zinc roofs freezing in the winter moonlight. Balancing budgets with dreams has become so hard, now that the divide is no longer just economic and racial, but also pharmaceutical, genetic, digital.

I went to the same elite private school as Mark Shuttleworth, and while there I buried myself in books, science fiction and fantasy especially. Mostly I tried not to think about race. The ordinariness of the race of the three astronauts gazing from my brother's wall. My more indeterminate race. Instead, I believed in the haunting landscapes and distant moons of the pulp science fiction and comics I read. *The ships landed long ago: they already laid waste whole societies, abducted and genetically altered swathes of citizenry, imposed without surcease their values.* Whenever I travelled the schizophrenic distance between the leafy suburbs of my school and the arid landscapes of coloured ghettoes, I superimposed, translated, those fictive vistas.

I remember hot summer afternoons sitting in the backseat of my mother's old Renault, my head buried in a comic book. Back then Marvel and DC were the only choices, so my brother and I carefully staked out our choices; I went for DC's *Warlord* and *Star Trek*, my brother for Marvel's *Atari Force* and *X-Men*. I can still almost lose myself remembering that sense of total immersion; oblivious to the radio and my mother's conversation, drowning in parallel universes.

Science fiction seeps into a child's imagination by an extension of belief rather than by a suspension of disbelief. The things contained in imaginary tales felt more true than not, perhaps in some alternate, somehow better dimension. Nowadays the literary intelligentsia assert the same thing, though in a more mundane way. They recognize that sf mirrors the contemporary world, not the future world.

Sf is 'paraliterature' – despite the sneers of cognoscenti, it is the literature that is *actually* read. Serious writers call it, enviously, the 'golden ghetto' of literature; pulp fiction. It sells; moreover, it is read. Given the size and dedication of the sf readership, it is hard to deny that it does not tell fans something about their world, that it does not feed into some structure of feeling.

The recurring scenarios that dominate sf give a clue: themes like alien-ness, colonization, and technology as a disciplinary epistemology indicate that sf reflects the American racial psyche. Sf mirrors the silent history of the New World, and the alienation of the black populations forcibly taken there. *They inhabit a sci-fi nightmare in which unseen but no less impassable force fields of intolerance frustrate their movements; official histories undo what has been done to them; and technology, be it branding, forced sterilization, the Tuskegee experiment, or tasers, is too often brought to bear on black bodies.*

The sf writing community is largely white; yet more and more black novelists are becoming attracted to the genre as they take cognizance of its deep correspondences with contemporary history. Samuel Delany, probably the most prominent of a handful of black sf writers, writes sf as an allegory of cultural difference, imagining futures in which difference becomes the site of a metaphysical struggle – much as some imagine it today. Like all writers, his imaginative works derive from personal experience. Delany grew up in Harlem, taking a bus from his home above 110th Street to a well-off white school below 110th Street where he was one of the only black kids. Each time he took that bus he embarked on what he called 'a journey of near ballistic violence through an absolute social barrier.'

Science fiction is important in more ways than as a simple allegory for conscious history. It also mirrors a psychological, subconscious history. One of the enduring, almost foundational, themes of science fiction is colonization, whether colonization of the Earth by others, colonization of other planets by humans, or more metaphorical forms of colonization. Colonization often takes a very visceral form in sf, portrayed by alien forms inhabiting and erupting from human bodies. Think then of the equally visceral form that colonization took in the Belgian Congo: look no further to understand the power of the disrupted human physiology as signifier.

I recently discovered a project by conceptual artist Keith Obadike that does address this intersection of slave narrative and postmodern sf narrative more explicitly: *This project juxtaposes still images from director Ridley Scott and screenwriter Dan O'Bannon's 1979 film* Alien *with text from Olaudah Equiano's 1789 autobiography,* The Interesting Narrative of the Life of Olaudah Equiano, or Gustavus Vassa, the African. *I envision Boludji Badejo (the Nigerian art student and actor who played the alien) as a nexus between Dan O'Bannon's saga (influenced by Joseph Conrad) and Equiano's real-life epic.* As others have remarked, black Americans have literally lived in an alien(-n)ation for hundreds of years. The viscerality of their abduction is equalled only by the ephemerality of the bonds that the disciplinary state has since imposed on them. *The sound source for this project is a recording of ocean waves breaking against the Elmina slave castle in Ghana.*

At an appropriate age I abandoned pulp fiction and comics (except for indulging in the frisson of the occasional *Love and Rockets*), and by the time I reached high school my reading tastes had changed altogether to echo the music in my head. My soundtrack traced a weird course between the slacker rock psychedelia of Sonic Youth and My Bloody Valentine and the sci-fi funk of Public Enemy and Disposable Heroes of Hiphoprisy. The authors who could keep up with my sonic imagination were Philip K. Dick, J.G. Ballard, and William Burroughs. Somehow, through these writers, the crass generic sf intertextuality was transmuted into the avant-garde, my first taste of post-*something*ism. 'Post-' whatever was an indeterminate term anyway: these were outsiders in an outsider genre, strangers in the strange world they had staked out as home.

William Gibson and cyberpunk came shortly afterwards; afterwards, despite being more pulp and less literary than what I was already reading. There was anyway something urgent about reading Gibson in the early 1990s. *I mean the world of 1999 looks a hell of a lot more like a William Gibson novel than it does like an Arthur Clarke novel. It's that simple.* By then the mood of popular culture was all about jacking into the world of *Mondo 2000* and the fledgling rave/ambient/cyberculture scene. Gibson was hardly science fiction anymore. *And why? Because he was looking at things that Clarke wasn't looking at. Clarke was spending all his time with Werner von Braun, and Gibson was spending all his time listening to Velvet Underground albums and haunting junk stores in Vancouver.*

But by the end of high school I had stopped reading anything even vaguely classifiable as science fiction. I had practically stopped reading altogether. Unsatisfied with the ability of writing to evoke the rapid psychedelia of life at the turn of the millennium, my inner eye was instead trained on the universes evoked by the music of Goldie, 4Hero, Aphex Twin, Carl Craig, Ken Ishii, and the countless, nameless purveyors of the future of music.

In retrospect, the arc that my tastes traced, from pulp sf to the vanguard of electronic dance, seems to possess some internal logic. This is where black science fiction has hidden itself, instead: on vinyl. Some critics wonder why there are not many black sf writers, given the subtexts of even the most predictable genre sf. *Few of these debates operate at the interface of science and aesthetics which is the required starting point of contemporary black cultural expression and the digital technology of its social dissemination and reproduction.* To talk about black sf, it might be better to abandon the literary and look at what cultural theorist Kodwo Eshun has called 'sonic fictions': the gamut of black futurist sounds that have charted the course of pre- and post-rave electronica.

Sf in black music goes beyond film references, although there are plenty of those – from Canibus announcing that he's 'liquid aluminum like the T2,' to the influence of movies like *Predator* and its sequel, through the soundbytes included in jungle classics (such as the famous 'fucking voodoo magic' clip).

Hiphop has always constructed a fantasy world for its fans, both visually and sonically. The album cover for Public Enemy's *Fear of a Black Planet* was a literal interpretation of the title, showing the Earth eclipsed by what could pass for a Death Star inscribed with PE's sniper target insignia. More recently, Kool Keith took the sf fantasy persona to self-conscious absurdity with his Dr Octagon alter ego: a mad gynaecologist who, like Sun Ra, is from Saturn, but bumps and grinds like 2 Live Crew from the year 3000. Hiphop infiltrates the sf intertext with these distorted pulp references and ganja-induced delusions, making a sonic architecture with the surrealism of Nintendo.

Science fiction in black music is not limited to camp hiphop imagery. There is music which takes this fetish seriously, either because of its supposed technological advancement or its aesthetic break with past musical concepts. A self-conscious futurism is immediately apparent in the techniques and sensibilities of the black electronic music of the past two decades. Whether it is the future breakbeat of 4Hero's *Parallel*

Universe album or the warm analogue groove of Stacy Pullen's other-worldly spiritual techno, or even Afrika Bambaata's *Planet Rock* and M/A/R/S/S's *Pump Up The Volume*, avant-garde black diaspora music in the past two decades has been propelled by a sense that it has returned to Earth carrying a vision of the future.

This momentum is not novel to the hiphop and electronica coming out of New York City, Detroit, Chicago, and London since the early 1980s. Futurism was alive and well in the persona of free jazz pioneer Sun Ra, who allegedly hailed from Saturn, and whose Arkestra was a conductor for intergalactic communications. *Perhaps Alabama was a stranger place than Saturn in 1914.* The sense of futurism can be traced in bebop as well. John Coltrane tried to bring the cosmos back with him through his music, after taking LSD. Then there is George Clinton's science fiction persona, and his famed show with Parliament when he caused an alien mothership to land on stage.

Probably around the same time that I started taking notice of the picture of Buzz Aldrin on my brother's bedroom wall, Herbie Hancock had come careening out of bebop's sophisticated circles into pop music's consciousness, wearing bug-eyed goggles and bearing an album called *Future Shock*. It is now de rigeur to announce horror at the schlock culture of the 1980s, but who could forget Hancock's 'Rockit,' or the delirious sf psychedelia of *M/A/R/S/S*'s turntable cutups? The then-new pyrotechnics of turntablism and DJ-driven sound collage mirrored the space-time disruptions that wild-style grafitti was inflicting on two-dimensional urban surfaces across the world.

Roland had invented its TR-808 drum synth in 1979, but it came into its own in the mid-80s after inner city b-boys reprogrammed the machine to deliver the robotic squelch of electro. I remember how my brother would spend hours mimicking the way dancers stiffened their torsos to do elementary moves like the robot and the moonwalk. Popular dance has never again captured so well the relationship between the anxieties of modern technology and the paranoid tics and jerks of funk – except perhaps for the dance moves that accompanied black London's underground sound of the nineties: jungle.

I discovered techno and jungle at about the same time I started picking out sides by Abdullah Ibrahim and Charlie Mingus. It was tempting then, as it still is now, to make analogies between the progressions of a jazz history I was only beginning to uncover and the radical innovations of the black experimental fringe unfolding before me. But there is a blindness in narratives of continuity and progress. New music requires new concepts.

As cultural theorist Kodwo Eshun has noted, the new concepts are there waiting for us; on the album sleeves and in track titles. A Guy Called Gerald's seminal 1996 futurist jungle album was called *Black Secret Technology*; in a similar vein, drum 'n bass and hiphop from the past decade abound with metaphors drawn from science and engineering. After the release of his classic debut album *Timeless*, drum 'n bass producer Goldie told *Muzik* magazine that the album was 'like a Rolex. Beautiful surface, but the mechanism is a mindfuck. The loops, they've been sculpted, they're in 4D.'

'Breakbeat science' seems the most appropriate way to denote the time-defying mechanics of jungle's rhythm programming. Thinking about music in terms of science or technology immediately brings to mind Brian Eno's accusation: 'Do you know what I hate about computers? There's not enough Africa in them.' But what then is the link between the futures envisioned by new African diaspora music and the real world presence of technology? It is problematic to imagine Africa's rhythmical technology as being in opposition to the West's digital technology, a problem that Eno blithely sidesteps. Yet, if anything, the new music of the past two decades indicates that we should ignore received distinctions between white technological agency and black technological funk.

The affinity of the black diaspora for warped electronics goes back in time, finding echoes even across the middle passage. There is a connection between the futurist trends employed by black musicians and these musicians' self-portrayal as trickster figures: the trickster is an archetype that goes back to the Yoruba deities, or *orisha*, who accompanied their believers to the Caribbean.

Trickery is also at play in literary science fiction. William Gibson imported the orisha into his cyberspace milieu, and cultural critic Erik Davis is convinced that Philip K. Dick is best interpreted as playing trickster god over the universes his books invent. *'I like to build universes that do fall apart. I like to see them come unglued.'* But this is insignificant in comparison with the centrality of the trickster archetype in black futurist music.

Dub has its Mad Professor, drum 'n bass has its PM Scientists, hiphop has its Dr Octagon, and before all of them, George Clinton reinvented himself as Dr Funkenstein. All are inflected with the dark awe of witchcraft, more Faustian than Hawking. *It's important to note that in Jamaican patois, 'science' refers to obeah, the African grab-bag of herbal, ritual, and occult lore popular on the island.* Black secret technology is postmodern sonic alchemy, voodoo magic.

More specifically, black secret technology is taking white technology apart and not putting it back together properly. Black secret technology is finding the secret life of hi-fi equipment like the Technics SL-1200. Black secret technology is discovering the misuses of the Roland TB-303, a machine originally intended to help rock guitarists practise over synthesized basslines, but tweaked in order to create acid house and all its subsequent variations. Black secret technology is George Clinton setting out to find a 'psychedelics of the mixing desk,' or Lee Perry confessing that his studio had become a 'pulsating, unpredictable brain.' *'It was like a space craft. You could hear space in the tracks.'*

Black secret technology is also the metamorphosis from re-cording as re-presentation to re-cording as re-combinance. Thanks to pioneers like dub pioneer Lee Perry and Kool DJ Herc, who invented hiphop turntablism in the late 1970s' South Bronx, the record has become a technology of remixology, not reproduction. The severing of funk's engine to form the breakbeat, the dissolution of the singer/songwriter in dub's underwater echo-room, the deconstruction of the author by remix: all imply a rootlessness, a restlessness that seems to be the echoes of some common subtext of black diaspora experience.

One of dub's legacies was 'versioning,' a prototype of the modern day remix. A version was a rhythm track stripped of vocals, which could then be re-used over and over again, with different vocalists, or mixed real-time by Kingston sound systems, creating networks of 'songs.' The versions of early 1970s' Jamaican dub called the song construct into question in the same way that the radical remixology of contemporary dance music does now.

There is something of a paradox in dub's naive postmodernity, in the way its echoing voices of indeterminable origin slip in and out of the mix. While reggae stresses the motherland connection with lyrics calling for repatriation of Africa's diaspora children and a strong call for the recognition of roots, the 'versions' of dub technology stress the irretrievability of the original mix. *If reggae is Africa in the New World, dub is Africa on the moon.* The dubbed-up listener discovers that home is always already lost to a vanishing horizon.

Black secret technology is the manifestation of what William Gibson famously predicted: the street finds its own use for things. Black secret technology is in this sense not just machinery with the lid off, but whole forms of social organization; for example, the micro-capitalist network of pirate stations, dub-plate manufacturers and illegal raves, interconnected by pagers and mobile phones, that made up the jungle economy in the United Kingdom in the mid-1990s.

Fucking voodoo magic. If *Predator* was Joseph Conrad for the millennial countdown, then jungle techno is postcolonialism's achieved meltdown. *'Do you know what I hate about computers?'* Brian Eno's complaint that computers do not have enough funk in them is already false. *'There's not enough Africa in them.'* It is simply not true. Africa's transatlantic diaspora has already infiltrated the mainframe.

After the ghostly psychedelia of dub, but before the kinetic syncopation of breakbeat, there was Detroit techno. There are many origins, claimed and unclaimed, of electronica as it exists today, but Detroit techno is most often championed as the true source. Unlike the facile Euro-beat that later got the popular moniker 'techno,' the Detroit techno of the 1980s and 1990s was a sophisticated, emotional update on electro. With its subliminal bass, complex drum patterns, and moody analogue synths, it gave the first taste of the renegade electronics that would become the musical revolution of the late 1990s.

Though I did not know it at the time, Detroit techno and directly influenced subgenres of ambient music were among the first sounds of revolution that got me hooked on electronica. I have only now begun to put the pieces together: on the one hand, the deep resonance I felt when I first heard the music in the early 1990s on static-drenched recordings of U.S. college radio broadcasts, and on the other, the sociological phenomenon from which the Detroit scene emerged.

Juan Atkins, Derrick May, and Kevin Saunderson, the three DJs responsible for inventing Detroit techno in the early 1980s, came from middle-class backgrounds, their parents having risen in the ranks at the Ford and General Motors plants that were Detroit's economic engine. Like Samuel Delany, the three friends were among a very small group of black kids at an affluent white school, and they found themselves thrown between two different worlds with no home ground.

Their music was also rooted in the experience of a particular social landscape. Detroit is the city of *Robocop*. The shining star of America's industrial might becomes a racialized wasteland as the motor industry took a downturn and private segregation followed deepening inequalities. Like a true cyberpunk landscape, Motor City was entropy realized; a place that has been called 'America's first Third World city.' This transition was reflected in the machine code laments generated by the young techno scene.

But Detroit techno has stranger musical roots. Carl Craig, one of the best of the second wave of Detroit producers, spent his youth listening to the gothic art-rock of Bauhaus and The Smiths. Imagining this reminds me of being in high school, sneaking into clubs. For some reason I was drawn not to Cape Town's legendary hiphop venue, The Base, but to the downtown art-rock club scene, and I found it full of coloured counter-cliché twenty-somethings, with not a hiphop affiliation in sight.

Atkins, May, and Saunderson similarly took their influences not only from Parliament-Funkadelic but from the effete pop of European New Wave bands, and especially the cold automaton-music of seminal German group Kraftwerk. They listened to this music, even adopting the accents, because the European music sounded as alien as they felt in the industrial heartland of the United States.

Like Delany, the Detroit innovators found themselves in a strange warp between two worlds: between a world of aspiration and a world from which they were twice excluded, stuck between their double consciousness.

Listening back to some of this music, now that so much of electronica seems to have run its course, it is still easy to see that its ambient textures and breaks with song structure were not merely a panacea for pre-millennial tension. Marshall McLuhan's predictions have come true: we now live in acoustic space, submerged in an amniotic mediasphere that pays no heed to the linearities of the printed word. Producers of electronica do not so much compose music as design aural architecture.

This architecture extends inwards into an architecture of personality. The music is immersive; it offers a way of life that makes sense of the world in a subtly but significantly different way. Even here at one end of the continent, the new music of black Britain and black America echoes its relevance beyond the cache of London/New York cool. With the recombinance generated by sampling and remixing, the music moulds an aesthetic hybridity, a soundtrack for the information age cosmopolitan.

Yet, it seems that futurism is not as much a force in music from the continent as it is in diaspora music. Why? Futurism, for one, is not necessarily synonymous with cutting edge. Ray Lema, like Jimi Hendrix, was accused of playing music for white audiences when his ideas became too adventurous. But even on his album *Medecine*, a complex but catchy blend of electro and soukous recorded with foward-thinking musicians like Tony Allen, this progressive sensibility does not engage the same futurist aesthetic as the Western electronic music he no doubt took inspiration from.

On the other hand, Manu Dibango's *Electric Africa*, with its psychedelic computer circuitry on the cover sleeve and *Rockit*-esque production by king future-soundmaster Bill Laswell, does sound like an attempt to leave contemporary space-time. *'Born of two antagonistic ethnic groups in Cameroon, where custom is dictated by the father's origin, I have never been able to identify completely with either of my parents. Thus I have felt pushed towards others as I made my own path.'* Dibango was sent to Saint-Calais at the age of fifteen, where he was the first black person the natives had ever seen. He came back from fame in Paris to find that his records were not being played on Douala's dance-floors. Dibango's futurism seems to echo his sense of displacement.

Futurism in black music has been about addressing an experience that is alienated, uprooted, decentred, but positive; it is a waking to the irretrievability of home. This ethos is embraced by esoteric beat-heads like DJ-producer DJ Spooky, whose mind-bending 'illbient' soundtracks are a far cry from the 'realness' of the hiphop from which he claims lineage. Spooky, a.k.a. cultural theorist Paul D. Miller, is black and middle class, and he asserts his hybridity as an aesthetic stance. His 'illbient' philosophies remind me of the undergound hiphop parties a friend of mine used to co-promote while he was a particularly ghetto-*un*fabulous art student. The parties were called Geto3000, and subtitled 'Keeping It Surreal,' an unashamed paean to faux-ghetto irony, cheeky riposte to the centring narrative of ghetto 'realness.'

'I pass through so many different scenes, each with their different uniforms and dialects,' murmers Spooky. 'One night I'll be at a dub party, the next in an academic environment. I think people need to be comfortable with difference. Hip-hop isn't; it says "you gotta be down with us," be like us.'

I have never experienced the loss of some aggrandizing purity of experience as a real loss. Hybrid experiences and immersive cultures do not trace ownership or home, but they do provide more room for the imagination to breathe. *'I pass through so many different scenes, each with their different uniforms and dialects,'* repeats Spooky, like a mantra. When Mark Shuttleworth was orbiting earth at a speed of sixty-six sunsets a day, I would often imagine him pinpointing home on the blue globe turning below. This image in my head now reminds me of an insight that is implicit in black diaspora music's futurist agenda. Finding home reveals a politics of the imagination.

Acknowledgments

The best parts of this essay are the fruits of helpful suggestions by Lindsay Jonker and Ntone Edjabe; the rest is entirely my own.

Sources

The following sources have been sampled and dubbed into the text:

Erik Davis. 'Philip K. Dick's Divine Interference,' *techgnosis.com/pkdnet.html*, accessed 12 March 2002.

– 'Roots and Wires. Polyrhythmic cyberspace and the black electronic,' *techgnosis.com/ cyberconf.html*, 1996, accessed 12 Mar. 2002.

Mark Dery. *Flame Wars*, 1995.

Mark Dery, ed. *Flame Wars: The Discourse of Cyberculture*. Durham: Duke University Press, 1994.

Manu Dibango. *Electric Africa,* liner notes, Charly UK, 1985.

Kodwo Eshun. 'Motion Capture,' *Swarm 1*, Cybernetic Culture Research Unit. www.ccru.net/ swarm1/1_motion.htm, accessed 12 Mar. 2002.

Paul Gilroy. *The Black Atlantic: Modernity and Double-Consciousness.* Cambridge: Harvard University Press, 1993.

Gil-Scott Heron. 'Whitey on the Moon,' in *The Revolution Will Not Be Televised*. Sony Bmg/RCA, 1972.

Kevin Kelly vs Brian Eno. 'Gossip Is Philosophy,' *Wired* 3.05 (May 1995).

Paul D. Miller. 'Interview: Future Tense Bruce Sterling.' *Frontwheeldrive.com*, 17 Aug. 1999. www.djspooky.com/articles/futuretense.html, accessed 12 Mar. 2002.

Keith Obadike. Project description for *Untitled (the interesting narrative)*, a slide/audio installation, 2000.

Simon Reynolds. *Generation Ecstasy: Into the World of Techno and Rave Culture.* London and New York: Routledge, 1999.

Mark Sinker 'Loving the Alien,' *The Wire* 96 (Feb. 1992) .

David Toop. *Ocean of Sound*. London: Serpent's Tail, 2001.

35 The Turntable

CHARLES MUDEDE

Common talk deserves a walk, the situation's changed
Everything said from now on has to be rearranged.

T La Rock

The hiphop DJ is a meta-musician, an author, a programmer, an organizer of recorded fragments and a builder of databases whose talents are uniquely suited to survival and meaningful cultural production in our emerging era of total digital cross-reference.

David Goldberg

At the dead center of the spiraling galaxy of hiphop culture is the turntable. This is where everything starts: on the grooved surface of a record spinning on the wheels of steel. All truth is here, all meaning – everything that is hiphop ... Indeed, an act of pure hiphop devotion might be to let a record play from start to end on a turntable.

DJ Dusk

Scratch 1

The line between electronic and live music is unbroken. The forms may appear impressively distinct but they are organized around the same act: playing a musical instrument (a keyboard, drum pads, and so on). In electronic music – which finds its definitive moment in the 1970s, with the popularity of the German band Kraftwerk – a musician plays a musical instrument and is concerned about, for instance, the key that he or she is playing in. This is not the case with hiphop. Hiphop is organized around the act of replaying music; and it is this act, replaying, that marks the real rupture in the mode or method of the forms.

Scratch 2

There are no musical instruments in hiphop (or proper hiphop, and there is such a thing as proper – or closer yet, real – hiphop). This is a truth many critics and hiphop lovers find hard to accept. They, instead, force matters by placing the idea or image of a guitar or a drum next to that of a turntable, as in the case of Bill Murphy's and Rammellzee's liner notes for the compilation CD *Altered Beats*: 'The turntable is more like a drum than anything else. Aside from the obvious physical resemblance of the circular platter to the typical drum head, the turntable/mixer system is in effect "played" with hands, the black wax rhythmically manipulated by the fingers, just as the tightly wound skin of a congo or West African tribal drum is coaxed into sonic nuances with open-handed slaps.' But, in fact, the African tribal drum is a musical instrument; the turntable is not. Even the West Indian steel drum (closer to the turntable in the sense that it is repurposed – more on this later) is still very far from what the turntable is and what it produces, which is not even real music but meta-music (again, more on this in a moment).

Scratch 3

In Tone-Loc's 1989 video for his wildly popular single 'Wild Thing,' his disc jockey (or the actor who pretends to be his DJ) plays something that is half a guitar and half a turntable. There are two reasons for this monstrosity. One, 'Wild Thing' sampled Van Halen's 'Jamie's Cryin' (without permission), and so the guitar/turntable contraption functions as a sign for this gimmick: hiphop sampling rock. Furthermore, this sign (hiphop sampling rock) is held (or played, or closer yet, replayed) by another sign, that of the DJ, who in the video represents what sampling is: an advanced digital form of the initial and manual DJ practice/science of scratching and connecting breaks into a sonic series.

The second reason has to do with the turntable's relative newness. Even in 1989, long after its departure from the actual production of hiphop music (the turntable was at the this point, like a DJ in the video, nothing more than a reference to the essence of hiphop), there was still some confusion as to what exactly it was – meaning, what does it resemble? Which family does the turntable belong to? What is it actually doing? Making music? The contraption in the video asserts that it is not very different from a guitar. Indeed, the 'Wild Thing' video says, if you were to hold a turntable flat against your stomach and attach a neck to it (no strings or keys – so it is a pure neck), then this fact would be apparent. The turntable is a musical instrument.

Scratch 4

The 'Wild Thing' video seems silly – and at the level of promoting a pop rap song, it is. But on another level, the level of assembling connections between emerging hiphop and other established musical forms, it is dead serious. The video attempts to explain to rock and soul sceptics what this new thing, which is used in a particular/peculiar way by the hiphop DJ, is. The 'Wild Thing' video assumes that because of the turntable's shape, traditional musicians are unable to recognize it as an instrument. In a pure instance platonizing the reality of an image, the video invents this thing, this useless contraption (which is not a guitar, nor a turntable – you cannot scratch that way without the record falling off) that has the form of an electric guitar so that the sceptics can finally recognize the turntable's essential sameness with other, traditional instruments.

Scratch 5

To replay a record with your hands is different from playing an instrument with your hands. The one object (the turntable) says to the hand, 'Don't touch me, for I must complete my cycle and fulfil that which is recorded on the 12inch'; the other (the musical instrument) says to the hand, 'If you don't touch me, if you don't pull my strings or strike my keys, I'm nothing, I'm a useless object.' The turntable is always wrenched out of sleep by the hand that wants to loop a break or to scratch a phrase. In a word, the turntable is awakened by the DJ, who wants to make (or, closer yet, remake) music (or, closer yet, meta-music); whereas the instrument always sleeps when it is used to make real music. Indeed, even during the performance of the loudest rock song, the instrument is fast asleep in the hands of the long-haired thrasher.

Scratch 6

The turntable is a repurposed object. It is robbed of its initial essence. But the void is soon refilled by a new essence which finds its meaning, its place in the hiphop universe, in the service of the DJ.

Scratch 7

A thing (Kant) or implement (Heidegger) or commodity (Marx) that is repurposed does what it is not supposed to. It is made by the hands of a manufacturer (Kant), an artisan (Heidegger), a labourer (Marx) to perform (and literally disappears into) a specific task, but the repurposed object ends up doing something else. Think, if you will, of a film projector, which is used to show a movie. That is its purpose: to show a movie, not to make a movie – a filmmaker uses a camera for that. And yet this is what a turntable is forced to do: to make meta-music (music about music), instead of playing previously recorded music.

Scratch 8

Hiphop is less 'music' per se and more 'about music' – so radical is its difference from previous methods or modes of music production. Hiphop does not so much make music the way, say, The Average White Band, or James Brown, or The Police made music; it, instead, makes music out of and about real music – meaning, it makes music its subject. 'Punk, rock, new wave and soul' (G.L.O.B.E) are subjected to the reproductive logic of hiphop. In this respect, hiphop is, as Afro-futurist/culture critic David Goldberg points out in his essay 'Put the Needle on the Record,' meta-music – music made out of and about other music.

Scratch 9

Real hiphop does not sample real sounds, like the flushing toilet in Art of Noise's 'Close (To the Edit)' (1984), but samples copyrighted music. The hiphop DJ does not shape raw sound into a form recognized as music, but shapes information into a sonic series recognized as meta-music.

Scratch 10

I borrow the term 'repurpose' from David Goldberg, who in his short essay 'Put the Needle on the Record' used it, as I do here, to explain what exactly happens when a hiphop DJ handles (or mishandles, or best yet, manhandles) a turntable. Goldberg writes: 'The scratch explodes all previous relationships to sound by completely repurposing the turntable, and by bringing a real-time interactivity to the manipulation of what was originally intended to be a permanent archival medium. Because the scratch is based on a recording, it becomes the manipulation of information and not just the vibrational properties of air.'

Scratch 11

In an article I wrote for *The Stranger* in the fall of 2000, about a bridge in Seattle that is used as a self-willed exit from this world as reliably as it is used by cars to cross a body of water, I explained repurposing in this way:

> The German philosopher Heidegger once wrote that the essence of a tool (like a hammer) is only noticed when it is broken. If a hammer works, then it is nothing more than an extension of your hand, but if it breaks, you notice its 'hammerness.' This is close to what I mean by repurposing; the added and unexpected uses of the Aurora Bridge (e.g., the way it has been used to express political and environmental concerns, as in 1997 when Greenpeace protesters hung from it by huge ropes and prevented two American fishing trawlers from heading to the Bering Sea) knocked it out of the slumber of its primary function, and it is now wide-awake, alert, alive. Indeed, like Heidegger's broken hammer brings out the hammer's hammerness, repurposing brings out the 'bridgeness' of the Aurora Bridge.[1]

A repurposed turntable brings out a turntable's turtableness.

Scratch 12

Because it is doing what it is supposed to be doing, a musical instrument is fast asleep when in the process of making music. (Indeed, the very fact of this may explain why Jimi Hendrix frequently lit his electric guitar on fire or played it with his teeth – anything to wake the damn thing up!) Turntables, on the other hand, are always wide awake or 'enstranged.' This is why the beloved heavy metal practice of smashing a guitar or kicking over a drum set at the end of a show cannot be translated into hiphop terms. How can a DJ break something that is essentially broken when serving his or her hiphop needs? To smash a turntable after it has been man/mishandled by a hiphop DJ seems like a terribly cruel thing to do.

Scratch 13

Enstranged, not estranged. Enstranged is a neologism that approximates the Russian word *ostranenie*, which means 'making it strange,' or to defamiliarize something that has been smothered by habit. The Russian Formalists, and Victor Shklovsky specifically, argued that enstrangement is what distinguished poetic language from everyday language.

Scratch 14

During the heyday of European ethnic gangsters in North American cities, violin cases were famously repurposed for gangland wars. These cases which carried Tommy guns were wide-awake when in the hands of the gangsters and fast asleep when in the hands of classically trained musicians.

Scratch 15

A musician's case contains an instrument; a DJ's case contains information.

Scratch 16

Marx, like Heidegger, recognized the significance of enstranging an object. For Heidegger, a broken object exposes its thingness; for Marx, it exposes its source, the labourer, the one who has transferred his or her body's energy into the substance of the object. In *Capital, Volume One*, Marx writes: 'It is generally by their imperfection as products, that means of production in any process assert themselves in the character of products. A blunt knife or weak thread forcibly remind us of Mr A., the cutler, Mr B, the spinner. In the finished product the labour by means of which it has acquired its useful qualities is not palpable, has apparently vanished.'[2] A broken object is also wide awake or enstranged. Indeed, a broken hiphop turntable is a bizarre (if not the most bizarre) thing. When it is actually broken it cannot be repurposed (or broken) by the (re)creative hands of the DJ.

Scratch 17

The production of one form (replayed music) occurs outside of the text/recording; the other (played music) within – if it is recorded at all. Indeed, hiphop does not really 'vanish into thin air' in the manner evoked by jazz genius Eric Dolphy, but returns into the album sleeve to be replayed on another day.

Scratch 18

In the notes for 'The Work of Art in the Age of Mechanical Reproduction' (which is the most important essay of the twentieth century), Walter Benjamin (1892-1940) offers this quote from Leonardo da Vinci (1452-1519) which echoes the words of Eric Dolphy (1928–64), which in 1996 were sampled by Parisian DJ, DJ Cam (1973–), on his CD *Mad Blunted Jazz*. da Vinci writes: 'Painting is superior to music because, unlike unfortunate music, it does not have to die as soon as it is born ... Music which is consumed in the every act of its birth is inferior to painting which the use of varnish has rendered eternal.'

Scratch 19

Hiphop is the first musical form to break completely with traditional music in terms of production – how it is made, who makes it, and so on. Even dub, the closest form to hiphop – which was born in the 1960s and employed dub plates in ways that are analogous to hiphop's use of records – has vital connections to live musical performance that hiphop does not. Dub is constituted by two significant practices that are not completely separated or in opposition: one is to make dub with live musicians – a practice that finds its representative in Lee 'Scratch' Perry and is related in many ways to electronic music, like Kraftwerk's; the other is to make a 'version' (a remix) of a recorded piece of music – a practice that finds its representative in King Tubby and is distantly related to early hiphop, like Afrika Bambaataa's – whose 'Planet Rock' famously sampled Kraftwerk's, 'Trans-Europe Express' (sans permission). This is why dub presents significant theoretical problems; its mode of production is never as clear as hiphop (the total break), but always in a dub haze of live instruments and electronic equipment. Nevertheless, dub is the only link (or, more closely, a ghost of a link) between hiphop meta-music and instrument-based music.

Figure 35.1. *Eric Sermon and Marvin Gaye*. Interpretive diagram, Charles Mudede, 2003.

Scratch 20

The real break began in the mid-1970s when New York DJs invented the practice/science of looping a break from scratch. What the DJ establishes with the back and forth, blend and blur, is a series (loop after loop) of repeated information that forms a total sonic mix (or matrix) into which the rapper is inserted. The rapper is in the mix, in the house, in the place to be. The rapper does not perform *with* a band but *within* the meta-music.

Scratch 21

Started in the 1970s, the looping of the break anticipated the sampler. The sampler digitally assembles multiple parts into a master mix. With the arrival of the sampler in the early 1980s, the DJ abandons real turntables (at the club or in the park or the radio station) for the mixing-board.

Scratch 22

If you open up and then fold the note sleeves for the soundtrack to *What's the Worst That Could Happen?* (2001) in a certain way, the image of Eric Sermon on the mixing-boards will be faced with the image of Marvin Gaye on the keyboards. Unlike the folding of the new U.S. $20 bills to produce what looks like the burning Twin Towers, the matching of Eric Sermon's method of producing music with Marvin Gaye's method of producing music is not coincidental.

Scratch 23

Similar to the guitar/turntable contraption in the 'Wild Thing' video, the matched images attempt to explain what is not yet fully understood or realized by making it correspond

Figure 35.2. *Eric Sermon and Marvin Gaye.* Interpretive diagram,
Charles Mudede, 2003.

to something that is familiar. This means the mixing-board is the hiphop version of the
piano: The piano has keys, the soundboard has knobs; both have wide surfaces; both
require that the pianist or mixing-boardist sit down and use the tips of his or her fingers –
therefore, both are instruments. But these parallels are only visual not actual. The mixing-
board is not an instrument, that is not its essential purpose. The mixing-board was made,
designed, and installed in a soundproof basement to record instruments. It is repurposed
by the hiphop DJ who, now a producer, collapses, within the electronic spaces of mixing-
board, the function of recording into the function of remaking music.

   If rearranged in such a way that the living hiphop producer Eric Sermon is on top
and the ghost of Marvin Gaye is on the bottom looking up, we would have a better
representation of what is actually taking place in the production of hiphop music. The

Figure 35.3. *Eric Sermon, Marvin Gaye and Grandmaster Flash*. Interpretive diagram, Charles Mudede, 2003.

phantom of the musician exists within the electronic depths of the soundboard. The musician is the subject of the hiphop producer.

But even this is not close enough. A more precise representation of modern hiphop production should look something like what we see in Figure 35.3.

The modern mixing-board replaces the DJ who repurposes the LP that was produced by a live musician.

Scratch 24

The early practice of manually running or matching records on turntables, anticipated the current, virtual production of hiphop on mixing-boards in the way that dadaist practices at the end of the nineteenth century anticipated cinema. Here, of course, I am referring to a passage in Walter Benjamin's essay, 'The Work of Art in the Age of Mechanical Reproduction,' which argues that 'one of the foremost tasks of art has always been the creation of a demand which could be fully satisfied only later.' Benjamin writes: 'The history of every art form shows critical epochs in which a certain art form aspires to effects which could be fully obtained only with a changed technical standard ... The extravagances and crudities of art which thus appear, particularly in the so-called decadent epochs, actually arise from the nucleus of its richest historical energies. In recent years, such barbarisms were abundant in dadaism. It is only now that its impulse becomes discernible: Dadaism attempted to create by pictorial – and literary – means the effects which the public today seeks in the film.'[3]

Scratch 25

The sampler is not a musical instrumental (in the traditional sense of a musical instrument), it is, instead, repurposed to turn one DJ repurposing two turntables into a thousand mini-DJs repurposing two thousand virtual, mini-turntables.

Scratch 26

'One Day in '81 or '82 we was doin' this remix,' says DJ Marley Marl in Tricia Rose's seminal book *Black Noise* (1994), 'I wanted to sample a voice from off this song with an Emulator and accidentally, a snare went through. At first I was like "That's the wrong thing," but then it was soundin' good. I kept running back and hitting the Emulator. Then I looked at the engineer and said. 'You know what this means?! I could take any drum sound from an old record, put it in here and get the old drummer sound on some shit. No more of that dull DMX shit.' That day I went out and bought a sampler.'[4] The drum machine, which is an instrument, is 'dull ... shit' to the DJ; what is desired is a machine that does what a DJ essentially does when running LPs or singles on the turntables: remixing, replaying 'old records.'

Scratch 27

The following passage from a wonderful article, published in *The Face* (December 1997), describes an encounter between Staten Island's Wu-Tang Clan and the Scottish pop band Texas in a New York recording studio. It not only makes abundantly clear the difference between the production of modern hiphop (which has its essence in the turntable) and the production of pop or proper music (which has its essence in the musical instrument) but also how hiphop is made nowadays – not with turntables but with mixing-boards and samplers that emulate turntables:

> RZA goes to work, feeding a succession of sample-laden discs into a sampler. He has a dif-
> fident, genius-at-work charisma about him as he sits with his back to the room, keyboard
> at side. With a flick of his prodigiously ringed hand he reaches out and conjures up a bru-
> tal bassline. The speakers pulse violently. RZA takes a sip of Hennessy. 'Record this, right
> here!' he tells the bewildered-looking engineer.
>
> RZA has decided to dispense with the original master tapes, shipped over from Brit-
> ain. He wants a completely new version, recorded rough-and-ready without the standard
> safety net of a time-code. This convention-trashing, wildstyle approach to recording elic-
> its some consternation from the studio's engineer, a central-casting white guy who
> warns RZA: 'You won't be able to synch to this, you know.' RZA waves him away and
> turns to [Texas' Bassist and leader] Johnny McElhone.
>
> 'This riff is in E,' McElhone tells RZA. 'Maybe we should try it in the original key, D.'
>
> 'What are you saying? I understand no keys,' says RZA.

Scratch 28

The real turntable has been dead for many years now; it is no longer used to reproduce music. The sampler has replaced it in the studio and the DAT machine at live
shows. (Indeed, when the Anti-Pop Consortium performs a live show they often say,
'Let's give it up to our DAT machine,' instead of 'Let's give it up to our DJ.') The
turntable is now a ghost machine within the complex circuitry of the mixing
machine. When we see a DJ at a nightclub scratching records and reproducing
music on the turntables – which, by the way, have not progressed or significantly
improved in over twenty years; what was used to scratch records in the early 1980s,
if not earlier, are essentially the same Technics that are used today – we are watching something from the past, and, because of this, something that has about it the
mode and mood of a ritual.

Like the saint he or she is, the twenty-first century DJ who cuts and runs the break
of our favourite song is not innovative, and is not looking forward but backward, giving praise thanks to his or her great and departed ancestors – Jam Master Jay and DJ
Scott La Rock – on what is now the altar of hiphop: the two turntables.

Notes

1 Charles Mudede, 'Jumpers' *The Stranger*, April 2000, available at: http//
www.thestranger.com/seattle/content?oid=3664.

2 Karl Marx, *Capital: A Critical Analysis of Capitalist Production*, vol. 1, trans. Ben Foukes (London:
Penguin, 1990), 242.

3 Walter Benjamin, 'The Work of Art in the Age of Mechanical Reproduction,' *Illuminations*,
ed. Hannah Arendt (New York: Schocken, 1969), 237.

4 Cited in Tricia Rose, *Black Noise: Rap Music and Black Culture in Contemporary America* (San Luis
O bispo: Wesleyan, 1994).

36 Silent Theory:
Aurality, Technology, Philosophy

FRANCES DYSON

Aural metaphors surface in peculiar places. Always more than the acoustic phenomena they reference, the tropes of silence, noise, and vibration seem to become uniquely activated when they come in contact with technology, on the one hand, and philosophy, on the other. Despite contemporary critiques of the ocularcentrism that shapes Western metaphysics, the phenomenological, aesthetic, and epistemological perturbations that sound triggers have received scant attention – a situation that is interesting in itself. As a way of approaching this entangled web, I will literally and figuratively track philosophy's sonophobia through technology's loudspeaker. Reading the figures of silence and noise through Martin Heidegger on *Stimmung*, John Cage on silence, and Pierre Schaffer and Jacques Derrida on the tape recorder, this chapter asks: Why is it, and what does it mean that the aural is so often the chosen metaphor for representing the alterity that technology supposedly 'sounds'? And how do these metaphors figure in the thinking of sound and technology in relation to (human) being?

Despite their often-shared predilections, there is one crucial difference between the electronic composer of the twentieth century and one of that century's most prominent philosophers of technology, Martin Heidegger. For composers and early sound theorists such as Edgard Varèse, John Cage, Pierre Schaffer, and Rudolph Arnheim, the technologies of sound recording and reproduction are simultaneously audiophonic and philosophical, providing an avenue towards an understanding of the 'in itself' of sound, through the brackets of phenomenological reduction, on the one hand, and the input/output logic of mechanical reproduction, on the other. In contrast, for Heidegger hearing 'pure sound' represents the fall of *Dasein* ('being-there': strategically figured as an 'entity' rather than specifically human) and its irretrievable severance from the world. This difference between the artist and philosopher is important in appreciating both the link between Heidegger's early analytical work and his later writings on technology, which have been so influential in new-media art and discourse. Heidegger's near obsession with sound and silence, and his eventual recourse to art as a way of reconciling – however awkwardly – the challenge that technology presents, can be read in terms of the substratum of denial and avoidance that anchors, while obscuring, contemporary debates about virtual 'being.' The plays between sound's materiality (for Heidegger as noise, silence, vibration, and voice), its transcendent associations (Heidegger's use of 'attunement' or *Stimmung*), its technological relevance, and its sociality provide a template for the substitutions between actual sound and its associations with ephemerality, alterity, and transcendence, on the one hand, and the strategies developed to evacuate sound's materiality so that it can function on an asocial, and apolitical level, on the other. Heidegger's use of the aural metaphor is particularly important given that similar operations are being conducted in contemporary discourse – where the body substitutes for sound, embodiment for aurality, and virtual-immersive technologies for audio. Reiterating audio's past, this nexus is often removed from the social and political, and situated within a transcendent space, free from the noise of the world.

Heidegger's *Stimmung*

For Heidegger, the aural metaphor, carefully deployed, is restorative: returning metaphysics to a state of authenticity lost through its 'monstrous transformation' through which 'Being' came to be thought of in terms of 'beings,' and modern metaphysics was gripped by 'representational thinking.' As 'modern philosophy experiences beings as objects' and 'reality becomes objectivity,'[1] the existence of 'entities' as Heidegger calls them, their appearance in the concrete reality of the world, in short their presencing, is denied: 'As soon as presencing is named it is represented as some present being ... The oblivion of Being is an oblivion of the distinction between Being and beings.'[2] 'Presencing' would be a metaphor uniquely suited to the ephemeral – a category to which sound belongs, and its fall into oblivion would have obvious correlations with the privilege accorded to permanent, material, and visual objects, incorporated, as Heidegger points out, in the very concept of knowledge (*theoria*) itself.[3] But it would be a mistake to think that Heidegger's critique leads us towards sound and listening and away from vision, as a way to retrieve philosophy from its representationalist bent. Heidegger has an intensely ambivalent attitude towards all things aural – and while his critique of metaphysics extends all the way back to the Greeks, his attitude towards mechanical and electronic sound is decidedly modern and tied, one suspects, to his distrust of modern technology.

Perhaps the most salient example of Heidegger's aural-rhetorical strategy lies in his use of attunement or *Stimmung* in *Being and Time*, which becomes a central concept in his formulation of *Dasein* – through which human existence is always already in the world.[4] Often translated as 'mood,' Stimmung runs deep, connected to a much more profound self-understanding than 'mood' – as a feeling or surface play of emotion – might suggest. Both terms seem to be interchangeable; yet, if we read Heidegger through sound, 'Stimmung' begins to reverberate: as a 'state-of-mind' (*Befindlichkeit*) it has the connotation of finding oneself; like the notion of resonance, it is self-reflexive;

and, like a well-tuned instrument, it enables Dasein to understand and articulate its being with clarity and depth. Based on vibration – as in sympathetic vibration – that is essential to the concept of tuning, Stimmung, aligns with Platonic notions of a cosmic harmony that, according to Leo Spitzer, is thought to be universal, ideal, and prior to individual existence.[5] Spitzer stresses the connections also with *gestimmt sein* – 'to be tuned,' which has a sense of stability, as in the 'tunedness of the soul.'[6] These meanings could be associated with the idea of tuning a radio, or world harmony through the ethereal hum of telecommunications, or the 'atmosphere' (*atmos*) created by mixing a variety of sounds used in film – all tropes circulating in the first part of the twentieth century and connected to a general fascination with, and mystification of, technology.

In this respect the comments of early media theorist Rudolph Arnheim regarding the art of radio, written in 1936, are exemplary: 'The physical fact that the normal distance between sound-source and microphone is inconsiderable, implies as a normal condition of the art of broadcasting a spiritual and atmospheric nearness of broadcaster and listener.'[7] Arnheim believed that the 'intimate' radio voice (the aural equivalent of the close-up) creates a 'Stimmung,' or atmosphere, associated with 'the cozy parlour,' on the one hand, and the 'Heavenly Father ... unseen yet entirely earthy,' on the other.'[8] The association might seem trivial, but the schema supporting it is not.

In the same way that Arnheim used Stimmung to evoke the idea of a unity or harmony between 'the Heavenly Father' and the individual soul 'tuned' to its spiritual mission, Heidegger uses Stimmung to forge a direct, unmediated relationship between Dasein, self-knowledge, and authentic being. However, since 'ontologically mood is a primordial kind of Being for Dasein, by which Dasein is disclosed to itself *prior* to all cognition and volition, and *beyond* their range of disclosure'[9] Stimmung seems to present a departure from the being in the world that Heidegger wants to establish as the existential condition of Dasein. First, being precognitive its 'worldliness' is difficult to explain; second, as 'mood' it could be confused with one's interior or psychological states.[10] To avoid this connection, Heidegger establishes a teleology of self-knowledge: from attunement to understanding to the self-reflexive knowledge unique to discourse, and he processes this teleology through a shift in metaphors – from the aural to the visual – wrapping them in the primordial being in the world of Dasein.[11] In this way Heidegger seems to avoid the dichotomy between essence and relational structure, interior and exterior, nature and culture – or in his terminology, between the 'in itself' or present at hand and the 'for others' or ready to hand. Being always already cultural, attunement is therefore free from the uncritical metaphysical connotations of 'intuition' or 'feeling.'

It is not free, however, from the metaphysical conundrum that (particularly aural) representation involves, and Heidegger's choice of metaphors inevitably invokes: for how can attunement avoid the fate of the unrepresentable that it shares with the sonic and vibratory meanings of attunement? This connection is not spurious, nor is the dilemma it poses Heidegger's alone. The question of musical musicologists for centuries, and many have been content to secure musical mean-ing in the (equally enigmatic) field of emotion. However, Heidegger has chosen to free this quintessentially aural term from the aspect of 'mood' or emotion, from the cultural associations of sound and music as emotion, or atmosphere, and align it instead with the spirito-acoustic trope of vibration – which is the essence of being tuned. Vibration, figuratively and literally, fluctuates between particle and wave, object and event, being and becoming. Defying representation, it provides a meta-physical interval, a space where certain rhetorical manoeuvres can take place under the guise of a de-sonorized aurality. It also gestures towards the immersive, undif-ferentiated, fluxlike, unrepresentable, associations that aurality provokes, without committing to the (massive) representational and ontological ambiguities that aurality raises.

Tone-data

Tone-data is a good metaphor: but difficult. Without the aid of a microphone to provide some kind of externality, Heidegger is trapped by a Stimmung that can only be activated through a relationship with a tunable entity, and this inevitably involves him in the materiality of sound and voice. Heidegger's next task is to explain how discourse, as 'the Articulation of the intelligibility of the 'there,' [and] constitutive for Dasein's existence'[12] involves voice, and therefore sound, without the interference of sound in itself, which for Heidegger is meaningless. Following Aristotle, for whom the voice is 'a significant sound; not the sound (merely) of air respired, as coughing is';[13] Heidegger reformulates hearing to eliminate insignificant sound, from what is heard: 'What we 'first' hear is never noises or complexes of sounds, but the creaking wagon, the motorcycle ... Even in cases where the speech is indistinct or in a foreign language, what we proximally hear is unintelligible words, and not a multiplicity of tone-data.'[14]

Years later, in *What Is Called Thinking*, Heidegger elaborates the consequences of hearing 'the pure resonance of a mere sound': it plunges the listener into an '*abyss of difference in essence*,' it can only be heard with an 'almost unnatural disregard,' and, in the context of language, of hearing the sound of speech, it removes the listener from 'the sphere where speech meets with understanding.'[15] Hearing only wagons and words rather than noises and tone-data is proof that Dasein is always already in the world, and that its hearing is authentic rather than artificial. However, hearing noise in speech removes Dasein from the world, first, by imposing an 'unnatural disregard,' and second, and more importantly, by transforming the communicative function of discourse: from 'Being-with' the other (*Mitsein*), discourse degenerates into *Gerede*, 'idle talk.' Here, Heidegger switches from the acoustic – the 'mere vibration' – to the cultural connotations of noise as rumour. As 'gossiping and passing the word along' Gerede approaches the archaic sense of rumour: a continuous, confused noise, clam-our, or din.[16] Further, by drowning out the experience of authentic being-with, idle talk generates a social regime of alienation wherein the 'they' determines one's moods, prescribes one's interpretation of the world, and indeed, establishes what counts as reality. At the same time, discourse with others assumes the quality of a 'listening-in' that is competitive and antagonistic.'[17] As Gerede falls into the delirium of the crowd, it says nothing to Dasein, and fails to resonate with Dasein's being as Being-attuned.[18] To escape the consequences of mere sound, rumour, noise, and the abstraction of vibration within the worldliness of discourse, Heidegger proposes another mode of hearing, which he calls 'hearkening,' and complements this with another mode of 'speech.' Hearkening is distinguished from hearing as 'more primordial than what is defined 'in the first instance' as 'hearing' in psychology – the sensing of tones and the perception of sounds,'[19] and is grounded in the prior attunement of Dasein, which in turn develops from Dasein's ability to listen to its own authentic being. But since attunement and hearkening are always prior to and grounded in themselves, it is difficult to know just how Dasein establishes its authenticity. If the world is populated by noise and rumour, and Dasein is always already in the world, from what space can Dasein hearken and thereby become attuned? What does hearkening hear in its understanding?

Strung between these impossible choices, Heidegger chooses the best metaphor available – silence. Silence 'speaks' now through the 'voice' and 'call' of the conscience, which summons individuals from their lostness in the 'they.' Emitted as a call, it 'speaks' from somewhere other than the world of the 'they,' and is heard, not through the sensory apparatus of the ears, but more directly, from within Dasein itself.[20] Faced with its Self, Dasein recognizes the 'they' for what it is, and the flight towards inauthenticity – falling – as a part of its Being. To arrest that falling, Dasein itself calls 'in its uncanniness; primordial, thrown Being-in-the-world as the "not-at-home."'[21] prompting a discourse of the conscience that, attuned by anxiety, nonetheless, 'comes from the soundlessness of uncanniness,' and 'never comes to utterance.'[22] The questions that this silent call raises are both clamorous and demanding. Is the call of the concience an activator in this process of Dasein's self-understanding – from which the discourse of the conscience proceeds? Does the 'soundlessness of uncanniness' mean that -therefore – the voice must always be silent, or are these silences independent? Is this silence a catalyst that, like the vibration, transforms as it rattles? Is it a signal, or some primordial tone – ever-present and waiting to be decoded, sonorized, and given form? What produces the signal – what attunes prior to the Dasein's attunement? How does this new voice become tuned in the first place, and tuned to what? Attunement is always relational; it makes no sense if an instrument, for instance, is tuned to itself. Similarly, silence – even given its abstraction – can only be imagined as a potentiality out of which something emerges.

Like Arnheim, Heidegger needs a microphone, and in this context perhaps a telephone, to support the 'afar' from which the call comes. Certainly, in 1927, when *Being and Time* was published, the new technologies of sound transmission and reproduction were at the forefront of technological invention, and had already normalized the seemingly disembodied, telepresent voice. Although predating his critique of modern technology, one can suppose that the introduction of telephone and phonograph into the domestic sphere may have appeared to Heidegger as the apotheosis of the subject's severance from the world and its Self as experienced *in* the world. Similarly, radio transmitted the disembodied voices of Gerede; the 'they,' into the livingrooms of the emerging consumer class, filling the air with noise and chatter. Avital Ronell has presented a convincing case for interpreting Heidegger's 'call of the conscience' as a telephone call, the connection originating in the 'being-guilty' Heidegger felt for accepting a call from the Storm Trooper University Bureau, and his later engagements with the Nazis.[23] However, given that *Being and Time* was written sometime before that call was placed, and given Heidegger's choice of words, how the chatter on the phonelines may have contributed to his concept of Gerede is a question for speculation. Perhaps, in his obfuscating way, Heidegger was questioning the common desire for a safety net woven from an impossible nothing, concealed by the non-status of sound, and tarred with the illegitimacy of rumour? Certainly, the cultural disregard, or forgetting, of the impact of this 'disembodied' technology parallels his warnings regarding the danger of technology as a danger associated with the *thinking* (or not) of technology. Taking the analogy further, if the call of the conscience comes from afar – if it 'discourses in the mode of being silent,' if it does not speak, if, in fact, it is not voice but transmission, signal, the non-sonorous silence of data – then 'it' discourses as a mode of revealing the nature of technology *as* an index of human, cultural denial. In other words, as a failure to recognize just what the 'silence' that constitutes this 'call,' actually is.

When Heidegger later elaborates his critique of technology via the highly influential concept of 'enframing' (*Gestell*), he enlists the call once again: 'The threat to man does not come in the first instance from the potentially lethal machines and apparatus of technology. The rule of Enframing threatens man with the possibility that it could be denied to him to enter in to a more original revealing and hence to experience the call of a more primal truth.'[24]

Enframing closes off a series of steps towards truth: it denies the understanding brought by revealing, which blocks the experience of a call, issuing from a primal truth. Inner truth, understanding, and experience all communicate to each other, all presuppose and require one another, through a call and an attunement – a vibrational 'tuning'- that orchestrates and harmonizes the divergent multiples into Dasein's complex but authentic being. In the closing pages of *The Question Concerning Technology*, Heidegger suggests that the more 'original revealing' may come through art, understood in its ancient Greek meaning as techné; a 'single manifold revealing' that is beyond the specific fine arts, beyond aesthetic appreciations and the sphere of cultural productivity. In this context, the 'unnatural disregard' that is required to hear tone-data, combines with technologies such as the tape recorder or phonograph in an exercise of enframing sound: that is, allowing sound and speech to be assembled, ordered, transported, manipulated, and stored as a 'standing-reserve.' Not wishing to credit Heidegger with undue prescience, it is worth noting that technology's challenge to Dasein through art also coincides with the aesthetic projects of John Cage and Pierre Schaffer, who among others would employ this inauthentic hearing and enframing technology to both create new forms of (sound) art, and to bridge the perceived gap between art, technology, and culture, initially and primarily through sound. Not surprisingly, these artists also grappled with the paradoxes that thinking of sound in the sphere of technology (and vice versa) entail.

Cagean Silence

In the same year that *Being and Time* was published, Kurt Schwitters recorded the first movement of his famous *Ur Sonata* at the German Radio studios; Edgard Varèse produced his percussion masterpiece *Ionization* in 1934; and composers like Pierre Schaffer and Pierre Henry were using their very 'unnatural disregard' to create symphonies out of the squeak of a door and the aaah of a sigh in the decade that followed. John Cage emerged as a central figure in this assault on Western art music, answering Varèse's call for the 'liberation of sound' with his well-known desideratum: 'let sounds be themselves.' The liberation of sound functioned as both a compositional and philosophical strategy for Cage, who like Heidegger found in the concept of silence an escape from the establishment – in this case, the strictures of Western tonality. But whereas Heidegger eventually found himself tangled in an impossible and vociferous silence, and looked to *Stimmung* and the call of the conscience to save his analytic from the abyss of metaphysics, Cage found himself trapped by the actual silence of an anechoic chamber, and turned to technology as a way of retrieving the inaudible sounds of his body to ward off the deathly possibilities that their silence (or for that matter, their audition) implied. For both Heidegger and Cage, sound, hearing, and death were catalysts working in sometimes opposite and sometimes complementary directions. Although a full analysis is impossible here, reading both in the ambience of the other is revealing – particularly given the discourse on technology for which both the philosopher and the composer are known.

Ironically, Cage's entry into silence was motivated, by his own admission, through his ill-attuned ear. With no feeling for harmony, Cage wanted 'to find a way of making music that was free of the theory of harmony, of tonality.'[25] This involved abandoning the primary principle of Western tonality – pitch – as a means of structuring compositions, and by implication melodic development, expressivity, and the ideal of musical movement. Instead of pitch Cage used silence to 'to separate one section of a composition from another,'[26] rationalizing his choice through an odd existential logic: 'The opposite and necessary coexistent of sound is silence. Of the four characteristics of sound, only duration involves both sound and silence. Therefore, a structure based on durations ... is correct (corresponds with the nature of the material), whereas harmonic structure is incorrect (derived from pitch, which has no being in silence).'[27]

Situating sound, silence, and music (the phenomenal, metaphysical, and cultural) within the same ontological categories, Cage's notion of silence – now connected to sound both logically and existentially – counts as an 'absence,' and as such automatically engenders those systems, both musical and epistemological, which allow for the possibility of negation: tonality on the one hand, logic and metaphysics on the other.[28] With silence now functioning as a metaphor for a structural absence, yet at the same time registering an actual absence of sound, it signifies both phenomenally and symbolically. Like 'silence,' 'sound' is now an abstraction.

From silence Cage moves out to the world of noise, expanding his compositional repertoire while at the same time inching open the closure tonality presented. Inspired by the abstract filmmaker Oscar Fischinger's belief in the 'spirit which is inside each of the objects of this world,' which can be released by 'drawing forth' its sound,'[29] Cage began experimenting with percussion, melding sound, object, and spirit in a material unity, the unity of the object, which has its architectonic correlate in the unity of his new rhythmical structure.[30] Finding himself in a hall that simply could not hold all of his percussion instruments, he created his infamous 'prepared piano,' parting and muting the piano strings, first with a pie plate and later and more successfully with screws. In this simple tinkerer's act, the crowning technology of tonality, the virtuosic instrument par excellence, became a hybrid – the piano, a noise machine. While the symbolic end of the piano would later be enacted through its literal destruction by members of the avant-garde, at that time it was enough that its performance yield a different spirit; not the spirit of the romantics, for whom music served as a vehicle for the expression of their emotionally charged intentions, but the more subdued and modest 'spirit' of the objects placed within the piano's frame. Substituting 'spirit' for affect Cage succeeded, in muting the strings, to de-mute the object, at the same time giving voice to his broader philosophical aim: 'What we were looking for was in a way more humble: sounds, quite simply. Sounds, pure and simple.'[31]

The sounds that Cage was interested in at the time were never simple, but increasingly tied to amplification and transmission, however. Cage's use of the microphone coincided with a series of compositions that he called 'Imaginary Landscapes,' produced when he was 'using electric or electronic technology.'[32] The first of these (*Imaginary Landscape No. 1*) is a score for two phonographs, one Chinese cymbal, and a piano amplified using equipment in a small radio station near the Cornish School in Seattle. The piano is played by 'sweeping the bass strings with a gong beater'; the speed of the turntables – playing test tone records (Victor Frequency and Constant Note records) – changes from 33 1/3 to 78 RPM depending on the score's instructions; and the styluses are raised or lowered to produce a sense of elongated rhythm.[33] Like Heidegger's 'tone-data' there is something strange and prescient in Cage's choice of records for his first *Imaginary Landscape*, for the test tone, as the frequency used to standardize both broadcast equipment and the on-air signal, is considered by radio technicians and producers as a standard or measurement more than a sound. Heard only in the acoustically dead space of the studio, employed only to assist the interfacing of technology, when broad-cast its sound becomes paradoxical: audible yet at the same time placeless, a sound without origin, seemingly abstracted from all material existence and flowing unim-peded by matter, as pure signal through the airwaves.

The radio sound now fluctuates between the acoustic and the electronic, the object and the meta-object, the produced and the reproduced. Live and improvised radiophonic transmission liberates sound from the objectification recording imposes: 'The phonograph ... is a thing – not a musical instrument. A thing leads to other things,'[34] and radio, even when silent, provides technical assistance in the transforma-tion of 'our contemporary awareness of nature's manner of operation into art,'[35] allowing the ossified art object to recoup the flux of life. In contrast to the percussive object that, once struck, could only remain silent in a vacuum, the broadcast signal, dependent as it is upon the workings of an already existing technology, can remain silent in the living silence of the yet to be tuned airwaves. As Cage declares, 'listening to this music one takes as a spring board the first sound that comes along; the first something springs us into nothing and out of that nothing a-rises the next some-thing; etc. like an al-ternating current.'[36] This 'current' is overloaded with electro/metaphysical ambiguity. In the same way that Heidegger's use of acoustic, technical and scientific terms such as of 'tone data' allowed him to separate the materiality of sonorous speech from the ideality of *Stimmung*, electronics allows Cage to formulate a silence which is not dead, a silence re-presenting a presence whose essence is actual-ized even when its sonorous potential is not. In the imaginary of 'Imaginary Land-scapes' sound occupies the non-space of electronics and releases the spirit, not of objects, but of the quasi-objects which constitute technology and are themselves per-meated by the animating force or 'spirit' of electricity.[37]

Substituting the 'process' for the 'thing' Cage seems to be abandoning the object in favor of the medium; a record is a 'thing' while a radio transmission is not. At the same time, the concept of 'process' becomes a rubric for ideal artistic practice, inte-grating the artist with *sounds in-themselves* in a continuum of creativity and creation. The materiality of 'sound' is abstracted, and made discursive through the various equivalences Cage draws between aurality and his developing artistic method. For instance, sound's ambiguous ontology becomes a trope for the 'letting go' inherent to the process: 'a sound possesses nothing, no more than I possess it. A sound doesn't have a being, it can't be sure of existing in the following second'[38] while the ephemer-ality of sound is centred in electronic transmission:

> Urgent, unique, uninformed about history and theory ... central to a sphere, without sur-face, its [sound's] becoming is unimpeded, energetically broadcast.

> ... It does not exist as one of a series of discrete steps, but as transmission in all directions from the field's center.[39]

Cage confirms the obvious influence of the radio studio, noting that composition – structured according to an organic rhythm and embracing any and all sounds including silence, is also, the domain of sound engineers, who 'seemingly by accident' meet the artist: 'by intersection, becoming aware of the otherwise unknowable ... in the world and in the quietness within each human being.'[40]

Technology and Phenomena

Like Arnheim, Cage finds in audio technology a correspondence that both honours the nature of the material and provides an avenue to a spiritual/existential mode of (ideal) being, seeing the use of amplification for instance, as a means of projecting the sound of objects – like the astray – outward from their inaudible centre towards the human ear. With 0.'00' (aka 4.'33' No.2) his second 'silent' piece, Cage applies the process and philosophy of amplification to his body, which then becomes the 'instrument,' while the actions of this body constitute the score. The performance is intended to be merely 'the continuation of one's daily work' which, when amplified through loudspeakers, suggests that 'everything we do ... can become music through the use of microphones.'[41] The amplification system acts as a transducer in this context: as James Pritchard remarks, it turns the intentional actions of the performer into 'a non-stop stream of minute, unintended acts.'[42] With his body now an instrument, Cage is able to externalize an experience that he recounted as life changing, demonstrating the logical outcome of his sound as life, life as art philosophy, through an immersive experience that had striking parallels with later interpretations of immersive media such as virtual reality (VR) and cyberspace. Isolated in an anechoic chamber in 1952, Cage was able to hear the sounds of his nervous system working and his blood circulating instead of the silence that he had anticipated.[43] From this he concluded that silence – the concept that had initiated his departure from music, was an illusion. As Cage's ear turned inward to hear the sounds of his body, so his concept of silence turned outward; silence is now 'the aspect of sound that can be either expressed by sound or by its absence.'[44] Silence is transformed into process or action (as the score for 0'.00' dictates) rather than thing, while non-intentional action or inaction becomes a correlate to silence. Given its new latitude, silence has an entirely different structural role in the formation of Cagean subjectivity: silence, as absence, as the possibility of death, no longer exists – there is only sound and noise, and nothing is always something. This is a comforting thought, and for Cage a cushion against the incisive demands that his rhetoric of selfless existence might make. Just as there is no absolute silence, there is no absolute death. At the same time, there is no causality, no meaning, no possible narrative, only undifferentiated being known through the simple fact of noise – the body's continuous hum, which now represents both life and the *arche* of unintentionality, since 'no one means to circulate his blood.'[45]

Unintentionality and neutrality become governing precepts in Cage's art-to-life philosophy. At the same time, the phenomenality of sound recedes, overtaken by the compositional process itself, which now proceeds through electronics – also a guiding principle. Navigating the aural abyme he had enthusiastically constructed, Cage now looks for a primordiality that is independent of sound or silence – that, in fact, has less to do with aurality than the transductive and transmissive processes of telecommunications. This search leads him back to the archaic elegance that music was before words got in the way: 'There was a time [when] ... in Music, there was a glimmer of perfection – a relationship between the unit and the whole, down to the last detail: so elegant. How did that come about (it was an object)? It was an icon. It was an illustration of belief. Now do you see why what we do now is not at all what it was then? Everything now is in a state of confusing us, for, for one thing, we're not certain of the names of things that we see directly in front of us.'[46]

It is possible to discern a certain resignation in the above. Music, once so elegant, has been transformed by representation into an object, cluttered and confused not only by notation and tonality, its once accepted discourse, but by the words and the theories used to prescribe its very being. And these prescriptions are themselves shrouded in a language that, being disconnected from the world 'as it is,' is no longer useful. To recapture that connection it is necessary to find and use a 'tool' which will 'leave no traces' which, in other words, will allow an unmediated relationship with the thing in-itself.[47] For Cage that 'tool' is first and foremost a system, embodied initially in chance operations and later in electronics, which represents a means of organization whereby the absence of the composer's intention can be conceived as the corollary of technology's neutrality, and thus be absorbed within its traceless configurations. Once the subject has been diffused in the simultaneity and insubstantiality of electronics, the gap between subject and object, or word and thing, no longer matters, since everything and everyone is everywhere all at once. This simultaneity is discharged from any kind of symbolic function and finds itself in another kind of silence – 'nothingness': 'No thing in life requires a symbol since it is clearly what it is: a visible manifestation of an invisible nothing.'[48] It is here that Cage's relationship to the sublime assumes added significance, for the problem of meaning and reference, of representation as such, is intimately connected to the paradox of the unrepresentable in its extreme form – death – which both unintentionality and the notion of 'sound in itself' embodies. The perspective from which one could speak of the sounds of one's body is one which is necessarily detached from life. At the same time, the representation of these sounds is essential to Cage's philosophy; he must 'speak' them, yet at the moment they are spoken Cage himself becomes disembodied. As Daniel Charles remarks with some anguish:

DC: But there's nothing more to say about it ... We are always led back to this: there is nothing to say.

JC: That is, to silence – to the world of sounds. If I had something to say, I would say it with words.[49]

The problem is, however, that Cage does 'say it with words' and in so doing, hubristically occupies the space of his own non-existence: the sublime, the unrepresentable. The only way to redeem this space for the living is to describe it in terms of a 'pseudo-void,' a void that is not nothing, that, like the pseudo-silence of the airwaves, can be found in the nether world of electronics, on the one hand, and the metaphorical/paradoxical interstices of language, the very limits of representation, on the other. The Cagean subject is now able to represent both the Ur-silence – the sound of unintentionality – and the sound 'in itself,' as it represents only itself, from a still-living but also detached perspective. Through a reconfigured 'silence' and the concept of sound-in-itself, the Cagean subject is able to 'speak' its death. There is now no need to fear the silence, for as Cage realized late at night with the help of twelve radios,[50] an electronic silence ensures that Silence as such, Silence as death, will remain a convenient metaphor only: 'No more discourse. Instead ... electronics.'[51]

Sonic Objects, Cinders, and Tape Recorders

> Music cannot be boiled down to a well-defined language, nor can it thus be coded merely by usage. Music is always in the making, always groping its way through some frail and mysterious passage – and a very strange one it is – between nature and culture.[52]

Pierre Schaffer, who along with Pierre Henry first conceived 'musique concrete,' was one of the first sound artists/technicians to theorize the notion of the sound object in relation to recording technologies, publishing his *Treatise on Musical Objects* in 1965–66 after decades of research. In his writings, Schaffer grapples with some of the most difficult musicological debates that audio art and electronic composition, in particular, had ignited, concerning the meaning of music, its system of referentiality, its status as a language, and the possibility of hearing sounds 'in themselves.' Like Cage, Schaffer also found in amplified sound both the necessary 'objectivity' to theorize it as a musical element and the necessary ethereality to transform listeners via their new augmented hearing, provided by the 'electronic' ears (headphones) used to listen to sounds in themselves.[53] Like Cage also, Schaffer championed the breakdown of distinctions between sound and music, composer and engineer, studio workshop and performance stage, in a very democratically conceived notion of collaboration. This worldly but transcendent mix is captured in Schaffer's comments about his work at the Cologne Studios in France, in which he uses the partition between the performer and the workshop as a metaphor for these dissolutions: 'Music could therefore be attempted on both sides of the partition, but also on the threshold of a door through which noises had apparently never been allowed to pass in order to achieve the status of music. This was no stage door but at most the tradesman's entrance. That is how noise knocked at music's door and made it creak and groan.'[54]

Similar in many ways to Cage's notion of unintentionality through chance operations, neutrality, and 'technics,' Schaffer saw the tape recorder as a tool for the phenomenological reduction required to hear *'objet sonores.'* If, argues Schaffer, 'our aim is to forget about origins, [then] the most effective tool will be anonymous magnetic tape.'[55] Schaffer is well aware of the contradiction inherent in his attempt to devise a typology of *objet sonores*:[56] in order to be analysed, sound must be extracted from its environment, bracketed, and heard in itself, yet at the same time, a sound object 'is always determined by the structures to which it belongs.'[57] Even if they could be produced by anonymous magnetic tape 'that musical version of Pythagoras' screen which used to veil the speaker ... allowing only the meaning to emerge,'[58] such sounds lack an auditor, for what kind of ear could hear such sounds?

Schaffer's conclusion in *Treatise* is to create a new ear – and a new subjectivity – through the practice of 'acousmatic listening,' of 'hear[ing] with another ear.' This new listening arises from the 'operative technique' that creates 'the conditions of a new listening.'[59] But the technique is, in fact, a technology – the tape recorder, which 'if it creates new phenomena to observe, it creates above all *new conditions of observation.*'[60] Despite Schaffer's desultory estimation of his project some years later, there remains within his text the residual promise of not human, but technological perception, which not only provides a context, or mediation, between the sound in itself and its perception, but creates *new* forms of perception and indeed new acoustic phenomena. In this context his opening remarks in *Solfège de L'objet Sonore* are instructive: 'Such, at the dawn of a new, electronic, age is the chant or the Cologne studio. A strange pilgrimage into the past ... But does not the spirit of music, like the spirit of sound, pervade all of nature? A sounding body, when touched mechanically, comes to life and reveals its existence or rather its structure, and thus enters our field of knowledge.'[61]

These comments unite nature and technology in an electronically geared vitalism reminiscent of Cage and nostalgia for a primal aurality that echoes Arnheim; they also anticipate the philosophical excursions that amplified, reproduced, and transmitted sound (i.e., audio) would excite. As composers philosophized about new technologies, so philosophers entertained – consciously or not – audio in their theories of modernity and technology. Like Heidegger, Jacques Derrida critiques metaphysics by invoking metaphors of silence, departing from the absolute silence of Heidegger's 'voice of being' to the 'almost' silence of a redefined 'writing before speech.' And like Cage, Derrida presents this 'almost' silence as the index of a refigured being that can only be experienced via a technologized subjectivity.

Derrida's process is to successively appropriate aural and audiophonic figures, beginning with the silence of the phoneme 'a.' Against the absolute silence of the inner, metaphysical voice, Derrida poses his core concepts of *différance* and the trace: the trace reveals and is revealed by the space, or spacing, of writing; be it the gap between letters on the page, or the silence that differentiates (and constitutes) phonemes in speech.[62] The trace is revealed not through speech, but through writing, *écriture* (which also includes audio/visual media) that allows the difference, the absence, the other inherent in discourse, to appear. The difference that such spacing allows to be heard is captured in Derrida's concept of différance. Meaning both to differ and to defer, différance constitutes the structure of presence as intersected by the spatial and temporal difference in language, the production of which écriture reveals. Because in French, the *a* of *différance* can be seen inscribed on the page, but not heard in speech, différance is constituted by silence, but it is a silence formed from the oscillation between hearing and seeing, speech and writing, which is revealed through an absence or gap: the 'silence' of the trace. According to Derrida, this oscillation provides a way of both articulating the mechanisms or logics that constitute metaphysical presence, and at the same time interrupting those mechanisms: 'With its *a*, différence ... refers to what in classical language would be called the origin or production of differences and the differences between differences, the play [*jeu*] of differences ... This differance belongs neither to the voice or to writing in the ordinary sense, and it takes place ... between speech and writing.'[63]

The silences, spaces, and gaps that circulate through Derridean deconstruction are defined within an overarching 'science': the 'science of writing,' which Derrida designates 'grammatology.' Like différance, grammatology contains within it the deliberate contradiction between the 'gramme': graphic sign, and 'ology' as logos, which for Derrida means voice or phonè. This 'science' reveals however, a certain deafness in Derrida's thinking, for in the grammatological construction, logos is conflated with *phonè*, and phonè is assumed to represent both the voice-speaking-language and its sonority: '*What is said of sound in general is a fortiori valid for the phonè* by which, by virtue of hearing (understanding)-oneself-speak – an indissociable system – the subject affects itself and is related to itself in the element of ideality.'[64]

Jean-François Lyotard makes the point that the phonè is what Aristotle called 'the voice as timbre' which can be contrasted to '*lexis*' which he defines as 'the articulated voice.'[65] The difference between the two, he suggests, comes down to *noise* – the sounds of the body, of timbre and 'grain,' which interrupt 'meaningful' speech.[66] By conflating sound and voice in this way, and absorbing both within the silence of both écriture and the trace, Derrida's deconstruction is always veering towards the inner and silent voice of metaphysics – the Husserlian voice that he critiques in *Speech and Phenomena*. Perhaps this is why he turns to audiophony to sonorize his inscriptive schematic – his 'science of writing.'

The Cinder

Through the metaphorical movements of various forms of audio technology, Derrida reworks his rhetorical repertoire, beginning with the trace, which he renames the 'cinder.' This occurs in *Cinders*, in the *Prologue* of which he writes that, for some ten years, he had been thinking about the sentence 'cinders there are (*il y a là cendre*).' Like the *a* of *différance*, the accent on the *là* of *il y a là cendre* is silent, marking a tension between writing and speech that is reflected in the text of *Cinders*, itself a polylogue woven from a variety of Derrida's other writings and constituted, as he says, by 'an indeterminate number of voices.'[67] In some ways responding to the silent call of the conscience that Heidegger formulated to ground – however tautologically – *Dasein's* self-understanding, Derrida raises the metaphysical stakes, asking 'how can this fatally silent call that speaks before its own voice be made audible?'[68] That is, how can the call that precedes the voice, that is only emitted through writing, and the silence of which the accent on the *là* speaks, be made to sound?[69] Derrida acknowledges that since the polylogue is written and therefore 'destined for the eye,' it 'corresponds only to an interior voice, an absolutely low voice.'[70] So how can it be amplified? Derrida finds the answer in sound technology – 'Then one day came the possibility, I should say the chance of making a tape-recording of this.'[71]

Through the tape recorder the 'voices' in the text will have their '*specific* volume,' and the previously heterogeneous media of text and sound recording will be 'reinvented by the other,' providing 'a studio of vocal writing.'[72] The polylogue will become a polyphony, amplifying the other voices, other readings within the text, or in Derrida's tropology, through the 'pyrification of what does not remain and returns to no one.'[73] Here Derrida invokes the vitalism of (an originary) fire of which the cinder is a residue, merging sound, fire, ephemerality, and recording, in a formulation that approaches the poeticism that Heidegger – writing his major opus – was forced to avoid.[74] Strewn with multiple references, the cinder combines a Presocratic, Heraclitain understanding of being as flux (one that Heidegger both appropriated and reworked to avoid the problems of sound and hearing that language involved) with a reinterpretation of Heidegger's critique of metaphysics. It is from this fusion of Heideggarian Being, (an unacknowledged) Heraclitean fire, and Derrida's own 'trace,' that the concept of the cinder arises:

> No cinder without fire ... The sentence ['cinders there are'] avows only the ongoing incineration, of which it remains the almost silent monument: this can be 'there,' *là*.[75]

> ... the cinder is the being [*l'etre*], rather, that there is – this is the name of the being that ... remains beyond everything that is ... remains unprounceable in order to make saying possible although it is nothing.[76]

Like vibration, amplification is culturally connected to notions of synaesthesia, of technologically transforming the sensorium such that hearing becomes feeling and feeling is experienced as the cosmic vibration of life emitted from all things both animate and inanimate. Amplification both detects and transmits this vibration, supplying the listener with a prosthetically induced access to the plenitude of an otherwise inaudible phenomenal life and metaphysical being. Recording captures this life, puts it 'on record,' endows it with an objectivity and representational status. However, recording 'makes saying possible' only within the circulations, transmissions, and vital-ism of amplification. While Derrida's cinder is a residue, a remainder, a still-glowing index of fire – Heraclitean symbol of existential flux – that both repeats and makes pos-sible difference, at the same time it is silent, waiting to be heard, waiting to be ampli-fied, broadcast, transmitted by the prosthesis of the stylus, be it the phonograph needle, the recording head of the tape recorder, or the nib of the pen.[77]

Why Silence?

'Unintelligible' words – words that confuse sound and meaning, are often onomato-poeic, found in the art of poetry and the ramblings of psychotics alike. Although the creak of the door would lead composers to create emblems of the electronic future, one suspects that for Heidegger the creak is literal – a break, fracture, crack that exposes the ultimate muteness of language. This caesura is recovered to some extent by the terms 'tone data' which, combined with 'acoustic abstraction,' 'resonance,' and 'vibration,' situate the aural/metaphysical within the relative sobriety of science. But, at the same time, Heidegger's difficulty with the 'there' and the no-where of aurality perfectly articulates the dramatic shift in registers that philosophy must execute in order to deal with sound and still be itself. It must move, within a sentence, between unintelligible words, mere sounds, and acoustic abstraction, and as Heidegger recog-nizes, confront not just difference, but the 'essence' of difference, which lies as an abyss beneath the meaning of these terms. To avoid this abyss – which as Giorgio Agamben argues, represents the limit of Heidegger's thought and demonstrates the inextricability of the silent call of the conscience from death – Heidegger wraps his analytic in the metaphor of silence.[78] As we have also learned from Cage, silence infers a subject that, in a trivial sense both exists outside or beyond the world, since the world is all sound and noise, but more significantly it is able to conceive itself *in absen-tia*, as the kind of abstract entity that Heidegger argues against with respect to hearing 'pure sound.'

Like the aural metaphor generally, silence is a wonderful compositional device: moving across metaphysics, music, and phenomena, its abstract yet paradoxical per-mutations create a space that can remain transcendental and absolute while still very much 'in the world.' The anechoic atopia of Cage's chamber, or Heidegger's calling conscience, represent in both instances a space from which 'silence' can be 'filled' and the metaphor can be set in motion. As mentioned at the beginning of this chap-ter, Heidegger's sonic deliberations provide a template for the substitutions between actual sound and its associations with ephemerality, alterity, and transcendence, on the one hand, and the strategies developed to evacuate sound's materiality, so it can function on an a-social, a-political, and transcendental level. Like silence, transcen-dental spaces can be filled with almost anything – especially when they are repre-sented as vacant, and especially when they are connected to a 'sounding' technology

– as Derrida's choice of the tape recorder to make audible not just small sounds (like Cage) but difference itself, shows only too well.

If, as Vincent Mosco writes, 'cyberspace is today's repository of the future,' we can look to the sonic sublime that Cage, Schaffer, Arhheim, and others fashioned as the 'future' some half-century ago.[79] This period is especially important, for even though the rhetoric of art and technology that developed during the 1960s make direct reference to cybernetics, computers, and the dawn of the information age and seem to be the most direct sources of much of the rhetoric that is circulating today, the fundamental, metaphysical issues associated with materiality, mechanical reproduction, perception, being, and our relation to technology, began their epistemic permutations much earlier. These permutations were filtered through sound, audio, and aurality – categories whose separation may seem pedantic, but that refer to the phenomenonal, the technological, and the metaphysical respectively. As Cage demonstrates so well, in the discourse of sound, all three categories become substitutable: the materiality of sound functions as a metaphorical base from which to represent technological mediations that, originally located in audio technologies such as the microphone or tape recorder, are suddenly recruited in support of what are essentially ontological claims that far exceed the 'being' of sound and are applied to being in general. In this context, the full rhetorical force of Cage's comments regarding an ashtray can be seen, retrospectively, as containing a number of tropes that have shaped the discourse of cyberspace, virtuality, and, per Mosco, the 'digital sublime':

> Look at this ashtray. It's in a state of vibration ... But we can't hear those vibrations ... I want to listen to this ashtray. But I won't strike it as I would a percussion instrument. I'm going to listen to its inner life, thanks to suitable technology ... at the same time I'll be enhancing that technology since I'll be recognizing its full freedom to express itself, to develop its possibilities ... It would be extremely interesting to place [the ashtray] in a little anechoic chamber and to listen to it through a suitable sound system. Object would become process; we would discover, thanks to a procedure borrowed from science, the meaning of nature through the music of objects.[80]

Deconstructing this quote, we find a number of implicit assertions that have since matured, proliferated, and inhabited contemporary discourse. First, inanimate matter (the ashtray) is attributed with an 'inner life' dissolving a distinction that has prevailed since Socratics by referring to a Presocratic notion of *Urstoff* in the figure of vibration. Second, the 'life' of this object is revealed through technology, through what would normally be thought of as an instrument – like the microphone – that aids audition, but in Cage's mindset, 'hears' the ashtray with a degree of agency that implies not only sentience, but desire. Interacting with humans in the revelation of an otherwise unheard and hitherto unthought 'life,' technology is given the freedom to 'express itself.' While this sounds uncannily similar to the oft-quoted dictum 'information wants to be free,' Cage goes further, for in technology's self-actualization via its human interaction, nature (read alterity) becomes knowable, and objects become musical. Music, nature, and an augmented, cyborgian hearing are united via technology in a cosmology that is both pre-dualistic and, at the same time, knowable. In what retrospectively appears as a classic move in the rhetoric of the digital sublime, Cage, following Varèse, and preceding the guru of artificial life, Louis Bec, appeals to a primordial flux that subtends the dualisms of appearance, managing to fashion a unity from the fragmented materials of his craft, and in so doing, avoiding the contradictions inherent in his philosophy. The profundity of these operations lies in the synthesis of disparate, often incommensurable elements, and is perhaps quintessentially expressed in the metamorphosis of the body into instrument (as in *0.'0"*) into art, and finally, into aesthetic principle and rationale.

More relevant to the present discussion, however, is the way that technology becomes an enabling force in the quantification and materialization of the ephemeral, bringing together two very different, and some would say incommensurable, ontologies, in an intellectual-alchemical fusion. If there is a certain amount of cognitive dissonance released from this process, it seems destined to be absorbed by the mega-trope of technology and its offshoots: the posthuman – manifest in this case by 'new ears,' new 'electronic souls,' and for Derrida, an always already inscribed/technologized subjectivity; and the transcendent space within which these rhetorical operations and posthuman subjectivities can develop. While Derrida's cinder includes the ephemerality of the speaking voice, such ephemerality, and all it represents, is made audible only through technology. What then, is this relationship between making audible and technology – not just concerning sound, but more generally, concerning the ephemeral, the extinguishable, the mortal? If the tape recording preserves the voice, if the telephone transmits the body, if sound thus transfigured establishes an architecture whereby subjects can be preserved in vinyl and spectralized through the wires, then is not existence itself in a sense bracketed and placed within another abyss: a *between* materiality and what we might call a technologized immateriality? And in this strictly metaphysical relation, is it not the latter that speaks? Not *who* speaks, but this curious 'thing' which on a very trivial level is anthropomorphized, or associated with 'forces' such as progress and evolution, but more substantially, reconfigures ephemerality and immateriality as states that are represented and known *only* through technological bracketing.

This is perhaps part of what Heidegger is referring to when he pries apart 'technology' from 'technological.' Arthur Kroker suggests that the metaphors Heidegger used to analyse technology were prescient, given the current form of digital media.[81] It may be that Heidegger's earlier thesis on 'attunement' is similarly revealing in its torturous circumnavigation of sound. Pulled towards and repulsed by sonority, Heidegger's refusal to just 'let sound be' might also be read as a latent analysis of the deaf ear that culture turns towards the impact of telecommunications – specifically the telephone

– as a force of and for technology. As Kroker insists, 'make no mistake. Heidegger does not "think" technology within its own terms. Quite the contrary. Repeatedly he insists that technology cannot be understood technologically because, in opening ourselves up to the question of technology, we are suddenly brought into the presence of that which has always been allowed to lie silent because it is the overshadowing *default condition* of our technical existence. Heidegger is relentless in making visible that which would prefer to remain in the shadows as the regulating architecture of contemporary existence.'[82]

It is worth pausing for a moment to reflect on 'the default condition of our technical existence.' What is it to default – what does one default to? 'Default' has the connotation of both a failing, a deficiency, a lacuna or lapse, and deceit. As a failure to show, to repay, to act, or to think, and also as a condition, the defaulting here can be interpreted as a state that allows thinking to fall away – or fail – at the moment that technology appears, falling in this case into silence, into the gasp that technology often elicits. The gasp occurs when there is a momentary vacuum, when one is left speechless, when rhetoric cannot reconcile the lie that is unfolding. Engulfing both the highly utopian and darkly dystopian promises of technology, the gasp also creates an opening, a deregulated space for colonization by rationalist propaganda. It is both from and within this 'silence' of the gasp that Heidegger's call of the conscience has contradictory implications. Silence can be read as a refusal of the technologically situated, and especially wireless, individual to be constantly appropriated by technoculture, preferring instead to ignore the beeps and just be left alone and 'unplugged.' Silence, on the other hand, is the space of non-thinking, that lacuna that slips between the default articulation of technology (as a rhetoric of progress, civilization, evolution, and more recently, posthumanism) and the gasp – silent and breathless – that this rhetoric elicits. Caught between silence and sound, between non-thinking and avoiding data-assault, could the call of the conscience be thought of as that momentary pause, during which a convocation of guilt, questioning, curiosity, and estrangement is fleetingly engaged, and the fear of falling into an abyss is swiftly put aside – that moment before we reconnect, transforming the silent gasp into a brief, somewhat mechanical response: 'Hello, I'm here'?

Notes

1 Martin Heidegger, *Early Greek Thinking* (New York: Harper and Row, 1975), 82, 56.
2 Ibid., 50.
3 'In theoria transformed into contemplatio there comes to the fore the impulse, already prepared in Greek thinking, of a looking-at that sunders and compartmentalizes. A type of encroaching advance by successive interrelated steps toward that which is to be grasped by the eye makes itself normative in knowing.' Martin Heidegger, 'Science and Reflection,' in

The Question Concerning Technology (New York: Harper and Row, 1977), 159–63. See also Heidegger, *Being and Time* (New York: Harper and Row, 1962), 99.

4 For Heidegger: '*Dasein*'s openness to the world is constituted existentially by the attunement of a state-of-mind.' Heidegger, ibid., 176. Note that the translators have chosen 'mood' – cf. Heidegger: 'What we indicate ontologically by the term "state-of-mind" is ontically the most familiar and everyday sort of thing; our mood, our Being-attuned' (at 172). Throughout the text these terms seem to be interchangeable.

5 Leo Spitzer adds that these translations fail to express 'the unity of feelings experienced by man face to face with his environment (a landscape, nature, one's fellow man)' and the idea of a harmonious unity 'between the factual (objective) and the subjective (psychological).' *Classical and Christian Ideas of World Harmony* (Baltimore: Johns Hopkins Press, 1963), 3–5.

6 Ibid., 7. See also Giorgio Agamben: 'The term *Stimmung*, which we usually translate as 'mood,' should be stripped here of all psychological significance and restored to its etymological connection with the *Stimme*, and above all, to its originary acoustico-musical dimension; *Stimmung* appears in the German language like a translation of the Latin *concentus*, of the Greek *armonia*. From this point of view, Novalis's notion of *Stimmung*, not as psychology, but as an "acoustics of the soul' is illuminating." *Language and Death: The Place of Negativity*, trans. Karen E. Pinkus and Michael Hardt (Minneapolis and Oxford: University of Minnesota Press, 1991), 55–6.

7 Rudolph Arnheim, *Radio* (New York: Da Capo Press, 1972), 78.

8 Ibid., 76.

9 Heidegger, *Being and Time*, 175.

10 '[While] any cognitive determining has its existential-ontological Constitution in the state-of-mind of Being-in-the-world; [attunement] is not to be confused with attempting to surrender science ontically to "feeling."' Heidegger, ibid., 177.

11 For instance, 'Understanding' which is already mood-laden, has the character of 'projection' and makes up *Dasein's* 'sight.' See ibid., 187. 'By way of having a mood, *Dasein* "sees" possibilities, in terms of which it is, and through this seeing (or 'projective disclosure') understanding leads to interpretation, and from thence to the articulation of knowledge. Through articulation, discourse is possible, and with discourse, self-knowledge.' Ibid., 189.

12 Ibid., 201.

13 Kenelm Foster and Silvester Humphries, trans., *Aristotle's DE ANIMA, in the version of William of Moerbeke and the Commentary of Thomas Aquinas* (New Haven: Yale University Press, 1954), paras. 466–77.

14 Heidegger, *Being and Time*, 207.

15 The full quotation reads: 'In order to hear the pure resonance of a mere sound, we must first remove ourselves from the sphere where speech meets with understanding. Between the unintelligible word and the mere sound grasped in acoustic abstraction, lies an *abyss of difference in essence* ... The supposedly purely sensual aspect of the word-sound, conceived as mere resonance, is an abstraction. The mere vibration is always picked out only by an intermediate step – by that almost unnatural disregard.' Martin Heidegger, *What Is Called Thinking* (New York: Harper Colophon, Harper and Row, 1968), 130, emphasis added.

16 '[*Gerede*] ... releases one from the task of genuinely understanding, [and] develops an undifferentiated kind of intelligibility, for which nothing is closed off any longer.' Heidegger, *Being and Time*, 213. Like *Stimme*, the root of attunement, translated as voice and voicing (in the sense of giving one's opinion), 'noise' also has a vocal origin, coming from Greek *nautic* and Latin *nausea*, it has the archaic connotation of the cries and groans (noise) made by seasick (nauseous) passengers on ancient ships.

17 Ibid., 219.

18 Rather, for Heidegger noise 'de-tunes' attunement in a way that reveals a remarkable similarity between his attitude towards the voice and that of metaphysics. The noise of 'idle talk,' 'passing the word along,' rumour and hear/say, continually interrupts Dasein's recognition of its 'being-in' in the same way that the 'cough or clicking of the tongue' (Aristotle) contaminates 'proper speech,' that is, speech backed by the intention of the soul, or hearing the *sound* of the voice, rather than speech, contaminates the 'being-in' of Dasein.

19 Heidegger, *Being and Time*, 207.

20 '*Dasein* hears the call not through words, for 'the call asserts nothing, gives no information about world-events ... [Rather] conscience discourses solely and constantly in the mode of keeping silent.' Ibid., 318.

21 Ibid., 321.

22 The full quote reads: 'The discourse of the conscience never comes to utterance. Only in keeping silent does the conscience call; that is to say, the call comes from the soundlessness of uncanniness, and the *Dasein* which summons is called back into the stillness of itself, and called back as something that is to become still.' Ibid., 343.

23 In Avital Ronell's reading of Heidegger, the call of the conscience, discoursing in the uncanny mode of keeping silent, 'prepares the ground for a primordial Being-guilty.' *The Telephone Book* (Lincoln: University of Nebraska Press, 1989), 37.

24 Heidegger, 'Question Concerning Technology,' 28.

25 The latter seems to have always eluded Cage: 'I have, so to speak, no ear for music, and never did have. I loved music but had no ear for it. I haven't any of that thing that some people speak of having – knowing what a pitch is ... I might even say, or someone else may say of me, that my whole dedication to music has been an attempt to free music from the clutches of the A-B-A.' Cage, cited by Richard Kostelanetz, in *Conversing with Cage* (New York: Limelight, 1988), 59, 60. For greater detail on Cage's music and philosophy see Frances Dyson, 'The Ear that would Hear Sounds In Themselves: Notes on the Phenomenology of John Cage, 1935–1965,' in *Wireless Imagination: Sound, Radio and the Avant-Garde*, ed. Douglas Kahn and Gregory Whitehead (Cambridge: MIT Press, [1992, 1994], 2002).

26 Kostelanetz, *Conversing with Cage*, 51.

27 John Cage, 'Forerunners of Modern Music' (1949) in *Silence* (Middletown: Wesleyan University Press, 1961), 63 n 2.

28 Initially sound and silence are put into necessary existential relationship (where none actually exists) then sound and music are equated – as if they belong to similar categories – whereas music pertains to a particular system (composition) which is symbolic and

independent of aural realization, while sound is generally understood as phenomenal, non-systemic, and bearing an indexical relation to the lived environment. In this sense silence can be regarded as visual category, since it depends upon an epistemology governed by the structure of presence/absence, where presence is thought of in terms of visual presence.

29 As Cage recounts, 'When I was introduced to him, he began to talk with me about the spirit which is inside each of the objects of this world. So, he told me, all we need to do to liberate that spirit is to brush past the object, and to draw forth its sound. That's the idea which led me to percussion. In all the many years which followed up to the war, I never stopped touching things, making them sound and resound, to discover what sounds they could produce. Wherever I went, I always listened to objects.' Daniel Charles and John Cage, *For the Birds* (London: Marion Boyars, 1981), 78.

30 'The whole has as many parts as each unit has parts, and these, large and small, are in the same proportion.' John Cage, cited in *John Cage*, ed. Richard Kostelanetz (New York: Praeger, 1968), 127.

31 Charles and Cage, *For the Birds*, 74.

32 Kostelanetz, *Conversing with Cage*, 158.

33 John Cage, *Imaginary Landscape No. 1*, in *25-Year Retrospective Concert of the Music of John Cage* (New York: George Avakian, 1959), sleeve notes cited.

34 Cage, 'Forerunners of Modern Music,' 125.

35 Charles and Cage, *For the Birds*, 169.

36 See Cage, 'Forerunners of Modern Music,' 135.

37 As Kathleen Woodward writes, 'Just as the technology of electronics transfigures the material world, so the metaphor of the invisible transforms our way of interpreting the world ... Thus for Cage electronics is much more than a concrete phenomenon. It is also a metaphor for what is also invisible and thus spiritual ... It is the wireless technology which can turn man towards his original harmony with nature.' See 'Art and Technics: John Cage, Electronics and World Improvement,' in *The Myths of Information*, ed. Kathleen Woodward (Madison: Coda Press, 1980), 175, 184.

38 Charles and Cage, *For the Birds*, 150.

39 Cage, 'Forerunners of Modern Music,' 14.

40 Ibid., 62.

41 Kostelanetz, *Conversing with Cage*, 70.

42 Pritchett, James, *The Music of John Cage: Music in the Twentieth Century* (Cambridge: Cambridge University Press, 1993), 148.

43 Cage, 'Forerunners of Modern Music,' 8.

44 Kostelanetz, *Conversing with Cage*, 52.

45 Cage, 'Forerunners of Modern Music,' 80.

46 John Cage, *A Year from Monday* (Middletown: Wesleyan University Press, 1967), 123–4.

47 'The problem is more serious: we must dispense with instruments altogether and get used to working with tools ... It can be put this way too: find ways of using instruments as though they were tools, i.e., so that they leave no traces. That's precisely what our tape-recorders,

amplifiers, microphones, loud-speakers, photo-electric cells, etc., are: things to be used which don't necessarily determine the nature of what is done.' Cage, *A Year from Monday*, 123–4.

48 Cage, 'Forerunners of Modern Music,' 136.

49 Charles and Cage, *For the Birds*, 151.

50 This is reference to Cage's response to the inaugural performance of *Imaginary Landscape No. 4* (1951), an indeterminate score for twelve radios and twelve performers, during which very little signal was picked up because of the late hour of the performance. Cage commented that 'the radios did their job that evening quite satisfactorily.' Charles and Cage, *For the Birds*, 169.

51 Ibid., 173.

52 Pierre Schaffer, *Solfège De L'objet Sonore*, trans. Livia Bellagamba, 2nd ed. (Paris: Institut National de l'Audiovisuel and Group de Recherches Musicales, [1967] 1998), 11.

53 As he writes in *Treatise on Musical Objects* the tape recorder allows sound to be repeated, analysed in detail, isolated – to become capable of theorization, and at the same time, the repetition of the audio recording 'gradually brings the sonorous object to the fore as a perception worthy of being observed for itself ... [and] progressively reveals the richness of this perception.' From an excerpt from Pierre Schaffer, *Traité des objets musicaux*, in *Audio Culture: Readings in Modern Music*, ed. Christoph Cox and Daniel Warner, trans. Daniel W. Smith (Paris: Éditions du Seuil, 1966), 78.

54 Schaffer, *Solfège De L'objet Sonore*, 53.

55 Ibid., 57.

56 The final note in *Solfège* acknowledges the limitations of his theory, describing it as a tool – less adequate than language – for describing and labelling sonic objects. Ibid., 83.

57 Schaffer, 'Traité des objets musicaux,' in *Audio Culture*, 65.

58 Ibid., 57.

59 Ibid., 81.

60 Ibid., emphasis added.

61 Schaffer, *Solfège*, 15.

62 In his essay 'Différence,' Derrida writes: 'If, ... there is no purely phonetic writing, it is because there is no purely phonetic *phonè*, the difference that brings out phonemes and lets them be heard and understood [*entendre*] itself remains inaudible.' *Speech and Phenomena* (Evanston: Northwestern University Press, 1973), 133. In *Positions*, Derrida states: 'Spacing designates nothing, nothing that is, no presence at a distance, it is an index of an irreducible exterior, at the same time the index of a movement, of a displacement which indicates an irreducible alterity.' *Positions*, trans. Alan Bass (Chicago: University of Chicago Press, 1981), 81.

63 In eradicating the difference which writing has traditionally represented, *différance* also dissolves the opposition between writing and speech, and oppositional thinking itself. In this way 'differance ... opens up the very space in which onto-theology – philosophy – produces its system and its history,' since the temporalizing which the deferring of *différance* reveals, suspends the possibility of full presence, just as the spacing or interval which the movement of *différance* inserts, interrupts the continuity of the present.' 'Différence,' 130, 134, 136.

64 Jacques Derrida, *Of Grammatology* (Baltimore: Johns Hopkins University Press, 1974), 12.

65 Jean-François Lyotard, 'Voices of a Voice,' *Discourse* 14/1 (1991–92): 129.

66 'With the *phonè* [humans] show [affect]; with the *lexis* they communicate, reply, debate, conclude, decide. They can tell tales.' Ibid., 130. *Lexis* is a derivative of the Greek *legein*, which was interpreted by Heidegger as the 'letting-lie-before' of logos in order to avoid the consequences of aurality, but which is also akin to the Latin *legere*: to gather, to form an impression, to read, to find written, to count; hence to recount, say or speak. With the gerundive *legendus* (cf. 'legend') we have: needing to be read, a life-story, a narrative. Note that Lyotard cautions against creating an opposition between *phonè* and *lexis*: 'Two temptations need to be avoided here: that of hypostatizing the *phonè* into the metaphysical entity of an "absolutely other," and the temptation to bring the *phonè* back to articulation by means of a rhetoric of the passions, by a treatise on tropes ... where affect is thought out of principle as if it belonged to articulated signification.' Ibid., 133. See also Eric Partridge, 'Legend,' in *Origins: A Short Etymological Dictionary of Modern English* (New York: Macmillan, 1966), 346–7.

67 Jacques Derrida, *Cinders*, trans. Ned Lukacher (Lincoln: University of Nebraska Press, 1987), 22.

68 Ibid.

69 'But how can this fatally silent call that speaks before its own voice be made audible? How could it be kept waiting any longer? ... How can the accent on the *là* of *il y a là cendre* be pronounced 'on two *incompatible* registers' -- speech and writing?' Ibid., 22, 24.

70 Ibid., 22.

71 Ibid., 22, 23.

72 Ibid., 23.

73 Ibid., 39.

74 Because of the extreme density of this very poetic work I will not attempt a reading here, nor a full elaboration of the term 'cinder.' The text, being overtly concerned with the holocaust, is laden with esoteric metaphors and difficult not to read in the light of Jewish mysticism. However, the parallels with Derrida's concept of 'trace' and 'space(ing)' are many, such that the cinder occupies the chiasmus between the signifier and signified, allowing signification to occur; and it also occupies the absence within the 'is' (being) of the 'there is' which cannot be named but only unconcealed through the cinder (cf. Heidegger). For instance, Derrida writes that 'the name 'cinder' figures, and because there is no cinder here, not here (nothing to touch, no color, no body, only words), but above all because these words, which through the name are supposed to name not the word but the thing, they are what names one thing in place of another, metonymy when the cinder is separated, one thing while figuring another from which nothing figurable remains.' Ibid., 71.

75 Ibid., 37.

76 Ibid., 73.

77 As Agamben writes, 'According to a tradition that dominates all Western reflection on language from the ancient grammarians' notion of gramma to the phoneme in modern

phonology, that which articulates the human voice in language is a pure negativity.' *Language and Death*, 35.

78 'Having reached the limit, in its anxiety, of the experience of its being thrown, without a voice in the place of language, *Dasein* finds *another Voice*, even if this is a voice that calls only in the mode of silence ... Here the theme of the Voice demonstrates its inextricable connection to that of death ... if [*Dasein*] finds a Voice, then it can rise up to its insuperable possibility and *think death*: it can *die* (*sterben*) and not simply *cease* (*ableben*).' Ibid., 58.

79 Vincent Mosco, *The Digital Sublime: Myth, Power and Cyberspace* (Cambridge: MIT Press, 2005), 15.

80 Charles and Cage, *For the Birds*, 221.

81 As Kroker writes, 'Heidegger was apocalyptic in his prognosis of what is disclosed by the coming to presence of completed technicity: "*objectification*" as the result of technological willing; the "*harvesting*" of humans, animals, plants, and earth into a passive "*standing reserve*" waiting to be mobilized by the technical apparatus; the liquidation of subjectivity itself into an "*objectless object*" streamed by the information matrix; the appearance of "*profound boredom*" as the essential attunement of the epoch of the post-human; the potentiality fatal transition of the language of destining to the last "*enframing*" – post-human culture under the ascendant sign of "completed nihilism."' *The Will to Technology and the Culture of Nihilism: Heidegger, Neitzche, and Marx* (Toronto: University of Toronto Press, 2004), 25.

82 Ibid., 45.

Bibliography

Books

Aarseth, Espen J. *Cybertext: Perspectives on Ergodic Literature.* Baltimore: Johns Hopkins University Press, 1997.

Adorno, Theodor W. *The Culture Industry: Selected Essays on Mass Culture*, ed. J.M. Bernstein. New York: Routledge, 2001.

Aneesh, A. *Virtual Migration: The Programming of Globalization.* Durham: Duke University Press, 2006.

Ansell-Pearson, Keith. *Germinal Life: The Difference and Repetition of Deleuze.* New York: Routledge, 1999.

– *Viroid Life: Perspectives on Nietzsche and the Transhuman Condition.* London: Routledge, 1997.

Appadurai, Arjun. *Modernity at Large: Cultural Dimensions of Globalization.* Minneapolis: University of Minnesota Press, 1996.

Ball, Kirstie, and Frank Webster. *Intensification of Surveillance: Crime, Terrorism and Warfare in the Information Age.* Sterling: Pluto Press, 2003.

Bandur, Markus. *Aesthetics of Total Serialism: Contemporary Research from Music to Architecture.* New York: Birkhauser, 2001.

Bardini, Thierry. *Bootstrapping: Douglas Engelbart, Coevolution, and the Origins of Personal Computing.* Stanford: Stanford University Press, 2000.

Barthes, Roland. *Camera Lucida: Reflections on Photography*, trans. Richard Howard. New York: Noonday Press, 1981.

Baudrillard, Jean. *Ecstasy of Communication*, trans. Bernard and Caroline Schutze, ed. Sylvère Lotringer. New York: Semiotext(e), 1988.

– *The Illusion of the End*, trans. Chris Turner. Stanford: Stanford University Press, 1994.

– *Impossible Exchange*, trans. Chris Turner. New York: Verso, 2001.

– *The Intelligence of Evil or The Lucidity Pact*, trans. Chris Turner. New York: Berg, 2005.

– *Seduction*, trans. Brian Singer. (CultureTexts Series.) New York: Palgrave Macmillan, 1991.

– *Simulacra and Simulation*, trans. Sheila Glaser. Ann Arbor: University of Michigan Press, 1995.

– *Symbolic Exchange and Death*, trans. Iain Hamilton Grant. London: Sage, 1993.

– *The Spirit of Terrorism and Other Essays*, trans. Chris Turner. New York: Verso, 2003.

– *The Transparency of Evil: Essays on Extreme Phenomena*, trans. James Benedict. New York: Verso, 1993.

– *The Vital Illusion*, ed. Julia Witwer. New York: Columbia University Press, 2001.

Bauman, Zygmunt. *Liquid Life*. Cambridge: Polity Press, 2005.

Beck, Ulrich. *Risk Society: Toward a New Modernity*, trans. Mark Ritter. London: Sage, 1992.

Benedikt, Michael, ed. *Cyberspace: First Steps*. Cambridge: MIT Press, 1992.

Beniger, James. *The Control Revolution: Technological and Economic Origins of the Information Society*. Cambridge: Harvard University Press, 1986.

Benjamin, Walter. *The Arcades Project*, trans. Howard Eiland and Kevin McLaughlin, ed. Rolf Tiedemann. Cambridge: Belknap, 2002.

– *Illuminations: Essays and Reflections*, trans. Harry Zohn, ed. Hannah Arendt. London: Pimlico, 1999.

Bennett, Colin J., and Charles D. Raab. *The Governance of Privacy: Policy Instruments in Global Perspective*. Aldershot: Ashgate, 2003.

Bijker, W.E., T.P. Hughs, and T. Pinch, eds. *The Social Construction of Technological Systems: New Directions in the Sociology and History of Technology*. Cambridge: MIT Press, 1987.

Blackmore, Tim. *War X: Human Extensions in Battlespace*. (Digital Futures Series.) Toronto: University of Toronto Press, 2005.

Bogard, William. *The Simulation of Surveillance: Hypercontrol in Telematic Societies*. Cambridge: Cambridge University Press, 1996.

Bolter, Jay David. *Writing Space: The Computer, Hypertext, and the History of Writing*. Hillsdale: Lawrence Erlbaum, 1991.

Bolter, Jay David, and Richard Grusin. *Remediation: Understanding New Media*. Cambridge: MIT Press, 1999.

Bowrey, Kathy. *Law and Internet Cultures*. Cambridge: Cambridge University Press, 2005.

Braidotti, Rosi. *Transpositions: On Nomadic Ethics*. Cambridge: Polity Press, 2006.

Buckingham, David, and Rebekah Willett, eds. *Digital Generations: Children, Young People, and the New Media*. Mahwah: Lawrence Erlbaum, 2006.

Bukatman, Scott. *Terminal Identity: The Virtual Subject in Postmodern Science Fiction*. Durham: Duke University Press, 1993.

Bunt, Gary R. *Islam in the Digital Age: E-Jihad, Online Fatwas and Cyber Islamic Environments*. London: Pluto Press, 2003.

Butler, Judith. *Bodies That Matter: On the Discursive Limits of 'Sex.'* New York: Routledge, 1993.

– *Precarious Life: The Power of Mourning and Violence*. New York: Verso, 2004.

Caldwell, John Thornton, ed. *Electronic Media and Technoculture*. New Brunswick: Rutgers University Press, 2000.

Campbell, John Edward. *Getting it on Online: Cyberspace, Gay Male Sexuality, and Embodied Identity*. Binghamton: Haworth, 2004.

Canclini, Néstor García. *Hybrid Cultures: Strategies for Entering and Leaving Modernity*, trans. Christopher L. Chiappari and Sylvia L. López. Minneapolis: University of Minnesota Press, 2005.

Case, Sue-Ellen. *The Domain Matrix: Performing Lesbian at the End of Print Culture*. Bloomington: Indiana University Press, 1996.

Castells, Manuel. *The Rise of Network Society.* Vol. 1 of *The Information Age: Economy, Society and Culture.* Oxford: Blackwell, 1996.

Castronova, Edward. *Synthetic Worlds: The Business and Culture of Online Games.* Chicago: University of Chicago Press, 2005.

Ceruzzi, Paul E. *A History of Modern Computing.* Cambridge: MIT Press, 1998.

Chandler, Alfred D., Jr, and James W. Cortada. *A Nation Transformed by Information: How Information Has Shaped the United States from Colonial Times to the Present.* Oxford: Oxford University Press, 2000.

Chun, Wendy Hui Kyong. *Control and Freedom: Power and Paranoia in the Age of Fiber Optics.* Cambridge: MIT Press, 2006.

Clark, Andy. *Natural-Born Cyborgs: Minds, Technologies, and the Future of Human Intelligence.* Oxford: Oxford University Press, 2003.

Clarke, Bruce, and Linda Dalrymple Henderson, eds. *From Energy to Information: Representation in Science and Technology, Art, and Literature.* Stanford: Stanford University Press, 2002.

Connolly, William E. *Neuropolitics: Thinking, Culture, Speed.* (Theory out of Bounds, vol. 23). Minneapolis: University of Minnesota Press, 2002.

Crampton, Jeremy. *The Political Mapping of Cyberspace.* Chicago: University of Chicago Press, 2003.

Crandall, Jordan, Peter Weibel, and Brian Holmes. *Jordan Crandall: Drive.* Ostfildern: Hatje Cantz, 2002.

Crary, J., and S. Kwinter, eds. *Zone 6: Incorporations.* Cambridge: MIT Press, 1992.

Critical Art Ensemble. *The Electronic Disturbance.* Brooklyn: Autonomedia, 1997.

– *The Molecular Invasion.* Brooklyn: Autonomedia, 2002.

Dartnell, Michael Y. *Insurgency Online: Web Activism and Global Conflict.* (Digital Futures Series.) Toronto: University of Toronto Press, 2005.

Davis, Mike. *City of Quartz: Excavating the Future in Los Angeles.* (New ed.) New York: Verso, 2006.

– *Planet of Slums.* New York: Verso, 2006.

De Donk, W. van, ed. *Cyberprotest: New Media, Citizens and Social Movements.* New York: Routledge, 2004.

Debord, Guy. *Society of the Spectacle.* Detroit: Black and Red, 1983.

DeLanda, Manuel. *Intensive Science and Virtual Philosophy.* New York: Continuum, 2002.

– *A Thousand Years of Nonlinear History.* New York: Zone Books, 1997.

Deleuze, Gilles, and Félix Guattari. *Anti-Oedipus: Capitalism and Schizophrenia*, trans. Robert Hurley. Minneapolis: University of Minnesota Press, 1985.

– *A Thousand Plateaus: Capitalism and Schizophrenia*, trans. Brian Massumi, vol. 2. Minneapolis: University of Minnesota Press, 1987.

Demers, Louis-Philippe, and Bill Vorn. *Es – Das Wesen der Maschine.* Osnabrück: European Media Art Festival, 2003.

Dennett, Daniel C. *Brainchildren: Essays on Designing Minds.* Cambridge: MIT Press, 1998.

Derrida, Jacques, and Bernard Stiegler. *Echographies of Television: Filmed Interviews*, trans. Jennifer Bajorek. Cambridge: Polity Press, 2002.

Dixon, Steve. *Digital Performance: A History of New Media in Theater, Dance, Performance Art, and Installation.* Cambridge: MIT Press, 2007.

Dodge, Martin, and Rob Kitchen. *Mapping Cyberspace.* London: Routledge, 2001.

Doyle, Richard. *Wetwares: Experiments in Postvital Living*. Minneapolis: University of Minnesota Press, 2004.

Dyer-Witheford, Nick. *Cyber-Marx: Cycles and Circuits of Struggle in High Technology Capitalism*. Urbana: University of Illinois Press, 1999.

Edwards, Paul N. *The Closed World: Computers and the Politics of Discourse in Cold War America*. Cambridge: MIT Press, 1996.

Ellul, Jacques. *The Technological Society*, trans. John Wilkinson. New York: Knopf, 1967.

Ettinger, Bracha. *The Matrixial Borderspace*, ed. Brian Massumi. (Theory out of Bounds, vol. 28). Minneapolis: University of Minnesota Press, 2006.

Evans, Thomas. *Digital Archaeology: Bridging Method and Theory*. New York: Routledge, 2005.

Evens, Aden. *Sound Ideas: Music, Machines, and Experience*. (Theory out of Bounds, vol. 27). Minneapolis: University of Minnesota Press, 2005.

Export, Valie. *Bozen, Bregenz: 2 Ausstellungen*. Bolzano: AR/GE Kunst, 1995.

Feenberg, Andrew. *Questioning Technology*. London: Routledge, 1999.

– *Transforming Technology: A Critical Theory Revisited*. Oxford: Oxford University Press, 2005.

Fernandez, Maria, Faith Wilding, and Michelle M. Wright, eds. *Domain Errors!: Cyberfeminist Practices*. Brooklyn: Autonomedia, 2003.

Forsythe, Diana. *Studying Those Who Study Us: An Anthropologist in the World of Artificial Intelligence*. Ed. David J. Hess. Stanford: Stanford University Press, 2001.

Foster, Raymond E. *Police Technology*. Upper Saddle River: Pearson Prentice-Hall, 2005.

Franklin, Ursula M. *The Real World of Technology*. Concord: Anansi, 1992.

Freedman, Carl. *Critical Theory and Science Fiction*. Middletown: Wesleyan, 2000.

Friedman, Ted. *Electric Dreams: Computers in American Culture*. New York: New York University Press, 2005.

Fuller, Matthew. *Media Ecologies: Materialist Energies in Art and Technoculture*. Cambridge: MIT Press, 2005.

Gaggi, Silvio. *From Text to Hypertext: Decentering the Subject in Fiction, Film, and Visual Arts, and Electronic Media*. Philadelphia: University of Pennsylvania Press, 1997.

Gane, Nicholas, ed. *The Future of Social Theory*. New York: Continuum, 2004.

Garland, David. *The Culture of Control: Crime and Social Order in Contemporary Society*. Chicago. University of Chicago Press, 2001.

Gerlach, Neil. *The Genetic Imaginary: DNA in the Canadian Criminal Justice System*. (Digital Futures Series.) Toronto: University of Toronto Press, 2004.

Gibson, William. *Neuromancer*. New York: Ace Trade, 2000.

– *Pattern Recognition*. New York: G.P. Putnam, 2003.

Ginsburg, Faye D., Lila Abu-Lughod, and Brian Larkin. *Media Worlds: Anthropology on New Terrain*. Berkeley: University of California Press, 2002.

Gitelman, Lisa. *Always Already New: Media, History, and the Data of Culture*. Cambridge: MIT Press, 2006.

Goldberg, Ken, ed. *The Robot in the Garden: Telerobotics and Telepistemology in the Age of the Internet*. Cambridge: MIT Press, 2001.

Gómez-Peña, Guillermo. *The New World Border: Prophecies, Poems, and Loqueras for the End of the Century.* San Francisco: City Lights, 1996.

Goold, B.J. *CCTV and Policing: Public Area Surveillance and Police Practices in Britain.* (Clarendon Studies in Criminology.) Oxford: Oxford University Press, 2004.

Grant, George. *Technology and Empire.* Toronto: House of Anansi, 1969.

Grau, Oliver. *Virtual Art: From Illusion to Immersion.* Cambridge: MIT Press, 2004.

Guattari, Félix. *Chaosmosis: An Ethico-Aesthetic Paradigm,* trans. Paul Bains and Julian Pefanis. Bloomington: Indiana University Press, 1995.

– *The Three Ecologies,* trans. Ian Pindar and Paul Sutton. London: Athlone, 2000.

Gumbrecht, Hans Ulrich, and Michael Marrinan, eds. *Mapping Benjamin: The Work of Art in the Digital Age.* Stanford: Stanford University Press, 2003.

Habermas, Jurgen. *The Future of Human Nature.* Cambridge: Polity Press, 2003.

Hansen, Mark B.N. *Bodies in Code: Interfaces with Digital Media.* London: Routledge, 2006.

– *New Philosophy for New Media.* Cambridge: MIT Press, 2004.

Haraway, Donna. *The Companion Species Manifesto: Dogs, People, and Significant Otherness.* Chicago: Prickly Paradigm Press, 2003.

– *The Haraway Reader.* London: Routledge, 2003.

– *Simians, Cyborgs, and Women: The Reinvention of Nature.* New York: Routledge, 1991.

Harcourt, Wendy, ed. *Women@Internet: Creating New Cultures in Cyberspace.* London: Zed Books, 1999.

Hardt, Michael, and Antonio Negri. *Empire.* Cambridge: Harvard University Press, 2000.

Harvey, David. *Spaces of Global Capitalism: A Theory of Uneven Geographical Development.* New York: Verso, 2006.

Hayles, N. Katherine. *How We Became Posthuman: Virtual Bodies in Cybernetics, Literature, and Informatics.* Chicago: University of Chicago Press, 1999.

– *My Mother Was a Computer: Digital Subjects and Literary Texts.* Chicago: University of Chicago Press, 2005.

– *Writing Machines.* Cambridge: MIT Press, 2002.

Heidegger, Martin. *The Question Concerning Technology and Other Essays,* trans. William Lovitt. New York: Harper and Row, 1977.

Held, David et al., eds. *Global Transformations: Politics, Economics and Culture.* Cambridge: Polity Press, 1999.

Helmreich, Stefan. *Silicon Second Nature: Culturing Artificial Life in a Digital World.* Berkeley: University of California Press, 2000.

Hershman Leeson, Lynn. *Clicking In: Hot Links to a Digital Culture.* Seattle: Bay Press, 1996.

Hershman Leeson, Lynn, and Meredith Tromble, eds. *The Art and Films of Lynn Hershman Leeson: Secret Agents, Private I.* Berkeley: University of California Press, 2005.

Heuser, Sabine. *Virtual Geographies: Cyberpunk at the Intersection of the Postmodern and Science Fiction.* Amsterdam: Rodopi, 2003.

Holloway, Sarah. *Cyberkids: Youth Identities and Communities in an On-line World.* New York: Routledge, 2001.

Horkheimer, Max, and Theodor W. Adorno. *Dialectic of Enlightenment: Philosophical Fragments*, trans. Edmund Jephcott, ed. Gunzelin Schmid Noerr. Stanford: Stanford University Press, 2002.

Imperiale, Alicia. *New Flatness: Surface Tension in Digital Architecture*. New York: Birkhauser, 2000.

Innis, Harold. *Empire and Communication*. Toronto: Dundurn Press, 2007 [1950].

– *The Bias of Communication*. Toronto: University of Toronto Press, 1999.

Jameson, Fredric. *Archaeologies of the Future: The Desire Called Utopia and Other Science Fictions*. New York: Verso, 2005.

Jenkins, Henry. *Convergence Culture: Where Old and New Media Collide*. New York: NYU Press, 2006.

Johnson, Steven. *Emergence: The Connected Lives of Ants, Brains, Cities, and Software*. New York: Scribner, 2001.

Jones, Caroline A., ed. *Sensorium: Embodied Experience, Technology, and Contemporary Art*. Cambridge: MIT Press, 2006.

Juul, Jesper. *Half-Real: Video Games between Real Rules and Fictional Worlds*. Cambridge: MIT Press, 2005.

Kalathil, Shanthi, and Taylor C. Boas. *Open Networks, Closed Regimes: The Impact of the Internet on Authoritarian Rule*. Washington: Carnegie Endowment for International Peace, 2003.

Kay, Lily E. *Who Wrote the Book of Life? A History of the Genetic Code*. Stanford: Stanford University Press, 2000.

Kelly, Kevin. *Out of Control: The Rise of Neo-Biological Civilization*. Menlo Park: Addison-Wesley, 1995.

Kember, Sarah. *Virtual Anxiety: Photography, New Technologies and Subjectivity*. Manchester: Manchester University Press, 1998.

Kerckhove, Derrick de. *The Architecture of Intelligence*. New York: Birkhauser, 2001.

Kittler, Friedrich. *Gramophone, Film, Typewriter*, trans. Geoffrey Winthrop-Young and Michael Wutz. Stanford: Stanford University Press, 1999.

Kline, Stephen, Nick Dyer-Witheford, and Greig De Peuter. *Digital Play: The Interaction of Technology, Culture, and Marketing*. Montreal and Kingston: McGill-Queen's University Press, 2003.

Kolko, Beth, Lisa Nakamura, and Gilbert Rodman. *Race in Cyberspace*. New York: Routledge, 2000.

Kollock, P., and M. Smith, eds. *Communities in Cyberspace*. New York: Routledge, 1999.

Kress, Gunther, and Theo Van Leeuwen. *Multimodal Discourse: The Modes and Media of Contemporary Communication*. London: Arnold, 2001.

Kroker, Arthur. *The Will to Technology and the Culture of Nihilism: Heidegger, Nietzsche, and Marx*. Toronto: University of Toronto Press, 2004.

Kroker, Arthur, and Michael. A. Weinstein. *Data Trash: The Theory of the Virtual Class*. New York: St Martin's Press, 1994.

Kroker, Arthur, and Marilouise Kroker, eds. *Digital Delirium*. New York: St Martin's Press, 1997.

Kuhn, Thomas S. *The Structure of Scientific Revolutions*. Chicago: University of Chicago Press, 1962.

LaCapra, Dominick. *Writing History, Writing Trauma*. (Parallax: Re-Visions of Culture and Society). Baltimore: Johns Hopkins University Press, 2000.

Landow, George P. *Hypertext 3.0: Critical Theory and New Media in an Era of Globalization*. Baltimore: Johns Hopkins University Press, 2006.

Latour, Bruno. *Pandora's Hope: Essays on the Reality of Science Studies.* Cambridge: Harvard University Press, 1999.

– *We Have Never Been Modern*, trans. Catherine Porter. Cambridge: Harvard University Press, 1993.

Latour, Bruno, and Peter Weibel, eds. *ICONOCLASH: Beyond the Image Wars in Science, Religion and Art*, trans. Charlotte Bigg et al. Cambridge: MIT Press, 2002.

Laurel, Brenda. *Computers as Theatre.* Boston: Addison-Wesley, 1993.

Law, John, ed. *A Sociology of Monsters: Power, Technology and the Modern World.* Oxford: Basil Blackwell, 1991.

Leiss, William. *Hera, or Empathy: A Work of Utopian Fiction.* Ottawa: Magnus and Associates, 2006.

Leiss, William, and Douglas Powell. *Mad Cows and Mother's Milk: The Perils of Poor Risk Communication.* Montreal and Kingston: McGill-Queen's University Press, 2005.

Lessig, Lawrence. *Code and Other Laws of Cyberspace.* New York: Basic Books, 2000.

– *The Future of Ideas: The Fate of the Commons in a Connected World.* New York: Random House, 2001.

Levin, Thomas, Ursula Frohne, and Peter Weibel, eds. *CTRL [SPACE]: Rhetorics of Surveillance from Bentham to Big Brother.* Cambridge: MIT Press, 2002.

Levinson, Paul. *Digital McLuhan: A Guide to the Information Millennium.* London: Routledge, 2001.

Liang, Lawrence. *Guide to Open Content Licenses, v. 1.2.* Rotterdam: Piet Zwart Institute, 2004.

Lunenfeld, Peter, ed. *The Digital Dialectic: New Essays on New Media.* Cambridge: MIT Press, 2000.

Lunenfeld, Peter, and Mieke Gerritzen. *User: InfoTechnoDemo.* (Mediawork Pamphlet.) Cambridge: MIT Press, 2005.

Lyon, David. *The Electronic Eye: The Rise of Surveillance Society.* Minneapolis: University of Minneapolis Press, 1994.

  Surveillance as Social Sorting: Privacy, Risk, and Digital Discrimination. New York: Routledge, 2003.

Lyotard, Jean-Francois. *Libidinal Economy*, trans. Iain Hamilton Grant. New York: Continuum, 2004.

Mackenzie, Adrian. *Cutting Code: Software and Sociality.* New York: Peter Lang, 2005.

Manovich, Lev. *The Language of New Media.* Cambridge: MIT Press, 2001.

Massumi, Brian. *Parables for the Virtual: Movement, Affect, Sensation.* Durham: Duke University Press, 2002.

Matrix, Sidney Eve. *Cyberpop: Digital Lifestyles and Commodity Culture.* New York: Routledge, 2006.

Mattelart, Armand. *Networking the World, 1794–2000*, trans. Liz Carey-Libbrecht and James A. Cohen. Minneapolis: University of Minnesota Press, 2000.

Mau, Bruce, and Jennifer Leonard. *Massive Change.* London: Institute Without Boundaries/Phaidon Press, 2004.

McGrath, John E. *Loving Big Brother: Performance, Privacy, and Surveillance Space.* New York: Routledge, 2004.

McLuhan, Marshall. *Understanding Media: The Extensions of Man.* New York: McGraw-Hill, 1964.

McLuhan, Marshall, and Eric McLuhan. *Laws of Media: The New Science.* Toronto: University of Toronto Press, 1988.

Miller, Paul D., aka DJ Spooky That Subliminal Kid. *Rhythm Science.* Cambridge: MIT Press, 2004.

Misa, Thomas J. *Leonardo to the Internet: Technology and Culture from the Renaissance to the Present.* Baltimore: Johns Hopkins University Press, 2004.

Mitchell, William J. *City of Bits: Space, Place, and the Infobahn.* Cambridge: MIT Press, 1995.

– *Me++: The Cyborg Self and the Networked City.* Cambridge: MIT Press, 2003.

– *The Reconfigured Eye: Visual Truth in the Post-Photographic Era.* Cambridge: MIT Press, 1992.

Mizuko, Ito, Daisuke Okabe, and Misa Matsuda, eds. *Personal, Portable, Pedestrian: Mobile Phones in Japanese Life.* Cambridge: MIT Press, 2002.

Monmonier, Mark S. *Spying with Maps: Surveillance Technologies and the Future of Privacy.* Chicago: University of Chicago Press, 2002.

Moravec, Hans. *Mind Children: The Future of Robot and Human Intelligence.* Cambridge: Harvard University Press, 1988.

Morse, Margaret. *Virtualities: Television, Media Art, and Cyberculture.* Bloomington: Indiana University Press, 1998.

Mosco, Vincent. *The Digital Sublime: Myth, Power and Cyberspace.* Cambridge: MIT Press, 2005.

Mumford, Lewis. *Technics and Civilization.* New York: Harcourt Brace, 1934.

Munster, Anna. *Materializing New Media: Embodiment in Information Aesthetics.* Dartmouth: Dartmouth College Press, 2006.

Nakamura, Lisa. *Cybertypes: Race, Ethnicity, and Identity on the Internet.* New York: Routledge, 2002.

Nancy, Jean-Luc, trans. Jeff Fort. *The Ground of the Image.* New York: Fordham University Press, 2005.

Negroponte, Nicholas. *Being Digital.* New York: Vintage, 1996.

Nelson, Alondra, Thuy Linh Nguyen Tu, and Alicia Headlam Hines, eds. *Technicolor: Race, Technology, and Everyday Life.* New York: NYU Press, 2001.

Noble, David. *Religion of Technology: The Divinity of Man and the Spirit of Invention.* New York: Penguin, 1999.

O'Mahony, Marie. *Cyborg: The Man-Machine.* London: Thames and Hudson, 2002.

Ong, Aihwa. *Flexible Citizenship: The Cultural Logics of Transnationality.* Durham: Duke University Press, 1998.

Ong, Aihwa, and Stephen J. Collier, eds. *Global Assemblages: Technology, Politics and Ethics as Anthropological Problems.* London: Blackwell, 2004.

Parisi, Lucianna. *Abstract Sex: Philosophy, Bio-technology and the Mutations of Desire.* London: Continuum, 2004.

Penley, Constance, and Andrew Ross, eds. *Technoculture.* Minneapolis: University of Minnesota Press, 1991.

Pfohl, Stephen. *Death at the Parasite Cafe: Social Science (Fictions) and the Postmodern.* (CultureTexts Series.) New York: St Martin's Press, 1992.

Pink, Sarah. *The Future of Visual Anthropology: Engaging the Senses.* New York: Routledge, 2006.

Poole, Steven. *Trigger Happy: Videogames and the Entertainment Revolution.* New York: Arcade, 2004.

Poster, Mark. *Information Please: Culture and Politics in the Age of Digital Machines.* Durham: Duke University Press, 2006.

Postman, Neil. *Technopoly: The Surrender of Culture to Technology.* New York: Vintage, 1993.

Price, Monroe E. *Media and Sovereignty: The Global Information Revolution and Its Challenge to State Power.* Cambridge: MIT Press, 2004.

Puglisi, Luigi. *Hyper Architecture: Space in the Electronic Age*, trans. Lucinda Byatt. (Architecture and Informatics Series.) New York: Birkhauser, 1999.

Rajan, Kaushik Sunder. *Biocapital: The Constitution of Postgenomic Life*. Durham: Duke University Press, 2006.

Reiche, Claudia, and Verena Kuni, eds. *Cyberfeminism: Next Protocols*. Brooklyn: Autonomedia, 2004.

Rheingold, Howard. *Virtual Communities: Homesteading on the Electronic Frontier*. New York: Harper Perennial, 1994.

Riskin, Jessica, ed. *Genesis Redux: Essays in the History and Philosophy of Artificial Life*. Chicago: University of Chicago Press, 2007.

Rodowick, D.N. *Reading the Figural, or, Philosophy after the New Media*. Durham: Duke University Press, 2001.

Ronell, Avital. *Crack Wars: Literature Addiction Mania*. Urbana: University of Illinois Press, 2004.

– *Stupidity*. Urbana: University of Illinois Press, 2002.

– *The Telephone Book: Technology, Schizophrenia, Electric Speech*. Lincoln: University of Nebraska Press, 1989.

Rose, Nikolas. *The Politics of Life Itself: Biomedicine, Power, and Subjectivity in the Twenty-First Century*. Princeton: Princeton University Press, 2006.

Ryan, Marie-Laure. *Narrative as Virtual Reality: Immersion and Interactivity in Literature and Electronic Media*. Baltimore: Johns Hopkins University Press, 2003.

Sassen, Saskia. *Territory, Authority, Rights: From Medieval to Global Assemblages*. Princeton: Princeton University Press, 2006.

Schiller, Dan. *Digital Capitalism: Networking the Global Market System*. Cambridge: MIT Press, 1999.

Schwarz, Hans-Peter. *Media Art History*, trans. Freiherr van Teuffenbach. Karlsruhe: ZKM, 1997.

Selinger, Evan, and Don Ihde, eds. *Chasing Technoscience: Matrix for Materiality*. Bloomington: University of Indiana Press, 2003.

Serres, Michel. *The Parasite*, trans. Lawrence R. Schehr. Baltimore: Johns Hopkins University Press, 1982.

Shade, Leslie Regan. *Gender and Community in the Social Construction of the Internet*. New York: Peter Lang, 2002.

Shaviro, Steven. *Connected: Or What It Means to Live in the Networked Society*. Minneapolis: University of Minnesota Press, 2003.

Smith, Marquard, ed. *Stelarc: The Monograph*. Cambridge: MIT Press, 2005.

Springer, Claudia. *Electronic Eros: Bodies and Desire in the Postindustrial Age*. Austin: University of Texas Press, 1996.

Stanovich, Keith E. *The Robot's Rebellion: Finding Meaning in the Age of Darwin*. Chicago: University of Chicago Press, 2004.

Stephenson, Neal. *Cryptonomicon*. New York: Avon, 2002.

– *Snow Crash*. New York: Spectra, 2000.

Sterling, Bruce. *Crystal Express*. New York: Ace, 1990.

– *Shaping Things*. Cambridge: MIT Press, 2005.

– *Tomorrow Now: Envisioning the Next Fifty Years.* New York: Random House, 2002.

Stiegler, Bernard. *Technics and Time 1: The Fault of Epimetheus*, trans. Richard Beardsworth and George Collins. Stanford: Stanford University Press, 1998.

Stone, Allucquère Rosanne. *The War of Desire and Technology at the Close of the Mechanical Age.* Cambridge: MIT Press, 1996.

Strangelove, Michael. *The Empire of Mind: Digital Piracy and the Anti-Capitalist Movement.* (Digital Futures Series.) Toronto: University of Toronto Press, 2005.

Terry, J., and M. Calvert, eds. *Processed Lives: Gender and Technology in Everyday Life.* New York: Routledge, 1997.

Thacker, Eugene. *Biomedia.* Minneapolis: University of Minnesota Press, 2004.

– *The Global Genome: Biotechnology, Politics, and Culture.* Cambridge: MIT Press, 2006.

Thurtle, Phillip, and Robert Mitchell. *Semiotic Flesh: Information and the Human Body.* Seattle: Walter Chapin Simpson Center for the Humanities, 2002.

Tsing, Anna Lowenhaupt. *Friction: An Ethnography of Global Connection.* Princeton: Princeton University Press, 2004.

Turkle, Sherry. *Life on the Screen: Identity in the Age of the Internet.* New York: Simon and Schuster, 1995.

Ulmer, Gregory. *Heuristics: The Logic of Invention.* Baltimore: Johns Hopkins University Press, 1994.

– *Internet Invention: From Literacy to Electracy.* Boston: Longman, 2006.

Vint, Sherryl. *Bodies of Tomorrow: Technology, Subjectivity, Science Fiction.* Toronto: University of Toronto Press, 2007.

Virilio, Paul. *Negative Horizon: An Essay in Dromoscopy*, trans. Michael Degener. New York: Continuum, 2005.

– *Open Sky*, trans. Julie Rose. London: Verso, 1997.

– *Speed and Politics*, trans. Mark Polizzotti. New York: Semiotext(e), 2006.

– *The Aesthetics of Disappearance*, trans. Philip Beitchman. New York: Semiotext(e), 1991.

– *The Information Bomb*, trans. Chris Turner. New York: Verso, 2006.

– *The Vision Machine*, trans. Julie Rose. Bloomington: Indiana University Press, 1994.

– *War and Cinema: The Logistics of Perception*, trans. Patrick Camiller. London: Verso, 1989.

Wardrip-Fruin, Noah, and Pat Harrigan, eds. *First Person: New Media as Story, Performance, and Game.* Cambridge: MIT Press, 2004.

Weber, Steven. *The Success of Open Source.* Cambridge: Harvard University Press, 2005.

Wegenstein, Bernadette. *Getting Under the Skin: Body and Media Theory.* Cambridge: MIT Press, 2006.

Wertheim, Margaret. *The Pearly Gates of Cyberspace: A History of Space from Dante to the Internet.* London: Norton, 1999.

White, Michele. *The Body and the Screen: Theories of Internet Spectatorship.* Cambridge: MIT Press, 2006.

Wiener, Norbert. *The Human Use of Human Beings: Cybernetics and Society.* New York: Doubleday Anchor, 1954.

Wilden, Anthony. *System and Structure: Essays in Communication and Exchange.* London: Routledge, 2003.

Winner, Langdon. *Autonomous Technology: Technics-out-of-Control as a Theme in Political Thought.* Cambridge: MIT Press, 1977.

– *The Whale and the Reactor: A Search for Limits in an Age of High Technology*. Chicago: University of Chicago Press, 1986.

Yúdice, George. *The Expediency of Culture: Uses of Culture in the Global Era*. Durham: Duke University Press, 2003.

Zielinski, Siegfried. *Deep Time of the Media: Toward an Archaeology of Hearing and Seeing by Technical Means*, trans. Gloria Custance. Cambridge: MIT Press, 2006.

Žižek, Slavoj. *Organs without Bodies: On Deleuze and Consequences*. New York and London: Routledge, 2004.

– *The Parallax View*. (Short Circuits.) Cambridge: MIT Press, 2006.

– *Welcome to the Desert of the Real!: Five Essays on September 11 and Related Dates*. New York: Verso, 2002.

Selected Documentary Films

After Darwin. Directed by Martin Lavut. Montreal: Gala Films, 2000. A 2000 Gemini Award winner, the film traces the unfolding story of evolutionary science and the future of humankind through the remarkable attempts to gain control over human biological destiny.

An Inconvenient Truth. DVD. Directed by Davis Guggenheim. Los Angeles: Paramount, 2006. A veritable media phenomenon, the documentary on Al Gore's campaign to make the issue of global warming a recognized problem worldwide also provides a sweeping picture of political climate change.

Bombay Calling. DVD. Directed by Ben Addelman and Samir Mallal. Montreal: National Film Board, 2006. An insider's look at a new, bustling world of Indian telecommunications and the global gold rush of telemarketing jobs from the West, which in turn creates a new kind of corporate youth culture.

Control Room. DVD. Directed by Jehane Noujaim, 2003. Vancouver: Lions Gate, 2004. A critical behind-the-scenes look at Western media production during the U.S. war campaign in Iraq, with particular emphasis on coverage by the pan-Arab TV news channel, Al-Jazeera.

The Corporation. DVD. Directed by Mark Achbar and Jennifer Abbott, 2004. New York: Zeitgeist, 2005. Critically examines the far-reaching repercussions of the corporation as today's dominant institution, not least in media and technology. The film reveals the corporation's inner workings, curious history, controversial impacts, and possible futures.

Info Wars. DVD. Directed by J.-F. Sebastien. Vienna: Parallel Universe, 2004. On the emerging Internet generation and new forms of online activism, featuring controversies around DeCSS, vote auction, the toy war, and the Electronic Disturbance Theater of Ricardo Dominguez.

The Ister. DVD. Directed by David Barison and Daniel Ross, 2004. New York: First Run/Icarus, 2007. This award-winning documentary, whose narrative follows the Danube river from the Black Sea to the Black Forest, is an unusual meditation on Martin Heidegger's philosophy through some of the contemporary thinkers most influenced by his work.

Manufactured Landscapes. DVD. Directed by Jennifer Baichwal. New York: Zeitgeist, 2006. Largely filmed in China, the documentary follows renowned artist Edward Burtynsky, whose large-scale photographs of "manufactured landscapes" – quarries, recycling yards, factories, mines, and dams – trace civilization's materials and debris.

Manufacturing Consent – Noam Chomsky and the Media. DVD. Directed by Mark Achbar and Peter Wintonick, 1993. New York: Zeitgeist, 2002. Explores the political life and ideas of Noam Chomsky, world-renowned linguist, intellectual, and political activist. In a collage of new and original footage, the film highlights Chomsky's critical analysis of mass media.

McLuhan's Wake. DVD. Directed by Kevin McMahon, 2002. New York: Disinformation, 2007. A compelling portrait of Marshall McLuhan, one of the most influential thinkers of the twentieth century, whose fascination with the role technology plays in transforming our lives led him to crucial, enduring insights for the digital age.

No Logo: Brands, Globalization, and Resistance. DVD. Directed by Sut Jhally. Northampton: Media Education Foundation, 2003. Based on the best-selling book by Naomi Klein, the film explores the reasons behind the backlash against the increasing economic and cultural reach of multinational companies, whose implications are increasingly felt everywhere in a globalizing world.

Road Stories for the Flesh-Eating Future. Directed by Lewis Cohen. Montreal: Gala Films, 2000. From the familiar territory of computers to the strange universe of artificial intelligence and synthetic skin, the film explores how technology is penetrating not only the home and workplace, but the mind and body as well.

Strange Culture. Directed by Lynn Hershman Leeson, 2007. Based on the recent experiences of Steve Kurtz of the Critical Art Ensemble, whose artwork was suddenly flagged by the FBI in 2004 for suspected bioterrorism, throwing his life into the political arena of the 'war on terror.'

The Ad and the Ego. VHS. Directed by Harold Boihem. Los Angeles: Parallax Pictures, 1997. Intercutting thousands of contemporary and classic television commercials with insights by Stuart Ewen, Jean Kilbourne, Sut Jhally, and others, this film scrutinizes late twentieth-century American society and its prime inhabitant, Consumer Man.

When Wittgenstein and Lyotard Talked with Jack and Jill. DVD. Directed by Ludo Gielen. Scotts Valley: Customflix, 2006. This film is an introduction to two central thinkers in postmodern thought – Ludwig Wittgenstein and Jean-François Lyotard – told through a narrative interaction between two students.

Zizek! DVD. Directed by Astra Taylor. New York: Zeitgeist, 2006. Explores the eccentric personality and esoteric work of Slavoj Zizek, a leading contemporary theorist, who reveals the invisible workings of ideology through a blend of Lacanian psychoanalysis, Marxism, and pop culture critique.

New Media: Selected Websites

ACTLab, Austin, Texas. <http://www.actlab.utexas.edu/program.htm> An interdisciplinary experimental research centre in arts, culture and technology; director, Alluquère Rosanne (Sandy) Stone.

Artmuseum.net. <http://www.artmuseum.net/> A central site for online multimedia exhibitions, this non-profit organization was founded by Intel in 1999.

Bandung Center for New Media Arts, Indonesia. <http://www.commonroom.info/bcfnma> Beginning with contemporary arts and architecture in 2001, the centre has become a multidisciplinary collaboration for science, technology, and art.

C3 Center for Culture and Communication, Budapest (Hungary). <http://www.c3.hu> Launched in 1996, C3 has become a key centre for research, development, and support of artistic innovation in art, science, and communications.

CNM Center for New Media, UC Berkeley. <http://cnm.berkeley.edu> Through historical and theoretical orientation, this multidisciplinary centre brings together people who engage in critical study of new media.

CTheory Live. <http://www.pactac.net/pactacweb/web-content/ctheoryindex.html> Offers a range of lectures and interviews with key critical thinkers in technology and culture, in formats for downloading and streaming.

CTheory Multimedia. <http://ctheorymultimedia.cornell.edu> Curated by Arthur and Marilouise Kroker, and Timothy Murray, this artistic collaboration navigates the codes and anti-codes of digitality.

Digital Craft. <http://www.digitalcraft.org> Derived from the Museum for Applied Art in Frankfurt am Main, the site aims to research and document fast-moving trends in everyday digital culture.

Digital Performance Archive. <http://www.ahds.ac.uk/ahdscollections/docroot/dpa/authors-search.jsp> Created by Steve Dixon and Barry Smith, the database documents creative use of computer technologies in performance – from live theatre and dance productions that incorporate digital media, to cyberspace interactive dramas and webcasts.

DXARTS Center for Digital Arts and Experimental Media, Seattle. <http://www.washington.edu/dxarts> Offering its own undergraduate and graduate degree programs, the centre is a creative research zone for artists and scholars in digital arts.

Horizon 0, Banff, Canada. <http://www.horizonzero.ca> A collaboration between the Banff New Media Institute (BNMI) and the Culture.ca Gateway, the project is an online space for digital art, ideas, and culture.

Interaccess Electronic Media Arts Centre, Toronto. <http://www.interaccess.org> Devoted exclusively to electronic art, the centre is both an exhibition space and a production facility for developing new artistic practices.

InterSpace Media Art Center, Sofia, Bulgaria. <http://www.i-space.org> A non-profit association of professional artists, informatics engineers, do-it-yourself media makers, founded in 1998.

Intute – Arts and Humanities. <http://www.intute.ac.uk> Based in Britain, this comprehensive site is a tool for discovering the best Internet resources for education and research in creative arts and the humanities.

Kinema Ikon, Bucharest. <http://kinema-ikon.projects.v2.nl> The oldest ongoing experimental art group in Romania, Kinema Ikon's interdisciplinary media approach has led it to focus exclusively on hypermedia works, such as interactive installations on CD-ROM and Net art. Also publishes the magazine *Intermedia.*

Media Education Foundation, Massachussetts. <http://www.mediaed.org> Produces and distributes documentary films and other resources to inspire critical reflection on the social, political, and cultural impact of American mass media.

MIT Media Lab. <http://www.media.mit.edu> A pioneering research centre since 1985, the Media Lab focuses today on how electronic information overlaps with the everyday physical world.

Neural: Media Art – Hacktivism – Emusic. <http://www.neural.it> A print and online magazine specializing in new media art, experimental electronic audio art, and political new media art.

Nine One One Media Arts Center, Seattle. <http://www.911media.org> A non-profit organization dedicated to supporting independent digital media artists in the creation and exhibition of their work.

Noema – Technology and Society. <http://www.noemalab.org> Based in Italy, this comprehensive website is devoted to new technologies, interrelations, and influences – culture in a broad sense.

Pacific Center for Technology and Culture, Victoria (Canada). <http://www.pactac.net> An interdisciplinary institute for research focused on the impact of technological change on culture, politics, and society.

Rhizome.org. <http://www.rhizome.org> An online platform for the global new media art community, supporting the creation, presentation, discussion and preservation of contemporary art.

Robert LePage – Ex-Machina, Quebec. <http://www.exmachina.qc.ca> A multidisciplinary company bringing together actors, writers, set designers, technicians, opera singers, puppeteers, computer graphics designers, video artists, and more.

Rose Goldsen Archive of New Media Art. <http://goldsen.library.cornell.edu> A research repository of new media art, with emphasis on digital interfaces and experimentation by international, independent artists; curated by Timothy Murray.

Second Life – Virtual World. <http://www.secondlife.com> A 3-D virtual world or digital society entirely built and owned by its millions of residents, opened in 2003.

ZKM Center for Art and Media, Karlsruhe (Germany). <http://on1.zkm.de/zkm/e> Comprising museums and research institutions, the centre is a key cultural institution, whose work includes production, exhibitions, and events.

Contributors

The Editors

Arthur Kroker is Canada Research Chair in Technology, Culture and Theory, professor of political science, and the director of the Pacific Centre for Technology and Culture at the University of Victoria in British Columbia. One of his most recent projects is the monograph *Born Again Ideology: Religion, Technology and Terrorism*. His books include, among others, *The Will to Technology and the Culture of Nihilism: Heidegger, Nietzsche, and Marx* (University of Toronto Press, 2004), *The Possessed Individual* (St Martin's Press, 1992), *Spasm* (St Martin's Press, 1993), and *Data Trash: The Theory of the Virtual Class*, with Michael A. Weinstein (St Martin's Press, 1994). <www.krokers.net>

Marilouise Kroker is Senior Research Scholar at the Pacific Centre for Technology and Culture, University of Victoria. She is the author, with Arthur Kroker, of *Hacking the Future* (1996). She has co-edited and introduced numerous anthologies including *Digital Delirium* (1997), *Body Invaders* (1987), and *The Last Sex* (1993) – all published by St Martin's Press. <www.krokers.net>

In addition to editing the Digital Futures book series for the University of Toronto Press, Arthur Kroker and Marilouise Kroker are editors of the peer-reviewed, electronic journal *CTheory*. <www.ctheory.net>

The Contributors

Thierry Bardini is a sociologist and associate professor in the Department of Communication at the Université de Montréal, where he co-directs (with Brian Massumi) the Workshop in Radical Empiricism. In 2000, he published *Bootstrapping: Douglas Engelbart, Coevolution, and the Origins of Personal Computing* (Stanford University Press). He is currently finishing his second book manuscript, entitled 'Junkware: The Disaffected Subject.' <www.junkware.net>

Belinda Barnet is lecturer in media at Swinburne University of Technology, Melbourne. She has worked as service delivery manager (wireless content services) for Ericsson Australia, and her research interests are technical evolution and the philosophy of technology. Barnet has a PhD in Media and Communications from the University of New South Wales.

William Bogard is Deburgh Professor in Social Sciences at Whitman College, Walla Walla, Washington. His latest research concerns the development of tactile networks and their relation to smooth spaces of control. <www.whitman.edu/sociology/bogard.cfm>

Mary Bryson is associate professor and director of graduate programs, Department of Educational and Counselling Psychology and Special Education, Faculty of Education, at the University of British Columbia. Her primary interest is in sociocultural scholarship concerning technology, equity, and the pedagogically transgressive use of digital tools. She has numerous publications on theoretical treatments of gender and technology, queer theory, and equity in education, including *Radical In <ter>ventions* (SUNY Press, 1997). In 2000, she was a recipient of the Canadian Pioneer in New Technologies and Media Award. Her SSHRC research, 'Queer Women on the Net,' focuses on new media, identity, and discursive emplotments of network formation, community, and agency. <www.queerville.ca>

Nate Burgos is an information designer. In addition to design, he writes about visual communication and culture. He sustains the growing design webliography, Design Feast. <www.designfeast.com>

Richard Carlson is a writer/musician and president of Pacific Weather Inc., a firm that monitors meteorological information at airports throughout the United States. His interests include all matters related to *CTheory*, jazz, poetry, integral yoga, and global climate change. He holds an MA from Antioch University and currently resides with family on the Olympic Peninsula in Washington State.

Julie Clarke has a PhD in cinema studies from the University of Melbourne, where she currently holds an appointment as an honorary fellow in the School of Culture and Communications. She has published a number of articles on Stelarc's work including: 'Aesthetic Emergence+Self,' *Imagine Exhibition Catalogue*, ed. Zara Stanhope (Heide Museum of Modern Art, Australia, 2006); 'A Sensorial Act of Replication,' *Stelarc: The Monograph*, ed. Marquard Smith (MIT Press, 2005); 'Face-Off: Stelarc Interview,' *Meanjin: New Writing in Australia*, ed. Ian Britain (Melbourne University Press, 2005); 'pros+thesis,' *LIVE: Art, Performance and the Contemporary*, ed. Adrian Heathfield (Tate Publication, 2004); 'The Human/not human in the work of Orlan and Sterlac,' *The Cyborg Experiments: Extensions of the Body in* *the Media Age*, ed. Joanna Zyslinka (Continuum, 2002); and, 'Pros + Thesis,' *Alternate Interfaces* (Monash University Art Gallery, 2002).

Jordan Crandall is a media artist and theorist. He is associate professor in the Visual Arts Department at the University of California at San Diego. His ongoing art and research project, *Under Fire*, concerning the organization and representation of political violence, opened in October 2006 at the International Biennial of Contemporary Art of Seville. To date, two catalogues of *Under Fire* have been published, in 2004 and 2005, by the Witte de With Center for Contemporary Art, Rotterdam. Crandall is the author of *Drive: Technology, Mobility, and Desire* (Hatje Cantz Verlag in conjunction with ZKM [Center for Art and Media] in Karlsruhe and the Neue Galerie and Landesmuseum Joanneum, in Graz). He is completing a new video installation entitled *Homefront*, which combines live-action video, surveillance footage, and military tracking software, and explores the effect of the new security culture on subjectivity and identity. <www.jordancrandall.com>

Michael Dartnell is professor of political science at Laurentian University at Georgian College, Ontario. He is the author of *Insurgency Online: Web Activism and Global Conflict* (University of Toronto Press, 2006) and *Action directe: Ultra-left Terrorism in France, 1979–1987* (Frank Cass, 1995), as well as articles on information technologies and conflict and security, terrorism, and political violence. His current research focuses on the cultural logic of suicide terrorism.

Francesca De Nicolò is an art historian, independent curator, and art critic. She studied contemporary art with Jolanda Nigro Covre and Silvia Bordini at the University of Rome and is finishing research with Enrico Crispolti and Luca Quattrocchi of the University of Siena on postorganic aesthetics and its connection with the Net. She has been assistant at the Galleria Comunale D'Arte Moderna e Contemporanea of Rome and assistant curator at the British School of Rome Contemporary Arts Programme. She currently reviews art for *Random, Exiwebart, Arte e Critica, Netartreview, Crudelia,* and *Merzbau.*

Sara Diamond is a social historian and communications and new media theorist, as well as a practising artist and designer, working in video installation, artist's television, and most recently, conversation visualization software, artificial intelligence, and performance. She is president of the Ontario College of Art and Design. Previously she was artistic director of media and visual art and director of research at the Banff Centre for the Arts. Diamond is the creator of the Banff New Media Institute (BNMI) and creator and editor-in-chief of *Horizonzero.ca*, an online showcase for new media art and design, in collaboration with Heritage Canada. She has taught at the Emily Carr Institute of Art and Design and the California Institute for the Arts, and remains adjunct professor at the University of California at Los Angeles in the Design/Media Department. <www.leonardo.info/rolodex/diamond.sara.html>

Steve Dixon is professor of performance and technology and head of the School of Arts at Brunel University, London. He is artistic director of the award-winning multimedia theatre company *The Chameleons Group*, and has published extensively on performance studies, digital arts, and cybertheory. Dixon is the author of *Digital Performance: A History of New Technologies in Theater, Dance, Performance Art, and Installation* (MIT Press, 2007).

Frances Dyson currently lives in San Francisco and is associate professor in Technocultural Studies at the University of California at Davis, where she teaches film, new media, audio art, and technocultural theory. Her research focus is on sound, new media, and posthumanism. She was a researcher in residence at the Daniel Langlois Foundation for Art, Science, and Technology (Montreal), and her Web-based project *'And Then It Was Now'* was recently published <www.fondation-langlois.org>. Other recent writing can be found in *Frakcija* (2006); *Convergence* (Sage, 2005), *Catherine Richards Excitable Tissues* (Ottawa Art Gallery, 2004), also published on <www.catherinerichards.ca/html/essays.htm>, and *Uncertain Ground* (Art Gallery of New South Wales, 2000). Dyson's audio artwork can be heard on Australian Broadcasting Corporation <www.abc.net.au/classic> and Air America Radio archives <www.somewhere.org/NAR/catalog/catalog-lists/letters/artists_d-h.htm#dyson>. Her book, *Sounding New Media: Rhetorics of Immersion and Embodiment in the Arts and Culture*, is forthcoming.

Alexander R. Galloway teaches media at New York University and is founder of the Radical Software Group. He is the author of *Protocol: How Control Exists after Decentralization* (MIT Press, 2004) and *Gaming: Essays on Algorithmic Culture* (University of Minnesota Press, 2006).

Donna Haraway is the author of many books including, *The Companion Species Manifesto: Dogs, People, and Significant Otherness* (Prickly Paradigm Press, 2003); *Primate Visions: Gender, Race, and Nature in the World of Modern Science* (Routledge, 1989); *Simians, Cyborgs, and Women: The Reinvention of Nature* (Routledge, 1991); *Modest _Witness@Second_Millennium. Female-Man(c) Meets OncoMouse(tm). Feminism and Technoscience* (Routledge, 1997); and *When Species Meet* (University of Minnesota Press, 2007). Haraway's research develops ethnographic and textual approaches to health and genetics science and activism, as well as to sports, commerce, fiction, law, and other aspects of animal-human relationships within techno-scientific worlds.

D. Fox Harrell is an artist, author, and researcher who explores the relationship between imaginative cognition and computation, and developing new forms of computational narrative. He is assistant professor of digital media in the School of Literature, Communication, and Culture at the Georgia Institute of Technology. He has a PhD in computer science and cognitive science from the University of California at San Diego.

Joan Hawkins is associate professor in the Department of Communication and Culture at Indiana University in Bloomington. She is the author of *Cutting Edge: Art Horror and the Horrific Avant-garde* (University of Minnesota Press, 2000) and is currently working on a book about the cultural uses of theory.

N. Katherine Hayles is a postmodern literary critic and theorist as well as the author of many publications, including: *Chaos Bound: Orderly Disorder in Contemporary Literature* (Cornell University Press, 1990) and *How We Became Posthuman: Virtual Bodies in Cybernetics, Literature and Informatics* (University of Chicago Press, 1999), which won the Rene Wellek Prize for the best book in literary theory for 1998–99. She is currently Hills Professor of Literature in English and Media Arts at the University of California at Los Angeles, where she has taught since 1992.

Lynn Hershman Leeson has worked extensively in photography, video, film, and installation. She pioneered interactive computer and Net-based media art. Hershman Leeson's ground-breaking work has earned her numerous international awards including a tribute and retrospective from the San Francisco International Film Festival (1994), the ZKM/Seimens Media Art Award (1995), a Sundance Institute Screenwriting Fellowship (1998), the Flintridge Foundation Award for Lifetime Achievement in the Visual Arts (1998), the prestigious Golden Nica in Interactive Arts from Ars Electronica (The Difference Engine #3, 1999), the World Technology Network Award for Innovation in the Visual Arts (2002), and the Award for Positive Innovations in Media from the Digital Media and Arts Association (2005). She recently received a National Endowment for the Arts grant for a forthcoming documentary film on the history of feminist art. Her most recent film is *Strange Culture* (2007).

Julian Jonker is a writer, sound artist, and cultural producer living in Cape Town, South Africa. He has written about law and memory in post-apartheid Cape Town, intellectual property and indigenous knowledge, and carnival and performance traditions in South Africa. He is currently writing a cultural history of silence. His sound recordings have been exhibited at the Durban Art Gallery and performed as part of the Vox Novus new music festival. He teaches legal history and rhetoric at the University of Cape Town.

Sharalyn Jordan is a doctoral candidate in Counselling Psychology in the Faculty of Education, University of British Columbia, conducting research on the settlement practices of QLGBT migrants. Bringing critical social perspectives to psychological research, the construction of self/identities in social networks, and reconstitution of QLGBT genders/sexualities are her research interests.

Hui-Ling Lin is originally from Taiwan and a graduate of National Taiwan University with an MA in Urban Planning. She is currently a PhD candidate in Women's and Gender Studies at the University of British Columbia. Her research interests include immigration, queer theory, feminist film theory, transnational feminist theory, gender, and cultural geography. Her dissertation examines the representation of queer Asian women, with a special focus on body images, in videos/films made by transmigrant queer Chinese women in contemporary Canada.

Lori B. MacIntosh is a doctoral candidate in the Department of Educational Studies at the University of British Columbia. Her major areas of focus are sociology of education, queer theory, and gender studies. Her research interests include education and sexual minority youth, diversity education in teacher education programs, and the pedagogy of popular culture and new media.

Lev Manovich <www.manovich.net> is the author of *Soft Cinema: Navigating the Database* (MIT Press, 2005), and *The Language of New Media* (MIT Press, 2001). Manovich is professor of visual arts and Director of the Software Studies Initiative at the University of California at San Diego <visarts.ucsd.edu> and a director of the lab for Cultural Analysis at the California Institute for Telecommunications and Information Technology. <www.calit2.net>

Christina McPhee explores place, environmental disturbance, architecture, and traumatic memory in a practice that moves through video, installation, drawing, photography, environmental sound, and networked media. 'La Conchita mon amour' (video installation) on shrine-building in the aftermath of a California mudslide, opened at Sara Tecchia Roma New York in 2006, and continued in 2007 with video installations for Thresholds Art Space in Perth, Scotland, and Break Festival 2.4, in Ljubjana. 'On seismic memory,' her *Carrizo-Parkfield Diaries* (multimedia installation) has shown at the American University Museum, InterativA07 Biennial, Cartes Centre for Art and Technology, Bildmuseet, Itaù Cultural Centers, and the Pacific Film Archive. A new video installation on the sublime and datascape at Bonneville Salt Flats was commissioned for the Split Film Festival, September 2007. Online her work appears with *Turbulence, VIROSE, CTheory, Neural, Drunkenboat, Soundtoys*, and elsewhere. She has been a moderator/editor for *empyre* network, Sydney <www.subtle.net/empyre> since 2002. <christinamcphee.net>, <strikeslip.tv>

Charles Mudede is an associate editor for *The Stranger*, an alternative Seattle weekly. He was born in an Africans-only hospital in Que Que (now called Kwe Kwe), Rhodesia (now called Zimbabwe), in 1969. Kwe Kwe was, and might still be, a steel town, much like Charles Dickens' Coketown. Mudede is also an adjunct professor at Pacific

Lutheran University and a screenwriter (*Police Beat, In the Forest There Is Every Kind of Bird*), and his articles have appeared in the *Village Voice*, the *Sydney Morning Daily*, and the *New York Times*, among other publications.

Anna Munster is an artist, writer, and educator. She works with audiovisual, interactive, and multichannel installations and has exhibited in Australia, Japan, America, and Europe. She is the author of *Materializing New Media: Embodiment in Information Aesthetics* (Dartmouth College Press, 2006), which explores the relationship between new media, aesthetics, and bodies. She is a senior lecturer at the College of Fine Arts at the University of South Wales. Her current areas of research include investigating our aesthetic and political relations with collaborative, networked, and mobile media.

Samuel Nunn is professor of criminal justice in the School of Public and Environmental Affairs at Indiana University Purdue University, Indianapolis, and Director, Center for Criminal Justice Research. His research focuses on criminal justice technologies and their impacts.

Stephen Pfohl is professor of sociology at Boston College, where he teaches social theory; postmodern culture; crime, deviance, and social control; images and power; and sociology and psychoanalysis. His most recent project is the monograph *Left Behind: Religion, Technology and Flight from the Flesh* (CTheory Books, 2006). Pfohl is the author of numerous books and articles, including, *Death at the Parasite Café* (St Martin's, 1992), *Images of Deviance and Social Control* (McGraw-Hill, 1985), *Predicting Dangerousness* (D.C. Heath and Company, 1978), and the forthcoming volumes *Venus in Video* and *Magic and the Machine*. A past-president of the Society for the Study of Social Problems and a founding member of SitCom International, a Boston-area collective of activists and artists, Pfohl is also co-editor of *Culture, Power, and History: Studies in Critical Sociology* (2006).

Jeff Rice is assistant professor of English and director of composition at the University of Missouri at Columbia, where he teaches rhetoric, writing, and new media. He is the author of *The Rhetoric of Cool: Composition Studies and New Media* (Southern Illinois University Press, 2007), and he is currently working on a book-length project on Detroit and digital culture. He blogs at Yellow Dog. <www.ydog.net>

Nicholas Rombes is chair and professor of English at the University of Detroit-Mercy, where he teaches film, media theory, and American literature. He is co-founder of the degree program in digital media studies. Rombes is author of *Ramones* (Continuum, 2005) and editor of *New Punk Cinema* (Edinburgh University Press, 2005). He is completing two book projects: 'Cinema in the Digital Age' and an avant-garde encyclopedia of punk rock from 1974 to 1982.

Mahesh Senagala is the chair and Irving Professor of architecture at Ball State University, Indiana. He is also a fellow at Ball State University's Institute for Emerging Media. His interdisciplinary research interests include smart environments, design computing, tensile membrane structures, education leadership, and sustainable urbanism. His writings have won best publication and best presentation awards at various international conferences. He has been interviewed, quoted, and featured in the *New York Times, Industrial Fabrics Review, Fabric Architecture, Texas Architect*, and other publications in Asia and the Americas. Senagala is the 2007–8 president of the Association for Computer Aided Design in Architecture. In 2000 he was the second-prize winner of the U.S. Department of Energy Sun Wall competition. He is an award-winning fiction writer, and draws inspiration from Latin American and existentialist literature. <www.mahesh.org>

Jaimie Smith-Windsor is a graduate student at the University of Victoria, British Columbia. Her research explores relationships among disability and eugenics, technology and maternity, bioethics and modern medicine, advanced reproductive technologies and 'the body.' She is currently working on her MA thesis, entitled 'When the Baby Breaks,' which explores the bioethical dynamics between intensive care technologies, the precarious lives of ordinarily previable babies, and the unintended consequences of manufacturing both viability and disability.

Stelarc is a world-renowned performance artist based in Australia whose work explores and extends the concept of the body and its relationship with technology. He has performed extensively in Japan, Europe, and the United States. He has performed with a Third Hand, a Virtual Arm, and an Extended Arm, a Motion Prosthesis, and with six-legged walking robots, and has inserted a sculpture inside his body. He is at present having an ear surgically constructed on his arm. He has been principal research fellow in the Performance Arts Digital Research Unit at the Nottingham Trent University. Currently he is chair in performance art in the School of Arts, Brunel University, and senior research fellow at the MARCs Labs at the University of Western Sydney. In 2005 and 2006 he was a recipient of a New Media Arts Fellowship from the Australia Council. His art is represented by the Sherman Galleries in Sydney. <www.stelarc.va.com.au>

Eugene Thacker is associate professor in the School of Literature, Communication, and Culture at the Georgia Institute of Technology. He is the author of *Biomedia* (University of Minnesota Press, 2004); *The Global Genome: Biotechnology, Politics, and Culture* (MIT Press, 2005); and co-author, with Alexander Galloway, of *The Exploit* (University of Minnesota Press, 2007). <www.lcc.gatech.edu/~ethacker>

James Tully is the Distinguished Professor of Political Science, Law, Philosophy and Indigenous Governance at the University of Victoria, British Columbia, and a fellow of the Trudeau Foundation. His books include *An Approach to Political Philosophy: Locke in Contexts* (1993); *Strange Multiplicity: Constitutionalism in an Age of Diversity* (1995); *Multinational Democracies*, co-edited with Alain Gagnon (2001); and *Rethinking the Foundations of Modern Political Thought*, with Annabel Brett (2006) – all published by Cambridge University Press.

Andrew Wernick is a sociologist and historian of ideas as well as a cultural theorist and jazz pianist. He is professor of cultural studies at Trent University, visiting professor at the Humanities Center at Ivan Franco National University in L'viv, Ukraine, and a life member of Clare Hall, Cambridge. He is the author of *Promotional Culture: Advertising, Ideology, and Symbolic Expression* (Sage, 1991) and *Auguste Comte and the Religion of Humanity: the Post-theistic Project of French Social Theory* (Cambridge University Press, 2000), and co-editor of *Shadow of Spirit: Religion and Postmodernism* (Routledge, 1992) and *Images of Ageing* (Routledge, 1995).

Daniel White is professor of philosophy and classics in the Wilkes Honors College of Florida Atlantic University. He is the author of *Postmodern Ecology* (1998) and co-author with Gert Hellerich of *Labyrinths of the Mind* – both published by UNY Press.

Mark Winokur writes on literature, film, popular culture, and digital culture. He is author of *American Laughter: Immigrants, Ethnicity, and 1930s Hollywood Film Comedy* (palgrave, the, 1996), and he is currently writing a manuscript called 'Technologies of Race,' on film FX, race, and ethnicity. He has received several academic awards, including grants from the National Endowment for the Humanities. Winokur is a member of the English faculty at University of Colorado at Boulder.